I0813971

ALSO BY NATHAN KERNAN

POETRY

Poems, with art by Joan Mitchell (1992)

AS EDITOR

The Diary of James Schuyler (1997)

A DAY LIKE ANY OTHER

A DAY LIKE ANY OTHER

The Life of James Schuyler

NATHAN KERNAN

FARRAR, STRAUS AND GIROUX
NEW YORK

For Tom

Farrar, Straus and Giroux
120 Broadway, New York 10271

EU Representative: Macmillan Publishers Ireland Ltd, 1st Floor,
The Liffey Trust Centre, 117–126 Sheriff Street Upper, Dublin 1, DO1 YC43

Printed in the United States of America
First edition, 2025

Frontispiece photograph: Screened porch, Great Spruce Head Island, ca. 1968.
Photograph by James Schuyler. © The Estate of James Schuyler, Courtesy
James Schuyler Papers, Archive for New Poetry, Mandeville Department of Special
Collections, University of California, San Diego, La Jolla, California.

Owing to limitations of space, all acknowledgments for permission to reprint previously published material can be found on pages 477–479 in the Acknowledgments.

Library of Congress Control Number: 2025002808
ISBN: 978-0-374-28117-5

Designed by Gretchen Achilles

10 9 8 7 6 5 4 3 2 1

CONTENTS

A DAY LIKE ANY OTHER

PROLOGUE

TUESDAY, NOVEMBER 15, 1988

On a cold evening in November 1988, a crowd was assembling outside a nondescript loft building in New York's SoHo district. By 7:30, the line of people waiting to get into the Dia Art Foundation at 155 Mercer Street was snaking down to the corner and up Prince Street. There was a buzz of excitement as friends and acquaintances recognized one another, and casual passersby wondered what it was all about. In fact, the crowd was gathered for a reading by James Schuyler, a reclusive sixty-five-year-old poet who had never read in public before.

A hired town car pulled up in front of the building, and the slow-moving figure of the poet emerged, dressed in khaki slacks, a tweed jacket over a dark sweater, accompanied by his friends the painter Darragh Park, a tall, slim, strikingly handsome man with a mane of silver hair, and the editor Raymond Foye, curly-haired and boyish.

When the doors opened, the ground-floor space quickly filled to capacity. Folding chairs on a wooden platform provided slightly raised seating, with standees lining the back of the room. At the front a simple wooden table and chair were set before a plain blue backdrop. Looking around, members of the audience took stock of themselves, aware they were taking part in something special. The poet Peter Gizzi was struck by the diversity of listeners from across the city's cultural spectrum: "The uptown poets and the downtown poets, the *New Yorker* poets, the staple magazine poets were there. Editors of big magazines, big presses, little presses were there. Abstract painters, figural painters, composers, language poets . . . every clan came out to hear him."

After a brief welcome by Dia's director, Charles Wright, the poet John Ashbery introduced Schuyler, calling him a friend of such long standing and intimacy that "asking advice from him is only a step away from consulting oneself," and praised his work for being "written in what Marianne Moore calls plain American which cats and dogs can read. He makes sense, dammit, and manages to do so without falsifying or simplifying."

The reading that followed has entered the annals of New York poetry lore. Many in the audience knew of Schuyler's reclusive nature, which had prevented him from reading in public before, and his long history of mental illness, and some had heard tales of wildly eccentric behavior in his past. There was a mood of expectancy mingled with apprehension, and a sense of the audience holding its collective breath. Schuyler was impassive and outwardly calm, but in his very calm projected a certain vulnerability. He had been nervous about the reading beforehand and had been prescribed a beta blocker by his psychiatrist. "When about to enter a tumbrel, *always* take a beta blocker!" he wrote to a friend.

As Schuyler settled himself with his newly published book *Selected Poems* in front of him, put on his reading glasses, and took a drink of water, the painter Duncan Hannah recalled the room growing "dim, hushed, respectful," with a feeling of "everyone pulling for Jimmy."

"Past is past, and if one / remembers what one meant / to do and never did, is / not to have thought to do / enough?" Schuyler began with his first published poem, "Salute." With this short poem, spoken in his deep, slow, and deliberate voice, with a very slightly "blurred" or "thick" sound, due perhaps to his false teeth or to years of taking antidepressant medications, Schuyler put to rest any doubts about his ability to read effectively. The poem itself, with its evocation of past expectations and present quiet resignation, seemed to encompass the room, the listeners, the poet, and the occasion in a circle of timelessness. But it was with the third poem he read, the relatively long and discursive "Empathy and New Year," that he hit his stride. Written at the turn of the year from 1967 to 1968 while living with the Fairfield Porter family on Long Island, the poem is quintessential Schuyler, interweaving immediate sensual responses to weather and daily events with witty asides and reflections. When he read the lines "It's a shame / expectations are / so often to be counted on," there was laughter from the room, which clearly delighted Schuyler, and he chuckled along in response. This happened again throughout the reading: whenever there was audience laughter, Schuyler quietly joined in. When he came to the end of "Empathy and New Year," there was applause, the first poem to be followed by audience applause, but not the last.

As it became clear that Schuyler read very well indeed, both the crowd and Schuyler relaxed into enjoyment and appreciative concentration. The painter Trevor Winkfield, a longtime friend, recalled "everyone being 'rapt' as Jimmy read—we wanted to capture his every word, not miss a thing. The sense of [the] historic even was . . . very palpable. And Jimmy, I thought, read very well, very plain-spoken, like a truck driver giving traffic directions, no affectations or acting whatsoever." The poet and publisher Geoffrey Young also approved of the way Schuyler read "with no ornament, no dramatic effect, just unadorned directness." Douglas Crase recalled that once the reading had begun, "there was also the assurance of our poet's deep voice as he read, he who was supposed to be so nervous." To Eileen Myles, "Everybody on the planet was there and everybody was so happy and I just feel like I had never seen an event in New York like that. There was no animosity, it was all like openness, we were all there for something that we had never had before and it was very exciting."

When he came to the end of the forty-five-minute reading—all too soon—there was extended applause, which seemed to go on for several minutes. It started enthusiastically enough, but instead of tapering off after the expected few seconds, it went on, and on, and became self-perpetuating as people realized that it was lasting longer than usual and as a result continued it. Crase recalled, "Most vividly I remember the contented expression on his face when the audience burst into applause at the end, and how he kept us clapping by waiting a long time before he moved his books and signaled that we could shift our attention and break the spell. The acclaim was his due and he knew it. It was a great moment." As Myles put it, "And then that famous applause that just didn't end and that was so awkward and so beautiful. And Jimmy couldn't leave because people wouldn't stop applauding."

Geoffrey Young remembered that at the end "the crowd began to clap, and then clap some more, and then not stop but continue clapping, happily, enthusiastically, lovingly, for what surely lasted several long and amazing minutes. [Actually about one minute.] I looked at Ron [Silliman], he looked at me, and together we kept clapping, as did everyone. We'd never seen or heard anything like it . . . It was the palpable and considered and felt response to a man who'd been through a lot, had survived, kept his genius intact, and that evening, in his own voice, delivered a chunk of it to us . . . For which we were unabashedly grateful."

After the reading, Schuyler and about a dozen friends went to a nearby restaurant to celebrate, where Jimmy, often uncomfortable in that kind of situation, was "in a very good mood, and was very affable." He left soon afterward to return to his small apartment in the Chelsea Hotel. Two days later he wrote to his friend Anne Dunn with a report of the event, concluding without exaggeration, "I was a fucking sensation."

> Anyone who ever wants to write my biography will have his/her work cut out for her/him, since virtually no documentation or juvenilia exist. There is The Birth Certificate, The First Grade Report Card (F in all subjects: I was a late bloomer), The Passport: and? no diplomas, no degrees, maybe some postcards and a letter or two . . .
>
> —JAMES SCHUYLER, *Diary,* **August 3, 1985**

James Schuyler was one of the five poets usually considered to be the "first generation" of the so-called New York School of poetry. The term began as a joke, and continues as a fiction, but a useful one. John Ashbery, for one, protested against it but Schuyler eventually accepted it as inevitable journalistic shorthand, handy for designating a group of poets who, while certainly no "school" united by any actual or implied manifesto, were close friends and shared a time, a place, a larger circle of acquaintances, and at times a sensibility. While their poetry was quite distinct, the voices, in prose and sometimes in person, of the four male poets in the group in particular, Frank O'Hara, John Ashbery, Kenneth Koch, and James Schuyler, could be uncannily similar. Rereading the novel he co-wrote with Schuyler, *A Nest of Ninnies*, Ashbery claimed not to be able to tell in some cases which lines were his own and which Schuyler's; while Ashbery's own mother, listening from another room, once confused his speaking voice with O'Hara's. The letters that passed among these four share a tone of intimate hilarity, to the degree that the identity of the correspondents can almost seem interchangeable.

Rule-proving exceptions frustrate any absolute group identity for the first-generation New York School. Barbara Guest was the only woman. Koch was the only male heterosexual, the only Jew; Guest and Schuyler were the only non–Harvard graduates; in fact, Schuyler didn't graduate from college at all. Ashbery was the only one of the men who did not serve in the military during World War II. O'Hara died at forty, more than a quarter of a century before any of the others and half a century before the longest-lived of the five (Ashbery). Of these poets, Schuyler may have been the least known for most of his life, for a variety of reasons. Relatively late to publish, retiring by nature, he was plagued by mental illness intermittently, and lived long stretches outside the city. This began to change after the reading at Dia in 1988, and again after his death in 1991 and the release of his *Collected Poems* two years later. Since then the work has continued to gain new readers, bringing fresh, twenty-first-century perspectives, and to sustain longtime ones, who find themselves returning to it again and again.

I had discovered Schuyler's work in the early eighties and felt a close connection to its directness and lyricism, its wit and music, and, as Ashbery put it in his introduction to the reading, its quality of "inspired utterance couched in everyday terms." Through my job at an art gallery we had friends in common, and we'd been introduced briefly at a party in 1987. I was excited to be at the Dia reading, but I would never have aspired to know Schuyler if it had not been for two mutual friends, the artists Anne Dunn and Joe Brainard. First Anne brought us together for a quiet restaurant dinner in March 1990, then about two weeks later Joe took us both out to dinner near the Chelsea Hotel, where Jimmy lived. After the ice was broken I began to see Jimmy on my own; soon we were meeting about once a week, in his tiny apartment in the Chelsea, going out to dinner in the neighborhood or to a movie or an exhibition. Often, we simply spent time sitting quietly together in the two easy chairs that were, aside from a desk, a filing cabinet, and a single bed, the only furniture in his room. I loved hearing him tell stories about his past, which he too seldom did, and I too often failed to remember or to note down. Loving his work, and then him, together and separately, I wanted to know more about how it came about "that *he* / should grow up to be *him*," as he wrote of Darwin in "Empathy and New Year." When Jimmy died, on April 12, 1991, at the far too young age of sixty-seven, I felt a huge sense of loss, cheated not only of so much poetry that might have been written but also of a close but still new friendship.

Somehow I got it into my head that I wanted to write his biography. When I approached his executor, Darragh Park, with the idea, Park demurred. However, he did suggest I edit Schuyler's *Diary*, which I did and which was published by Black Sparrow Press in 1997. To accompany the notes for the *Diary* I prepared a chronology of Schuyler's life, and the research I did for this chronology gave me a head start when, six years later, Jonathan Galassi, Schuyler's editor and the publisher of Farrar, Straus and Giroux, commissioned a biography. Intervening projects and responsibilities have meant that the book took far longer than it might have. Yet having my life entwined with Schuyler's for so many years has been immensely enriching, and I am gratified finally to be able to present what I have learned to readers, who I hope will find like sustenance in it for themselves.

There are those who feel that biography is, at best, irrelevant to the work of an artist, which must "stand alone." I don't share this view, but even if I did, I would argue that James Schuyler may present a special case inasmuch as his poetry draws both implicitly and explicitly from his daily life and his past. My intention is to give information about a life, the life of a poet, his friends and milieu, and thereby to bring more readers to James Schuyler's work. This is not intended to be a critical biography; in discussing the poems, my aim is usually to restate what is self-apparent. But even while absorbing the details of Schuyler's life I would have the reader remember the caveat Schuyler himself sets out in "Hymn to Life" about the taxonomy of his beloved roses, "After learning all their names—Rose / de Rescht, Cornelia, Pax—it is important to forget them."

In referring to the poet in these pages I alternate between the formal Schuyler and the familiar Jimmy, the name by which I and most friends called him. However, he was also known as James or Jim to various people at various times in his life, especially his family, and occasionally I use those names as well.

[1]

A DREAM OF THE GREAT MIDWEST

1650–1923

James Marcus Schuyler was born in Chicago on November 9, 1923, the only child of Marcus James Schuyler, a newspaperman, and Margaret Daisy Connor, a politically active professional woman. Both came from Midwestern farming families. They met and married in Albert Lea, Minnesota, where Margaret was born and grew up, and where Marcus had recently come to work on a small weekly newspaper.

Although James Schuyler, from the age of four, grew up in Washington, DC, and in upstate New York, and spent most of his life in and around New York City, he retained a lifelong emotional attachment to an idea or "dream" of the Midwest. It is reflected partly in his love for writers such as Willa Cather, William Maxwell, and Hamlin Garland, whose novels and memoirs mirror the experiences of his own parents and forebears, and can perhaps be sensed, too, in aspects of his work, its unfussy diction and sense of expansiveness, and of a natural world populated with grass and flowers under eventful skies. Schuyler's first published work, the very short story "A Memory Haunts Me," has a Midwestern setting: "the mystery of a flat mountainless (its sadness, its sweetness) farmland." It draws on his own memory of the farm landscape surrounding Albert Lea, which he visited at least twice as a boy. With the oblique precision of a dream, the story relates the meeting between a country woman and a strange man, just arriving in town, whom she would marry—a transposed version, perhaps, of James's own parents' meeting in Albert Lea in 1921, and/or that of his maternal grandparents in 1887.

The name Schuyler (pronounced "SKY-ler") is of Dutch origin. The Schuyler family were early seventeenth-century settlers of New Netherland, and prominent in New York State before, during, and after the Revolutionary War, lending their name to a number of localities and geographical features. New York State alone has a town of Schuyler, a Schuyler County, Schuyler Lake, and Schuylerville, and there are other Schuyler place-names in the Midwest.

The history of the Schuylers in America begins with two brothers, Philip (1628–1683) and David Pieterse Schuyler (1636–1690), who immigrated from the Netherlands sometime before 1650. After landing in New Amsterdam, they both moved up the Hudson River, became fur traders, and helped establish the city of Albany. By the mid-eighteenth century, the descendants of both Schuyler brothers were wealthy landowners who in some cases exercised almost feudal manorial rights over their extensive properties. The famous General Philip Schuyler (1733–1804), the Revolutionary War hero and member of the Constitutional Congress and one of New York State's first senators, was a descendant of the older brother, Philip. His daughters, Elizabeth Schuyler Hamilton and Angelica Schuyler Church, were celebrated for their beauty, wit, and style. Elizabeth married Alexander Hamilton, the first secretary of the Treasury, while Angelica married a member of the British Parliament and was close to Franklin, Jefferson, and Lafayette. These historic family associations stirred James Schuyler's imagination, especially during his difficult adolescence, despite the fact that (as he may or may not have realized) he was descended not from Philip but his younger brother.

David Pieterse Schuyler was in Schenectady at the time of the Schenectady Massacre of February 8, 1690, when a band of French and Mohawk and Algonquin soldiers invaded what was then a small frontier fort, killing sixty people and taking twenty-seven back to Canada as prisoners. He escaped home to Albany but died there two days later, apparently of injuries sustained in the attack. Over the next several generations his descendants gradually emigrated westward across the state and into the Midwest.

David Pieterse's four times great-grandson, James Marcus Schuyler—James Schuyler's grandfather—was born in Syracuse in 1854, shortly before his parents moved west to a farm in Bremer County, Iowa, where he grew up. At age twenty-six he married Sarah Pound Brock, twenty-two and already a widow. Their son, Marcus James Schuyler, the poet's father, was born on a farm near Ottumwa, Iowa, on October 30, 1881. James Marcus died sometime around 1900, and in about 1907, Sarah married her third husband, Edward C. Pease, and moved with him and young Marcus to Ravenden, Arkansas. Pease died some decades later, and in January 1935, Sarah, at about seventy-nine years old, married her fourth husband, James Riddle, age seventy. She died in 1937, bequeathing her farm in Arkansas to her grandson. The money that James Schuyler realized from the sale of the farm enabled him to live in Italy for two years, a life-changing experience.

All too little is known about the poet's father. Marcus's childhood and youth on his parents' Iowa farm in the 1880s and '90s was probably not that different from Hamlin Garland's Iowa boyhood some twenty years earlier: a life of grueling work in a hard climate, amid stark natural beauty. Like many homesteaders, the Schuyler family moved frequently in search of better farming conditions. In 1885, when Marcus was three, they lived in Butler County, Iowa; by 1900 they had moved to Garfield County, Oklahoma, where Marcus, age eighteen, was still working on the farm. But sometime after his father's death and his mother's remarriage in 1907, Marcus left home and learned the printing trade. By 1913, he and his first wife, Effie, were living in Tulsa, Oklahoma, where Marcus was a printer on the local paper. Shortly after this, either the marriage failed or Effie died, and Marcus spent the next decade crisscrossing the Midwest from newspaper to newspaper. Sometime before May 1921, he moved to Albert Lea, Minnesota, where he got a job with the *Albert Lea Examiner.* There he met and married a vivacious local woman named Margaret Connor.

Named, with Midwestern pragmatism, after the surveyor who laid out the region in 1835, Albert Lea lies about ninety miles south of Minneapolis, just twelve miles north of the Iowa border. In the late nineteenth and early twentieth centuries, it was a market, meat-packing, and small-manufacturing center for the surrounding farm country, and the town, attractively sited at the junction of two lakes, continues to be a local hub.

Margaret Connor's grandfather John Slater was one of the town's early settlers and the patriarch of a large family. Born in Colne, England, in 1819, he came to the United States with his wife, Ann, and six children in 1854. By 1859, they had made their way to Albert Lea and established a homestead of 160 acres about two miles north of the center of the town. Four more children were born to the couple after their arrival in America, making ten in all, of whom eight survived to adulthood.

Ella Slater, James Schuyler's beloved granny Ella, was born in Albert Lea on October 29, 1863. She was the ninth child, the youngest to survive childhood, and a full generation younger than her oldest sibling, her sister Margaret, who had been born in England in 1843. At the time of Ella's birth Margaret was still unmarried and living at home, and over the next five years she helped their mother in caring for Ella, toward whom she always remained strongly attached and protective. In 1868, Margaret Slater married another Albert Lea farmer from England, John Godley. Godley prospered, eventually branching out into banking, and built a substantial house on the shore of Lake Albert Lea, which he named Linden Terrace. Although she died when James Schuyler was a toddler, Aunt Margaret's memory was regularly evoked in his mother's and grandmother's stories, through which she became a vividly imagined presence in James's childhood.

In 1878, John Slater and several neighboring farmers met to establish a new elementary school district for their area, and the following year sixteen-year-old Ella Slater became the new district's first teacher. She continued to teach there until 1887, when she married Frederick Connor, a young Englishman, recently arrived in this country and working as a hired hand on her father's farm.

James Schuyler never visited England, but he was a lifelong Anglophile. That was mostly due to his love of English literature, history, architecture, art, and gardens, but he also knew that his immediate forebears on his mother's side were English and Irish. Among his mother's keepsakes was a pair of yellowed *carte-de-visite* photographs showing a man in clerical dress and his wife, who were said to be Frederick Connor's parents. Family tradition held that Reverend Connor had been the vicar of no less a church than St. Martin-in-the-Fields in central London. The facts were slightly other.

Frederick Connor's father, Richard George Connor, was born in Dublin in 1806, earned his MA from Trinity College in 1832, and immigrated to England a few years later. By 1856, he was the chaplain of the St. Martin-in-the-Fields workhouse and almshouse located in Camden Town, far from the main church in Trafalgar Square. He and his wife, Elizabeth, both then aged fifty, were childless. The household also included a young servant, Jane Sheam, a farmer's daughter, age twenty-three. But Elizabeth died in 1862, and at some point a sexual relationship, consensual or not, developed between the chaplain and his much younger servant, and she became pregnant. Remarkably, on September 19, 1864, Rev. Connor, at age fifty-eight, married his servant Jane Sheam, age thirty-one and about six months pregnant.

The couple's first son, also named Richard George Connor, was born on December 6, 1864, but for appearances' sake, he was not baptized until ten months after the wedding. A second son, Frederick, James Schuyler's grandfather, was born to the couple on December 21, 1865. Seventeen months later, Rev. Connor died at (ca.) age sixty-one, leaving a young widow and two infant sons.

As a former servant who had married her employer, but now a clergyman's widow, Jane Connor's social position in mid-Victorian England would have been anomalous, even if it was not widely realized that her elder son had been conceived out of wedlock. It appears that after her husband's death she returned to live with her own family on their farm somewhere in the country.

As they reached the age of ten, Jane sent both Richard and Frederick to be educated at the Clergy Orphan School (now St. Edmund's School) in Canterbury, where they each stayed for about six years, absorbing to the best of their abilities the standard Classical education of the time, based on the study of Ancient Greek and Latin. Most of their classmates, all sons of deceased clergymen, were being educated to go to university and follow in their fathers' footsteps.

After his infancy in London and childhood spent on a farm, Frederick had arrived at a boarding school where he was, putatively, on equal social footing with other clergymen's sons. To their fellow students, Frederick and his brother may have seemed like country bumpkins, even assuming no one at the school ever discovered that their mother had once been "in service." And yet after six years of education among other young "gentlemen," Frederick may have felt equally out of place returning to his mother's family. It is hardly surprising that he decided to emigrate to the supposedly classless New World. In March 1882, at sixteen years of age, but claiming to be seventeen, Frederick took a steerage passage for New York on the Belgian ship *Rhynland*. He landed in New York on March 20.

It is not clear just when or why Frederick Connor made his way to Albert Lea, but it must have been reassuring for him to discover English farmers already there, and naturally he gravitated to them. According to family lore, he was working as a hired hand on the Slater farm when he met Ella Slater. Hired farmhands in the late nineteenth century were generally a rough, uncouth, and migratory lot and Frederick Connor would have stood out as a conspicuous exception to the rule. Charming and red-haired and fresh from England, with elements of what the Slaters and the Godleys would have recognized as an educated accent and gentlemanly manners, he won the heart of twenty-four-year-old Ella Slater. The couple were married on December 6, 1887, against the strong objections of Ella's father. They leased a farm in Albert Lea and bore three children, including Margaret Daisy, known in the family as "Maney," who would be the poet James Schuyler's mother.

Unfortunately, Frederick Connor was not successful as a farmer in the harsh and unfamiliar climate of Minnesota. In the fall of 1894, discouraged and apparently in debt, Frederick abandoned his wife and three young children and returned to England. Ella swallowed her pride and followed him, taking four-year-old Margaret with her. Margaret retained vague memories of the trip, which included a meeting with Frederick's younger half sister, Daisy, her namesake, and a visit to Windsor Castle.

Thinking herself unsuccessful in her mission to bring back her husband, Ella returned with Margaret to the United States alone in November 1894. But to her surprise, as family tradition has it, Frederick had actually been a stowaway on the same ship. Unfortunately, their reconciliation in Albert Lea did not last, and by the fall of 1895, Frederick was living apart from his family. On the night of Saturday, November 16, he appeared at a friend's house in a distraught state and asked to sleep in the granary. In the morning he was found dead there curled up on some blankets. He had committed suicide by drinking liquid morphine. He was twenty-nine years old. His daughter Margaret was five.

Throughout James Schuyler's childhood, his grandfather's suicide was never spoken of in the family. His second cousin Ruth Blunt did not learn of it until she was an adult; his half brother Fredric Ridenour did not know of it until his wife, Hilde, began to research the family tree, and it is unlikely that James ever knew the details of his grandfather's suicide.

First abandoned, now widowed at age thirty-two, Ella and her three small children returned to the family farm to keep house for her now widowed father. Her older sister Margaret stepped in to help raise Ella's children as she had earlier helped raise Ella herself. Margaret and John Godley's only son had died in infancy, and their surviving child, their daughter Anna, was grown and living away from home. With a big empty house on the lake, Margaret Godley was well placed to help her sister, and always took a special interest in her namesake, Margaret Connor.

John Slater died in 1901, and bequeathed Ella half of his original homestead, an 80-acre farm adjacent to his own. As soon as he was old enough to do so, her oldest son, Ralston, left school in order to work full-time on the farm. Margaret Godley's granddaughter Ruth Blunt recalled that Ralston, or Rally, was "truly a *wonderful* person" and "was quite young to take charge of [his mother's farm], but he did . . . He was always full of fun and neighboring farmers enjoyed, as well as respected him. I'm sure that the years that he and Aunt Ella lived on that farm together were among the happiest in her life."

James Schuyler's relationship with his mother was never easy, especially after his adolescence. Yet they were close at times, sharing a love of literature and nature. His last long poem, "A few days," begun while he was staying with her and she was in failing health, closes (later, in New York) with the news of her death at the age of ninety. Over the years she seems to have told him comparatively little of her life before her marriage to Marcus Schuyler. In some ways she seems almost to have been a different person then from the often stern and judgmental figure James knew.

While family pressures, and his own temperament, influenced Ralston's decision to cut short his schooling to run the farm, it was Margaret who had the aptitude, ambition, and opportunity for higher education. From her high school years through college, she stayed long periods in town with her aunt Margaret and uncle John Godley at Linden Terrace. Theirs was a cultivated and literate household, where learning was valued, and where, as Ruth Blunt recalled, "Dickens and Thackeray were read aloud in the evenings." At a time when college and, especially, postgraduate education for women was still somewhat unusual, the Godley family already had a tradition of it: Margaret Godley's daughter, Anna, graduated from Albert Lea College in 1891, served for three years as Dean of Women and professor of English at Buena Vista College, in Storm Lake, Iowa, and went on to complete a graduate degree at the University of Chicago in 1897.

Margaret Connor graduated from Albert Lea High School in 1908. After teaching for a year in the elementary school where Ella had taught, she enrolled in Albert Lea College, a small Presbyterian women's college, graduating with a BA in 1913. Margaret entered enthusiastically into the life of the college, where she took part in various clubs. Dubbed "Muggie" or "Muggs" by her classmates, she was known for her outgoing, demonstrative manner: a limerick written by a fellow graduate in the college yearbook includes the couplet, "There once was a senior named Mug, / Who was great on the kiss and the hug."

By 1916, Margaret had moved to Chicago, where the following year she was hired as a secretary in the Chicago office of the U.S. Food Administration, a branch of the Federal Trade Commission established on America's entry into World War I to oversee food production and distribution.

Chicago in the first quarter of the twentieth century was astir with political and artistic ferment. Here Margaret Connor developed a strong political awareness, due at least in part to the influence of her immediate employer, Stuart Chase. In 1917, Chase was an accountant and public administrator at the start of a long and illustrious career in public service and scholarship. Later a well-known economist and semanticist, and an advisor to Franklin D. Roosevelt, he coined the phrase "New Deal." On coming to Chicago from Boston in 1916, he worked for six months at Jane Addams's Hull House before going to the FTC. Chase and his wife, Margaret Hatfield Chase, his associate, Samuel W. Tator, and Samuel's wife, Irmagarde, all became friends with their bright, attractive contemporary Margaret Connor.

In January 1918, Chase organized a meeting at the Chicago Theater at which Jane Addams and the anarchist Lincoln Steffens both spoke, and Margaret was there, as she later told her son. Chase started the Chicago Fabian Club, which, like the original Fabian Society in England, was a place where people met to discuss socialism and Marxism; it's likely Margaret attended a talk there by Chase's friend and Harvard classmate John Reed.

Chase also stepped in as director of the Radical Book Shop, a famous meeting place for young political activists, poets, and writers from its founding in 1914 through the 1920s. After it was raided by the government in 1917, Chase reorganized its ownership and issued shares of stock, which he distributed to associates and friends, including Margaret. Sherwood Anderson, whose paintings were exhibited there in 1920, characterized the Radical Book Shop as "a hangout for political, religious and philosophical radicals." The young poet Kenneth Rexroth wrote of taking part there in "long discussions about that Revolution which then seemed so near . . . All day long the bookshop was a hotbed of argument." Given her growing political interests, her outgoing nature, her aspirational friendship with the Chases and the Tators, and the fact that she carefully saved her stock certificate among her keepsakes, it is likely that Margaret also took part in the shop's discussions and activities.

Like Jane Addams and some other early feminists, Margaret held antimilitaristic and pacifist views during World War I, and she faced expulsion from her Chicago rooming house for her principled refusal to knit socks for soldiers fighting in the war. Learning of this, Irma Tator wrote to suggest that she move in with them. The tone of the letter and its domestic details makes clear the warm friendship that had sprung up among the Tators, the Chases, and Margaret.

Margaret's job for the Food Administration ended with the Armistice in November 1918, but her interest in progressive politics and public policy remained. From December 1918 to spring 1919, she was the office manager for the newly founded Labor Party of Cook County, and managed the campaign of the party's candidate, John Fitzpatrick, in the six-way race for mayor of Chicago. The incumbent, Republican William "Big Bill" Thompson, finally won the closely watched election in April 1919, but Fitzpatrick's third-place result was considered something of a victory for the new party.

After the election, Margaret followed the Chases and the Tators to Washington, DC, where she worked for about two years as a secretary and publicist for the Farmers' National Council, a left-leaning lobbying group affiliated with the National Farmer Labor Co-operative Association. She also stayed politically active outside of work. In August 1920, the Nineteenth Amendment to the U.S. Constitution was finally ratified by Congress, giving women the right to vote. Six months before final ratification, the League of Women Voters was established as a nonpartisan forum to promote open discussion of current political issues. Margaret immediately joined the League and became an active member.

In December 1920, Stuart Chase was fired from the FTC as a result of intense right-wing machinations against him (and Samuel Tator), and in 1921 he moved to New York. Sometime during the first part of 1921, Margaret also left her job at the Farmers' National Council and returned to Albert Lea. It is hard to avoid the inference that she left because Chase, a man she clearly admired and on whom she may have had more than a crush, had gone. Her engagement and marriage, soon after her return to Albert Lea, to her next employer, Marcus Schuyler, another passionate crusader for social justice, has some of the earmarks of a relationship formed on the rebound.

The first half of the twentieth century was a golden age for American newspapers. In fiction and in countless movies of the 1920s, '30s, and '40s, images of newsrooms and reporters were an exciting staple of popular culture. Small local newspapers proliferated in the 1920s, and a town like Albert Lea, with a population of 8,056 in 1920, supported one local daily paper, the *Evening Tribune*, in addition to four weekly newspapers of various stripes, not to mention the fact that many in the town also read one or more of the Minneapolis papers. Most local papers were frankly partisan and combined national and international news and opinion with local affairs. Many of the writers of the Chicago Renaissance of the late teens and '20s, including Sinclair Lewis, Sherwood Anderson, and Theodore Dreiser, or later writers such as Ernest Hemingway, got their start writing for newspapers in Chicago or the Midwest. Marcus J. Schuyler's position as a Midwestern newspaper editor in the early 1920s puts him in illustrious, evocative company.

The *Albert Lea Examiner* was founded in December 1919 as a weekly aligned with the Farmer-Labor Party, a leftist political party prominent in Minnesota and the Midwest at the time. The (rather convoluted) motto of the paper was "If you are wrong you can't be too conservative; if you are right you can't be too radical." Judging from frequent pleas to its readers to support the paper's advertisers, its finances were never secure, which may have had something to do with the fact that it went through four editors in the first fifteen months of its existence. Finally, with the issue of May 26, 1921, "M. J. Schuyler" appears on the masthead as editor. Marcus Schuyler remained the editor (and later publisher) of the *Examiner* for at least a year and a half, much longer than any of his predecessors. Most of what little we know about Marcus Schuyler comes from whatever can be inferred from his writings in the *Albert Lea Examiner*.

James's memories of his father were few, but he recalled him as a "heavy, jolly, well-read man." The single surviving photograph of him shows a rather portly, rumpled figure with a bow tie and a happy smile, and seems to bear out the first two adjectives. That he was also "well-read" can be confirmed from his lively and opinionated literary references in *Examiner* articles and editorials. Most of Marcus's editorials are passionate, not to say overheated, statements of liberal positions on the political topics of the day. While national and international issues were addressed, most editorials were on issues specific to Minnesota or the Midwest, where there was a strong tradition of labor activism. On the editorial page in August 1921, Schuyler is vehement on many topics, among them the proposed new Minnesota sales tax: "There is no camafloge [*sic*] about the sales tax, it is a direct and unevasive shifting from the rich the rich man [*sic*] to the poor." In all his writings, Marcus Schuyler comes across as a wholehearted espouser of liberal causes, often lost ones, at times showing a wry, outraged sense of humor, although his angry, indignant tone can also seem over the top.

Marcus was quick to take up arms against literary as well as political reactionaries, and came to the defense of Sinclair Lewis and Sherwood Anderson, among others. On November 10, 1921, he praised *The Minnesota Daily Star* for having the courage to serialize Sinclair Lewis's *Main Street* in its pages, writing, "Smug citizens will be often shocked and sometimes grieven; the radicals will chortle with glee at the clear exposition of conditions that they long knew existed. *Main Street* may make you laugh, it may make you sore, and it may even make you cry, but there is one thing certain no matter how you react to Lewis' narrative—it will make you think—that is if your brain is not totally atrophied." His political views colored his literary ones, and he had a particular loathing of the then very popular but imperialistic Rudyard Kipling, a "jingler, and exploiter of trite slang," whom in one editorial he compared unfavorably with Twain, Harte, and "the peerless stylish Stevenson, whose pure, limpid and understandable English rolls out with the quiet force of some clear and mighty stream."

While the *Examiner*'s news articles and editorials often focused on anti-imperialist struggles in postwar Europe and labor issues at home, the paper was also very much a local, small-town miscellany. Not being a longtime resident, Marcus announced in a June 1921 issue that the paper was looking for new contributors of local news. Under the heading "News Writers Wanted," he wrote, "The Examiner wants to get news correspondents in every part of Freeborn County . . . What do you know about the happenings in your neighborhood? Has anyone died, eloped, been divorced, embezzled something, left the country, someone new moved in, had a fire, had a baby . . . sold a farm, been arrested . . . Well . . . sit right down and [write about] the happenings of your neighborhood and send them in to the Examiner."

Once she moved back to Albert Lea in early 1921, it wouldn't have taken Margaret Connor long to become aware of the *Examiner*, allied as it was with the Farmer-Labor Party she had been working for in Washington. Undoubtedly, she saw Marcus's call for contributions of local-interest news, and soon the paper was featuring social notes connected to her own family and friends, such as a tea party at Linden Terrace, or travels of the extended Slater family. But Margaret's talents, skills, and experience went beyond the social sphere, as Marcus soon realized, and she was hired as city editor of the *Examiner* in October 1921. In the short announcement of her hiring, Marcus Schuyler wrote, "Miss Connor brings to her work wide experience as a writer and a keen knowledge of economics that will prove a valuable asset to the Examiner."

By February 9, 1922, Marcus had apparently bought the paper, for the masthead on that date reads: "Published by M. J. Schuyler Editor; Margaret Connor City Editor." Two weeks later, on February 23, an equal partnership was announced: "Published and Edited by M. J. Schuyler and Margaret Connor." A month after that, Margaret and Marcus were married, and from the March 30 issue until the paper's demise eight months later the masthead read, "Published and Edited by M. and M. J. Schuyler."

When Margaret Connor and Marcus Schuyler married, he was forty and she thirty-one; they had known each other for about six months. What was Marcus's attraction for Margaret? The fact that he was "jolly" and "well-read" would have had strong appeal to "Muggs." And from Marcus's writings in the *Examiner*, one can sense his passion for social justice, which must have reminded Margaret of what she had admired in her friend Stuart Chase. After their marriage the pair continued to write, edit, and publish the *Examiner* together through most of the year. But sometime in November 1922, before they had been married eight months, the paper failed financially.

In later recollections Schuyler referred to his father as a "compulsive gambler" and believed that this failing led to his "losing his paper" and eventually to his parents' divorce in 1929. Whether Marcus or the newspaper declared bankruptcy in 1922 is not clear, nor is it clear how much of the blame for the paper's failure can be put to Marcus's gambling problem, and how much to the paper's perennial money shortage.

In mid-1923, Marcus and Margaret moved to Chicago. Losing the paper and leaving Albert Lea under a cloud of financial embarrassment less than a year into her marriage must have been a moment of bitter realization for Margaret—especially painful and shaming if her husband's obsessive gambling was the cause. If so, no doubt he made fervent promises of reformed behavior. Very likely it was Margaret who pushed for moving to Chicago, a city she knew well and had been happy in, and we can be pretty sure she was the dominant force in the relationship from this point on. Adding to both her anxiety for the future and her native optimism, as they left Albert Lea for Chicago, was the fact that she was pregnant.

[2]

LOVER'S LEAP LOST / ITS ROMANCE

1923–1935

Margaret and Marcus moved to Chicago in the summer or early fall of 1923, renting an apartment at 7261 Harvard Avenue, near Hamilton Park and the university. Marcus got a job with one of the local newspapers.

Their son, James Marcus Schuyler, was born at Auburn Park Hospital, at 7:20 in the morning, November 9, 1923. A "Baby Book," lovingly filled out by his mother, tells almost more than we want to know about James Schuyler's development in his first eighteen months—a life crowded with incident, indeed. He weighed a whopping 10 pounds at birth and was 19½ inches long. Jimmie (as his mother called him) had blue eyes, which changed later to brown, and reddish brown hair. At eleven weeks he "discovered hands." At sixteen weeks he could "sit up straight with back unsupported" and indulged in "much vocal exercise." At eighteen weeks he "observes color" and "yells to be taken."

James was a cheerful baby with a happy disposition who "always smiled! When he was three months he would laugh heartily." One is moved by the thought of this hearty infantine laughter, which seems of a piece with the deep, spontaneous laughter his friends knew later, and the ubiquitous laughter that would become, as one poet recalled, the characteristic medium in which New York School friendships and gatherings were lived. His favorite foods, his mother noted, were: "All foods!"

An early indication of Margaret's firm hand, and James's equally firm resistance, came at the age of six months, when he first said "Mamma"—"but was discouraged as his mother wanted him to say 'Mother.'" As a result, he refused to call her by name at all for nearly a year, and then at seventeen months called her "Mine." "At 15 months he called his Daddy 'Schuy,' the same as his mother did."

In the late summer or fall of 1924, when James was still under a year old, the family moved to Downers Grove, a suburb about twenty-five miles west of Chicago. James Schuyler stated in several interviews that Marcus edited and published his own newspaper in Downers Grove, but he was clearly confusing that with the earlier *Albert Lea Examiner*. Records show that the town's single newspaper, the *Downers Grove Reporter*, was neither owned nor edited by Marcus Schuyler.

"My earliest memory is of my father killing a snake on our front stoop. It was a big black snake, perfectly harmless I assume. It writhed and writhed and he kept hitting it and hitting it with a shovel. I was two at the time." James Schuyler's memories of Downers Grove, like most early childhood memories, are small and specific, and it is likely that in some cases they were stimulated or reinforced by snapshots he saw later. He incorporated some of these childhood memories into the posthumously published poem "Snapshot," and also refers to family snapshots in a short unpublished prose sketch in which he returned to some of the same images: "My mother's name was Daisy. She was beautiful with long brown shining hair. Somewhere there is a snapshot of me in my Indian suit and my mother seated on a low stool, drying her long hair in the sun. She wore it in a *chignon* on the nape of her neck." "My father's name was Marcus James Schuyler but he was always called Sky." "I also remember him cranking the car and getting awfully angry (which he almost never did) when the meter would not turn over. It was a black touring car."

The interlude in Downers Grove lasted about two years. By the summer of 1926, Margaret was already contemplating the drastic step of leaving Marcus. In August, she applied for admission as a graduate student in the Law School of the University of Chicago for the fall 1926 term. On the application she gave her "Permanent Address" as Linden Terrace, while she gave her mailing address as "General Delivery, Downers Grove, Ill" (rather than their home address). The selective job history

Margaret put down also omitted any reference to her work as city editor on the *Albert Lea Examiner*. That fall, Margaret returned to Albert Lea, taking James with her, to visit Ella and stay with Ruth Countermine Blunt, who had inherited Linden Terrace on Margaret Godley's death that year. The timing suggests that this may have been a temporary or trial separation from Marcus. Margaret was accepted into law school, but she never enrolled; she and Marcus reconciled, but only temporarily, as it would turn out.

The choice of Washington, DC, as the city for their new start must have been Margaret's, as a place she knew well and where she had friends. Initially, Marcus moved to Washington alone in 1927, while Margaret and Jimmy stayed in Albert Lea, but by 1928 the family was reunited and living at 114 F Street SE. Marcus was working as either a printer or a copy editor on a newspaper. James Schuyler was later under the impression that this was *The Washington Post*, but circumstantial reasons suggest it was more likely to have been the rival *Washington Times*.

Fronting directly onto the attractive, tree-shaded Garfield Park, 114 F Street SE is a narrow, two-story, late nineteenth-century row house in a pleasant Capitol Hill neighborhood. The house was probably divided into floor-through flats when the Schuyler family lived there. The elementary school where James would start kindergarten in the fall was in the next block of F Street, also facing the park. It was an ideal situation, and there was every reason for the family to be happy and thrive there.

In about 1928 (from the context, perhaps Palm Sunday, April 1), James had what he considered his first visionary religious experience, when a woman named Mabel took him to a Catholic church service for the first time. The "vision," as he attempted to describe it later in two poems, was fleeting, moving like haze or "an arrow" in his heart, leaving him with only a vague memory of "a room where all was gray," but with it a profound and lasting sense of mystery and the power of grace. When they got home, his father asked, memorably but to Margaret's pious indignation, "Did the / priest come riding in on his ass?" The *double entendre*, the only known direct quote of Marcus's speech, begins to suggest the irreverent wit of his personality.

Another of James Schuyler's most vivid memories of his early childhood in Washington, which he described at length many years later in "The Morning of the Poem," was a trip he took with his mother to visit her friends the Golds on their farm in rural Virginia. At the farm, James swam naked in a brook with another little boy, watched men rebuilding a barn, helped feed chickens and pigs, watched as cream was skimmed from milk and then made into "the very best" homemade ice cream, enjoyed Virginia Gold's blueberry muffins, and went on an expedition "up a hot dusty road" with some farm women, who, in the late 1920s, still wore old-fashioned sun bonnets, to gather wild pokeweed, which was later cooked and eaten with fried ham. At the end of the visit, Mr. Gold, in his Model T, drove Jimmy and his mother to the train back to the city.

On August 27, 1928, tragedy struck the Connor family in Albert Lea when Margaret's older brother Ralston died at thirty-nine from injuries sustained in a grisly accident on his farm. Deeply mourned by his family and the community, he was described in a newspaper account as "one of the most successful farmers of the county [who] operated a fine farm in which he took a great pride and had hosts of friends both in the city and the country." Ella was stoic, writing to Margaret: "Shall we, darling, be *willing* to let him go? believing that he knows and understands. I feel that it is all right with him and I know comfort will come to us as it always has to me . . . I am glad you have Schuy and Jimmie to comfort you." Shortly after this she wrote to her young grandson, noting that he, Jimmy, was lucky to have both his mother and his father.

Unfortunately, that would soon change. Within the year, Marcus's gambling problem had reasserted itself. Working late nights at the paper, he would play poker with his cronies before going home. What most infuriated Margaret was his habit of borrowing money from her friends to make up his losses. During the summer of 1929, a season of tears and recriminations, the couple separated and Marcus moved out. Very likely Margaret had exacted promises of good behavior from Marcus as a condition of rejoining him in Washington in 1927. When he relapsed, Margaret was unforgiving and contemptuous. Marcus was reduced to tears by his own shame and remorse, combined with the scolding of his wife and the resulting breakup of his family. For the five-and-a-half-year-old Jimmy, it was deeply disturbing to see his father crying as his mother "taunted" him for what she termed his "weakness."

At some point that summer, Marcus unexpectedly appeared and took Jimmy out of school or away from home. The details, including Marcus's intentions, are unclear, but Jimmy was left with a memory of riding on a streetcar with his father until they were apprehended and he was removed from the streetcar by the police. His confused impressions of the incident were alluded to in a (posthumously published) poem about his father, entitled "Heroic Shape," which seems also to reach back still earlier to Jimmy's first childhood memory of his father, with its cryptic reference to the snake that he killed, suggesting that even to the very young Jimmy his father's behavior and words seemed irrational:

> Then, in the asexual embrace of a summer
> trolley (the conductor trailed his foot
> swinging along the footboard: clink, clink:
> dimes and tokens) it seemed under a boy's
> beret you said about warming a cold snake.
> How black you were in that white, white city.
> Since, many springs flower-fruit the wisteria
> on the passing wall, and lover's leap lost
> its romance, but you, black, black, still
> speak of the snake in sparks and clangings.

This disturbing episode must have confirmed Margaret's resolve to file for divorce, as she did on September 20, 1929, on grounds of "desertion." She was granted sole custody and child support of $12.50 a week. The divorce agreement contained a clause enjoining the defendant (Mark Schuyler) from "molesting the plaintiff and said infant child and from interfering and intermeddling with the care, custody and control of said child."

James Schuyler, in later interviews, attributed his parents' marital difficulties to his father's gambling habit, a succinct explanation for Margaret to have given him when he was a little older, and no doubt a true one, whether or not additional problems existed. Medical opinion is divided on whether pathological gambling should be considered an "addiction" similar to chemical addiction, or an impulse control disorder, relating it to other mental disorders such as schizophrenia. Dr. Edmund Bergler, best known for controversial views on homosexuality, linked gambling addiction to masochism: the gambler wants to lose. Certainly Marcus Schuyler lost all that he held most dear: his family, his newspaper, and no doubt many jobs along the way, due to his gambling disorder.

The divorce of his parents, which Jimmy experienced as a series of tearful confrontations followed by his father's disappearance (and the strange episode on the streetcar), was deeply traumatic, of course, but at the time, as we would say now, he "internalized" it. This response would become a pattern throughout his life: to withdraw into himself, into silence and passivity, in the face of trauma or adversity. When, later in life, James Schuyler occasionally spoke or wrote about his childhood in Washington after the divorce, he said virtually nothing about the divorce itself or its effect on him as a very young child. But once or twice he revealed that he actually thought of it as a defining event, tracing his future mental ills back to the divorce: "To be children of a broken home is bad news: ask me—six mental hospitals . . ."

By November 1932, Marcus was living in Baltimore and working as a proofreader. Soon after that he moved back to the Midwest and resumed his peripatetic ways. He died from a heart attack in June 1942 at the age of fifty-nine, in the pressroom of the *Jackson* (Michigan) *Citizen Patriot*. Jimmy may never have seen him after the divorce was finalized and Margaret remarried. As he grew up, his biological father became an increasingly distant figure, but a correspondingly potent abstraction. During his difficult adolescence his absent father's image provided a counterforce to his uncongenial and all-too-present stepfather in at least two ways: as a writer and journalist, whom he could look to as a role model when he became interested in writing himself, and as the bearer and bestower of a historic and glamorous name (meaningful especially in New York State, where Jimmy then lived). In relations between Jimmy and his mother, Marcus took on a different kind of invisible presence: a pathetic failure in whose footsteps Margaret at times clearly feared her son would follow. The very timing of Marcus's sad and lonely death, at a time when Jimmy was flunking out of college, seemed designed to underline her fears, and possibly his own, of some sort of unspecified "weakness" of character inherited from Marcus.

In the fall of 1929, when Jimmy was five, Margaret and he moved across the city to an apartment in the Valley Vista apartment house at 2032 Belmont Road NW, near Rock Creek. This was a tonier area than F Street, with a slightly suburban feeling: winding leafy streets, big brick houses standing in spacious yards, and along Connecticut Avenue a series of dignified apartment buildings such as the Valley Vista. The contrast in surroundings reinforced Margaret's sense of a break from her old life with Marcus. Ella, lonely and at loose ends in Albert Lea, came out from Minnesota to be with Margaret and Jimmy at this time and lived with them for the next several years.

After the wrenching loss of his father, preceded by puzzling and painful domestic scenes, Jimmy was solaced and distracted by the presence of his grandmother. In interviews, while he never spoke directly about the emotional effect of his parents' divorce, he did always mention the beneficent presence of his "gentle Grandma Ella" in his life at this time. A former schoolteacher, she was able to engage the boy's curiosity to his (and our) lasting benefit. She read aloud to him, and taught him about the natural world: Schuyler credited his lifelong sensitivity to plants and birds to Ella's influence: ". . . 'those / birds,' she / would have said, / 'are starlings. / They came from / England.' Or / 'This is a / monarch butter-/ fly.'"

He later described her as a "wrinkled woman who wore a cloche hat in two shades of velvet; who taught me the Lord's Prayer . . . who would not kill a living thing—except butterflies: those by the legion, arranged on cotton wool in silk stocking boxes; who taught me how to multiply when nobody else could; who took me to a creek in Chevy Chase to see a touch-me-not in bloom, and, later to see it again and experience what happens when you touch the pod and the miraculous ejaculation of the seed; and more, so much, much more."

Ella's literary taste was grounded in the classics of nineteenth-century fiction and poetry. In Schuyler's poem "Quick, Henry, the Flit," there is a reference to Ella reading James the traditional English ballad "Chevy Chase" and part of Sir Walter Scott's *Ivanhoe* out of *Journeys Through Bookland*, a popular ten-volume illustrated anthology of excerpts from the then-accepted canon of great literature, suitable for reading to children. That volume also included poems by Wordsworth, Whittier, Tennyson, Longfellow, Amy Lowell, James Whitcomb Riley, and Alexander Pope, and prose excerpts by Hawthorne, de Quincey, Dickens, Irving, Cardinal Newman, Virgil, and Homer, among others. James had an unusually receptive mind and his early exposure to these works, superficial as it was, laid a foundation for his lifelong love of English literature, as well as contributing in certain ways to his self-image. Blending in unconscious memory, perhaps, with the direct experience of natural phenomena under Ella's tutelage, would have been his identification with the eponymous boy of John Greenleaf Whittier's "The Barefoot Boy," with his:

> Knowledge never learned of schools,
> Of the wild bee's morning chase.
> Of the wild flower's time and place,
> Flight of fowl and habitude
> Of the tenants of the wood;
> How the tortoise bears his shell,
> How the woodchuck digs his cell,
> And the ground-mole sinks his well

The issue of "boyishness" would be a subtheme of Schuyler's novel of childhood, *Alfred and Guinevere*, in which the quieter Alfred is led astray by the naughty Stanley, who incites Alfred to go swimming in Rock Creek and starts a fire, and which mentions the Ernest Thompson Seton novels of woodcraft. Boyishness would eventually become a fraught subject in relations with his stepfather, Berton, and by extension his half brother. Later it would crop up in a quite different way with his friend and fellow poet Frank O'Hara, with whom he would exchange poems touching on the subject in the 1950s.

In addition to awakening him to literature and natural beauty, Ella took him to museums: the Freer Gallery of Art, the Corcoran Gallery of Art, the Smithsonian Institution, and the Natural History Museum. He had his first direct exposure to the art of painting at the Corcoran Gallery, which was filled with nineteenth-century academic works, such as Emil Renouf's *The Helping Hand*, showing a small girl ineffectually attempting to help her fisherman father ply a heavy oar, which Jimmy recalled as the first painting that stuck in his mind. The Smithsonian Museum was then a single collection housed in the current Natural History Museum building, where the jumble of disparate impressions was itself stimulating. Jimmy recalled later: "The Spirit of St. Louis, it's so small and delicate and silver like a fish, hangs over your head with the hall of the Presidents' Wives on your right and all that lace, it must be the world's greatest collection of Colt revolvers, the life of the living bee behind glass, and models: how the Chicksal [*sic*] poisons the well (with arrows) and Battles and Formations of the Great World War in Tootsie toys: 'Your Uncle Fred,' Granny said, 'was on a mine-sweeper just like that.'"

Ella had a store of old-fashioned sayings and modes of conduct derived from her Midwestern, Presbyterian background, which impressed themselves lastingly on young Jimmy. Several of her characteristics are shared by the grandmother in *Alfred and Guinevere*—the only character, Schuyler claimed, based on life. Many of the grandmother's utterances were undoubtedly actual remarks of Ella's:

"You mustn't answer a question with a question, dear."

"Nobody wants to have stories they feel they ought to hide. Secrets are very, very unpleasant . . . A secret is something you deliberately hold back. No gentleman does that."

Granny is someone with a special reverence for Sundays: a day when it is "a very bad thing" to fight or go to the movies.

"We mustn't care too much about worldly possessions. All the little Jesus child had for toys were the shavings in his father's carpentry shop."

To which the sharp little Alfred/Jimmy answers: "Does it say it in the Bible?"

One can imagine Ella's perhaps conflicting feelings as she came to be with her only daughter, whose husband had behaved badly and whom she had just divorced. Ella's own husband, of course, had also behaved badly, abandoning her with three small children, and soon thereafter had killed himself. Whether or not Ella approved of Margaret's decision to divorce her husband, she was there to support her and her grandson.

James was a sensitive child, and from the warm way he later remembered Ella, it's clear that there was great empathy between them. Jimmy was too young to understand completely what was going on, but he understood emotionally. His father had gone. His mother was unhappy, bitter, and stern. His grandmother was there, supportive and loving in ways that stirred his creative imagination, trying and perhaps only partly succeeding in concealing from him her own deep sadness at the recent death of her son. Jimmy felt the dampened intensity behind her quiet focus on birds, flowers, insects, the art and the airplanes and the First Ladies' dresses in the museums—her focus on him, in fact, but channeled through these extraneous things. Not only was his love of the natural world and of the richness of art awakened, but also a sense of how love for nature and beauty and art could embody, while holding back, deep but unspoken emotions. In all of it was a "gentle influence" which he felt and remembered for the rest of his life.

In about 1930, Margaret met Fredric Berton Ridenour, the man who would become her second husband. It is possible that they met through a couple also living at the Valley Vista Apartments, an architect named Eldred Mowery and his wife. In 1930, Eldred Mowery and Berton Ridenour, as he was known, were colleagues working on a renovation of the White House, Mowery as architect and Ridenour as construction engineer. The Mowerys, having made Margaret's acquaintance at the Valley Vista, may have indulged in a little matchmaking by introducing her to Berton, who was also divorced. Conversely, Margaret might have met Berton elsewhere, and he could have recommended the apartment building to her because his colleague already lived there.

Ridenour was born in 1892 and grew up in Washington, DC. After high school he completed various college-level courses in technical subjects, including two years of civil engineering, and had studied contract law at Columbia University Extension, but he never earned his engineering certificate. Before the onset of the Depression, this was no particular handicap, but soon it became one. However, when Berton Ridenour met Margaret Schuyler he was enjoying one of his professional high points.

The West Wing had been damaged by fire on Christmas Eve 1929, and the renovations and rebuilding took place in 1930.

Eldred Mowery was born in Minnesota and earned his MA in architecture at Harvard in 1914. His wife, Irene Ketchum, a graduate of Radcliffe, was from an "old" Massachusetts family. They had two children, a daughter, Faye, a few years older than Jimmy, and a son, Eldred Jr., a few years younger, who became his occasional playmates. The children and their parents and their whole upper-middle-class way of life exerted a strong appeal on the imagination of young Jimmy.

The Mowerys' apartment at the Valley Vista was furnished with family heirlooms and souvenirs from their European travels, including an ancient marble fragment carved with egg-and-dart decoration that sat on Eldred Sr.'s desk. It fascinated Jimmy, who believed that it came from the Parthenon, and later recalled that it was "the first image I ever had of Greece (I mean an image substantial enough to pick up in your hand)." Another prized artifact in their apartment was a carved panel from a Breton cupboard-bed showing a lady in medieval costume. The recollection of this stately figure may have contributed to his decision to give the Arthurian name of Guinevere to the girl in the novel that he later based on the Mowery children.

The precocious Mowery children both fascinated and intimidated James: they went to private schools; they had been to Europe on a ship. Although Faye Mowery in old age did not remember Jimmy, he retained memories of her and her brother, which eventually merged into a kind of wishful identification when he wrote his novel *Alfred and Guinevere* in the mid-1950s. Meeting the Mowery family at a time when his own family was so recently broken up presented an idea or ideal of family life to contrast with his own. They appeared not only stable (although this would prove deceptive) but gave off a kind of comfortably cultured aura, which Jimmy somehow recognized even at the age of six or seven, and unconsciously came to associate with emotional well-being. The Mowerys were the first of several surrogate families that James would be attracted to throughout his life, and into which, to one degree or another—usually figuratively but in one case literally—he would move. One such family, the Fairfield Porter family, was similar in certain ways to the Mowery family, which may partly explain why he reached back to this early part of his childhood for inspiration to write *Alfred and Guinevere* when he first became close to the Porters.

Directly across from the Valley Vista Apartments is a wooded area descending precipitously to the bed of Rock Creek, spanned by the Connecticut Avenue, or Taft, Bridge. Because of its height, about 136 feet above Rock Creek gorge, and the lack of tall guardrails, the Connecticut Avenue Bridge was a notorious suicide spot. One day Faye and Eldred, playing in the park beneath the bridge, came upon a recent suicide, a Black man who had jumped to his death from above. Luckily they weren't the discoverers of the body: there was already a small crowd, and they were shooed away, but it was an exciting experience that they related to Jimmy, then aged about seven, on whom it made a huge impression, all the more so for being experienced indirectly, imagined and pondered on from their description. It formed the invisible nucleus of *Alfred and Guinevere*, in which the incident is barely hinted at until being somewhat clarified in the penultimate chapter.

Alfred and Guinevere, which Schuyler began in 1954 and was published in 1958, provides some insight into the moods and undercurrents, if little or no concrete detail, of his early childhood years in Washington. The novel is a strange and brilliant hybrid: told entirely in direct conversation and in the words of Guinevere's diary and letters, its lack of external narrative or ostensible viewpoint, aside from the characters' own voices, gives it a feeling of being untethered. *Alfred and Guinevere* does not so much reveal Schuyler's childhood as conceal it—a screen of words gliding over feelings of loss and anxiety. References to divorce and family separation, as perceived (or misperceived) by young children, float over and through the seemingly soufflé-light novel. When the children's father leaves the family to go to Europe on business, it is never really clear to the children or the reader whether he is leaving permanently, a situation that echoes the family histories of both the Ridenours and the Mowerys.

Margaret and Marcus Schuyler's divorce was finalized on August 7, 1931, and on October 21 Margaret and Berton were married. Margaret and Jimmy and Ella moved into Berton's house at 4404 Stanford, a small two-story bungalow on a quiet street in Chevy Chase, Maryland. In the side yard, Berton constructed a rock garden. Jimmy, in the late poem "Three Gardens," described it in a way that suggests some of his stepfather's later harshness: "from schist / to granite to / you name it, sort of a giant hunk / of conglomerate . . . it was a *rock* garden, / a garden of rocks, but not / Kyoto style."

Berton Ridenour, the hardworking, down-to-earth construction engineer, was in some ways the antithesis of the passionate, left-wing, and, as it proved, irresponsible Marcus Schuyler, and one can understand Margaret's attraction to the kind of stability he appeared to represent. Berton, while not a political figure, was close enough to the Hoover administration that he and his family were invited to the annual White House Easter Egg Hunt in 1931, where Jimmy was photographed on the South Lawn. Margaret's political loyalties would be tested in the summer of 1932 when the Bonus Marchers' encampment on the Mall was destroyed and burned by orders of President Hoover. The Bonus Marchers, some 43,000 strong, were unemployed veterans of World War I who were demanding early redemption of their army service bonuses and had set up shantytowns in Anacostia Flats and on the Mall, vowing to remain there until their demands were met. Margaret's youngest brother, Fred, who was a WWI veteran (but not a marcher) stood to benefit once the bonuses were paid. Jimmy saw the encampment, and its destruction by fire made a lasting impression on him. For his part, Jimmy "loved" living in Washington as a boy; he was excited to know that he was in the capital of the country, and, as he later recalled, he thought "all those ugly white buildings were very beautiful."

Berton: give him credit. In marrying Margaret, he took on not only a moody stepson, but also a live-in mother-in-law. Although there were serious problems between them later, James Schuyler said that Berton Ridenour was a conscientious stepfather to him at the beginning: "When I was young, before Berton lost his money and before Fred was born, he did make a real effort to be a father to me." Ridenour had been married and divorced twice before, and the only child from his previous marriages, a son, had drowned tragically at the age of twelve. However docile and nice Jimmy apparently was as a young child, his very existence must have been both a sadness to Berton and a second chance.

In September 1930, Jimmy entered first grade. In his diary, Schuyler would later recall having received an "F in all subjects" in his early school grades, but his first-grade report card does not paint quite so dire a picture. In the first period of the fall semester, Jimmy did receive an F in reading, of all subjects, but advanced to Ds in the two grading periods that followed. On the nonacademic side, Jimmy's Cooperation, Courtesy, Industry, Promptness, Neatness, Fairness, and Thrift were all found satisfactory, but his Self-Reliance was seen to be in need of improvement. Throughout his school life, Jimmy's grades would vary widely and unpredictably, often depending less on the subject itself than on the degree of engagement a particular teacher was able to inspire in him.

Moviegoing was an early passion and would remain one to the end of Schuyler's life. Margaret was untypically lenient in allowing Jimmy to go into downtown Washington by himself to the movies for the Saturday matinees, although she always preapproved his choice. Movie houses in those early days of talkies retained elements of vaudeville in the form of live shows presented onstage before the feature film: on one especially memorable occasion Jimmy was treated to "the floor show from the Paradise nightclub in New York . . . one stately beauty after the other, each wearing feathers in her hair, a train, and a *cache-sexe*."

In 1931, Ella took Jimmy to see the recently released biopic *Alexander Hamilton*. At eight years old, Jimmy didn't get much from the movie itself, recalling it as "blueish people in costumes standing around talking to each other," but afterward, walking home with Ella, she explained to him that as a Schuyler descendant, he was related to Hamilton's wife, and thus to Hamilton himself, "in real life, and in history." This gave him the sense that he "had a name to live up to," causing "a surge of pride as we walked up the sidewalk between the yellow bricks of the Valley Vista Apartments and Rock Creek Park." Although the family relation to that branch of the Schuyler family, while real, was distant, a sense of family pride became important to the boy, having just lost his birth father, and again later in adolescence, when he was figuring out his identity in a high school and family environment that was in many ways unsympathetic.

In the fall of 1932, Jimmy entered third grade in the Chevy Chase public school. It was at this time that his last name was changed from Schuyler to Ridenour. Although, according to Schuyler, the change was never effected legally, he would be known as James Schuyler Ridenour until October 1947.

For unknown reasons, the family didn't live very long in the pleasant house at 4404 Stanford, and in 1933 they moved back across the District line to "La Reine" apartments at 5425 Connecticut Avenue. They were living there when Margaret and Berton's son, Fredric, was born on May 20, 1933. Jimmy was nine and a half years old by this time, old enough to take a measured interest in the baby as an amusing novelty, and was willingly enlisted to help watch him. Once the young Fredric had joined the family, the Connecticut Avenue apartment was too small to accommodate Ella as well, and she moved back to Albert Lea, while Margaret settled into the role of a conventional stay-at-home wife.

The Depression was in full force in the early years of Margaret and Berton's marriage and the Ridenour family did not have an easy time of it financially. Berton's employment history reflects that of the Great Depression. In 1927, his annual salary as a contractor was $11,000; from 1927 to 1934, the period during which he worked for the White House, and met and married Margaret Schuyler, he earned a minimum of $7,800 a year.

But by 1934, the construction business had been at a standstill for several years, and Berton left Chevy Chase for a desk job with the Federal Housing Administration in Buffalo, New York, at a salary of $4,600 a year. The period when Berton was alone in Buffalo job hunting may have been stressful for Jimmy, who could not have known for sure that he was coming back, a situation that is mirrored in *Alfred and Guinevere*, when the children's father goes away for an extended business trip and the children worry about a possible divorce. Happily, in 1935 Berton sent for Margaret, Jimmy, and Fredric, and the family was reunited.

[3]

THE LANDSCAPE SHIMMERED

1935–1941

Within a year of moving to Buffalo, Berton left the FHA to work as an underwriter for the Buffalo Savings Bank, a job he held for about three years. The family moved to an apartment in the Windsor Apartments at 703 West Ferry Street, a large, brick, vaguely neo-Colonial building with an attractive garden courtyard.

The most significant event of Jimmy's two years in Buffalo occurred early in seventh grade, when he met his first real soulmate, Bernie Oshei. Shy to begin with, Jimmy was all the quieter for being the new kid in his class. He spoke in a soft voice with a slightly southern accent and locutions, for which his classmates sometimes teased him. Once, when he didn't hear something the teacher said, he replied with a quaint, interrogatory "Ma'am?" and the rest of the class tittered. "Maybe that's when I started liking him," Oshei later recalled. Bernie was instinctively drawn to Jimmy, sensing in him a fellow "sissy" who he felt was less adept at "passing" in the straight world than Bernie himself. As he got to know him better, he was also increasingly impressed with Jimmy's intelligence.

Oshei's family was prominent and well-to-do in Buffalo. Bernie's uncle had purchased a patent for the automobile windshield wiper and established the Trico Corporation to manufacture the device, while his father owned a plastics company. Bernie's mother, Hortense Chittenden, a descendant of one of the city's original settlers, had died in 1922, the year Bernie was born. The family was Roman Catholic, which became a point of special interest for young Jimmy: on and off throughout his life, ever since his visionary experience at Mass as a young child, he would contemplate converting to Roman Catholicism. In a conversation that Oshei recalled as occurring "very early on" in their friendship, Jimmy spoke approvingly of W. H. Auden's "becoming a Catholic," and Bernie remembered being puzzled by James's interest, asking himself, "Why would anyone want to be a Catholic on purpose?"

Bernie and Jimmy were best friends for the next five or six years. Their friendship foreshadows Jimmy's later platonic relationships with Chester Kallman, John Ashbery, Joe Brainard, and others. That Jimmy found a queer soulmate at a young age helped him to be relatively comfortable with his homosexuality as he began to recognize it in himself. With each other's support, the two boys were able to explore their queer or "sissy" personas: egging each other on, they "enjoyed" being sissified together. They shared a love of movies and movie fan magazines, especially those featuring the many glamorous female stars of the 1930s. Fay Wray was one of their idols, and Jimmy once read in a magazine article that whenever she entered a room she looked straight ahead and walked with a "gliding" motion. Sometimes Bernie would catch Jimmy trying to emulate this walk and tease him: "You're gliding!" Wisecracking Joan Blondell was another favorite, and when her movie *Gold Diggers of 1937* opened in downtown Buffalo, Bernie and James were driven to the theater in style by a "rich cousin" of Bernie's in his Silver Wraith Rolls-Royce. Jimmy, already something of a dandy at age thirteen, was proudly wearing his new porkpie hat.

The boys also devoured the glamorous high-fashion magazines of the time, with the result that both Jimmy and Bernie decided they wanted to be fashion designers when they grew up. "I was a real *Vogue—Harper's Bazaar* . . . freak," Schuyler later wrote. "It used to drive my step-father up the wall and out the window when he found a stash of such like mags in my room. And they did have great artists—Eric, Bérard . . ." For exposure to more mainstream visual art James and Bernie visited the Albright Art Gallery (later the Buffalo AKG Art Museum) together, where James drank in its collection of nineteenth- and early twentieth-century paintings, including works by Matisse, Picasso, and the Impressionists.

Jimmy conceived a romantic attachment to the idea of Bernie's evocatively named mother, whose photograph stood in a frame on Bernie's bureau. He once brought a stem of fragrant freesia to place as an offering beside it, as he recalled in a late poem, "On the Dresser." The gesture introduces a pattern of sorts, enacted in various ways throughout his life, whereby Jimmy would deflect some of the affection—maybe too strong—that he felt for his friends onto people close to them: their mothers, when he was young, and their progeny when he was older.

On April 27, 1936, when he was twelve, Jimmy came home from school to find his mother holding a telegram. "Your grandmother is dying; *and you never wrote her that letter*," she told him, turning an occasion for shared grief into a guilt-making accusation. Ella had been taken to the hospital in Albert Lea with pneumonia and was not expected to live. Margaret, Berton, Jimmy, and little Fred made the long drive out to Minnesota, crossing Lake Michigan by ferry. But on May 1, soon after they arrived, James's grandmother Ella Connor died at the age of eighty-three.

This was apparently the only time Jimmy visited the town since his mother took him there as a toddler in 1926. As the family gathered at Linden Terrace, Jimmy wandered about the house disconsolately, taking note of an "armadillo shaded study lamp," a frieze of painted grapes around the dining room ceiling, and an old-fashioned wind-up Victrola, all of which seemed to breathe an atmosphere of family secrets and mustiness. He browsed through an old copy of *The Victor Book of the Opera*, and walked down to the edge of the lawn where it met Lake Albert Lea and looked out at the water. At the funeral in the flower-banked Presbyterian church, Jimmy was shown Ella in her open coffin, surprised at how much younger she looked than when he had last seen her. He kissed her "rouged and icy cheek" and felt a frisson go through him. During the ceremony he burst into unstoppable tears.

A little over a year later, in August 1937, James's paternal grandmother, Sarah Riddle, died in a "diabetic coma." Sarah Pound Brock Schuyler Pease Riddle had lived to the age of eighty-nine or ninety, outliving three of her four husbands. According to a neighbor, writing to Margaret at the time of her death, "She always talked about Jimmie and would have liked to have seen him . . . She said she wanted Jimmie to have her farm." Sarah Riddle's farm in Arkansas was indeed bequeathed to him, and later that year, when he was thirteen and his brother, Fred, about four, the family made another long drive, to rural Arkansas to make a start at settling the estate. The farm was in the hills, "in the middle of nowhere." At one point on the way, as Fred later remembered, the car got stuck in a creek bed and had to be pulled out by a mule. Once they finally arrived, someone took a shotgun from the wall, went outside, and shot a goat, which was then roasted in the fireplace for dinner. The farm was eventually sold in September 1947.

In the spring of 1937, just after Jimmy completed the eighth grade, the Ridenour family moved to East Aurora, New York, about twenty-five miles southeast of Buffalo. At about the same time, Berton lost his job with the Buffalo Savings Bank and started his own business as a freelance construction manager. Most likely Margaret inherited some money after her mother's death the year before, which would have helped with the purchase of the house there. In any case, the mortgage, in the amount of $5,800, was in her name.

East Aurora, with a population of about 5,253 in 1940, has probably not changed greatly in appearance since then, consisting as it does of mainly nineteenth- and mid-twentieth-century houses on leafy streets, grouped around a main street lined with useful shops. In Jimmy's day these included Vidler's, an old-fashioned general store (still there); Closs's flower shop, which the adult Schuyler loved to patronize; and Frank Sipprell's photography studio, where sooner or later everyone in town came for a portrait. Though he later disparaged East Aurora for its provinciality and missed the urban stimulations of Buffalo and Washington, it was on the whole not such a bad place in which to grow up.

Setting East Aurora apart from other suburban towns is its having been the home of the Roycrofters, a utopian community of craftspeople established by the essayist and letterpress printer Elbert Hubbard in 1895. Inspired by the English designer and social reformer William Morris, he believed in the "improving" nobility of handwork, and attracted a community around him of like-minded craftspersons in various media, including metalwork, woodwork, stained glass, and ceramics. By 1910, the Roycroft Campus had grown to include about five hundred artisans housed in at least eighteen buildings, in addition to the Arts and Crafts–style Roycroft Inn, where public events were held and distinguished visitors stayed. Hubbard and his wife died in the sinking of the *Lusitania* in 1915, and with inevitable changes in taste the community declined. The Roycroft Inn barely managed to stay in operation during Jimmy's years in East Aurora.

The Roycroft Campus sits at the center of town, directly across from what was then East Aurora High School. Although many of the Roycrofters' stone and timbered buildings were in disrepair by 1937, the campus was still an impressive and distinctive presence. While Bernie Oshei found the Roycroft campus "depressing," Jimmy came to appreciate its special atmosphere—one building was modeled on Wordsworth's cottage at Grasmere—which, he later said, imparted "a certain romance" to his life. He developed an early appreciation for the handcrafted objects made at the Roycroft workshops: "oaken planks, hammered copper, tooled leather, all of that," and the respect for materials they communicated arguably told on his own aesthetic sensibility.

The Ridenours' modest two-story bungalow-style house at 784 Chestnut Hill Road was only a few blocks from the center of town. It stood in a large lot, with room for Berton's vegetable garden in the back, as well as an undeveloped, wooded gully, where Jimmy set up a tent on a platform. There, alone or with Bernie, he would retreat to read and escape from the rest of the family, and they often spent the night.

If anything, Jimmy's friendship with Bernie Oshei grew stronger after the move to East Aurora, and most Saturday mornings Bernie got up at dawn and rode his bicycle from Buffalo to stay for the weekend. Bernie really loved the backyard tent, which was just big enough to sleep two. Bernie had some feelings of sexual attraction for Jimmy, but he never felt they were returned. The boys never experimented sexually together during their hours alone in the tent, although Bernie got the feeling that Berton suspected or assumed that they did. As a result, Bernie was conscious of trying to act butch in front of Berton, and on one occasion this led to his killing a harmless snake to impress him. Afterward, both he and Jimmy were horrified by the realization of taking a life, but Berton made Bernie follow through on the act by instructing him on how to skin the snake, nail the skin to a board, and "tan" it with salt. Bernie and Jimmy both recognized that the episode stemmed from an attempt to mimic stereotypical "boyish" or macho behavior. In a similar vein, Jimmy told Bernie of his admiration for a tough local youth who had set fire to a vacant lot nearby. Bernie couldn't tell whether Jimmy admired the kid himself or simply the "assertiveness" of the act of vandalism. A variation of the transgressive fire-setting theme would feature in *Alfred and Guinevere*, when Alfred and his naughtier friend Stanley accidentally set fire to the gully where they have a club.

Mainly because of the ten-year difference in their ages, but also due to different interests, Jimmy and his younger brother, Fred, were never especially close. As Fred later put it, "We were more friends than brothers." They shared responsibility for a dog, a smooth fox terrier named Nipper, who would sometimes accompany Jimmy and Bernie in the tent and on their tramps in the woods. Nipper was a tireless hunter of rats, mice, and moles, and would dig up Berton's lawn to get at them. Nipper "hated" Berton, and no doubt the feeling was mutual.

Berton had creative impulses that were mostly unfulfilled, but he found partial outlet for them by making watercolor paintings for his family, and, chiefly, as a keen gardener. Although Jimmy would become a good gardener himself much later in his life, Berton's garden at this time meant only hated chores: as a teenager, he would say, he had been "a gardening slave" to Berton's hobby. The garden was ambitious and included irrigation trenches, asparagus beds, and grapevines. Vegetables and fruits preserved by Margaret lined shelves in the basement. To Bernie, Berton's garden was a revelation: being able to eat salad greens, homegrown tomatoes, and other fresh vegetables straight from the garden was an experience new to an urban child of the '30s.

Although Jimmy's relationship with his stepfather had been good when he was younger, that changed after the Depression and the move to East Aurora. As his career and income tanked, Berton became "quite nutty and very cruel," and by the time Jimmy entered adolescence there was often terrible friction between them. Jimmy resorted to fictional parallels to describe the situation, comparing Berton to David Copperfield's cruel stepfather in one interview, and in another equating his childhood to "a novel by Dostoyevsky!" But Jimmy was never terribly specific about just what form this cruelty took, beyond a pervasive climate in the home of disapproval and disdain, and Berton's refusal to let him have a library card. To friends he confided simply that he had felt "unloved" in his childhood. A scene of simmering resentments erupting into sudden violence in Schuyler's story "The Home Book" may reflect underlying tensions or an actual episode in the Ridenour household during his youth. The story describes a woman who, exasperated at passive-aggressive needling by her "second husband," throws a plate at him, which smashes against the wall.

Due to his lack of formal certification, there were times when Berton was without work or had to take low-paying jobs for which he was overqualified. The work he did get often meant he had to travel long distances away from home. It must have been during one such low point that, according to Schuyler, he made a half-hearted attempt at suicide. As Jimmy recalled in a 1975 letter to his sister-in-law Hilde:

> You probably saw him at his worst plenty of times, but you still can't imagine what he was like in the 30s. Once he went in the garage, shut the doors and turned on the car engine. Neither Mother or I made a move (Fred was too young to know what was going on). After a while the big phoney turned off the engine and came in the house, giving mother and me each a special dirty look and went up in the attic.

Bernie Oshei liked Margaret, although he came to feel she, too, was hard on Jimmy. She was a stickler for proper table manners, and her unbending nature had already been in evidence when Jimmy was first learning to talk, and she insisted that he address her as "Mother" rather than "Mama." Jimmy retained disjointed but disturbing memories of her harsh treatment of his father during the divorce, as he mentioned to Bernie, and Jimmy himself would be subject to similar treatment later. To Bernie, it sometimes seemed she was watchful for and overly sensitive to any incipient signs in James of the kinds of character "weaknesses" that had led her first husband astray.

But it was possible to get away from all this. Just a few blocks from the house, real country began, and the boys loved to explore what is now Majors Park, or swim in Cazenovia Creek, sometimes at night, as Schuyler recalled in his long retrospective poem "The Morning of the Poem":

I wish it was 1938 or '39 again
and Bernie was sleeping
With me in the tent at the back of the yard
the time we got up
In the starry night and went downhill,
down Olean road, downhill again
And through the pasture where the cows coughed
and exhaled warm breath,
Barefoot among the cow flops (Dutchman's
razors) and stands of thistles and
Buttercups the cows won't eat [. . .]

sharp cropped
dewy grass between toes to where Cazenovia
Creek made a big bend and the warm and muddy water was deep
enough to swim in. Starlighted silent
Ripples as you stroke: the thick black shapes against the
black are old big trees: Bernie climbs
Up into one and dives: night air is loudly shattered by a
splash . . .

The two boys also continued to share enthusiasms for the books, magazines, and movies they were discovering together, and formed plans and fantasies for the future, some inspired by what they read. In response to a special January 1938 issue of *Architectural Forum* devoted to the work of Frank Lloyd Wright, Jimmy exchanged his former ambition to be a fashion designer for a new one—to be an architect. Of course, other factors contributed to this interest, including his recollections of the attractive and interesting Mowery family, along with, in a competitive spirit, the fact that Berton had originally wanted to be an architect himself. Berton, however, was quick to put a damper on the idea, telling Jimmy that he would never succeed as an architect, since he could not draw. An article the boys read in *Esquire* about how it was possible to live very cheaply in South America inspired a shared fantasy of moving to Guatemala when they were older. As Bernie later observed, this was, more than anything else, an indication of how skeptical of and unengaged they already were with the idea of finding a place for themselves in the conventional adult world of the United States in the mid-twentieth century.

Both boys were avid readers, and the experience of discovering and recommending books to each other was an important part of the friendship. From the stories of Saki (H. H. Munro) they went on to the early novels of Evelyn Waugh and Somerset Maugham, Elinor Wylie's *Jennifer Lorn* and *The Venetian Glass Nephew*, Harold Nicholson's *Some People*, Logan Pearsall Smith, Oscar Wilde, and Julian Green.

For a boy of fifteen living in suburban upstate New York, Jimmy's reading was both worldly and idiosyncratic. Wilde, Saki, Maugham, Nicholson, Green, Logan Pearsall Smith—in fact, with the possible exception of Evelyn Waugh, all of the male prose writers he and Oshei mention reading in high school were gay. The queer slant of Jimmy's early reading did not escape his mother's sophisticated eyes. When, at an unknown age, Jimmy informed Margaret that he was gay, her response was "Just because you like Oscar Wilde, it doesn't mean you have to do all those things." Most of his favorite writers were English and wrote with a careful attention to their prose style, which tended to be clear and elegant, if sometimes mannered. Once Jimmy had decided to be a writer (of prose), he consciously modeled his prose on that of his heroes, and his heroes' heroes. For example, he said, "I was very affected by reading Somerset Maugham's *Summing Up* in my teens. In that book he describes how he really tried to learn by copying out long passages of Dryden's prose. I did the same thing, only I chose Walter de la Mare and Cardinal Newman." He also traced his habit of stitching together sentences with colons, often in evidence in his long poems of the 1970s, to his high school reading of Harold Nicholson's *Some People*.

One afternoon when he was about fifteen or sixteen years old, while lying in his backyard tent and reading Logan Pearsall Smith's memoir *Unforgotten Years*, Jimmy experienced a life-changing epiphany. In the first part of the twentieth century, Smith was a well-known literary figure, famous for a book of rather precious short prose sketches called

Trivia. Unforgotten Years, published in 1939, tells how when Smith was a young man growing up outside Philadelphia in the early 1880s, he and his family became friends with the aged Walt Whitman, who used to travel from his home in Camden, New Jersey, to stay with them, and how through his friendship with Whitman, the youthful Smith became aware of his own vocation as a writer. While reading this in his backyard tent, as Jimmy later recalled, "I looked up and the whole landscape shimmered, and I said, 'Yes, that's it.'" In that moment, he realized that, "rather than an architect, I wanted to be a writer and *would* be one."

In reconstructing his youthful epiphany in several interviews, Schuyler conflated elements from different passages in Smith's book, including Smith's own description elsewhere of reading Ruskin while "lying out of doors in the grass one late summer afternoon," when he too looked up from his book to see "the blue sky and the golden architecture of the unmoving summer clouds" and felt his "first experience of conscious aesthetic enjoyment." What also stayed with Jimmy was Smith's characterization of Whitman's vision of the artist's vocation as "receptivity to experience, and . . . a complete surrender to it, combined with a patient effort to grasp its deepest meaning in significant words . . . the ability to embody in words some one of Nature's aspects,—the sea's voice, for instance, or the breath of its salt fragrance, or even, as he himself had said, 'the undulation of one wave.'"

In retrospect one can almost hear and see Schuyler's whole oeuvre rippling outward in concert with these words, and his youthful response to them. The "notion of receptivity to experience, and of a complete surrender to it" would become central to Schuyler's nature and poetic project, while the description of the "sea's voice" will echo later in "The Crystal Lithium." The fact that for Jimmy the "landscape shimmered" gives the episode the character of a visionary experience, and links it with the religious vision of his early childhood and the later religious visions that occurred during certain of his psychotic episodes.

However, no writings from Jimmy's adolescence have survived or can be identified, aside from conjectural, unsigned newspaper articles and two childish early poems. Bernie did recall a novel he had written set in East Aurora, which included a character based on a local, macho guy who worked as an auto mechanic, to whom Jimmy was strongly attracted and who was friendly toward him. (He told Bernie, "I can imagine some girl burrowing her face into his crotch.") Bernie was horrified when Jimmy told him that he had burned this early novel; still, it is not clear whether it was written while they were still in East Aurora or in the early 1940s, when they were both living in New York.

East Aurora High School, an imposing two-story Federal-style brick building, was both literally and figuratively at the center of town, also drawing students from the surrounding farm country. The Future Farmers of America had a large presence on campus, as did classes in "homemaking" and the manual trades, but there was also a strong humanities and arts program.

Looking back as an adult, Jimmy was consistent in recalling his unhappiness in high school. "I really didn't fit in and wasn't very happy growing up in East Aurora . . . There wasn't anyone like me who liked to read books and who was interested in art." Nonetheless, "fit in," in the sense of not drawing attention to himself, was exactly what Jimmy tried to do, and he was rather successful. The few fellow students who could recall James Ridenour at all remembered him as quiet, unobtrusive, and "very smart." Music and drama were taken seriously at East Aurora High School, and in his junior and senior years, Jimmy took part in a couple of theatrical productions, serving on the Properties Committee and Costume Committee, and singing in the chorus of sailors in *The Pirates of Penzance*. Russell Drosendahl, who was also in the production and became friendly with him, confirmed that he was "quiet, but not standoffish." Sally Ingalls (Rohrdanz), who worked with him on the school newspaper and in some of the musical productions, recalled Jimmy as something of a dandy: he "wore a different collar and tie-pin from the other fellows"; "he was unique." His careful attention to his wardrobe and appearance, borne out in photographs, may have been one way he sought to provide himself with a sort of protective covering of conventionality, reinforcing a natural dignity and reserve. Indeed, the East Aurora High School yearbook for 1941 records that James's classmates voted him the "Most

Dignified" graduate in his senior year, and the "Class Prophecy" foresaw that he would end up as the local district attorney.

Jimmy gravitated toward two fellow students in particular who shared his interest in writing. In the fall of 1939, at the beginning of their junior year, the school newspaper gossip column linked James Ridenour and Mary Nenno romantically, noting that they were in the habit of walking to school together, "just too too of-e-ten." Nenno was one of the star pupils of the class of 1941: in addition to being editor in chief of the school paper, she was president of Quill and Scroll Club, assistant editor of the yearbook, a member of the National Honor Society, and a member of the debating team and of the varsity girls' tennis, soccer, basketball, badminton, volleyball, and baseball teams. Her ambition as stated in the yearbook was "to ride the Washington Merry-Go-Round," an ambition she later achieved. She did not marry, and may have been a lesbian. Between her and James there could have been a slight, perhaps unconscious, tendency to use the other as a "beard"—walking each other to school may have allowed other students to assume (as the gossip item would suggest) they were in some sense "going together."

In his junior or senior year, Jimmy fell in love with a fellow student, Paul Sipprell—who as it happens also went out with Mary Nenno at one time. Sipprell, whose father was a portrait photographer in town, and whose aunt, Clara Sipprell, was a well-known Pictorialist photographer in the early twentieth century, was a year older than James and Mary and attended East Aurora High School as a "post-graduate" student specializing in journalism. There is quite a bit about him in "The Morning of the Poem." As a handsome, smart, slightly older student, Sipprell had a certain glamour. He won a national high school essay contest and was apparently their English teacher "Luther Smeltzer's pet," which made James jealous. According to Jimmy's own account in "The Morning of the Poem," Paul recalled the younger boy's advances ruefully when they met in New York several years later: "I couldn't take it: / it was too heavy; you put on too much / Pressure." Jimmy's pursuit seems to have lasted much of his senior and perhaps junior years, encompassing a "winter of / Silent midnight walks in deep snow." Craftily, Jimmy made friends with Paul's parents and sent roses to his mother, who then invited him to dinner. Jimmy accepted the invitation, to Paul's chagrin, and, for once, was not shy but instead held forth about his "Schuyler descent and who Alexander / Hamilton married."

One night in the summer of 1940, Bernie and Jimmy snuck into Paul's bedroom and woke him up in the middle of the night. "He was furious but got / Dressed and came out to the Roycroft Inn and got mildly drunk / on gin and Squirt." Although Bernie did not share Jimmy's attraction to Paul, Paul was "nuts about Bernie," and Jimmy shamelessly used his friend as bait. If not on that occasion, it appears that Jimmy and Paul did have sex, for Schuyler describes his cock in "The Morning of the Poem" (not very enticingly), and seventeen was the age when he had his first homosexual experience, or so he told navy authorities later. Calling Paul, as he does, "The very first . . . the one in high school," also suggests there was a physical dimension to what was otherwise a one-sided romantic affair. But one day, "It was over: I passed him on the street and looked at him un- / sheepishly and said, 'Hi, Paul,' he was startled into saying / 'Hello' for the first time in a year." A few years later they met in New York, where they were then both living and making their way in "queer ('gay,' if you prefer) New York." Sometime in the late 1950s or '60s, Sipprell was murdered in New York City.

Meanwhile, throughout Jimmy's senior year, the school gossip column continued to link him with a series of young women. Jimmy always had many close women friends, so there is no reason to suppose he didn't enter into the high school dating scene in a relatively straightforward way, which may account for his somewhat puzzling entry under the heading "Ambition" in the senior class yearbook: "To go steady with *two* girls at once" (an ambition that struck Sally Rohrdanz as distinctly odd, since she remembered Jimmy as someone who was not known to date many girls).

It was the beautiful Dorothy (Dottie) Flanagan whom Jimmy took to the senior prom in June 1941. Dorothy was "very luscious with long dark auburn hair—a page-boy bob, I guess," Schuyler later recalled. To the prom she wore "a strapless dress of electric blue satin and had gold dust brushed through her hair." Dottie Flanagan had taught Jimmy how to inhale cigarettes one summer night at her house, after he, a novice smoker, had tried to show his sophistication by lighting up with her.

"You're not inhaling!" she accused. What with smoking alone with boys and her beauty and her daring prom dress, Dorothy Flanagan would no doubt have been considered "fast" at the time. She was also, Jimmy remembered, "about the first girl in our class to get married."

The most meaningful engagement Jimmy had with high school life came through his senior-year work on the school newspaper, *High School Highlights*. Published under the supervision of Luther Smeltzer as a special section in the local weekly newspaper, the *East Aurora Advertiser*, *High School Highlights* achieved remarkable professionalism, almost on a par with the mainstream paper into which it was inserted. Jimmy was credited as an "assistant editor" and "chief copyreader," and contributed articles on various subjects. Working on the newspaper was the only extracurricular activity Jimmy listed on his application to college in 1941, where he stated that as a senior he worked there an average of seven to eight hours a week.

Disappointingly, the articles in *High School Highlights* were, with very few exceptions, unsigned, so none can be attributed with certainty to James Ridenour. Several focus in rather Schuyler-like ways on mundane aspects of school life, such as items in a student's desk or the dust and detritus swept up by janitors. If some articles sound uncannily like "Current Events," Jimmy's 1957 short story written in the voice of a high school journalism student, this proves only that he was an excellent mimic of the style of high-school-age writers in general. In addition to whatever writing he did, Jimmy's experience as chief copyreader helped him develop editing skills that would prove useful with his New York School colleagues. One could say that the communal, collaborative nature of Jimmy's earliest prose writings, in what was literally a school, anticipates the close social involvement that was so much a part of New York School writing in the 1950s, and which makes some of their works seem, while hardly interchangeable, at least closely related.

Of course, many future writers (and nonwriters) worked on their high school newspapers, but for Jimmy, it carried emotional weight. By changing his ambition from being an architect to being a writer, and then taking the step of joining the school newspaper, Jimmy rejected his stepfather's professional world in favor of that of his absent natural father. Looking ahead, we will see that the poet Schuyler would internalize and use many aspects of newspapers (and magazines) in his mature work. Genres of newspaper prose are lovingly parodied not only in "Current Events," but also "Ron Padgett," "A Picnic Cantata," and "What Ails My Fern." The heterogeneous, collage-like nature of newspapers is emulated implicitly in many other works, while the dated, daily nature of newspapers is reflected in the great many Schuyler poems that bear dates and immortalize particular days.

The intellectual high point of high school for James came in his senior English classes with Luther Smeltzer, the only teacher Jimmy mentions in his work or in his reminiscences, aside from his college English professor, Florence Hoagland. Jimmy entered his class with a definite and sophisticated, if eccentric, literary canon of his own, based on his and Bernie's readings. In his recollections about Smeltzer he is a bit condescending toward his teacher's more conventional tastes, but he recognizes areas where Smeltzer gave him a wider view.

Schuyler credited Smeltzer with opening "windows for me on / flowering fields and bays where the water greenly danced, / Knifed into waves by wind: the day he disclosed William Carlos / Williams to us, writing a short and seemingly / Senseless poem on the blackboard." Smeltzer also piqued Jimmy's interest with a mention of James Joyce's *Ulysses*. However, when Jimmy asked after class for more information about *Ulysses*, which had been banned in this country as obscene until 1933, Smeltzer chuckled and said, "When you're in college it will be time enough." Annoyed by Smeltzer's coy hypocrisy, Jimmy went to Buffalo and, as he related in "The Morning of the Poem," bought a copy of the book from Otto Ulrich's bookshop, where John Bernard Myers, later a prominent figure in the New York art and poetry world, then worked as a salesclerk. Jimmy recalled him as a "big white whale" who loomed over him one day as he was reading in a corner of the shop, and said "You look like an interesting boy," and gave him a copy of his magazine, *Upstate*. Jimmy's rumored possession of *Ulysses* lent him unwonted status in the eyes of the high school jocks, normally oblivious to his very existence. He managed to get the book into the house, past his suspicious stepfather, by telling Berton it was a socially conscious book "about poor people in Ireland."

Despite Smeltzer's introducing him to William Carlos Williams's poetry, Jimmy did not read him in earnest until he was in college, when he especially loved the "complete freedom" in his work. Through anthologies he also discovered Marianne Moore, Wallace Stevens, T. S. Eliot, Robert Frost, Edna St. Vincent Millay, D. H. Lawrence, and other modernist poets. Lawrence and Stevens had probably the most impact, and over the next few years he came to feel he had memorized *Harmonium* and *The Man with the Blue Guitar* and *Ideas of Order.*

While Whitman, the person, was central to Jimmy's decision to become a writer, he did not actually read him in depth until later, although he was exposed to him through Mark Van Doren's *An Anthology of World Poetry*, which he described as one of his "sacred books" in high school (and where he also first read Thoreau). For Jimmy's purposes, the *idea* of Whitman, as reflected in the prose of Logan Pearsall Smith, more than sufficed as an inspirational figure of the (queer) Writer. As he said, he was inspired "not so much by reading only, but by the idea of who he was, and what he was."

With the new decade came national changes that directly affected the Ridenour family. In anticipation of American involvement in World War II, the government began a huge military base construction program. In 1940, Berton got a job as a construction supervisor on the navy barracks at Great Lakes, in Waukegan, Illinois, on Lake Michigan. He, Margaret, and young Fred left East Aurora to live there during the construction. Rather than uproot Jimmy during his senior year, it was decided that he would stay and board with a neighbor family, the Harriets. The job in Waukegan lasted until 1941, but after that Berton was sent to work on another barracks construction project, in the Panama Canal Zone, and again, Margaret and Fred accompanied him, leaving James back in East Aurora.

By then, Bernie Oshei, a year older, had left home and gotten a job at the Bell Aircraft assembly plant in Wheatfield, New York, north of Buffalo. When the war started, he enrolled in the Air Corps. Jimmy and Bernie would resume their friendship when they were both living in New York after the war, but never again with their teenage level of intimacy.

In about 1940, when they were living in Waukegan, Margaret and Berton joined the Church of Christ, Scientist. Margaret eventually became a Christian Science practitioner, the equivalent of a priest. Jimmy, who in 1938 had bowed to family tradition and was confirmed as a Presbyterian—despite undefined yearnings toward the Catholic Church, and a contrary youthful atheism (derived, he said, from reading Maugham's *Of Human Bondage*)—never joined, and attended Christian Science services with the family only a few times. Jimmy came to detest the Christian Science church, saying that "it does kill people," but at the same time recognizing that it saved Berton's sanity and helped his mother.

James Ridenour graduated from East Aurora High School on June 24, 1941. That summer, while his family was still away, he worked at the Silver Dairy. He was disappointed that it paid so little, in comparison with a job at Bell Aircraft, but to work there one had to be eighteen. He later recalled "vividly wanting to be 18" for that reason—although of his actual eighteenth birthday later in the fall, by which time he was in college in West Virginia, he remembered nothing.

[4]

CURSES FLAP INTO THE SKY LIKE STARLINGS

1941–1943

In his senior year in high school, Jimmy won a scholarship to Bethany College, a small liberal arts college in Bethany, West Virginia, affiliated with the Disciples of Christ, a Protestant evangelical denomination (now the Christian Church). While the school is well regarded, and accepts students of all religious backgrounds, the choice remains something of a mystery. No doubt the $200 scholarship, renewable for four years, played a part in the decision. Jimmy visited the school with Margaret and Fred the summer after his high school graduation, and on September 18, 1941, he enrolled.

Bethany is located in the little triangle of the state that juts up between the western border of Pennsylvania and the eastern edge of Ohio. Jimmy later described the college as "an attractive group of buildings on a small steep hill" designed in a neo-Gothic architectural style based on that of Edinburgh.

He joined the Sigma Nu fraternity—another odd decision. Underclassmen did not usually live in the fraternity house, and surviving fellow Sigma Nu brothers did not recall whether Jimmy did, but he may have lived there in his second year. He would eat there in any case, and he also spent a lot of time playing bridge there, which he later claimed was his main activity during his college years.

Jimmy was lonely and unhappy throughout his year and a half at Bethany. Whatever sense of freedom and relief he may have initially felt at getting away from East Aurora soon gave way to feelings of depression, reflected in an accumulation of failing or incomplete grades. For someone who had decided to be a writer (journalism was his "Preference of Vocation" as stated on his transcript), the freshman and sophomore course requirements, which included biology, mathematics, physical education, and heavy doses of economics, must have been discouraging. In his first semester he earned four Fs, and from there his grades got no better. At the end of each of his first two semesters, he was put on academic probation.

Academically and intellectually, the only bright spots of his time at Bethany were his courses in Shakespeare and in Victorian literature with Dr. Florence Hoagland, the head of the English department, in which he earned a B and an A, respectively. As he later put it, "I was very influenced by a wonderful woman named Dr. Florence Hoagland . . . who encouraged me in a wonderful way."

A lesbian who lived with her friend Margaret Carrigan in one of the women's dormitories, Hoagland held expansive ideas about education, based on the teachings of Alfred North Whitehead, believing that it should engage the "imaginative, the intellectual and the ethical life" of her students. The poet May Sarton, with whom she was having a long-distance love affair and who gave a talk at Bethany in November 1942, described her as "a large great *sun* of a woman, one of the great givers." Jimmy kept in touch with Hoagland after he left Bethany, and sent her a copy of a poem by Wallace Stevens when he was in the navy—presumably "The Idea of Order at Key West." According to Jimmy, she was "thrilled by it." His apparent confidence that she would appreciate the poem as he did suggests a close emotional understanding between them, if surely unspoken or projected on his side. Hoagland died in an automobile accident in 1946 at the age of forty-five.

Jimmy seems to have gotten along well enough with his classmates and made several casual friends. Jesse Barton, a classmate and fellow member of Sigma Nu, recalled him primarily as a "quiet," "sensitive," "moody," "introspective" boy who smoked far too much and kept to himself, but would sometimes join in long nighttime walks out of town to drink beer at a roadhouse called Emily's. Robert Golbey, another Sigma

Nu brother, saw him as "a quiet, introspective young man who was not happy at school," although he was "as bright as any student that I can remember." To Golbey, he seemed out of place at Bethany, which was "not a place where there were many New Yorkers." Golbey was struck by the fact that Jimmy never mentioned his family, and that it seemed as though he had "no place to go back to." This was quite true for much of 1942, when Berton and Margaret were in Panama. Feeling sorry for him, Golbey invited him to spend a weekend with his family at their home on Long Island that summer. Afterward, Jimmy sent Golbey's mother a thank-you gift: a copy of Stendhal's novel *The Red and the Black*. Golbey remembered thinking it a distinctly odd gift.

Jimmy developed mild crushes at Bethany on some of his oblivious, presumably straight, male fellow students and fraternity brothers, including William Stophel, who also recalled being struck by his obvious unhappiness. Stophel's girlfriend, Nancy Sebring, a journalism major, was a somewhat closer friend, and on Sundays the two of them traveled off campus together to attend Catholic Mass.

At that time and place, most of his fellow students would have been relatively naïve about the full range of human sexuality. Robert Golbey, for example, who became a doctor, was "virtually ignorant of the existence of homosexuality" while at Bethany. Despite the fact that Jimmy had been sexually active since the age of seventeen, the prospect of sexual activity with his fellow students and fraternity brothers was highly unlikely, not to mention dangerous. At the same time, his classmates' naïveté made them oblivious to any homosexual activity that Jimmy and others did manage to get up to, including Jimmy's casual relationship with the college librarian, E. Hugh Behymer. Then in his early thirties, Behymer (pronounced "BE-hymer") regularly socialized with the students, such as Bill Stophel and Nancy, who called him "Bee" and regarded him as "lighthearted . . . more like a friend than the teachers would be." Jimmy, always a voracious reader, would have found the library a welcome refuge, and his friendship with Behymer very likely began there, or in the fraternity house, where Behymer often attended parties. Thirty years later Jimmy recalled sneaking into Behymer's house one night to keep a sexual rendezvous and feeling his way in the darkened hallway, "not knowing which bedroom was his, which his sister's (also a maiden lady), finding the right one, tiptoeing out to his car, drive to the woods, suckage."

Although Jimmy was not happy at Bethany, in retrospect he claimed to be glad he had gone there, at least in one sense. Something about it reinforced his sense of his own identity as a deracinated Midwesterner. He realized this only later, when, at a party, the painter Alex Katz mistakenly assumed he had gone to Harvard, like John Ashbery, Frank O'Hara, and Kenneth Koch. When Jimmy clarified that he had actually gone to Bethany ("this little dump in West Virginia"), Katz brushed it off, saying, "Nah, you're Harvard." Jimmy did regret at times that he had not had a Harvard education like his friends, with the chance to learn French, for example, "in a proper manner." But in that moment, he realized that he was "actually proud of *not* being 'Harvard,'" that he had a different background, "in the way that Sherwood Anderson might have been proud of not being 'Harvard.'"

On December 7, 1941, the Japanese attacked Pearl Harbor and the United States entered World War II. Jimmy, still in his first semester at Bethany, heard the news while playing bridge in the Sigma Nu house, or so he claimed. A month earlier he had turned eighteen, making him eligible for the draft.

On his way back to East Aurora for Christmas break that winter, Jimmy stopped in New York City. This was his first extended visit to the city, which he had been drawn to since his suburban adolescence, when he had regularly and avidly pored over the entertainment listings in *The New Yorker*. He stayed at the West Side YMCA, at 5 West Sixty-third Street, where he took advantage of the ready availability of casual sex. He recalled in "A few days": "I was in the shower / when a hunk walked in. I got a hard-on just like that. / He dropped his soap / to get a view of it and in no time we were in bed in / his room. Sure was / a change from West Virginia." He saw (or thought he saw) Alice Faye, a blonde singing film star of the previous decade, eating dinner at a popular Times Square Chinese restaurant called Ruby Foo's. Later, the sighting, and the odd music of the combined names, would inspire a poem, "Alice Faye at Ruby Foo's" (1959), giving impressionistic glimpses of the city in that first month of the war, when a newly anxious populace feared that "almost any night they might just bomb / the Hotel Henry Hudson" (a famous hotel for military personnel on West Fifty-seventh Street), yet so full of possibility that even cinema idols were human and available, like "Alice Faye // smiling and smiling in the flaming night."

In what turned out to be a futile attempt to make up the necessary credits to stay in school, Jimmy remained at Bethany for the summer term of 1942. That June, his father died of a heart attack at the age of fifty-nine. This news, added to his depression and the prospect of flunking out and being drafted, may well have set off a severe anxiety attack similar to those he experienced later during periods of stress and trauma. Although there is no record of Jimmy experiencing a nervous breakdown prior to 1951, it seems possible that his early story "The Forty-First and Youngest Brother," published in *Accent* magazine in 1951, may obliquely record an undiagnosed breakdown at Bethany College in 1942. "The Forty-First and Youngest Brother" has the clarity and intensity of a lived visionary experience. It is set in a dreamlike version of Bethany college's "gables" and "towers," where the unnamed protagonist is one of forty-one "brothers." In the story, he is visited by his dead father's ghost and undergoes a Christlike "crucifixion" and rebirth, consistent with pervasive Christ imagery and identification in Jimmy's documented breakdowns.

In December 1942 (or earlier), Jimmy registered for the draft, and went for his physical examination in Wellsburg, West Virginia, on January 13, 1943. He was found to be in perfect health and classified 1-A. At the end of the winter 1942–43 term, Jimmy received an F in six of his eight subjects (which included not one but two economics courses) and was, in the words of his official transcript, "denied the privilege of further registration at Bethany College." On January 28, 1943, he withdrew. This put an ignominious end to his college career.

On his way home to East Aurora in February 1943, Jimmy stopped again in New York City. He visited the gay bars, including Pop Tunick's, at 978 Second Avenue between Fifty-second and Fifty-third, which had been a popular working-class Irish bar since at least the 1930s, but by the '40s was predominantly a gay bar in what was then becoming a gay neighborhood. Jimmy was besotted at the time with Lena Horne's rendition of Noel Coward's "Mad About the Boy," and was playing it repeatedly on the jukebox one night when he and a tall, handsome Finnish

American serviceman and Spanish Civil War veteran named Bill Aalto caught each other's eyes and picked each other up. (Later Aalto would tease Jimmy about his playing of the song that night, thinking it typically "East Fifties queen / taste.") Aalto, too, was just passing through the city, on leave from Fort Ritchie in Maryland, where he was an instructor in guerrilla warfare and tactics. They weren't together long: Aalto had to get back to Fort Ritchie, and Jimmy to East Aurora to resolve his own military situation. But they must have exchanged addresses.

On April 8, 1943, Jimmy went from East Aurora to Buffalo and volunteered for a two-year tour of duty in the navy to preempt being drafted into the army. He was then 5 feet 8 inches tall, weighed 149 pounds, and had brown hair, blue eyes, and a "ruddy" complexion. On enlisting he was assigned the rank of Apprentice Seaman SV-6 with a salary of $50 a month. After a week at home in East Aurora he was sent to Sampson Naval Training Station, on Seneca Lake, one of central New York's Finger Lakes, where he went through three months of basic training.

Frank O'Hara, Jimmy's future friend and fellow New York School poet, would also undergo basic training at Sampson one year later, and like Jimmy went on from there to sonar school in Key West, Florida. O'Hara's letters home survive, unlike Jimmy's; and O'Hara also wrote an early prose poem about his war experiences, "Lament and Chastisement." In O'Hara's words, Sampson Naval Training Center looked "more or less like a prison camp." Recruits began their day at 5:00 a.m. by running laps around "the Grinder," an athletic field next to the barracks. They then moved on to a regimen of four-hour watches, mess duty, shooting instruction, drilling, educational movies. Spare-time activities included boxing matches, rowing contests on the lake, and "smokers" (at which there was no smoking).

In the regimented environment of the training camp, even someone as outgoing as O'Hara found it necessary to tamp down his personal identity beneath a veneer of outward conformity. In "Lament and Chastisement," O'Hara wrote, "Now that we were broken in and we all looked the same so nobody could tell anybody else from anybody else . . . Nothing to do but say this isn't really me because the real me slipped away before you got here." As gay men, both Frank and Jimmy had reason to avoid attracting unwanted attention. Recruits, drawn from all over the country, could at times be intolerant of others different from themselves: African Americans were segregated into their own troops, and anti-Semitism, as O'Hara wrote, was fairly common. Officially, homosexual or effeminate behavior was despised, even though the same-sex atmosphere of the barracks and shower room held strong undercurrents of unacknowledged, or partially acknowledged, homoeroticism. O'Hara mentions an apparently simpleminded youth who regularly masturbated publicly in the showers, and another boy who "showed off" in the showers and was discharged for homosexuality. "Without exaggerating at all the [undesirable] discharge will ruin him," O'Hara wrote to his family. Yet O'Hara apparently did manage to engage in some surreptitious oral sex under the covers with fellow recruits at Sampson, and Jimmy may have done the same.

During basic training, aptitude tests were administered to the recruits to determine which of them might have useful abilities. Jimmy was found to have a sensitive ear and was assigned to be trained as a sonar operator, and on July 6 was transferred to the Fleet Sound School in Key West, the southernmost island of the Florida Keys. For both Jimmy and Frank O'Hara, who was also assigned to sonar school a year later, Key West was their first experience of a tropical environment, and both later included impressions of it in their work. O'Hara's "Lament and Chastisement" describes the town: "There are bars all up and down and you drink rum or vodka, sometimes brandy-and-vodka, but the scotch is watered . . . // . . . The sky is nearer to the earth in Key West than anywhere else. The moon is bigger in Key West than anywhere else . . . There are also a number of lovely night sounds, but the military police are mean."

Jimmy's memories (written from a greater distance of time) are a little more abstract, and possibly idealized: "Key West! / The beautiful white houses / With the louvered upstairs, downstairs porches, / the heavy oaks densely hung / With Spanish moss, the tall blue-blacks with / hauteur and disdain, beyond / The chain fence, in their eyes and carriage . . . the barracuda and the angelfish, / stars like the Koh-i-noor / And a full moon reflecting back the star-encrusted / sea, a face- / Enveloping moon . . ." Jimmy certainly had sexual adventures in Key West, at least off the base. In "The Morning of the Poem," he recalled "walking under the palms on liberty in / 1943 with a soldier / I had just picked up and in my sailor suit some- / thing stony as the / Washington Monument I wanted to hide from the / officer coming toward me: I / Guess I was afraid he'd see it, get the picture / of what was about to and in fact / Did happen, and send me back to base." Jimmy also recalled a slightly similar kind of sexual exhibitionism to what O'Hara observed at Sampson, remarking on the self-conscious attention that fellow recruits gave to a "short skinny boy in the barracks at Key West with the enormous cock behind which he would come from the shower with an air of disclaimer and acceptance. The hooting and teasing he got was not without good-natured pride: after all, it lived in our barrack. And overhead, day and night, the big fans revolved."

Sonar, a kind of underwater radar, is the reading of sound waves reflected from undersea objects to determine their location and characteristics. Trainees were first taught the rudiments on a shore-based console that mimicked shipboard echo-sounding. After that came training at sea: recruits were roused at daybreak to board dilapidated World War I–era ships, where they learned to interpret the different characters of the reflected "pings" from various obstacles: "sandbar, whale, school of fish, submarine, wake of another ship, etc. and chart its length, depth and movement." As a contemporary sonarman recalled, "Even though he was but an enlisted man, the sonarman's judgement was crucial to the ship's safety, because it was his 'call' to analyze the contact . . . and pass his judgement to the officers." It was nerve-racking work.

Jimmy completed his five-week training course as a radioman on August 14, 1943, the twentieth in his class of sixty-five trainees, and was advanced to the rank of Soundman Third Class [SoM3c]. From the Amphibious Training Base outside Norfolk, Virginia, he was transferred to New York City on September 28, and assigned to the destroyer USS *Glennon*, which he boarded on October 2. The *Glennon* (DD620) was a brand-new vessel, launched the previous year and put into service guarding convoys of troops and supplies crossing the Atlantic. She was a ship of about 1,600 tons and 350 feet in length, manned by 16 officers and 260 enlisted men. Each transatlantic crossing took approximately ten days.

For the first eighteen days after Jimmy joined the ship, the *Glennon* was engaged in exercises along the East Coast. She departed again from

New York on October 21 as part of a convoy of nine or ten ships en route to Belfast, Northern Ireland. On the first night out of port, one of the other blacked-out ships in the convoy, the USS *Murphy*, was accidentally struck by a commercial oil tanker and cut in half. The forward section of the *Murphy* sank, but the aft section remained afloat, surrounded by many survivors struggling to stay alive in the frigid water. The *Glennon*, alerted by the failure of the *Murphy* to respond to radio communications and seeing "sparks and lights in the vicinity," rushed back to the scene and stayed to rescue 107 survivors from the sea. But 35 officers and men from the *Murphy* were drowned. The *Glennon* then towed what remained of the ship back toward port, until it was taken in hand by rescue vessels and brought back to the Navy Yard. Whatever role Jimmy played in the rescue of USS *Murphy* survivors from the cold waters of the Atlantic (the only "action" he is known to have seen in his truncated term of service), it must have been creditable, for he later mused in his diary, "I was brave and I proved it that day on the USS *Glennon*." But the horrific nighttime scene, with men dying in front of his eyes illuminated by eerie searchlights, stayed with him, and about ten years later he wrote a sonnet about it:

A GRAVE

While we who wished to help stood helplessly by,
a stranger, whom we neither knew nor loved (saw,
simply, as one of our kind), sank from sight,
drowning, gave up what we value most, our life.

If then between the shifting ocean and sky,
in whose two blacknesses he had seemed the flaw,
had been driven and drawn, tearing night from night
to show us his death's beyond, and ours, a knife!

which did not happen. His agony,
we who stood and watched the threatened promise kept,

could not share, even in fearful sympathy.
Searchlights moved upon the uninjured ocean.
Now he was part of that lighted blackness, slept
in what the screw of our ship set in motion.

The *Glennon* continued on to Belfast without further incident and, after a week in port, returned to the States. Jimmy marked his nineteenth birthday on board, and nine days later, on Thursday, November 18, the *Glennon* docked in Bayonne, New Jersey, where she remained for a period of approximately two weeks. While in port, the crew would generally be divided into three groups of officers and men, which would rotate in taking days ashore, so that each group ended up spending about one day in every three in port on shore leave: a total of around five days for Jimmy, in this case.

After the bleak, cold, and sometimes frightening experience of being stuck on a cramped ship in the North Atlantic, New York's lights and activity, not to mention its sexual possibilities, must have been heady indeed. Picking up a *New Yorker* when he hit town, Jimmy would have noted a mind-boggling array of entertainment on offer: Paul Robeson, José Ferrer, and Uta Hagen were starring in a "magnificent" production of *Othello*; *Oklahoma!* was in its original run with Alfred Drake and Celeste Holm; Mary Martin was playing in *One Touch of Venus*, and Ethel Merman in *Something for the Boys*. At Café Society Uptown, Hazel Scott and Mildred Bailey were performing with Teddy Wilson's orchestra; Frank Sinatra was singing at the Waldorf-Astoria; Roger Stearns was playing piano at the 1-2-3 Club; Count Basie was at the Lincoln Club; Benny Goodman was at the New Yorker Hotel; and Tommy Dorsey's Orchestra was at the Pennsylvania. Billie Holiday and her trio were at the Onyx Club on West Fifty-second Street, a few doors down from the Three Deuces, where Art Tatum and Ben Webster were playing.

Many of these jazz performers and clubs are mentioned in Jimmy's later poems, letters, and diary, including Mildred Bailey, Art Tatum, Teddy Wilson, Roger Stearns and the 1-2-3 Club, Café Society Uptown, and Billie Holiday, and it is likely that he heard one or two of them during this, his first leave in New York from navy service, although most of his clubgoing came later, when he returned to New York to live the following year. He also visited the Astor Bar, in the Astor Hotel at Times Square, which was well-known during the war as a place for military men (and women) to meet admirers of both sexes. Like certain hotel bars in other large cities during the war, it catered to a partly gay clientele without being an obviously gay bar. It also generated an aimless crowd of late-night cruising extending into the surrounding streets, as young sailors and soldiers on leave, and unused to hard drinking, desperately attempted to enjoy their few hours of liberty.

The details of Jimmy's desertion from the navy at the end of November 1943 are obscure but can be pieced together from a later account. On the *Glennon*'s last night in harbor, November 29, Jimmy was scheduled to stay aboard and be on watch. At the last minute, however, a comrade who was scheduled for shore leave but for some reason was unable to go asked him if he wouldn't like to go ashore in his place. Jimmy of course was happy for another night ashore and went. But having started the evening later than usual, he stayed up drinking later than he was accustomed to, got very drunk, maybe got picked up, then passed out someplace. By the time he awoke it was morning and he realized he had missed curfew. Panicking, he stayed where he was.

Jimmy was reported officially missing the next morning, November 30, and the *Glennon* departed on December 1 for New London and more exercises up and down the East Coast. She returned a few days later before starting on her next trip across the Atlantic on December 5. Jimmy was still missing, and at this point his onboard possessions were inventoried and put ashore.

It was not all that unusual for sailors to overstay leave and miss curfew; had he gone back to the ship he would have been mildly disciplined and able to rejoin the *Glennon* for her next transatlantic convoy. In June 1944, six months after Jimmy's desertion, the USS *Glennon* took part in the Allied invasion of France. On June 7, she shelled the mainland in support of troops advancing toward Quinéville, but the next day she struck a mine and was badly damaged. During efforts to salvage the ship, a salvo from a German shore battery hit the ship, and on June 10 she sank, with losses of twenty-five dead and thirty-eight wounded. If Jimmy had not gone AWOL, he might have been one of the sailors killed on June 10, in which case there would never have been a poet named James Schuyler.

Jimmy later stated he went through a "kind of breakdown" at this time, and that this led to his desertion. But in the version he told his friend Tom Carey in the 1980s, he made it sound as if his desertion was more or less accidental, or anyway alcohol-induced. The truth is probably a combination of the two. It would hardly have been surprising if he had had some sort of breakdown on board the *Glennon*. Surrounded by uncongenial companions, beset by frightening storms, stressed by the responsibilities of his job, not to mention the very real possibility of submarine attack, he did experience severe depression, which, as he told a psychiatrist at the time, prompted thoughts of suicide. The actual and ongoing "breakdown," however, could have been just as much a result as a cause of his desertion, and probably manifested itself as an attack of severe anxiety, of withdrawal and passivity, brought on by the realization of what he had done, and seeing no very good way clear of it.

Whether the cause or the result of his desertion, this breakdown or attack of panic continued to freeze his will, and he remained at loose in New York City for a total of twenty-nine days. What he did in those twenty-nine days—where he stayed, whom he met, how he survived—is mostly unknown. Almost certainly, he spent at least some time living at the West Side YMCA at 5 West Sixty-third Street, which was known as gay-friendly and inexpensive, and where he had stayed on previous visits to New York. Starting with just the uniform on his back and whatever small amount of money he happened to have with him, he would have needed a protector, or protectors, to help him get by, and being the young, handsome sailor boy that he was, would not have lacked for them.

The name of one older man he met during this time was revealed by Jimmy in a fragmentary recollection, included in a letter of August 1971 to Ron Padgett—the only firsthand account he left of the AWOL episode:

> In '43 Sidney Gittler entrusted his cute sailor found-object to a "friend" who took me to meet a lady lush in "volunteer" uniform who once starred in a flop musical: her big number, Roxy Rose. She, we, got bad . . . drunk and she did her number. Hubby came home to his star looking [pissed], "friend" took me to the Everard

baths—and me still "19" well, just 20, maybe—yes, 20—where I grooved with a nifty soldier and, Ron, I can feel those dogtags this minute . . .

Sydney Gittler (d. 1991, age eighty-five) was at the time a buyer at either Bloomingdale's or Macy's, and became known after the war as a designer of women's suits and coats. The aimless passivity with which Jimmy characterizes his younger self in this short passage, along with the fact that he had apparently established a relationship with an older man (by about fifteen years), suggests that this episode must have taken place while he was adrift and AWOL in the city. Describing himself in the third person as a "cute sailor found-object," Jimmy increases the distance between the young sailor of 1943 and his 1971 self. Gittler and he must have picked each other up somewhere—perhaps at the Astor Bar—and remained together long enough for Gittler to "entrust" him for an evening, like the sex object he was, to somebody else, and Jimmy passively went along.

It was generally known that if a serviceman stayed away for more than thirty days his legal status would change from mere "straggler" to "deserter," and make him liable for much more severe penalties. If Jimmy communicated with his parents, there is no record of it. But someone seems to have suggested he see a psychiatrist, not only for help with what must have been acute depression and anxiety, but also as a strategic move. If he could get a doctor's letter attesting to his disturbed mental state, it might carry weight when he tried to explain his desertion to the navy authorities. Thus it was that on December 23, and again on December 28, Jimmy was examined by Dr. Charles R. Hulbeck, a psychiatrist at 415 East Fifty-eighth Street. Hulbeck provided Jimmy with the following letter for navy authorities:

To Whom it May Concern:

This is to certify that Mr. James Ridenour who was born on November 9, 1923 at Chicago, Ill. came to my office twice, on December 23, and on December 28, 1943. Mr. Ridenour contends that he has been suffering from depressive spells which made it

> hard for him to attend to his duties and sometimes were so strong that he had suicidal ideas.
>
> Mr. Ridenour has been an active homosexual for years and though he does not know whether his depressions have any connection with these homosexual inclinations it is clear to him that they are an expression of a general feeling of frustration which has been growing during the last year.
>
> Though I am unable to commit myself as to the truth of Mr. Ridenours statements it seems to me that the past history of the patient makes him recommendable for a thorough psychiatric examination.

Hulbeck's cautious letter must have disappointed Jimmy for failing to argue more strongly that his mental illness or "depression" caused his desertion, and should therefore be a mitigating factor in considering it. The revelation of his homosexuality would get him out of the navy, he knew, but it would not prevent his being punished for being AWOL, and, moreover, the "undesirable" discharge that came with the admission of homosexuality could seriously damage his future employment prospects. To posterity, however, the letter's relative lack of engagement is disappointing for an additional reason. Charles Hulbeck in an earlier life had been none other than the Dada poet and performer Richard Huelsenbeck, whose stream-of-consciousness and pure sound poetry placed him as one of the pioneer inventors of Dada in Switzerland during the First World War, along with Hugo Ball, Hans Arp, and Tristan Tzara. But of course, Jimmy was not yet a poet and Huelsenbeck was working under another name and profession, and the exchange passed without the recognition of any common interests.

How was it that in his search for a doctor, Jimmy happened to land on a chief instigator of one of the most revolutionary and influential art movements of the twentieth century? Pure coincidence does not seem possible. Yet it may have had less to do with Hulbeck/Huelsenbeck's Dada credentials than with his personal history of antimilitarism. Thirty years earlier, at the start of World War I, Huelsenbeck, who was German, had persuaded a doctor friend to give him a series of medical certificates, exempting him from military service on mental health grounds, which enabled him to join his friend Hugo Ball in Zürich and invent Dada rather than become a nameless casualty of the slaughter.

Circumstantial evidence suggests one possible intermediary in the rather unlikely person of a Viennese émigré painter named Maximilian Mopp (1885–1954). Known in Austria as Max Oppenheimer, Mopp had been a prominent Expressionist painter in pre–World War I Vienna, rivaling Kokoschka and sharing a studio with Schiele. Provocatively homosexual, he had affected a "decadent," dandified persona, given to wearing a black abbé's cassock and carrying an antique tasseled walking stick. His pre-1914 mythological and biblical-themed paintings take one aback even today with their depictions of blood and violence imbued with homoeroticism. Mopp knew Huelsenbeck from Zürich, where he had also spent World War I, taking part in Dada performances at Cabaret Voltaire and exhibiting a painting in the first Dada exhibition. Immigrating to New York in 1939, he lived until his death in the Hotel des Artistes on West Sixty-seventh Street, eking out a living from the occasional portrait commission. "Every evening," according to Huelsenbeck's memoir, *The Dada Drummer*, Mopp walked to the nearby West Side Y to play chess and socialize with young men there. It is more than likely that Jimmy was living at the Y at this time, and certain that it was one of his haunts.

It is not hard to imagine Mopp, fifty-eight at the time, taking an interest in a handsome, troubled young sailor (who tended to be attracted to older men) hanging around the West Side Y. Learning of Jimmy's predicament, he could have recalled that his old acquaintance was now practicing psychiatry under the name Hulbeck, and reasoned that his own medical deferments from military service would make him sympathetic to Jimmy's case and lead him to write a report that might convince military authorities to excuse his desertion. While there is, as yet, no documentary evidence that Jimmy and Mopp met, a strong point in favor of such a meeting, and for Mopp as the link between Jimmy and Hulbeck/Huelsenbeck, is the circumstance that he was surely the only person within Jimmy's very limited social milieu at the time who not only knew Hulbeck but would have known that he had received two psychiatric deferments from military service in World War I. In fact, since Hulbeck probably did not maintain close ties with Mopp in New York, it could very well have been Jimmy who told him about Mopp's daily visits to the West Side Y, in the course of explaining how he knew him.

Unfortunately for Jimmy, however, and his hopes for a sympathetic medical advocate, Dr. Hulbeck was homophobic, in both of his personas. The references to Mopp in *The Dada Drummer* are slighting and refer darkly to his "sexual problems" with a tone of distaste, which seems to have carried over to the decidedly cool attitude toward Jimmy evident in his letter. A bit later, in a paper called "Emotional Conflicts in Homosexuality," read at the New York Academy of Medicine in 1947 or '48, Hulbeck declared, "Homosexuality develops from character neurosis. It seems clear that the homosexual shows all the characteristics of a neurotic personality—for example, compulsive aggressiveness, submissiveness, detachment, neurotic pride, and self-hatred . . . Characteristic of this sexualization of neurotic needs is the absence of mutuality between partners which is present in adult, healthy love." Since homosexuality was not removed from the American Psychiatric Association's list of mental illnesses until 1973, Hulbeck was in line with conservative psychiatric opinion of the time, but he seems to have had something of a bee in his bonnet on the subject. In 1969, while comparing popular misperceptions of Dada and existentialism in his memoir, Huelsenbeck wrote: "For the average brain, existentialism is identical with 'doing one's own thing totally'—rape and murder, homosexuality, and the like."

At 11:05 a.m. on December 29, the day after his second and final visit to Dr. Hulbeck, Jimmy, in uniform, surrendered to the authorities at the Navy Receiving Station on Pier 92 (West Fifty-fourth Street). Clearly, he realized that if he stayed away thirty days or longer he would be classified as a "deserter" rather than simply AWOL, which would have been a much more serious crime. As it was, he waited until the last possible moment, having been absent for a period of "29 days, 3 hours and 35 minutes," according to a note in his file, and he was indeed classified as a "straggler" rather than a "deserter."

Jimmy was sent to the temporary U.S. Navy prison, or brig, on Hart Island. The 101-acre Hart Island, situated in Long Island Sound a few miles north and east of Manhattan, has a checkered history. At the end of the Civil War, it was briefly a federal prison camp for Confederate soldiers. In 1868, it was purchased by the City of New York for use as a potter's field, which it still is, with burials there carried out by prisoners from neighboring Rikers Island. At different times in the nineteenth and twentieth centuries it also housed a tuberculosis hospital, an insane asylum, a boys' reformatory, a women's prison, a drug abuse center, a shoe factory, and a Cold War intercontinental missile base.

During World War II, the greater New York City area was a busy navy harbor, teeming with thousands of sailors on shore leave in the city. Disciplinary problems were inevitable, and beginning in April 1943, and until to the end of the war, a portion of Hart Island was requisitioned by the navy as a disciplinary barracks. During its wartime use as a prison camp, the island held about sixty buildings of various kinds, including a mess hall, heating plant, firehouse, butcher, commissary, laundry, garbage disposal plant, hospital, visitors' house, theater, officers' quarters, kennels, and two churches. Remnants of many of these buildings stand today as crumbling brick ruins, overgrown with foliage.

Prisoners were sent there either to await court-martial or a disciplinary hearing, or, in the case of minor infractions, to serve out their sentences. At least half of the Hart Island inmates were judged by the military doctors to be "emotionally unstable, some neurotic, some psychopathic." Nonetheless, most of the men would eventually be returned to active service, since their transgressions were usually not serious enough to warrant their permanent removal from the war effort. Inmates were held there for no longer than a year; sailors convicted of serious crimes were sent on to military prison elsewhere. Still, it was a hard, grim, isolated, and creepy prison environment. Security was relatively inconspicuous because of the island's isolation, but armed guards with German shepherd police dogs patrolled the island at night.

Prisoners were wakened at 5:30 a.m. and worked six hours a day at manual labor, which in frigid January, when Jimmy was there, was confined to shoveling coal, doing roadwork, and digging up and freeing from frozen ground the remaining gravestones of a former Civil War cemetery, the final phase of a project begun in 1941 to reinter the remains in Cypress Hills Cemetery in Brooklyn. If no useful work could be found, prisoners were assigned to Sisyphean make-work, such as shoveling coal pointlessly from one pile to another. It was freezing on the island, and prisoners were within tantalizing sight of the everyday normality of Westchester County or Long Island. After lunch the men were assigned to additional tasks, or else "drilling." They slept in barracks with bars on the windows, and lights-out was at 9:30.

Without identifying the location or the situation, Jimmy later gave impressions of the prison in a section of his story "The Infant Jesus of Prague." Here again, as in the "sailor found-object" letter to Ron Padgett, he employed the third person, not letting on that he was one of the prisoners involved:

> Across the water lies the shore and its houses, folded like a fan. In the deep coal barge out of the January river wind bearing gulls, a prisoner turns his hands, his palms red through the palms of the cheap black wool gloves the shovel handle wears out so quickly.
>
> Swinging up, the laden bucket spills lumps of coal. At the centre the boards are shoveled clear and gleam gray and silver. Or it is another day on another part of the island, shaped like a stone dividing a stream. Among the concrete grave markers a pale fire, its flames almost invisible in the sunlight. With crowbars, the prisoners try to break the grave markers from the frozen earth. Or they are in the mess hall, eating cake that tastes of soap, or there is nothing for them to do and they shovel a coal pile from where it is to a place next to it. Secretly, quickly, five share a cigarette. Curses flap into the sky like starlings, fall on them like frozen starlings.

Hostile and humiliating interviews and examinations took place at the prison. On one occasion, Jimmy overheard a sneering receptionist tell his or her boss over the intercom, "The fairy's here." In time, he was examined by the "Psychiator" [*sic*], who filed the following report on January 7, 1944:

> The subject gives a history of active homosexual practices since the age of 17. For a time he was able to control these homosexual impulses but recently they have been a very disturbing element in his makeup.

> Examination reveals findings to substantiate the diagnosis of homosexuality. He has effeminated mannerisms and urges toward oral perverse activity. His reason for going AWOL was directly related to homosexual urges and activities.
>
> Because of this diagnosis it is felt that he is not suitable for retention in the Naval Service.

Exactly what sort of "examination" Jimmy was subjected to in determining the "diagnosis" of homosexuality, is not known. However, some of the tests that the historian Allan Bérubé records as being used by the U.S. military during World War II to determine sexual orientation included inserting tongue depressors into the throats of suspected homosexuals to test their gag reflexes, on the theory that gay men did not show a gag reflex due to "the repeated control of the reflex during the act of fellatio." Rorschach inkblot tests were also sometimes given, as well as "biological tests" of male and female hormone levels in urine.

Another report in Jimmy's file states that the punishment recommended—Summary Court Martial—had been dropped, "in view of the report of the Psychiatric analyses." In other words, they saw no point in trying him on the charge of being AWOL, since his diagnosis of homosexuality made him ineligible to return to active duty anyway. On January 19, he was released from detention with an Undesirable Discharge. Before being released, he had to sign the following statement: "I hereby admit that I am homosexual and of no use to the U. S. Naval Service. I have been fully informed that I am to be discharged from the U. S. Naval Service with an UNDESIRABLE DISCHARGE because of unfitness. [signed] James Schuyler RIDENOUR." He was furnished with a set of civilian clothes and a travel allowance to get him to Buffalo and banned from further service in the military.

Jimmy seems to have gone into what might be called psychological shock. Like someone who survives a terrible accident and feels as though he is standing outside himself, Jimmy was able to take in where he was and what he was doing, but as though it were happening to another person. What he was left with was a series of visual and sense impressions, such as those he described in "The Infant Jesus of Prague." This kind of retreat into deep passivity would remain his survival strategy throughout his life in times of setback, illness, anxiety, and depression. At times it led him into almost indescribable depths of squalor and self-destructive behavior. But it also may be connected to his uncanny ability to "transcribe" the physical world in a seemingly unmediated way. In his poem "Unlike Joubert," this Keats-like state of "negative capability" is associated with the impossible idea of being able to "think nothing."

The ordeal was not only traumatic, but shameful and embarrassing, and throughout his later life Jimmy told very few of his friends anything about it. John Ashbery, his close friend in the 1950s and later years, who had his own traumatic draft interview in 1945, was one of the few in whom he confided. In the 1970s, he told his psychiatrist, Hy Weitzen, about the experience, explaining that it was the root cause of his lifelong fear of "doing anything in front of a crowd of people," and hence his inability to give public readings for most of his career. He also told his dearest friend of the 1980s, Tom Carey, about the episode, emphasizing its somewhat ridiculous aspects (getting drunk and passing out) rather than its more painful ones.

Jimmy's reunion with his family in East Aurora was not a happy one. But perhaps he was in no fit state to note it. According to his mother, he arrived home in a "disturbed condition." His brother, Fred, only ten at the time, had earlier been proud to see James's name on a wooden signboard in front of the high school, listing the graduates who were serving in the war. Now he observed his brother's depressed and withdrawn state and noticed that he had "the shakes," causing his hands to tremble visibly. These nervous tremors would return throughout Jimmy's life in times of emotional stress. Over the next few weeks, Berton and Margaret tried to make sense of the triple whammy of James's homosexuality, his depression, and his desertion. Berton wrote to the navy requesting that his psychiatric records be sent to the family doctor in Buffalo. Margaret, despite her pacifist views during World War I, showed limited sympathy with her son now. One can perhaps understand her distress, based on fears that Jimmy could have inherited some tendency to character "weakness," either from his father, Marcus, the obsessive gambler, or from her own father, Frederick Connor, whose desertion of his family in 1895 and subsequent suicide were never fully acknowledged or understood. Under the pressure of these family ghosts, Margaret became an exponent of what would later be called "tough love." She was verbally cruel to her son after his dismissal from the navy, much as she had been to Marcus when he succumbed to his gambling compulsion, and accused Jimmy of cowardice, in effect, telling him that he should have had "the guts" to remain in the service.

On March 30, Margaret took matters into her own capable hands and wrote the following letter to the commanding officer of the Hart Island Disciplinary Barracks.

> Re: James S. Ridenour SOM 3/c 3114
>
> Dear Sir:
>
> I am the mother of James S. Ridenour, SOM 3/c (3114) who was discharged from the Navy about the 13th [*sic*] of January, 1944.
>
> When James came home and we ascertained he had been discharged with the notation "undesirable"—and had been told some of the facts, such as the one about his being A.W.O.L., examination by a psychiatrist, and subsequent dismissal, we considered it wise to take some time for observation of him before taking the matter up with you.
>
> Two months have elapsed and James has been here at home with no work except the duties we have given him about the house. Although he was in a disturbed condition when he arrived, he manifests no such symptoms now; and we are convinced the disturbance was the normal result of disobedience with its subsequent fears that any normal person would have experienced. He was no doubt greatly upset or he would not have been A.W.O.L., but we do not feel he was abnormal or subnormal to the point of being permanently unsuited for his work. Also we feel that since he is not yet twenty-one he is neither old enough nor wise enough to make decisions for himself that will mitigate against his best interests all his life.
>
> Is it possible for James to be re-instated in the Navy? Subject of course to whatever discipline the Navy feels necessary under the circumstances.

I realize the Navy is not an institution for developing wayward youths, and that in order to be a good Navy man a boy must possess the qualities of true manliness that make the highest type of citizen. To these points as well as others you and your staff gave consideration. I only ask that this case be reconsidered if it is in any way possible for I know you would not only add one more trained man to an effort that needs them now; but for the future you would add a more worthwhile citizen to a world that needs real men.

Sincerely,
Margaret Connor Ridenour

The commander at Hart Island replied with a suggestion that she redirect her letter, with one from James himself, to the Bureau of Naval Personnel in Washington, DC, "as the matter is entirely out of the hands of the local Naval officers." This she did on April 11. James's letter is as follows:

Dear Sir:

On January 19 of this year, I was discharged from the U. S. Naval Service as "undesirable" because of "unfitness" (Article D-9112 (2) (3) Bureau of Naval Personnel Manual). Since that time I have lived at home, not working, and have attempted to make a readjustment in my own mind and attitudes toward the cause of my discharge. Whether this condition is inherent or one which is acquired, I do not know. I am convinced, however, that I have destroyed it in myself.

Since the foregoing was the only reason for my discharge, and since I believe it no longer exists, I am writing to ask if there is any way in which I can be reinstated in the Navy.

I understand that there is a shortage of trained and experienced enlisted men. While it is true that I was in the Navy only eight months and six days, I did in that time, finish boot training, and the training at the Fleet Sound School, Key West, and served for several months on the USS Glennon, DD 620. This, perhaps may make me somewhat more valuable than one who is untrained and without Naval experience.

My service number was 8054702 and, at the time I was discharged, I held the rating of Soundman Third Class.

Respectfully,
James Schuyler Ridenour

It seems clear that this letter, with its improbable claim that Jimmy had cured himself of homosexuality, was actually written by Margaret. Whatever worries Jimmy may have had about the possible repercussions of his undesirable discharge, we know that he was primarily "relieved" to be out of the navy, as he later recalled. That he would consent to sign such an abject document has nothing to do with his true feelings or his self-knowledge, but everything to do with the passivity that would remain, to a greater or lesser extent, his response to anxiety and setbacks. In any case, this attempt to reenlist failed, and Jimmy received a form letter from the navy dated April 20. His reinstatement was "not authorized" and his discharge, which had been "legal and regular in all respects, is now the record of an accomplished fact." To the preprinted form letter a typed postscript added, "Your patriotic offer to serve again is appreciated."

But by the time the letter was received, Jimmy had already moved to New York City.

[5]

GOSSIP AND OPERA

1944–1947

Jimmy had apparently managed to keep in touch with Bill Aalto, the former Abraham Lincoln Brigade veteran whom he had met at Pop Tunick's bar the previous winter, and by late April 1944, they were living together in Bill's apartment at 163 East Seventy-first Street. Jimmy got a job working at NBC for the Voice of America, while Bill, who had been invalided out of the US army after the loss of his right hand in a training accident, was studying European history at Columbia on the G.I. Bill.

New York would be Schuyler's home for the rest of his life. Years later, even after the changes of subsequent decades had overlaid his first impressions, the New York of the mid-'40s would remain, as he would write in 1988, "*my* New York." It was a city where the El still rumbled and clattered up the middle of Third Avenue, dominating the Upper East Side neighborhood where he first met and lived with Aalto (the El ran directly in front of Pop Tunick's), creating a strange netherworld of angular shadows below; it was a wartime city, swarming with servicemen on leave and looking for a good time; a city where social mores and expectations had been changed and were changing still in the social upheaval and aftermath of war. It was a city of possibility, where a beautiful woman glimpsed in a Chinese restaurant in Times Square might or might not be the movie star Alice Faye; where the light and air and crowds and buildings James had read of in stories by Cheever, O'Hara, or Maxwell could be stepped into, as could the clubs on Fifty-third Street, where a person might drop in one evening and hear Billie Holiday or Mildred Bailey sing.

The next five years of Jimmy's life would be dominated by his tumultuous relationship with Bill and his friendship with Chester Kallman, his best friend through the 1940s. Along with Kallman's longtime partner, the poet W. H. Auden, they formed a quartet within a particular circle of friends, mostly gay men, surrounding Auden and Kallman. Jimmy's engagement with this group foreshadows in some ways the close friendships he formed in the next decade with fellow New York poets and their painter friends.

Bill Aalto was a complex, colorful, and ultimately tragic figure. He was born out of wedlock on July 30, 1915, in New York City to Elsa Akkola, a Finnish immigrant employed as a domestic servant. He never knew his father, William Alstrom, who left soon after Bill was born. Elsa was a proud, educated, and politically engaged woman who found her work a grating humiliation. As he grew up, Bill became increasingly embittered about his mother's social degradation and his own illegitimate birth, both of which he traced to the capitalist system. Throughout his life, his anger regularly erupted in violent outbursts. Elsa raised Bill in the Bronx as a single mother until he was twelve, when she married Otto Aalto, who adopted Bill and gave him his name. Bill hated his stepfather, who beat him, and would probably have left home earlier than he did (at age nineteen or twenty) if Elsa hadn't insisted he stay to complete his education.

From the age of fourteen, Bill worked at various jobs to help support the family. A voracious reader, he was never to be seen without a book or two in hand, and spoke Finnish and Spanish (even before going to Spain) in addition to English. He also wrote poetry. Politically active, he joined the American Communist Party Youth Movement in about 1934 or 1935, and the Communist Party itself in 1937.

Like idealistic young people all over the world, Bill was moved by the struggle of the Spanish people to resist the military coup, initiated in 1936 by General Francisco Franco, that threatened to overthrow the democratically elected Spanish government. In February 1937, he sailed to Spain to join the American volunteers of the Abraham Lincoln Brigade fighting on the side of the Spanish Republic. He was recruited directly into the Republican Army's guerrilla forces to fight behind the enemy's lines—one of only three or four Americans, and very few non-Spaniards, chosen for this dangerous and elite work, as his biographer, Helen Graham, has pointed out.

Aalto advanced quickly in the ranks and was promoted to Captain of the 230th Brigade by 1938. At the end of the Civil War, both the CPUSA and the Comintern graded him politically and militarily outstanding. Bill was assigned to missions of intelligence-gathering and sabotage, mostly in southern Spain, where he was joined by Irving Goff, a fellow Lincoln who went through most of the war with him. Bill and Irving are acknowledged to be among the three or four Lincoln Brigade members on whom Hemingway based his fictional hero, Robert Jordan, in *For Whom the Bell Tolls*. Like Jordan, Aalto and Goff rigged train lines and bridges to explode when they were driven over. In May 1938, the pair led a daring raid resulting in the liberation of three hundred Republican prisoners of war from the rebel fortress of Carchuna on the coast near Granada. Caught behind enemy lines, they survived by swimming out to sea at night under fire, remaining in the water for several hours, then scrambling their way along the shore for three days, until they finally made it back to Republican lines. The exploit was much celebrated in the Republican press and propaganda at the time.

Bill's departure from Spain after the defeat of the Republican cause, in one of the last groups of Lincoln Brigade members to get out, was covered in *The New York Times* of January 20, 1939. The article described Aalto as the leader of the returning veterans and the "hero" of the Carchuna jailbreak—"the Partisans' outstanding feat in the war." Back in the States, Aalto spent the next two years engaged in a series of odd jobs and lecture tours on behalf of the Spanish Republican refugees. During one of the tours, Aalto impulsively decided to declare his homosexuality to Irving Goff, who was shocked and uncomprehending that someone like Bill Aalto, big, macho, and heroic, could be queer.

In October 1941, Aalto was drafted into the U.S. Army and began basic training. A few months later, in early 1942, William ("Wild Bill")

Donovan, the head of the newly formed Office of Strategic Services (OSS, the forerunner of the CIA), started recruiting former Lincoln Brigade veterans to join local resistance groups behind the lines in occupied Europe, and Aalto began training with this elite guerrilla group. But thanks to Goff, his homosexuality was common knowledge among his fellow trainees, who met privately and insisted that Donovan remove him as a "security risk." Donovan disagreed, but in the end he complied and Aalto was kicked out of the unit. He was transferred to Fort Richie in Maryland, where he was assigned to train regular army officers in guerrilla methods. He had been there for almost a year when on September 29, 1943, a trainee froze holding a live grenade. Bill grabbed it, but it exploded before he could get rid of it, blowing off his right hand and part of his forearm. He spent the next several months at Walter Reed Hospital in Washington, where he taught himself to write with his left hand, and in February 1944, he was invalided out of the army.

Bill Aalto went back to New York and in March 1944 enrolled in Columbia University to study European history, while he continued to write poetry, as well as reviews and articles for the American Marxist monthly, *New Masses*. At Columbia, he cut a striking figure, even as he consistently played down his heroism and sacrifice. Fellow students in these years included Allen Ginsberg, Jack Kerouac, and Jimmy's future friend John Hohnsbeen. Aalto makes a brief cameo appearance in Kerouac's *The Subterraneans* as "the famous one-armed Nick Spain."

In the poem "Dining Out with Doug and Frank," Jimmy gives an account of how he met Bill Aalto at Pop Tunick's bar, without saying when it was. However, in 1948, Jim and Bill gave the winter of 1942–43 as the date of their meeting, meaning that they had met, however briefly, before Bill lost his right hand and Jimmy went AWOL. This can be indirectly confirmed by considering how quickly Jimmy got settled in New York, with a lover, an apartment, and a job in April 1944, even as Margaret was still trying to have him reinstated in the navy. It must be that Jimmy and Bill had kept in touch since the preceding year, and Bill now came to Jimmy's assistance. The Voice of America was associated with the OSS, and "Wild Bill" Donovan, who had been reluctant to exclude Aalto from the OSS guerrilla group, leading to the loss of his hand, could well have contacted Bill with an offer of help when he got out of the hospital. Bill was settled at Columbia and didn't need help himself, but Jimmy did. Donovan's backing would have persuaded the VOA administration to hire Bill's friend, despite his undesirable discharge, which would likely have been disqualifying otherwise.

By late 1945, Bill and Jim had moved to a walk-up railroad apartment in Greenwich Village at 63 Downing Street, near the Catholic church of Our Lady of Pompeii, whose Italianate steeple they could see from their kitchen window. The apartment was a typical New York cold-water flat of basically two rooms: a kitchen, which doubled as a living room, and a bedroom. There was a toilet down the hall. Jimmy was making about $50 a week, while Bill had his pension of $138 a month. Jimmy considered Bill to be his first friend of his own generation who was a serious writer, even though his writing was politically motivated and they had "terrible fights about it." This was Jimmy's first real home of his own, and a place where he and Bill were able to establish a shared domestic life and entertain friends for simple meals.

James Schuyler Ridenour, as he was still known, was twenty years old in the spring of 1944. He was handsome in a boyish way: his finely drawn mouth, slightly upturned nose, and hint of a cleft chin lent him a quiet sexual allure. But the depression he was already said to have exhibited at Bethany had only been exacerbated by his experiences in the navy, his desertion, and his imprisonment on Hart Island, leaving him shy and withdrawn.

Bill Aalto, by contrast, exuded confidence and charisma. He, too, was handsome, with straight dark hair slicked back from a high forehead and large soulful eyes: "A dark / Finn who looked not unlike / a butch version of Valentino," according to Jimmy. But he added, "Watch out for Finns. They're / murder when they drink." Most people were initially attracted by Bill's good looks and intensity, but beneath the surface was an emotional volatility, which was apt to find an outlet in angry outbursts. As the novelist Donald Windham observed, he was "always on the defensive against being hurt." To some people, such as the painter Bernard Perlin, it seemed he had a chip on his shoulder, with a tendency to "brandish his stump."

Bernie Oshei, who reconnected with Jimmy in New York and met Aalto, compared him to "an Auden without wrinkles" and likened his stares to "being looked at by an eagle." When drunk he could be violent and frightening, and there are many stories of him throwing glassware, china, and food and on one occasion angrily tipping over an entire luncheon table when he took offense at some seemingly innocuous remark. Another time he bodily picked up Chester Kallman's college friend from Ann Arbor, Dorothy Farnan, and threw her across the room. Bill's camp name was "Big Edna," which some thought derived from Hurricane Edna (1954), or from the volcano Mount Etna, in reference to his volatile temper. But very likely it was simply a funny, rather dykey-sounding name to give this big, sensitive bruiser of a gay man. (One can hear Kallman's wit in this.)

Bill was not only violent in public settings, but also at times an abusive lover: in a retrospective poem, Jimmy recalls, "Perhaps he'll / bat me one again." Over time, or at times, Jimmy became complicit in Bill's abusive behavior, which may have devolved into something approaching a consensual sadomasochistic scenario. Such, anyway, is the inference to be drawn from an unpublished poem, dating from a few years after the relationship had ended. It exists in several versions, one of which reads:

All I ever found you were in five years
of kissing, fighting, traveling and lies
the night we met you spread before my eyes.
You even promised we would part in tears.

You promised we could make a kind of hell
for each other, and we did. You taunted
me with what I was and what I wanted.
In return, I admit I paid you well.

It's said that it takes two to make a rape
or kiss, or hug, or home, or family.
We should know, who raveled our history,
it takes the world to give one life its shape.
When the match struck the box and we caught flame,
we were such each thought, here's one I can blame.

The complicity and reciprocity of an S&M "contract" is suggested in the lines "it takes two to make a rape" and "You taunted / me with what I was and what I wanted. / In return, I admit I paid you well."

Through Bill, Jimmy got to know Chester Kallman, whom he had first met casually in the Astor Bar during his brief navy service. How Chester and Bill knew each other is not clear: possibly through a sexual encounter. Chester's quick and irreverent wit, New York City savvy, blond good looks, and passion for music and poetry captivated Jimmy. For the next six or eight years, he considered Chester to be "much" his closest friend, only to be supplanted by John Ashbery and Frank O'Hara after he got to know them in early 1952.

Chester Kallman was born in Brooklyn in 1921. His mother died when he was four and he did not get along with his stepmother, but remained close to his father, Edward, a dentist. Brilliantly precocious from an early age, his passions were poetry, opera, cooking, and sex, not necessarily in that order. In 1939, he and his boyfriend at the time, the poet Harold Norse, attended a reading by W. H. Auden, Christopher Isherwood, Louis MacNeice, and Frederic Prokosch. Sitting in the front row, they both flirted outrageously with Isherwood and Auden, who had just come to the States together. After Isherwood gave the boys his card, Chester went to the British poets' shared hotel room and met Auden. By his second visit they were lovers, and they would remain together for the rest of their lives. The relationship was never a monogamous one, especially as far as Chester was concerned, and after Chester stopped going to bed with Auden in about 1941, it became nonsexual. Still, it was the central domestic relationship of both their lives, and became, especially for Auden, who gave much thought to such matters, a kind of marriage.

Wystan Hugh Auden was of course one of the great poets and characters of the twentieth century. As an Oxford undergraduate, his brilliance and erudition already attracted acolytes and detractors, and his first book, *Poems*, published in 1930, established him as the era's most promising young poet. In January 1939, he and his close friend Isherwood traveled to the United States together, and when World War II broke out later that year, they decided to stay. Both eventually became American citizens, although Auden returned to England to take a post at Oxford at the end of his life. When Jimmy met Auden in the summer of 1944, he was teaching at Swarthmore College in Pennsylvania. At this point Auden didn't have his own place in New York, and on his visits to the city he spent most of his time at Chester's apartment, sometimes sleeping rolled up in the rugs on the floor "with a bottle of red wine and a plate of boiled potatoes" beside him.

Over the next several years, Chester Kallman's tenement apartment, above a Balkan restaurant at 129 East Twenty-seventh Street, near Lexington Avenue, became the social center for his and Wystan's young gay friends, and Jimmy and Bill were frequent visitors. The fourth-floor walk-up was notoriously squalid. Painted a "dim and dusty blue," it had two grimy windows facing Twenty-seventh Street, with a skylight in the ceiling that had been painted over in compliance with wartime blackout regulations. Beneath the windows sat a mattress, with a sofa on one side "of a color undistinguishable because of the dust and cigarette burns" and a fireplace on the wall opposite. The coffee table was stained with dark red circles from wineglasses and held a large ashtray overflowing with cigarette butts. In the corner stood the all-important phonograph, its arm tied together with string, and on every possible surface in the room were stacks of 78 rpm records.

Auden loved not only Chester's youth, charm, and physical attributes, of course, but also his bright intelligence, wit, and poetic gifts, and part of the attraction for him was that Chester was someone he felt he would be able to help and, to a degree, mold. Auden had paid for his year of graduate study at the University of Michigan, but Chester's real education was living with "Miss Master," as he called Auden. And yet, as Auden's biographers acknowledge, Chester also contributed to an enlargement of Auden's own sensibility. Auden valued Kallman's critical faculties, and sometimes took his advice about his work. Chester was also helpful to Jimmy, who in recalling his beginning attempts to write short fiction, credited him as "the person who most encouraged me to write."

Chester's own poetry Jimmy later characterized as "constipated." Undoubtedly it suffered both in its style and its reception from his personal closeness to Auden. Most seem to agree that Kallman's best works were the opera libretti he wrote with Auden, beginning with their collaboration with Igor Stravinsky on the opera *The Rake's Progress*, which they began in 1947.

Chester Kallman was a major opera queen, and one can credit Chester's infectious enthusiasm with making opera a large part of the lives of his entire circle of friends, including Jimmy, whose period of greatest interest in it coincides with their friendship. Auden had grown up with a love for the operas of Mozart and Wagner, but had had relatively little exposure to the Italian operas of Verdi, Bellini, Rossini, Donizetti, and Puccini before meeting Chester, who immediately set about to remedy the omission. Within a year of their meeting, Auden wrote to a friend, "My chief luxury is the opera." "When Chester shared with you his love of music, it somehow overflowed from him to you and pervaded your life," wrote Dorothy Farnan. Chester's visitors were invariably treated to whatever opera recordings he was obsessed with at the moment, at top volume: mounting the stairs to Chester's apartment while the music was blaring was like climbing into Kirsten Flagstad's very throat, according to his friend William Weaver. Alan Ansen, another close friend, intended to make Chester the central character of an unfinished novel, whose themes were "homosexuality, partygoing and the opera."

Chester was also what we would now call a sex addict, exhibiting a seemingly insatiable need for casual sex with mostly blue-collar, often straight or bisexual men. "Chester was really *dedicated* to sex. Dedicated," claimed his good friend John Hohnsbeen. But at the same time he was "the most enchanting man in the world, the best cruising partner on God's earth." He and Jimmy "were marvelous together. But almost everybody was good with Chester, he brought out the very best. He was such a funny, funny man." Yet "he was *so* self-destructive, and made poor Wystan *so* unhappy."

In addition to Jimmy and Bill Aalto, the group around Kallman and Auden included William Vinson (1916–1979), William Weaver (1923–2013), David Protetch (1921–1969), John Hohnsbeen (1926–2007), and Alan Ansen (1922–2006). Most were not writers, or at least not yet: Vinson was a navy officer and would become a virologist; Protetch, also a naval officer during the war, would become a doctor and Auden's trusted physician; Hohnsbeen was a student at Columbia, later an art dealer;

Weaver, an aspiring writer, would in time make his name as a translator from Italian; and Ansen, the only one of the group not originally a friend of Chester's, was a graduate student who sought out Auden and became his sometime secretary, and would become a poet and teacher. When he was with Chester and his younger gay male friends, Auden, by day a public intellectual in a now nearly vanished sense, could let down his hair, gossip, discuss the homosexual experience with the deep seriousness he gave every topic, and express, somewhat giddily, his queer persona. He and Chester made a game of bestowing camp nicknames not only on themselves and their friends, but also on Dorothy Farnan (who had begun an affair with Chester's father, and thus became "Miss Mistress"), God ("Miss God"), and even abstractions ("Lily Law") and inanimate objects ("Sheila Sugar").

The close "sisterly" bond between Jimmy and Chester, who were known by the camp names "Dorabella" and "Fiordiligi" after the two flighty sisters in Mozart's opera *Così fan tutte*, brought them into a kind of foursome with their respective lovers, Bill and Wystan, who, though not as close as Jimmy and Chester, had in common their service in the Spanish Civil War, where Auden had served as an ambulance driver. Auden's impassioned 1937 poem "Spain" became a rallying cry for British intellectuals to the Loyalist cause, but he later disowned it as "meretricious" and it did not appear in his *Collected Poems* as issued in his lifetime. The mood of disaffection with righteous posturing and partisanship that caused Auden to do so was an attitude he shared with Bill, whose heroic and celebrated deeds were matched by his refusal to brag about them.

In *Così fan tutte*, as all of their circle were well aware, the sisters' lovers are two soldiers who march off to war, but sneak back in disguise to test the girls' faithfulness by each attempting to seduce the other's lover. Most likely the "Dorabella" and "Fiordiligi" camp names date from the spring of 1945, when Wystan went to Germany with the rank and uniform of major in the U.S. Army to take part in a special Pentagon mission, interviewing civilians about the effects of the Allied bombing. He returned to New York at the end of that summer, bragging to friends that he was "the first major poet to have flown the Atlantic." With Aalto already strongly identified with soldiering, the plot of *Così fan tutte* would have put into the air unspoken or playful conjectures, if nothing more, about whether there might be anything physical between Chester and Bill, or Jimmy and Wystan.

The world of grand opera overlaid their lives. Chester had a habit of entering a room speaking in quotations from Italian opera, such as Amina's first act entrance from *La Sonnambula*, "Care compagne, e voi, / Teneri amici . . ." ("Dear companions and you, my good friends"), and often found (or created) parallels between his tumultuous love affairs and the fates of tragic operatic heroines. Auden, too, shared an opera-saturated worldview, telling Alan Ansen, rather revealingly, "I've decided that opera represents the willful display of emotions. And it's so odd how the characters always manage to fall in love with unsuitable people." He compared himself to the Marschallin in Richard Strauss's *Der Rosenkavalier* in his resigned acceptance of Chester's affairs, and specified that Siegfried's Funeral Music from *Götterdämmerung* be played at his funeral, as it was. After Jimmy and Bill had broken up, Jimmy instinctively summoned a situation and character from opera (Violetta examining herself in the mirror in Verdi's *La Traviata*) as a parallel to Bill's narcissistic attitude. In this fervid operatic context, even imaginary dalliances between Auden and Jimmy or Chester and Bill could have been all but real to them and their friends.

Jimmy's friendship with Auden, while never as easygoing as his with Chester, in time became warm and close. He later described Auden as "a very intimidating person" whom "it was impossible not to be in awe of" but at the same time "a sweetie" and not at all "stern." In the years of their closest friendship, from about 1945 to 1952, Auden was on several occasions unusually generous to "beloved Dorabella," but Auden was notably generous to many people. One mutual friend in the early 1950s, Helen Burckhardt, believed that they had been lovers, which is unlikely, but it's possible there may have been gossip to that effect at one time. We would know more about the friendship if Auden had not as a matter of principle thrown away all personal letters, as a corollary to asking his friends not to save his own to them. Of course, anyone who got a letter from Auden did save it, but he threw away those he got in return, including Jimmy's. "Please thank Jimmy for his [letter]," writes Auden to Chester in the spring of 1949. "The account of the Carnavale was divine." Divine or not, it went straight into the wastebasket.

Auden's *The Age of Anxiety*, subtitled "A Baroque Eclogue," is a book-length narrative poem in alliterative verse written in the voices of four characters who meet in a bar in wartime New York. Auden began writing *The Age of Anxiety* in the summer of 1944, within a month of meeting Jimmy and Bill, and traces of both Bill and Jim can be found in the early sections of the poem: Bill in aspects of both the disillusioned older clerk, Quant, and the air force pilot, Malin, and Jim in the sailor Emble. (Rosetta, the poem's female character, is thought to have been based partly on Rhoda Jaffe, a woman with whom Auden had a brief affair in the 1940s.) When it was published in 1947, Auden intended to dedicate it to Bill and Jimmy, but Chester wouldn't let him, saying Auden was always trying to "steal his friends. Later I realized I was just as glad that *The Age of Anxiety* wasn't dedicated to me," Jimmy recalled. "I had enough problems by then." In the end, Auden dedicated the work to John Betjeman.

Emble is a handsome but insecure young man who, "Having enlisted in the Navy during his sophomore year at a Mid-Western university . . . suffered from that anxiety about himself and his future which haunts, like a bad smell, the minds of most young men . . . In certain cases—his was one—this general unease of youth is only aggravated by what would appear to alleviate it, a grace of person which grants them, without effort on their part, a succession of sexual triumphs. For then the longing for success, the doubt of ever being able to achieve the kinds of success which have to be earned, and the certainty of being able to have at this moment a kind which does not, play dangerously into each other's hands."

One of Emble's early interior monologues describes being at sea in a long transatlantic convoy when one of the ships is struck by a torpedo, casting men into the sea to freeze and drown before the eyes of the survivors:

The blast killed many; the burning oil
Suffocated some; some in lifebelts
Floated upright till they froze to death;
The younger swam but the yielding waves
Denied help; they were not supported,
They swallowed and sank.

As we know, Jimmy had witnessed and taken part in a similar disaster while serving on the *Glennon*, and it's likely that he related this experience to Auden, who could have used it as a source for Emble's initial monologue, spoken by a character otherwise inflected by Jimmy's general demeanor. With this in mind, the first part of Emble's monologue, with its sense of watchfulness coupled with descriptions of sounds heard through ocean water ("webs of . . . sad sound"; "the insensible ocean . . . moaned"; "Strained with gazing / Our eyes ached, and our ears . . . Kept their care for the crash . . .") might suggest a sonar operator's experience as imagined by the poet.

Reading Emble's monologue together with "A Grave," Jimmy's own response to the incident, produces a sense of déjà vu. Not only are their themes and certain images comparable, but the formal diction, frequent alliteration, and syllabic lines of Jimmy's poem seem reminiscent of the diction, vocabulary, alliteration, and syllabic lines of Emble's monologue. Although the correspondences are hard to pin down exactly, one might note a few: "The insensible ocean" (Auden), "the uninjured ocean" (Schuyler); "They swallowed and sank" (Auden), "sank from sight / drowning" (Schuyler); "Miles without mind" (Auden), "night from night" (Schuyler); "Kept their care" (Auden), "kept / could not share" (Schuyler); "over water webs of brightness" (Auden), "part of that lighted blackness" (Schuyler). (The words *slept* and *kept* are adjacent in Auden's poem, separated by a line break, and are end rhymes in the final stanza of Schuyler's poem.) It is as though Jimmy, recalling the event over ten years later, also heard Auden's earlier version of it in his mind's ear: his own experience refracted through Auden's imagery, vocabulary, and cadences: unconscious echoes that tie his version of the event to Auden's, and indirectly confirm him as its source.

In many respects, the 1940s in New York continued to be an age of anxiety even after the war ended. Jimmy's first months in the city with Bill were dominated aurally by the sound of the elevated trains that ran up and down Third Avenue, half a block from their apartment, whose "roar" he once appeared to conflate with the trains transporting Jews to extermination camps in eastern Europe. Through his job at the Voice of America, Jimmy was better informed than many people at that time about the Holocaust and other events of the late wartime and early postwar period. One especially dramatic moment occurred on July 15, 1945, when the first atomic bomb test was broadcast on the air. There was a concern that the unprecedented explosion might somehow "set off a chain reaction that would destroy the world." Jimmy's job was to listen to the transmission and—"if the world wasn't destroyed"—run the recording down to the studio.

Jimmy worked for the Voice of America, out of the NBC offices at Rockefeller Center, for about three years, from the spring of 1944 until October 1947. His job there was purely clerical and consisted of keeping an ongoing "log" of broadcasts as they went out on the air. It was not a creative position, and his day job provided no outlet and little time for his own writing. The job did provide enough downtime to look out the window, however, always a favorite occupation. As he recalled in "A few days": "I remember the years / at NBC, looking / discontentedly out at grimy Sixth Avenue, waiting for / the time to pass." Close attention to the passing of time was in fact the essence of Jimmy's job at NBC; the noting and logging of "air time" was his daily occupation, and in a larger sense anticipates his poetic practice, when one considers the transcriptive or "log"-like aspects of his work: the many poems titled with a specific date; their sense of being lived in real time, or "now" ("Now it's tomorrow, / as usual"; "Now, this moment / flows out of me / down the pen and / writes").

Jimmy's life in the 1940s was not focused on work, however, but on his social life with Bill, Chester, and their friends. When they didn't gather at Chester's apartment, they met at bars such as the San Remo or the nearby McDougal's on McDougal Street. The San Remo was a favorite of writers and artists and not exclusively gay, but did have a large gay clientele. It was "a kind of crazy place where you could talk to anybody and anybody could talk to you and you never knew who was going to turn up there," as William Weaver recalled. The '40s were also a golden age for New York City nightclubs, such as Café Society Uptown and Café Society Downtown, the 1-2-3 Club and Spivey's Roof, where

Jimmy developed his ear for the jazz vocalists and pianists, including Mildred Bailey, Billie Holiday, Art Tatum, and others, who would later be evoked in his writing.

In July 1945, Jimmy and Bill drove to Canada for a two-week vacation, stopping in Montreal and Quebec on their way to a rented cabin near Lac St. Jean, about 120 miles north of Quebec. There is a possibility that this cabin and its surroundings were the remembered location evoked in Jimmy's first published poem, "Salute": "that field / the cabin stood in." This first vacation, just over a year after he and Bill had moved in together, when they were still in the first flush of their love, sharing a simple cabin in a beautiful, wild place far from any city, was indeed a past worth remembering and saluting, even or especially after it had all come apart.

The following summer, Auden and his friends James and Tania Stern jointly purchased a small unwinterized beach house in Cherry Grove on Fire Island, and for the next couple of years this would be Wystan and Chester's summer getaway. Fire Island is a long narrow strip separated from the south shore of Long Island by the Great South Bay. Cherry Grove, already a lively gay summer resort in the 1940s, is about midway down the island and is reached by a short ferryboat ride across the bay. That and the fact that there are no roads or cars on most of the island give it a sense of apartness belied by its relative proximity to the city. Auden, who hated the summer heat in New York, loved Cherry Grove's cool breezes and simplicity, and apparently learned to put aside his strong work ethic while there—while Chester found the sexual opportunities almost overwhelming. With a reference to the seductive and lethal "Flower Maidens" of Wagner's *Parsifal*, Auden wrote to Rhoda Jaffe, "The truth is, the bar here is a little too much for him. I call it Klingsor's Magic Garden." In August, Jimmy came out to Cherry Grove in time to help cheer up Chester after his latest unhappy love affair. Auden continued, "It was not I that did the boohing and hooing but Chester, who hit a rough trough in his manic depressive cycle. Now he is riding the wave and Jimmy Ridenour is here for two days."

In November 1946, the essayist Cyril Connolly came to the United States for the first time, intending to travel to various parts of the country and record his impressions for a special double issue of *Horizon*, the epoch-defining literary magazine he edited. His first stop was New York to see his old friend Auden. Auden met him at the boat, took him to lunch, then left him at the Holliday Bookshop at 49 West Forty-ninth Street, a small chic store that specialized in books imported from England. Connolly condescendingly described the store—a valued resource for Anglophile New Yorkers at the time, where Jimmy would work in the early '50s—as "an oasis where carefully-chosen books are sold like hand-made cushions." The next day, Wystan and Chester invited Connolly to an intimate dinner on Twenty-seventh Street with Bill and Jimmy. After two days of what he had been complaining of as American glitz and inauthenticity, Connolly was pleased to be back in a more bohemian atmosphere. His *Horizon* article reports:

> At last the luxury of poverty; stairs, no lift, leaking arm-chairs, a bed-sitting-room with bath-kitchenette curtained off, guests with European teeth (who was it said that Americans have no faces?), a gramophone library, untidy books not preserved in card-board coffins, an incompetent gas stove—and an exquisite dinner cooked and served by C[hester]. Clam-juice mixed with chicken broth, chops with a sauce and lima beans, lederkranz cheese and pumpernickel, dry Californian wine. Argument afterwards about poetry interspersed with selections from Wystans favorite operas. They are many.

Jimmy and Bill were the guests with "European [i.e., imperfect] teeth," as Wystan told Alan Ansen. (One of Emble's lines in *The Age of Anxiety* is "My teeth need attention.") In a slightly different reminiscence of the party, Connolly wrote that the conversation that evening revolved around "poetry and Lorca. Mysticism and fucking, according to Wystan, are the two extremes where man forgets himself and art consequently can't be made." Jimmy was also struck by Auden's words and remembered them as: "One cannot write about either end of the somatic scale: fucking and mystical love," adding that Connolly then proposed the Spanish mystic poet St. John of the Cross as an exception. No doubt Bill's presence and the research he was doing at Columbia for a book on the history of Spain helped steer the conversation to Spanish poets.

In October 1946, Auden began a series of lectures on Shakespeare at the New School, where Alan Ansen was one of his students. They became friends, and after class, Ansen would sometimes accompany Auden back to the small apartment he had recently rented on Cornelia Street in the West Village, or to Twenty-seventh Street. Ansen made extensive notes of their conversations, from which he later published excerpts as *The Table Talk of W. H. Auden* (1989). The book, along with Ansen's unpublished notes for it, provides a remarkable picture of what it must have been like to spend time socially with Auden in the late 1940s, when he was with his younger queer friends. Auden's pronouncements and conjectures were wide-ranging, erudite, iconoclastic, and funny. Gossip and opera loomed large, as Jimmy remembered, but Auden argued that even gossip could be a creative endeavor.

During Ansen's first visit to Wystan and Chester on Twenty-seventh Street, Chester tested his opera knowledge by playing excerpts from Donizetti's *Lucia di Lammermoor*, Glück's *Paride ed Elena*, and Rossini's *La Gazza Ladra*. Soon, "two other fairies drifted in": Bill, who is described as "fairly tall, rugged, prominent nose, mutilated hand, blue shirt," and Jimmy, "baby-face[d]" and wearing a gray suit. On a later visit he found Bill and Jimmy there again, this time listening to Schumann's song cycle *Dichterliebe* (*A Poet's Love*) set to poems of Heine, followed by Puccini's *La Bohème*.

Ansen gives candid glimpses of Chester's complicated sex life. "Chester seems to have hit a new peak by bringing home three sailors together Thursday," he notes in May 1947. On another occasion, Ansen accompanied Chester to a bar where he "made up with the sailor who'd beat him up the Sunday before" prior to going on to the Everard Baths. A good share of the group's conversation, as reported by Ansen, concerned not only their sexual conquests but also their run-ins, or near misses, with the authorities on account of their activities in restrooms and other public places. Auden warned Ansen, "They always have vice squad men in plain clothes either in the shop [restroom] or planted out of sight. Chester almost got into trouble that way. A friend of ours [Bill Aalto] was caught doing it with a minor in a tea-room [public toilet]. The vice squad man was hiding in the caretaker's room, The judge gave him a year and then suspended sentence because he was a veteran and had lost a hand. The minor was just as guilty as he was."

Auden devoted much thought and analysis to the subject of homosexuality, and it was a frequent topic among his friends in the 1940s. He told Ansen about a male brothel he used to go to in New York before the war called Matty's. "That was when people weren't making so much money. It was three dollars and mutual." He also told Ansen, "There's a good deal of [homosexual activity] on board [navy] ships," which was something he may have heard from Jimmy. In January 1948, Auden accompanied Ansen and Chester to court after Chester, or perhaps both of them, had been arrested for lewd behavior. "The judge was very nice (they asked Chester how much he was making before fining him)."

Though Jimmy was promiscuous, there is no evidence to suggest that "Dorabella's" promiscuity approached the level of "Fiordiligi's." Jimmy was, after all, living with Bill in some semblance of settled domesticity. Still, Jimmy and Bill were not sexually exclusive. Bill's arrest for having sex with a minor in a public bathroom seems to have taken place in 1947, while Jimmy was being treated with penicillin for syphilis at New York Hospital in the same year. Jimmy, having been introduced to the Everard Baths during the war, was a regular patron for much of his life, and it's possible that he continued going there during his relationship with Bill.

The idea of leaving New York and going to live in Italy began to take shape in the summer of 1947, when Jimmy learned that the farm he had inherited ten years previously was finally able to be sold. It brought $6,000, with Jimmy keeping $4,000, and his mother, for some reason, getting the remaining $2,000. What better use for the windfall than going off to Europe, where living was cheap and they could "goof off and be somewhere beautiful," as Jimmy later claimed, for as long as the money held out? Also, more seriously, there Jimmy could pursue his writing and Bill conduct research for the history of Spain he hoped to write.

When they went to apply for passports in June, both Bill and Jimmy had issues in determining what names to use. Bill's old passport for Spain had used his birth name, William Aalstrom. However, his new one was issued in the name Aalto, which had become his legal name when his mother's husband Otto Aalto adopted him as a boy. Jimmy, on the other hand, found, or claimed, that his name had never in fact been legally changed to Ridenour when his mother married Berton. Whether or not this was true, he submitted only his birth certificate to the State Department, giving his name as James Schuyler, taking this opportunity to cast off his stepfather's name. It felt like a rebirth.

[6]

WE ALL LAY ON THE ISLAND BEACH TOGETHER

1947–1948

"October's bright blue weather" was on full display on the afternoon of October 20, 1947, when Jimmy, Bill, Wystan, and Chester made their way to Hoboken, New Jersey, and the Holland America Line dock. Jimmy and Bill boarded one of the line's smaller passenger ships and the foursome said their goodbyes, with promises to meet later in Italy.

During the nine- or ten-day crossing, Jimmy went on deck and watched the water churning in the ship's wake, feeling the sense of occasion. His ambition, which he hoped to realize in Italy, was to write fiction—short stories and a novel. He had no thoughts yet of writing poetry. Meanwhile, his change in name held tremendous significance, and not only because "It's good to / have your own name," as he later deadpanned in "A few days." By resuming the name he had been born with, he transformed with a single stroke his unhappy high school years, aimless college years, and the trauma and disgrace of his navy expulsion, into a life lived by another person.

Bill's self-transformation had begun with his entering Columbia in 1944, graduating in 1947. While in Europe, he was planning to conduct research for two separate books: one on the theory and tactics of guerrilla warfare, the other a general history of Spain and the Mediterranean. Although Auden doubted Bill's ability to see either of his book projects through, telling him, "You're never going to write that book," he helped with practical suggestions and contacts, giving him the name of a Professor Passonatti of Yale, who suggested he work in Florence and gave him a list of possible contacts there. Following this advice, the pair settled on Florence as their destination, but they would stop in Amsterdam and Paris on the way.

The ship docked in Rotterdam on about October 30, and Jimmy and Bill immediately made their way to Amsterdam. There they stayed for a week or two—long enough to hear an "astringent" orchestral concert at the Concertgebouw, and for images of the chilly, autumnal city to be impressed in Jimmy's memory, later to be incorporated into several poems:

> Amsterdam belongs to the clerk in black,
> who, with briefcase and a bunch of crimson roses,
> boards the sadly lighted tram,
> withdrawing from the far-off dying sunset
> station square, as night
> clangs down and into place . . .

Jimmy basked in his newfound freedom from the drudgery of working at the Voice of America and being able to spend his afternoons at leisure, "free to be a slightly / drunk tourist, eyeing / the man-made wonders along the Amstel . . ."

They then spent two or three weeks in Paris, during which they rented bicycles and made a pilgrimage to what Jimmy later claimed were "all of the towns mentioned in Henry James's *A Little Tour in France*." While they could not have actually visited *all* the many towns across France that James described in his classic travel book, "is / not to have thought to do / enough?" as the poet asks in "Salute." A more realistic itinerary might have included the cathedral town of Tours and the chateaux of Blois, Chambord, Amboise, and Chenonceau, all within a few miles of one another in the valley of the Loire.

On December 1, a night train brought them across France and through the Alps, and they woke to find themselves in Italy. When Bill and Jimmy emerged from Santa Maria Novella station in Florence, they discovered the center of the Renaissance city largely in ruins. Three years previously, on the night of August 3, 1944, hoping to slow the advance of American and British armies, the Germans blew up five of the city's six bridges, sparing only the Ponte Vecchio. They compensated for that omission by dynamiting all the streets leading up to the bridge on either side of the river. In 1947, most of this damage had yet to be repaired, although temporary Bailey bridges had been erected in place of the Ponte Santa Trinità and the Ponte alla Carraia.

Despite the ruinous state of the city, and the exhaustion of the people after war and hardship, preceded by years of Fascist rule, there was a mood of optimism in the air. "Early post-war Italy was glorious," wrote the novelist Sybille Bedford. "One embraced the people for whom the springs of life were flowing again; they were at one with the staggering beauty of what there was to see, *everywhere*, dawdling in the sun, the sweet air, the new near quiet. Petrol was scarce, the Vespas and rattling trams were joyful toys, their noise another attribute of being alive."

Gore Vidal, who first went to Italy in January 1948, wrote of the exodus of young American writers to postwar Italy. "Rome was strange to all of us. For one thing, Italy had been sealed off not only by war but by Fascism. Since the early thirties, few English or American artists knew Italy well." Certainly Bill, Jimmy, and Chester Kallman had never been to Italy, but more surprisingly, neither had Wystan.

The enthusiasm of American and British writers, artists, and travelers for Italy was reciprocated by the Italians, who to a greater or lesser degree extended to these new, young (and relatively free-spending) visitors a continuation of the welcome with which they had greeted the liberating Allied armies. The young Americans who came to Italy after the war, according to one young Italian student who would soon meet Jimmy and Bill, had a particular "smell" and a refreshing air of optimism and energy.

In addition, the Latin world was more accepting of male homosexuality than the Anglo-Saxon, and for American gay men, the relative sexual freedom in Italy was especially welcome in contrast to the atmosphere of entrapment and persecution that was prevalent in New York in the 1940s and '50s. Tennessee Williams came to Italy in February 1948 (also for the first time), and was soon writing enthusiastically to his friend the novelist Donald Windham, "Honey, you would love Rome! . . . The pin-cushions [i.e., male buttocks] have been justly celebrated by artists for many centuries and there is nothing I can add to the statements of Michelangelo except a corroboration in modern times. I have not been to bed with his David but with any number of his more delicate creations, in fact the abundance and accessibility is downright embarrassing . . . Of course it usually costs you a thousand lire but that is only two bucks . . . and there is never any unpleasantness about it."

After settling into a pensione near the Pitti Palace, both Jimmy and Bill enrolled in classes at the University of Florence to study Italian language and culture. Jimmy eventually found the classes "superficial and boring" and withdrew, but Bill continued to attend, as far as their busy traveling schedule permitted. In time, both acquired at least a rudimentary knowledge of Italian. During his sojourn, Jimmy was introduced to the poetry of Giacomo Leopardi and the stories of Giovanni Verga, and by the end of his stay, was considering translating some of Verga's stories. A longer-lasting interest was Leopardi, several of whose poems Schuyler would translate in the late '50s.

One rainy night soon after they arrived, Bill Aalto was out walking amid the rubble of Via Por Santa Maria when he met a handsome young art student named Piero Tosi. Tosi, seventeen or eighteen at the time, was studying at the Accademia di Belle Arti. He was immediately taken with Bill's physical grace, stature, and indefinable American aura, which contrasted with the gray poverty of the postwar city. "He had that facility of rapport, like a gift given to him by life," Tosi recalled. "He was always smiling, happy. I remember perfectly the impression he gave me, with a raincoat, a cigarette in his mouth or parked behind one ear, books under his arm. I was not aware, for example [at the first meeting], that he was missing one hand." Retrospectively, Tosi compared Bill's "staggering charisma" to the film persona of William Holden. They arranged to meet the following day at the pensione. But to Tosi's dismay, when Bill appeared he was accompanied by Jimmy, who made an entirely different impression, as he did on many who met them as a couple. In comparison with

Bill, he seemed fragile, timid, and "closed." Crestfallen to learn of Jimmy's existence, Piero attributed Jimmy's reserve to an unspoken jealousy. In fact, Jimmy may have been unaware of or unconcerned by Piero's attraction to Bill, and while Tosi always preserved an unconsummated "amorous friendship" with Bill for the several years that he knew him, there was never, reportedly, any physical relationship between them. As Piero became more familiar with Jimmy's natural reticence, a warm friendship sprang up between them as well.

In the evenings Piero often met Jimmy and Bill at Caffè le Giubbe Rosse, a famous meeting place for writers and artists in the early twentieth century and in the years before and after World War II. Both Jimmy and Bill impressed Piero with their informed curiosity, their thirst "to know Italy in that moment, to know the literature, to know the current cinema . . . They were organized and they always knew where to find the most beautiful places"—not only the major tourist sights but the lesser-known Florentine museums, such as the Museo Bardini and Museo Horne. They were scarcely less interested in the popular culture of the day, and the three of them made a beeline to see the new movie *L'Onorabile Angelina*, starring the riveting Anna Magnani and with the young Franco Zeffirelli in a small role. This was, of course, a thrilling period for film in Italy, and all three were "wild at the idea of seeing La Magnani and Italian cinema: Rossellini, Visconti, de Sica." Soon Tosi himself would begin a long and brilliant career in the film industry, as the preeminent costume designer for Visconti and other Italian directors.

One reason Jimmy appeared silent and withdrawn when he first met Piero, aside from his habitual shyness, could have been because he was worried about what appeared to be a recurrence of the case of syphilis for which he had been treated shortly before leaving New York. In January 1948, Jimmy went to Zürich to see a specialist about his problem. He stayed in the "snow-white" Hotel Storchen beside the Limmat River—"with a river in front and a carillon almost in bed with me," as he wrote later. Once he saw the doctor, however, Jimmy's ailment was diagnosed as genital herpes—early symptoms of which are similar to those of syphilis. As we learn from "The Morning of the Poem," he was given a prescription for what he described as "eye salve" and sent on his way.

Relieved, Jimmy stayed to explore Switzerland on his own for about two weeks. "Drunkenly" leaning on the balustrade of a bridge one evening, he was picked up by an older, gray-haired man, with whom he spent several nights. He turned out to be the manager of one of the big hotels in Zürich, and treated Jimmy to romantic dinners in the evenings, followed by a box of *marrons glacés* sent to him at his hotel every morning. From Zürich, Jimmy went to Geneva and stayed at the Hotel de l'Ecu, basking in the knowledge that he was again following in the footsteps of Henry James, who had famously stayed there.

As he had done earlier in France, Jimmy continued to seek out connections to the European travels of Henry James, the quintessential expatriate American novelist of the nineteenth century. Florence was not, for him, the city of the Medici, but a place where one of James's heroines might have lived, identifying with her to the point of absorbing imaginatively her memories and impressions. "To walk up to / Bellosguardo, to look / and wonder and remember / what I never knew!"

Back in Florence, Jimmy set to work on a novel (of which no trace remains) while Bill spent the first months of 1948 attempting to set up interviews with both right-wing figures and former Italian Partisans for his book on guerrilla warfare. In February they traveled to Rome, where they spent most of their time with Donald Downes (1903–1983), an old acquaintance of Bill's from the OSS.

It was Downes who had given Donovan the idea of recruiting former Lincoln Brigade veterans into the OSS for guerrilla activity in occupied Europe. After the war he moved to Italy, where he became a correspondent for various American newspapers and magazines and also wrote novels, his memoir, and cookbooks. He became closely involved with promoting neorealist Italian cinema, and, according to Franco Zeffirelli, provided important material assistance to underfinanced Italian film companies by supplying directors such as Rossellini with top-quality black-and-white film stock, which he pilfered from American news crews. At this time he was trying to raise money to enable Visconti to finish his neorealist masterpiece *La Terra Trema*. Tennessee Williams, who was living in Rome that winter, met Downes soon after his arrival and described him as "a gentleman of international connections who looks like a pleasantly depraved Roman emperor such as Tiberius and talks like a character out of Dashiel [*sic*] Hammett."

Downes knew everybody in Rome "both in high and low strata," according to Williams. Through him, Bill and Jimmy found themselves on the periphery of the postwar Italian film renaissance, meeting Zeffirelli, among others, who was one of Downes's closest friends. Downes also helped Bill seek out former Partisans and others he thought might be able to help in his research, including Gino Bardi, a left-wing Italo-American journalist and translator, who dined with Bill and Jimmy one night and then took them on a tour of Roman nightlife. Of course they also saw several operas during their stay.

From Rome they journeyed south to Amalfi with Downes and another American friend of his, Gordon Rollins, a rich gay American expatriate and flamboyantly eccentric dabbler in the arts, to spend about a week in the Hotel Luna. The Hotel Luna was built around the thirteenth-century cloister of a former Franciscan convent and had been famous since Wagner's time for its beautiful setting, lovely garden, and illustrious guests. While in Amalfi they also visited Robert J. Ullman, another OSS acquaintance of Bill's and a close friend of Downes's and Zeffirelli's, whose nearby villa was spectacularly perched on a cliffside in Positano.

When they returned to Florence in April, Jimmy and Bill took a six-month lease of a furnished apartment in a fourteenth-century building at 29 Via dell'Erta Canina on the south side of the Arno, near the beautiful medieval church of San Miniato al Monte. The apartment was furnished with antique-style furniture and had a small walled garden, presided over by a "giantly ancient cypress / of dark and towering smoke" from which a nightingale sang, sometimes keeping Jimmy awake nights. As he later wrote to Kenneth Koch, "After the first wild surmise it was interesting to just lie in my witty bed with its brocade cover in my trecento bedroom and listen to it carrying on while some pre-flood moon light drenched the well worn trecento bricks; not to speak of me! Interesting! It was bliss."

In mid-April, Jimmy and Bill traveled to Milan so that Bill could interview the novelist Elio Vittorini about his anti-Fascist activities during the war, and while they were there, see *Tristan und Isolde* starring Kirsten Flagstad at La Scala. As it happened, the visit coincided with an important national election in which a Communist and Socialist coalition was widely expected to win, causing panic among some American expatriates, including Frederic Prokosch and Gore Vidal, who fled (temporarily) to France and Egypt, respectively, and the U.S. government itself, which was illegally funneling money to the opposing Christian Democrats. Vittorini was thus too busy to see Bill, but the pair made a side trip to Genoa and Rapallo on the Ligurian coast, and also saw Verdi's *Un Ballo in Maschera* before returning to Florence. Contrary to expectations, the Christian Democrats won the election, but the political climate remained unstable, causing problems for Bill and Jimmy later that year.

Jimmy and Bill had been keeping in touch with Wystan and Chester over the winter, and as soon as they were settled in the apartment they extended an invitation for them to visit. On April 7, 1948, Chester and Wystan sailed on the *Queen Mary*, stopping first in England for several weeks. On April 27, they stayed overnight in Paris, where they ran into Christopher Isherwood and his lover, Bill Caskey, and had cocktails with them at the Ritz. Isherwood, who had been present when Auden first met Chester in 1939, gives a picture of them at this moment in his *Diaries*:

> I get to like Chester much more as he grows older. He must be around thirty now [he was twenty-seven], and he looks all of that, with stooped shoulders and big pouches under his eyes. Indeed, he is getting to look more and more like Wystan. He is very funny, and so anxious to be friendly that it is quite touching . . . As for Wystan, he's quite middle-aged, with a thick waist and such a sad anxiously lined face . . . Wystan still fusses and rags anxiously at Chester, and screws up his eyebrows when he fears that Chester will say or do something tiresome or upsetting to his plans. Chester teases him, of course. But, watching them, you feel: "They're together, now, till the end."

On April 28, Wystan and Chester arrived in Florence to stay with Jimmy and Bill. Auden immediately fell in love with the country. "Italy is pure heaven, lovely buildings and lovely sexy-looking people," he wrote. He had told Isherwood that while in Italy it was their intention to "see all available operas during the summer," and they lost no time in getting started. In their first week the foursome made a two-day trip to Rome to see Bellini's *I Puritani*. Back in Florence, there were performances at the Maggio Musicale, Florence's annual spring music festival, which had just been revived after the war. Bill and Jim introduced their friends to Piero Tosi, and they all became regulars at Caffè le Giubbe Rosse. Tosi did not speak English, so their conversations were in makeshift Italian: all four Americans had a fund of flowery Italian recalled from opera to draw upon. Tosi was impressed at how the group "spoke of opera constantly," and with the way they "spoke an Italian crossed with the texts from operas."

Chester photographed Wystan and Jimmy standing by the Arno overlooking a ruined Florence, and Jimmy alone, at the open door to the Erta Canina apartment. Jimmy sent a print of this picture to his mother, inscribing on the back a quotation from the Bible that makes clear his sense of this time as one of hopeful new beginnings: "Taken outside the entrance to my house in Florence, by Chester. My shirt is hanging out because I had just climbed up Erta Canina. 'I have set before thee an open door & no man can shut it.' Rev. 3:8."

In the three weeks or so he stayed with Jimmy and Bill, Auden wrote two poems, "The Managers," responding to Medici splendor, and "For T. S. Eliot," a commissioned sixtieth birthday tribute, and worked on a third, "In Praise of Limestone," which he completed later on Ischia. Schuyler typed these poems for Auden, as he would others later. When Wystan wasn't looking, Jimmy and Bill used to go through the wastebasket and retrieve his discarded drafts, until Wystan learned of this from Chester and started burning his drafts instead. He took great pleasure in doing it, saying, "My dear, I feel like an ambassador burning secret papers!"

On May 21, Auden's old friend Brian Howard and his red-haired Cockney boyfriend Sam Langford arrived in Florence, and shortly thereafter Wystan and Chester left with them for Rome and Ischia, the then relatively unspoiled island close to Capri in the Bay of Naples. Howard (1905–1958), of American parentage but brought up in England, had been the most famous and flamboyant of the "bright young things" of

London and Oxford in the 1920s. Aspects of his self-conscious dandyism, insouciant wit, and prickly charm had contributed to fictional characters created by Evelyn Waugh, Nancy Mitford, Cyril Connolly, and other writers. But aside from some minor poems, his own promise was largely frittered away in pranks, parties, drink, and drugs. By 1948, Howard had become conspicuously a "failure" in life in inverse proportion, one might say, to the degree to which he had a "successful" alternate life as a character in other people's fiction and memoirs. Though alcoholism could make him a difficult and disagreeable companion, he was mostly kept in line by the younger Langford. Auden, who had known him since the '30s, remained a loyal friend. Nonetheless, he later wrote, "he was, inside, I think the most desperately unhappy person I have ever known."

Jimmy and Brian Howard disliked each other almost on sight. Schuyler, when meeting someone for the first time in this period, was often reserved to the point of seeming hostility, while Howard's 1920s airs and affectations, especially when magnified by drink, were no doubt an acquired taste. To Jimmy, Brian seemed "an arrogant drunk," and after spending time with him decided that he was also "the most / bored and boring man / I ever met." The remark makes a deceptively simple but astute point, connecting Howard's deliberate show of fashionable disengagement and discontent with his failure to create anything lasting. In a way, Jimmy, with his own, albeit very different, tendency to social disengagement, may have seen Howard as a kind of object lesson, and his antipathy may have been partly motivated by elements of recognition. Young though he was, Jimmy was already something of a failure himself: a failure at college and in the navy, and a failure so far at producing any writing to speak of.

Auden, Kallman, Howard, and Langford arrived on Ischia by May 25. They made directly for Forio, at the far end of the island from the main landing at Porto, and put up at the Pensione Nettuno, where they had rooms with balconies looking directly onto the bay. Auden found it to be "one of the loveliest spots on earth . . . Everyone is very poor and with nothing to do but religious processions and fishing."

Jimmy and Bill joined them on about June 10 and stayed until June 25. It was an idyllic time, with hikes up into the green interior of the island, where farmers gave them simple meals; visits to coastal hot springs, followed by swims in the nearly effervescent Mediterranean water: the realization of an ideal Italy, as Langford wrote, of "blue skies, lemons, olives, vineyards and tiny green lizards that sun themselves on the rocks and scamper away when one approaches."

Auden settled down to work immediately, writing for two hours most mornings and again after lunch. It was now that he completed his poem "In Praise of Limestone," evoking the landscape of England, Italy, Ischia, and the Naples region. One day Brian Howard accused Auden of being "more a moral than a visual poet" and "challenged him to write a visual poem." In response, Auden wrote "Ischia," which he dedicated to Howard. The poem is largely an apostrophe to the island, celebrating its beauty, pleasures, and relaxed pace: "My thanks are for you, / Ischia, to whom a fair wind has / brought me rejoicing with dear friends // from soiled productive cities. How well you correct / our injured eyes, how gently you train us to see / things and men in perspective / underneath your uniform light."

Howard, touched by this gift and fully appreciating the honor ("though," he wrote to his mother, "I should like to have achieved immortality on my own!") responded in kind with a poem of his own, which presents a fairly sentimental "photograph" of the group of friends on the beach, ending "They turn to face the sun, and my machine. / Where they have always been. They will always be there." The poem includes glimpses of Auden (who "Made poetry mean things again"), Kallman ("a second poet"), Langford ("the youngest / Of all"), and Bill Aalto ("a hero, there / With a hand missing"), but not Schuyler.

Writing much later as the last survivor of the group, Schuyler conjured up a similar image, but in more disillusioned terms:

WE ALL LAY ON THE ISLAND BEACH TOGETHER

We all lay on the island beach together
now they are gone. Brian and his friend
the red head each dead of his own hand.
Leukemia took Bill, Wystan and Chester

passed on, as they say, in sleep. I bid
them adieu. The beach view we say was of
water and winking into sight the distant hills
that environ Naples where the lurking beggar
was aptly known as No-Nose. She got the money
that she begged for. Brian was
an impossible man, an arrogant drunk. Bill
had high ideals he never could live up to.
Perhaps only Wystan was in an angry way
serene. Each face, not excepting mine,
was eroded by booze. We took a group
trip, I and the others, from an island
to an island and on to Sorrento, Amalfi,
Pompei and Naples and back to Forio. We
knew our way quite well. Now except myself
the sightseers are gone, dead and gone.
Good day, good night.

(Actually, Sam Langford did not commit suicide but died accidentally in 1958, and a despondent Howard killed himself a few days later.)

The first stop on the group excursion Schuyler mentions was the neighboring island of Capri, a glamorous resort since Roman times. Auden hated it and compared it to Palm Beach. Like all visitors, they gravitated to the *piazzetta*, where they ran into the poet and novelist Frederic Prokosch, an acquaintance of Auden's from the '30s (and a fellow participant at the 1939 reading in New York where Wystan and Chester first met). From the evidence of his autobiography, *Voices* (1983), Prokosch took himself very seriously and assiduously cultivated the acquaintance of more famous writers. Auden teased him by campily introducing the others as "Lady Howard," "Madame Kallman," and "Baroness Aalto." Prokosch described Bill as "a handsome young man whom they called 'Big Edna.' He had a face like a pirate's and only a single hand."

The group took the ferry across the bay to Sorrento, and from there traveled by bus to Amalfi, where Jimmy and Bill introduced the group to Donald Downes and Robert Ullman, who invited them to a sumptuous lunch at his romantic Villa Treville. As described by Franco Zeffirelli (who owned it later), the villa was "hidden from Positano by a spur of limestone rock [next to] a cascade falling sheer down the cliff" and was set amid "a riot of Mediterranean vegetation, pines, flowers, trees, cacti. Through the foliage were romantic glimpses of Positano, an opera set with dramatic mountains behind it, over which the occasional clouds of summer mist poured like dry ice." Walking down the steep cliff steps, amid terraces planted with orange trees, Chester paused to break off a sprig of myrtle and transmute the moment into operatic terms, as was his wont, quoting Goethe's poem of yearning for Italy, "Kennst Du das Land," and its French version, from Ambroise Thomas's opera *Mignon*:

> Connais-tu le pays où fleurit l'oranger?
> Le pays des fruits d'or et des roses vermeilles . . .

Shortly after the group returned to Ischia (via Pompeii) Auden came to the momentous decision to take a long-term lease on a house on the island. A little way out of the center of town, the house had three bedrooms, two living rooms, and a huge kitchen, and was set in a large vegetable garden. The rent was $230 a year, which, as he put it to Jaffe, was "less than 3 months rent of my Greenwich Village closet. I feel so giddy and excited." Part of the plan was that Jimmy and Bill would stay in the house and care for it over the winter while Wystan and Chester were in New York.

Within a few days the three couples went their separate ways: Bill and Jimmy returned to Florence, Brian and Sam traveled to England, and Wystan and Chester, after finalizing the house arrangements, went back to Florence on July 7 to spend another week with Jimmy and Bill, before continuing on to Venice, Salzburg, and England. During this part of the visit, the foursome made a day excursion to Bologna, a city that Jimmy and Bill had become fond of during previous visits, loving its archway-covered streets and its marvelous traditional food. One night at Caffè le Giubbe Rosse, Auden invited Piero Tosi to accompany him back to New York, discreetly slipping money for the ticket under his saucer. Tosi, with no English and a lifelong distaste for travel, somewhat regretfully declined.

Auden sailed back to New York in early September, alone. Chester stayed behind in Paris, and eventually decided to remain in Europe all fall and winter.

As soon as they got back to Florence at the end of June, Jimmy and Bill applied to the authorities for extensions of their six-month *permessos di soggiorno*, or temporary residence permits. They didn't give much further thought to what was normally a routine matter and took a short sight-seeing trip to Pisa and Lucca, "whose striped churches tell the striped churches of Florence where to get off." But on August 17, an official from the town hall, or *questura*, called on them with the shocking news that their requests had been denied and that they were ordered to leave the country in two weeks. This unexpected setback was connected to recent political events: on July 14, Palmiro Togliatti, the head of the Italian Communist Party, had been severely wounded in an assassination attempt. Countrywide rioting resulted, followed by a general strike. Many political observers feared that after losing the April elections the Communists would now use the pretext of the attempt on Togliatti to stage a coup. By August, the situation had cooled, but Bill's history as a Spanish Civil War veteran, which led the authorities to believe he was a Communist Party member, combined with his visits to various left-wing political figures in the course of his research, had raised eyebrows at the Foreign Ministry. It turned out that both he and Jimmy had been under police surveillance for some time.

On August 18, Bill and Jimmy filed separate written depositions with the American consulate in Florence, attesting to their status as writers and cultural tourists who were not members of the Communist Party and had no intention of meddling in Italian politics. (Bill had long since drifted away from the Party.) Jimmy ended his on a defiant note: "If the embassy of our country is informed of the details behind this charge, I wish them to be relayed to me, that I may deny them *specifically*, and thus attempt to keep my record—as a citizen of the United States traveling abroad—clean of what I can only regard as, to me, dangerous libels."

The following day, Bill and Jimmy were interrogated separately by American authorities at the consulate. For both, the situation brought back unhappy memories and fears. For Bill, it reawakened a lifelong paranoia and deep-seated resentments of unjust treatment extending back to his mother's exile from Finland. For Jimmy, of course, the interview replayed traumatic memories of his navy interrogations in 1943. The couple tried to blur the true nature of their relationship by stating that Jimmy was simply a live-in "secretary and assistant" to Bill, necessitated by Bill's physical impairment. The subterfuge was not completely successful, as a confidential memo to the State Department in Washington makes clear: "Mr. Schuyler appears to be a young man of extremely weak personality and, while admittedly there is no factual information to support this belief, it is not considered unlikely that both he and Mr. Aalto are abnormal persons who find each other's company mutually satisfying. The records pertaining to Mr. Schuyler's discharge, if available to the Department, may possibly contain corroboration for this suspicion." (As indeed they would have.)

The whole business was of more than passing concern to Auden, who wrote to Rhoda Jaffe on August 30, "Poor Bill and Jim are in trouble in Italy, as they are suspected by the *Italians* of being Reds and may get thrown out. Annoying for me as I was counting on them to take my villa in Ischia." At the beginning of September, Bill and Jimmy traveled to Rome to enlist the help of Donald Downes, who had top-level connections in the Italian government. Downes contacted Ferruccio Pari, a former Resistance leader, former prime minister of Italy, and now a senator, who got in touch with the undersecretary of the interior, Achille Marazza, and wrote back on September 20 that Aalto's residence permit would be "extended indefinitely." That took care of the matter as far as the Italian authorities were concerned. But American officials under J. Edgar Hoover's FBI pursued further investigation of Bill relentlessly over the next several years. When pressured to reveal the names of other Party members, he refused to cooperate. In retaliation the FBI had Bill's VA pension withheld, making him financially dependent on Jimmy (and Auden) until they broke up in 1949.

Jimmy and Bill remained in Rome for much of September, where they stayed in an apartment belonging to Donald Downes on Via della Vite, to which they would return on and off over the next year. Early in the month Downes introduced them to the young American novelist Donald Windham, who was spending the year traveling in Italy, and they all dined together at Alfredo's restaurant on Piazza Santa Maria in Trastevere. Downes drove a big American station wagon and his appearance on the piazza produced "a regular floor show" of neighborhood boys vying for his attention. For Windham, as for Tosi earlier, it was Bill who initially made the stronger and better impression, and Jimmy who seemed a bit distant. However, over the next couple of weeks, the trio of Windham, Jimmy, and Bill became inseparable, dining together almost every evening, and soon Jimmy and Donald became especially close.

On the 22nd, Jimmy and Bill returned to Florence to close up the Erta Canina apartment. After they left, the landlord inspected the apartment with Piero Tosi and wrote a formal letter, complaining of extensive damage to the upholstery and the fact that five dinner plates and numerous other pieces of china were missing. In light of later events, this missing chinaware may be seen as silent testimony to the domestic violence that seems to have characterized the Aalto-Schuyler household.

On October 7, Windham accompanied Bill and Jimmy on a rainy bus ride to Naples. From there Bill and Jimmy planned to get the ferry to Ischia to take up residence in Auden's house. In Naples that night, the three men took a long, meandering walk through the byways of the city. To Windham, who had never been to Naples before, the mad concatenation of the nighttime city, with its shops displaying mounded animal and fish carcasses, surreal window displays of "horrifying glass and metal lamps, religious pictures, bottles and kitchen utensils," and bonfires burning in the streets and squares had the quality of a dream.

The next morning, after a visit to the Archaeological Museum, Jimmy and Bill tried to convince Donald to cross over to Ischia with them, but he decided to stay in Naples for another few days, and saw them off on the ferry. They were planning an extended stay.

[7]

MEN ARE SUCH BOYS

1948–1949

The winter climate in the Mediterranean is cool and rainy, and when Jimmy and Bill returned to Ischia on October 8, 1948, the island presented a very different face from the summer. In June, they had only been able to make a cursory inspection of the house that Auden had rented. Now, along with Chester, who had spent the past month in Paris, the three of them were faced with figuring out how to live in what was basically a fisherman's house—charming and commodious but rather primitive.

Set off from Via Santa Lucia (now Via Monterone) by a high whitewashed wall, the house, of pale pinkish stucco, stood in a large garden planted with tomatoes, onions, and other vegetables, grapevines, and a fig tree. Exterior steps led up to the main floor and a terrace where meals were taken in good weather. The house had three bedrooms, two living rooms, a very large kitchen, a bathroom, and, on the top floor, two rooms that had been partly destroyed in an earthquake, leaving them roofless. Ischia being a volcanic island, the house came with its own hot spring, providing "unlimited water" for washing.

Despite the charm of its terra-cotta tile floors and white stucco walls, deliciously cool in the summer, the house was drafty and difficult in winter. Cooking was done over a charcoal-fired stove, which had to be coaxed alive every morning. Drinking water was drawn from a well in the garden and carried inside. Chester was a good cook, however, and rose to the challenge.

Quite soon the island's off-season isolation started to get on their nerves. Since Chester had decided to stay in Forio for the time being, there was no need for Jimmy and Bill to be there full-time, and during October and November they went back and forth to Rome several times, separately or together. Staying in Via della Vite, near the Spanish Steps, Jimmy would daily walk past the apartment where Keats had died, now a museum, but the idea of entering the room where the impoverished and dying poet had endured such an "agony" of "real hostility, real superstition, real penury" was unthinkable and he never visited. At some point that fall, Jimmy met a young man named Rino Oscari who worked in his uncle's grocery shop in the Parioli district, and they began a casual love affair.

In late November, Jimmy sought treatment for a painful anal fistula and case of hemorrhoids. For as long as possible he tried to avoid an operation, with a prescription for opium suppositories and a doughnut-shaped inflatable cushion, on which he perched throughout Luchino Visconti's acclaimed production of *As You Like It* at Teatro Eliseo. Rendered as *Rosalinda, O Come vi Piace*, it featured sumptuous décor by Salvador Dalí. (Much later, Jimmy would enjoy declaiming in his basso profondo voice the famous lines from the second-act monologue in their Italian version: "*Tutto il mondo è un paloscenico . . .*") The surgeon finally insisted that an operation was necessary, which took place in the first week of December, performed under local anesthetic and morphine, which caused hallucinations: "monstrous- / ly real, obscene, / filled with fear and strangers. // Across from my bed, a / crucifix looked much too / like a dancer dancing . . ."

When it was over, Rino Oscari came to see him and they "held hands and giggled." The hospital windows gave onto the kind of bleak postwar urban landscape immortalized by Italian neorealist cinema: "tangled bob-wire and / a bombed-out building: / an illustration / of the death of cities." When he was discharged from the hospital, Donald Downes picked him up in his station wagon and with Oscari they drove to the beach at Ostia, where they "gathered the Christmas / mistletoe and sea- / strawberries, saw / the wintry sadness of the gray sand / beaches, driving back / heard *Norma* on the radio." Auden sent money to help pay for the operation, adding in a letter to Chester, "I do hope our beloved Dorabella has survived the surgeon's irreverent touch."

While in Paris, Chester had reconnected with a friend from New York, Charles Heilemann, a decorative artist teaching advertising design in the Parsons School overseas program. Jimmy may have joined Chester in Paris for a brief visit in the fall of 1948 and met Charles there too; if not, they met now, in December, when Charles came and visited them on Ischia.

Auden's earlier encounters with Charles had apparently not been warm, and Chester delayed telling Auden that Charles had come to Ischia. Once he did, Auden seemed to believe that they were having an affair—and possibly they had been: "I am very glad you have mentioned Charlie at last. I knew he was with you and was hurt at your reticence. Naturally I drew the obvious conclusions. I'm not sure that—despite your protestations—I don't still but, so long as he is paying his way, that is your and his business." However, it was in fact Jimmy and Charles who were becoming involved, and would soon begin an affair. It's not clear how long Charles stayed in Ischia this first time—perhaps only a week or so, perhaps into January—and their growing mutual attraction, in any case, went unacknowledged in Bill's presence. But they continued the relationship through letters after Charles returned to Paris.

At Christmas, Jimmy sent Wystan a "sweet Christmas card" and was assured in return that he, Auden, would be prepared to help him and Bill if they found themselves in financial need. With the unexpected costs of Jimmy's operation, added to the fact that Bill's pension had been stopped, they did, and Wystan accordingly sent Jimmy the generous sum of $200 as a Christmas present.

By early 1949, Jimmy and Bill's relationship had become severely strained, and life was becoming difficult in the house in Forio. The weather was cold and bleak, food was limited in variety, and the radio was on the blink, but wine was all too cheap and plentiful, and drinking brought out all Bill's bad temper, aggression, and resentment. Soon Bill got wind of Jimmy's budding relationship with Charles, and this led to numerous violent incidents. Jimmy later told of one "huge fight" on Ischia, when he ran into the bedroom in tears and Bill followed him in and dumped a plate of food on his head. Many people heard later, probably from Chester, that Bill had hit Jimmy over the head with a grappa bottle during one of their fights, "nearly killing him." As Dorothy Farnan put it, "When [Bill] was drunk—and he was drunk much of the time—he was an enraged bull. All his resentments surfaced. He threw Wystan's crockery against the walls of the little house at Via Santa Lucia 22, and he smashed the furniture . . . From time to time he threatened to murder first [Jimmy] and then his host, Chester, and he came close to doing so."

One night, around the first week in February, Bill, who had, as usual, been drinking heavily, became maudlin and paranoid, and started crying and accusing Jimmy of "not loving him." Jimmy got fed up and threw his full dinner plate to the floor, at which Bill became enraged and picked up a big carving knife and started chasing Jimmy around the kitchen table. "He was serious and so was I," Jimmy later wrote. Trapped in a house on a remote island, with an unstable, violent, heavy drinker, Jimmy and Chester became truly frightened. When going out in the evening, leaving Bill alone, Chester made a point of hiding the carving knife, telling Jimmy, "Men are such boys." They resorted to locking themselves in a bedroom at night to protect themselves from Bill's rages. Jimmy's nervous anxiety became acute and brought about a reoccurrence of the physical tremors that had appeared after his navy disciplinary hearing and imprisonment on Hart Island. Months later, "any reference" to those frightening times was still unsettling enough to reawaken Jimmy's trauma and bring on "strain and tremors of emotions," according to Chester.

The high drama of all this caused a flurry of letters back and forth between Auden in New York and Chester and Jimmy on Ischia. Unsurprisingly, Jimmy was determined to break up with Bill, and was considering returning to New York, but Bill was trapped on Ischia without his pension. In New York, Auden was trying to help sort out Bill's finances, but to speed things along decided to lend them money himself. On February 7, he wrote, "Dear Jimmy, Just an immediate practical matter. However or whenever or if ever we can get Bill's affairs straightened here, it will take ages, so I have written my bank asking them to send you $500 in cash by air mail so that you [can] get your ticket or whatever." This was a lot of money; Auden was a generous man.

Auden's letter to Chester a few days later, on February 13, 1949, makes explicit reference for the first time to Jimmy's affair with Charles Heilemann as the cause of Bill's rage:

What do Bill and Jim respectively intend to do? I understood from Jimmy's letter that he wished to return to the US to look for a job. About B[ill], it is a little embarrassing for me. I can't *ask* him to leave when his money arrives . . . But entre nous I should prefer it. (Incidentally, my dear, it sounds as if there wasn't a piece of crockery left in the house.)

I am still not clear how serious the J[im]—C[harlie] affaire is, at least on J[im]'s side. The only occasion in the histoire as recounted by you in which I think they both were in the wrong was in their denials. (You know, *sweetie*, how I hate *that*!!) Incidentally, I think you were overly severe about B[ill]'s anxiety to know who started it. To *this* neurotic girl, it seems only too natural a question.

A week later Auden again wrote to Chester: "My desires are a) that Bill go. b) that Jimmy stay as long as he likes," and informed Chester that, instead of cash, he is sending Jimmy the $500 in traveler's checks. At the end of the letter, Auden drew a little picture of a hand pointing, with the words "BILL MUST GO."

Three days later Auden wrote again: "I want you or Jimmy or better still both to stay. If you will say you want to stay, but cannot if Bill does, I shall order him to leave . . . I don't want to be left either alone with Bill, or completely alone, and would much appreciate it if either you or Jimmy or both would stay on."

On March 3, one problem, at least, was resolved, when Auden sent the five hundred dollars to Jimmy. Most if not all of it went to Bill, allowing him to leave the island and Jimmy's life. From Rome, Bill wrote a series of passionate letters to Jimmy expressing his unquenched love and hope of being reconciled. The letters went unanswered. Bill remained in Italy another two years, where he formed a relationship with a young Italian, Franco Zuardi. In early 1951, the two of them made their way to the south of France, then Paris, where they lived a hand-to-mouth existence, while Bill struggled unsuccessfully to have his pension reinstated. Finally, the FBI caused the State Department to rescind his passport and he was forced to return to New York in about 1953. He then lived for several years in a cold-water apartment in a run-down building on the far

West Side, in bohemian squalor, surrounded by boxes of clippings and files, volatile and unpredictable as ever.

Jimmy later expressed his conflicted feelings about Bill and their affair most poignantly in a section of the poem "Dining Out with Doug and Frank," and in the unpublished sonnet beginning "All I ever found" quoted earlier. In the summer of 1950, a year after they broke up, he wrote about the affair and its end in a letter to Piero Tosi, who remained in touch with Bill for several years. The letter, which compares Bill to the tragic heroine of Verdi's opera *La Traviata*, and casually predicts the first line of his first published poem, "Salute," was composed in rudimentary Italian, which lends it a stilted quality; ellipses are in the original:

> Please do not give my address to Bill. I know that I too was to blame in that episode, but something past is past, let it die: but he writes and writes me, when all I want is a bit of peace. I'm not a Violetta like he, and I don't want to be always looking in the mirror . . . yesterday is not dead, but at the same time, yesterday is not today, and what interests me is today . . . I know that life has not turned out for him as he dreamed it would when he was a young man, I know that: but the thing that he is not able to understand is that lovers and friends cannot do the work of God or will (as you would say).

Auden's earlier prediction was all too accurate: Aalto never finished his history of guerrilla warfare, or his history of Spain and the Mediterranean, and died of leukemia on June 11, 1958, at the age of forty-two. He was given a military funeral and was buried in Long Island National Cemetery with three friends in attendance. Jimmy ran into him by chance only once or twice in New York in later years. When Bill was dying and asked to see him, Jimmy did not go, being still too traumatized, he said, by the events of February 1949.

Early in April, after Bill had gone, Charles Heilemann returned to stay in the house for several weeks and began his now-acknowledged affair with Jimmy. In looks, Charles was no "Valentino," but he was pleasantly handsome in his own Spencer Tracy–ish way, with a rather block-shaped head, a chunky build, red hair, and a ruddy complexion. Born in Brooklyn in 1918, he was about five years older than Jimmy. His artistic facility was recognized early and he went to Parsons School of Art, graduating in 1937, followed by graduate work at the Paris branch of Parsons. In 1941, he enlisted in the army and rose to the rank of lieutenant. After returning from Paris in 1949, he taught at Parsons for many years.

Meanwhile, other interesting visitors from New York were preparing to descend on Ischia. In late March, Truman Capote, his lover Jack Dunphy, Tennessee Williams, and his lover Frank Merlo all chanced to be in Rome together. The publication the previous year of Capote's much-anticipated first novel, *Other Voices, Other Rooms*, had caused a sensation in New York, in part because of the languorous, "come-hither" pose of the boyish author in the photograph on the back cover. He and Dunphy, also a novelist, were in search of a congenial place to work for the summer. Tennessee Williams was at the height of his early success: *A Streetcar Named Desire*, which had won the Pulitzer Prize in 1948, was still in its initial two-year run on Broadway, following the almost equally successful *The Glass Menagerie*. The Italian production of *Streetcar*, *Un tram che si chiama desiderio*, directed by Luchino Visconti, had recently opened in Rome. Williams and Capote were warily friendly. On about March 23, the four of them drove down to Naples together in Williams's Jeep, and the next day both couples made their way to Forio.

Williams and Merlo stayed for about two weeks, long enough to meet Jimmy, Heilemann, and Chester and hear all about the recent drama. In a letter to Donald Windham in New York, Williams seems to view it all as a mash-up of one of his own plays and his story "One Arm":

> The English-speaking colony consisted, aside from our party, of Chester Kallman (the perennial Auden lover), and a wee wisp of an American belle whose lover had practically beaten her to death with a bottle of Grappa the week before we arrived and she was still looking happily dazed. The lover had left the island and had written to ask if it was really true that they were through? The

> lover, incidentally, had only one arm. There was so little to gossip about that we discussed the Grappa-beating almost the entire two weeks. I had a feeling, from the look on Chester's face, that he had somehow managed the whole thing and that it was only the beginning of far more intricate and violent and far-reaching events to come. The island is an extinct volcano, but plenty seems to be popping or going to pop.

Williams's description of Jimmy as a "wee wisp of an American belle" seems not only a projection of one of his own emotionally fragile female characters, but must also reflect Jimmy's still-traumatized condition, on top of his habitual shyness. Ever the dramatist, Williams was inclined to "test" people and note their reactions. On one occasion, Jimmy later recalled, while they were all sitting in Maria's café, Williams unexpectedly threw an orange at Jimmy, which, being caught off guard, he fumbled and dropped. "Jimmy ca-n't ca-atch," teased Tennessee in a singsong voice.

Capote loved the island, finding it "the strangest, most haunting and beautiful place," and a good place in which to write, and he and Dunphy stayed until June. During this time a warm friendship developed between Truman and Jimmy. Windham was also a friend of Capote's, and wrote to him asking for news of Jimmy and Bill. Capote replied on April 12:

> Well, that is a story. They have divorced and in the most dramatic of fashions. According to Jimmy, Aalto is insane, has been insane for a very long time, all of which bothered him not one whit until one night about two months [ago] when Aalto tried to kill him. My private suspicion is that there is a great deal to be said on both sides. Jimmy, who is still here, is carrying on an affair with a tiresome little party named Charles Heilleman [*sic*], Aalto is living in Rome, and sends Jimmy three letters a day, which may be a sign of insanity, but I, the hopeless romantic, think it very sweet, for all the letters say is I love you, come back! come back!

Auden arrived in Naples on Saturday, April 16. Jimmy and Chester crossed over to meet him there, and Jimmy's 1974 poem "Wystan Auden" describes him getting off the liner wearing "black and a homburg," and greeting them with the information that he had just read "*all* of Doughty's *The Dawn in Britain*" (the 1906 epic poem in six volumes by the author of *Travels in Arabia Deserta*). The next day was Easter Sunday and the island celebrated with traditional rustic pageantry and fireworks. The following day, they took a picnic to the country, as was traditional for Easter Monday. Auden was adjusting to getting water from the well and making his morning coffee over the charcoal stove.

The island was already being "discovered," and there was now a small, changing colony of idle gay American expatriates, or "remittance men," living in the town, who hung out at Maria's bar drinking and gossiping. Chester was amused by them, but they "horrified" Wystan and he avoided them as much as he could. Charles Heilemann also rubbed Auden very much the wrong way.

Auden's analysis of Jimmy's relationship with Heilemann, as expressed in letters to friends in New York, is astute, in Auden's own slightly self-absorbed way. He seems to give little thought to what Jimmy might have seen in Heilemann or gained from the relationship, but mainly faulted Heilemann for monopolizing Jimmy and for turning himself and Jimmy into a single, seemingly self-sufficient unit, scornfully referred to by Auden as "Jimmy-Charlie." "The only emotional problems" in the household, as he wrote to Rhoda Jaffe, "are to do with Jimmy-Charlie (J's new friend). Charlie, whom I think a lower middle-class bore, is very possessive and has successfully isolated Jimmy from us. There are always being little incidents, trifling in themselves, but symptomatic—eg buying their own little box of sardines (one for Him one for Her) and not offering them to us."

Auden believed that he could detect not only an unspoken regret on Jimmy's part for taking up with Heilemann, but also Jimmy's silent awareness of Auden's belief. He wrote to a friend (May 2):

> In the house are me, Chester, and Jimmy-Charlie. There is tension because in his heart of hearts Jimmy knows that we know that he knows that he has made a mistaken choice. This puts up a barrier between Chester and he who have been the closest of sisters which is rather painful. (The tension expresses itself in little symbolic

> acts.—Buying their private eggs for breakfast—not helping peel potatoes etc.) It is lucky that there is another and very nice sister, Bernie Winebaum, who has his meals with us. She is very tactful and cheers us all up.

That Auden would claim the ability to read and commune with Jimmy's "heart of hearts" suggests an unusual degree of identification with him (recalling his earlier omniscient viewpoint in reading the thoughts and motivations of the sailor Emble). In fact, Auden sounds jealous—and it was probably Charles's awareness and misinterpretation of this jealousy that made him jealous in turn, and caused him to give his friend Helen Burckhardt the idea that there had once been a love affair between Jimmy and Wystan.

This was Auden's first summer in the house at 22 Via Santa Lucia, and set the pattern for his future summers there over the next several years. Auden liked an orderly life. He got up at 7:00 and divided the day into carefully timed periods of work (9 a.m. to noon and 4:30 to 6:30 p.m.), meals, drinks at Maria's café in the village before lunch and again after dinner, sunbathing on the beach in the afternoon, "martini time" before dinner, and finally bed at 10:00. Not for nothing was his next book titled *Nones*, after one of the canonical hours into which the early Church divided the day.

When the members of the household went into town for their daily aperitif at Maria's, they might run into various local characters or visiting friends and acquaintances, such as the German painter Eduard Bargheer, Truman Capote and Jack Dunphy, and occasionally the pianist duo Arthur Gold and Bobby Fizdale and their close friend the poet and dance critic Edwin Denby, who were living together on Ischia that summer. These three would become important in Jimmy's life a few years later when they became reacquainted in New York, but at this time they only met in passing.

Jimmy liked Truman Capote and valued his criticism of his writing. But Auden was annoyed by his mannerisms, blithe self-assurance, and almost everything else about him, although he held a grudging respect for Capote's work ethic (and appreciated their shared disdain for Charles Heilemann). One day Auden and Jimmy went down to Maria's for their customary pre-lunch aperitif, where they joined Capote, who was reading Stendhal's *The Red and the Black*. How did he like it? "Well," Truman said, "I'm really quite disappointed. The transitions are so clumsy." Auden was outraged at the presumption of the upstart Capote to criticize the great Stendhal as though they were on equal footing. All the way back to the house, "just white with rage," Auden kept repeating "The cheek! The cheek!" According to Jimmy, the encounter inspired Auden's poem "Under Sirius," or at any rate its lines "pottering shades, querulous beside the salt-pits, / And mawkish in their wits."

Another time, Capote and Jack Dunphy went over to Naples for the day and returned bearing such tokens of civilization as "a record of Mickey Rooney singing 'Treat Me Rough' and a bottle of something called Old Lady Gin, which was made in Trieste." Capote then gave a cocktail party and served martinis. He traveled with a portable record player and a collection of popular recordings, and at the height of the party, when he put on a record of Ethel Merman singing "Life Is Just a Bowl of Cherries," it all became too much for Auden, who leaped up from his chair to demand, "Take it off! Take it off! It's the *jungle*!"

Once Charles Heilemann returned to Paris, the situation at the house became easier. It was during this summer that Jimmy did most of the typing for Auden that has led to the somewhat misleading idea that he was Auden's "secretary," or rather, that that was the basis of their relationship. Jimmy had already typed two or more poems for Auden in Florence in 1948. But the period when he did the most typing for Auden was during the summer of 1949, when Auden was preparing *Nones* for publication. Although Jimmy saw this as primarily "an act of friendship," he did tell his mother he was getting paid a small amount for it, writing, "I'm earning my pin-money this summer typing for Wystan. He has just finished a longish poem, 'Memorial for the City,' about the City of God. Extremely interesting."

The poems in *Nones*, which have been dated by Edward Mendelson to the years 1946 to 1950, mark a dividing point for some critics between "early" and "late" Auden. Many of the 1948–49 and 1950 poems would have been written on Ischia, because Auden wrote most of his shorter poems when he was away from New York, but it does not necessarily follow that Jimmy typed only the ones that were written there. It was Auden's habit to hand Jimmy groups of manuscript poems at a time, and some of these would have been earlier poems that Auden was gathering and revising for publication. According to Jimmy, in fact, he typed up "almost the entire manuscript" of *Nones*.

Jimmy later said that, as he typed Auden's carefully constructed, poised verse, he told himself, "Well, if this is poetry, I'm certainly never going to write any myself." He clarified that he was "awed by the technical intricacy, the skill, the rhymes, the writing in meter: everything that's professional and traditional in Auden's verse." Jimmy, of course, had been familiar with Auden's poetry for many years, so its formal qualities were not new to him. Why this disavowal of them now? Clearly it is because he, in fact, *was* thinking of writing poetry by this time. In two of his recountings of this moment, Jimmy goes on to cite D. H. Lawrence's very different and seemingly casual free verse poems as a counter-inspiration: "It was very liberating to pick up a book of poems by somebody like D. H. Lawrence and not have to do these things." When, a few years later, Jimmy wrote his first poems, Lawrence would be his most explicit influence, or so he claimed. At the same time, Jimmy later wrote that typing Auden's poems and "the experience of so strong a creative gift was, and continues to be, powerfully stimulating."

Jimmy and Auden were perhaps closer at this period than either really acknowledged. If Auden could claim to see inside Jimmy's "heart of hearts" in the matter of Charles Heilemann, Jimmy likewise assumed—imaginatively and temporarily—Auden's authorial persona as he typed and retyped his poems. For someone with a mind as retentive as Schuyler's, this was, as he said, "powerfully stimulating." Even though he consciously rejected Auden's style, glimmers of this identification periodically returned to him in later years, especially when he came to write a series of formal, Audenesque poems in the mid-1950s, including "A Grave," a poem in which Schuyler seems to reimagine his own experience through the prism of Auden's version of it. Auden himself wrote about the peculiar intimacy of transcribing poetry, and imagined a future in which "an established poet would take on a small number of apprentices who would begin by changing his blotting paper, advance to typing his manuscripts and end up by ghostwriting poems for him."

Whatever specifics of the craft of poetry Jimmy may have learned, absorbed, or rejected from his close familiarity with Auden's verse might not have been as important as the opportunity to simply be "inside" the physical fact of the poems through typing them. Even as he was consciously rejecting, for himself, many of the formal and traditional aspects of Auden's verse, he was being made familiar, to his fingertips, with the poem as a physical object, with the extending, breaking, and "turning" of lines, the architecture of stanzas, the shape of the poem on the page. He learned to make a poem before he wrote a poem.

In June, Jimmy joined Charles Heilemann in Paris for a few weeks. Before he left, in late April, Truman gave a campy "dance-ball" on the rooftop of his Ischia pensione in honor of the much-publicized visit of Britain's nineteen-year-old Princess Margaret to the island. Paper lanterns were strung across the roof and a punch of the local sparkling wine, *lacrimae christi*, was served. Jimmy, Chester, and the young poet Ralph Pomeroy all came in drag. "Rather amusing," commented Capote to a friend.

Paris in the summer of 1949 was full of American expatriate writers and artists, gay and straight. The gay contingent included Capote, Ralph Pomeroy, Bernie Winebaum, and several other of Jimmy's acquaintances from Ischia. Coming from a quiet island, the gay scene in Paris was somewhat eye-opening to Jimmy: "I have *never* seen such a concentration of queens anywhere. At first it's a little terrifying, but after a while one rather takes for granted the idea that the majority of men bend backward at the knees. Why not?" Gay nightlife was split in its loyalties between two bars, La Reine Blanche and the Bar Montana, where Jean Genet was sometimes to be seen, and catty gossip might get around to the Duchess of Windsor, whose conquest of Edward VIII was attributed to the fact that "they say she's a circus in bed."

It was during this Paris visit that Jimmy had a brief encounter with the Franco-American novelist Julian Green. Browsing in Gagliani's bookshop on Rue de Rivoli one day, he noticed and caught the eye of a handsome older man (aged forty-nine), who, seeing that Jimmy's American passport was sticking out of his back pocket, said to him, "You shouldn't let your passport show like that, or someone may steal it." They fell into conversation and went somewhere to have a drink together. However, as soon as his new acquaintance told him his name, Jimmy was "appalled." Julian Green's novels of solitary, religious, troubled, often gay young men had meant so much to him growing up that he became tongue-tied and wanted only to get away as quickly as possible, and did so. It was, in fact, a very *Greenien* response.

Jimmy returned to Ischia by mid-August, in time for the visit of an old friend of Auden's, Cuthbert Worsley, who arrived with his young friend, John Richardson. Worsley was then the assistant literary editor and drama critic of the *New Statesman*. Richardson, the future biographer of Picasso, had spent the early part of that summer traveling with Douglas Cooper, a rich collector and scholar of Cubism, and would soon begin a long romantic relationship with him; his friendship with Worsley was platonic.

One afternoon when the group went into the village for the customary aperitif, they ran into some of the so-called remittance men, causing Auden and Worsley to flee back to the house, while Chester, Jimmy, and Richardson stayed behind to join in the gossip. Richardson was tall and ruggedly good-looking, a hunk, and was very taken with Jimmy's "dazzling" beauty, which struck the Englishman as "a completely new image" of "American sexuality," "like a sort of sailor off duty." Despite, or because of, Jimmy being "very quiet"—"almost psychotically quiet"—Richardson sensed in him an "erotic intensity." He and Jimmy began making eyes at each other from almost their first meeting.

The second or third night of the visit, Jimmy pulled his mattress out onto the terrace and the two made passionate love under the fig tree. Richardson later described the encounter as one of "intense, rough sex," and "*fairly* heavy S and M" during which he felt "something pent-up in Jimmy . . . and we both just let it kind of rip." "[Jimmy] took a passive role, but a very active part in his passive role," and in doing so, brought out in Richardson an inclination to violent sex he had not, until then, recognized (but would subsequently pursue).

Sex and violence. Violence had been an element of Jimmy and Bill's everyday relationship; most likely, it had some part in their sexual relationship as well. Or, conversely, it could be that the domestic violence—the thrown plates, the blows, the brandished knives—was an outlet for violence *not* expressed in the bedroom. Richardson's experience could point either way: on the one hand it seemed as though Jimmy was initiating him in modes of rough sex to which he, Jimmy, was already accustomed; at the same time, it seemed as though he was expressing something that had been "pent up." There are no indications that S&M behavior played a significant part in Jimmy's sexual activity for most of his life, despite the fact that Richardson (on the basis of the one extraordinary experience) felt that masochism was "a huge part of his sexuality." Much later, however, in the early 1970s, S&M practices would figure prominently in a three-year relationship with one of Jimmy's greatest loves.

At some point in the midst of it all, Jimmy drew Richardson's attention to the house behind. "Look." There outlined in the moonlight were the heads of Wystan and Chester peering down at them from one of the roofless rooms at the top of the house. "Don't stop," said Jimmy.

The next morning, Richardson found himself in disgrace and felt pressured to leave because he had behaved so "appallingly." Despite the fact that "everybody was fucking somebody—Wystan had a boyfriend, Chester had a boyfriend, God knows what was going on," there seemed to be "unwritten rules in the house" that he had transgressed. Richardson was given to understand that Jimmy's emotional state was too fragile to be stirred up as he had done. According to his reading of the situation, Jimmy and Wystan's relationship was "complicated," and Wystan "had a kind of grappling iron into him." Jimmy was still recovering from the trauma of Bill's attacks, and dependent on Auden's protection, and here was Richardson "coming in and undoing all their good work." For the remainder of their visit, Worsley and Richardson stayed in a pensione in town. For Richardson, the memory of that night—"a night I'll never, ever, ever, ever forget"—retained its radiant glow and a sense of being, a "rite of passage" for the rest of his long life, even though Jimmy and he never reconnected, neither on Ischia nor in later years when they were both living in New York.

It appears that Jimmy and Charles had earlier formed a habit of pulling their mattress outside to sleep and make love on hot Ischia nights, and this was not the first time Chester and Wystan had spied the goings-on from above. As a result, they came up with a new camp nickname for Jimmy and Charles. Playing on the title of a popular 1944 Italian movie, *Le sorelle Materassi* or *The Mattress Sisters*, they henceforth became "The Mattress Girls" to Wystan and Chester.

A short time later, on August 25, Jimmy left Italy, sailing from Naples and arriving in New York before the end of the month. On the ferry taking him across the bay from Ischia to Naples he met a young American vacationer named Morris Golde, who would later become a lively member of his circle of New York friends, and later still of great practical assistance in difficult times. Golde retained lifelong memories of that initial, fortuitous meeting. "We hit it off right away. He was thin, good-looking . . . He was just lovely . . . What I found charming was a kind of curious manner and behavior . . . in a sense involved with himself but also full of manners and listening . . . listening in a way that affected him." Golde was also aware that Jimmy "was sad that day. It was one of the reasons I loved him. There was this beautiful sadness about his face."

Sad he must well have been. He was returning, after an absence of two years and on the cusp of a new decade, to an unknown and possibly unwelcoming New York: jobless, moneyless, homeless, without having completed the novel he was said to have been writing, and with, if anything, only a few short stories to show for his two years' work abroad. He had lost one lover under traumatic circumstances that were still fresh, and acquired another, less dashing but more stable. On the other hand, he carried with him a wealth of sense impressions that would enrich and inform his poetry for the rest of his life.

[8]

SALUTE

1949–1951

Schuyler was back in New York by September 1, 1949. Chester Kallman planned to stay in Europe for the foreseeable future, and had told Jimmy that he and Charles Heilemann could stay in his apartment on Twenty-seventh Street. Unfortunately, this meant displacing Billy Vinson and John Hohnsbeen, who had been living there for the past year, and there were "somewhat strained relations" until Hohnsbeen found a place of his own. Introduced to the group by Vinson shortly after graduating from Columbia in 1948, Hohnsbeen was working at the Buchholz Gallery for the well-known German émigré art dealer Curt Valentin. He and Jimmy and Chester, once Chester returned from Europe in 1950, would all become close friends.

The Twenty-seventh Street apartment had undergone several transformations since Chester's day. David Protetch had spruced it up a bit when he and Chester were roommates in 1945, and Vinson and Hohnsbeen had made further improvements. Now Charles, a design and interiors professional, continued the transformation, painting the walls a light brown, the better to show off some of the new paintings he had done in Paris.

In addition to Hohnsbeen and old friends like Vinson and Protetch, Jimmy kept in touch with the new friends he had met in Italy: Donald Windham and Truman Capote. The change in lovers, however, had a somewhat dampening effect on Jimmy's relationship with Auden. Charles, for his part, felt Auden's dislike, and returned it with interest. Others also found Charles a somewhat surprising choice as a lover.

To Hohnsbeen, he seemed "the most *unlikely* person" for Jimmy to be involved with, and felt that his "explosive energy" sorted oddly with Jimmy's "comparative serenity: they were the most bizarre pair."

Auden had kept close tabs on Chester's apartment during the previous winter and had often visited Vinson there to cadge a meal and listen to "Mary Music"—Chester's phonograph and all his records were still there. It was also the place where he customarily spent holidays and his birthday. With Jimmy and Charles living there, Wystan no longer felt welcome to drop in unannounced. He resented the cooler atmosphere, and was hurt that he hadn't been invited to Christmas dinner there, as had been traditional.

Things went no better in the new year. On January 6, 1950, Auden wrote to Kallman: "Have not seen Jimmy and Charlie since Christmas Eve. Would like to hear records *occasionally* but wait to be invited—needless to say, I am not." On February 17, he reported he was "giving my birthday party at the Mayers' this year, no suggestion having emanated from 129 that I might have it where I am used to having it. Have invited the Mattress girls but with not too much warmth in my heart, I must admit."

Jimmy's first priority when he was back to New York was to find a job. Fortunately, John Hohnsbeen alerted Jimmy to an opening for a gallery assistant at the Kleemann Gallery, located across the street from the Buchholz Gallery, at 65 East Fifty-seventh Street between Madison and Park Avenues. Jimmy was hired and started work there in October 1949.

The Kleemann Gallery was established by another German refugee, Henry Kleemann, in the mid-'30s. The firm operated in both the primary and secondary markets, in that it exhibited a roster of living artists, but also sold work by whatever more famous or "blue chip" artists it could get its hands on. The living artists who showed at Kleemann in the '50s tended to be decorative, minor School of Paris figures, such as Claud Venard or Marcel Vertès, while secondary-market artists whose works passed through the gallery over the years were a very mixed bag indeed and included European modernists like Dubuffet, Klee, and Jawlensky, but also American painters such as La Farge and Eilshemius.

The job of assistant in a small art gallery is likely to include an array of disparate tasks, such as greeting customers, answering the phone, running errands, and preparing artworks for shipping. In a few of these areas Jimmy excelled; in most he did not. He was good with his hands, and quick to pick up certain manual skills, such as mat cutting. But his shyness, combined with a skeptical attitude toward the commercialization of art in general, meant that he was not a great success in the social aspects of the job. In addition, he did not get along well with Kleemann, whom he later characterized as "utterly unscrupulous and awful" and who was said by others to be a difficult employer. Writing to Piero Tosi in the summer of 1950, Jimmy expressed his distaste for the venal, provincial atmosphere of the gallery, lying just beneath the veneer of (would-be) good taste and refinement. Kleemann, he said, was a jerk, and the art he purveyed was "art of Paris from thirty years ago," which he "sold like cold-cuts: slices of Picasso, slices of Matisse, of Bonnard, of Gris, etc." In addition to the social hypocrisies endemic to art dealing, Jimmy was put off by other shady practices to which he was sometimes a reluctant party, as when Kleemann asked him to slip original drawings or watercolors into art books to mail them abroad, and thus avoid customs duties.

Auden came to dinner at Jimmy and Charles's on March 2, 1950—only the fourth time he had been invited there since their return the previous fall, as he bitterly noted. After they ate, Charles fell asleep "in protest." By that time, Jimmy had already "walked out on his job" at the gallery, although there are suggestions from other sources that he may have been working there again later, and perhaps into 1951.

During the summer of 1950, Charles Heilemann was in Mexico, teaching in the Parsons summer session there. Jimmy spent most of that time with Hohnsbeen, sharing a tiny wooden beach house in the dunes of Wainscott, Long Island, a small hamlet between East Hampton and Bridgehampton. The house, which was without electricity, stood about three hundred feet from the ocean among vast stretches of potato fields. In a letter to Tosi, he compared the flat eastern Long Island landscape to that of Emilia, the countryside surrounding Bologna, except that on Long Island "nothing but potatoes are growing, kilometer after kilometer, potatoes, potatoes, potatoes . . . and very far away some trees, like a seventeenth century Dutch painting."

With Charles away and Hohnsbeen still unattached (he would soon begin a ten-year relationship with the architect Philip Johnson), Jimmy and Hohnsbeen were enjoying their sexual freedom. "Our closest period, of course, was that long summer in 1950," Hohnsbeen recalled. "He was so beautiful, too, gorgeous. And sweet and shy. Already we all drank too much, already. That was a very heavy drinking period. Everybody drank all the time. And although we didn't have a car or anything, there was a bar . . . on the highway . . . It was walking distance, a long walk, but we managed to do it quite a lot. And then of course we'd pick up various people. It was a good, good, good summer."

David Protetch, who had completed medical school and was doing his residency at Kings County Hospital in Brooklyn, was also "around a lot" that summer, according to Hohnsbeen, and it's likely that this was when what Jimmy later described as "sort-of an affair" with him took place. During much of the week, however, Jimmy was alone in Wainscott, and took advantage of the solitude to write. In addition to working on a group of short stories, he also wrote a letter to Tosi expressing his pleasure at being in the country and a dark view of the city to which he was soon to return: "New York, that terrible city, city of the living dead, of sensuality without love, where people have eyes of glass, feet of rats, and soiled hands . . . aspirin and chewing-gum and whisky and a deeply silent sadness: you don't know how sad the skyscrapers are, not like tall men but like women who weep."

In September, Jimmy and Charles were evicted—or rather, Chester was, as the tenant of record—from the apartment on Twenty-seventh Street. For the next several months they lived in a series of short-term rentals, until finally moving into their own apartment at 873 Second Avenue at East Forty-seventh Street by August 1951.

The new apartment was a fifth-floor walk-up tenement, entered through the kitchen, which also contained the bathtub, while the toilet was in a separate room off the common hall, shared with the apartment next door. The floors had a pronounced tilt, and heat was provided by a "Clow" gas-fired steam heater that had to be kept filled with water in the winter. The living room had a view down into the park in front of the UN Building, now called Dag Hammarskjöld Plaza.

Little is known of Schuyler's activities between the summers of 1950 and 1951. Presumably he was being supported by Charles. He did some more typing for Auden, including his translation of Jean Cocteau's play *Knights of the Round Table* ("a minor work which got no better in English," according to Jimmy). And he had begun writing poetry in addition to stories. When he showed Auden some poems at this time, his advice was quite specific: "He sort of looked at the first one and said, 'Don't ever use ampersands.'" He also advised him "not to separate a modifier from its noun, like 'red'—end of line—'rose'. Auden said, 'It's very tempting, my dear.'" Jimmy also showed his stories to Capote, who was "much more helpful in his criticism than Auden ever was," Jimmy later said. "He was very astute and would always point out something good, that he thought was effective." In particular, Capote's comment that he wrote "very good endings" boosted his confidence.

In April 1951, Jimmy submitted a story titled "In White, Like a Bride" (unlocated) to *Accent*, a literary magazine published by the University of Illinois. *Accent* was one of the most prestigious American literary journals of the 1940s and '50s, and first published many of Wallace Stevens's poems, for example. The story was turned down, but it must have been an encouraging rejection, for Jimmy submitted four more stories about a month later, and three of these very short stories were accepted and printed in the Summer 1951 issue—Schuyler's first publication.

In August, he submitted again to *Accent*—this time seven poems, the first Schuyler is known to have written as an adult. None were accepted, however, and most are lost or unidentified, although some may have been revised and published later under other titles. At the end of August, he submitted another story or poem to *Accent*, "The Mushroom Gatherer's Familiar" (also lost or unidentified), which was likewise rejected.

We can form a partial idea about these early poems based on the assumption that the posthumously published "Amsterdam" and "Evening" are the same poems that were sent to *Accent* under those titles. The unpublished "Rome, December 1948" might also have been written around this time or shortly afterward. Together they suggest that many basic characteristics of Jimmy's poetic voice—and indeed some aspects of a shared New York School idiom—were present in his work from the first. One might grossly oversimplify these aspects and say they present a kind of near-conversational insouciance, with touches of wit or occasional light whimsy. These poems also corroborate Schuyler's assertion that the clearest conscious influence on his first poetic attempts was the poetry of D. H. Lawrence. It is not hard to imagine Schuyler taking to heart Lawrence's short introduction to *Pansies* (1929), in which he writes of his short poems as fleeting *pensées*, or "casual thoughts": "I offer a bunch of pansies, not a wreath of *immortelles* . . . A flower passes, and that perhaps is the best of it."

"Evening," as published posthumously in *Other Flowers*, is a strange poem. One is not sure how to take its odd naïveté (nor can one be sure that this is the version he sent to *Accent*). However, it does show some affinities with the poems in *Pansies*, in its matter-of-fact brevity and animal-world subject matter. There are also similarities of tone between it and another—more successful—early Schuyler poem, "At the Beach," which was probably written in 1951 and was published in *The New Yorker* a year later. "Amsterdam" is a more assured work, and seems fully Schuylerian, starting from a personification of the city as a lady adorned with golden bracelets of "hemicycular canals" bestrewn with floating yellow elm leaves, before moving to a straightforward and highly evocative description of the early fall of night.

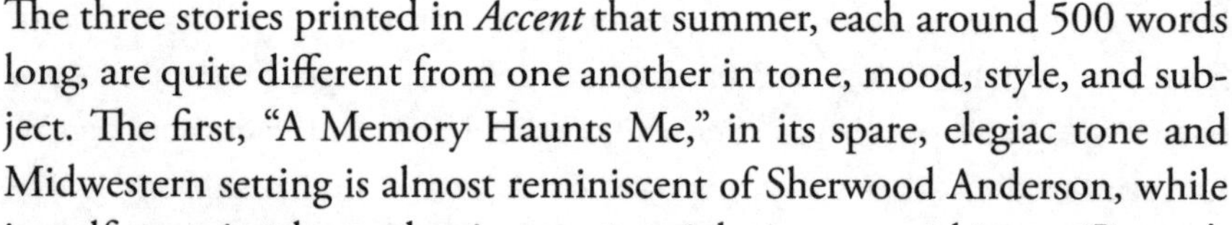

The three stories printed in *Accent* that summer, each around 500 words long, are quite different from one another in tone, mood, style, and subject. The first, "A Memory Haunts Me," in its spare, elegiac tone and Midwestern setting is almost reminiscent of Sherwood Anderson, while its self-consciously modernist syntax might owe something to Jimmy's reading of Gertrude Stein, or even Joyce.

A MEMORY HAUNTS ME

Certain haunting figures, certain people at certain moments, what they look like, and their mystery, say the solitary descender from the train at a small unpeopled junction, alone and his valise, the

> train is fading, is gone away, just him and the surround him flatness of the all perspective landscape, a man with a valise walks off into infinity; or say, a woman, what a woman thinks of while she's washing dishes, this woman with the ingrown eyes.

The story lightly sketches an unhappy marriage between the man who got off the train and a local woman, and ends with the woman finishing the dishes and turning off the light. "A Memory Haunts Me" might recall a family legend of how Ella and Frederick Connor met, spun from childhood impressions of his grandmother's farm in Albert Lea, a locale that was indeed haunted: by the ghastly death of his uncle Ralston, the desperate unhappiness of his grandfather Frederick, and the hard lives of his Slater forebears.

The second story, "The Mouse Party," concerns a small boy named Alfred who has a magic adventure at night when he gets out of bed and follows his pet mouse downstairs into the mouse's cage, which expands to become a sunlit lawn. Alfred has a sister named Guinevere, and of course they are, if only in name, forerunners of the title characters of Jimmy's first novel. The story is almost embarrassingly arch, but nonetheless has a hallucinatory, Alice in Wonderland quality that is oddly compelling.

"The Forty-First and Youngest Brother," the third story in the group, likewise is fantastic in mood, but in place of Lewis Carroll, it breathes a kind of 1890s aestheticism, like a decadent Oscar Wilde or Baron Corvo fairy tale. Along with certain *fin de siècle* mannerisms (such as inverted word order and words like *orison*), it leans toward a kind of crypto-masochistic Roman Catholicism with a final religious redemption like those sometimes found in tales by Wilde and his followers.

Upstairs in a dormitory, forty brothers sleep, while downstairs, "the forty-first and youngest brother" hones a knife and performs a solitary dance that "invoked his father's ghost." The knife comes alive and "slit his throat with its stinging blade and flew out of the house." The boy follows the fleeing knife, now a "minnowing" multitude of knives, up a frozen hill, where "shattering snow-crust cut his wrists and knees." After reaching the top, his knife wound heals, the sun rises, and he "knelt and made a brief orison." "The sun's first melting ray" carried him back to his own bed.

Jimmy's natural father died in June 1942, while James was at Bethany College. The word *brothers*, which at one time in Jimmy's life would have unambiguously meant "fraternity brothers," also argues for a dream-transformed Bethany College background. The story juxtaposes fairy-tale elements (the "youngest brother," flying knives, snow) with various Christian archetypes—the number forty, the lonely vigil on the hilltop, the stigmata-like wounds to wrists and knees, the magical healing of the knife wound, the character's resurrection—which contribute to the sense that the protagonist is a Christ figure or saint. He may also represent Jimmy himself, or a self-image that will manifest itself in periods of mental illness, when he declares himself to be Jesus Christ. Suggestions of violence and suicide hang over the story. As stated earlier, there is no record of Jimmy undergoing an undiagnosed psychotic break while at Bethany, but this story suggests that he may have.

In spring of 1951, Jimmy received his author's copy of *Accent*. After he had finished reading and rereading his own stories, he turned to the rest of the magazine and found himself rather disappointed with the other contributions, until he came to a poem called "The Three-Penny Opera" by one Frank O'Hara that seemed fresh and vital. He had never heard of the author, and since the contributors' notes said that he lived in Michigan, he did not imagine they would meet.

Through various mutual friends, including Auden and Chester, Jimmy had recently reencountered John Bernard Myers, his old acquaintance from the Otto Ulbrich Bookshop in Buffalo. Myers had moved to New York in 1944, and six years later opened the Tibor de Nagy Gallery at 219 East Fifty-third Street. His business partner, De Nagy, an aristocratic Hungarian, managed the practical end. The gallery quickly became an indispensable element of New York's postwar cultural landscape, showing young artists such as Larry Rivers, Grace Hartigan, Jane Freilicher, Helen Frankenthaler, and many others.

Myers had acquired a copy of *Accent* and immediately phoned Jimmy to congratulate him. "You never *told* me that you were a *poet*!" Myers enthused. "Oh," said Jimmy, "you liked my stories?" "They're not stories, they're *poems*!" At that Jimmy became rather self-conscious, and mentioned that the only other work in the magazine that he liked was "The Three-Penny Opera," by Frank O'Hara. Myers could barely contain himself: "My dear, it's *too* extraordinary, he's sitting here in the room with me now!" O'Hara, a friend of Myers's through his painter friends, was visiting for the summer from Ann Arbor, where he was attending graduate school at the University of Michigan. Before he and Jimmy had a chance to meet, however, O'Hara returned to Ann Arbor.

Jimmy, Charles, and Charles's friend Helen Burckhardt spent the summer of 1951 in a small primitive cabin in Pikes Falls, Vermont, a tiny hamlet in the Green Mountain National Forest. Helen, who would also become a good friend of Jimmy's, was a graphic artist and textile designer, born in Basel, Switzerland, in 1911, into a distinguished Swiss family, from the respectable weight of which she and her younger brother, Rudy, had been eager to escape. She had a sort of "Garbo-esque simple beauty," according to her sister-in-law Edith Schloss, or, as another friend put it, "looked a lot like Julie Harris, [and was] very, very interesting, and amusing and talented." After spending several years as assistant to the artist Jean Arp in France, with whom she was unrequitedly in love, she moved to New York in 1950 and worked as secretary to the writer Max Lerner.

The novel Jimmy was said to have been working on that summer is lost or unidentified, like so many others. When the trio returned to the city in the fall, Jimmy may have gone back to work for Kleemann. Most likely, he was being supported by Charles.

In later recollections, Jimmy said that he first met John Ashbery in 1950 at a party given by Fred "Butch" Melton and Wilber Pippin, a couple known in the 1940s and '50s for their large, predominantly gay male cocktail parties. Pippin was a writer, while Melton, a photographer, was the ex-lover of Jimmy's friend Donald Windham, and had moved to New York with him from Georgia. The writer Joe LeSueur, a frequent guest, described their parties as "a gay salon, the likes of which I'd never seen and would never see again," and noted that they were paid for by "no less a presence" than Lincoln Kirstein, the co-founder of the New

York City Ballet. It must have been through Windham that Jimmy was invited, while Ashbery's introduction to the pair had been through his Harvard friend the photographer George Montgomery.

Jimmy said he met Ashbery toward the end of one of these big Melton and Pippin parties, when John was probably "a little drunk because he had the giggles, and I think that's why he doesn't remember meeting me." Ashbery then "bragged about his record collection and the fact that some radio station was going to broadcast excerpts from it." At the time, Jimmy decided he was "rather silly and snooty. Little knowing that he was to become the person I love the most in the whole world."

Ashbery, who indeed did not remember this earlier encounter, recalled, rather, that they were already friends when they attended another of Melton and Pippin's parties together in 1952. In his recollection, he and Frank O'Hara first met Jimmy on October 1, 1951, after the opening of Larry Rivers's first solo exhibition at the Tibor de Nagy Gallery.

Rivers was a charismatic twenty-eight-year-old painter, formerly a jazz musician, who had started painting seriously a few years previously, after he met and had an affair with Jane Freilicher. Rivers was sexy, talented, funny, and bisexual. Both John Bernard Myers and Frank O'Hara were in love with him, and Rivers to some degree played them against each other, but he was half in love with O'Hara himself, and after their affair the two would remain close friends and sometime artistic collaborators until O'Hara's premature death. The party was held downtown in Rivers's studio on St. Marks Place, where Jimmy was thrilled to find himself rubbing shoulders with artists like Willem de Kooning, and to overhear him arguing with Nell Blaine the perennial question of "whether a serious artist could morally support him- or herself by doing commercial art work." While Jimmy was standing around with a drink, a young man "with a prominent broken nose, receding hair . . . wearing [khakis], a Shetland sweater and white sneakers" approached "and said 'Hello. I'm Frank O'Hara,' to which he added, 'You're Jimmy Schuyler.'"

Later, Jimmy was unable to remember much of what they talked about at that first meeting, except that, as usual, he said very little himself. "But that was never a problem with Frank, who usually had the ball and was running fast." One topic they discussed was an article in the latest issue of *The New Yorker* about André Gide's wife, who, in her bitterness at his treatment of her, had burned his letters. O'Hara's reaction to this was "Well, I never liked Gide, of course, but I never realized before that he was a *complete shit*!" At one point John Ashbery came up and joined the conversation—"loomed" over them, as Jimmy later put it. Jimmy was "intrigued by him, too, and the two of them seem to be rather intrigued by me. Magic moments." In addition to this heady first exposure to the wit and fun of these two handsome young poets, what thrilled Jimmy most was the serious interest they took in him as a fellow poet, something he had never before experienced in this way. Both poets had read his work in *Accent* and heard about him from John Bernard Myers. Jimmy ended the evening feeling "completely ecstatic." But before he was able to build on these promising introductions, his ecstatic feelings would find an unhappy outlet in a serious nervous breakdown leading to his first psychiatric hospitalization.

On October 12, Jimmy stopped in to visit John Hohnsbeen at the Buchholz Gallery. To Hohnsbeen's surprise and growing dismay, Jimmy was declaring to anyone who would listen that he was Jesus Christ—specifically, the Infant Jesus of Prague. At first, Hohnsbeen thought it was a joke, but gradually he realized that it wasn't, especially when Jimmy began "making these little sermons . . . to various people, and especially the clients who came in the gallery."

At about 5:00 that same afternoon, Jimmy visited Donald Windham. Saying he had something "very important" to tell him, he proceeded to harangue him for the next ten hours in a heightened state of manic ecstasy. He described everything he had seen on the way to visit him in an obsessive and minutely observant way, "knitted with mathematically exacting revelations and coincidences," yet none of these myriad details seemed to "lead to anything," Windham recalled. When he said he had "good news," Windham asked, "For whom?" "Everybody." The news was that "Judgment Day was near and that he had talked with the Virgin Mary yesterday afternoon and been presented with a package of Du Maurier cigarettes by her."

Windham, too, was at first unsure whether to take all this seriously and that it wasn't some elaborate game, but he soon became worried by an undercurrent of violent or apocalyptic imagery in Jimmy's talk, which woke fears that he was building up to an announcement that he had just murdered Charles or Wystan or done something equally terrible. Jimmy finally left at 3:00 in the morning, "no less elated and calm than when he arrived." Later that morning, Windham heard from Charles that Jimmy had been taken to Bellevue, the public mental hospital on New York's far east side.

The Infant Jesus of Prague is the name given to an elaborately begowned eighteenth-century Spanish doll kept in a church in Prague, where it is greatly revered. About a year later, Schuyler wrote the prose poem "The Infant Jesus of Prague," which he characterized as "a rather cryptic description of a nervous breakdown." The first short section of the work seems to coincide with how Windham described his speech that October day:

> One afternoon there were hollow far explosions, within thunder, and fire-torn wire trash baskets, messages, understanding.
>
> The shell cracked.
>
> Number: zero to one closed the ring. Duality, eleven, the Roman two. Triads, tridents. Four spun on its unseen center, five, a star, spinning zero, the sun. Etcetera.
>
> Hints, garbled saints, conversion of Jews. Clues in what was laughed at, imprisoned, tolerated, ignored, unnoticed.

As in later psychotic episodes, and in the "The Forty-First and Youngest Brother," Schuyler, or the protagonist, identifies with Christ:

> He gave his smiles as blessings, platitudinous tracts their readers would look from and laugh, "So that's how it is. It had a meaning all along" . . . For it was horrible, that they might pray him, mind and soul, into the heart of a doll: bottled, worshipped, that they might run freely in flesh fresh from laundries. [. . .]
>
> * * *
>
> "I go alone in the city, passing through the crowd that doesn't know . . ."

From Bellevue, Jimmy was transferred to Payne Whitney Westchester, the suburban branch of the psychiatric hospital attached to New

York Hospital (now New York Presbyterian), where he spent approximately nine weeks. Often referred to as "Bloomingdale" after its address on Bloomingdale Road in White Plains, the hospital is situated on an attractive campus with many beautiful old trees. Auden footed the bill for Jimmy's stay. Once he was well enough to receive visitors, there were many, including Charles and Wystan, Donald Windham, Billy Vinson, John Hohnsbeen, Truman Capote, Helen Burckhardt, Bernie Oshei—even Marianne Moore. (Chester was in Europe.)

Hohnsbeen and Capote traveled up together to Westchester, where they found Jimmy doing handicrafts: "braiding belts and Indian beaded moccasins and all that stuff . . . They were nice, nice belts, and he gave each of us one." Judging by Jimmy's letters, he spent a lot of the time playing cards, gin rummy, and bridge, and wrote to Hohnsbeen, "When I get out of here I'm going to make a collage of playing cards just for the fun of attacking them with scissors. Snip snip snip." He also reported that he was taking boxing lessons.

Marianne Moore, whom he had met through Auden, was his most "entrancing" visitor. "Entrancing and somehow a little terrifying, since I don't really know her at all. During our visit I had a faint recurrent wish to say, 'Miss Moore, don't you sometimes think Wystan's full of crap?' But I wrassled with Satan and threw him." A week later, Moore mailed him a warmly inscribed copy of her recently published *Collected Poems*.

The desperately serious mental illness that led to Jimmy's hospitalization tended to be trivialized or glossed over by him, and even by some of his visitors. Helen Burckhardt, who traveled up to the hospital with Auden, recalled his saying to her as they were leaving, "Quite a bunch of mad queens in here, aren't there?"—as though mental illness were some kind of flamboyant, eccentric performance. Once he was on the mend, Jimmy's own depiction of the period somewhat disingenuously conflates the illness, which had been frightening for his friends, with the cure, while seeming to recognize its creatively liberating potential: "Whatever it was it happened very quickly and seems terribly worth while having had happen. I'll call it a nervous breakdown, and say that I feel better now than I have in years, only a certain *tristesse* at sundown, a longing for the cold blaze of a martini and some familiar faces, conversation about something other than football, TV and bridge."

By late November, Jimmy had improved enough to begin writing poems. But the poems he wrote now were different from those he had written before. The first poem he wrote in the hospital was called "Salute," and according to Jimmy it was directly inspired, especially in its form, by O'Hara's "The Three-Penny Opera," the poem that had appeared in *Accent*.

O'Hara's poem refers, of course, to the Brecht-Weill musical, and is both longer than and quite different in character from "Salute." What Jimmy took from it was its "broken" form and its informal tone. Discussing the two poems in 1977, Jimmy explained:

> If you look at ["Salute"] carefully and then read Frank's poem "The Three-Penny Opera," you'll see that my form is entirely taken from Frank O'Hara, particularly breaking a line where it would seem logical not to break it, and leaving such things as a dangling "a" or "the" . . . What I loved in Frank's poem, aside from the glitter of style of it, was this broken rhythm. It was almost like listening to jazz, or the kind of jazz that someone like Prokofiev might write.

Both poems achieve their "jazzy" rhythm by breaking lines at places that might seem counter to the natural flow of speech or expectation. Both poems break a word just before an "-ing" suffix: "Air- / ing old poodles" ("The Three-Penny Opera"); "Like that gather- / ing of one of each." ("Salute"). "The Three-Penny Opera" is written in a conversational tone to which Jimmy also responded, and which helped him find and trust his own voice.

From the hospital, within a week or so of writing it, Jimmy sent a copy of "Salute" to the *New Yorker* poetry editor, Howard Moss. A year older than Jimmy, Moss was a poet, but is also known for his twenty-seven-year editorial career at the magazine, having started there as fiction editor in 1948. Jimmy's letter of November 27 included two poems; one, "The Double Gallery" (lost or unidentified), was written before his breakdown, he says. The other, "Salute," is described as "the only writing I've done here, since."

Moss did not accept either poem, but instead forwarded "Salute" to another editor, Arabel Porter, whom Moss was advising in the selection of poetry for a new literary periodical, *New World Writing*, to be published by New American Library. After learning of this, Jimmy suggested that Moss and Porter also consider the work of his new acquaintance Frank O'Hara, whom he described as "one of the Young Harvard set . . . What I've seen of his poems I've thought awfully good." Moss and Porter took Jimmy's recommendation, and both "Salute" and O'Hara's "Poem" ("The eager note on my door said 'Call me'") were accepted for publication in the first issue of *New World Writing*. Jimmy was still in the hospital when he got the good news. On December 31, he wrote to Moss, "I'm pleased about the poem: how wonderful to be in something brand new, and that is not (I confess this pleases me) printed on an old ditto machine in a converted loft on East West Street." Jimmy eventually received payment of $7.50 for "Salute" at the going rate of fifty cents a line.

New World Writing was indeed a mainstream venue for Jimmy's first published poem. For this inaugural issue, Arabel Porter had elicited work from some of the big names of the day, and "Salute" appeared alongside contributions by Christopher Isherwood, Louis Auchincloss, Tennessee Williams, Flannery O'Connor, Thomas Merton, Rolfe Humphries, Shelby Foote, Gore Vidal, Wright Morris, William Gaddis, Howard Nemerov, James Laughlin, and others. The fact that a mass-market reprint house like New American Library was bringing out a serious literary magazine for new writing—fiction, poetry, and criticism—attracted media attention, and *Time* reviewed that first issue, albeit tepidly: "The selections are devotedly serious, they reflect solid craftsmanship, they are only rarely arresting." *New World Writing* would go on to be a highly regarded literary vehicle through the 1950s and '60s, publishing chapters from the books that became *Catch-22* and *On the Road*.

Throughout December, Jimmy sent Moss additional poems, including the still-unpublished "Rome, December 1948," an elegy, "Harold Ross," and two untitled short poems, beginning "Good days and bad . . ." and "Having felt so extremely . . ." One of them, Jimmy said, had been written eighteen months previously, which would date it to the summer of 1950. This could have been "Rome, December 1948" or "At the Beach," the poem that was eventually accepted by Moss and published in *The New Yorker* in July 1952.

SALUTE

Past is past, and if one
remembers what one meant
to do and never did, is
not to have thought to do
enough? Like that gather-
ing of one of each I
planned, to gather one
of each kind of clover,
daisy, paintbrush that
grew in that field
the cabin stood in and
study them one afternoon
before they wilted. Past
is past. I salute
that various field.

The significance of "Salute" within his work was acknowledged by James Schuyler throughout his life. It was the title poem of his first (limited edition) book of poems, and the concluding poem of his first commercially published book of poems, *Freely Espousing*. Late in life, when Jimmy gave a series of remarkable public readings, he invariably led off with "Salute."

"Past is past." The poem begins with a truism almost trite. But as a piece of homespun wisdom, it is possible that the expression came to him through the trio of remarkable women who helped shape his childhood: his mother, his grandmother, and his great-aunt Margaret Godley. Plainspoken sayings by all three eventually made their way into Jimmy's work, passed down through his mother, who, he recalled, "always had a ready proverb."

The phrase is also a kind of near-palindrome, as Eileen Myles points out, both in itself and in its repetition at the end of the poem. Actually, the entire poem is in a sense palindromic, with, at its center, the generative (retrospective) "eye" of "I planned," cupped on either side by the pair of nearly identical phrases, "gather- / ing of one of each" and "to gather one / of each," and with "past is past" and the title itself occurring both at the beginning and near the end of the poem. One might diagram the quasi-palindrome of key phrases thus, in the order in which they occur:

Salute
past is past
gather one of each
I planned
gather one of each
past is past
salute

Pared down to this core, "Salute" reveals a crystalline inner structure, holding, as it were, a mirror up to itself. It is centripetal like a flower, and if we study it as we would a flower, our action reflects that of the poem's narrator.

The poem presents an event that, while we are told it did not actually happen, is nonetheless the poem's primary image: the poet picking wildflowers in a grassy meadow on a summer day and systematically studying them as they wilt. This reader has always envisioned the narrator lying prone in a summer field, an image that held deep associations for Schuyler, extending back to his first awakening to what he "meant / to do," while he was lying in his backyard tent and looked up from the book he was reading to see the landscape "shimmer" before his eyes. The book in his hands then, of course, was Logan Pearsall Smith's *Unforgotten Years*, with its similar epiphany occurring when Smith recalls his youthful friendship with Walt Whitman, whose *Leaves of Grass* begins with the poet lying in a field and contemplating "a spear of summer grass." Again there is the sense of endless mirroring, here coupled with the idea of a continuing literary legacy, specifically of queer male writers.

As Whitman wrote in "Salut au Monde!": "Who are they you salute, and that one after another salute you?"

In Italian, the primary meaning of *salute* is "health," as Jimmy well knew. Titling his breakthrough poem, written in a hospital, with a word connoting health implies a connection in Schuyler's mind between (mental) health and this poem, and, perhaps by extension, the writing of poetry in general. With few exceptions, Schuyler's poetic voice seems a paradigm of calm sanity, in contrast to his intermittent breakdowns, periods of delusional behavior, and sometimes messy, on-the-edge existence.

The poem itself, and the believable nature of Schuyler's work in general, convince us that "that field / the cabin stood in" was a real place. Although it's not possible to pinpoint the setting with certainty, there is circumstantial evidence to suggest that Jimmy was thinking of the cabin he and Bill Aalto rented near Lac St. Jean in northern Quebec in the summer of 1945. He had already used the phrase "*una cosa passata è passata*" ("something past is past") in a letter to Piero Tosi, where it referred to his failed relationship with Aalto. In the letter, Bill is described as someone forever looking into a mirror—a metaphorical mirror of self-doubt—and with being obsessed with his own unrealized talents and ambitions, as well as the failed relationship with Jimmy. Although he had not seen or spoken to Bill in over two years, theirs had been the longest and most important romantic and sexual relationship in Jimmy's life up to that point; he, and a place where they had been happy together years before, might well have been in Jimmy's mind as part of the personal stock-taking that would have followed his breakdown.

In seeming to favor imagination over action, the central question of the poem ("is / not to have thought to do / enough?") touches on an important problem of Jimmy's own life and sensibility. Compared to many poets, James Schuyler was a late bloomer. In November 1951, he had just turned twenty-eight. He did not have a job and was being supported by his lover. It had been at least twelve years since he had made the solemn decision to be a writer, lying in that East Aurora field, and he still had little to show for it except the three very short stories published in *Accent*.

If the poem is in part a personal reckoning, it begins with resignation and the suggestion that maybe to have meant to be, say, a writer was somehow a creative act in itself. Suggesting otherwise was the object lesson of Bill Aalto and others (Chester, perhaps) who never lived up to creative ambitions they originally set themselves. And now Jimmy had the positive inspiration of an exciting new friend, Frank O'Hara, whose work had shown him in practical, formal terms a way to go forward.

Though the poem's surface narrative suggests that it might be acceptable not to follow through on many ambitions, the poem itself, by its very existence, implies the opposite. The solid fact of the poem contradicts its own ambiguous message. The writing of "Salute" changes everything, even the past, even "Salute." In the poet's very act of resigning himself to not having done what he meant to do, he finally does it. The lovely, sad, possibly "unhealthy" dream that anything at all is possible, a dream that can be kept alive only by never actually settling on the thing to be done, is dissolved. In its place is the far more satisfying act of writing the poem, with all the unexpected discoveries and transformations to which the actual putting of words to paper can miraculously lead.

Jimmy was "ever so much better" by late December, as Wystan reported in a letter to Chester. On Christmas Day, he was allowed to come home for the day and was released for good on about January 7, 1952.

The hospital set conditions, or strong recommendations, before releasing him. According to Jimmy, "It was decided in the hospital that it was very important that I be self-supporting and also that it would be better if I lived alone," and that "it was a requisite of my leaving the hospital that I have a job." These statements corroborate the supposition that Jimmy had been supported by Charles at the time of his hospitalization in October, and probably had been ever since he quit the Kleemann Gallery in 1950. Requiring that he get a job seems only sensible, but to recommend that he live alone is much less straightforward. Assuming that this was indeed the hospital's recommendation, it must have been the result of disclosures Jimmy made in therapy about the nature of the relationship, which may have been based in an unhealthy dependency on Charles. Early in 1952, Jimmy would end the relationship, "somewhat to mutual regret."

The question of a job was soon settled. Through John Hohnsbeen, Jimmy had become friends with Stuart Preston, the art critic for *The New York Times* from 1949 to 1965. Preston learned of an opening at the Periscope-Holliday Bookshop on East Forty-ninth Street and suggested that Jimmy apply for the job. He was hired to begin work in the middle of January.

Before he started his new job, Jimmy visited his parents in East Aurora for a week or so. He flew to Buffalo and back—very likely his first experience on a plane. "I can't think where I got the courage to get into an airplane; I nearly died of fright on the trip up," he wrote to Moss. From East Aurora he sent Moss his first collaged poem, incorporating items from the local *Suburban Reporter and Shopping Guide* and issues of *National Geographic.*

Jimmy had been back home in New York for a week when, on the evening of January 14, 1952, Donald Windham came to visit him for a drink after dinner. In addition to Charles, Wystan and John Hohnsbeen were also there. Jimmy, according to Donald, looked "plump and bored," and Windham was struck by "how, in the presence of certain people, all evenings seem the same." To Jimmy the gathering may indeed have seemed like the same-old-same-old, and if he appeared bored, he could have been feeling impatient for his new life, with new friends, to begin.

[9]

I WAS A POET

1952

James Schuyler's close friendships with John Ashbery and Frank O'Hara, which began in early 1952 and lasted, in O'Hara's case, for most of the decade, and in Ashbery's to the end of Schuyler's life, determined the direction of his life and work. Jimmy himself was the first to recognize this. As he said later, "Both John and Frank were very encouraging and made me feel that I wasn't just a poet who was being tested but that I was a poet. That was perhaps one of the most, if not the most important moment of my life; to be accepted by people of whose work I was absolutely certain."

Frank O'Hara and John Ashbery had met as Harvard undergraduates in the spring of 1949. At a party in Cambridge celebrating the opening of an exhibition of watercolors by Frank's roommate, Edward Gorey, John heard, rising over the hubbub, a nasal voice that sounded to him uncannily like his own, expressing a thought uncannily like one of his own: "Let's face it, *Les Sécheresses* is greater than *Tristan*." The idea of preferring a short cantata (recently performed on campus) by the modern French composer Francis Poulenc, who at the time tended to be regarded as a lightweight, to Richard Wagner's larger-than-life operatic *Gesamtkunstwerk* would have struck most informed listeners as absurd—a provocation, but a serious one, and it was instantly recognized by John as implying a whole armature of other aesthetic preferences: wit, intelligence, and a "French" lightness of spirit over ponderous, self-important Germanic heaviness. The speaker was, of course, Frank. John went over and introduced himself, and thus began their close friendship.

John Ashbery was born in Rochester, New York, in 1927 and grew up on a farm in the small upstate community of Sodus. Farm life was often uncongenial to the sensitive, bookish boy, and when he could, he took refuge with his maternal grandparents at their house in Rochester, where his grandfather was a professor of physics, and later at their home in Pultneyville on the shore of Lake Ontario. John began writing poetry as a precocious eight-year-old and to publish while in prep school at Deerfield, Massachusetts. By the time he went to Harvard, he was clear in his vocation. Until he met Frank, Kenneth Koch was John's closest poet friend at Harvard, and the two of them had been showing each other their poems for the past year. But Koch had graduated in the class ahead of him.

Frank O'Hara was born in Baltimore in 1926 and grew up in an Irish Catholic family in Grafton, Massachusetts, a small town about thirty miles west of Boston. Passionate in high school about poetry, James Joyce, and music, he hoped to become a pianist and took courses at Boston's New England Conservatory. The war interrupted his plans, and on graduation from high school in 1944 he enrolled in the navy, serving in the Pacific during the war. After demobilization in 1946, he went to Harvard on the G.I. Bill, where his main interest shifted from music to poetry.

Frank and John were inseparable in the short time that remained of the 1949 term before John graduated. Frank was a year older, but because of his navy service he still had one more year of college until his own graduation in 1950. Having visited New York the previous year, John knew he wanted to live there, and headed straight for the city after graduating. Kenneth Koch had moved to New York the year before and said John could stay in his apartment for a few weeks; the upstairs neighbor, a young painter named Jane Freilicher, would give him the key. She did, but it would take several meetings for the shy poet and the sardonic painter to recognize each other as soulmates. Born in Brooklyn in 1924, Jane possessed a laid-back urban wit and sophistication that soon made her a muse for all three of the Harvard poets and, in time, Schuyler as well. After a short stint working at the Brooklyn Public Library, Ashbery was accepted in the MA program at Columbia. He devoted much of the next year to hanging out with Freilicher, her boyfriend Larry Rivers, and other painters, including Nell Blaine, Alfred Leslie, and Grace Hartigan, while corresponding with O'Hara in Boston and exchanging visits with him.

In the fall of 1950, O'Hara was accepted into the graduate program at the University of Michigan at Ann Arbor and moved there for the year. Meanwhile, Kenneth Koch went to Italy on a Fulbright, and then moved to California, entering the graduate program at UC Berkeley, so for the next year John was without his two Harvard friends in New York.

Frank O'Hara's definitive return to New York to live, the following August, was felt by John, Jane, and Larry Rivers to be the one thing necessary for their adult lives to begin, to "kind of cobble everything together and tell us what we and they were doing," as Ashbery wrote later. By that time, Frank's poem "The Three-Penny Opera" had appeared in *Accent*, and he had had his indirect "meeting" with Jimmy through the intermediary of John Bernard Myers. He moved in with a former Harvard roommate, Hal Fondren, sharing his apartment at 326 East Forty-ninth Street, and in November he got a job at the front desk of the Museum of Modern Art.

After Charles moved out, Jimmy continued to see him socially for the next several years, but Charles had become peripheral to his life as his new poet and painter friends became central to it. Jimmy now found himself without a live-in lover for the first time since he came to New York to live with Bill. As he later recalled, "I had never really gone out on the streets or into the bars, except secretly, behind my lovers' backs, and I was looking forward to having some fun on my own." Fun was sought at bars downtown in Greenwich Village, chiefly the San Remo, the Old Colony, and even the Cedar Tavern, which was not a gay bar but a lively scene for artists and writers. Closer to home were the many popular gay bars around Third Avenue in the East Fifties, many of them named after birds—the Blue Parrot, the Golden Pheasant, the Swan—so that they were collectively referred to as the "bird circuit."

A reluctance to give up his newfound sexual liberty may have contributed to Jimmy's ambivalence about a new relationship he did enter into at this time, with the poet and dance critic Edwin Denby. Jimmy and Denby first met briefly when they overlapped on Ischia in the summer of 1949. They had several mutual friends through whom they could have remet in New York, including Auden, Helen Burckhardt, and John Bernard Myers. By the time John Ashbery was seeing Jimmy regularly, early in 1952, he was already having an affair with Denby.

Edwin Denby was slender and angular, white-haired, elegant and patrician in demeanor, with skin, according to Jimmy, "the color of silvery parchment." Restrained and austere, he spoke in a "whisper." A full twenty years older than Jimmy, he had been born in 1903 in China, where his father was a diplomat. Denby dropped out of Harvard and went to Germany, where he toured with a modern dance troupe, and began writing and publishing libretti, essays, and poems. In Europe in the late '20s and early '30s, he met various members of the international avant-garde, including Virgil Thomson and Aaron Copland. In Switzerland in 1934, he fell in love with Rudy Burckhardt, a twenty-year-old Basel photographer; the two of them came to New York in 1935 and moved into an industrial fifth-floor walk-up loft on Twenty-first Street, which would be Denby's home until he died in 1983. Denby and Burckhardt's circle soon grew to include "the most interesting and lively people in the late thirties, actors from the group theater, dancers, writers, composers . . . all still young and unknown," wrote the artist Edith Schloss, who later married Burckhardt. At the suggestion of Aaron Copland and Virgil Thomson, Denby began to write dance criticism, which he raised to a fine art with his precise observation and stylish writing. But he was primarily a poet, whose books, *In Public, In Private* (1948) and *Mediterranean Cities* (1965), had a deep if subtle influence on his younger poet friends.

Rudy Burckhardt was the love of Denby's life but was not gay himself, and after he married Schloss in 1946, he moved out of the loft, but continued to use the darkroom he had set up there. Denby's loft was an extension of his character in its Spartan elegance. White and spacious, with a skylight, a wall of north-facing windows, and a gray-painted floor, it contained little furniture aside from a double bed covered with an Indian bedspread, some plain wooden chairs, and a long dining and work table constructed by his next-door neighbor, Willem de Kooning, using steel plumbing pipes for legs.

In many ways, Denby was a delightful person to have an affair with. He was modest about his poetry, his cosmopolitan background, and his worldly connections, and eager to share his love of dance and performance with a sensitive and appreciative lover like Jimmy. Their time together was marked with many evenings at the New York City Ballet, where his intimate knowledge of the dance and dancers expanded Jimmy's critical sensibility in general, and appreciation of dance in particular.

Because the affair ended badly, and both parties eventually wrote about its aftermath, albeit cryptically, more is known about the end of the relationship than about its beginning or middle. What seems clear, however, is that Jimmy felt some ambivalence from the beginning. When John Ashbery first learned of the affair, he sensed that Jimmy was already having "second feelings" about it; and for some reason Jimmy told Jane Freilicher that they were not sleeping together. That the affair was in fact physical in nature is shown most clearly by a letter of condolence, written to Rudy after Denby's death, in which Jimmy writes: "I loved Edwin and he loved me. Of course it was wonderful to go, say, to the ballet together; it was even more wonderful (or it is to remember) a frank erotic sensuality that we both thoroughly enjoyed." What is not in doubt is the intensity of Denby's feelings for Jimmy, which could feel overwhelming. Being the object of Denby's attentions was, as Jimmy vividly put it, "like having an x-ray fall in love with you." The poet Anne Waldman, who was close to Denby later, sensed that Denby's love for Jimmy remained "a vulnerable spot" for him many years after their affair had ended, "something unrequited that haunted him."

Schuyler's position in relation to his new poet friends was somewhat anomalous. He was a few years older than the "Harvard Wits," as Ashbery, O'Hara, and Koch were sometimes known, and in certain ways more worldly. Although both Frank and Kenneth Koch had served in the war, neither had experienced anything comparable to Jimmy's imprisonment on Hart Island, not to mention the tumultuous five-year relationship with Aalto. He had been an intimate member of W. H. Auden's domestic circle and had rubbed shoulders with other literary celebrities. Yet in other ways he was less sophisticated than they; he had not much of a college education, nor the years of dedicated writing and critiquing one another's work that John, Frank, and Kenneth had begun at Harvard. Although none of them had yet published much, John and Frank were more practiced poets than Jimmy. Yet as a relative novice, by mid-1952 he had already published in *Accent* (for which John envied him) and *New World Writing*, and was the first member of their group, by many years, to publish in *The New Yorker*.

The importance of John, Kenneth, and Frank's friendship for Jimmy extended beyond their recognition of him as a poet, central as that was. What made the friendships particularly stimulating was the access he gained to a social milieu of artists and other poets. Kenneth, who would return to New York and meet Jimmy in the middle of the year, described that milieu as a series of "dramatic occasions," when "a new poem, or a new painting was enough, sparked by Frank, to have us all in turmoil, until we'd read, seen, appropriated, or in some way adjusted and learned to live with whatever it was."

> Jimmy was a regular part of our "gang." There were other people in it, but the friends I thought about every day were Larry Rivers, Jane Freilicher, John Ashbery, Frank O'Hara, and Jimmy. In the social realm if you invited one of us to a party, you were likely to get us all, plus one or two more. We were always showing each other our work—poems, plays, stories, paintings. We were each other's main audience and so in time each other's main inspiration.

While Frank's and John's personal sensibilities were similar, and even their distinctly nasal voices could sound identical (leading Jimmy at one point to accept a lunch date with John, as he thought, only to find it was Frank who had phoned him and who turned up at the restaurant), the two poets related in quite different ways to Jimmy and their other friends. Frank, with his outgoing nature, was the catalyst for the group, which included not only Jimmy, John, Kenneth, and Barbara Guest, but also the painters: Jane Freilicher and Larry Rivers above all, but also Michael Goldberg, Al Leslie, Alex Katz, Grace Hartigan, Joan Mitchell, Nell Blaine, Elaine de Kooning, and Helen Frankenthaler.

Bursting with brilliance and high spirits, Frank was never still, never not "on." Even his low points were expressed in torrents of tears. His job at the MoMA information desk, in these early years, was low-key, and in quiet moments he was free to write or read. The first time Jimmy visited Frank at the ticket counter, he found him sitting with a yellow legal pad in front of him, writing in "gigantic" longhand a poem called "It's the Blue," with next to him a copy of André Breton's *Young Cherry Trees Secured Against Hares*. Frank reserved his formidable energies for his social and cultural life: "going to parties, movies, and the New York City Ballet; drinking at the San Remo and the Cedar; sitting around with friends at home"—and of course his writing. Frank gave the impression that writing poetry was of a piece with this social activity, as his longtime friend Joe LeSueur wrote, "part of life and not separate from it so that he had to shift into high gear to get ready for an esthetic experience. He was in high all the time, high on himself, and his every waking minute, regardless of what he was doing, was vital, super-charged, never boring if he could help it." Jimmy recalled an occasion when he and Frank and Joe LeSueur were home having coffee one morning and the others began to tease Frank about his ability to write a poem "any time, any place." Frank glared, went into the bedroom, typed furiously for a few minutes, then reemerged having written "Sleeping on the Wing."

Frank had a gift for friendship and for maintaining old friendships. Jimmy described him as "an enchanter": "He always had charm, he always had something witty to say, he could completely control a whole roomful of people. It was quite staggering to experience this." But he was also a "great giver. Any time a young poet wanted to know something, Frank would just start talking and tell him all about it."

Between Jimmy and John Ashbery, the friendship was quieter, somehow more individualized, and steadier. "John always made me feel that I was right there and he was right there . . . a friend, a companion, a fellow wit." Jimmy felt it was a compliment of a high order indeed when, one night while they were hanging out beside the jukebox at the San Remo, John said to him, "I'd rather stand here exchanging *limp* remarks with you than go out and pick somebody up."

John in turn was somewhat dazzled by Jimmy's good looks—"everybody considered him the handsome member of the New York School"—and had "sort of had a crush" on him when they first became friends, but he was too shy to say anything to him about it, so "nothing ever came of it"—except their close and long-lasting friendship. At the time, this took the form of their seeing each other several times a week, often taking walks together along the East River, and in the evenings going to movies or concerts, ending up at bars such as the San Remo or the Old Colony (which they referred to as "The Lost Colony") or the "bird circuit" on Third Avenue.

The Periscope-Holliday Bookshop, where Jimmy started work in January 1952, owed its double-barreled name to the merger of two of the many small bookstores that used to thrive in the East Forties and Fifties near Fifth Avenue: the Holliday Bookshop, long known for its stock of books imported from England, and the nearby Periscope Bookshop, whose owner, Robert Vanderbilt, merged the two shops in the old Holliday location on Forty-ninth Street.

Jimmy worked there for the next several years, and as jobs go, it was a congenial one. Vanderbilt was a "generous" employer, Jimmy later conceded, in tolerating his less than assiduous work habits. The store had a club-like atmosphere and was an informal gathering place, where visiting British writers and celebrities—such as Noel Coward, the Sitwells, or the Duchess of Windsor—were likely to drop in. "How delightful it used to be," Jimmy recalled, "when Alec W[augh] came bouncing and bubbling into the Periscope Bookshop: quite the opposite, obviously, of his brother." Of course Jimmy's own friends frequently dropped in as well. John Ashbery, who was working on lower Fifth Avenue at the Oxford University Press, often took a taxi uptown to visit Jimmy at the store for an extended lunch, and was so frequently late in getting back that it inspired a line in his short play *The Coconut Milk*: "I relax in my lateness." Jimmy did complain about his supervisor, Brayton Lewis, a fussbudget who would sometimes make him stay late to dust the stock, and whose coy expressions (such as that he was going to "waltz over" to, say, the post office) remained a source of private jokes between Jimmy and John long afterward. On the other hand, the stock was wonderful for browsing in during quiet moments, and he was even able to do some writing there when Brayton was out.

When they first met Jimmy at the Larry Rivers opening, neither John nor Frank had read more than the three stories in *Accent*, yet somehow they felt a strong and seemingly instantaneous bond. Nonetheless, Jimmy was nervous when he first showed John and Frank a selection of his poems early in 1952. These poems included "Salute" and "Rome, December 1948," possibly "At the Beach," and no doubt some of the unidentified poems that he had sent to *Accent* in 1951. In any case, to Jimmy's immense satisfaction, they approved, recognizing not only his distinct gifts, but a kinship to their own sensibilities.

They were not usually in the habit of verbalizing this sensibility in any explicit way, but it was understood amid the humorous repartee of their meetings and (soon enough) correspondence. When Ashbery first read Schuyler's "Rome, December 1948," which begins with a bang—"Hemorrhoids / like the misery of gnat-stung Io / drove me from Ischia to Rome"—he responded, not losing a beat: "Marie, Marie, hold on tight!" (quoting from "The Waste Land"). Direct conversations about one another's poems were most often couched, like this, in irony and humor. Perhaps the closest any of them came to verbally acknowledging a common aesthetic was when one of them veered from it, as when, a few years later, Jimmy experimented with formal verse, to John's expressed disapproval.

What they did share were enthusiasms for the work of poets they considered in some sense inspirations or predecessors, as well as antipathies for most of the mainstream contemporary American poets of the day. Jimmy was nothing if not well-read, but both John and Frank were better informed about modern and contemporary French poetry, and broadened his knowledge and understanding of figures like Guillaume Apollinaire, Pierre Reverdy, André Breton, Max Jacob, and others. Soon

John would begin his study of the French proto-Surrealist Raymond Roussel, whose work he then introduced to his friends. A natural occasion for such discussions was when John and Frank would stop by to visit Jimmy at the bookstore, and interesting-looking books would be pulled from the shelves for perusal. A poet who was very important to them all at this period was Boris Pasternak, whose selected writings were then available in English only in a New Directions translation by Babette Deutsch. Jimmy cited his line "waving a bough of fragrance" as a favorite for the way it takes "a metaphor beyond a metaphor." Pasternak's autobiographical memoir, *Safe Conduct*, also impressed Jimmy for its strong evocation of the kinds of physical memories that would become a part of his own poetic approach.

In the USA of the 1950s, the predominant mode of poetry was academic and masculinist, as seen in the work of writers like Robert Penn Warren, Robert Lowell, Randall Jarrell, John Berryman, Theodore Roethke, Delmore Schwartz, and others. Even at their best they appeared to be stodgy, humorless, and overly formal, at least to Kenneth, John, Frank, Jimmy, and Barbara, and to other young poets, including the Beats and the Black Mountain poets. Jimmy and his friends did read and look to the canon of modernist poets of the previous generation, particularly "the greats," as Jimmy called them: William Carlos Williams, Marianne Moore, Wallace Stevens, Ezra Pound, T. S. Eliot. And of course his friend Auden was ubiquitous, "like the common cold," as he put it. In a letter reflecting on his and his friends' shared influences in the 1950s, Jimmy elaborated:

> I doubt if any very direct connection can be found between Moore and anyone. I wanted to write like her, but her form is too evolved, personal and limiting . . .
>
> Eliot made the rules everyone wants to break.
>
> Stevens and Williams both inspire greater freedom than the others, Stevens of the imagination, Williams of subject and style.
>
> Pound I wonder about. Like Gertrude Stein, he is an inspiring idea. But a somewhat remote one. A poem like Frank's "Second Avenue" might seem influenced by the *Cantos*, but Breton is much closer to the mark.

Later, when asked about his own early influences (rather than those of the group), he answered:

> Marianne Moore and Elizabeth Bishop very much. The Italian poet Leopardi. I wish English were as musical as his Italian, but it isn't. And Walt Whitman's "Song of Myself." Also Wallace Stevens very strongly and Boris Pasternak . . . Most of all, Frank O'Hara and John Ashbery.

In considering the essential difference between the so-called New York School poets and not only the poetry establishment to which they were reacting, but also contemporaries such as James Merrill, Richard Wilbur, Adrienne Rich, Anne Sexton, Robert Creeley, Donald Hall, and even the Black Mountain poets and the Beats to some degree, one might look to the influence of the visual arts—specifically the Abstract Expressionist movement of the 1950s, followed by Pop Art and other tendencies of the 1960s, with whose practitioners the poets were in constant social contact. "There were so many exciting things going on in the art world, we didn't want to miss anything," John Ashbery recalled. As Jimmy wrote, "New York poets, except I suppose the color-blind, are affected most by the floods of paint in whose crashing surf we all scramble." What they valued most in Abstract Expressionist painting was an ethos of spontaneity and improvisation. For Jimmy and his friends, the writing of a poem was not the execution of a predetermined idea, or not entirely, but a process of discovering where the poem would take them as they went along. As Kenneth Koch liked to say, "The next line should always be a surprise."

Through John Myers, Jimmy, Frank, John, Barbara Guest, and Jane Freilicher all became friends with John Latouche, the gifted theatrical producer and lyricist who wrote the song standards "Lazy Afternoon" and "Taking a Chance on Love," among others. Beginning in the 1940s, he held a "salon" in his apartment on East Sixty-seventh Street, where luminaries from Broadway, Hollywood, and the theatrical and musical worlds mingled with poets and artists, and soon Jimmy and his friends were all going there regularly.

Jimmy heard both Frank and Barbara Guest read their own poems for the first time at a party at Latouche's apartment in the spring of 1952. Barbara read first, and Jimmy was greatly taken with her "gnomic" work. Guest's poems had caught the attention of John Ashbery when they appeared in *The Partisan Review* the previous year, and he had introduced himself to her. Born in 1920 in Wilmington, North Carolina, she was three years older even than Jimmy, and not always included in the bibulous parties or sharing in the irreverent humor of Frank and his friends; but her image- and language-centered work made her a kindred spirit, and she regularly published alongside her four male friends in journals such as *Folder*, *Semi-Colon*, and *Locus Solus*. By early 1952, she was an editorial associate at *Art News* and contributing regular reviews to the magazine, an involvement with visual art that consistently informed her poetry.

The audience listened to both poets in what Jimmy described as "the kind of non-committal trance thought so suitable for hearing verse"—until Frank read "Easter," a poem containing a few graphic sexual references. Overt sexual allusions were not often encountered in poetry at the time, and several members of the audience expressed shock, including the gallery owner Betty Parsons, who, as a lesbian, was additionally offended by the reference to "women who use cigars." On that or another evening, Jimmy, wandering in the apartment looking for the bathroom, opened a door and found himself confronted with Latouche's lover, Kenward Elmslie, stark naked, shaving. It remained Jimmy's "primal image" of Elmslie.

Early in the year, Jimmy wrote his first and longest play, *Presenting Jane*. The original title was *Presenting Jane Freilicher* (in reference to the 1943 movie *Presenting Lily Mars*, starring Judy Garland). At Jane's request, Jimmy took her last name out of the title; nonetheless, the immediate inspiration for the play was Jane's upcoming first exhibition at Tibor de Nagy, for which she was busily painting at the time: the first line is, "JANE: Critics promulg. I am filled with fear like a taxi." Although the play soon goes to strange surreal directions, it remains on one level an homage to Jane and to the wit and talent for which the poets loved and admired her.

The early plays of John, Frank, Kenneth, and Jimmy may be the quintessential works of their putative "school," in that they sometimes seem inspired by the repartee typical of their social gatherings (at which they were occasionally performed). As the poet Michael Brownstein observed, the New York School was all about talk, all about laughter. Among the many diverse influences behind the poets' impulse to channel some of this talk and laughter into playwriting in the early 1950s were Hollywood movies of the 1930s, the dialogue-driven novels of Ivy Compton-Burnett and others, and the plays of Gertrude Stein. John wrote his play *The Heroes* in 1950, shortly after arriving in New York. He recalled that he "just sat down and wrote it." It probably inspired Frank to write his first play, *Try! Try!*, subtitled "A Noh Play," which he did in early 1951 or late 1950. Jimmy had never written a play before, and probably never thought to until he met John and Frank. What the plays of the New York School poets emphatically do not emulate (unless to parody) are the self-consciously "poetic" verse dramas (or translations) by such poets as Archibald Macleish, Christopher Fry, and Richard Wilbur—although that was precisely what the name of the Cambridge group that first staged many of these plays, the Poets' Theatre, led some early audience members to expect. Founded at Harvard in 1950 by Molly Howe, Richard Wilbur, Lyon Phelps, and others, the Poets' Theatre's first performance, on February 26, 1951, was a quadruple bill of Frank's *Try! Try!* (with sets by Edward Gorey), John's *Everyman* (with incidental music composed by Frank), Richard Eberhardt's *The Apparition*, and *Three Words in No Time* by Lyon Phelps. John came up from New York and played the role of "John" in *Try! Try!*.

In New York, Judith Malina and Julian Beck's Living Theatre opened its first production, Gertrude Stein's *Doctor Faustus Lights the Lights*, at the Cherry Lane Theatre on December 2, 1951. John and Frank knew Malina and Beck, to whom John immediately offered *The Heroes*, which they produced in August 1952. Meanwhile, both John and Frank appeared in the Living Theatre's next production, Pablo Picasso's play *Desire Caught by the Tail*, which opened in February 1952, in which they made "a madly funny pair" as two dogs who ran around the stage bow-wowing through almost the entire play. Enjoyable as this was, even more meaningful for Jimmy was the curtain-raiser, Gertrude Stein's extremely short and nonlinear play *Ladies Voices*, which influenced him "immediately and directly" both in the plays he would himself soon write and in certain of his poems.

There is no action to *Presenting Jane*, per se, and the play consists of alternating short speeches delivered by characters to whom he gave the names of his friends: "Jane," "John," and "Frank." Jimmy described it as "sort of a Dada play. The characters simply exchanged inane, sometimes witty, sometimes silly, sometimes poetic remarks." Aside from several references to the art of painting made by "Jane," the speeches can seem to be interchangeable between the characters, just as in real life the originals shared a similar sense of wit, and even vocal mannerisms. However, intimations of their individual personalities do emerge, as though variations of these lines had actually been uttered by the real Jane, Frank, or John.

JOHN: I want to change these limericks to a haiku.
FRANK: I ignore that. There's more to painting than covering a flat surface.
JANE: Stick in a penny, out comes the gum. It's impossible not to love you, cactus. You give the aperçu its old meaning. What more could a good education do for a stable of polo ponies?
JOHN: The glorious milksops forgive you in the library stacks. I see you turn down an invite to Castle Duino, and wonder about the square white card in your hip pocket.
JANE: Everyone has a published secret.
FRANK: If I go as Leda I'll come as a swan. A temple bell, a churchwarden, a safety catch. A leaden silence flaps Worcester down stream and a sandpaper block scours mares tails in its sky by the colonial steeple local yokels called Betsy's leap. Talk to me about lily of the valley bulbs. Red is for ketchup the way zippers are for flies or a well in a desert where twenty clumsy mules jostle in harness.
JOHN: Reading my diary I recaptured our old depression. The vision goes untold, like a suitcase left in a train.
JANE: I always wanted to give a grand piano a good kick.

The longest speech in the play belongs to "Jane" and strings together a series of fantastic dream episodes and images:

Then a dead bird fell, and the bells' tongues, and the shoes.
"Nothing good will come of it," at which cry of mine the world opened out like a mountainous pancake and giraffes drew home the sublime limousine.

Jane's soliloquy is followed by a series of quick free-association exchanges of single words and short phrases, with "Jane" having the last word:

FRANK: Bats in the belfry.
JOHN: Crabs in the crotch.
FRANK: Mercedes McCambridge.
JOHN: Toby Wing.
FRANK: Sex.
JOHN: Sox.
FRANK: I.
JOHN: O.
JANE: U.

Free association as a technique for accessing the unconscious was something Schuyler had presumably been exposed to in a psychiatric context by this time, but here it is more suggestive of Surrealist verbal parlor games and the collaborative writing practices that would be increasingly important in New York School activity. The collaborative ethos in a larger sense—that is, the strength and inspiration that the poets and painters derived from one another's works and friendship—is evoked by the concluding three lines of this exchange, read as "I owe you." Ending on what is literally a promissory note, the play gives notice of the future accomplishments of the as-yet virtually unpublished New York School.

Conspicuously absent from *Presenting Jane* is any character called "Kenneth." Kenneth Koch was born in Cincinnati in 1925 and served in the war before entering Harvard. After graduating in 1948, he moved to New York to get a graduate degree at Columbia, but had been away from

New York for the past year, first on a Fulbright scholarship in France, and then in Berkeley at the University of California. He and Jimmy did not meet until he returned to New York in the summer of 1952.

While he was away, Kenneth had heard reports from John about a new poet on the scene, and was initially rather displeased to think that someone else had joined what had previously been an exclusive trio of Harvard poets. His introduction to Jimmy took place in the Periscope-Holliday Bookshop, on a warm Saturday afternoon. Jimmy had hoped to get off work early, but Brayton had charged him with cleaning a bunch of heavy reference books. When John and Frank appeared, with Kenneth in tow, Jimmy was dirty, hot, and cross, and felt that Kenneth was "rather cool" toward him. They all went out to dinner, but even there, Jimmy continued to be "very conscious of the fact that while Kenneth was not exactly snubbing me, he also was not making any friendly overtures."

Jimmy had already read some of Kenneth's poems and had liked them, but not as much as he liked John's and Frank's. Koch, likewise, "felt uncertain at first that he was as good as we all were. . . . I thought our little crowd of geniuses was just the greatest and I was reluctant to admit someone new." But soon he realized that "Jimmy was irresistible and so was his poetry," and they became close friends. "It was one of the great experiences of my life, just to talk to him," Kenneth said. "He wasn't, as a conversationalist . . . someone who wants to turn the conversation to himself, or to any 'subject' either." "Jimmy was the best listener in the world . . . because whatever you gave him came back set in gold, he would turn it into something wonderful, and then you'd have *that* to talk about."

At times, Kenneth could be defensive about his own heterosexuality when surrounded by gay poets. Later, he acknowledged that "hearing about homosexual stuff . . . really sort of made me anxious when I was in my twenties." Frank called this attitude a symptom of Kenneth's "H.D.," or "homosexual dread." In time, as Kenneth became more relaxed about the matter, he noticed that Jimmy was the most matter-of-fact about the specifics of gay sex. While Frank was sensitive around what he assumed was Kenneth's "H.D." and John did not tell Kenneth he was gay for years, "with Jimmy there was no pretense." "Frank didn't really seem interested in talking about physical details; he seemed more interested in love. Jimmy was interested in both. He was interested in what you did with your mouth and your hands."

Jimmy also came to know Kenneth's girlfriend and future wife, Janice Elwood, who was studying for a graduate degree in English at Harvard when Kenneth returned to New York, but was living with him by about 1953. "Janice loved Jimmy," recalled Kenneth, "she just loved him, and I think he loved her too." Among other qualities, Jimmy admired her tremendous intelligence: once the couple's daughter was old enough to go to school, Janice went back to work as an editor, working on one book with Noam Chomsky. Later she returned to graduate school and earned simultaneously both a law degree and a degree in physics.

John Bernard Myers, again and always in the thick of things, gave a copy of *Presenting Jane* to John Latouche, who was greatly taken with it. He arranged for John, Frank, and Jane to read the play aloud to him, and then decided that he should make a movie of it. To Jimmy it seemed unbelievable that anyone would want to make a movie of his "short nonsense play." Latouche originally wanted Maya Deren to direct it, admiring her 1943 film *Meshes of the Afternoon* for its enigmatic, poetic mood and handcrafted black-and-white cinematography. Deren instead recommended her lover, a young recent Berkeley graduate named Harrison Starr. Latouche borrowed a house in East Hampton on Georgica Pond belonging to a friend, Lenore Pettit, and it was there, over the course of two weeks in July 1952, that the filming took place. In addition to Touche (as he was called) and Starr, the group in the house included, at different times, Touche's former lover, Harry Martin; his new lover, Kenward Elmslie; Jane Freilicher, John Ashbery, Frank O'Hara, and Jimmy. John Myers was in charge of cooking for the group, and brought his lover, the theater director Herbert Machiz.

The movie was filmed without sound from a scenario by Touche. The action, which bears no discernible relation to the text, consists of various scenes of Frank, John, and Jane arriving at the house (in Touche's convertible), walking about, reading, swinging a tennis racket, sitting at a table while Jane draws, all reaching a kind of climax when Jane appears to walk on the surface of the pond toward the camera (actually supported by an unseen plank). Jimmy pops up throughout as what he called "the writer-spy," observing the other characters, who do not acknowledge or seem to see him.

"I suppose there has never been a more disastrous event than this very simple undertaking," Jimmy later recalled.

> Everyone quarreled with everyone else, no one co-operated, Touche was in a rage, always bawling everybody out; he especially took it out on John Bernard Myers. In the middle of one of Touche's bawlings-out, John managed to break the refrigerator by shutting the wrong door. Touche said, "John, that's so *typical* of you! It's exactly what you *always do*!" John, for once, had no comeback.

Jane remembered the two-week period of the shooting as being "like a Marx Brothers movie."

> I think that John Latouche sort of felt taken advantage of, because we were all there sort of freeloading and having a great deal of fun . . . John [Ashbery] was getting very annoyed with the sort of restrictions that were being placed on us by John Latouche. I remember he was washing the dishes and instead of putting them to dry he dropped them on the floor, each one.

Jimmy came out for about a week, spending most of his time with John, who stayed in a shed behind the house where "he found a lot of ladies' dresses . . . and would keep appearing in drag expecting great acclaim for each new outfit." Larry Rivers had rented a separate house nearby and matters became "very steamy" for a while, with Jane and Frank both competing openly for Rivers's attentions.

Never completed, the film was considered lost for some sixty years, until the extant footage was tracked down by Ashbery's biographer, Karin Roffman, in 2013. However, in the fall, Latouche gave a Halloween party where rough footage may have been screened, as it would be at a production of the play itself in 1953.

The painter Fairfield Porter had met Jane during a studio visit that spring, in preparation for reviewing her first solo exhibition at Tibor de Nagy for *Art News*, and had fallen under her spell. Learning that she and her friends were in the Hamptons that summer, Porter invited the group to dinner at his big rambling house in nearby Southampton. Jimmy had met Porter in the city the year before with the Burckhardts but had not particularly liked him. Misunderstanding his brusque manner and lack of social graces for patrician aloofness, Jimmy thought him "a cold rich snob." This time, he got a more complete sense of Porter and his family, and his perspective turned around. During dinner, Porter and his old friend the photographer Walter Auerbach got into a passionate argument, and after a "severe teasing" from Auerbach, Porter "suddenly exploded in total rage and began yelling and screaming at him." This startling show of passion humanized Fairfield for Jimmy. Meanwhile, as the evening drew on, two-year-old Katie Porter was wandering around the house, with Fairfield's wife, Anne, somewhat ineffectually in pursuit, saying in her distinctive whisper, "I'll put you to bed, dear, as soon as I've made your bed."

One night Frank drove Jimmy and John out to the house in Latouche's convertible, and while Frank drove, Jimmy and John wrote two collaborative poems, "Out at Lenore Petit's" [*sic*] and "The Rash." Both poems were composed in a manner reminiscent of the free-association exercise in *Presenting Jane*, the two poets taking turns making contributions in response to the previous line. Jimmy later had doubts about them both, "but it was fun writing them and it was my first experience at doing a collaboration."

At the end of the weekend, Jimmy and John caught a ride back into the city with the cinematographer Harrison Starr, who also had his father along. The poets, bored in the back seat, decided to write a collaborative novel. "It was Jimmy who suggested it," John recalled. "Well, how do you do that?" "It's easy. You write the first sentence." John wrote "Alice was tired," and then, passing a yellow legal pad back and forth, each wrote a sentence or two, or a whole paragraph, continuing from where the other had left off. In 1952, the Long Island Expressway had not yet been completed, and much of the route followed smaller roads. Going through Smithtown, they passed a white house with green shutters and decided they would have their characters live there.

> Alice was tired. Languid, fretful, she turned to stare into her own eyes in the mirror above the mantelpiece before she spoke.
>
> "I dislike being fifty miles from a great city. I don't know how many cars pass every day and it makes me wonder."
>
> Marshall smiled at her and continued to remove the plastic covers from a number of dishes he had just extracted from the icebox. Kicking out her housecoat, Alice moved to the kitchen table and picked up a chicken wing.

The resulting collaborative novel, *A Nest of Ninnies*, is a masterpiece of understated wit, playing off fictional conventions and esoteric cultural references, among much else. The process was improvisational—they let the story, such as it is, develop from speech to speech, page to page. It begins, as so many of Jimmy's poems seem to do, with the writer(s) simply "looking out the window": in this case a car window. Noticing a suburban house, the poets begin to imagine the life lived in it—a life not too dissimilar, in the abstract, from lives they themselves had left behind in upstate New York. Alice's first line of dialogue, in a novel that consists mostly of dialogue, is to remark wistfully and indirectly on *them*, the two poets passing out of her ken in one of the "I don't know how many cars" that make up the ceaseless traffic past her house. Jimmy and John would continue "exchanging *limp* remarks" in the fictional personas of Alice, Marshall, their neighbors Mr. and Mrs. Bridgewater, and their children Fabia and Victor, and an ever-increasing cast of characters, whenever they got a chance for the next sixteen years until they finally finished the novel in 1968.

Later in the summer, Jimmy spent a couple of weeks with Edwin in a primitive shack on the dunes in the Peaked Hill region of Provincetown, near another shack occupied by Rudy Burckhardt, Edith Schloss, and their two-year-old son, Jacob. There were at the time several such isolated former fishermen's shacks on the dunes, all without electricity or running water, owned by Hazel Hawthorne, a famous Provincetown character known as the "Dune Queen," who let them out to artists and writers.

Jimmy included a brief description of the setting in his 1952 story "The Home Book":

> In among the dunes, where the shacks seemed more sheltered though they were not . . . the surf sounded like a freight train passing in the distance of a hot farmland night. Breakers threw pebbles at gulls and sandpipers; and the rippled trail of a snake ends abruptly on the flank of a dune in a small patch of turmoil.

Midway between the two shacks was a sheltered hollow with a hand-pumped well, the only source of fresh water for both cottages. Jimmy and Edith met there most late afternoons. Occasionally they sat for a minute in the fading light, saying little except to point out to each other the names of some of the dune wildflowers they found. Jimmy knew most of their names, as Schloss recalled: "Dusty miller silvergray and yellow; wormwood velvety; little sedoms; the clumps of wild rose and beach plum bushes." Schloss sensed that the vacation was idyllic for Jimmy, but all too soon it ended, sending him back to the city and his job.

At the end of the summer of 1952, Hal Fondren moved out of the apartment he and O'Hara had been sharing at 326 East Forty-ninth Street, and Frank invited Jimmy to move in. Located between First and Second Avenues, it was a sixth-floor, two-bedroom walk-up, larger and nicer than where Jimmy was—no more bathroom down the hall. The front door opened onto a narrow living room facing toward First Avenue, with two sunny bedrooms off to the right with views to the East River and the UN Building. The expansive view, John Ashbery remembered, was "the nicest thing about the apartment."

This would be his and Frank's home for the next five years, and a frequent gathering place for all their friends. For Jimmy, who was shy and retiring in most social situations, the greatest effect of the move was being drawn into the daily and nightly whirlwind that was Frank's social life. "That really is the beginning of a very happy period in my life, because I loved living with Frank," he recalled.

One fine August afternoon in 1952, Edwin Denby took Jimmy and John to meet his friends the piano duo Arthur Gold and Robert (Bobby) Fizdale, who lived in Snedens Landing, a small town on the west side of the Hudson about twenty miles north of the city. It seemed to John that Denby wanted to "exhibit his prize," i.e., his much younger boyfriend, to his friends.

Gold and Fizdale were internationally known in the 1950s for their performances of music written for two pianos. They were then renting a large Victorian house called the "Ding Dong House," ornamented with gingerbread carving, surrounded by lawn, a grape arbor, and a garden on a bluff directly overlooking the river. Handsome, witty, and very sociable, they were also great cooks and hosts and had many glamorous friends among the musicians, actors, dancers, and artists of the "haute bohemia" of 1940s, '50s, and '60s New York. Formerly romantic partners, they were now simply professional partners, but still lived together, with, at times, their respective lovers. At this time Gold was unattached, but Fizdale was living intermittently with a decorator named Arthur Weinstein.

This first lunchtime encounter was a great success. In fact, according to John, Jimmy and Arthur Gold almost immediately became "very interested in each other," as did John himself and Bobby Fizdale. That visit was followed by invitations for the two poets to visit on their own. One such visit was commemorated in Jimmy's amusing sestina "Le Weekend." Seeming to record a particular visit (though it most likely includes incidents from several), it has Bobby baking a cake for Arthur, croquet being played, and Jimmy falling down the back stairs into the kitchen.

Unacknowledged in the poem are the love affairs that had started to develop between Gold and Jimmy and between Fizdale and John. John's affair with Bobby was relatively brief, lasting until Weinstein eventually forced Fizdale to choose between them, and he chose to stay with Weinstein. Apparently Jimmy and Arthur's much longer love affair also started shortly after they met that August, at least in a casual way, but was deepened through their exchange of letters over the winter, while Arthur was on a five-month concert tour in Europe with Fizdale. In October, soon after arriving in Europe, Arthur wrote to Jimmy, putting forth a tentative invitation: "Dear Jimmie, This surprises me as much as it surprises you—I just wanted to say good-bye or is it hello—and I guess what I'd like you to do is write to me." By December 7, 1952, which is the date of Schuyler's earliest surviving letter to Gold, there seems to be what Victorian novelists might call an "understanding" between the two of them: the salutation is "Arthur lamb" and ends: "Absolutely everyone sends you his or her love. Of course I sent the most. Ever Thine, Jimmy . . ." It would remain to the spring of 1953 for the romance to flower in person.

[10]

MUSIC, SWIMMING AT NIGHT, PLAYS, POEMS, LOVE AND QUARRELS

1953–1954

Inspired by the Poets' Theatre in Cambridge, John Bernard Myers and Herbert Machiz established the Artists Theater in 1953, aiming to produce plays by poets with sets by Tibor de Nagy Gallery artists. Their first production, which opened in February at the Theatre de Lys on Christopher Street, was a quadruple bill featuring *Presenting Jane*, with a set designed by Elaine de Kooning and a projection of footage from the summer's filming in East Hampton. Jimmy's was the shortest play on the bill, alongside Tennessee Williams's *Auto-da Fé*, Frank O'Hara's *Try! Try!*, with a set by Larry Rivers, and Kenneth Koch's *Red Riding Hood*, with a set by Grace Hartigan.

Judith Malina attended a preview with Frank, who watched his own play with "nervous excitement" and held her hand "as if he were in a dentist's chair, happy when I responded feelingly." Of *Presenting Jane*, she noted only: "The three characters, Frank, John and Jane, speak the language of ephemera." Jimmy, for his part, found the production "horrible thanks to Herbert." Although Machiz had a flair for directing light Broadway comedies, "he didn't have a *clue* about poets' plays," according to the poet Tony Towle, yet ironically that is what he is remembered for, thanks to his association with Myers. Schuyler tried to interest Malina and Beck in producing *Presenting Jane* at the Living Theatre, writing "I long to see Judith as Jane," but to no avail.

Gold and Fizdale returned from Europe in the first week of March, and by the 15th, Jimmy and Arthur had begun or resumed their love affair with a new commitment to each other. One problem remained, however, in the form of Edwin Denby, and they dreaded and delayed telling him about it.

Gold and Fizdale were then at the height of their fame. Arthur Gold was born in Toronto in 1917, and met the slightly younger Fizdale in about 1940, when they were both studying piano at Juilliard. They played a wide repertory but were best known for championing twentieth-century French and American music, and within the rather recherché area of four-handed piano music, commissioned works from many of the major composers of the day, including Francis Poulenc, Aaron Copland, Samuel Barber, Darius Milhaud, and John Cage. According to Ned Rorem, "Half the valid music for two pianos in the twentieth century is because of their existence." Known collectively as "the Boys," the common perception about them as individuals was that Gold was the testy or difficult one, with an acerbic wit that could turn cruel, while Fizdale was more easygoing and domestic. As one friend put it, "[Gold] was snippy and very bright and show-offy, as to how funny and witty and superior he was . . . But Bobby, contrariwise, was just *adorable*, from top to bottom. He couldn't have been nicer." The very prevalence of this assessment inevitably prompted a contrary view, with some saying that Gold was actually the nice one, despite a critical manner, while Fizdale "*seemed* much nicer but probably wasn't."

Jimmy and Arthur's attachment became intense right away. Gold was generous and loving in his relationship with Jimmy, but could also be bossy and manipulative, which answered Jimmy's need for a more dominant partner. Kenneth Koch, recalling the relationship, felt that "Arthur . . . was the stern one who told Jimmy he had to work, sort of a disciplinarian in sort of a silly way. I think he believed he brought order into Jimmy's life."

Arthur was eager to support, exploit, and to some degree direct Jimmy's poetic gifts, and quite early in the relationship, he arranged for Jimmy to write the text for a work for duo pianos and four voices to be set to music by Paul Bowles. Bowles, whose first novel, *The Sheltering Sky*, had been published in 1949, is now thought of primarily as a fiction writer, but he originally made his reputation as a composer, a disciple of Aaron Copland and Virgil Thomson, and he continued to compose music well into the 1950s. The singer and philanthropist Alice Esty provided the funds for the commission, which would become *A Picnic Cantata*, and is dedicated to her. Schuyler began work on the text in mid-April, referring to it in letters to Arthur as "the Mass." On slow days he was even able to work on it in the bookshop.

In mid-April, Gold and Fizdale left for a tour of the southern United States, and for a period of two weeks, at the height of what he called his "new happiness," Jimmy wrote to his new lover nearly every day and sometimes twice a day. The letters express his exuberance and optimism at his new affair: "I know who I want, I want you, I want you to want me, you do, I want to feel we will want and have each other for a long time, we will." The letters also give a day-by-day report of his activities for those two weeks, exemplifying the intensity of his social life in the mid-'50s: there was lunch with Ashbery and a hirsute and ring-bedecked Edward Gorey; dinner with Chester; a cocktail party at Stuart Preston's; a cocktail party at John Hohnsbeen's (where he and Jane Freilicher met the English painter Lucian Freud); a concert of music by Henri Sauguet at the Museum of Modern Art, featuring the soprano Leontyne Price and the dancers Maria Tallchief and Todd Bolender; a concert performance of Monteverdi's opera *The Coronation of Poppea* with Edwin Denby and Jane Freilicher; and much else. A highlight of the two-week period was a performance at Juilliard of Mozart's *Così fan tutte* with Martha Flowers (who would appear in *A Picnic Cantata* the following year), "much the best" in the role of Fiordiligi. Even more stimulating was the exhibition of Dada art at the Sydney Janis Gallery—a museum-quality selection of more than two hundred items, which he visited with John Ashbery and Barbara Guest on his lunch hour, and again two days later, and which made a great impression on all three of them. Even the catalogue was a Dada work, designed by Marcel Duchamp and printed on a single sheet of paper crumpled up into a ball, so that one needed to flatten it out to read it. When he got back to the bookstore, Jimmy was inspired to write a one-page Dada play, *The Gunga Den, or, Chez When*, incorporating excerpts from his and Gold's recent letters, which he signed "Marcel Schwitters."

The Dada exhibition, and especially the Kurt Schwitters collages it included, reinforced both Jimmy's and John's preexisting interest in collage as a tool for writing poetry. Schuyler had made a collage poem as early as January 1952, which he sent to Howard Moss. He could have been aware by now that the psychiatrist he saw as Charles R. Hulbeck in 1943 was also the Dada poet Richard Huelsenbeck (who contributed an essay to the Janis Gallery catalogue), but having deeply repressed that whole period, he may not have made conscious note of the fact, and did not mention it to John. Certainly John, with an interest in Surrealism going back to his childhood, was already quite aware of Dada aims and techniques. Several months before seeing the exhibition, in December 1952, Ashbery and Schuyler collaborated on a literally collaged poem, "Controls," by cutting up unconnected lines of text out of magazines and gluing them in rows down a page.

Literary collage, by which one may mean either or both the use of purely found materials and/or the juxtaposition of seemingly unrelated elements, often resulting in disjointed syntax and imagery, would remain central to both poets' work. Where Ashbery (to oversimplify) might use collage as a metaphor for the way we experience the world, Schuyler used it more pragmatically, to transform humble materials into something fresh and harmonious. "I like an art where disparate elements form an entity," Schuyler wrote in 1969, specifically citing Schwitters, whose collages, he said, "always compose a whole striking for its completeness." Two mid-'50s works that Jimmy identified as collage poems are "Walter Scott" and "A New Yorker." Both seem to repurpose snippets of text from outside sources, rearranged by the poet. A broader sense of the use of collage can be found in the title poem of his first commercial poetry book, *Freely Espousing*, which "marries" various weather observations, private memories ("Quebec! what a horrible city"), historical events ("excavating the battlefield where Hannibal whomped the Romans"), quotations from remembered conversations, and pronouncements about literary diction ("it is absolutely forbidden / for words to echo the act described; or try to. Except very directly / as in / bong. And tickle. Oh it is inescapable kiss").

Jimmy had seen Edwin Denby a number of times while Arthur was away, but had still not told him about his and Arthur's new relationship. Shortly after Gold's return, the pianist took the brave step of going to see Denby in person to give him the news. This formal courtesy didn't help, and Denby became infuriated and hit Gold. Later that evening, when Rudy Burckhardt came over to Denby's loft to use the darkroom, he found Denby lying on his bed alone in the dark, motionless and traumatized. "He was very white. 'Edwin, are you alright?' cried Rudy. Edwin was quiet. Then he said tonelessly, 'I smacked him. I have felt weak ever since.'"

Denby's anger must have been exacerbated by the fact that at some point in the past, he had been unrequitedly in love with Gold himself, to the degree that he once threatened to throw himself out the window over him, or so Gold told Joe LeSueur. Denby focused most of his rage at Gold, but he was also very angry with Jimmy, and later expressed his feelings in a "revenge" poem which includes the stanza:

> The blazing sun of August sweeping wide
> Burns open secrets that a heart would hide
> "Arthur" the loyal, brother of beauty "James"
> Of treason and of filth become the names

Somehow, the fact that John Ashbery had also been present when Jimmy met Arthur, and that he remained Jimmy's close confidant, caused Denby to feel that John, too, was complicit in the "betrayal," and he came in for a disproportionate share of Denby's wrath. In an angry phone call, Denby announced that he was cutting off relations and never wanted to have anything more to do with him. According to Jane Freilicher, Edwin "went berserk." "He was kind of off his rocker for a number of years, he was so filled with animus." As John recalled, "He could be extremely unpleasant, however everybody sort of remembers him as a sort of genial Uncle Wiggly. I don't think he ever forgave Arthur and probably Jimmy either, although he probably wanted to keep open the channels of communication with Jimmy."

At the end of April, Gold and Fizdale (with Arthur Weinstein) again took up residence in the Ding Dong House. Jimmy spent as much time there as he could that spring and summer, and he remembered it as a particularly happy period. For a while he became a commuter, working at the bookstore during the day and driving back and forth with a neighbor or taking the bus to Snedens, and staying out there on his vacation and days off.

The Ding Dong House was furnished in a casual way with hand-me-downs and antiques, including a pair of pier glasses in carved gold frames that faced each other at opposite ends of the living room, multiplying the light and everyone's reflections. The room also contained two grand pianos, where Gold and Fizdale practiced for several hours a day. This could be too much of a good thing, and Jimmy would retreat to the other end of the house to write while they were practicing. Even there he could still hear the "thunder" of the two pianos.

The Gold and Fizdale social circle consisted of a stellar group of fellow musicians, performers, and artists. Dropping in for a meal or staying the weekend might be the composers Aaron Copland, Samuel Barber, Gian Carlo Menotti, Leonard Bernstein, Virgil Thomson, or Ned Rorem; choreographers Jerome Robbins and George Balanchine and his wife, the dancer Tanaquil LeClerq; actress Ina Claire; singers Lotte Lenya and Tova Frisch; and many others. Jimmy was a quiet presence, as always, and wasn't "included all that much in conversations." This didn't bother him, however, as he loved listening to the urbane talk, and he helped with the cooking.

Frank O'Hara came out for one memorable weekend, and a group decided to drive out to Coney Island for the day. Jimmy was scared and miserable on the famous roller coaster there, but Frank, typically, was exhilarated by it. Driving back, Frank was still somewhat punch-drunk from the park and sped up as he came into the driveway, pretending he was about to run into Fizdale and several others standing there, but stopped just in time. Fizdale and Gold were frightened and angry at this recklessness, and Jimmy assumed that this would be the last time Frank would be invited out to Snedens Landing. On the contrary. At breakfast the next morning, Fizdale sidled up to Schuyler and said, "I *very* much like your friend, Frank O'Hara!" Later that day, when Jimmy walked into Fizdale's bathroom, he was surprised to find Bobby and Frank in the tub, happily taking a bath together. For the rest of the summer, to Jimmy's great delight, Arthur Weinstein was off the scene and O'Hara and Fizdale enjoyed what would turn out to be a summer romance. There was a witty symmetry to the arrangement, noted with amusement at the time: the two poet-roommates having simultaneous affairs with the two duo-piano partners. The tandem love affairs had the incidental effect of bringing Jimmy and Frank closer together, emphasizing a sort of brotherly feeling that they seemed to have shared, particularly around this time.

Frank was an excellent pianist himself, having studied piano and composition in college. When the pair of professionals were not at their instruments, he often played for long periods. Fizdale was astonished one day to hear from the other room "some Rachmaninoff or Liszt piece being dashed off at the piano" and assumed that Gold was playing, only to come in to find that it was Frank, who he hadn't even realized could play. This summer was the period of Frank's life when he came closest to reconnecting with his early musical interests, and it shows in some of the references to musical forms, and to piano music in particular, in poems he wrote at the time. Living with the pianists had an influence on Jimmy's work as well, giving him not just a greater familiarity with the literature of the piano, seen in later poems such as "Hoboken," "Scriabin," "Grand Duo," and others, but also an insider's view into the workaday practice of pianists, particularly the intimate collaboration, almost amounting to mindreading, required of duo pianists—insights somewhat applicable to his ongoing collaboration with John Ashbery on *A Nest of Ninnies*.

Jane Freilicher and her husband, Joe Hazan, were renting a house in nearby Nyack that summer, and there was much coming and going between the two houses, including one weekend when Fairfield and Anne Porter were visiting Jane and Joe. This was Jimmy's third meeting with Fairfield, who surprised him again with his unselfconscious behavior when he saw the artist reading casually while lying on the bare flagstone terrace. "I didn't know Fairfield at all well at that point. I didn't realize that simply lying on the ground or rug or a floor or a stone or beach was utterly natural to him."

The pianists had been given the use of a swimming pool belonging to some neighbors, whose house opened onto a stone terrace directly above the edge of the Palisades. Sitting there, one had the sensation of being up among the treetops, looking over and through "very old and ancient trees" to the river and the far shore, a setting that gave Frank the idea for his play *The Houses at Falling Hanging*. One evening, after a visit to Nyack, they all drove back to Snedens Landing and to the neighbor's house with the pool, where they took off their clothes and went swimming in the moonlight. Jimmy later recalled that idyllic summer evening, and "how ravishing Jane looked, naked in the moonlight with her rather large breasts, slipping into the water. Frank dove and dove and dove. There's no way to describe what a marvelous swimmer he was: small pool, deep and turbulent ocean: Frank was always ready for it."

Frank's grace and confidence extended to other areas of his life, such as dancing at parties, and driving. To Jimmy he was "the most brilliant driver I have ever known: completely confident, completely relaxed, completely in control, smooth, rather speedy but he never drove too fast." Jimmy now decided he ought to learn to drive himself. He took out a learner's permit and started taking occasional lessons from Fizdale, but they were both too nervous and the lessons were not a success. Then Frank "took over" and "suddenly it was all magic." Frank's skill and confidence behind the wheel "became infused" in his pupil, and Jimmy happily drove O'Hara all around the neighborhood of Snedens Landing. Franz Lehar's operetta *The Merry Widow* was playing on the car radio as they returned to the house one day, and for some reason this suddenly seemed terribly funny and they broke into gales of infectious laughter.

"What a very good time, what an absolutely marvelous time, we all had that summer!" The tone of Jimmy's recollections of the summer of 1953 suggests that a good part of the glow through which he remembered it was due to the fraternal closeness he felt at that time to Frank, whose physical beauty had struck him early in the friendship and of which he never lost the sense.

At the end of the summer Gold and Fizdale departed for their usual fall and winter tour in Europe. It was a blustery, overcast day when the poets drove the two pianists to the airport and then returned to the empty house, where they found the maid closing up. She had always seemed slightly hostile to Jimmy and Frank before, but now she became "warm and rather tearful" as their presence "reminded her of friends: a house that always means music, swimming at night, plays, poems, love and quarrels." The two poets hitchhiked back to the city while reminiscing about the past few months and their friends: Grace Hartigan and her "natural generosity" and the "*beaux yeux*" of Jane Freilicher. When they got home, they wrote poems and letters to their respective lovers, before going out to an opening at Tibor de Nagy, and on to the San Remo.

The rest of the autumn of 1953 was a bit of a letdown, at least in Jimmy's memory. One day Stuart Preston called to invite him and Frank to a Halloween party. They went to a thrift store and bought long black mourning veils and hats, and proceeded to the party on the Upper East Side, where they put on their veils in the vestibule. Preston answered the door kilted and in full Highland regalia, and all of the other guests were also dressed very elaborately, "like Pierrots and that kind of thing. The effect that we had was stunning! We filled them with loathing and hate. I was drinking a martini under my veil when I turned to Frank and said, 'Get me out of here!'" They then went downtown to a big loft party where the only other person in drag was the poet James Merrill, wearing his maid's dress with some sort of "schmatta" wrapped around his head, who exclaimed, "My *dears*, I'm so *glad* to see you!" "The evening for me ended in snow," Jimmy later reminisced, "and going home with someone in lederhosen who was rather fun. When I left his house I left my veil and hat on the hood of a car."

Jimmy and Frank were gradually getting to know Fairfield Porter. They invited him for dinner in their apartment in November, when Frank cooked hamburgers and sautéed potatoes, and they found the usually reserved Fairfield to be, for once, "entrancingly warm." He confided to them his troubled feelings about his oldest child, Johnny, who was developmentally challenged with what was later recognized as a form of autism.

Fairfield Porter was born in 1907 in Chicago to a wealthy, intellectual family with New England roots. His father was an architect with an inherited income and his mother a social reformer and occasional poet, who passed on a love of poetry to her five children, of whom Fairfield was the fourth. Originally named John Fairfield Porter and known as "Johnny" until the age of three, he suffered lasting emotional trauma when, at the birth of his younger brother in 1910, his parents inexplicably "stole" the name John and gave it to the new baby. While at Harvard, Fairfield realized he wanted to be an artist, even though he felt he had "no talent." He subsequently studied at the Art Students League in New York for two years, where his developing interest in social justice found expression in the social realism taught there by Thomas Hart Benton and others. During a year of travel and study in Europe he developed a strong but chaste attachment to a young male English student, which he came to recognize as evidence of his bisexuality. After returning to the United States he reconnected with Anne Channing, whom he had met in 1931, and in 1932 they were married.

Anne Channing was born in 1911 to a distinguished Boston clan of progressive thinkers, including the founder of Unitarianism, William Ellery Channing, and was educated at "dame schools" in Boston and at Bryn Mawr and Radcliffe. As a teenager she became aware of her dual vocations as a poet and a person with deep religious feelings, the latter at odds with her family's tradition of rational intellectualism. In 1955, she would convert to the Catholic Church. Her poetry expresses a love of the natural world, steeped in quiet religious conviction. After the 1930s, when several poems appeared in *Poetry*, Anne hardly ever published her work, or showed it to people outside her family until she was in her eighties, and then reluctantly. Shy and recessive, she gave the impression of being "very domestic and very quiet," speaking in a "little birdlike voice" scarcely above a whisper. Yet when she did speak, it was often to deliver a pertinent remark with a sharp, "mordant" wit.

The newlyweds moved to New York's Greenwich Village, where Fairfield struggled to make a go of his painting. From the beginning there were conflicts in the marriage over the question of children: Anne wanted them and Fairfield didn't, realizing that the responsibilities of rearing children would impede his freedom as an artist. When their first child, a girl, was stillborn, Fairfield was "relieved" and said so. Their eldest surviving child, Johnny, was born in 1934. He was difficult from infancy and it soon became evident that he had serious developmental problems. Despite his initial ambivalence about children, Fairfield "poured himself out" (in Anne's words) working with him and with teachers, doctors, and caregivers in an attempt to get through to Johnny. Over time, he did appear to make some difference in the child's social awareness, but nonetheless Fairfield always felt he had "failed" his son, which he somehow connected to feelings that he was himself a disappointment to his own father. Two other sons, Laurence and Jeremy (known as Jerry until he later changed his name to Richard), were born in 1936 and 1940, respectively, followed by a daughter, Katharine or Katie, in 1949, and another daughter, Elizabeth, in 1956.

In the year of Katie's birth, the family moved to Southampton, about ninety miles from the city near the eastern end of Long Island, a village somewhat uncomfortably poised between exclusive seaside resort community and market town for the surrounding potato farmers. Artists had long been drawn to the area, too, attracted by the quality of coastal light, including mid-twentieth-century New York painters such as Jackson Pollock, Lee Krasner, Willem de Kooning, and many others.

As a painter Fairfield was slow to arrive at the painterly naturalism for which he is now known, his early work having been in a dour social realist vein, and his development hampered by tending to Johnny's needs. With the change of scene to Southampton, coinciding with Johnny being sent to live with a foster family on a farm in Vermont, Fairfield was free to paint full-time. Soon his subject matter became more domestic in focus: depicting members of his family and friends in intimate interiors, as well as the landscape of eastern Long Island or coastal Maine, where the family spent summers. From about 1952, partly inspired by Jane Freilicher, Larry Rivers, Alex Katz, and other younger painter friends, Fairfield's palette and brushwork lightened, and all of them, though painting figuratively, were inescapably influenced by the bravura paint handling of the Abstract Expressionists, especially Willem de Kooning.

As much as Fairfield Porter was influenced by and an influence on the young painters he met at this time, he was perhaps even more intrigued by their poet friends, not least the three gay ones: Ashbery, O'Hara, and Schuyler. Since his marriage, Fairfield had given every appearance of having settled down to family life with Anne and their children. He'd had a serious extramarital love affair with a woman, Ilse Hamm, in the early '40s (and Anne reciprocated with an openly acknowledged affair of her own in 1944), but apparently none with men. Getting to know the gay poets, with their relatively insouciant approach to homosexuality, seeing them working and living unencumbered by spouses or children, gave Fairfield a vision of what his own life as an artist might have been if he had followed a different path. He began writing poetry himself.

Fairfield had long maintained a New York City studio separate from his family home, and after the move to Southampton in 1949, he rented a small cold-water apartment on the Lower East Side where he could also stay overnight when he came into the city to review exhibitions for *Art News*, as he began to do in 1951. On these occasions he often had dinner with his poet and artist friends, but they also visited him regularly in his family setting in Southampton.

When Gold and Fizdale returned from Europe in early January 1954, they rented an apartment in the Chelsea Hotel on West Twenty-third Street. Still working at the bookshop, Jimmy began dividing his evenings and weekends between living with Gold at the Chelsea and Frank at the Forty-ninth Street apartment, to which he fled to get away from all the piano practicing.

Gold and Fizdale's aesthetic was rooted in the neo-Romantic or neoclassical milieu of the 1940s, and '50s, as exemplified by the composers they commissioned. Their taste in poetry ran along similar lines: Arthur Gold admired Auden, James Merrill, Robert Lowell, and especially his good friend Elizabeth Bishop. In addition to arranging for the commission of *A Picnic Cantata*, Arthur, in his "bossy" way, wished to influence the direction of Jimmy's poetry and suggested that he should try writing in traditional forms. It wasn't bad advice, perhaps; Jimmy's pointed disdain of "the rhymes, the writing in meters, all that was traditional and professional in Auden's verse" showed a certain fascination with it, which might have been something to be worked through rather than ignored. With Arthur's encouragement, then, in the early and mid-'50s Schuyler wrote several sonnets, villanelles, and sestinas. He later said he found working in such forms "very easy to do, when I put my mind to it," but in the end decided it wasn't right for him, and for the most part he did not include these poems in his collections. The best of them retain a certain awkwardness that deliberately subverts the limitations of their formal structures.

For Schuyler the concept of formal verse led directly back to Auden, as is especially clear in his two best-known poems of this group, the sonnet "A Grave," and the villanelle "Poem" ("I do not always understand what you say"). "Poem," in fact, could be read as a response to Auden's 1940 villanelle "If I Could Tell You." Both poems are addressed to an unidentified "you" and explore a theme of miscommunication between intimates, which the reiterative structure of the form effectively supports. Where Auden's poem ends: "If I could tell you, I would let you know," the conversation is picked up, as it were, in the first line of Schuyler's villanelle, "I do not always understand what you say" (both lines being repeated four times in their respective poems). The poems also share one of their two alternating end-rhyme sounds, as well as specific end-rhyming words. Schuyler's poem ends:

> We talk together in a common way.
> Art, like death, is brief: life and friendship long.
> I do not always understand what you say.
> What is, is by its nature, on display.

Jimmy's good friend Darragh Park believed that "Poem" referred to Fairfield Porter. This is supported by a later mimeographed typescript of the poem bearing a dedication to Fairfield (which does not appear in any published version). However, at the time the poem was written, in the mid-'50s, Schuyler's friendship with Fairfield was still in its formative stages, and the poem includes lines that do not seem to accord with Fairfield's modesty and forthrightness: "I sense a heaviness in your light play, / a wish to stand out, admired, from the throng." The writer Wayne Koestenbaum makes a strong case for the poem being addressed to John Ashbery, whose work was famously opaque, and who, while open in his homosexuality among friends, was long determined to prevent its being known publicly: "You would hate, when with me, to meet by day / What at night you met and did not think wrong." In the end, the "you" of the poem is probably a composite, inspired by various friends and lovers.

Jimmy's makeover as a formalist poet seemed so complete for a while that John became irritated at what he perceived as a defection from their shared commitment to experimental verse, and when they met, would ask sardonically, "Have you written *anything* lately that will interest *me*?" "Poem" could also be understood as a defiant response to this question.

Jane and Paul Bowles returned to New York from their home in Morocco for the long-awaited production of Jane's play *In the Summerhouse*, with incidental music by Paul, which opened on December 29, 1953. Jimmy saw it when it opened and again on January 13, with, as he reported to O'Hara, "no diminishment of enjoyment." Jane Bowles's dry language was an influence on both Jimmy's ongoing collaboration with John, *A Nest of Ninnies*, and on *A Picnic Cantata*.

Schuyler's collaboration with Paul Bowles, *A Picnic Cantata*, is scored for two pianos, percussion, and four female voices. Like "Salute," the work begins with a folksy saying: "falls to the floor, / comes to the door." Who comes to the door is a friend inviting "you and she" to go for a Sunday drive into the country. Reviewers who called the text "nonsense" were incorrect, of course. The text has a clear and simple narrative: The travelers drive to Hat Hill Park, and while they eat their picnic, they read the horoscopes, advice to the lovelorn, and garden sections from the newspaper. On the way home they see the evening star "set / in the peel of the moon, / a bit of ice / in an ice-tea sky. // Look at the outline / of the city. / No wonder our lives / have their ups and downs." Like many of the poems Jimmy was writing in the early '50s, *A Picnic Cantata* is partly in collage form, or perhaps faux-collage, with its made-up excerpts from several newspaper features.

The premiere performance of *A Picnic Cantata* took place at Town Hall on March 23, 1954, as part of a Gold and Fizdale concert that included the New York premiere of Francis Poulenc's Sonata for Two Pianos, also written for the pair. The two works were recorded by Columbia Records that year. Paul Bowles's prediction, in a letter to Tennessee Williams, that none of the reviews of the *Cantata* would prove to be "bright enough to matter" was sadly borne out. The best of them, signed "H. W. L." and appearing in the April 14 issue of *Musical Courier*, reported: "This sophisticated and rather non-sensical supersecular cantata provides the kind of fun supplied in Gertrude Stein's poems. It has rhythm and the charm of the night-club stage. The performances were superb." Schuyler's friends were enthusiastic, at any rate. Frank reported to Ned Rorem that "the Bowles Cantata was very charming and the girls as well as the boys performed brilliantly and with vivacity. I liked the piece very much and of course Jimmy's text as just plain words." At the after-party he and Jimmy had an "exchange of affection which is one of the high points in my last few years," as Frank wrote to Jane Freilicher. "He is an angel and a pearl of price, isn't he? The cantata is one of those perfect things—how do you two do it?"

All four of the singers, Martha Flowers, Gloria Davy, Mareda Gaither, and Gloria Wynder, were Black, students of Florence Page Kimball at the Juilliard School. Kimball, who taught voice at Juilliard for forty-six years, was responsible for training a remarkable number of Black classical singers in mid-century, most famously Leontyne Price, Betty Allen, and Flowers herself. Two years earlier, Flowers, Davy, and Price had been cast by Virgil Thomson in a revival of his and Gertrude Stein's opera *Four Saints in Three Acts*, which, like the original 1934 production, had an all-Black cast, due to Thomson's belief that African Americans had better diction and moved better onstage than white singers of the day. Flowers, though, credited the casting of *A Picnic Cantata* more prosaically to the direct influence of Florence Kimball, who was, in Flowers's words, "very much aware" of the lack of opportunities for Black classical singers, and "did a lot to try to get her students of color to have places to perform and opportunities to perform." Kimball was a good friend of the pianists, and Fizdale was the accompanist for her classes at Juilliard.

Jimmy attended rehearsals for the *Cantata*, but he did not interact much with the singers. Flowers recalled him simply as "a very charming man" who spent most of his time with the pianists. Nonetheless, he came to consider Flowers a friend. Up to this point, Jimmy had had relatively little social contact with African Americans. There are no Black faces among the senior class photos of East Aurora High School in 1941, Bethany was an all-white college in 1942, and the U.S. armed forces were not desegregated until after Jimmy's naval service. Knowing Flowers and the other singers, even slightly, was one reason he was at pains later to remove the most common racial slur from an early draft of his novel *Alfred and Guinevere*.

Two days after the performance at Town Hall, Jimmy's short play *Shopping and Waiting: A Dramatic Pause* was performed in Cambridge at the Poets' Theatre, directed by Frank's friend V. R. ("Bunny") Lang. It was panned in the *Harvard Crimson* as "scarcely more than an esoteric joke." There is no record that Jimmy or any of his friends went to Cambridge for the performances.

None of these poets published much in the early 1950s. Their work did not conform to mainstream tastes, which gave them the freedom to write undisturbed by the expectations of anyone besides their friends. From time to time one of them would be published in *Poetry*, or *Accent*, or *The Partisan Review*, or the *New Directions Annual*, but these were mostly one-offs and did not make any kind of collective impression. It was their artist friends who were the first to appreciate their work, due in no small part to the series of chapbooks published by John Bernard Myers at the Tibor de Nagy Gallery starting in the early '50s. These included Frank O'Hara's *A City Winter*, with illustrations by Larry Rivers, in 1952, and Kenneth Koch's *Poems* with prints by Nell Blaine, and John Ashbery's *Turandot*, illustrated by Jane Freilicher, both 1953. (Later came Barbara Guest's *The Location of Things*, with Robert Goodnough images, in 1960, and finally, in 1966, James Schuyler's *May 24th or So*.) In the mid-'50s, the Tibor de Nagy Gallery also put out nine issues of the leaflet-style periodical *Semi-Colon*, with work by Jimmy, John, Barbara, James Merrill, and many others.

Aside from the Tibor de Nagy Gallery, one of the first outlets to recognize the New York School poets and artists as a group and to regularly publish their poetry, prose, and visual art was Daisy Aldan's *Folder*. The first issue, Winter 1953, included Jimmy's poem "Royals" and the play *Shopping and Waiting*, along with work by Frank, John, Kenneth, Aldan herself, James Merrill, Jean Garrigue, William Weaver, and others. The inaugural issue also contained three multicolored screen prints by

Grace Hartigan—but credited to "George" Hartigan, a name she briefly adopted in an attempt to circumvent art-world sexism. Jimmy's story "The Infant Jesus of Prague" appeared in the second of the publication's four issues in this format.

These little magazines and gallery publications were all very well, but Arthur Gold had other ambitions for his talented lover. The idea that Jimmy might write a novel, which, if successful, could lead to greater recognition, not to mention financial independence, was another of his helpful suggestions. With Gold's support, Jimmy decided to take the summer of 1954 off from the bookshop in order to start writing the novel that would become *Alfred and Guinevere*.

Several factors came together at this time to suggest the subject and tone of a novel that would evoke the setting, and indirectly the traumas, of his childhood in Washington, DC. One was a "dopey" childhood diary of the painter Grace Hartigan, which she read to Frank and Jimmy one day when they were visiting her studio together in 1952 or 1953. "Mostly it was a weather report," Hartigan recalled, but it also recorded the names of movies she had seen, followed by the cast, and invariably the comment "It was swell." The deadpan earnestness put them all into "hysterics" of laughter, and influenced Schuyler's decision to begin his novel with Guinevere's diary.

But the main inspiration for the setting and the mood of the novel were his boyhood memories of the Mowery family. Arguably, these memories were reawakened by Jimmy's first extended visit to the Porter family for a weekend in June 1954. In his thank-you letter to Anne and Fairfield he wrote, "Arthur and I liked visiting you very much. I liked our wing of the house . . . I liked the meals, the drives, the walks, talks and beach. I like sitting under your big trees . . . And I love your family."

There were several intangible correspondences between the Porter and Mowery families that could have stirred Jimmy's imagination. Both Fairfield and Eldred Sr. had Midwestern roots, and both went to Harvard; Fairfield's father was an architect, as was Eldred; both Anne Porter and Irene Mowery came from WASP Boston or Cambridge backgrounds and attended Seven Sisters colleges, giving them similar, genteel accents. In addition, the shared social backgrounds of the two families lent their homes common physical characteristics, with family heirlooms and hand-me-down furniture. At the time, the Porters had two children living at home: their son Jerry, thirteen, and five-year-old Katie.

Like childhood itself, the plot of *Alfred and Guinevere* is difficult to perceive, harder to summarize. There is no direct narration, only dialogue and the "untrustworthy" voice of Guinevere's diary and letters. Beneath the surface of Guinevere and Alfred's sibling rivalry, the ins and outs of Guinevere's competitive friendship with her neighbor Betty, and Alfred's adventures with his friend Stanley, all accompanied by the wise admonitions of Granny, lie darker issues and themes, indirectly felt. In the first chapter the children come upon the body of a Black man who had jumped from the "suicide bridge" near their home, but after vague hints throughout the book, this disturbing event is made clear only in the final chapter. Still more lightly touched on is the theme of family separation and divorce. When their father goes on an extended business trip, the children latch onto the idea that their parents are going to divorce. Beneath their bravado, one senses genuine anguish, though they do not express it. The book ends, however, with Alfred, Guinevere, Mother, Granny, and even Uncle Saul all on board a ship to Europe to join Daddy there—the threat of divorce, if it ever was real, seemingly dispelled.

As he worked on the book, Schuyler was keenly aware of the challenge of writing simultaneously in two registers: "the implied story" as opposed to "the story that gets invented page by page." Despite his struggles, the first draft of the novel was completed relatively quickly, but revisions requested by the publisher kept Jimmy tied to the book for several years.

That summer, Gold and Fizdale brought Jimmy (and Arthur Weinstein) along on their annual European tour. Jimmy was excited to be going back to Europe again. "I keep forgetting I'm going, and then when I remember, I feel thrilled. I'm afraid for me Europe will always be followed by an exclamation point." They landed in Cherbourg on August 9, and spent a few days in Paris before making their way to Austria to visit Florence Kimball, who summered there, and attend the Salzburg Festival. Schuyler was ambivalent about Austria, although he found the Alps "very beautiful, especially in the evening, when the light goes up the buildings and then up the valley and onto the tops of the mountains," as he wrote to Porter. Not much of a hiker, Schuyler's primary experience of the mountain scenery was from the towns, or through the train window: "You didn't *visit* the alps?" someone later asked him. "No, but I saw from the train they were black / and streaked with snow." By the end of August, after a short train ride across the mountains, they were in Venice.

The city, which he had never visited before, was a revelation, even somewhat overwhelming at first. "I'm really so foolishly pleased with such vast extents of Venetian art, that it's [like] falling into a bottomless pit of delight," he wrote to O'Hara. "I can't tell you how much my legs ached last week or, what's more remarkable, how little I minded." The group rented a ground-floor apartment near the Zattere, where Jimmy stayed for almost two months. He perceived subtle changes in the celebrated Venetian light as autumn drew on: "It's marvelous to have gotten to know Venice well, and then have it turn in a day into something so much more beautiful—all the hard whites have turned to cream and roses, and the dry stucco colors have gotten as rich as autumn leaves." He reveled in the luxury of being able to loaf and quietly absorb the uneventful minutiae of daily life, as though Venice were a place like any other.

Images and aesthetic principles derived from his stay in Venice would be felt throughout his later work. In a letter to Fairfield from the end of September, he wrote, "I am so delighted by Venice, that my experiences have become like a lump of pink marble, that I can hardly bear to break apart to exhibit . . . Venice has given me the sense of a new idea (or the freshening of an old one) of how far art can go without artifice or inflation, without sacrificing anything that makes it personal, without diminishing its scale, color or intensity. I mean something as simple as the connection between people seen in a window at evening, and the figures in a Bellini." The idea of the "connections" between fleeting sense impressions would stay with him and be expressed most explicitly in his poem "February," written not long after his return to New York.

Although Jimmy was focused on the old Venice, of churches, museums, and architecture ("Venice itself," as he put it), the city was abuzz with contemporary art and culture that month: not only a Twentieth Century Music Festival that brought Virgil Thomson, Ned Rorem,

Leonard Bernstein, and others in Gold and Fizdale's circle to the city, but also the Venice Biennale. The highpoint of the Biennale was the mini-retrospective of twenty-six de Kooning paintings in the American Pavilion, including a painting on loan from Fairfield, a close friend of de Kooning's since the '30s. Jimmy, although he had yet to write any art criticism, was perceptive about the experience of seeing these examples of "the new American painting" in a European context, and observed that the de Koonings "looked so much 'quieter' than I would have expected; they seemed to make no extra theatrical bid, beyond that of denseness and quality."

After Gold and Fizdale departed for a concert tour on October 17, Jimmy went to Rome, intending to stay there for two months of concentrated work on *Alfred and Guinevere*. At the beginning of his stay, William Weaver was there to give him dinner, amuse him, and take him out to parties, but Weaver soon went off to Vienna and Jimmy was left to spend rather lonely evenings, reading or going to the movies. At the English bookstore he bought copies of Keats's poems and letters and Matthew Arnold's poems, noting wryly to Jane Freilicher, "I meant my gloom to strike a lighter note than this—maybe it's because I went to see 'Waterfront' last night, then read in bed Keats' last letters and all about his death." A few days later, on his thirty-second birthday, it was rainy and had turned colder, and "the cheeriest thing" he had done was to "read Keats's 'Hyperion' over and over." His work on *Alfred and Guinevere* was not going well.

Gold, Fizdale, and Weinstein arrived in Rome on November 12, and they all moved into the Villa Aurelia at the American Academy in Rome, where Gold and Fizdale had been invited for a short residency. The pianists gave a concert at the Teatro Argentina, Rome's principal concert hall, playing the Poulenc Concerto for Two Pianos and Orchestra (1932) with the St. Cecilia National Academy Orchestra, followed by a party given by the American expatriates John and Ginny Becker in their apartment in the Palazzo Caetani. Jimmy was happy to be swept back up in the "high-class wining and dining" that was life with the Boys, comparing the social ambiance to a play by Ronald Firbank: "I met Respighi's widow and Casella's widow. Italy has not changed much since the days of Princess Zoubaroff." When a lady from Los Angeles at one dinner party asked him, "Are you just writing a novel or are you—if you'll excuse my expression—trying to prove something?" he merely gave her his "Mona Lisa laugh." There were slightly discordant moments, as when, at a dinner given by the arts patron Mimi Pecci-Blunt in her family's palazzo, a Madame de Beaumont asked whether he agreed that "nowadays, so few young people seem interested in maintaining their beautiful homes." "Maybe it costs too much money," Jimmy suggested. "No, no, no, I don't mean that," the lady replied—"as I might have deduced from the beads on her fingers and the rings in her ears," he wrote.

Later, he did manage to buckle down and make some progress on his novel. By December 2, he wrote to Fairfield that he had "finally a feeling of its having an end, which I shall be relieved to reach." He had also written "a couple of poems." Although he claimed he was "not pleased with them," this verdict may have changed over time, for in January he sent Frank his new poem "A Head." It is a curious poem for him to have written at this moment, and a powerful, strange poem for any period of his work. From its opening lines, "A dead boy living among men as a man / called an angel," which is reminiscent of "The Forty-First and Youngest Brother," and specific musical allusions common to "The Mouse Party," one would think it had been written at the time of "Three Stories." In its description of a "boy" it is also a rather dark pendant to the untitled poem "The boy who walks with his head up," which Jimmy had included in a letter to Frank from Venice at the end of September. The latter apparently precipitated O'Hara's autobiographical poem of this same year, which he dedicated to Schuyler, "Poem" ("There I could never be a boy"). While "The boy who walks with his head up" incorporates a portrait of O'Hara, with a reference to a frightening incident in March when he was shot by an intruder on the staircase of 326 East Forty-ninth Street, "A Head" is much more ambiguous and its subject is likely Jimmy himself in a depressed mood—a self-portrait looking in the mirror and contemplating the contents of "this head where thought repeats / itself like a loud clock."

At the beginning of December, Jimmy joined Gold and Fizdale in Genoa at the Hotel Splendide et de la Ville. Here he wrote to Fairfield, with layered references to Marianne Moore, Henry James, and Rilke: "I like writing in a hotel room. It combines a nice sort of privacy with, if not 'accessibility to experience,' at least the feeling that 'if I should cry' (I don't know why these quotations are running around in my head) while none of the angel orders would hear me, the chamber maid might . . . And how it's rained since I left Rome. All up the coast, after La Spezia, there were torrents dashing into the sea off the cliffs and making a wide earth colored band, like a beach of water in the milky blue and blue-green." The letter inspired Fairfield to write a sestina, "Genoa," which appropriates imagery of the solitary hotel room and the rain dashing against cliffs to become both a collaboration and nearly a love poem: "Each one of us in his separate room . . ."; "Who can resist the dissolving power of water?"

After Christmas, Jimmy and the others went on a whirlwind trip to Sicily, with stops in Palermo, Monreale, and Agrigento. In Palermo's Pinacoteca, Jimmy was moved by Francesco Laurana's early Renaissance bust of Eleanor of Aragon, which he found to be "as beautiful as any work of art I've ever seen," and remained a touchstone for him in his subsequent years as a reviewer. From Palermo they took a train to Agrigento and its famous Greek "squat temples, / too much restored, too picked at." On the way back into town they passed a "*manicomio*," or insane asylum, causing Jimmy to experience a slight frisson and wonder: "is / Sicilian mental hygiene / really up to date?"

Three days after returning to Rome, Jimmy wrote to Fairfield, "My impressions of Sicily seem to have sunk inside me like a ball of tin foil, but I hope I'll soon have a few quiet moments in which to smooth them out and look at them." All too soon the group began to make ready to leave again, for Paris by way of Vicenza, Trento, Milan, Strasbourg, and Baden-Baden, all cities in which Gold and Fizdale were to give concerts.

On January 28, 1955, Schuyler, Weinstein, and the pianists sailed home on the French liner *Liberté*, landing in New York on February 3. Fizdale and Gold now had an apartment at 333 Central Park West, but it was not big enough for all four men, especially if two of them were practicing at two pianos all day. Before leaving, Jimmy had written to ask Frank if he could return to the Forty-ninth Street apartment, and he was welcomed home.

[11]

BETWEEN THESE LINES I WRITE YOUR NAME

1955–1956

Jimmy was happy to be rooming part-time with Frank again, and he quickly got back into the swing, with social events almost every night. The friendship with Fairfield Porter had deepened too, through their exchange of letters. Fairfield's third exhibition at the Tibor de Nagy Gallery had opened the day Jimmy arrived, but he made up for missing the opening by seeing the show four or five times that month. He felt the work showed "new ease, a directness and lightness, that's enchanting."

In the spring, Arthur Gold sublet a floor-through apartment in a brownstone on East Sixtieth Street from the painter Leonid Berman and his wife, the harpsichordist Sylvia Marlowe, and Jimmy divided his time between living there with Arthur and coming back to Forty-ninth Street during the day to write. The apartment was filled with paintings by Leonid, his brother Eugène Berman, and Pavel Tchelitchew, all "neo-Romantic" painters, highly fashionable in the 1940s. It was with glee that the "first thing" Jimmy did on moving into the apartment was to take down the neo-Romantics and replace them with the work of his friends: a Jane Freilicher and a couple of Fairfield Porters.

Jimmy's poem "February" was written at Forty-ninth Street on the last day of the eponymous month. It followed an earlier attempt to write a poem in a regular form based on his memories of his visit to Sicily. That poem, however, "turned out laborious and flat." As he related later, he then looked out the window and "saw that something marvelous was happening to the light, transforming everything. It then occurred to me that this happened more often than not (a beautiful sunset I mean) and that it was 'a day like any other,' which I put down as a title. The rest of the poem popped out of its own accord."

When Frank came home from work that afternoon, bringing Fairfield with him, Jimmy read the new poem to them. They both "made fun of it, which was a terrible put-down" and caused Jimmy to have doubts about it himself, although, he told an interviewer, "later on I decided it was a perfectly OK poem." In fact, it remains among the most frequently referenced of his poems as an illustration of his full presence in the moment of observation. An account of its writing, carefully recorded in a letter to a reader, suggests something of the poem's significance to him. With "February," Jimmy comes to a conscious recognition of the poetic territory that was his: not the constricting formal prosody that Gold advocated, but free verse put to the service of careful and fluent observation in real time. "Looking out the window," yes, but also acknowledging what he could not see, including feelings and "involuntary memories." The effect is not so much descriptive, as one of putting the reader in the position of making the same discoveries, at the same time, as the poet. As he wrote, "Often a poem 'happens' to the writer in exactly the same way that it 'happens' to someone who reads it."

A chimney, breathing a little smoke.
The sun, I can't see
making a bit of pink
I can't quite see in the blue.
The pink of five tulips
at five p.m. on the day before March first.
The green of the tulip stems and leaves
like something I can't remember,
finding a jack-in-the-pulpit
a long time ago and far away.

[. . .]

It's the yellow dust inside the tulips.
It's the shape of a tulip.
It's the water in the drinking glass the tulips are in.
It's a day like any other.

While his main priority this spring was finishing the first draft of *Alfred and Guinevere*, Schuyler also worked on translations of Giacomo Leopardi's poems. "In Rivers language, I'm bugged on Leopardi," he wrote to Barbara Guest in July 1955. None were published in his lifetime, despite encouragement from Guest, then the poetry editor of the *Partisan Review*, and other friends. His translations to some degree seek to work against the intrinsic musicality of the poet he called "the most musical poet in the most musical language." By selectively retaining the word order of the original Italian, Schuyler's versions can run counter to conventional English syntax, bumping the reader up against the words themselves, to achieve a plain-hewn quality consonant with the pain within Leopardi's plangent music:

blind rests the night,
and singing, with a sad melody,
a wagon driver salutes the last ray
of the fled light
which before had led him on his way

Jimmy identified with the solitary, melancholic Leopardi: his lifelong ill health, isolated upbringing, and self-education by immersion in his father's extensive library. Around the same time as the translations, he wrote an homage to Leopardi, "Distraction: An Ode," incorporating memories of his visits to Naples in the late '40s (where Leopardi spent his last years) and comparing it with the tenemented streets of New York, both overseen by the "icy whiteness" of the moon.

Throughout the spring, Jimmy and Frank O'Hara were, as John Ashbery put it, "enjoying a domesticity" in the Forty-ninth Street apartment, "subject to interruption by the periodic return of The Boys." In March, Jimmy helped Frank put together a manuscript of new work to submit to the Yale Younger Poets Series, an annual competition for poets under the age of forty who had not yet published a book of poems. The prize was publication by the Yale University Press, and the judge was W. H. Auden. Jimmy advised Frank on the selection and the final composition of his submission, a collection similar to the book Frank would publish in 1957 as *Meditations in an Emergency*, which Jimmy again helped with—or, as Frank later put it, subjected to his "clippers, pruners and . . . grafting equipment." John also submitted a book to Yale, and after a certain amount of intrigue, owing to the fact that both manuscripts were rejected by the initial screeners, Auden awarded the prize to Ashbery's book *Some Trees*, which was published the following year with Auden's introduction.

In the meantime, John, Jane Freilicher, Joe Hazan, Grace Hartigan, and the photographer Walter Silver drove down to Mexico together on May 28, for about eighteen days. It was John's first visit to any foreign country, and inspired his poem "The Instruction Manual," which he wrote in his office at McGraw Hill, where he now worked, a few days after getting home. Learning on his return the exciting news that he had won the Yale prize, John then added the poem to the manuscript of *Some Trees*, and it became a kind of instant classic among his friends, affectionately parodied by Jimmy in a letter to Kenneth Koch that August, for example. John also found out that he had been awarded a Fulbright Grant to study that fall in France, where he planned to translate modern French poetry.

In June, with Jimmy spending most of his time with Gold on Sixtieth Street, Joe LeSueur moved into the Forty-ninth Street apartment with Frank. LeSueur was a twenty-year-old writer with blond movie-star good looks who had been close to Frank since they met at John Ashbery's New Year's Eve party in 1951. He and Frank would end up rooming together for about ten years, and remained close friends until the end of Frank's life. They were not lovers, contrary to what many believed, but rather, as we'd now say, "friends with benefits," who did have casual sex together from time to time. At Jimmy's recommendation, LeSueur also took over his old job at the Periscope-Holliday Bookshop.

At the beginning of July, Jimmy finished the first draft of *Alfred and Guinevere* and, with a sense of relief, sent it to Harcourt Brace. How he came to choose that publisher is not clear, but it may have been through Barbara Guest's connections at the *Partisan Review*, whose managing editor, Catherine Carver, was also an editor at Harcourt. By the fall, Carver had tentatively accepted the book, subject to extensive revisions.

With Gold and Fizdale tied up in the recording studio all summer, Jimmy was now eager to get out of town. He decided to take Fairfield Porter up on his earlier invitation to visit him and his family on Great Spruce Head Island.

Great Spruce Head is an island of about 350 acres in Penobscot Bay off the coast of Maine, which Fairfield's father bought for $10,000 in 1912 as a summer retreat. Rising to an altitude of about 220 feet, it is covered in spruce forest interspersed with inland meadows, with coves and rocky beaches around the perimeter. Soon after buying the island, James Porter built a large, somewhat unusual house on a prominent point near the shore. Over the years, two of Fairfield's three brothers, Eliot and John, and their sister, Nancy Straus, built their own smaller houses on the island, leaving Fairfield and his family, by default, in possession of the ungainly but charming big house. Although imposing in scale and design, the house was strictly a summer residence without insulation and with only intermittent electricity provided by a generator. The interior was dominated by a large, central, double-height living room, with the kitchen, bathroom, and several small bedrooms tucked away in two-story wings at either end. Heated only by fireplaces and a wood-burning stove in the kitchen, the house was designed not only with a healthy New England obliviousness to cold and discomfort, but with the presumption of servants to fire the stove and cook meals on it, as had been the case in Fairfield's childhood. Now, however, the grueling housework fell to Anne.

Jimmy's first visit didn't start well. Taking the bus from Penn Station at 2:00 a.m. on July 15, he missed his connection in Boston, and arrived in Camden some fifteen hours later, "chafed, constipated, cranky and with incipient piles." At Camden he was met by Fairfield and his brother John, who owned the only motorboat in the family, the *Kittiwake*. The trip across Penobscot Bay took about ninety minutes, during which Fairfield gave a running commentary on the geography of the bay, pointing out the various islands as they came into view. As Jimmy wrote thirty-three years later to his friend Tom Carey, "Little did I suspect what the future held."

After the long ride across the bay, the island feels quite isolated. At the center of a small archipelago of still smaller islands, it seems to face out toward the Atlantic with the mainland several miles away at its back. The main house was virtually unchanged since Fairfield's childhood, and had an atmosphere in some respects typical of a relaxed New England summer cottage and in other ways unique to the Porter family. The central room was ringed by a high mezzanine on which was attached a dragon banner from a long-ago children's pageant, as well as one of the large toy sailboats made for the Porter children; a large plaster cast of a panel of horses from the Parthenon frieze hung over the fireplace; and in the corners were overstuffed bookshelves where well-loved volumes belonging to Fairfield's parents, brothers, and sister mingled with more recent ones brought by his own family and friends. An old wind-up phonograph and some 78 records of opera, classic, and popular music stood in the corner. Meals were eaten on a screened-in porch with a view of the bay and the neighboring islands.

For Jimmy, it was love at first sight: he called it "one of the most beautiful places I've ever been," and said, "A week here is like a month anywhere else in its breadth, depth and general spaciousness." Writing to Frank, who was planning to visit later, he added, "I won't attempt to describe it, just come & come soon."

Fairfield painted the first of his many portraits of Jimmy during this visit, a particularly sensitive one showing him sitting on the screened porch, gazing directly at the painter (viewer), wearing a yellow shirt that seems to hold and concentrate the light from outside the porch. Fairfield wrote to Frank: "Jimmy is writing a new novel, and sometimes I hear him typing and often I hear a woodpecker and think it is he. He loves to canoe, and has been in the water, swimming slowly around for a time with a smile on his face, and remarking very gently after a bit, 'Why Fairfield, it's the coldest thing I ever felt.'" In the evenings Fairfield and

Jimmy took turns reading aloud Keats's long narrative poems "Lamia" and "Hyperion." The sculptor Richard Stankiewicz, who was also visiting, found the poems puzzling: "Jim and FP seem not to consult me or take my opinions after these readings but are not offensive about it."

Jimmy's first letter to Fairfield after his return to New York on August 13 stated, "It's really impossible to tell you how much I liked visiting you and Anne and staying on the island. I've never enjoyed any company or place so much." Two days after he got back, Jimmy saw Frank into a cab en route to his own visit to Maine. Frank, too, was entranced by Great Spruce Head and the Porter way of life there. He brought with him his new play, *The Thirties*, a spoof of Hollywood films of that decade, which he read to the family. It was dedicated to John Ashbery, who later said he liked it best of all O'Hara's plays. Tragically, Frank lost the only copy, along with his typewriter and the rest of his luggage, at Penn Station when he got back to the city, terribly fulfilling the prophecy of a line in *Presenting Jane*: "The vision goes untold, like a suitcase left in a train."

The trajectory of the emotional history between Jimmy and Fairfield was never linear or cut-and-dried. At this point, one could say that Fairfield was already in love with Jimmy, based on the tone of the portrait he painted on the island and of the tender references to Jimmy in his letter to Frank, whether or not he was ready to acknowledge it to himself. Perhaps it even began earlier, while Jimmy was in Italy and Fairfield wrote his sestina "Genoa."

After he had been back in the city for a couple of months, Jimmy wrote to Fairfield, attempting to defend himself against the latter's accusation that it was always he who had to initiate social contact. Undoubtedly Fairfield's serious demeanor was not always in tune with the energy of his younger friends, who weren't always in the mood to socialize with him when he came into the city. This led to some hurt feelings for Fairfield, who sometimes felt they were avoiding him. Jimmy's attempt to refute this sounds slightly defensive. "Often, when it has been you who called, wasn't it because we had arranged it so beforehand—as often at my suggestion as at yours—on the grounds that you would be out during the day?" More to the point, Jimmy sensed a self-consciousness on Fairfield's part about the age difference between them, which he sought to counter: "I'm also rather put out by this youth and age stuff. In so far as

I think of you as 'older,' I feel honored and benefited by your friendship; but if it turns out that you feel odd in bestowing it, I feel snubbed. I don't think of you as 'older' so much as I do a friend who has had a life very different from mine." At the going-away party for John Ashbery, who was moving to France for his Fulbright, Fairfield confirmed sternly to Jimmy that he "knew damn well he could" come visit him in Southampton, and Jimmy now said he would do so soon, and followed through within a week or two.

That fall, Jimmy began reviewing exhibitions for *Art News* magazine, taking over the position from Frank O'Hara. O'Hara had originally started reviewing after quitting his front-desk job at MoMA in December 1953, but having rejoined the museum in a curatorial position in January 1955, he now found he had no time to do both. Schuyler would write regularly for *Art News* until 1961, and occasionally after that.

Art News in the 1950s was experiencing a golden age under the editorship of Thomas B. Hess, a Yale graduate in French art and literature who had worked briefly at MoMA before joining the magazine in 1945. Hess developed close relationships with the downtown Abstract Expressionist painters and was especially important in promoting the work of Willem de Kooning. At that time, it was *Art News* policy to review, if briefly, every gallery exhibition in New York—the New York art world still being small enough for that to be possible—and Hess's brilliant idea for obtaining cheap and lively copy for these myriad reviews was to hire poets and painters to write them. This gave *Art News* reviews, at their best, a remarkable freshness of observation and language. Fairfield Porter had begun reviewing for the publication in 1951, and continued until becoming art critic for *The Nation* in 1959. Other writers on the masthead during Jimmy's years there included Barbara Guest, Edith Schloss, the painters Paul Georges, Lawrence Campbell, and Elaine de Kooning, novelist Parker Tyler, and critic Irving Sandler.

If there was an overarching ethos to the *Art News* short reviews at the time, it was perhaps expressed by the editor in chief Alfred Frankfurter, who told Fairfield early on, "Just report . . . The best criticism is simply the best description." Jimmy picked up the idea quickly. He had read a lot of art history (introducing Ashbery to the writing of the English critic Adrian Stokes, for example) and had become familiar with the aims and terminology of contemporary art through his many painter friends and his experiences looking at art with them. Schuyler's reviews are distinguished by the kind of close, idiosyncratic observation and concise construction that also characterize his poetry. The limitations of the form and the exercise in careful looking lend his reviews a beautiful consistency, and the best of them come to an almost sonnet-like resolution:

> Al Jensen [Tanager], who was born in Guatemala City, lived in California, studied painting in Munich and Paris and now lives in New York, said of his abstractions in his show last month that they were done from autobiographical recollections. This could be seen in the color, soft and tranquil, and in the heavy outlining of forms, at once isolating and connecting them, the way the context of vivid memories is dim or lost. That they were abstract saved the pictures from tiring privacy or over-intimacy; and the treatment of surfaces (the paint in some places had shrunk and rippled, in others it was put on with pieces of paint skin in it) secured them to the physical present. The few without the heavy outlines implied a further radiance, beyond whatever is oppressive in memories.

In January 1956, Frank O'Hara took a leave of absence from the Museum of Modern Art and moved to Cambridge to accept a six-month "Poet-in-Residence" position at the Poets' Theatre. With Frank and John both away and Arthur Gold on tour in Italy for two months, Jimmy grew close to the painter John Button and his lover, the pianist Alvin Novak. The couple had recently moved to New York from Los Angeles, and by the summer of 1955 were part of the extended group orbiting around Frank, glimpsed dancing in a gay bar in O'Hara's poem "At the Old Place," and sleeping peacefully in "Poem" from 1955 ("Johnny and Alvin are going home, are sleeping now / are fanning the air with breaths from the same bed"). LeSueur attempted to describe John Button's appeal thus: "Slight, wiry, of medium height, John Button had neat, smallish features, mischievous brown eyes, not very good teeth . . . but he was the possessor of such peppery wit, insouciant charm, and sexual allure that those of us under his spell were like so much putty, stripped of all objectivity, not qualified to assess his sheer physical attractiveness." Alex Katz compared him with James Dean in looks, and felt he was less committed to his art than to his social and sexual life. "He was the life of the party, a real firecracker."

Although Button had studied at the Hans Hofmann School, he was not an abstract painter but a fairly straightforward, if reductive, realist. Four or five years younger than Larry Rivers and Jane Freilicher, Button was less advanced in his career than they and all the more willing to regard Fairfield Porter, who liked him and his work, as a mentor. Jimmy began writing to Button during numerous visits to the Porters in Southampton, and during a visit to Frank in Cambridge that spring. Full of wit, joy, and vivid observation, the letters trace the birth and growth of a major infatuation.

Almost immediately after arriving in Cambridge, Frank began to regret the decision to come, missing New York and feeling oddly dissociated from his present life, although there were compensations, mainly catching up with his old friends Violet "Bunny" Lang and George Montgomery. The highpoint of his time there was the production of John Ashbery's play *The Compromise, or Queen of Cariboo*, which ran from April 4 to 21. Jimmy drove up with Jane Freilicher and Joe Hazan in early April to stay with Frank for about two weeks and see the play.

The Compromise is a very funny parody of 1930s Rin Tin Tin movies and westerns about Royal Canadian Mounties, such as John would have seen as a child. However, it is probably unplayable today because of its casually accepted racial stereotypes and exaggerated pidgin English dialogue, discordant when seen printed on the page in a serious work of literature. Frank was credited as Executive Producer and also played the Author of the Play, who, in what he called a "Pirandelloesque touch," comes on at the end and gives a speech resolving, by deliberately not resolving, the impossibly tangled plot. Violet Lang played Daisy Farrell, a saloon dancer with a heart of gold; George Montgomery and the young poet John Wieners had small roles.

Wieners, then twenty-two, had spent three months at Black Mountain College the previous spring studying with Charles Olson, and would return there in the summer of 1956 to study with Robert Duncan. Both O'Hara and Schuyler got to know him during the production and liked him and his poems. He had not yet published his work professionally, and O'Hara sent his poems to Barbara Guest (for the *Partisan Review*), to John Bernard Myers (for *Semi-Colon*), and, at Schuyler's suggestion, to Daisy Aldan (for *Folder*). Myers printed "With Mr. J. R. Morton" in the final issue of *Semi-Colon*, which was Wieners's first appearance in print outside of undergraduate work. Jimmy kept in touch with Wieners by letter for a couple of years afterward.

Jimmy loved Cambridge. As Frank reported to Kenneth, he "looks rested and chummy, keeps saying he likes Cambridge because it's so flat." George Montgomery often made a third in their excursions to the movies, or to drink beer in a local bar. Taking inspiration from Frank's ability to write anywhere, it was in the bar that Jimmy began the "Four Poems" he would later publish under that title, dedicated to O'Hara.

It's 4:30 in Cambridge

and I have a slight headache
on one side only just
enough for a drink.

What a long time since I wrote a poem.

Montgomery was a Harvard contemporary and close friend of O'Hara's and Ashbery's. A photographer and a poet, he also designed the posters and fliers for the Poets' Theatre. On April 11, Montgomery drove with Frank and Jimmy out into the country to Lexington. The day was cold but sunny, and the two poets "sat on rocks in a woods and wrote poems and got all PINK," while Montgomery took photographs. The poem that Frank wrote was "On a Mountain." Jimmy's was "With Frank and George at Lexington":

The snow has footsteps in it
like wet cement; a cowlick
is in a tuft of last year's grass;

cars fly by like bees; and so on.
A big quill hat bends an evergreen
introspectively down.

It feels good here.

Jimmy initially included "With Frank and George at Lexington" with the "Four Poems" dedicated to O'Hara, writing to Al Leslie, "I do seem to have this all or nothing feeling about them." That feeling obviously changed at some point, and "With Frank and George at Lexington" was published by itself in Schuyler's first book, *Salute* (1960), while the "Four Poems" were not published until 1965. In fact, "With Frank and George" is distinct from the other four in an important way: it is not about John Button. The dedication to Frank and the several references to him in the "Four Poems" are sincerely meant, but also red herrings. The bigger presence in the poems is actually an absence, that of Button, with whom Jimmy had come to realize he was in love.

In the first of the "Four Poems," Schuyler writes, "It's nice here thinking about all the men / who have one name in common" (i.e., John Button, John Ashbery, John Wieners, John Myers) and then: "Between these lines I write your name / in the name of each hair on your chest." In the second poem, "Mass. Ave., Cambridge, Mass.," after describing the view from the window of "this flat brick city / you might like," he confesses, "It's odd, having an emotion / so much bigger than yourself." The fourth poem, "Frank! Frank!," beginning "Afternoon of indecision . . . ," expresses the poet's "mixed emotion" over the prospect of leaving Cambridge and O'Hara and the pleasant life he had found there, to return to New York, Gold, and the painful decisions that his newfound love for Button imply: "suppose my heart tore in two."

From the time of Jimmy's return from Cambridge into the fall of 1956, his primary emotional focus was this love, expressed largely through letters and poems. For the moment, however, Gold was still on tour in Italy, and it is possible that either at this time, or even before Jimmy went to Cambridge, he and Button slept together. The situation was awkward and painful because both were in relationships, and Jimmy felt torn, guilty, and at first reluctant to confess the depth of his feelings. During the first month after his return to New York, while he wrote to Button regularly, he did not speak of his growing love. When he finally did so, it was in the form of a poem, which was also a kind of love letter, "Having My Say-So," which he held on to for a month before he finally handed it to Button at a party.

The love poem is an inherently self-exposing genre that occupies a clearly established position in James Schuyler's oeuvre, along with its corollary, the elegy. Schuyler's work in both genres owes something to the impetuous and irresistible onrush of "feelings" characteristic of many of O'Hara's poems, though tempered by Schuyler's greater reticence and, often, self-reflexive contradictions. "Having My Say-So," with its sometimes long lines, loping rhythm, and confiding voice and tone, undoubtedly shows the effect of Jimmy having just spent ten days with Frank, yet ultimately it does not sound much like O'Hara; the sense of performance and bustle of many O'Hara poems is replaced by a voice of quiet, sometimes uncomfortable ingenuousness.

> Surely it's undignified for a gent to want to take another gent
> bouquets, and absurd?
> Just as surely I could not care less.
> Surely it's an incredible invasion of someone else's privacy to sit
> around writing unsolicited poems to and about him?
> Well, as you-know-who would say,
> I'm sorry but I just can't help it I feel this way.
> Deeply.

Over half of the poem is taken up with a close physical description of Button (supporting the premise that they had slept together by this time), ending with a slightly Leopardian apostrophe to the moon: "Moon! look down and see the small dark pit of your reflection on this pale shaded plain of flesh."

On May 11, Gold and Fizdale returned from Italy, "tired, rather tan and not excessively contented." For July and August 1956, Schuyler and

Gold, with Fizdale and Arthur Weinstein, had arranged to rent the Porters' house at 49 South Main Street in Southampton while the family was in Maine. Fairfield and Anne Porter's fifth child, Elizabeth, had been born on Easter Sunday, April 1, and Jimmy went out to Southampton at the end of May to meet the new baby and to be oriented in the workings of the house.

Back in New York, Jimmy finally gave Button the love poem. At approximately the same time, he also mailed him a letter that begins, "I don't know why I have to tell you this today (but I do)—perhaps it's because when I look out into the fog all I can see is the hairs on your adorable chest. I'm terribly in love with you, and have been for such a long time, ever since the first time Frank took me to your apartment . . . I've looked at you a lot since then and there isn't anybody else in the world I want to look at; or want, for that matter."

There were, of course, several problems with this love. One was his relationship with Arthur Gold, now going into its fourth year. Another was Button's relationship with Alvin Novak. A third was John Button's essentially promiscuous nature, which, to more than one observer, made the affair an exercise in futility from the beginning. As an acquaintance said, "[Jimmy] was *mad* for him! And he pursued him, pursued him, which is really like trying to catch a butterfly. John Button was darling, he was beautiful, he was so sweet and so cute—and he slept with absolutely everybody! . . . Kind of a very unfortunate person to fall in love with." But as summer got under way, there was enough to-ing and fro-ing among all the parties to keep any painful decision at bay.

During one of Jimmy's visits to the Porters this spring, Fairfield suggested that he accompany him to Maine when he went up to open the house, as he customarily did ahead of Anne and the family. Jimmy, who was becoming aware of Fairfield's amorous feelings toward him, had "no comment" about this invitation when he reported it to Frank, other than that he had deflected it with a countersuggestion that he take John Button instead. As Fairfield did.

Button, too, was enchanted with the island, and had a productive visit, completing a number of paintings and relaying his impressions in amusing letters to Jimmy. Jimmy, writing to Button on the island, referred to his earlier declaration with a light touch: "I hope that poem I forced on you at Howard's didn't embarrass you: I'd written it a month before and not liked it, then I looked at it and seemed rather to like its silliness. At least the apostrophe to the moon seemed just, since alongside you I find it about as attractive as a dried pea . . . Give my love to Fairfield (that's a way of speaking), and I send you all my love (that's the truth)."

Button's response to Schuyler's epistolary courtship was warm, but not fully reciprocating: "'That poem,' you forced on me at Howard's was—let's face it—how can I do anything but blush and feel strong and creative when you say such nice things. I loved it." Much later, he characterized himself at this time as "a young and somewhat snotty new-comer, from California, and completely unresponsive to Jimmy's feelings, though I certainly admired him and wanted to be his friend." So he claimed in hindsight, yet his letters to Schuyler from the actual period of the infatuation paint a different picture, and seem intended to encourage rather than to douse Schuyler's feelings.

In another letter from mid-June, Jimmy attempted to envision a future that could somehow include both Button and his present relationship with Gold: "I think in the fall my life will be adjusted in a way that I can see you more (if you like, I hope you like), but right now there have been too many obligations, and the obligations are too real." Despite the difficulties, he continued, "what does make me happy . . . is that you've refreshed something about me that had gotten awfully dry, I scarcely know what to call it, my creativity or my self-esteem as an artist. I went through more than a year when nothing I wrote gave me any satisfaction, and when most of what I did write wasn't nearly the best I'm capable of."

Complicating Jimmy's feelings further was the fact that at the same time, Fairfield Porter was coming to a realization of his own: that he was in love with Jimmy. While Fairfield was in Maine this summer, he and Jimmy carried on a lengthy and intricate correspondence. One or two key letters have been lost, but sometime in late June, Fairfield wrote to Jimmy with some sort of declaration of love. Apparently, in his response, Jimmy was disturbed and dismissive, both of the content and by the fact that it was written in a letter rather than spoken. In his rejoinder to Jimmy's reply—which is where the surviving correspondence picks up—

Fairfield refers to Jimmy's own declaration by letter to Button. "I sent my letter because my missing you became unbearable, and I could neither speak nor hold my piece. You would not have adopted a superior moral tone to me if I had been able to speak what I was forced to write or else keep bottled up. You wrote John [Button] a letter when you could have spoken to him: when you could have been direct you chose to be indirect. I had no choice." Fairfield continues: "As to my measuring the immeasurable etc., I agree that that is a quality that is tiresome; I hope I get over it. I do not want to be everything to you, I wanted to be that which you said John was to you, which is not everything."

Fairfield's use of the past tense indicates that Jimmy had rejected his advance, and that Fairfield accepted the rejection. Jimmy's answer to this letter, however, was apparently conciliatory enough to stir up his feelings again. Typically, Fairfield ties himself in knots of scruple: "You have the power . . . of making me extremely happy. When I do not hear from you in answer to a letter of mine it makes me feel that I don't exist. When I hope for and do not find a letter from you, I get restless and depressed and want to break things and damage myself. . . . My rudeness comes from an attempt to get rid of those positive feelings that are unwelcome to you. The forcing of myself to be unnatural requires violence. Since my conscience finds these positive feelings to be my best ones, whatever I can substitute for them will seem inferior: you find me wicked for both my positive feelings and the negative ones that I substitute for them: when I feel wicked in relation to you, I lose hope and purpose; I can hardly concentrate."

In closing, Fairfield weighs separate categories of love: "As for me, I love you very very much. Anne and I send our love to you and Frank, and I include John and Alvin." A postscript brings matters further along: "I just got your second note in the mail. It makes me awfully happy. Last night, I was up, and feeling good, because I had heard from you, I was outdoors, talking to Kenneth, about the sunset and the birds; and Kenneth said to me, 'You have such an air of new life, of beginning again, of taking an interest in things. I am so glad you are well at last.' It was my emotional health he was talking about: I was feeling happy about you again."

It may be relevant to note that during this period Schuyler, Porter, O'Hara, and many of their friends were reading Marcel Proust's multivolume novel, *Remembrance of Things Past* (as it was then called), and references to various characters and situations from the novel are dotted throughout their correspondence of the late '50s. Being immersed in this material contributed to the way Porter, for one, framed his feelings for Schuyler, and Schuyler, to a lesser degree, his for Button. In one of his letters from that summer, Porter refers to yet another letter, which he burned without sending, "The letter I wrote you one day all day . . . was about Proust and about writing, about what musicalness can be, about John A's, Kenneth's, Frank's and your poems, about the pollen blowing from the spruce trees, about Balbec, Maine, northern California, Oregon and Norway, about my relief when after the awful bitchy musical party at Mme de St. Euverte's Swann fell out of love, and my elation and hope."

Meanwhile, the realities of both Jimmy's and Button's domestic situations kept them mostly apart, as Jimmy found himself reabsorbed in the busy social life of the Boys: "They do tell funny stories and scream a lot, and what more can one get out of social life I should like to know?" he wrote to Button. But inevitably, the strain of being in love with another man began to show in his day-to-day life with Gold. In late June, Jimmy seems to have almost deliberately goaded Gold into a disagreement by staying out all night with a casual trick after a dinner at Chester Kallman's. Jimmy made light of the matter in an amusing letter to Button: "I'm in the dog house today; which means A[rthur] isn't speaking to me, or barely. It would be better, much, if he weren't at all."

On July 2, Gold and Fizdale's two grand pianos were moved into the Porters' Southampton house, as they, Jimmy, and Arthur Weinstein prepared to take up residence for the summer. Jimmy reported to Fairfield, "Everything about the house is fine (not to say beautiful and a joy). Arthur W. prowled through [the house] like a cat-detective and is already to line up a membership for you in the IDA (interior decorators assoc)." Jimmy was writing in Fairfield's studio, continuing to revise *Alfred and Guinevere*, and rereading Proust alternately with the *Divine Comedy*.

This calm would not last. Shortly after Button returned from Maine, Novak announced that he was moving out of their shared apartment. This was for reasons of his own, and although he had sensed something between Jimmy and Button, the parting was amicable. It did increase the psychological pressure on both Jimmy and Button, however.

Jimmy and Button had anticipated getting together during the month of July. A couple of Button's letters to Schuyler mention looking forward to "July" (in quotes) as though it were a private code word referring to their finally sleeping together, which by this time had become a matter freighted with such import as to be anxiety-producing. In one of his letters from Maine, Button writes, "I want to talk to you concerning my serious doubts about 'July.'" That was before Novak decided to leave Button; his action changed the dynamics by leaving the field open for Jimmy, which was both exciting and terrifying. Writing to Button shortly after learning of Novak's decision, Jimmy replied, "We never spoke of the serious doubts you wrote me about. They don't have to be serious, dear, all it takes is a scruple."

Button replied, "Jimmy, I can't even think about 'July' I'm so scattered . . . I just can't do anything to disturb your marvelous feelings and that moment just before going to bed with you is going to be a dilly— I'll scream and giggle and hide my head up my ass and take baths and try to get it up and I won't be able to and I—oh you're my favorite, you adorable boy, and I just can't face you when I'm all undressed. // Please don't ever stop loving me. I couldn't bear that any more than I could go on if God's beautiful sky stopped being."

John Button and Frank came out to Southampton on July 11 and stayed three days at Larry Rivers's house, really to see Jimmy. One night Jimmy stayed up late with Frank, talking over the whole dilemma with him, "the most marvelous devil's advocate a chap could ask for." But apparently the long-anticipated consummation of the affair was not a roaring success, judging from Jimmy's comments in his next letter to John: "I feel so certain I could make you happy; sex, too (that was the one thing I shut Frank up about: he just doesn't know. Why shouldn't people who're in love be cockshy and virginal? That's the way love is for people who are shy about their deep feelings. I can't tell you how strange it made me feel to walk into that room and see you all naked—it was so personal!)"

From the city, Button and O'Hara wrote a very silly and camp collaborative letter to Schuyler. Jimmy's reply treads a fine line between responding in kind to their flights of extravagance and actual mania: "No matter what I manage to tell you, it won't be the right things—and I'll leave out all the connection—and forget that if I say *this* it won't make sense because you don't know that—besides, you're not an Aztec, why should you want a bloody heart dropped in your lap? 'For heavens' sake stop hacking at yourself or we'll never get to the movie . . .'"

Jimmy's state of mind was beginning to affect him physically: one minute a sense of surplus energy, the next: "I feel like a dirigible made of solid platinum all coated with Van Dyke brown." Waking up disoriented in the night to use the bathroom, he took the wrong door and fell down the back stairs, scraping the skin off his thigh and hurting his ankle.

On the evening of July 20, Jimmy confronted Gold about his unhappiness in their relationship, and told him that he was going to go back to New York. He didn't bring his feelings for Button into it, but wrote to Button, "There's been a real estrangement between us for a long time. If Arthur's upset, he's also relieved. We haven't said we're breaking up, though that in effect is what it is. I feel distressed, but greater than my distress is my certainty that I'm doing the right thing." He then wrote to Frank, asking if he could come back to Forty-ninth Street to live again. Frank's answer was instantaneous and encouraging: "Just received your letter a few minutes ago and, although I haven't had time to reflect, I thought I'd write right away to say YEZ! come!"

Jimmy returned to Forty-ninth Street on July 29, getting a ride with Larry Rivers. They arrived at an inauspicious moment, however, and found Frank in desperate straits. He had just heard that his friend Bunny Lang died unexpectedly in Boston from Hodgkin's disease, and he was nearly hysterical from grief. Jimmy had been anticipating unburdening himself to a sympathetic ear, and instead it was he who had to do the commiserating: "Frank cried and cried. Frank cried for weeks."

Over the next two weeks, things went from bad to worse. On August 7, John Latouche died after falling down the stairs at his farmhouse in Vermont. The following weekend, hoping to get away from so much sadness and anxiety, Jimmy and Frank went to stay with Morris Golde on Fire Island. Golde was a genial gay businessman, a friend and supporter to his many poet, artist, and musician friends, who regularly gave big lively parties in his garden apartment in the Village. His beach house was located in the small community of Water Island, at the isolated eastern end of Fire Island. The day after they got there, after a night of heavy drinking, Jimmy began to suffer an extreme anxiety attack, feeling as though his head was "full of gas." Golde managed to get him some tranquilizers and Jimmy retreated to the bedroom and didn't emerge for the rest of the visit, while Frank brought meals in to him and "took care of him like a twenty-four-hour nurse."

Sunday morning brought still more bad news, when the front page of *The New York Times* carried a report of the death of Jackson Pollock in a car accident on Long Island the previous evening. As soon as Jimmy got back to the city that Sunday, he called his old friend David Protetch, who was able to get him some more powerful tranquilizers. Both O'Hara and Button urged him to seek psychiatric help, which he soon did.

With Joe LeSueur away in California for the summer, Frank was glad to have company on Forty-ninth Street. Jimmy also resumed his old job at the Periscope-Holliday Bookshop for three or four weeks, ending when LeSueur returned in mid-October.

During the busy months of August and September, while Jimmy was both reviewing and working at the bookstore, his emotional life was also quite complex. He had begun seeing a psychiatrist regularly; was dealing with Frank's swings of emotion; disentangling his life from that of Arthur Gold, who was baffled and hurt by their abrupt breakup; fending off a series of epistolary declarations of love from Fairfield Porter, while striving to maintain a close friendship with him; and, not least, trying to get his love affair with John Button, in which he had invested so much hope and expectation over the previous several months, off the ground.

At a moment when his optimism was cresting, Jimmy wrote an enthusiastic letter to John Ashbery in Paris, announcing his newfound happiness with Button. This was the first inkling Ashbery had of Jimmy's love for Button and the news struck him as "quite strange," since Jimmy and Button had, as far as he knew, simply been friends for some time already, and the letter itself sounded to him to be "totally manic." Nonetheless, he replied, "I am thrilled and delighted. When two people one loves fall in love it makes one feel all warm and good inside. However I must say that it struck me with the unexpected force of an I. Compton-Burnett denouement, when couples who have barely exchanged three words during the course of the book suddenly appear and announce their engagement."

But by the end of August, it was clear that the relationship was not working out, and on September 2, Jimmy called a halt to a love affair that had never really begun, writing, "Your physical rejection of me is too wounding and continuous for me to bear it. (The serious things in life are almost always funny: you made a movement of withdrawal from me in bed this morning that so angered and hurt me that I would have gotten up and dressed and left—except I was feeling too dopey from my sleeping pill to be bothered.)" Nonetheless, after a short cooling-off period, they remained friends to the end of Button's life.

Jimmy's new psychiatrist, Dr. Frederick Loomis, was apparently the first psychiatrist he had seen with any regularity outside of a hospital. As he wrote to his mother in November, "Since last September I have been in psychoanalysis. Now that I am in it, I can see that it would have helped me a lot had I tried it sooner. Live and learn!. Psychoanalysis, like quite a few other things in life, is not exactly free. In a very real sense, 'it costs as much as you think it costs.' It also costs cash." In a letter to Kenneth Koch that fall, Jimmy gave a jocular impression of his sessions with Dr. Loomis: "How shy one is, so earnest to please and delight; one's little winning ways and gaucheries . . . Perhaps I will become heterosexual like the French! Or multi-faceted, like a rose!"

To John Ashbery, Jimmy characterized his sessions with Dr. Loomis as the high point in an otherwise dreary period. As part of his new regime, he gave up both drinking and casual sex. It is not clear how long this period of sobriety lasted—probably not very long. Still, his acknowledgment of a drinking problem was important and prescient. Excessive drinking was ubiquitous in the social life of his poet and artist friends, so it had been all too easy to overlook what would continue to be an issue in Jimmy's life.

August did bring one piece of good news, when Jimmy learned that Harcourt Brace had formally accepted the revisions of his novel *Alfred and Guinevere* and offered him a contract. Over lunch to discuss the terms, his new editor, Dan Wickenden, also suggested that the book be illustrated to make it "more of a package." Jimmy was initially appalled at the idea, but agreed in the end, and went so far as to suggest possible artists. As a first novel, and a very short one, the advance offered was "piteously little."

In mid-October, Joe LeSueur returned from California, and the living situation at 326 East Forty-ninth Street grew difficult. The apartment had two bedrooms, but the one that had originally been Jimmy's, later LeSueur's, and was now Jimmy's again, was quite small. When Jimmy invited himself back at the end of July and obliviously moved back into his old room, it meant that LeSueur, on his return, was relegated to sharing Frank's room (and bed).

The cramped conditions were bad enough, but worse was Jimmy's morose behavior. With the dashing of his hopes for a satisfying relationship with Button, coupled with the realization that he could no longer rely on Gold's emotional and financial support, Jimmy sank into depression. According to LeSueur, Jimmy was no longer the "warm, witty, immensely attractive person he was when I first knew him in 1952 . . . He was now more dead than alive." In his depression, Jimmy spent much of the time sleeping, which created a "dispiriting atmosphere." He developed a passion for buttermilk, leaving "empty, buttermilk-encrusted glasses" around the apartment for LeSueur to pick up. Worst of all were the "black looks" he gave to LeSueur and Frank: "chilling" and "demonic" stares that made them feel almost as though he wanted to kill them. "And perhaps he did."

Years later Jimmy himself recognized some of the difficulties of the situation. "As soon as I found a psychoanalyst I sort of fell apart, and that, I think, began to put pressure on Frank that he found very hard to take. I mean he'd come home and I'd be, you know, in a hot tub or I'd be in bed or something . . . There was a great deal of tension between Joe and myself, and Frank sort of kept out of it and said, 'As far as I'm concerned, this is between the two of you.' The idea being that somebody had to go. Well I had no place to go except that apartment, and even though it would have been perhaps the right thing for me to leave, I mean where was I to leave to?"

This was Frank's and his friends' first direct experience of one of Jimmy's serious bouts of mental illness and they had no precedents for dealing with it. Both Joe and Frank noticed that along with Jimmy's apparent depression, which was expressed passively (or passive-aggressively), there were also more alarming symptoms: the hostile stares described by LeSueur and a "liberated aggressiveness" that Frank noted in a nuanced letter to Kenneth at this time, which ended, "I am clinging to my self-interest like Ishmael to his spar."

Finally, what had become an impossible situation came to a head one Sunday afternoon early in January 1957, while Jimmy was napping, as usual, and Joe said to Frank, "mildly, keeping my voice down, 'I don't think three people can live together . . . I think I'd better get a place of my own.' Frank said, 'Don't leave without me.'" They took the first place that was offered to them, a cold-water third-floor apartment at 90 University Place, near Twelfth Street, and moved out in mid-January, leaving Jimmy alone on Forty-ninth.

[12]

YOU SEE ALL THESE FRUSTRATING THINGS HAPPEN

1957–1960

A week into the new year, Frank and Joe started moving their things to University Place. It seemed the only solution to what had become an untenable living situation, but no one was happy about it. Joe and Frank resented leaving Forty-ninth Street, while for the introverted Jimmy, their moving out meant the loss of something rare: "And then it was my turn to cry a great deal, because I was profoundly attached to Frank, and that was really the end of my close friendship with Frank. We were always friends but it was never the same again."

For years afterward Jimmy blamed LeSueur for taking Frank away from him, but in time he came to accept that Joe "had not done anything mean towards me; he had as much claim on Frank as I did; he had as much claim on the apartment as I did . . . At the same time, it was Joe that [Frank] was really fondest of." Others, including O'Hara's old friend Larry Osgood and even LeSueur to some degree, were surprised at O'Hara's alacrity in dropping Schuyler at a time when he was clearly ill. As LeSueur wrote, "Frank was capable of great compassion, he was very good in an emergency, you couldn't find a better friend. But if someone went off the deep end, his gift of sympathy went out the window . . . Frank couldn't get away from Jimmy fast enough." Osgood "had the feeling, and I think it was shared with some others, that Frank just deserted him, you know, did not do much to help him at that point. And

I frankly held that against Frank." Jimmy himself, in hindsight, felt that Frank's distancing himself had a lot to do with his own fear and mistrust of mental illness and psychoanalysis.

Their departure was hard for Jimmy, but as in other episodes of anxiety and setback, he found himself at first unable to fully take it in. Writing to Kenneth in mid-January, he had nothing to say about the change in circumstances. He wrote primarily, it is true, to send his condolences on hearing the news that Janice Koch suffered a miscarriage in Florence in December. "Your December news made me cry," he wrote, itself an indication of his fragile condition.

In fact, it would seem that the shock of Frank and Joe's departure jolted Jimmy, at least partly, out of the funk of lethargy and self-pity he had been in—that combined perhaps with a certain sense of relief. After all, the bad vibes that had been emanating so strongly from him in the past two or three months would have been reflected back in feelings of resentment and anger coming from Frank and Joe, and now that destructive circular dynamic was cut. His continuing work with Dr. Loomis may have helped him to take himself in hand to some degree.

He had plenty to keep him busy, including a full schedule of reviewing for *Art News*. He also spent the early months of 1957 refining his revision of *Alfred and Guinevere*. His editor had suggested that the book be extended with an additional chapter to give it a more dramatic or conclusive ending, but Schuyler disagreed: "By that point, the story has either made its effect or it has not . . . part of the pleasure of a short work is its brevity." He also declined to take up a suggestion that the ages of the children and the location and year of the story be specified.

Jimmy clearly enjoyed the challenge of writing in the voice of a child, and further exercised his gift that April with "Current Events," a short story narrated by a boy of about thirteen. The story takes the form of the unnamed boy's report on his eighth-grade class field trip to the state capitol. The perfectly judged tone of overwritten ingenuousness, with the occasional charmingly skewed syntax, very much reminiscent of certain articles in his own high school newspaper, is a marvel of creating and inhabiting a character solely through a written voice.

By now, Jimmy's love for John Button had resolved into a comfortable friendship, characterized by many evenings spent quietly watching old movies on television in Button's apartment. Button, one of the few of the group who had a TV in 1957, regularly hosted viewings of such classic Hollywood films as *Grand Hotel*, *Dinner at Eight*, and *Trouble in Paradise*, or lesser ones starring Kay Francis, Alice Faye, and other beloved actresses, movies that had been relatively inaccessible since their initial release in the '30s but were now being broadcast on television. At the same time, Schuyler was seeing a lot of Button's ex, Alvin Novak, who had moved to Hoboken, New Jersey. Jimmy especially enjoyed riding the ferry across the Hudson to visit him there, taking in the view of lower Manhattan from the boat and then the views of the Hudson from Novak's apartment, or walking along the waterfront and eating at a clam house there.

In addition to reviews and "Current Events," in the spring of 1957 Jimmy wrote a number of significant poems, including three with musical references, "Hoboken," "Hudson Ferry," and "Rachmaninoff's Third," that reflect to some degree Jimmy's friendship with Novak, who was a pianist. In both "Hoboken," dedicated to Novak, and "Hudson Ferry," Jimmy includes images of his ferry trips across the Hudson, of Hoboken itself, and of Novak's loft, with its view of "the Hudson instead of a pet dog / instead of a yard." The nominal subject of "Hoboken" (published in the chapbook *May 24th or So*, and in a variant version, "So That's Why," in *Other Flowers*) is Novak's playing of Chopin, but the overriding subject of both poems is the elusiveness of everyday experience, and the impossibility—or possibility—of "capturing" it in poetry, when the very words for things are secondhand or come with baggage of preconceived associations. In "Hudson Ferry," Schuyler writes, "you can't talk about the weather / it's like saying my lady's damask cheek." In "Hoboken," even the word *Chopin* is off limits: "you can't just say / Chopin / and leave it in the air / like an unfrosted Mazda light bulb / burning: someone will want to put a muffler / around it or a pleated paper shade." Even harder to attain is the quality of undistracted attention required to write—lack of which, or the distractions themselves, then become the subject (as in "February"). "Hoboken" begins:

I was going to write you a poem
about Hoboken and you playing Chopin
but I can't write it now

you see all these frustrating things happen

I know exactly how I felt
how the poem felt when I was going to write it
you know, that was when I should've

today—look at it—
it might as well be L. A.
with smog off the cold Pacific

but that posthumous étude!

Like "Salute," "Hoboken" is about a poem (a gathering) that was never written (never made), but which becomes, *faute de mieux,* the poem we are reading. The seeming impossibility of a "pure" response to experience, unmediated by language even as it is transmitted through language, makes Schuyler look deeper and more closely both at external events, and the tides and eddies of his own consciousness. As he writes in "Hudson Ferry," "you can't get at a sunset naming colors / the depth the change the charge deep out of deep / the flaring upward what it nails on houses . . ."

"Rachmaninoff's Third" (dated April 2, 1957, on the typescript) is dedicated to Frank O'Hara. Socially, there was no overt break right after Frank moved out, and to the degree that there were some feelings of constraint, the poem could be considered a sort of peace offering (a successful one, if so, for they visited the Porters in Southampton together one weekend later that month). The original title, "Radio's Oldest," suggests that he happened to hear Rachmaninoff's Third Piano Concerto, a perennial warhorse of the classical repertory, on the radio one day, and the "exorbitant intimacy" of the music reminded him of Frank and his passion for the composer. He hoped somewhere he, too, was "listening / to your city station" at the same time, along with the "8 million" other inhabitants of New York, "living in harmony" with the music. An interest in radio as a communal flow of information is a minor theme through Jimmy's poetry, while the collage aspect of the poem points back to work of a few years earlier. The closing lines (lacking full stop): "We'll shoot the rapids / on Rogue River / before they build that dam," while not necessarily addressed to O'Hara, imply, if taken with the dedication, a poignant hope for future adventures with him.

The way the broken-up lines of "Rachmaninoff's Third" are spaced and separated on alternate sides of the page could be seen as a visual reference to the dialogue between piano and orchestra of a piano concerto:

a moment and
                        over and with
the picking strings
                            Horowitz enters
accurate and fully
                            singing

The format relates more directly, however, to Charles Olson's ideas of "Projective Verse," which had been brought to Jimmy's attention through correspondence that spring with John Wieners. Wieners had decided to publish a small literary magazine, *Measure*, and in March or early April got in touch with Jimmy and Frank for contributions. Over the next months, Jimmy sent him at least twelve recent poems, which Wieners commented on in some detail in letters in April and June. Of "Hoboken," for example, Wieners wrote, "And one *can* say / Chopin / and leave it in the air. Dont make doilies for yr hard chair, or cushions. Give it to us hard . . . There is enough breakthrough there, that shd keep you working until 1960. Form-wise . . . Letting the image set in the word said."

In his comments, Wieners referred to his former teacher's ideas about the importance of "breath" in poetry, specifically in determining line breaks, and in composition by "field," spreading words across the entire page, rather than using traditionally measured lines and stanzas. While in later years, Schuyler dismissed the idea that he was influenced by Olson's theories about "breath" per se (or his poetry), he did acknowledge that the open arrangement of lines across the page in works of 1957–59 was influenced by Wieners's suggestion that he "try using that field that he used."

Olson's essay makes connections between composition by "field," musical notation, and typing. Because of the inherent constrictions of the typewriter, he writes, "For the first time the poet has had the stave and the bar a musician has had . . . he can, without the convention of rime and meter, record the listening he has done to his own speech." Whatever Jimmy may have thought about Olson, he would have responded to the notion of writing poetry as a form of "listening," and the typed sheet viewed in relation to musical notation. Jimmy was an expert typist, composed on the typewriter as often as not, and the concept of the poem as a physical, typographic object had long been a given for him. Schuyler also acknowledged Mallarmé's typographically dispersed poem "Un Coup de Dés," first published in English in the final issue of *Folder* in 1956, as an influence on these poems.

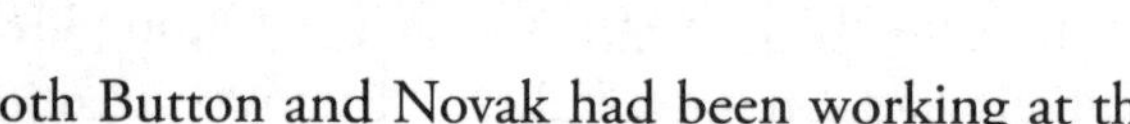

Both Button and Novak had been working at the ticket counter at the Museum of Modern Art since the previous year, and they had been encouraging Schuyler to join them there. Finally he applied and was hired, starting in about May 1957.

The museum then was much smaller and more familial than the large corporate enterprise it was to become. It was also open seven days a week, and at first Jimmy worked a six-day week, including Sundays, which left him only one day to visit galleries and write his reviews. Working at the front desk were about ten employees who rotated shifts, so that five or six would be on duty at any given time. With Button and Novak working there too, O'Hara dropping in regularly from the administrative offices, and various friends stopping by all day, the lobby of MoMA became in effect an extension of the New York School. As Novak recalled, "We used it as our social playground." Jeanne Keyes Youngson, a young woman who worked at the front desk from 1951 to 1958, also remembered her years there as hugely enjoyable because of the laughter and camaraderie of the poets and painters she befriended on the job and others who would visit: Fairfield Porter, who was there "half the time," and Larry Rivers, "more than half the time," Arnold Weinstein, "full of life and vim and vigor," handsome Joe LeSueur, Edward Gorey in his "rat fur" coat, rings, and sneakers, who often came to see the movies downstairs, and Grace Hartigan, who grew jealous of Youngson's friendship with O'Hara. To Youngson, Jimmy was someone who "if he liked you he would warm up to you immediately, I mean it was like you had been friends forever."

Working there also, of course, gave Jimmy and his friends the opportunity to immerse themselves in the collection on their breaks, or watch the movies being screened there daily. You could run down to the auditorium on break and see twenty minutes of whatever movie was playing, and go back at different times over the next few days so that eventually you saw the whole film.

Jimmy's regular job at the museum helped ease the loneliness he felt after O'Hara left Forty-ninth Street. In time, however, his attitude to the job grew a bit casual, and he was frequently absent or late. When he was, Novak and the others "tried to cover for him as much as possible. But it was so amusing the way he would treat it . . . he was so 'above it' somehow . . . it was funny how he *couldn't* come into work. And it just didn't occur to us that there was something seriously wrong, because he had this wonderful amusing and detached way: 'God knows, I *tried* to get out of bed, but . . . it just wasn't possible. And, darling, if you do come to visit, would you bring me a cherry Coke?'"

The summer of 1957, the first since his split from both Gold and O'Hara, and the different social scenes they had each provided, was not a very happy one for Jimmy. Even going out to Water Mill to visit Jane Freilicher and Joe Hazan, who were renting a house there, or to see other friends in the country, was impossible due to his work schedule. "Everyone except one is in the Hamptons this summer," Jimmy complained to John.

He could look forward to John's return from France at the end of August to stay with him, and in anticipation, he took some time to spruce up the perennially shabby Forty-ninth Street apartment, going so far as to paint the living room and the bathroom. John arrived on September 2, 1957, his two-year Fulbright Fellowship having expired, and stayed on Forty-ninth Street for a few days before going to visit his parents on their fruit farm in upstate New York. He had decided to get a graduate degree in French from NYU, and when he returned from upstate later that month, he lived with Jimmy on Forty-ninth Street until about June of the following year, dividing his time between taking courses downtown and teaching elementary French at New York University's campus in the Bronx.

During his time on Forty-ninth Street, John observed only a few, far milder symptoms of the depressive behavior that had so disturbed Frank and Joe LeSueur ten months earlier. He did notice that Jimmy was smoking too much, and in his mild way he wrote him from his parents' house: "I hope you are feeling OK and that your nerves are better. Did you ever think of cutting out smoking?" Other than his increased smoking, and a reluctance to get up in the morning to go to work, Jimmy's lingering depression simply "took often the form of his kind of withdrawing" from social activity.

Starting in about November, John, at Jimmy's suggestion ("It's really very easy!"), began his own stint of writing reviews for *Art News*. They also managed to do some work on *A Nest of Ninnies* at this time, and they visited the Porters in Southampton together, where Fairfield painted a double portrait of them, looking pensive as though paused in their collaborative endeavor: Jimmy sitting on a flower-patterned sofa, in profile with his left hand up to his face, and John on a chair in front of him to his right, facing forward but a little askance, with arms crossed.

During the previous year in Paris, John had fallen in love with and begun living with Pierre Martory, a poet, novelist, and journalist for *Le Monde Diplomatique*. In April 1958, on the way back from an assignment in Puerto Rico, Pierre stopped over in New York to stay with John and Jimmy on Forty-ninth Street for about a week. Jimmy became very fond of Pierre, and greatly enjoyed his lively wit and conversation peppered with amusing Franglais. But John and Pierre understandably tended to keep to themselves, which reawakened anxieties for Jimmy. At night, the lovers could sometimes hear him sobbing violently in the next room. John attributed these crying jags to Jimmy's feeling "sort of excluded" from their relationship. At that point it was assumed that John would complete his degree and continue to live in New York indefinitely, and in addition to simple jealousy or feeling left out, the appearance of Pierre must have raised fears in Jimmy that the situation between him, Joe LeSueur, and Frank O'Hara was replaying itself.

On the morning of April 15, 1958, during Pierre's visit, a serious fire broke out at the Museum of Modern Art—"one of the most horrible events in the life of anyone connected with the museum," Jimmy recalled. The fire started in the early morning before the museum was open. Jeanne Keyes Youngson first heard the news on the radio as she was getting ready to go to work, and turned on the television to see a friend of hers carrying Monet's *Water Lilies* out of the building. Later that day, John and Pierre happened to be walking up Fifth Avenue when they were startled by a huge number of fire engines "clanging by," and wondered where the fire was. When they got to Fifty-third Street, they saw that it was the museum. The sight of "flames shooting out of MoMA" was horrifying and "really surreal."

Jimmy got there that morning to find the fire mostly extinguished but a hectic rescue effort under way, as employees rushed to remove paintings from the galleries before they were damaged by smoke or water. As mere front-desk employees, Schuyler, Button, and Novak weren't allowed to go up into the galleries and help carry down paintings. "I only saved the money," Jimmy joked. A major Georges Seurat exhibition was in the museum at the time, with many important inter-museum loans, including *La Grande Jatte* from the Art Institute of Chicago—the sole time that it would ever be lent. *La Grande Jatte* barely escaped destruction when firemen's axes crashed through the wall it was hanging on from behind, just missing the painting. Most of the paintings survived, but one of the Monet *Water Lilies* was lost to smoke damage, and Larry Rivers's *Washington Crossing the Delaware* was also badly damaged. One workman died from smoke inhalation.

The museum was closed to the public for about seven months. For the first few days after the fire, Jimmy made himself useful doing "some rather random jobs, like sweeping up broken glass in the Department of Architecture," but shortly afterward, he was hired as an administrative assistant in the International Program, housed in offices down the street. Headed by Porter McCray, the International Program was a sort of unholy alliance of the Rockefeller family, the State Department, and the museum, with a mandate to promote American art and culture by organizing exhibitions and sending them to foreign countries. The corresponding Department of Circulating Exhibitions, also headed by McCray, organized exhibitions that toured in the United States. McCray was a charming West Virginian with a can-do attitude and the social skills of a diplomat who came to the Museum of Modern Art in 1947. He had a liking for Jimmy, which was reciprocated, and regularly cut him some slack during his years at the museum.

The first project Jimmy worked on in his new position was the traveling exhibition *French Drawings from American Collections*, which eventually came to the Metropolitan Museum of Art in New York in 1959. His work on this show was secretarial: filing and typing. Initially, Jimmy found the work "quite pleasant," and a refreshing change from the routine and public interactions of the front desk. But soon he was reporting to John Button, "It's fantastic how tiring these 9.30–5.30 jobs are! You just can't think. And it isn't as though it made any demands on one's *real* energies."

In the course of his visits to Alvin in Hoboken in 1957 and 1958, Jimmy became friends with his neighbor in the building, Esta Leslie, the wife of the painter Al Leslie, from whom she had recently separated. (Later they would divorce and she would marry the art critic Hilton Kramer.) Esta at this time was described as "precious," in that she had a distinctive personal style, wore lacy antique Victorian clothes, and was a wonderful and generous cook, who would bring delicious and elaborate leftover meals—"gorgeous casseroles, beautiful soufflés, blanquette de veau"—to Alvin and his friends. One of Esta's closest friends was a former art dealer named Donald Droll, and in the late spring of 1958 he and Jimmy began a love affair.

Donald Droll was born in Chicago in 1927. After graduating from Black Mountain College he came to New York in 1949, and got a job at the Charles Egan Gallery, where the year before Willem de Kooning had had his groundbreaking first solo show. When Donald and Jimmy met, he was working for a fancy Madison Avenue antique dealer and decorator, but would later return to his true calling as an insightful art dealer. Droll was good-looking in a pleasant, Midwestern way, with a sort of professional likableness, combined with a great sense of style and *savoir-faire*. He was known to be "tops in the taste department," making an art form of his living spaces, and projected an aura of stability that while possibly illusory, Schuyler would have been attracted to. He was similar in that regard to Charles Heilemann, and, as with Heilemann, his rather unemphatic personality was hard for some of Jimmy's friends to get a sense of, making the idea of them as a couple seem "very unlikely" to John Ashbery, for one. Droll himself told John he recognized there was an "evasive" aspect to his own character, an assessment with which John could not disagree.

Alfred and Guinevere finally came out in the spring of 1958, bearing a dedication to Arthur Gold. After the overlong period of rewriting and editing, its appearance could not help but feel somewhat anticlimactic for Jimmy. At the party for its publication, held in Elaine de Kooning's studio, virtually the whole of what we think of as the New York School appeared in a collaborative play, *The Coronation Murder Mystery*, written for the occasion by John Ashbery, Kenneth Koch, and Frank O'Hara.

Unfortunately, the book was not well understood. As a poet's novel, *Alfred and Guinevere* ran counter to the expectations of most fiction readers, and the misunderstanding was compounded by the line drawings by Paul Sagsoorian that illustrate it, which gave the impression that it was for rather than about children. Reviews tended to damn it with faint praise. Jane Cobb in *The New York Times Book Review* called it "an amusing book." The only meaningful review was that of Kenneth Koch in *Poetry* magazine, who wrote that the novel was not written in "poetic prose" but rather in language that has "transferred the excitements of poetry to his prose; something (witty or prosodic) is happening at every second."

Jimmy, who had somewhat naïvely hoped the book would bring in some money, was disappointed at its poor reception, and its publication came and went as unremarked-upon by him in his letters of that year as it was by the rest of the world.

John Ashbery returned to France late in June, ostensibly just for the summer, so he left most of his belongings with Jimmy on Forty-ninth Street. But in mid-September 1958, he learned that his parents had agreed to subsidize an extended stay in France so that he could continue his research there on Raymond Roussel. He had also begun to write for *Art News* and other publications as a Paris correspondent, and in the end he remained living in France with Pierre for another five years. But this would not become clear to either John or Jimmy for some time. After John left, Jimmy began living with Donald Droll in his apartment at 438 East Eighty-seventh Street, but wanting to keep the Forty-ninth Street apartment for John when he returned, he began to sublet it to a series of short-term tenants, including the former building super.

Jimmy's job at MoMA kept him in the city most of that summer, but at least now, with his Monday-to-Friday schedule, he and Donald Droll were able to make weekend visits to friends in the country, including Donald's friend Susan Weil in Connecticut, and Jane Freilicher and Joe Hazan in Water Mill. Jimmy and Donald were looking forward to renting the same house the Hazans rented when they left, until learning that the owner refused to rent to two men, prompting Jimmy to write John, "Do you suppose if I spent the entire time in drag and a simulated pregnancy we could pass?" (The painter Jane Wilson, who lived nearby with her husband, John Gruen, was pregnant that summer with their daughter, Julia.)

The museum reopened to the public on October 8 with a gala party. With the reopening, Jimmy was formally confirmed as a permanent employee in the International Program, and he began working on a survey, *Twentieth Century Italian Art from American Collections*, curated by James Thrall Soby and Frank O'Hara, for exhibition in Milan and Rome in 1960. He was greatly relieved to learn that his new status allowed him to enroll in the museum's health insurance plan, which would now pay half of his analyst's bills.

The job was flexible enough for him to be able to write poems at work from time to time. Two he identified as having been written at MoMA are "December" and "Fabergé." Titled after the Tsarist Russian jeweler famous for such uncannily realistic *objets d'art* as a sprig of lilies-of-the-valley made from pearls, gold, and jade leaning nonchalantly in a rock crystal glass of water, "Fabergé" begins, "I keep my diamond necklace in a pond of sparkling water for invisibility," and goes on to enumerate other objects of great value concealed within humble materials, or actually, within themselves, including "a rose made out of a real rose." The conceit of a "rose made out of a real rose," where the thing is identical with *itself* but at the same time somehow "made," may be broadly applied to Schuyler's work in general, anticipating the credo tucked into "The Morning of the Poem" years later: "How the thing said / Is in the words, how / The words are themselves / The thing said." As if to further this idea, the entire poem is placed between quotation marks: the poem itself made out of a "real" poem. "Fabergé" bears no dedication, but on some level its inventory of exquisite objects hiding in plain sight might be a tribute to Droll's sense of style and elegance. In the last line, the poem takes a bit of a turn and "real" emotion comes into it too: "I have nothing to cry about now I have you."

Jimmy's thirty-fifth birthday, on November 9, 1958, was celebrated with a "hearty spread" at Kenneth and Janice Koch's apartment. When the subject of his age came up, Janice laughingly quoted, "Nel mezzo del cammin" ("In the middle of [life's] journey"), the opening line of Dante's *Divine Comedy*. In fact, Jimmy would not live to the proverbial age of three score and ten; his life was already a little more than half over.

Feeling confident about the future of his relationship with Droll, Jimmy had planned to give up the lease on Forty-ninth Street at the end of February 1959. Yet the thought or the hope that Ashbery might yet return in the near future combined to keep him from finally letting go of the apartment. The situation grew more complicated in April when Jimmy received a letter from the landlord stating that the building had been sold to new owners, who intended to demolish it, and if he stayed on after his lease ran out in the fall, he would be considered a "stuatory tenant," "which doesn't sound very nice."

After the patchy summer the previous year, Jimmy and Droll decided to share a house in Southampton with the Kochs for the summer of 1959. The rental, known as the "Bungle House," included an orchard and a separate residence in a made-over barn where they would sleep. They started going out there for weekends in June, and planned to spend the whole of Jimmy's vacation there in August.

The month started out well, with Jimmy, Donald, and the Kochs enjoying what Frank O'Hara called "one of those lovely summer Ivy Compton Burnett relationships, now that they are sharing a kitchen, bath and barn." O'Hara and LeSueur were planning to come out to visit over the weekend of August 15, but a conflict arose at their end, and before a new visit could be scheduled, the idyll had broken up. On the evidence of a rambling, six-page letter that Jimmy sent in July to the painter Leland Bell, who was about to visit Europe, packed with breathless suggestions about gaining entry to private art collections in Paris and what to see in London (where he had probably never been), Jimmy was approaching a manic episode.

Droll had become disturbed and frightened by Jimmy's increasing mental instability over the summer, and also his drinking, which led on one occasion to Jimmy getting up drunkenly in the night and urinating in the corner of the room. Things came to a head over the weekend when Frank was supposed to visit, and Jimmy and Donald had a fight and broke up. They both precipitously left Southampton, leaving Kenneth liable for the remaining month's rent, which caused a slight rift between him and Jimmy for a time. Jimmy took refuge with Alvin Novak in Hoboken for the rest of August. He was bitter and defensive about being left, complaining somewhat hysterically to John, "Anyone who combines maximum frigidity with total hypocrisy laced liberally with cock-teasing and deceit is not my ideal beau." The emotional and practical repercussions of the breakup would linger for the rest of the year and well into 1960.

For the month of September, Jimmy house-sat in John Button's apartment at 28 East Second Street while Button was away on an extended trip to California. There, Jimmy took guilty pleasure in Button's television set, which he now found to be "an insomniac's torture and delight, particularly on those evenings when I found myself rushing home a little early to catch a chopped-up Laurel & Hardy or an Our Gang festival, and not winding up until the wee hours with Norma Shearer on the late-late."

While living on Second Street, Jimmy got a report from John Ashbery of seeing Gold and Fizdale several times in Paris, and their playing for him Schubert's *Grand Duo* in C major for piano four hands, opus 140. John called it "a simply staggering masterpiece . . . they play it marvelously and bring out its gigantic quality." In reply, Jimmy recalled having heard the pair play the work earlier: "It is sublime. How I envy you both," and later that day he wrote the poem "Grand Duo." Dedicated to Gold and Fizdale, it begins with imagery recollected from their trip to Austria in 1954, and moves up, down, out, and across memory, consciousness, and the page to enter into the exalted spirit of the music, without ever attempting to mimic it or be "musical" in any obvious way. Description yields to lyricism, to pedagogy, to exhortation; memory to present sensuality:

> Rain lashed the windows of a careening train.
> Tunnels,
> boulders, crevasses. Vapors and clouds parted on
> blue.
>
> *
>
> Art is formality, courtesy, passion, control, practice,
> rehearsing the unrehearsed
> art is no is
> melodiously
> repeated endlessly
> varies naturally
> Sweet basic monotone
> heavens of gray
> melt away

With Button's return from California at the beginning of October, Jimmy moved back to the now sadly abandoned and dilapidated Forty-ninth Street apartment. The building's demolition, originally scheduled for November, was repeatedly being postponed. Most of the other tenants had moved out, a dismal and depressing situation that also caused all "the roaches and silverfish [to] seek hospice in friendly apartment 37," he wrote to John. Adding to the "quite sinister" atmosphere, the street entrance to the building was chained and padlocked. One evening Schuyler accidentally locked himself out; an unhelpful locksmith sold him a hacksaw blade without the handle, with which it took him an hour and a half to saw through the chain. Although the process "made enough noise to set all Pierre Boulez's hairs aquiver," Jimmy wrote, evoking the atonal French composer, it was disconcerting that "not so much as a head peeked out" to see what was going on. He seems to have been unable to take decisive action to find a new apartment—a kind of paralysis in the face of necessity.

Reading remained a refuge. In November, Jimmy sent John his new poem, "Money Musk," inspired by some of his current reading, eclectic as always, and dedicated to Janice Koch in recognition of her Midwestern background. Literary references focusing on the Midwest include Hamlin Garland's memoirs, William Dean Howells, Theodore Dreiser, the historian Henry B. Fuller, and Willa Cather, but there are also classic mystery writers and characters: Tod Claymore, Gideon Fell, Miss Marple, Sherlock Holmes and Dr. Watson. The welter of names become ciphers standing for content the reader can grasp only imperfectly, not resolving into anything definite, other than "a dream of the great Midwest," as the poem puts it. John Ashbery found the poem "simply marvelous," and compared it to "eating one's way through a box of Whitman's Sampler chocolates with no diagram to tell you what the fillings are—some of the names in your poem are hard, others creamy, chewy, bitter-sweet, peanut, etc. . . ."

A love of evocative, odd names was a shared interest of John and Jimmy, who invariably used humorous pseudonyms in writing to each other: an ongoing roster of temporary camp names borrowed from obscure actors, writers, public figures, or even concepts. Written that same month, "Alice Faye at Ruby Foo's" recalls Jimmy's 1941 Christmas in New York at the beginning of the war, when he saw, or thought he saw, the '30s movie star Alice Faye eating in a Chinese restaurant in Times Square. The memory is presented elliptically, leaving the impression that what the poem is mostly "about" is the dissonant euphony of the conjoined names, Alice Faye and Ruby Foo.

By now, the poets were beginning to be recognized as, if not a "school," a distinct if loosely associated group, and various projects came to fruition at the end of the 1950s and start of the new decade that seemed to confirm this.

The most influential was the anthology *The New American Poetry*, edited by Donald Allen and published by Grove Press in 1960. The book brought together and sought to identify and differentiate various, sometimes overlapping, strands of postwar American poetry, including the Beats and the Black Mountain poets and the New York School poets. Under the latter rubric (called by Allen simply the "New York Poets") were grouped the expected Ashbery, Guest, Koch, O'Hara, and Schuyler, with the addition of Edward Field. The book confirmed and to a degree codified what was already clear but not widely recognized: the existence of a lively new kind of postwar American poetic energy, transcending to some degree regional and stylistic differences. Most of Allen's "new" poets were born in the 1920s or '30s, but the book did include a few older figures, including Charles Olson, by implication the spiritual father of the trends that Allen posits. The book was in part intended as a challenge to the 1957 anthology *New Poets of England and America*, edited by Donald Hall, whose American selection presented a completely different group of poets of the same generation, writing in more traditional forms, including James Merrill, Richard Wilbur, Anthony Hecht, John Hollander, W. S. Merwin, Adrienne Rich, James Wright, and others.

Schuyler is represented by four poems and his essay on poetics, "Poet and Painter Overture." The jacket copy of *The New American Poetry* makes comparisons among Abstract Expressionist painting, jazz, and American postwar poetry; Schuyler's essay goes further, describing the New York poets as working in a kind of symbiotic relationship to the New York painters. The essay ends: "Of course the father of poetry is poetry, and everybody goes to concerts when there are any: but if you try to derive a strictly literary ancestry for New York poetry, the main connection gets missed." The anthology was widely reviewed, including on the front page of the *New York Herald Tribune* by Marianne Moore, who included Schuyler among the handful of poets she singled out for praise, and quoted from no fewer than three of his poems—"Salute," "February," and "Freely Espousing"—an extraordinary distinction considering that the book included some 209 poems.

In 1959, John and Kenneth encouraged John's friend Harry Mathews to underwrite the publication of a new literary magazine, which they would call *Locus Solus* after one of Raymond Roussel's novels. Mathews was an American poet and novelist who lived most of the year in Paris, where he gained the distinction of being the only American included in the French avant-garde literary group *Oulipo*, whose patron saint, as it were, was Roussel. Mathews had recently inherited $20,000, and decided to invest about a quarter of it in starting *Locus Solus*. Jimmy was invited to be the fourth editorial partner on the basis of John's and Kenneth's enthusiastic recommendations. The idea was that the three poets would take turns editing each issue, and they decided that the first was to be edited by Schuyler, in part because (as Mathews later put it) "he was less severe than Kenneth, and less affected by sometimes imaginary courtesies that John felt toward other writers."

The project coincided with a period of intermittent emotional instability for Jimmy, however, which made for some awkward interactions between him and Frank and Kenneth. Frank made some rather pointed complaints to John and Kenneth about some of the work that Jimmy wanted to include in his issue, citing a bias toward what he called "Chelsea," meaning Rudy and Edith Burckhardt and Edwin Denby, who all lived in lofts in that neighborhood. In the end, a play by Rudy and poems by Denby did make the cut, but a story by Edith did not.

The first issue of *Locus Solus*, dated "Winter, 1961," was released at the end of 1960 and also included poems by Kenneth, John, Frank, Barbara Guest, and Anne Porter, along with two California poets (also included in *The New American Poetry*), Ebbe Borregaard and Robin Blaser, in order, as Jimmy put it in a letter to Blaser, "to leaven the New York School in-group." Jimmy's own contribution was his story "Current Events." The story was met with universal delight, and in March 1961, it was awarded a prize of $300, one of forty given annually by the Longview Foundation for literature published in "little" magazines. In 1962, Jason Epstein at Random House offered to publish a "book of sketches similar" to "Current Events" if he should write more of them. Unfortunately, Jimmy never did.

In 1960, when Barbara's chapbook *The Location of Things* was published by Tibor de Nagy, Jimmy became the only one of the five New York poets who had not yet published a solo book of poems. This situation would be remedied in 1961 when the Tiber Press—the partnership of the poet Daisy Aldan, her husband, Richard Miller, and his lover Floriano Vecchi that had put out the four issues of *Folder* in the mid-'50s—published a beautiful and ambitious suite of four oversized *livres d'artistes* by Ashbery, Koch, O'Hara, and Schuyler, each illustrated with color serigraphs by one of their abstract painter friends: Joan Mitchell with Ashbery, Al Leslie with Koch, Michael Goldberg with O'Hara, and Grace Hartigan with Schuyler.

Hartigan recalled that "the poets were assigned to the painters, almost, by Floriano," and she was happy to be paired with Jimmy, whom she had known since 1952. The artist/poet teams did not collaborate directly: in Schuyler's case, the poems were written independently, and a few had already been published. Hartigan recalled, "I did the prints, and I didn't do them in relationship to any poems. I just did what I was doing then." The result was a landmark in artists' book production, combining beautiful design and fine printing with contemporary art and poetry. The decision to present the poets in the context of Abstract Expressionism (of the so-called second generation) rather than, say, realist work by Freilicher, Rivers, or Porter, was smart, serving to emphasize qualities of improvisation and open-endedness in the poetry over descriptive or "personal" concerns. The addition of Barbara Guest would have reinforced these connections and it was unfortunate that she was not included.

The four volumes (each measuring almost 18 x 15 inches) were cozily encased together in one slipcase, issued in an edition of 225 copies, signed by the artists and the poets, and priced at $300. Because this put his first book of poems effectively out of reach of most readers, Jimmy reprinted most of his poems in later books.

Fairfield Porter reviewed the set in the September-October 1961 issue of *Evergreen Review*, questioning (typically) the basic premise—"One wonders about the whole series, is this done for the artists' or the poets' sake? Do the prints enhance the poems, or the poems glamorize the prints?"—but making astute observations about all eight artists and poets and their works' interactions on the page. Jimmy's fifteen poems, which take up noticeably less space (and fewer pages) than the others, were described by Fairfield as "contemplative and compressed." He adds, subtly conflating Rimbaud's famous dictum "I is another" with Schuyler's poem

"Fabergé": "Even when he says 'I,' the 'I' is a third person, as though he were invisible in the presence of his object."

Jimmy was having a hard time resigning himself to the finality of his breakup with Donald Droll, and there were occasions when they met socially, when he put Droll under some emotional pressure to reconcile. This had the contrary effect of making Droll even more leery of becoming involved again. One night toward the end of December 1959, Schuyler went out first with Droll for a drink, followed by dinner with Edwin Denby. "The more things change," he noted ruefully to John Ashbery. "Although I think it is most unwise of me to keep seeing D., since he quite plainly doesn't want to go to bed with me and this causes me to go home and cry or else fret furiously. The mere mention of his name is enough to make my analyst turn to stone."

Forty-ninth Street had become virtually uninhabitable, but Jimmy seemed unable to overcome his apathy and depression to do anything about it. Finally Fairfield Porter provided the solution. For the past two years, Fairfield had been renting an apartment on the Lower East Side at 500 East Eleventh Street, to use when he came to the city, and which he was now sharing with his son Jerry, who had run away from boarding school. When early in 1960 he learned that the painter Philip Pearlstein and his wife were moving out of their apartment at 181 Avenue A, across the street from his own apartment, Fairfield arranged for Jimmy to take it over. On March 1, 1960, he moved in.

[13]

NOW AND THEN A HUMAN BEING

1960–1962

One Eighty-One Avenue A had been built as a typical tenement of four or five stories, but after a fire some years earlier the upper floors had been removed, leaving only the commercial ground floor and the floor above, which had been converted into an open loft with its own street entrance and stairway. The space was long and narrow: about 50 feet deep by 15 feet wide, with the kitchen at the back. The question of John Ashbery's return from France and the disposition of his belongings was still up in the air, so Jimmy took anything of value (books, records, artworks) with him to Avenue A, but left furniture and much else behind.

Now that they were close neighbors, Jimmy's friendship with Fairfield entered a new phase. To be sure, Jimmy had always stayed friendly with Fairfield during the four years since his epistolary declaration of love, visiting him and Anne in Southampton and remaining very much engaged with his life, work, exhibitions, and family. But Jimmy's move downtown changed the equation, coinciding as it did with his increasing neediness. Having rescued Jimmy from a situation that he had appeared incapable of solving by himself, Fairfield now took on a certain degree of responsibility for him.

If Jimmy was needy in practical ways, Fairfield was in his own way emotionally needy. In a letter to Jimmy written in early July 1960, Fairfield confided his feelings of dissatisfaction with his recent painting, which he says is "bad like me. My badness consists of a lack of courage . . . all is muddiness, and muddier and muddier the more I adjust . . . I have to be open to discovery, and also I have to be able to distinguish *before* the discoveries are made, between genuine and false ones." The letter also enclosed a mildly homoerotic poem, "The Young Man," which he says recalls his first meeting with John Ashbery in 1952, and Fairfield asks, "Do you think it is too homosexual?" The conjunction of the two seemingly unrelated topics suggests an unspoken question: whether Fairfield's homosexual urges may be a "genuine" or a "false" discovery, and whether to deny them is due to "a lack of courage" or makes him a bad person. Jimmy's reply, written the following day, does not acknowledge such a reading, but instead seems designed to counter his self-absorption with a series of sharp admonitions, almost veering into the kind of "megalomania" Frank O'Hara would soon experience from Jimmy: "An easy way of getting in touch with me, when you are in town, is simply to slip a note through the slot of my door & say when & where I may be able to call you. Also, you can always write to me at the Museum . . . Mr. James Schuyler / Guest Director / Department of Circulating Exhibitions . . ." He added, "Ask Anne if she thinks you are 'bad' . . . You try to get too much done. Stop barking & acting like a terrible tempered Mr. Bang [?] & enjoy your family & friends."

Jimmy's letter also included very specific suggestions, not to say commands, concerning such things as the fencing in the yard at 49 South Main Street, and the location of the trash incinerator, almost as though he were claiming a place in the household. Yet in reply, Fairfield, rather than showing offense, saw nothing odd in Jimmy's bossiness, but instead claimed to like it, telling him, "I love to get an advice filled letter from you . . . I will consider it all quite seriously."

Soon after moving downtown, Jimmy met Fairfield's friend the painter Bob Dash, who had shared a studio with Fairfield on Fourteenth Street for a while and now lived nearby. Dash was born in New York City in 1934 and went to the University of New Mexico, where he wrote poetry and was the editor of the literary magazine. On moving to New York, he wrote reviews for *Arts* magazine and *Art News*, where he met Fairfield as a fellow reviewer. Fairfield encouraged his return to his earlier avocation of painting, and he had his first gallery exhibition in 1960.

Dash had a kind of insouciant, self-conscious brilliance that Jimmy increasingly came to enjoy and value. He was well-read in the kinds of literary byways Jimmy himself most enjoyed; he had studied the piano as a youth and was knowledgeable about music; his paintings, landscapes, and interiors, in the Porter manner, were serious and good; and he was always ready with amusing, highly opinionated, and intelligent talk, delivered in a quasi-British intonation, acquired, he claimed, from schooling in England. On Dash's side, he felt an instant rapport with Jimmy, whom he came to regard as a kind of "brother," despite the difficulties of social engagement with him during times of intermittent mental illness. If there were painful evenings when he might sit unresponsively and not say anything at all, at other times his remarks were expressed so beautifully and had such thought behind them that each was treasured.

Schuyler's poem "An East Window on Elizabeth Street," dedicated to Dash, was written in Dash's apartment one day while he was out, and is on one hand a quintessential Schuyler poem of "just looking out the window" and "transcribing" the unpretty urban landscape he saw there. In a sense, though, one could argue that a Schuyler poem of this kind is in a way about *not* seeing, or more accurately "unseeing," in that it appears to record the sensation of seeing something without the usual set of assumptions that allow us to know what it is, conjuring the strangeness of everyday appearances by means of unexpected metaphors and mental associations: not rivulets of puddled water but "rhizomes of wet"; ill-maintained tenements are "dental: / carious, and the color of weak gums"—the whole scene "an organic skin for the stacked cubes of air / people need." The gritty, slightly dystopian vision of "stacks, pipes, ventilators, tensile antennae" and a metal ladder climbing "five rungs above a stairway hood / up into nothing" makes it a kind of dark twin of the earlier, light-imbued "February."

In October of the previous year, Jimmy had been transferred to a new position at MoMA in the Department of Circulating Exhibitions, the domestic equivalent of the International Program, also headed by Porter McCray. His new offices were shared with George Montgomery, Waldo Rasmussen, and Adele Hoenig, while O'Hara and a new young colleague, Kynaston McShine, remained in the International Program.

With the change, Jimmy became more proactive, and in February wrote to McCray proposing an exhibition of drawings by the Italian American modernist painter Joseph Stella (1877–1946). The exhibition was approved, and Jimmy began to style himself "Guest Director" of the Department of Circulating Exhibitions in correspondence with friends. Whether this title was recognized at the museum is not clear.

The Stella show was Jimmy's focus at the museum for the rest of his time there, and his most, not to say only, notable achievement as a museum professional. In addition to coming up with the idea and writing the exhibition wall text (there was no catalogue), Jimmy helped his colleagues research the location of drawings and arrange the loans. The show debuted in an exhibition in the West Gallery of the ground floor of MoMA, running there from October 26 to November 13, 1960, before going on tour to fourteen museums across the country through the spring of 1962. It was the first museum exhibition to focus on Stella as a draftsman, and by doing so, set off a critical reappraisal of the painter, who had been well-known in the 1910s and '20s, but relatively overlooked in the years before and after his death in 1946.

Jimmy remained busy and active through the first half of the year. In addition to museum work, and ongoing correspondence with John Ashbery, Kenneth Koch, and Harry Mathews concerning *Locus Solus*, he also contributed about twenty reviews to *Art News* from February to May 1960. But after that the reviews ended, and starting in late spring of 1960, Jimmy began to act increasingly strangely, his moods alternating between busy mania and glum depression. This was particularly noticeable to Frank O'Hara, at the museum, where he bore the brunt of what he described in a letter to Ashbery as a "period of megalomania-paranoia" followed by a "rather sinister air of purposefulness about trivia." Having escaped Jimmy's foul moods on Forty-ninth Street three and a half years earlier, Frank was sensitive to any signs of their return, and must have had a horrible sense of being trapped in a déjà vu nightmare when they did.

During this time Jimmy wrote a somewhat hostile letter to John, caused, Frank believed, by his feeling that John had been insufficiently warm in welcoming the artist Philip Guston and his poet wife, Musa, to Paris in June. After hearing Jimmy go on about this at work, Frank had "wanted to slap him." Jimmy had also been barraging Waldo Rasmussen, the executive director of the Department of Circulating Exhibitions, with "little notes" complaining about Frank, and became enraged one day when Frank was slow to join him in his office to see a Frankenthaler drawing that he had just borrowed for a show. "Sometimes, though it seems hilariously funny—but those moments coincide with my not giving a shit for him, which is again depressing in itself," O'Hara wrote.

While it was certainly wonderful that Marianne Moore had given Jimmy's poems such prominent attention in her review of *The New American Poetry* in June, this too may have provided fuel for his "megalomania." At the same time, the fact that Moore had singled him out in preference to his friends made him feel conflicted about accepting the recognition, and there is almost no record of his direct reaction to it, aside from an appreciative note he wrote to Moore and a few ambiguous sentences in a letter to Anne Porter, where he writes, "Did you see what M. Moore wrote in last Sunday's *Herald Tribune*? . . . I want to go to a Minnesota lake and reflect, while composing a short thank-you note which will also defend my friends and point out a few mistakes and 'clue her in' on the secret history of THE NEW AMERICAN POETRY. // Is this too tart: 'Dear M. Moore: Thanx, Really, I am not a bit nicer than anybody else & I think F. O'Hara's *Why I Am Not a Painter* is swell. So does E. Bishop. So get with it before you miss the boat, Gratefully, JS.'" By "internalizing" and in a sense denying what should have been feelings of pride at this public recognition, Jimmy exacerbated unresolved notions of his self-importance.

As Jimmy was all too well aware, he had published less than Frank, John, Barbara, or Kenneth. A sense of grievance about this fed and was fed by his growing paranoia and megalomania, to the degree that he came unreasonably to blame Frank for "putting him in the shade as a writer" and "damaging his self-confidence." In fact, it appears that John Bernard Myers had long been interested in publishing a Tibor de Nagy chapbook with Jimmy, but according to Frank, it was Jimmy who "couldn't bring himself to let John Myers publish his poems," whether through lack of confidence, lack of material, an exaggerated sense of self-worth, or all three.

Yet even as his personal behavior began to exhibit strains and oddities, most of his letters, both personal and museum-related, and his reviews remained—with some exceptions—lucid and sane. Even at his most deranged, he could appear, and perhaps be, calm and rational in his writing. There was a discipline and a sense of performance in writing that he could harness, making it hard at times for anyone reading his letters—whether John, Fairfield, or the latter-day researcher—to reconcile their sensible tone with his actual behavior around the time of writing.

A year on, Jimmy was still mourning his breakup with Donald Droll, a situation all the more painful because they continued to see each other regularly as part of a social group that included Frank, Joe LeSueur, Kynaston McShine, Alvin Novak, John Button, and a new friend of Frank's, the poet Bill Berkson. Berkson was a nineteen-year-old student when his life was changed by a poetry workshop he took with Kenneth Koch at the New School in the spring of 1959. Kenneth took him to a party at Jane Freilicher and Joe Hazan's house, promising, "Frank O'Hara will be there and he will become like a germ in your life." This came to pass, and Bill's easygoing demeanor, talent, and good looks made him an instant success with the group, especially Frank, for whom the fact that he was heterosexual only added to his appeal. They enjoyed a close, quasi-amorous friendship that led to several poetic collaborations.

The realization that a reconciliation with Droll was impossible was finally brought home to Jimmy when Droll moved in with his new lover, Roy Leaf, in September. The unexpected force of Jimmy's feelings caused him to recall Edwin Denby's desperate feelings about *him* in 1953. As he wrote to Ashbery on September 30: "For the last few weeks my pillow has been rather a sodden mass. It really gave me quite a shock, and has even caused me to work quite hard; anything not to think. I would like to move to another city."

During this period Jimmy grew attached to a fellow employee at the museum, an administrative assistant in his office named Adele Hoenig. The exact nature of their relationship is hard to understand, but it's clear that Jimmy, along with the Porters and some of their friends, saw himself and Adele as, in some sense, a couple. John Ashbery believed that the relationship included a sexual component; Jimmy seemed to refer to this aspect, while simultaneously making light of it, when he boasted in a letter to John, "My life has not been all tears and anxiety; since I've done quite a bit of mousing around after pussy, with some success."

All agreed that Adele was genial, kind, greatly devoted to Jimmy and he to her. Kynaston McShine remembered her as "petite, fairly attractive, darkish," and felt that she was drawn to Jimmy, not only because he could be a charming and witty friend, but also as someone in need of help and support. "Jimmy had a real talent of being taken care of, and finding people to take care of him . . . I think Adele fell for him, and in a way became a caretaker." Bob Dash recalled her as "merry and sad; short; not terribly well-formed or well-featured; amiable; a doer; a handmaiden." He, like most of Jimmy's friends, was skeptical of a sexual involvement, but felt the relationship was based in a rather unhealthy way on Jimmy taking advantage of Adele's willingness to help him and put up with his bossiness, and that she misinterpreted his evident need for her as love. They remained close from the middle of 1960 through his hospitalization in 1961. By mid-1962, once Jimmy was living at the Porters', they drifted apart.

Over the summer and fall of 1960, Jimmy made many weekend and extended visits to the Porter family in Southampton, often bringing Adele. The family did not go to Great Spruce Head that year, due to perceived financial strains, which also led Fairfield to take back and sell the early de Kooning painting he had ambiguously either lent or given Frank years before. His abrupt and unexplained reclaiming of the work hurt Frank, who, unaware that Fairfield's inherited income had dwindled almost to nothing and that he was now supporting his family solely on the sales of his paintings, felt that if Fairfield had only explained to him what he needed the money for, he would have gladly relinquished the painting. But such a conversation would not have been in Fairfield's nature. The fact that Fairfield (whom Frank now dubbed "Foulfield") was at the same time providing comfort and support to Jimmy, humoring and encouraging, as Frank saw it, his dependency and imperiousness, added to his bitterness and colored in turn his feelings toward Jimmy himself.

Describing a long visit Jimmy made to the family that August and September, Fairfield wrote:

> Jimmy has been spending a lot of time here as you know, often with Adele . . . When he first came in August, Anne asked me privately, almost with tears in her voice, "Why is Jimmy so *thin*?" and to Katie she said, "Jimmy used to be one of our fattest friends." She has been inspired to cook all kinds of creamy eggy foods; and if something is gone from the icebox in the morning, she is very pleased, and says complacently that Jimmy ate it in the night.

Fairfield painted several paintings of Jimmy during these visits, including *Black Rocker*, in which he appeared with what Fairfield called "romantically hollow cheeks and longish curly hair." Jimmy also made little improvements around the house and painted the kitchen. During the August visit, he and Katie, now eleven, collaborated to create a charming booklet, "The Yvonne Clare Story," consisting of a title page and twenty-one sheets of colored construction paper, each bearing a single captioned photograph, usually of four-year-old Lizzie striking a dramatic pose. The work parodies the language of old-fashioned movie star fan magazines, such as those Jimmy and Bernie Oshei devoured in the 1930s, to describe the supposedly "ordinary" life of a Hollywood child star. The movies of Yvonne Clare have witty names and descriptions: "*Summer Bride*. Her radiantly shy smile suggests secret wishes." Reminiscent of the opening page of *Alfred and Guinevere*, the text was actually dictated by Katie, who may have read the novel by this time.

Jimmy idealized family life. He always took a vicarious pleasure when married friends had children, and seemed truly fond of them while they were little, celebrating their births and showering them with gifts on their birthdays. When the painter Alex's Katz's wife, Ada, went into the hospital for the birth of their son Vincent that summer, Jimmy sent her a voluminous package of books, including the final typescript of *Alfred and Guinevere*; the eighteenth-century Chinese novel *The Dream of the Red Chamber*; Boris Pasternak's *Selected Poems*; and an anthology, *German Stories and Tales*. The books were thoughtfully chosen, but there was also a too-muchness about the gift, as was often true of Jimmy's extravagant presents to children or to their parents.

On September 2, the Porter household and Jimmy attended John

Gruen and Jane Wilson's daughter Julia's second birthday party at their home in Water Mill, where Jimmy gave Julia an acrostic birthday poem, "J Is for My Name." Also in attendance were Larry Rivers, Arthur Gold, Bobby Fizdale (who baked a pink birthday cake for the occasion), Robert Rauschenberg, and a host of others. Gruen, a writer and photographer, and his wife, the painter Jane Wilson, knew everyone in the artistic and musical circles of the time, and over the years, Julia Gruen's birthday party at their home in Water Mill would become an annual gathering, much photographed by Gruen, helping to establish the mythos of the "New York School" of poets and painters, its various interconnections and ramifications.

Collaboration was in the air among the poets and painters of the group: in the following year, the much-anticipated Tiber Press books would appear, along with the next issue of *Locus Solus*, edited by Kenneth and devoted to collaborations, including four chapters from the still-unfinished *A Nest of Ninnies*. In about 1960, Jimmy collaborated with Bob Dash on a small group of poem-paintings. Their genesis was casual: Jimmy might be visiting Dash for lunch, and one or the other would say, "Do you feel like doing something?" Unlike in his collaborations with Grace Hartigan, the painter and the poet worked in tandem on the same surface at the same time. "I would give him a stick of charcoal," Dash recalled, "and he would scribble something." A couple of the texts were based in persistent feelings of loss after Jimmy's breakup with Droll, and one was explicitly dedicated "For D. D." They were included in an exhibition called *Poem Painting* in January 1962 at the Kornblee Gallery (along with collaborations by Frank O'Hara and Grace Hartigan, Larry Rivers and Kenneth Koch, and Barbara Guest and Mary Abbott), with a short text by Jimmy on the announcement brochure. Frank was at the opening and felt that the Schuyler/Dash collaboration dedicated to Droll was "mushy" as poetry as well as "a little too close to emotional blackmail for comfort."

After at least a month's absence, Jimmy returned to work at the museum in September with some initial optimism and energy. He finalized preparations for the Stella show, which opened on October 26, 1960, and was sent on its national tour in November. But by the late fall, his behavior was again intermittently odd and disturbing. He was stressed by his dealings with Harry Mathews over the issue of *Locus Solus* he was editing, and in a letter to the poet Robin Blaser he gave vent to his feelings of being under pressure from different directions: "I'm still a director of special exhibitions at the museum, an editorial whosis for *Art News*—a writer !?@* and now and then a human being." His relations with Frank continued to deteriorate, causing Frank to withdraw self-protectively, as he had earlier by moving out of Forty-ninth Street. By October, Frank was writing (presciently), "Fairfield has more or less adopted [Jimmy]—he spends part of each week there, usually quite more than the weekend—and I hear that the bossing that goes on in that poor benighted household is fearsome to behold. But I suppose it may provide an opportunity for sainthood to someone." That "someone" was, of course, Anne Porter.

By the end of 1960, Jimmy was seldom seen at the museum anymore, or anywhere else. He started locking himself into his apartment, or into the closet, refusing to answer the door. Old friends, including Jane Freilicher, grew worried at being unable to get him to respond.

Bill Berkson, who had gotten a job at *Art News* as an office boy, was sent downtown one day to pick up Jimmy's overdue reviews. He rang the buzzer repeatedly but there was no reply. Baffled, he telephoned Frank, who told him to phone Jimmy from the corner, which he did, and finally Jimmy opened the door. When Bill went upstairs to the apartment, there was Jimmy in his pajamas with tousled hair, "sort of a mess," standing in the midst of a chaotic scene of disarray and dirt. Berkson said, "Well, Jimmy, do you have the reviews?" A quiet "No" was the answer. Bill escaped as best he could, and reported to Tom Hess, "Mission *not* accomplished."

Sometime during these troubled months, Jimmy set fire to his apartment, apparently by smoking in bed. It was a measure of his confusion that he called the former tenant, an astonished Philip Pearlstein, to report it, waking him in the middle of the night. Pearlstein told him to call the fire department and went back to bed. Fortunately, the fire was quickly extinguished with minimal damage and no casualties. As he had in 1951,

Margaret Connor Schuyler, ca. 1920.
(Courtesy Ridenour Family)

Marcus Schuyler, ca. 1920.
(Courtesy Ridenour Family)

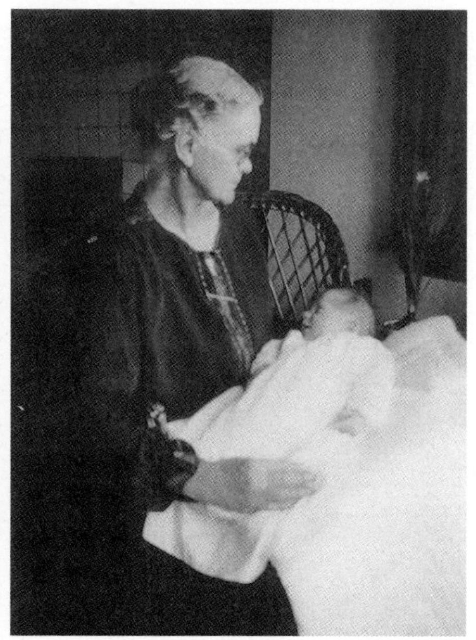

James Schuyler with Ella Connor, 1923.
(Courtesy Ridenour Family)

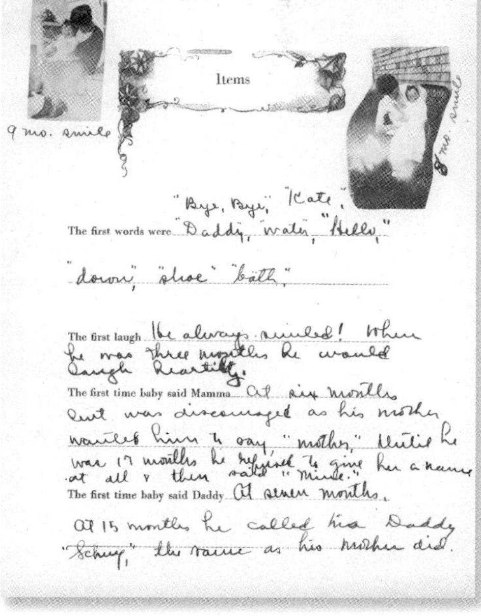

Items

9 mo. smile

9 mo. smile

The first words were "Daddy," "water," "Hello," "Bye, Bye," "Kate," "down," "shoe" "bath."

The first laugh He always smiled! When he was three months he would laugh heartily.

The first time baby said Mamma At six months but was discouraged as his mother wanted him to say "mother." Until he was 17 months he refused to give her a name at all & then said "Minie."

The first time baby said Daddy At seven months.

At 15 months he called his Daddy "Schuy," the same as his mother did.

Page from Margaret's "Baby Book," 1924.
(Courtesy Ridenour Family)

Margaret and James, Garfield Park, Washington, DC, ca. 1927. (Courtesy Ridenour Family)

ABOVE The Ridenour home at 784 Chestnut Hill Road, East Aurora, New York, in 1995. (Photograph by the author)

LEFT Portrait of James Schuyler by Sipprell Studio, ca. 1939. (Courtesy Ridenour Family)

Members of the Sigma Nu fraternity outside the fraternity house, Bethany College, ca. 1942 (detail). Schuyler crouching, third from right.
(Used by permission from Bethany College, T. W. Phillips Memorial Library, Archives and Special Collections, Bethany, West Virginia)

ABOVE LEFT James Schuyler at Key West, 1942. (Courtesy Ridenour Family)

ABOVE RIGHT William Aalto in front of VALB flag, ca. 1936–1939.
(Veterans of the Abraham Lincoln Brigade Photographs, Tamiment Library and Robert F. Wagner Labor Archives, NYU Special Collections, New York University, New York)

James Schuyler outside his apartment at 29 Via dell'Erta Canina, Florence, 1948. Photograph by Chester Kallman. (Courtesy Ridenour Family)

James Schuyler on Ischia, 1949. Photograph by Charles Heilemann. (Author collection)

Chester Kallman with James Schuyler, Ischia, 1949. Photograph by Charles Heilemann. (Author collection)

"We All Lay On the Island Beach Together," Ischia, 1949. From left to right: unknown, unknown, Chester Kallman, James Schuyler.
(Author collection)

Charles Heilemann, Ischia, 1949.
(Author collection)

W. H. Auden, Ischia, 1949. Photograph by Charles Heilemann.
(Author collection)

ABOVE Edwin Denby, ca. 1950. (Photographer unknown. Courtesy Angelo Torricini)

RIGHT *A Picnic Cantata*, album cover, Columbia Masterworks, 1954. (Courtesy Angelo Torricini)

Ding Dong House, Snedens Landing, New York, ca. 1953. (Photographer unknown. Courtesy Angelo Torricini)

Snedens Landing, ca. 1952–1953. Back row, from left to right: Arthur Gold, George Balanchine, Samuel Barber, Edwin Denby, John Ashbery; middle row: Bobby Fizdale, James Schuyler, Charles Turner; sitting front: Roger Baker, Arthur Weinstein. (Photographer unknown. Courtesy Angelo Torricini)

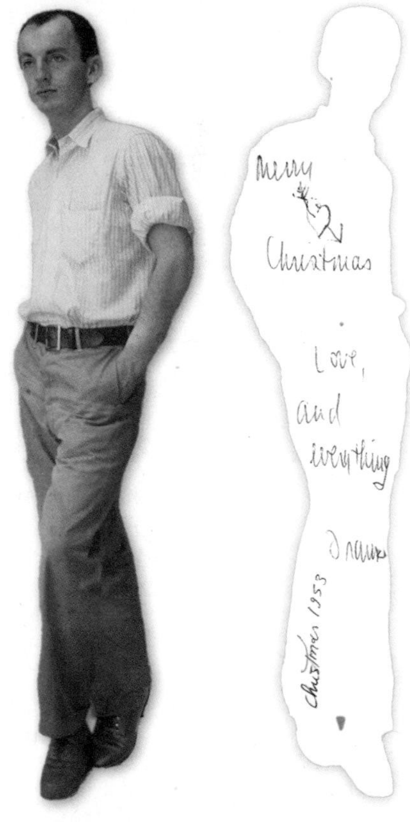

ABOVE Jimmy and Arthur Gold, Snedens Landing, ca. 1953. (Photographer unknown. Courtesy Angelo Torricini)

RIGHT Frank O'Hara. Both sides of a cutout included in a letter from Frank to Bobby Fizdale, 1953. (Photographer unknown. Courtesy Angelo Torricini)

Jimmy and John Ashbery. Photobooth pictures included in a joint valentine to Arthur Gold and Bobby Fizdale, 1953.
(Courtesy Angelo Torricini)

ABOVE Bobby Fizdale, James Schuyler, Jane Freilicher, ca. 1953.
(Photographer unknown. Courtesy Angelo Torricini)

RIGHT Kenneth Koch, 1958. Photograph by John Gruen.
(© Estate of John Gruen, 1958. Used by permission)

John Ashbery and James Schuyler, Great Spruce Head Island, ca. 1968. (Photographer unknown. James Schuyler Papers, Archive for New Poetry, Mandeville Department of Special Collections, University of California, San Diego, La Jolla, California)

Fairfield Porter painting on Great Spruce Head Island, ca. 1968. Photograph by James Schuyler. (© The Estate of James Schuyler, Courtesy James Schuyler Papers, Archive for New Poetry, Mandeville Department of Special Collections, University of California, San Diego, La Jolla, California)

Anne Porter, ca. 1944. Photograph by Ellen Auerbach. (Courtesy Jacob Burckhardt. © 2025 Artists Rights Society (ARS), New York / VG Bild-Kunst, Bonn)

Kenward Elmslie and Joe Brainard, 49 South Main Street, Southampton, New York, ca. 1968. Photograph by James Schuyler. (© The Estate of James Schuyler, Courtesy James Schuyler Papers, Archive for New Poetry, Mandeville Department of Special Collections, University of California, San Diego, La Jolla, California)

ABOVE John Button, Southampton, New York, 1958. Photograph by John Gruen. (© Estate of John Gruen, 1958. Used by permission)

LEFT Ruth Kligman, 1959. Photograph by John Gruen. (© Estate of John Gruen, 1959. Used by permission)

Fairfield Porter, *Portrait of James Schuyler*, oil on canvas, 48 × 42 inches, 1955. (Private collection. © 2025 The Estate of Fairfield Porter / Artists Rights Society (ARS), New York)

Great Spruce Head Island. Photograph by James Schuyler, ca. 1968. (© The Estate of James Schuyler, Courtesy James Schuyler Papers, Archive for New Poetry, Mandeville Department of Special Collections, University of California, San Diego, La Jolla, California)

RIGHT Fairfield Porter, *House with Three Chimneys* [49 South Main Street], oil on canvas, 22 × 21 inches, 1972. (Collection of Bronwen Hruska. © 2025 The Estate of Fairfield Porter / Artists Rights Society (ARS), New York)

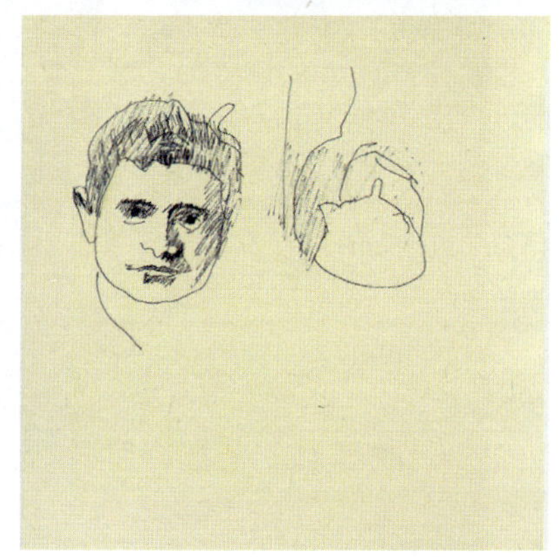

ABOVE LEFT Anne Dunn, *Portrait of Jimmy Schuyler*, mixed media on paper, 19 × 25 inches, 1974. (Courtesy Anne Dunn)

ABOVE RIGHT Fairfield Porter, *Portrait of Jimmy Schuyler*, September 27, 1970, ink on paper, 11 × 8½ inches. (Collection of the author. © 2025 The Estate of Fairfield Porter / Artists Rights Society (ARS), New York)

LEFT Joe Brainard, *Jimmy Schuyler*, pencil on paper, 14 × 11 inches, 1971. (Private collection. © The Estate of Joe Brainard)

RIGHT Alex Katz, *James Schuyler*, oil on linen, 60 × 36 inches, 1959. (Private collection. © 2025 Alex Katz / Licensed by VAGA at Artists Rights Society (ARS), New York)

BELOW Fairfield Porter, study for the cover of *Hymn to Life*, watercolor on paper, 18 × 25½ inches, 1973. (© 2025 The Estate of Fairfield Porter / Artists Rights Society (ARS), New York)

ABOVE James Schuyler, *Collage Made on Great Spruce Head Island*, leaves and wildflowers on paper, 7½ × 11½ inches, 1967. (Ron Padgett Papers, Beinecke Library, Yale University, New Haven, Connecticut. © The Estate of James Schuyler)

LEFT Darragh Park, study for the cover of *A Few Days*, oil on canvas, 17 × 13 inches, 1984. (Collection of the author. © The Estate of Darragh Park)

Crystal Lithium, Excelsior Springs, MO. Postcard that inspired the title "The Crystal Lithium." (Darragh Park Papers, Archive for New Poetry, Mandeville Department of Special Collections, University of California, San Diego, La Jolla, California)

LEFT James Schuyler, poet, in his room at the Chelsea Hotel, 1983. Photograph by Mary Ellen Mark. (© Mary Ellen Mark. All rights reserved)

BELOW Eileen Myles, 1981. Photograph by Irene Young. (© Irene Young)

BELOW LEFT James Schuyler and Raymond Foye, Chelsea Hotel, 1991. Photograph by Jeannette Montgomery Barron. (© Jeannette Montgomery Barron, 2025)

BELOW RIGHT Artie Growich and Darragh Park on the balcony of Schuyler's room at the Chelsea Hotel, 1991. Photograph by Jacob Burckhardt. (© Jacob Burckhardt, 1991)

RIGHT Tom Carey with James Schuyler, March or April 1990. Photograph by Duncan Hannah. (Courtesy Megan Wilson)

LEFT Barbara Guest, Geoffrey Young, James Schuyler, and Clark Coolidge after Guest's reading in Great Barrington, Massachusetts, November 20, 1988. (Courtesy Geoffrey Young)

BELOW LEFT James Schuyler with Anne Dunn after her exhibition opening at the Fischbach Gallery, 1989. Photograph by Jane Kitselman. (Courtesy Anne Dunn)

RIGHT James Schuyler with the author, Chelsea Hotel, April 4, 1991. Photograph by Tom Carey. (Courtesy Tom Carey)

Jimmy also began to suffer from hallucinations, including the distressing delusion that his bed was "full of pins." Anne Porter was under the impression, no doubt from something passed on to her by Fairfield, that he had attempted suicide, but this has not been independently confirmed. There were also windows of clarity, as when he wrote to his mother on February 11, 1961, that he had "alternately been working hard and not being very well" and as a result had "taken some time off & come out to stay with the Porters—Katie & Lizzie cheer me up." The visit must have helped, but not for long.

The news that Jimmy was ill spread among his friends. It became clear that he needed professional help, but no one knew quite what to do. At a Stable Gallery opening on January 23, Frank ran into Tom Hess, who had recently seen Jimmy and said he "looked terrible" and he was going to try to help him. It may have been Hess who alerted John Bernard Myers to Jimmy's situation, or it may have been Dash, whom Jimmy later credited with getting through to him and "digging him out" of the apartment during this crisis. In any case, it was the ubiquitous Myers who took on the logistics of getting Jimmy hospitalized.

Myers had been close to the poet James Merrill and his lover David Jackson for several years, and was acting as the secretary to the Ingram Merrill Foundation, which Merrill established in 1954 in order to give financial aid to writers. Although Merrill was gay and of the same generation as the New York School poets, and they had mutual friends, he was not part of their social scene, and his poetry, with its willfully Parnassian tone, was antithetical to theirs. Merrill had reservations about O'Hara and was "uneasy" about the possible influence of Ashbery's work on his own, but had a deep appreciation of Schuyler's poetry. At Myers's urging, David Jackson wrote to Merrill's own former psychiatrist, Dr. Thomas Detre, who had grown close to Merrill when he was his patient in Rome in the early '50s, and was now the head of the psychiatric department at Grace New Haven Hospital in Connecticut. Detre replied directly to John Bernard Myers on March 1, "While the Medical Center restricts admissions to the greater New Haven area, I would be more than glad to make an exception."

Detre advocated what was then a relatively new approach to psychiatry, treating its causes in the chemistry of the brain with medication rather than relying on classic Freudian talk-based therapy. Myers explained to Jimmy that because of his "artistry," and because Detre was "particularly interested in writers," the doctor would waive all personal fees, while the hospital fees ($30 a day) would be paid by the Ingram Merrill Foundation.

Jimmy entered the psychiatric ward of Grace New Haven Hospital around March 20, 1961, and remained there for about three months. Without access to hospital records, which have not been preserved, his diagnosis remains unclear. There was probably some uncertainty on the part of Detre himself, at least at first, as to whether Jimmy was schizophrenic, depressive, manic-depressive—or, as we now say, bipolar. In *Modern Psychiatric Treatment*, the psychiatric textbook that he co-authored in 1971, Detre wrote, "Patients in the manic phase of *manic-depressive disease* often resemble schizophrenics in that they, too, report accelerated thinking and a sense of unusual clarity . . . The distinction between the manic and the schizophrenic can be particularly difficult when the patient's prior or family history offers no clue." During a visit in mid-May, Fairfield Porter was given to understand, apparently by Detre, that Jimmy's illness "may have been schizophrenia."

Many of Jimmy's friends made the trek to New Haven to visit him, and his mother and stepfather even came down from East Aurora. Alex Katz was teaching at the Yale School of Art and came to see Jimmy several times. He found him to be perfectly coherent, showing no obvious signs of mental illness, but also remarkably changed, physically. The medications he had been prescribed and the sedentary regime had caused him to gain weight and become bloated. Earlier he had been quite handsome; Katz felt he bore a resemblance to the actor Dana Andrews, with his rather square-shaped head. Now, as it seemed to Katz, his illness had been made external and visible in a physical unattractiveness.

Frank O'Hara did not visit. Word got back to Frank that since his breakdown Jimmy had developed "quite a hate" for him, and he therefore determined that he was not going to write or visit unless Jimmy invited him to. "It is strange," Frank wrote, "to think that he and I will not be friends again, but that is my conclusion after hearing several unmalicious reports of his opinion of me. At first I thought that this was part of his illness, but now that he has improved it has only seemed to grow more articulate . . . I don't mean that I blame or dislike Jimmy for what's happened—anyone's actions can be interpreted as amiable or hostile depending on your point of view and perhaps mine more than most—but I don't see any use in either of us going through the strain of pretending we like each other as much as we once did." As to Jimmy's delusion that Frank had somehow interfered with his recognition as a writer, Frank rightly saw this as ridiculous, but added generously, "I don't think it's a particularly bad thing for him, even, since that sort of spleenish feeling may lead him to write more, and he always writes so beautifully. Perhaps I shall have the glamorous position of being the villain in some future *roman à clef* from his typewriter—I suppose Tony Curtis will play me in the movie, I'm so pushy."

When Jimmy first went into the hospital, Fairfield, who visited several times, gave him a small landscape painting as a kind of talisman to keep him company. Soon after, Jimmy wrote a poem about it, "A Blue Shadow Painting," dedicated to Fairfield. In its focus on the details of the painting before him and the way they recapitulate the actions of the painter in producing them, the poem responds, belatedly and indirectly, to Fairfield's letter of the previous summer about the act of painting, and by extension, the creative act in general. Expanding on Fairfield's realization that he has to be "open to discovery," the poem ignores his qualms about "muddiness" and inauthenticity by simply evoking the physical facts of the painting itself and how they were achieved: "The context . . . / in which, squelch, a brush lifted a load / of pigment from the thick glass palette, and, concentrated, / as though he saw neither the work in hand nor the subject, / the painter began"—while giving numerous instances of specific, unstable discoveries to be found in the finished work, translated from pigment to words:

It's like this: the orange assertions, dark there-ness
of the tree, malleable steel-gray blueness of the ground; and sky;
set against, no, with, living with, existing alongside of and part of,
the helter-skelter of rust brown, of swift indecipherables. The day
is passing, is past: mutable and immutable, came to live
on a small oblong of stretched canvas . . .

On or near the first day of summer, Fairfield picked Jimmy up from the hospital on his way to Maine and took him directly to Great Spruce Head Island, where the family would once again be spending the summer. Fairfield wrote to a mutual friend that he found Jimmy "well, cheerful and fat." According to Jimmy, Fairfield told him at the time, "I'll never let you down, Jimmy." To which Jimmy added later, "He never did."

In addition to being the first summer the family had been able to spend on the island in four years, it was also Jimmy's first visit since his original one in 1955. For several weeks they were alone in the house, while Anne, Katie, and Lizzie were in Massachusetts with Anne's mother, who was dying of leukemia. Fairfield had originally planned to join them, leaving Jimmy alone, but he realized that Jimmy was in no condition to fend for himself, and so he stayed. For both of them it was restorative just to be there together. Fairfield did a lot of painting and Jimmy mostly read and slept, gaining even more weight. In the evenings they read Dostoyevsky's *The Possessed* aloud.

At the end of July, Jimmy left to check in with the hospital in New Haven, the first of several visits he continued to make as an outpatient through the rest of 1961. From there he continued on to New York City, where he stayed a few days with the Kochs, all of them miserable in the city's summer heat. When he returned in early August, bringing Adele Hoenig, Fairfield had been joined by Katie and two of her teenage cousins. Jimmy took long walks in the woods and on the beaches with Katie and her cousins, taking note of their conversation for a new novel he was thinking about writing, once again using children's voices. As for actual writing, however, he was doing little or none, complaining to Dash, "I don't know when, since youth, I've felt so blocked or maybe just blah about it. Each day seems as though it will be the answer since the reply to why write? is usually, why not?" A week or two later, when Anne Porter returned with Lizzie after her mother's drawn-out death, Jimmy's reaction to her reappearance was less than welcoming: Anne recalled his face on her arrival as "quite expressionless." Evening readings progressed from *Nicholas Nickleby* to *Sense and Sensibility*.

Back in New York at the end of August, there was no question of Jimmy's returning to work at the Museum of Modern Art, but he did make an attempt to pick up where he had left off as a reviewer, hoping, somewhat optimistically, that he might be able to make a living from art writing. Half-humorously he wrote to John Ashbery, whose growing success as an art correspondent in Paris (in terms of activity, if not remuneration) he hoped to emulate, "I gather you are quite a powerful figure in the Paris art monde; I wish I were here . . . I'm going to do a paints a pix about Alex Katz, which will be fun, and Albers asked me to write an introduction to a book about him, which is fame of a small sort."

The Josef Albers book project didn't come through, but in December he did write "Alex Katz Paints a Painting," part of a regular series in *Art News* about artists at work. It appeared in the February 1962 issue, and is fresh, engaging, and totally Schuylerian. Like many of his poems, and his diary, the article is written in "real time," with a minute-by-minute report on the progress of the painting, interspersed with Katz's trenchant comments, random domestic vignettes, and Jimmy's own sometimes unrelated musings. If Katz was in a sense putting on a performance for Jimmy and his accompanying photographer, Rudy Burckhardt, Jimmy's ability to write the piece under observation was also performative, as Katz was quick to recognize. During the several hours that it took to paint the painting, Katz recalled, "Jimmy just took a pencil and wrote the whole thing, as I painted the picture. It was enough time for him to write it . . . It was quite a performance." The collaborative nature of the painting/writing session was carried further by the fact that Jimmy, Rudy, and Ada Katz were all pressed into service as models for the work being created. Titled *Incident*, it shows Jimmy standing between an unsmiling Ada and Rudy and writing in his notebook, like a detective taking down the facts of a crime or "incident": the observers collaborating to become the observed.

Although Jimmy felt that his mental health had improved following his "long vacation in New Haven," and with his weekly outpatient visits, socially he was having mixed success in coping with being back. In November, he seemed fine when he attended a party for John's friends Rodrigo and Anne Dunn Moynihan, visiting from Paris. Frank, who saw him there for the first time in about a year, found him "friendly and charming" although "enormous." But a few weeks later Frank saw him again at an opening where Jimmy appeared "very upsetting and had difficulty articulating," although Frank considered that this may have been partly due to the fact that he'd already had "a couple of martinis." They made vague plans to have lunch to discuss the future issue of *Locus Solus*, which Jimmy was editing, but he didn't follow up.

As his friendship with Frank continued to falter, his friendship with Bob Dash partly took its place, alongside a renewed friendship with Kenward Elmslie, whom he'd first met in 1952 when he was the lover of John Latouche. Kenward was born in 1929 and graduated from Harvard in 1950 but wasn't close to Frank or John there. His interests had been centered in musical theater, but he was also a poet, and in the late 1950s took the initiative to reestablish ties with John, Frank, Kenneth, and Jimmy. With funds he inherited as a grandson of the newspaper magnate Joseph Pulitzer, Kenward had recently established the Poets Foundation to provide financial assistance, quietly and anonymously, to poets, and he began to seek regular advice from Kenneth and Frank in identifying worthy recipients. Kenneth was particularly helpful, since he had just begun his forty-three-year teaching career at Columbia, where he would mentor a new generation of New York poets.

One of the first poets helped by the Poets Foundation was Jimmy, who received a $1,000 grant in December 1960. Chances are that Jimmy was aware that Kenward was behind the foundation, but generally the secret was well guarded. Kenward was a talented, original writer in his own right, possessed of a bright, sardonic wit and a sophisticated sense of fun. By the winter of 1961–62, his friendship with Jimmy had grown to include weekly bridge evenings with Kenneth and Janice Koch—an extension, for Jimmy, of the many hours of bridge he had recently played in the hospital. These sessions were so enjoyable that they soon taught the "demon game" to Jane and Joe Hazan and enjoyed alternate bridge evenings with the two couples. Kenward had a house in Westhampton Beach, near Southampton, and when the weather got warmer and the Hazans went out to the house they had recently built in Water Mill, the bridge evenings continued.

Locus Solus was beginning to lose steam. Once each of the editors had been able to put out his own issue, enthusiasm for continuing the project and its slightly ungainly editorial process ran thin, with only Schuyler editing a second issue. By December, Jimmy was already bemoaning to John that the issue was "having birth pains." In addition to "the Grand Old Men," Barbara, Kenneth, Frank, John, and Jimmy himself, the issue when it appeared in 1962 included work by figures from Jimmy's past such as Chester Kallman, Edwin Denby, John Wieners, and Daisy Aldan; new friends Bob Dash, Carl Morse, Ted Berrigan, and Kenward; as well as poets recommended by Harry or John: Gerard Malanga, Piero Heliczer, and Anselm Hollo.

At the end of January 1962, Jimmy was back at the Porters' Southampton house, and did not go into the city to attend the opening of the *Poem Painting* show at the Kornblee Gallery on the 21st. By now, he had his own designated room, upstairs at the back of the house, and was, as he wrote Harry Mathews, "writing poems very occasionally and mostly goofing off . . . The lake is frozen, the movies are dull. I read mystery stories and play foolish card games, which I enjoy, with the little girls . . . content to continue being a water lotus."

He had given up the Avenue A apartment during his hospital stay, and on his release moved into Fairfield's apartment on Eleventh Street, sharing it with his son Jerry—a rather directionless young man at this time, nominally attending City College. They were not compatible, and to make matters worse, the apartment was repeatedly broken into and robbed, and many of Jimmy's prized possessions were stolen, including paintings given to him by Alex Katz and Norman Bluhm, along with most of the books, records, and artworks, among them a painting by Fairfield, that he had been storing for Ashbery since he first left for France. The situation was disheartening and unstable.

In contrast, the generous and open-hearted Porters and their big white house on the quiet leafy street in Southampton beckoned irresistibly. Sometime in early 1962, Jimmy went out for a visit and failed to return.

[14]

BUT THIS IS NOT / YOUR POEM, YOUR POEM I MAY / NEVER WRITE

1962–1966

"Jimmy came for the weekend and stayed eleven years." By the early 1970s, when Schuyler had been living with the Porter family for about a decade, this was Anne Porter's well-worn reply to puzzled acquaintances who, observing the unusual situation, would hesitantly ask, "Is Mr. Schuyler a relative of yours?" Delivered in a voice no louder than a whisper, her answer was nonetheless pointed and, in a manner typical of the woman Jimmy once called "the wittiest person I know," deflected into wry humor a situation that started casually and warmly, but would gradually turn awkward, then painful, then traumatic over the course of those eleven or twelve years.

By mid-1962, if not earlier, it was somehow a fact that Jimmy was living at the Porters' house full-time. He would remember the years he lived with the Porter family as "much the happiest period" in his life. It was a decade in which he wrote such exemplary works as "Empathy and New Year," "A Man in Blue," "Buried at Springs," "The Cenotaph," "The Crystal Lithium," "Hymn to Life," and many other poems imbued with the physical presence of Southampton, Great Spruce Head Island, and the Porter household, not to mention Fairfield's paintings.

In retrospect, the relationship between Jimmy and Fairfield and Anne had an almost chemical or magnetic force of inevitability, when the "very needy" Jimmy came into the domestic circle of the "almost *pathologically* generous" Porters. It was the poet Larry Fagin who used the seeming oxymoron "pathologically generous" to describe Fairfield and Anne, whose own emotional makeups and family dynamics were certainly part of the equation. Jimmy's neediness was expressed through periods of crippling withdrawal and passivity, occasionally escalating to delusional, irrational, and hostile behavior, and can be attributed fundamentally to his mental illness, and to habits of reacting or adapting to it that became ingrained. His illness might originally be traced to a family legacy of depression and impulse control disorder, exacerbated by the childhood trauma of his parents' divorce and his stepfather's hostility; followed by the ordeal of his navy hearings and imprisonment on Hart Island; the assaults by Bill Aalto; and possibly other experiences. In particular, his difficult childhood and adolescence, marked by abandonment and withheld affection, led him throughout his life to seek out (consciously or not) stable surrogate families to attach himself to in one way or another. In addition, Schuyler had a history of being financially supported, at times, by romantic partners, notably Charles Heilemann and Arthur Gold. Fairfield Porter, in the dual role of quasi-lover and *paterfamilias*, fit the bill in both regards.

Fairfield had his own emotional neediness, stemming from a family and personal history that included a stern and remote father whom he felt he could never please; an autistic son he believed he had also failed; latent homosexual urges recently explored; and a conflicted attitude toward family responsibilities, which he perceived as an impediment to his vocation as an artist. In various ways and degrees, Jimmy's presence, at least initially, helped Fairfield come to terms with some of these needs and conflicts. For her part, Anne's humility, supported by deep religious feeling, was such that she often put others' perceived needs before her own, even as she might have occasionally misjudged or misprioritized them.

At first, taking Jimmy in didn't seem like such a big deal. Anne and Fairfield were long accustomed to inviting artist friends to live with them in troubled times. In 1952, Larry Rivers lived with the family for a couple of weeks after a suicide attempt. Later that year, the Rudy Burckhardt family also stayed for several weeks. That summer, Anne Porter wrote to her mother, "I hear that in the city we're called 'Porter's Rest Home for Broken Down New Yorkers.'" According to Robert Dash, "Anne and Fairfield were surrogate parents for a whole bunch of people. They completed the growing up process for innumerable painters and poets." But none of these previous visits came with the emotional complications of Schuyler's stay, or lasted nearly as long.

Fairfield's bisexuality was no secret to his wife. Before their marriage, he had conscientiously told her of his youthful love for another young man. It was also clear to the male members of the New York School, with whom he flirted, and in a few cases openly propositioned. One time after he had been to a party in the city for John Ashbery's birthday without Anne, she asked him how it was, and with typical lack of guile he replied, "I had a wonderful time! I kissed all the men." Fairfield took his reacknowledged bisexuality, as he took everything else, very seriously, even self-importantly, and it might have been out of earnestness—not "in memory of" his feelings, but out of a sense of responsibility toward them—that he made sexual advances to Jimmy and other younger men.

Fairfield had been in love with Jimmy since at least 1956, judging from his letters. His son Laurence, observing from the sidelines, compared his infatuation with Jimmy to his much earlier love for Ilse Hamm, a young German refugee who had been a caregiver for the Porter children in the early '40s, whom he pursued in vain and wanted to marry, and felt that in both cases his father had a "romantic fixation on the unobtainable." Indeed, the very intensity of Fairfield's infatuation (not unlike Edwin Denby's, perhaps) made it almost inevitable that Jimmy would resist it at first. In 1956, Jimmy had been in the process of ending his relationship with Arthur Gold and in love with John Button, and could not deal with Fairfield's feelings. But there had been much water under the bridge since then. Jimmy was attracted to older men, and to Fairfield in particular, and he could have been additionally motivated by love, generosity, and self-interest, in proportions unknown, to respond more favorably now to Fairfield's advances. Always, his feelings about Fairfield and their relationship remained fluid and complex. Whenever he wrote of them, it was in measured terms of deep long-term affection, intimacy, and love, but stopping short of giving a sense that this was a romantic or erotic passion on his part. In "The Morning of the Poem," Jimmy refers to Fairfield with an exactitude that sounds like understatement, as his "best friend," before continuing: "but this is not / your poem, your poem I may / Never write, too much, though it is there and / needs only to be written down / And one day will and if it isn't it doesn't matter: / the truth, the absolute / Of feeling, of knowing what you know, that is / the poem . . ."

With one or two exceptions, long after the fact, Jimmy never let on to friends that there was any kind of sexual relationship between him and Fairfield. Certainly there were no public expressions of "touching or intimacy or affection or any kind of complicity." Whatever sexual activity did occur took place when the two of them were by themselves, opening the house in Maine at the beginning of the summer, or in the fall, when they often went back together to pick up the paintings that had been left there to dry. It was not in either of their natures to be demonstrative anyway, and both Jimmy and Fairfield were keen to avoid causing hurt or embarrassment to Anne Porter and the children. Jimmy also had an independent relationship with Anne, whom he related to on her own terms, as a poet, a person of religious conviction, and someone with whom he shared an understated sense of humor.

Anne Porter knew that "F[airfield] and Jimmy had a very long and close relationship that was very important to them both," and this included, for example, a ritual of Fairfield going to Jimmy's room and kissing him "every morning to wake him up," because, as Fairfield explained to her, Jimmy liked to be awakened "by hand." But it "never occurred" to Anne to ask her husband just "how physical" the relationship was, and she "didn't assume anything one way or the other." While she was aware of a rivalry for Fairfield's love and attention, she "didn't think of it as a specifically sexual competition." For Anne, in fact, the conflict appeared more serious than that:

> I understood a little bit the supportive role that Jimmy had for Fairfield . . . [but] there was a danger to our relationship—Fairfield's and mine . . . concretely [. . .] It was hard for him to be a father, his own father had been so *bleak*. And I was very selfish, having all those children—I'm not sorry, but it was, you know. So this was someone who supported the other side of him [. . .] I would never write my [auto]biography, God help me, but I thought if I did I would start, "All my life I've wanted to marry my husband." And that about says it all. So that there was always a concrete, real danger that he wouldn't be able to stay with us . . . so to have someone like Jimmy around always constituted a real threat.

Jimmy recognized this aspect of the situation too, but coming at it from the other direction, felt that his continued presence in Fairfield's domestic life actually "saved" the marriage (as he wrote to Anne later) by providing Fairfield the creative support and close male companionship he needed without his having to leave Anne.

Jimmy took to heart Fairfield's promise—"I'll never let you down, Jimmy"—on picking him up from the hospital in 1961, and in time he came to regard 49 South Main Street as his home and himself as virtually a member of the family. Whatever the sexual aspect of the relationship, commitment had been proffered, and Jimmy in his neediness clung to it, while the principals continued to allow and encourage outsiders (and the children) to believe what they assumed and wanted to believe—that he was simply a friend whose weekend visits had somehow become abnormally extended. Jimmy probably half believed this himself at first, yet over time convinced himself that his was a sanctioned position, with its own rights and privileges. He usually had more sense and tact than to presume on these "rights," but other people could occasionally seem to recognize them unintentionally, even in ways very hurtful to Anne, as when hosts would blithely invite Jimmy and Fairfield to a party as a couple, and not Anne.

In Jimmy's life, as in Fairfield's, the relationship between them, with all its ambiguities, stood apart from any other. "Oh Fairfield, Fairfield," he lamented nine years after Fairfield's death, "of all of them, why did *you* have to die?"

In 1962, the Porter household consisted of Fairfield and Anne and their two daughters, Katharine, or Katie, then about twelve, and Elizabeth, or Lizzie, about six. The couple's three sons were not living at home: Johnny was with his foster family, Jerry was living in New York, and the middle son, Laurence, a professor of French, was married and living in Baltimore.

Southampton in the mid-twentieth century still retained much of the character of a conservative farm town, and growing up there was not easy for any of the Porter children. They felt socially isolated and sometimes ostracized by their peers in school because their father did not have a regular job but was an artist who worked at home (in a converted barn), and their house was apt to be filled with their parents' unconventional friends. Not to mention that their oldest brother was "crazy" and sometimes acted out publicly on his visits home. Both Porter girls combined precocity with shyness and seriousness, giving a sense of being not quite of their time—there was no television in the house, for one thing. To visitors they could seem silently critical or even otherworldly with their wide-eyed unflinching stares. Katie's favorite among her parents' friends was the ebullient Frank O'Hara, but the more withdrawn Jimmy also attracted her sympathy and affection early on.

At the beginning of his long residence with the family, Jimmy was a benign presence, whom the girls liked and who contributed in various ways to their growing up. Friends and acquaintances sometimes compared his position in the family to that of "another child," or "the older brother of the children or something." Dash characterized Jimmy's relationship with the Porter girls in the early years of his stay as one of "avuncular kindness," which they accepted and enjoyed at face value, while in some ways they recognized that "he was another child also." Katie recalled, "When I was a kid, he was sort of like a friendly adult figure in my life who did a lot of things with me that later on, I guess, I resented because I wish my father had done those things with me." Lizzie, too, had good memories of the first years of Jimmy's stay with the family: "He was sort of like an uncle who did fun things with me . . . It was easy for him to enter into a world of play and imagination and he did it very well." When she was about five or six, and Lizzie was having trouble learning how to tell time, which was affecting her schoolwork, it was Jimmy who had the idea of getting her a wristwatch of her own, and then she learned very quickly. "Neither of my parents thought of that," Lizzie recalled.

Although Johnny Porter was with the family only a few weeks a year, for Christmas and his birthday, his presence then was strongly felt. Johnny had a disarming childishness, and plentiful obsessions and quirks, combined with innate intelligence. He exhibited a sensitivity to language expressed in a fascination with corny puns ("toad's tools" / "toadstools") which he would repeat over and over loudly and with "a raucous laugh." Above all, Johnny was passionate about music, as something "raw and intoxicating . . . that made him feel much better." He had records of marches and polkas that he would play at full volume and dance to. Jimmy added to his enjoyment immeasurably by teaching him to use a tape recorder. Anne felt that no one other than Jimmy would have had the patience and empathy necessary to do so. In addition to music he also recorded all kinds of natural sounds: from crickets to the crashing surf at the beach. He loved to stand in the front yard of the house and play his recordings, waving his arms, singing at the top of his lungs and "varying it with whoops and growls / of wild ecstatic joy."

Jimmy liked Johnny and considered him a friend, although the relationship was slightly uncomfortable. As Anne conjectured, Jimmy "felt for him a little bit because Johnny was an outsider like Jimmy sometimes felt," and they were both "living on the margins because of mental illness." At the same time, as the allotted term (usually two weeks) of his stays would draw to a close, Anne always noticed "the *enormous* relief that Jimmy showed when Johnny was going to go home," and if any logistical problem arose that threatened to delay his leaving, Jimmy would suddenly become "an absolute genius in solving all the obstacles in the way of Johnny's departure."

The fact that Johnny had been sent away, and Jimmy was there instead, left the sense that a kind of substitution had taken place. Katie Porter, in recollection, felt there was almost a "trade off." Unable to give Johnny the care he needed, her parents, she felt, "wanted to do something for somebody they could help."

To one observer, the utter strangeness of Schuyler's long tenancy in the family was somewhat camouflaged by the offbeat character of the whole household. "Nothing about the Porters was ever normal in the sense that—it wasn't your average daily life." What with Fairfield's laconic utterances and stony silences, Anne's recessive, whispery nature, Johnny's acting-out, and the girls' elusive shyness, Jimmy's ambiguous status was kind of accepted as just one more idiosyncrasy. In this context, said another friend, Jimmy was "probably the most socially, quote unquote, normal of everyone there."

The big, white, fourteen-room Federal-style house at 49 South Main Street was built in 1836, and stood in the center of town, just a block from the main shopping street. Such was the still-rural character of the town that throughout Jimmy's time there, the next-door neighbors kept at various times a cow, horses, a pony, and a pig on their property. The spacious tree-shaded yard contained a large elm and a grape arbor and extended behind the house down to Lake Agawam.

The house was furnished in a deceptively casual way with an assortment of family heirlooms, set off by beautiful old Oriental rugs. The look of the interior was largely Fairfield's creation: he chose the wallpapers and personally mixed particular hues of paint for the walls, and since the colors and patterns of the rooms became prominent motifs in his paintings, his exercise of control over them can be seen, in a sense, as an element of his art. When visiting the house, Robert Dash always felt that he was "in the middle of a still life." In the kitchen dwelt the fearsome coal-fired Aga stove, which had to be kept burning day and night, summer and winter, to prevent the humid ocean air from rusting the interior and over which Fairfield became somewhat obsessive. As a concession to Anne, however, he had also allowed a "tiny, tiny" electric range to be installed. It was Fairfield, too, who had ordered pricey Schlumberger wallpaper for the upstairs hall, in a pattern of California wildflowers. By the time that Schuyler lived there, much of it had started peeling off the wall in great swaths.

The seemingly casual but actually rather austere physical environment of the house was also reflected in the Porters' manner of living. Dash sensed this contradiction when he spoke of the Porter house as a "wonderfully undisciplined, disciplined" place, where an apparently "casual way of living" nonetheless entailed "its own strictnesses." There was a steady stream of visitors, who were not necessarily catered to, but left to their own devices and expected to fit in. Recalled Dash, "I remember a third day I was spending there, Anne asked me how was everything in my room and I said, 'Everything's fine; I could have some sheets.' She said, 'Oh dear!' . . . There was always food at the Porters', and the rest was up to you, including your thoughts." When she was older, Lizzie enjoyed the long dinners with the likes of Elaine de Kooning, Frank O'Hara, Kenneth and

Janice Koch, Joan Mitchell, Michael Goldberg, and many others. Jimmy, she felt, was often at his best in such stimulating company.

Jimmy's room was in an extension at the back of the house over the kitchen, where its separation from the rest of the house gave it privacy. It was quite large, handsome, and sunny, with windows on three sides looking out at the garage and studio on one side, and overlooking on the south side a pear tree that every spring erupted in "wondrous" white blossoms. The room gave an impression of being "full of books," with bookshelves along the entire back wall and books on every available surface.

At the beginning of his stay, Jimmy contributed in various ways to the look and atmosphere of the house, rearranging furniture, acquiring rugs, and broadening Anne and Fairfield's cultural horizons, particularly in regards to music. After years of association with Chester Kallman and Gold and Fizdale, and spurred on by John Ashbery's adventuresome musical taste, Jimmy had become an avid collector of classical music records and brought a broad range of recorded music into the Porters' lives. Jimmy had a favorite armchair in the living room where he would spend hours sitting and reading or listening to music and "could get kind of inside himself." After Jimmy compared the sound of the speaker of their phonograph to a "Brillo Pad" in the poem "A Man in Blue," the Porters got a better phonograph.

Schuyler's poems have been described as highly visual or painterly, which is true enough, but possibly beside the point, and the prevalence of the claim may do the work a disservice to the degree that it could encourage readers to think of it as illustrative. But Jimmy himself declared in one interview that he "tried to write poems that were like [Fairfield's] paintings." What aspect of Fairfield's paintings did Jimmy want his poems to be "like," seeing that the paintings themselves are less "about" their bucolic subject matter than the imperfect correspondence between paint and visual perception? Jimmy had written very few poems during the past few difficult years, but two from the early 1960s, "A Blue Shadow Painting" and "Under a Storm Washed Sky" (both published posthumously in *Other Flowers*), show the influence of his new relationship to Fairfield. "A Blue Shadow Painting" takes as its subject the painting that Fairfield had given him and reconstitutes, in a sense, the original scene through imagining the process of its making, while "Under a Storm Washed Sky," dated December 8, 1962, in its close attention to the landscape and in particular the colors of shadows (a noted concern of Fairfield's), might also be describing a Porter painting. Or rather it seems to describe how the scene would be understood through what a painter could and could not indicate with paint, and by extension draws attention to the inherently limiting but at the same time transformative effect of verbal description: "An elm and its shadow are one. / The twigs of a pear tree are knotted / and glazed with light. The clothes pole / stands empty of purpose, a faint green / on its shadowed side. A cloud like a slice of mist / slides under the sun and the shadows momentarily fade . . ."

Forgetting, apparently, about these two poems, Jimmy later said that when the poet Ted Berrigan phoned him in the summer of 1963 to ask if he could publish "The Infant Jesus of Prague" in his new periodical, *C* magazine, he told him he hadn't been writing poems "for some years," but that Berrigan's call prompted him to start writing again. The first poem he wrote after that which he felt was "any good" was "A Man in Blue." The poem seems to encapsulate, among much else, Schuyler's feelings of contentment and security at 49 South Main Street, skirting big themes like "immortality," "ecstasy," and "life" with humor and images of dailiness.

"Under the French horns of a November afternoon," it begins, "a man in blue is raking leaves." The poem could be said to be set to the music of Brahms's Second Symphony, which is superimposed on the day, as for Schuyler "the day" is often a metonym, in a sense, for the poem in which it is taking place.

The Brahmsian day
lapses from waltz to march. The grass,
rough-cropped as Bruno Walter's hair,
is stretched, strewn and humped beneath a sycamore
wide and high as an idea of heaven

The first movement is imagined as "a family / planning where to go next summer / in terms of other summers." A painterly image then transforms its melody into "vocalese-shaped spaces / of naked elms" and "a copper beech / ignited with a few late leaves." The Brillo Pad reference is followed by a comic image of heaven seen from below "as a thick glass floor / with thick-soled Viennese boots tromping about on it." The vision dissolves cinematically back to the poet sitting in the living room at 49 South Main,

> Ensconced in resonant plump easy chairs
> covered with scuffed brown leather
> in a pungent autumn that blends leaf smoke
> (sycamore, tobacco, other),
> their nobility wound in a finale
> like this calico cat
> asleep, curled up in a breadbasket,
> on a sideboard where the sun falls.

The summer of 1962 was Jimmy's first full summer on Great Spruce Head Island, and his first as a more or less acknowledged member of the family. The island held an undeniable magic, which resided as much in the old family house and its evocative contents and smells, and the unusual family that lived there, as in the unspoiled landscape itself, and its setting in Penobscot Bay. One of the earliest poems Jimmy wrote in and about the island is "Penobscot," orienting the poet and the island in the bay, noting other islands visible nearby and some of their characteristics, all quite simply:

> Open water facing Bradbury snags fog in its spruce.
> Eagle has a meadow down its spine;
> Compass, a cave; Scrag, five trees.
> On Dirigo apples hang down into raspberries;
> nearby, a lilac. Many remember
> its old name, Butter, though Little Spruce Head
> only one man still calls Frenchman's.
> Birch-pale Beach has a chapel,
> Bear has sheep . . .

Part of the island's special charm was due to the primitive living conditions. Perishables were still kept in an old-fashioned icebox, supplied with blocks of ice that were delivered in the spring and had to be carried in from the icehouse, and all the cooking was done on a wood-burning stove. Meals were eaten essentially outdoors at a twelve-foot-long cypress table in one of the two screened porches that flanked the main room on both its long ends. The other porch was Fairfield's studio. Because of the way the house was centered around the large double-height living-family room, with the bedrooms on two mezzanine floors at either of its short ends, "acoustically it's like you're all in the same room," Anne recalled.

Outside, the beaches and inland meadows invited long walks and picnics. There were wild raspberries and blueberries and mushrooms to pick, and icy springs in the woods to drink from. The water in the bay was cold but swimmable in high summer, and the island could be circumnavigated by canoe or rowboat in an afternoon. Fairfield was often to be encountered in the woods or meadows, painting. And Jimmy was in his element. As Jane Freilicher observed, "His penchant for natural beauty, nature, was fulfilled up there . . . like being in a herbarium."

Evening entertainment consisted of reading aloud or playing parlor games, such as Dramatic Switchboard, a kind of verbal *cadavre exquis*, where each person thinks of a character and writes down a line of dialogue and stage directions, folds it over, and passes it on to the next player. "The result is sometimes surrealistically quite funny, and sometimes, alas, just dull," Fairfield wrote.

Late that summer, Alex and Ada Katz and their baby son, Vincent, visited for a few days from their summer home on the mainland. They felt that Schuyler did not enter wholeheartedly into some of the more Spartan aspects of the place, such as the family custom to eat breakfast outdoors on the screened porch. Penobscot Bay mornings can be quite chilly, even in summer, and Jimmy used to register a wordless protest by appearing wearing an overcoat or with a blanket wrapped around him, in which he would sit to eat his oatmeal. Often he stayed up late at night writing or reading and would only get up well after the rest of the family had breakfasted. Fairfield, fondly indulging the idiosyncrasies of his friend, wrote to Dash, "Jimmy asks to be waked up, but he sleeps usually half the day," and confided to another longtime correspondent, "I hear applause from the kitchen below, which means I think that Jimmy Schuyler has got up for breakfast."

Jimmy and John's correspondence had lapsed during Jimmy's hospitalization, but finally John wrote in February 1963, asking for confirmation of what he feared: that his records and other things had indeed been stolen from Jimmy's apartment. "I would love to renew our correspondence if you see no objection," John concluded, "as with a little effort we could easily outdo Voltaire and the Marquise du Chatelet. As well as finish feathering the 'Nest.'" Jimmy replied in March, confirming the thefts, and agreeing that they might try to continue to write *A Nest of Ninnies* by mail: "Would [writing] alternate pages work? I will if you will." The subject came up again several times in letters over the following two years, but the chemistry never seemed to be there to continue the novel remotely. They were able to resume writing the book only after John moved back to New York in 1965.

In early June 1963, Anne came down with hepatitis with a fever of 104 and was hospitalized for ten days, then confined to her bed at home for several weeks, delaying the family's move to Great Spruce Head Island that year to late July, and missing a Porter family reunion marking fifty years since the family spent its first summer on the island in 1913. While Anne was sick, Jimmy pitched in to help with the chores. As he wrote to John, "I'm sorry you weren't here to see me at the ironing board, pressing a little white first communion dress for Liz to wear in a Corpus Christi procession." Anne recalled that after ironing the dress he said to her, "Woman's work is never done, especially when a man is doing it." Jimmy also did the cooking while Anne was bedridden, and proved to be good at it. He had "certain knacks," such as a pasta dish with sautéed breadcrumbs that Jane Freilicher envied but could never duplicate. But he always seemed to get most pleasure from baking: buns, pies, salt-rising bread, and a caramel Bavarian cream cake "that would have satisfied the sweets craving of an entire kindergarten for a year."

In the wake of *Locus Solus* two other periodicals arose, very different from each other (and *Locus Solus*) but sharing some of the same interests: *C: A Journal of Poetry*, edited by the New York poet Ted Berrigan beginning in May 1963; and *Art and Literature*, jointly edited in Paris by Anne and Rodrigo Moynihan, Sonia Orwell, and John Ashbery from 1964 to 1967.

Berrigan had been a graduate student in Tulsa, Oklahoma, when he fell in with a group of precocious local high school students and poets: Ron Padgett, Dick Gallup, and the artist Joe Brainard. In the fall of 1960, Padgett and Brainard came to New York together, Ron to study at Columbia with Kenneth Koch, and Joe en route to art school in Ohio. By early 1961, Brainard had dropped out of art school and returned to New York City; a year later, Berrigan had also arrived to make his way as a poet in downtown New York. All three soon became acquainted with Frank O'Hara, who was always eager to meet and encourage younger poets.

C, which Berrigan began as a way to publish his and his friends' work, was one of the earliest "mimeo" magazines, assembled of mimeographed sheets stapled together, a quick, unfussy form of publishing that would become a hallmark of the growing activity around the Poetry Project at St. Mark's Church in New York's East Village. Most of the magazine's run of thirteen regular issues (ending in 1966), plus two special issues of *C Comics*, had cover art or illustrations by Brainard, lending the publication a distinctive visual identity. The magazine's involvement with the earlier generation of the New York School began with issue number 4, which included a large selection of Edwin Denby's poems. It was Denby who advocated for publishing Schuyler in *C*, whetting Berrigan's interest with a group of unpublished early poems and prose works. After "The Infant Jesus of Prague" appeared in 1963, Berrigan asked permission to publish Schuyler's story "The Home Book," as well as some of the poems Edwin had shown him. Jimmy agreed, and they appeared in February 1964, along with *Unpacking the Black Trunk*, a short play he had written in collaboration with Kenward Elmslie.

Art and Literature, which ran for twelve quarterly issues from March 1964 through spring 1967, featured poetry and fiction by both European and American writers, as well as regular features on art, with black-and-white reproductions printed in halftone on coated stock. John Ashbery was jealous that Berrigan had published "The Infant Jesus of Prague" in *C* and asked about "The Home Book" for *Art and Literature*. Despite having already given it to Berrigan, Jimmy also allowed John to publish it, thus it appeared in both publications in the summer of 1964. *Art and Literature* also published a selection from *A Nest of Ninnies* in 1967.

In December 1963, Joe Brainard returned from an unhappy sojourn in Boston, and moved into a back room in the poet Tony Towle's apartment on East Ninth Street, living a hand-to-mouth existence on the occasional sale of a drawing or collage. Frank O'Hara and Joe LeSueur were frequent visitors to Towle and Brainard, and Brainard, who up to then had been private about his sexuality, was stunned by the good-looking blond LeSueur. LeSueur in turn was much taken by the shy, gangly twenty-two-year old, and they began an affair—Brainard's first open gay relationship.

Joe and Jimmy met sometime in the spring of 1964, and not long after that, Brainard visited Schuyler at the Porters' house in Southampton. They quickly recognized each other as kindred spirits, although Brainard was some nineteen years younger, and that July they began a wonderful exchange of letters that would last until Schuyler's death. The fact that Brainard and Joe LeSueur were an "item" at this point briefly gave Schuyler pause, but it became moot that fall, when Brainard left LeSueur and began his lifelong relationship with Kenward Elmslie.

Joe Brainard (1942–1994) was that extremely rare person, an artist and a writer equally gifted and original at both; he was also a human being of unusual generosity of spirit and personal modesty. His visual art, modest in scale, consists of assemblages and collages, oil paintings, black-and-white ink drawings, and "alternative" comic strips done in collaboration with poets. His illustrations for books and flyers for poets numbered in the hundreds. As a writer, he is best known for the book-length prose work *I Remember*. Both his visual art and his writings feel "personal" rather than "professional" (in the sense that they are unslick, uncommercial, unformulaic), perhaps because both seem to come from his desire to be what he called "completely open." A confiding tone, close observation of the quotidian, and a shared collage sensibility, broadly speaking, are perhaps the most noticeable areas of overlap between the art of Schuyler and Brainard. Both had similar, understated senses of humor.

Jimmy and Fairfield got an early start on the summer of 1964, and were up on Great Spruce Head in May to open the house, ahead of the rest of the family. Anne was still in Southampton as late as June, when Fairfield wrote, "There are Quaker Ladies on the island, which are apparently also called bluets . . . Jimmy . . . does most of the cooking, making good brown bread, somewhat like the kind you sent Jerry, only no molasses. He makes a little too much cake and pie."

This was the summer Fairfield painted the large multiple-figure work *The Screen Porch*. In art historical terms a "conversation piece," conversation seems to be exactly what is lacking from it. The central figure is Jimmy, seated stolidly in a wicker chair reading, with Katie standing rather awkwardly on the left, and Liz in the middle with her back to the painter and one hand on the chair. Anne Porter stands at the far right, outside the screen, looking in at her family. The Porter family had a nickname for the painting: "Four Ugly People." Missing from the painting is Jerry Porter, who was with the family earlier in the summer, moody and saturnine, went into Camden with Fairfield one day, and at the last moment announced that he wasn't coming back to the island but was "going on a trip" without saying where. His disappearance left Anne, in particular, worried and unhappy. For the next several years he would travel the country, with unpredictable reappearances at home.

In July, Jimmy's stepfather, Berton Ridenour, died suddenly of a heart attack at the age of seventy. By the time Margaret's letter with the news arrived on the phoneless island, the service and cremation had already taken place. Considering his feelings about his stepfather, Jimmy's letter to Margaret after his death was full of empathy: "After so long a companionship, this must be a doubly great loss to you. I'm glad you have the certainties of a deep and strong religious conviction, which I know will now be an unfailing resource for you. Many, many memories came back, all revealing a man who took great joy in the natural world, and in its beauty." Writing about the event to Bob Dash, Jimmy expanded,

"It's made me feel serious and very mortal. And I've had a succession of memories, from my early childhood, of him, all showing his best & most admirable qualities, and that have come perfectly spontaneously. I didn't anticipate that."

Among the "admirable qualities" of Berton's that came back to Jimmy now was his love of gardening. Although Jimmy had resented being made a "gardening slave" to yardwork when he was an adolescent, he now began to take an interest in gardening himself, starting by planting nasturtiums and other summer annuals in old whiskey tubs placed around the house in Maine. "I'm gardening quite a lot, of the foxglove, forget-me-not, Iceland poppy style," he wrote to Bob Dash, who had recently bought a two-acre property in Sagaponack, Long Island, and begun to make a garden there, "Madoo," that would become nationally known. "You must put me on to some interesting books about it."

In the fall, Jimmy's gardening extended to 49 South Main, where most notably he planted many different varieties of roses, as he later celebrated in "Horse-Chestnut Trees and Roses" and other poems. During the mid-'60s, he was "a very good, *serious* gardener," Anne Porter recalled. One day she opened the refrigerator and was surprised to find a quart jar full of beneficent, pest-eating ladybugs, which Jimmy had put there, having read that if they were chilled before being released into the garden they would settle there and not immediately fly away to other gardens. Another time, she "peeked into the guest room next to Jimmy's room and there were little peat pots with seedlings in them all over the bed."

In December, John Ashbery's father died too, and he returned from France to upstate New York for the funeral. He spent most of December there, while Jimmy passed the holidays with his mother in East Aurora. This was Jimmy's first visit to his family in many years. His brother, Fred, and his wife, Hilde, whom he had met and married while serving in the army in Germany, also lived in East Aurora with their three children, and their presence greatly eased Margaret's transition to widowhood. While there had been no overt break between Jimmy and his mother, the visit still felt like a reconciliation. Both recognized the relationship had changed radically with Berton gone. After Jimmy left in January, Margaret felt a pang that she compared to losing her husband: "The house seemed very empty after you left, like when Berton was gone—after six months I still feel he must be getting back soon."

That spring, from March to May 1965, Schuyler's play *Shopping and Waiting* and his collaboration with Kenward, *Unpacking the Black Trunk*, were being performed on the weekends by the American Theater for Poets along with a changing array of other works. From its founding in 1961 by Diane di Prima, LeRoi Jones, Alan Marlowe, and others, until its demise in 1965, the theater presented a mix of short plays by poets, poetry readings, jazz and rock concerts, and dance performances in a series of small downtown spaces. The action of *Unpacking the Black Trunk* consists of three people taking odd items from a trunk in search of some unnamed object, accompanied by free-associative comments and recollections. *Shopping and Waiting* had a set by Alex Katz, while *Unpacking* was accompanied by a silent film by Ken Jacobs showing the actors going through the same motions. As di Prima recalled, "The timing and action between the two was always a little different, and that was part of what made it interesting."

On June 8, 1965, Fairfield had a bad accident when his car was struck by a train at a local crossing. The car was overturned and its rear end demolished. Porter, miraculously, escaped with only minor injuries, which nonetheless confined him to the hospital for four days. The accident inspired Schuyler's poem "Stun." It was a month before Porter was healed and his bandages came off, which meant that Anne was the driver when the family went up to Maine in early July, a journey that was "not without a touch of drama" from a few near collisions, due to Anne's being unaccustomed to freeway driving.

That summer was a particularly hot one, giving the island flora a prematurely autumnal look, as Jimmy noted: "The island is dry as a Gibson . . . When I look out in the early morning my time sense is all dislocated by the colors, pinks and dry beiges and pinky-gray, like September, so that even the mauve fire weed looks like asters. The island smells differently, the spinach in the garden looks like a dinky herb and wild strawberry, raspberry and blueberry picking will there be none. And the island is very, very beautiful."

The long period of living with the Porters and dividing his time between Southampton and Maine corresponds roughly to the period of Jimmy's closest involvement with the natural world as a subject. Nature in his poems is often endowed with human qualities and speaks to him directly. On July 26, 1965, Jimmy wrote a poem in celebration of a particular day, "Today." Written in the present tense and seemingly observed as it is being written, it begins with a typically Schuylerian metaphor of personified nature, "The bay today breaks / in ripples of applause." There follow a series of passively registered sights, sounds, events melded together in a wind that becomes, as elsewhere in Schuyler's work, a subliminal metaphor for consciousness, in which sounds become tactile, objects are voiced:

> The wind takes with it
> a wrack of voices: "the who?"
> and unintelligible shapes of phrases

The poem ends without a full stop, on a hanging, objectless phrase, implying a limitless continuance that could have been but did not happen to be "transcribed" by the poet:

> Everything chuckles and creaks
> sighs in satisfaction
> reddens and ripens in tough gusts of coolness
> and the sun smites

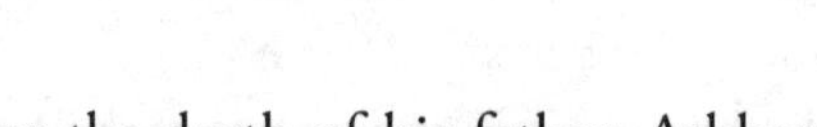

After the death of his father, Ashbery decided to return to the United States in order to be near his mother, and in November 1965 moved back to New York City to take a job as executive editor of *Art News*. John's return gave Jimmy strong motivation to start going into the city again, and he began the new year 1966 with an early January visit. He found John happy in his new job at *Art News* and although he missed Paris, it was also a relief (of a typically Ashberian kind) to no longer have hanging over him the fear that he would have to leave Paris and return to New

York. During the visit the two poets were finally able to continue work on *A Nest of Ninnies*. Ever since 1958, when Ashbery went back to Paris after his stay with Schuyler on Forty-ninth Street, work on the novel had come to a halt at the end of Chapter Four, leaving the characters in limbo and Jimmy with the feeling he had been "living in a storm-swept Florida nightclub for the last six and a half years." Now they were finally able to progress to Chapter Five, and would continue to work on the project whenever they got a chance. By this time, John had a publisher, Holt, and an editor there, Arthur Cohen, who was interested in the novel, which spurred them to set a goal of finishing the book by Christmas.

Later in January, Paul Bowles wrote to Jimmy to let him know that the Ingram Merrill Foundation had decided to subsidize a sequel to *A Picnic Cantata*: a second text by Jimmy to be set to music for voice and two pianos by Bowles and premiered by Gold and Fizdale. Jimmy worked on the commission over the spring but was not happy with anything he came up with until he got up to Maine that summer, and began going through a group of prewar English gardening magazines he found there, including back issues of *The Countryman* and another called *Industrial Archaeology*. Starting from various texts found in these magazines, he "collaged" the ten poems that make up the poem sequence "The Fireproof Floors of Witley Court" (later published in *A Few Days*), which was intended to become the Bowles commission. It was never completed, however, because Bowles, now devoted almost exclusively to fiction, never wrote the music.

In March 1966, Schuyler finally had a book of poems published by John Myers under the Tibor de Nagy Gallery Editions imprint. *May 24th or So*, a "slender volume" of twenty-eight pages containing fifteen poems, included four of the poems already published in the limited edition *Salute* in 1960, but otherwise consisted of more recent work, including "A Man in Blue," "Penobscot," and the title poem. As a small press publication in an edition of 300 copies, the book did not find distribution beyond the small world of the New York School poets and painters and their friends, but it was a long overdue acknowledgment of Schuyler's position among his contemporaries.

Jimmy spent the summer of 1966 on Great Spruce Head Island, where once again friends visited, including John Ashbery, coming for the first time. The Friday before his departure, Frank O'Hara called and invited Ashbery to lunch, but John had to wind up his affairs and straighten his desk before going away, and they postponed it for another time. John took the bus to Camden on Saturday, July 16, and was met at the station by Alex and Ada Katz, with whom he spent the weekend. On Monday, Jimmy, with Fairfield and John Porter, met John in Camden and took him across the bay on the *Kittiwake*.

Ashbery's visit with Jimmy and the Porters on Great Spruce Head was short but sweet—"like a dream come true to have you here," Jimmy wrote afterward, "and unfortunately as quickly passed." They did some more work on *Nest*. John "loved the island, loved walking around it." With Kenward Elmslie and Joe Brainard, who were visiting at the same time, they collected mussels from the far end of the island and made *moules marinière*. Kenward loved the island too, with its "pines, lichen, crabs, mussels, beaches, woody walks, porpoises, fog and the huge pleasure of being with Jimmy & Fairfield & Anne & Liz, who is the living embodiment of Bette Davis trapped inside a Henry James Screw child." John rode back with Joe and Kenward for a brief visit with them at their house in Vermont on his way to New York. When he got home on Sunday the 24th, he heard that Frank O'Hara had had an accident the previous night on Fire Island and was in a hospital on Long Island in serious condition. "And then I was very worried, but of course one didn't think that people were going to die. And then the next day I heard that he had."

That weekend, O'Hara and his lover, J. J. Mitchell, went out to Morris Golde's house in Water Island on Fire Island—the same house, at the remote eastern end of the island, where Frank had stayed with Jimmy in August 1956, shortly after the deaths of Bunny Lang and John Latouche, when Jimmy suffered an anxiety attack. On Saturday night, Golde, Mitchell, O'Hara, and the composer Virgil Thomson went dancing. Thomson and Golde returned home around midnight; O'Hara and Mitchell came back by beach taxi over the dunes in the early hours of Sunday morning. The taxi had a flat tire, and while they were waiting for it to be fixed, Frank, standing apart from the others in the darkness, was struck down by a speeding dune buggy and mortally injured. He died in the hospital in Mastic two days later. He was forty years old.

Frank's many friends were shocked, horrified, and deeply saddened by this senseless accident. New York's then-small and collegial world of younger artists, curators, poets, musicians, and writers was shaken. Jimmy too, though they had drifted apart, was "stunned by Frank's death." The news stopped "with a thump" his lighthearted work on the commission for Paul Bowles. He wanted to go back to Long Island for the funeral, but Anne and Fairfield thought this would be unwise, fearing that it might cause another breakdown, and in effect didn't let him go. Later Anne agonized over whether they were wise to have been so protective, or whether it wouldn't have been better for him "to go through the whole process."

"I too have been feeling stunned and very depressed about Frank's disappearance," wrote John to Jimmy. The funeral "was of course the grimmest event one can remember. Naturally everybody was squabbling about funeral arrangements and who would read, just as they did over Frank's attentions when he was alive. I had no desire to read and therefore was pressed into service. It was very strange seeing about 200 people who were all genuinely grief-stricken."

At the beginning of August, a week or so after the funeral, Janice Koch and her daughter, Katherine, arrived on the island for a six-day visit. Katherine and Lizzie, now both aged ten, were best friends, and Jimmy, as in other years, spent time with them, taking them on canoe trips "of the slow and stately sort which I prefer" around the island to distant beaches where all three would sit and contentedly read. Janice was able to give Jimmy firsthand news of the events surrounding Frank's death and burial, which eased his helpless sense of its abstract unreality caused by his being so far away. "She was somehow the best person to talk to, and hearing it all while coming out across the bay—a setting more real than claustrophobic NYC apartments or telephones—did finally make it seem credible, and not merely horribly improbable."

On August 27, five days before he and the family were due to leave Great Spruce Head and return to Southampton, Jimmy was in his room typing a letter to John. A wasp flew in; he waited until it landed, clapped a water glass over it, slid a sheet of shirt cardboard underneath, and released it out the window. The letter stops in "real time" to note the event.

The episode set Jimmy off into a poem about the day as he observed it and lived it going on around him, which became "Buried at Springs," an elegy to O'Hara, who had visited the island and stayed in the same room in 1955, and the invisible, inexorable passage of time in a place where time seems suspended:

it's eleven years since
Frank sat at this desk and
saw and heard it all
the incessant water the
immutable crickets only
not the same: new needles
on the spruce, new seaweed
on the low-tide rocks
other grass and other water
even the great gold lichen
on a granite boulder
even the boulder quite
literally is not the same

Frank's tragic early death would trouble Schuyler intermittently for the rest of his life. Jimmy always remembered that it was Frank's "Three-Penny Opera" and his subsequent, exhilarating friendship that changed both his work and his life's direction. But the fact that at the time of his death they were somewhat estranged made Jimmy feel that there were things unsaid between them—a lack of what we would now call "closure," which contributed to his writing several other poems to or about Frank in later years, and to his hallucinating Frank's presence during two of his subsequent mental breakdowns.

[15]

VAGABOND SHOES

1967–1970

Nineteen sixty-seven started off with a flurry of publishing activity, when in January Maxine Groffsky invited Jimmy to send her a group of poems for *The Paris Review*. Jimmy and most of his friends got to know Maxine after she appeared at the party celebrating the publication of *Alfred and Guinevere* in 1958, while still a college student. There she met the painter Howard Kanovitz, who introduced her to his friends and got her a job that summer at a branch of the Five Spot Café in Water Mill, Long Island. Her beauty, brains, and style captivated the New York School painters and writers, and she was quickly absorbed into the group. After an affair with Larry Rivers she "ran off" with Harry Mathews to Paris in 1962. There she became the Paris editor at *The Paris Review*, working with Tom Clark, the poetry editor, to publish both first- and second-generation New York School poets, including many who had appeared in *Locus Solus* and *C*. Jimmy sent her a group of five poems that were published in the next two issues.

Soon after, Groffsky approached George Plimpton, the magazine's publisher, and proposed that the newly formed book publishing arm of the magazine, Doubleday Paris Review Editions, release a book of Schuyler's poems. Plimpton agreed, and by May 23, Jimmy had begun to assemble the book that would be published two years later as *Freely Espousing*.

Now that John was an editor at *Art News*, he took the opportunity to commission feature articles from Jimmy on Franz Kline, Fairfield Porter, and Joe Brainard. The Porter piece appeared in the March 1967 issue, to coincide with his new exhibition at Tibor de Nagy. After an introduction refuting the criticism sometimes leveled against Porter's paintings that they glorified "bourgeois" values and tastes, the article moves into a strong exposition of the essential qualities of Fairfield's painting in terms that might in some sense be applied to the author's own poetry as well:

> The paint is not, however, merely a vehicle for description . . . The paint is itself a palpable fact that holds an imprint of life and infuses life into the image [. . .]
>
> Its art is one that values the everyday as the ultimate, the most varied and desirable knowledge. What these paintings celebrate is never treated as an archetype: they are concentrated instances . . . Their concern is with immediacy.

"Joe Brainard: Quotes and Notes" appeared the following month, to accompany the cover image, one of Brainard's multiflower "Gardens." As the title suggests, the piece borrows from Joe's own collage practice in being constructed as an assemblage of short texts: statements by Jimmy interspersed with his own studio notes and other "found" quotations from letters and conversations with Joe. As in his earlier "Alex Katz Paints a Picture," Jimmy was enlarging the parameters of art journalism and blurring the distinction between it and the rest of his work.

That spring, Ron Padgett invited Jimmy to submit work for an anthology of New York poets that he and David Shapiro were editing. The mainstream recognition of the group identity was significant, even as the poets and compilers themselves remained ambivalent about the designation. Jimmy sent Ron a large group of poems to choose from but wrote, "I hope . . . you aren't going to bear down too hard on The New York School (or use that term). It sounds, uh, insular, and somehow isn't altogether true." Ron agreed: "When I described the project as a collection of 'New York' poets, I too shuddered. I don't even know what New York is, let alone a New York poet."

When it was published by Random House in 1970 as *An Anthology of New York Poets*, illustrated with beautiful ink drawings by Joe Brainard, the book opened with no fewer than twenty Schuyler poems. The anthology is a cornucopia of riches, if of its time in that out of twenty-seven New York poets born between 1903 and 1947 only one is a woman (Bernadette Mayer). The exclusion of Barbara Guest in particular caused a minor scandal and some lasting resentment. Forewarned, Jimmy wrote to John Ashbery, anticipating Barbara's angry reaction: "I guess it's time to head for the hills."

In the summer of 1967, Fairfield, Anne, Katie, and Lizzie Porter took an extended trip to Europe instead of going to Maine. They were away two and a half months, and visited Naples, Rome, Orvieto, Florence, Venice, Paris, London, and rural Wales to see an old friend of Porter's. Although trundling around Europe with Fairfield, Anne, and the girls would not have been anything Jimmy really wanted to do, at the same time he could have resented the fact that he was not invited. Instead, he stayed in Southampton, joined there by Kenward and Joe for most of July. Joe was excited to be able to use Fairfield's studio and was beginning to work in oil paint.

No sooner had Fairfield, Anne, and the girls returned, exhausted, at the end of August than Jimmy left to stay with Kenward and Joe at the small clapboard farmhouse in Calais, Vermont, that Kenward had originally bought with John Latouche. Ron and Pat Padgett and their baby were also visiting. This was Jimmy's first visit of any length to Calais, and also the first time the Padgetts spent any extended time with Jimmy. Ron and Jimmy had met in about 1965, through Joe and Ted Berrigan, and began corresponding in 1966, when the Padgetts were living in France. On their return to New York in 1967 (following a stay in Tulsa) the friendship deepened. Jimmy enjoyed knowing another young family and appreciated Ron's poetry and wit.

Evenings were often spent sitting around the kitchen table making collages: "Joe has got everybody (including me) cutting pictures out of 1925 *McCalls* and pasting them on boxes and pieces of wood and things," Jimmy wrote. These "scissors-and-paste nights" in Vermont in the late '60s, often fueled by pot, would continue to be a hilarious staple of summers with Kenward and Joe. John recalled occasions when "we used to smoke a lot [of marijuana] at Kenward's and then just sit around laughing hysterically and reading aloud from this magazine, *Women's Household*, which was a very low-grade women's magazine that Kenward discovered."

Jimmy enjoyed noting the differences between the landscape, flora, and populace of northern Vermont and those of quasi-suburban Southampton and coastal Maine. Kenward and Joe took him to other towns and villages, such as St. Johnsbury, Hardwick, and the evocatively named Adamant, visiting antiques stores and farm stands along the way. These excursions inspired Schuyler's longest poem to date, "Now and Then," a 165-line tour de force incorporating—collaging—vignettes of Vermont landscape, weather notes, domestic trivia, and down-home New England speech. The unpausing flow in which these disparate elements are noted contributes to a run-on quality—the first full stop in the poem comes at line 55. Words, phrases, and images simultaneously jostle against and meld into one another in a manner that the poet Larry Fagin (speaking of Schuyler's early work in general) likened to the "jukes," or dodges and feints, of basketball players, the flow of imagery perpetually metamorphosing.

As in other works, Jimmy seems to get *inside* nature, personifying it and subjectifying it. "The spirit / of Gelett Burgess [the early twentieth-century nonsense poet] sets Mother Nature / gabbing. '*That's* my Actea pachypoda, dear, we / call it Doll's-Eyes.' Got up as smart / as ever in muck and dank she belches / —''Scuse: just a touch of gas.'" The harsh beauty of the New England landscape becomes entwined with the tough lives of occasionally sinister backwoods farmers and plainspoken shopkeepers, so that both partake of aspects of the other:

> . . . two men clearing shoulders
> of a narrow high-crowned road
> stacked poles were lately saplings
> the leaves on the slash gone limp, unstarched, unsized
> one man with one fierce eye and where the other should be
> an ill-knit cicatrix
> men who don't make much aren't much
> for spending what they do
> on glass eyes, tooth-straightening devices ("a mouth
> like the back of a switchboard"), nose jobs, dewenning operations
> a country look prevails
> and a vestigial fear of the evil eye lurks

"... my skin creeps ..."
[...]

... Quick and clear as the water
where cress grows the cold
breaks on the hills to the soft crash
of a waterfall beyond
a beaver pond
and slides on
flinging imaginary fragments of cat's ice
from its edges to flash
a bright reality in the night sky and it—
the cold—stands, a rising pool, about
Sloven's farmhouse and he dreams
of dynamite. A bog sucks
at his foundations. Somewhere a deer
breaks branches. The trees
say *Wesson. Mazola*
replies a frog.

Jimmy dedicated the poem to Kenward and submitted it that winter to *Poetry*, where it was published in the October 1968 issue. The poem elicited a fan letter from James Merrill, who praised its "extraordinary freedom of tone + subject" and a "feeling of intimacy *beyond* the need to say 'I' and so imply a division between you + your reader."

While in Vermont, Jimmy decided he wanted to show the Padgetts Great Spruce Head Island. They drove to Sunset and took the mailboat over to the island, where they stayed for three or four days. Ron called the visit "the most magical three days" of his life. None of the Porter family members were there, only the caretaker, and "there was nothing to do but just look and walk around." Jimmy and Ron wrote a collaborative poem, "Within the Dome." One day Jimmy picked a number of different wildflowers and leaves and made a collage of them by gluing them to a sheet of paper: a "gathering" of actual leaves and flowers on the page that looks back to "Salute" and "Fabergé" and forward to "The Trash Book" of 1970.

The weather as the end of 1967 approached was cold and gray, alternating between snow and sleet. Johnny Porter came home to visit that Christmas, as usual. Jimmy spent the days after Christmas and into the new year reading in his customary wide range, and enjoying the snowy weather, which "all came together" in his great poem "Empathy and New Year."

Written over New Year's Eve and New Year's Day 1967–68, "Empathy and New Year" recalls somewhat the earlier "A Man in Blue" in its domestic setting and deliberative pace, but in place of Brahms's Second Symphony, the poem is imbued with traces of Jimmy's recent reading. The poem opens with an epigraph from "The Scope of Anthropology," an essay by the French anthropologist Claude Lévi-Strauss: "A notion like that of empathy inspires great distrust in us, because it connotes a further dose of irrationality and mysticism." The poem itself begins with two conjoined references to Whitman, taken from the prose sketch "A Winter Day on the Sea-Beach" in *Specimen Days*, and the poem "Are You the New Person Drawn toward Me," from the Calamus poems. Later he mentions Charles Darwin's *Autobiography*. Part of the richness of the poem lies in ideas or emotions half-sensed beneath its surface of domesticity, some of which may derive from the texts Jimmy mentions, especially Lévi-Strauss's, which includes philosophical speculations on the nature of empirical knowledge and language. The concept of empathy is relevant to all, or to Jimmy's response to them, and lends emotional subtext to the poem.

"Are You the New Person Drawn toward Me" consists of a series of rhetorical questions addressed to a potential lover: "Do you suppose you will find in me your ideal? / Do you think it so easy to have me become your lover? . . . Have you no thought O dreamer that it may be all maya, illusion?" Schuyler refers only to this last, and counters it with "I / doubt it, though. Men are not / so inventive. Or / few are. Not knowing / a name for something proves nothing." This, in turn, may also be a rebuttal to one of Lévi-Strauss's statements: "It is impossible to discuss an object, to reconstruct the process of its coming into being without knowing first *what it is* . . ." (emphasis in the original)—a precept that Schuyler's work itself seems to disprove, here as in other poems—and is a reminder of how much of Schuyler's work is in dialogue with other poets, people, or situations. When Schuyler says "you" in a poem, usually there really is another person being addressed.

The first you in the poem is Johnny Porter, who comes to him at midnight to remark on the cyclical, predictable feelings of "letdown" following the elation of Christmas, a pattern roughly congruent to Jimmy's cycles of mania and depression: "It's a shame / expectations are / so often to be counted on." Schuyler follows this with a beautiful epigram: "who, knowing himself, would / endanger his desires / resolving them / in a formula?"

The second you in the poem is Fairfield, with whom Jimmy shares the kind of "reticence of intimacy" that he admires in Darwin's writing, as he notes in his diary entry of the same day. As they walk home from the movies in the aftermath of a snowstorm, the snow-laden branches overhead make "big disclosures," pointing up the lack of any such thing between the two of them. It would not have been in either of their natures to voice the pointed questions in Whitman's Calamus poem. Instead, they talk about the weather amid "Night / and snow and the threads of life / for once seen as they are, / in ropes like roots."

Although Schuyler makes light of New Year's resolutions in the poem, over the next few weeks he decided to make some himself, if not in so many words. He realized he needed to lose weight and went on a diet. And he also made the gesture of coming to grips with his sometime tendency to bossiness and ill humor, recognizing that he had been "too touchy lately, and sharp with Liz. It's something I needn't analyze but just stop." He also started a diary.

Jimmy kept his diary intermittently, with several changes of emphasis and direction, from January 1, 1968, through January 1, 1991, interrupted by a major gap from 1971 to 1984. Recalling later the genesis of the diary (temporarily forgetting a few entries at the beginning of the year), Jimmy said that he started it in the summer of 1968 on Great Spruce Head when he found himself in a poetry-writing slump and decided to force himself "to write *something* every day, and that would be a weather diary." "People," Jimmy said, "never get into it," which is far from true, but does convey a fair sense of the diary's essence in observation of the natural (and later, urban) world.

At Easter, Jimmy traveled with John Ashbery to visit his mother in Pultneyville, New York, getting a ride with Sophronus Mundy, a charismatic former marine whose mother lived near John's, and his lover, the painter Richard Hennessy. During the ride, John and Jimmy continued to work on *A Nest of Ninnies*, finally ending the book as it was begun, in the back seat of a car. Returning to the city they stopped in Elmira, New York, to see John's aunt and uncle. His aunt was a (not so) secret alcoholic, who kept disappearing into the kitchen during lunch to take swigs from a bottle of vodka she had hidden in the dishwasher—a circumstance Jimmy later borrowed for a character in his novel *What's for Dinner?*

After their return, Jimmy and John continued to correspond about *Nest,* deciding questions of an editorial nature: getting names right, cutting, fiddling with word or sentence order. The collaboration carried over into and enriched their friendship: their letters in particular got funnier than ever, each topping the other, so that their correspondence, too, became very much a collaborative work.

In the summer of 1968, Jimmy and the whole Porter family were excited to be in Maine after not having been there the year before, and Jimmy, Fairfield, Anne, Lizzie, and Lizzie's golden retriever, Bruno, all drove up together on June 24. "It's bliss to be here," Jimmy wrote to Joe, who was living at 49 South Main for the summer with Kenward, "especially since we've stopped assembling beds, sweeping, stretching canvases and the sun has come out."

They were soon joined by Laurence and Betsy Porter with their young son, Leon, and another couple with two little children, so the house was full indeed. Jimmy helped ease the kitchen burdens on Anne by baking popovers and a Swedish tea ring for which he invented a "memorable currant-cardamom filling (and how) [which] brought gasps from the Laurence Porters and friends."

For much of July, Jimmy was at work on a long poem, "The Cenotaph." At 177 lines, divided into three sections recording activities over a sequence of several days, it is slightly longer than "Now and Then." "The

Cenotaph" is dedicated to Kenneth Koch (who would visit in August) and is written in a wry, deadpan tone that is reminiscent of Koch's poetry in places, with a touch of Ashbery's "The Instruction Manual." The primer-like style also recalls the writings of Joe Brainard. The poem's three sections were originally separate poems that were later put together in a single work. Before they were assembled, Jimmy showed the first section, "Moneses Uniflora," to Kenneth, who made fun of it, saying, "There sure are a lot of smells in this poem." Jimmy viewed the subsequent dedication as a way "to get even with him."

Observations in the poem are stated in the driest possible manner, a beautiful and sometimes very funny deconstruction of both "fine writing" and narrative convention:

> We see seals.
> Boats go by.
> The stones hurt tender feet, so we walk on hands.
> It is easy: bodies are buoyant.
> The water is clear.
> It has thrown together some loose stones.

Formally, "The Cenotaph" might be seen as a response to the fluidity of "Now and Then." All of the full stops that are missing from the earlier poem have been put back into this one, and then some. The poem's disarming plainspokenness seems to acknowledge that the beauty, wonder, pleasures, and at times strangeness of life on the island are beyond the ken of mere art, and can best be expressed through the simplest, most artless means. The lack of narrative drama or buildup gives every statement the same weight, as though the events they describe were interchangeable, unimportant in themselves except as part of a fabric continually woven of experience and sensation.

The poem ends with a reference to the French historian and Resistance hero Marc Bloch, whose book *The Historian's Craft* Jimmy had been reading to Fairfield that summer while he painted:

> Suppose I found a bone in the grass and told you it is one of Marc
> Bloch's?

It would not be true.
No it would not be true and the sea is not his grave.
Noble, great, and good:
It is his cenotaph.

Defining the world-encircling sea as a cenotaph, or memorial, is to suggest the physicality of an uncapturable element, nearly an abstraction, in constant flux. Applied to Bloch in particular, it also calls to mind that historian's theory of "historical time" as simultaneously "a continuum" and also "perpetual change"—a concept from *The Historian's Craft* that Jimmy quotes in the article on Franz Kline he was also working on this summer.

It was a summer of familiar pleasures, but also new endeavors. Jimmy used some of his advance for *Freely Espousing* to buy a 35 mm camera, and he proved to be a good photographer, picking up the rudiments as readily as he did those of cooking and gardening. His photographs were mostly landscapes, still lifes, and interiors on Great Spruce Head, with few human subjects, and share with his poetry a sense of responding to the changing moment with deep attention but in an unforced way. Jimmy was modest about his achievements, and half-seriously wrote to Joe the following year, "There really isn't anything to photography except point and snap (I'm not sure that's true) . . . On the other hand, perhaps there isn't much more to poetry than point and snap."

In taking up both photography and his diary in the same year, both focused to some extent on Great Spruce Head, Jimmy was obviously aware of Fairfield's photographer brother Eliot Porter's books, *In Wildness Is the Preservation of the World* (1962) and *Summer Island* (1966). Both were large-format coffee-table books showcasing Eliot's highly skilled photographs of the island, its birds and its flora, the former taking as its text excerpts from the diaries of Thoreau, the latter Eliot's own reminiscences of his idyllic childhoods spent on the island. Porter worked mostly with a large format 4 x 5 view camera, entailing elaborate framing, exposure, and processing. In comparison, Jimmy's nifty little 35 mm rangefinder with its built-in light meter was indeed just a step above "point and snap."

Kenneth Koch and his daughter, Katherine, arrived on August 3 for a visit of ten days. For Katherine, who visited almost every summer from about 1966 through 1972, the island was "magic." As an urban child it was to her "very, very cool that there were no cars and no roads really to speak of, and no stores . . . It was kind of made for children: we could adventure out whenever we felt like on all the trails, seeing all the different beautiful forests and meadows and beaches." As an artist, she loved it when the group produced collaborative comic strips as part of the evening entertainment. A sheet of paper would be folded lengthwise and crosswise into sixteen squares, and the first person would make a drawing in one square and the second person would do voice balloons for the drawing, and the story would unfold improvisationally as the page filled. "Of course it was great having Fairfield Porter do drawings!" she recalled. "And Jimmy and Anne and my father, if he was there, do words."

As on previous visits, Jimmy enjoyed Kenneth's company, but at the same time he recognized that his outsized personality came with bluster, obliviousness, and occasional bad temper. But even these Jimmy seemed to enjoy, in a way, as fodder for amusing letters to his friends. To Ron Padgett, he wrote ahead of the visit, "The thought of Kenneth the Menneth (as Kenward lately called him) here is faintly alarming. He fills the house so with his Henry VIII impersonations and mad German scientist impersonations and cries for meals between meals, and types so fast and long (I especially resent that), and never helps with the dishes, and that's very annoying, since really you don't want him to help, as, dishwise, he's strictly a bull in a hoop-skirt." Whatever the drawbacks, Jimmy enjoyed having a generational peer around, especially such a lively one, who stimulated his own lagging sociability. The two poets took walks around the island and swam and sunbathed and showed each other new work in progress. Jimmy especially liked talking about "Literature with a capital L" with Kenneth, something most of his other writer friends didn't do. "I wish I could recapture the tone of those conversations," Kenneth later said. "There was always a chance when you were with Schuyler that some wonderful thing would happen . . . He would always take what I said seriously, always think about it, the response was always fresh . . . [To talk with him] was like an education and also like dancing."

Janice Koch did not accompany her husband and daughter on this visit, but at the end of it she joined Kenneth, Katherine, and Jimmy in a weeklong road trip to Nova Scotia. Kenneth drove with Janice beside him in the front seat, and Katherine and Jimmy in back (again inserted into another surrogate family). They spent a week exploring the province, driving to Cape Breton Island, the northernmost section, and made the circuit of the Cabot Trail to the lookout point on Cape Smokey. Everyone got along, despite Kenneth's occasional flares of temper—he "could get angry at the drop of a hat," his daughter recalled. Jimmy took evocative black-and-white pictures of the excursion. The bleak, windswept landscape of New Brunswick and Nova Scotia, its small isolated settlements, both like and unlike Maine, stimulated his imagination. "For the landscape, it's a must for all New England States lovers, but rather hard to describe—unless you can take the word 'empty' as the high praise I mean it to be."

By the late '60s, Jimmy was going into the city several times a month, to prepare an occasional *Art News* article, see John, Joe, and other friends, and not least, visit the Everard Baths. The novelist James McCourt recalled seeing him there around this time, "shuffling along the hall just like me." In addition to sex, there was also a friendly camaraderie among fellow patrons. Through their later friendship, McCourt learned that Jimmy felt very strongly "the intense satisfaction of the homosocial atmosphere of the baths."

In town, he usually alternated between staying with Kenward at his small house on Cornelia Street and with John Ashbery at his apartment on East Ninety-fifth, but as Jimmy increasingly took his welcome for granted, John began to find these visits a strain. Jimmy's habit of staying out all night at the baths and coming home in the morning only after John had left for work, then sleeping all day, did not accord well with John's nine-to-five schedule. Thus it was fortunate that early in 1968 Kenward bought a four-story town house on Greenwich Avenue, and dedicated the top-floor studio as a guest apartment for Jimmy. Helping to find and arrange nice things to decorate the house and achieve the "total eclectic looks" that Kenward and Joe were aiming for brought out

Jimmy's domestic streak. As Elmslie recalled, "He was a great practical help. He made himself useful that way." The house became Jimmy's unofficial New York base over the next couple of years.

March 1969 saw the publication, at last, of both *Freely Espousing*, Schuyler's first commercially published book of poems, with a cover collage by Alex Katz, and *A Nest of Ninnies*, published by Dutton. Considering that the book drew from some sixteen or seventeen years of writing poetry, the forty-two poems in *Freely Espousing* are a remarkably small group—in effect a "selected poems" of work up to that point. As John Koethe observed in his review in *Poetry* the following October, "Coming upon a mature body of work without much prior warning is always a perplexing experience requiring an accommodation . . . But in Schuyler's case this effort is amply rewarded, for not only is *Freely Espousing* a collection of extremely good poems, but it also embodies the sort of vision that periodically reawakens us to the infinite range of possibilities open to the poet." In fact, while a little more than half of the poems in *Freely Espousing* date from the 1950s, what seems to give the book its center are the more recent poems written after 1961, in Southampton, Maine, or Vermont. Although there was an unfavorable review in *The New York Times Book Review* by Guy Davenport (calling it "slapdash and talkative"), Schuyler had the last word: on the day it came out he wrote "Things to Do When You Get a Bad Review," a follow-up to his original, much-emulated "Things to Do."

The generally mixed reviews of *A Nest of Ninnies* were made up for, perhaps, by the appreciative one by W. H. Auden in *The New York Times Book Review*, who wrote that the book was "destined to become a minor classic," comparable to the work of Ronald Firbank, Lewis Carroll, P. G. Wodehouse, the "Lucia" novels of E. H. Benson, and *The Importance of Being Earnest*. It was also reviewed favorably, if not entirely to the point, in the daily *New York Times* by Thomas Lask, who liked the book's "unruffled, sec and witty style."

Arthur Cohen, Ashbery's editor at Dutton, gave a publication party for *A Nest of Ninnies*, which in effect became a celebration of *Freely Espousing* as well. It was well attended: Auden was there, along with many uptown literary and publishing figures, as well as downtown poets like Lewis Warsh, who recalled that it was a big party, teeming with people, and that Jimmy looked "happy and *beaming* . . . cherubic . . . like he was stoned," and as though "he just couldn't believe all the attention he was getting."

Fairfield Porter had accepted a teaching position at Amherst College, in Amherst, Massachusetts, for the academic year of 1969–1970. He and Anne invited Ron and Pat Padgett and their young son, Wayne, to live at 49 South Main Street during the family's year away, and they moved in over the summer, when the Porters were in Maine.

The weather was unusually hot and sultry. Much of Jimmy's writing this summer was focused on his diary, where his observations on the island and the weather were interspersed with interactions and conversations with the various Porters. He also continued his photography, willing himself not to be intimidated by Eliot Porter and his son, Stephen, whom he encountered one morning at the harbor, aiming an enormous telephoto lens at neighboring islands shrouded in fog, and letting him know by their manner that they did not wish for his company.

The summer of 1969 exposed a bit of tension between the families of Fairfield's siblings and Jimmy, whose presence they never quite understood or approved of. Although nothing, or very little, was ever said in that buttoned-up WASP environment, criticism and disapproval were in the air, and while Jimmy in letters to friends never referred directly to any bad vibes he may have gotten from the family, they may be inferred from his own negative comments. The more Fairfield and Anne and the girls interacted with the other islanders, the more Jimmy seems to have chafed at being stuck in their company, away from his witty friends, and he took to making fun of the other Porters in his letters, especially to Ashbery and Brainard. "Tomorrow," he wrote in July 1969, "the crabby Porter brother, Edward, is coming to stay—with Nancy [Straus], thank God—for several weeks. So is his astonishingly plain wife." Although earlier that summer he reported, "John P[orter] seems easier to get on with this year," he had to cap it with a put-down: "I suppose being the dumb Porter brother is not such an easy role to fill." The mean-spiritedness of some of these remarks is a symptom of a general darkening of Schuyler's mood in the late '60s, as the long extension of his stay with the family began to wear on all concerned.

Alex, Ada, and nine-year-old Vincent Katz visited the island for the second time this summer. Alex couldn't help observing Fairfield's strange relationships with his brothers and sister, and the sense in which being on the island was for him to be plunged back into his childhood, with all its insecurities and sibling rivalries intact. When Fairfield pointed out a low bridge where he had once jumped off and hurt his back, it took Alex a while to realize he was talking about something that had happened forty years earlier, when he was a boy. Katz got the sense that John Porter and the rest of Fairfield's brothers and sister saw Fairfield as "kind of a Sunday painter or something, it wasn't a serious occupation," and regarded most of his artist and poet friends in a similar light. But because Katz taught at Yale, which was "something real respectable . . . [Fairfield] pushed me in his brother's face, who taught at some junior high school [*sic*] . . . Their development seemed quite arrested."

Later in the summer, John Ashbery and Pierre Martory stayed for about three days. The visit was a particularly nice one; John was relaxed, and Jimmy found him to be an "easier guest" than on some occasions in the past, when he had been "worked up about crowding every second with pleasure and plans, conflicting plans at that." They both cooked up a storm; John made a rich lentil soup and Jimmy a large blueberry pie. John recalled, "There was always somewhat of a problem with food there, because everything had to be transported from Camden, and it had to be at the pleasure of Fairfield's brother, who wasn't all that pleasant." During this visit John had a growing sense that "Jimmy was not looked upon with great favor by the rest of the [Porter] family." On one uncomfortable occasion, Lizzie, out of the blue, asked her parents for the meaning of the word *parasite*. It had apparently come up in a conversation she had overheard at her uncle John's house, and Ashbery got the feeling "it might well have been referring to Jimmy."

By the late 1960s, Jimmy and his friends had begun to smoke marijuana more or less regularly. Pot added significantly to the hilarity of the collage-making evenings around Kenward and Joe's kitchen table;

in addition, within a few years, both Joe and Ted Berrigan would become increasingly involved with amphetamines, problematically so by the mid-'70s. During the summer of 1969, Jimmy was grateful for the occasional discreet package of joints from Joe, and when John visited in August, Jimmy asked him to bring both a bottle of scotch and some pot. Writing to Joe, he also mentioned his small stash on the island of "Voodoo Darkskin Love Beans," probably speed. No doubt the growing sense of alienation that the family felt from Jimmy in these years was, in part, due to his being stoned some of the time.

On August 27, Jimmy and the Porters left Great Spruce Head for Amherst, where Fairfield took up his job as a visiting lecturer and artist-in-residence. The family moved into a large clapboard house near the campus. Soon after they settled in, Jimmy left for another visit to Kenward and Joe in Calais, and for September and October 1969, he was traveling almost constantly between Amherst, New York, and Calais, with a quick trip to Maine with Fairfield to close the house and collect the new paintings, spending only a week or two in any one place. "I haven't come to light since Aug. 28th," he wrote to Ron Padgett on October 7: "vagabond shoes."

Jimmy liked Amherst, in a mild way. The house was near a nature preserve where he enjoyed walking, and not far from the Emily Dickinson house, which had opened as a museum in 1965. Being a college town, there were bookstores and no fewer than four movie theaters, in addition to retrospective film programs at the college itself. But a little of Amherst went a long way, and in late October Kenward returned to pick him up and take him back to Vermont.

He brought with him a new friend, Trevor Winkfield, who was visiting from England. Now best known as a painter, Winkfield was then a recent graduate of the Royal College of Art in London, and was editing a little magazine called *Juillard*, named after a character in Raymond Roussel's novel *Locus Solus*, through which he had already become epistolary friends with Kenward, Jimmy, and other New York poets. A few days after Trevor arrived in New York, Kenward decided to take him up to Vermont to see the fall foliage, stopping in Amherst to pick up Jimmy. Although they stayed only about an hour before they were on their way again, Anne served the travelers bacon and eggs, which seemed to Trevor "such an English thing to do." The group stopped again en route at a used-book barn, where Jimmy found a copy of the *Letters of Emily Dickinson*, which he bought for ten dollars and presented to Trevor. Trevor realized immediately that he "liked Jimmy enormously. He was a very easy guy to get along with, very funny and also very quiet . . . So we hit it off immediately. And also he was interested in so many different things, and he'd introduce you to so many, like he'd just introduced me to Emily Dickinson's letters . . . And the fact that I didn't really know this guy and he immediately bought me a book; that's the kind of thing he would do."

While he was in Vermont this time, Jimmy completed his first application for a Guggenheim Foundation grant. The grants are intended to support a specific project, and he proposed a book about Nova Scotia, building on his trip there the previous summer, to be written in a combination of prose and poetry. He secured recommendations from Kenneth Koch, John Ashbery, James Merrill, and the critic F. W. Dupee, but even as he put the application together, he braced himself for disappointment, adding to John, "I already feel quite depressed, as I look forward to being turned down."

John, who would write for all eight of Schuyler's eventual Guggenheim applications, began his recommendation with the words, "I think James Schuyler one of the best writers living." All of the other recommendations were equally strong (Dupee calling him "one of the two or three best poets of his generation").

Trevor stayed with Jimmy and Kenward for about a week before they all drove back to the city. On the way they stopped at a rather upscale restaurant, or what Trevor described as "a Vermont version of what a New York restaurant should be like." The trio "were so disgusted about the whole petit-bourgeois atmosphere of the place" that Kenward and Jimmy proceeded to stand in front of the restaurant's picture window and neck ostentatiously, in full view of the shocked restaurant patrons. "This was a total shock for me as well," Trevor recalled. "I'd never seen anything like that in London."

That fall, Joe Brainard sent Jimmy a work of prose he had completed called *I Remember*. Deceptively simple, the work is composed of a series of apparently random memories, mostly from childhood, each beginning "I remember . . ." It has become Brainard's best-known text and a classic of New York School—or indeed twentieth-century American—writing. Jimmy's response was immediate and prescient: "I think about *I Remember* all the time . . . It's a great work that will last & last—in other words, it is literature."

Jimmy spent Thanksgiving with his mother in East Aurora, and returned to Amherst for Christmas with the Porters. The change from Southampton to Amherst agreed with Fairfield: when Jimmy saw him on one of his returns that fall, he found him looking "ten years younger." He enjoyed teaching, and both he and Anne felt at home in the academic milieu of the town. Liz, too, was happier with school friends who were more compatible than those in Southampton. Christmas in Amherst was cold and snowy, but extremely beautiful. "We've had ice storms and snowstorms all on top of each other. Every twig and branch is coated with ice, and when the sun came out yesterday the effect was like nothing I've ever seen before—so dazzling," Jimmy wrote to Joe Brainard.

The summer of 1970 would be Jimmy's last on Great Spruce Head and, although he could not have realized this, an almost elegiac mood entered some of his writing about the island this summer. In a letter to Kenward on first arriving, he wrote, "The sun is shining on the sea, the yellow hawkweed is shining in the grass, and I feel as though yesterday I was sitting at this desk writing to Joe. As Lizzie said on the Kittiwake, 'Going to the island makes me feel schizophrenic.' Because it really seems as though no time had passed—there's a person who only lives here, and then there's someone else who lives in the inferior places. Scary and beautiful . . . I guess one does forget each winter the utter sameness of here as a place. It's not enough to be here and see it, I want to be it."

He resolved that summer to give up smoking dope, at least while on the island, and to go on a diet. He also gave up smoking cigarettes, but in compensation took up cigar smoking, which he thought might help him to lose weight. Soon, however, the strain of simultaneously dieting and not smoking cigarettes proved too much, and he gave up the diet—with the result (as he wrote to Larry Fagin) that he "instantly . . . gained

800 pounds and now look like something you find glowering in a back alley of Naples."

Continuing to explore ideas about the materiality of poetry, and inspired by Joe Brainard's assemblages, that summer Jimmy made what he called a "trash book," taking an empty address book and pasting in it various scraps of paper and natural materials, which he presented to Joe. He also created its counterpart in the poem "The Trash Book," dedicated to Joe: a collage of observations and phenomena that would be impossible to fit into any physical book: a "smear" of landscape, a half-remembered remark, concluding with an "involuntary memory" of a beer advertisement glimpsed at Emily's roadhouse in 1942, when Jimmy was flunking out of Bethany: "a cardboard / girl sitting on a moon in / West Virginia. She smiled / and sipped her Miller's."

At the beginning of July, Katherine Koch arrived to spend the month with Lizzie, followed a few weeks later by her father. As in the previous years, Jimmy enjoyed complaining humorously if rather bitchily in letters to Kenward and Joe of Kenneth's supposed faults. After Kenneth left, John Ashbery returned, accompanied by his new lover, Aladar Marberger, a charismatic art dealer about twenty years John's junior, who was the new director of the Fischbach Gallery. John and Jimmy had intended to start work on a new collaborative novel, but in the end it never got off the ground, largely because of the distracting presence of the hyperactive Marberger, who had charm but could be extremely abrasive. Though he enjoyed the visit, Jimmy found himself in the slightly uncomfortable position of third wheel, a rather reluctant witness to the acting-out of their relationship. "He and John have evolved a kind of Maggie and Jiggs style . . . When alone with me they also do quite a bit of Hubby and Wifey billing-and-cooing—I'm not a bit sure that I [don't] prefer the dish-throwing act." Part of the problem, Jimmy recognized, was that he was "a little bit jealous at not having John's full attention." In general, he also preferred "Pierre's Parisian style."

The Porters' car going back to Southampton that September was more crowded than ever, with Fairfield, Anne, Katie and a college friend of hers who had come up for a weekend, Liz, Jimmy, the golden retriever Bruno, and all their luggage. "Yes, when we travel we are the pitiful family you glide by on the freeway," Jimmy wrote sardonically to Joe, "the one with the playpen and mattress on the roof and a tarpaulin dragging in the road behind."

He was pleased to be back in Southampton rather than Amherst. This month, Fairfield made the momentous move from his longtime gallery, Tibor de Nagy, where John Myers's rather cavalier ways had long been an annoyance, to the venerable Knoedler Gallery, where Donald Droll was now the head of contemporary art. After a few weeks, Jimmy and Fairfield returned to Maine together to close up the house, and on September 27, Fairfield made a quick, informal drawing of Jimmy's head in ballpoint pen on a sheet of typing paper. On the same sheet he also sketched a teakettle, the chance juxtaposition subtly underlining the domestic nature of their relationship. A few days later, they returned to Southampton. Jimmy would never see the island again.

At the beginning of November, Jimmy, Kenward, and Joe drove back up to Vermont for a week's stay. Jimmy kept a record of the visit, written in a combination of prose and poetry (exploring a form he had intended to use for his unrealized Nova Scotia opus), which he published as "A Vermont Diary" in *The Crystal Lithium*. It is a tour de force of varying moods and tones, resolving organically by not resolving, another example of what Jimmy called "an art where disparate elements form an entity." The prose sections of the work are similar to other entries of his diary, although a new kind of thoroughness and narrative enters into a description of a long walk he took on November 6, perhaps thinking of how he might treat similar explorations of unfamiliar territory in Nova Scotia. In another entry, Jimmy appears to be channeling the "in the moment" aspect of Joe Brainard's diary writings, where he tries to nail down a passing moment as he writes it: "Kenward is right behind me taking wood ashes out of the fireplace to add to the compost. Actually, he is through doing that and is laying a fire, bringing big chunks of wood up from the cellar. Whippoorwill hops off the couch with a sneeze and gallops after him, then comes back to lie in some unexpected sunshine."

At the end of 1970, Katie Porter was twenty-one and Lizzie was fourteen. Jimmy had been living in their family for half of Katie's life, and most of Liz's. Katie had been away at college for the past four years, returning periodically for summers and holidays, and as an adult she now took an objective and highly critical view of the utter strangeness of Jimmy's continued presence, with an increased awareness of how it had distorted and damaged their family life: absorbing Fairfield's attention at their expense, and casting a pall over the house in Jimmy's depressed moods, which had become more frequent. Although Katie liked Jimmy and felt he had "so much to give" the family when she and her sister were younger, and she also understood something of what his friendship meant to her father, she knew it was time for Jimmy to leave. She was particularly concerned for Lizzie, now that she was older, and hoped she might be spared some of the hurt and confusion she herself had experienced as an adolescent due to Jimmy's presence.

Jimmy could still be charming and amusing, but often, now, he seemed sunk in his own world, exuding a sense of oppression and gloom that pervaded the house. Like Katie, Anne was particularly worried about the effect on Lizzie, who herself felt the situation was not right. She would come home from school to find him sitting in "his" chair in the living room, listening to Mahler and drinking a martini at four o'clock in the afternoon, "and I can almost see the black cloud over his head . . . he was just so depressed."

Anne had long come to feel that Jimmy needed to have a place of his own, and that by continuing to live with the family he was only becoming increasingly dependent. But it was Katie who was the catalyst in the family's decision finally to ask Jimmy to leave, and both she and Liz spoke to Anne, expressing their sense that the time had come. Katie was present when, in the fall of 1970, Anne brought the matter up with Fairfield and asked him to ask Jimmy to move out. When she did, Katie saw her father's face "turn white." But he agreed to do it.

Fairfield and Anne recognized the gravity of what they would be asking and were greatly troubled by the idea that to simply kick him out would devastate him, and might well trigger another nervous breakdown, not to mention the big question of whether he could realistically support himself after so many years of having been cared for. "We didn't want Jimmy to be destroyed," Anne later recalled. "We knew it was . . . an almost dangerous thing to ask him to separate from us." Before they actually approached him about it, Anne and Fairfield consulted several psychiatrists for advice "to find out what was safe," including Dr. Detre, who told them that while they had "saved his life," they had also done Jimmy a "disservice by letting him become so closed in in this situation." Anne, as was her nature, took this criticism to heart, but as was also her nature, she was not dissuaded from doing now what she knew was right.

The ocean beach was a mile from the house, and in all seasons Fairfield was known for taking long, brisk walks down South Main Street to the shore and then along the beach, sometimes with Jimmy. It was in the course of one of these long walks that Fairfield explained to Jimmy the family's concerns, and suggested it was time for him to leave. He must have couched the request in fairly mild terms, for Jimmy's reply, as Fairfield relayed it to Anne that evening, was "I'll think about it."

Think about it he did, for three additional, uncomfortable years. During that period there was an increase in Jimmy's visits to other friends, and, starting in 1971, the use of his own small apartment in the city as a pied-à-terre. There came a flowering of new poems, including some of the most ambitious work he had yet done, as though the request to leave had given him an unconscious desire to show the Porters what he was capable of. In particular, Jimmy wrote two major long poems during the period between the walk on the beach with Porter and his final departure from the house in October 1973. Both of them begin with imagery of a windy beach, in winter ("The Crystal Lithium") or spring ("Hymn to Life"), as though starting from that uncomfortable talk, unconsciously acknowledging it as a stimulus.

For the next several months, Jimmy's letters and diary continued on an even keel, and he did not deign to acknowledge the conversation in his prose or poetry. His emotional reaction to the gentle ultimatum was delayed until the following summer, when the realization that he was not to be invited to Great Spruce Head finally sank in.

[16]

PAIN DOESN'T HURT; IT'S A SENSATION, LIKE A KISS

1971

It was a cold winter, and when Jimmy got back to Southampton after spending Thanksgiving with his mother, he wrote a series of short poems and diary entries that made reference to the snowy weather:

> December 24, 1970: "It's snowing—flakes fat as feathers fall . . . There's a lot of twisting, turning, gusts and indecisions, all about to settle when they rise up like an alarmed flock from a field . . ."

He proposed collaborating with Trevor Winkfield on a "snow anthology," and sent him one of the poems he had written in December, "Poem," dedicated to Trevor and dated December 26, 1970. It begins: "The wind tears up the sun / and scatters it in snow." It is likely that "Self-Pity Is a Kind of Lying, Too" was also written in December 1970. That poem does not define the cause of the self-pity, but the fact that he had recently been asked to leave South Main Street would make Jimmy a good candidate to be feeling it. The poem ends with an image of bleak unprotectedness: "one day we'll / just have snow / to wear too."

Cold weather endured into the first two weeks of February, when Jimmy came into New York for another stay with Kenward. While in the city he caught a rare sight of his old friend John Wieners, in town to give a reading. Wieners had recently been hospitalized for mental illness, and Jimmy's attitude to him was complicated by feelings of identification and self-protective disapproval. As he wrote to Trevor, he "seemed in a truly awful state . . . I feel a great deal of sympathy, no, really, love, for John. I only wish that he did not believe, as he does, that what he has done to himself (with hard drugs, analysis resistance, the works) is somehow all for the Sake of the Good of Art. That, I am not buying."

In late March, John Ashbery invited himself out to Southampton for a weekend, to escape from a tiff he was having with Aladar Marberger. Things were never easy between Ashbery and the temperamental younger man, and to complicate matters, John was having a simultaneous affair with a handsome young Iranian American graduate student at Columbia, David Kermani. John had met David just three weeks after meeting Aladar and found him "very beautiful in all ways," quickly deciding he had made a mistake in getting involved with Aladar because he liked David much better. "I really feel bad about it because of Aladar," he wrote to Jimmy the previous July. But it was not easy for John, with his mingled diffidence and courtesy, to cut off ties suddenly with Marberger, and the two relationships existed in uneasy tandem for some time.

By this time, Jimmy was moving slowly toward a manic period. Although he was still in "denial" about the Porters having asked him to leave, and there was no open reference to it in his letters or poems, his anxiety found outlet in increased activity. For the time being this energy was channeled constructively into poetry. Unable to sleep one winter night in Southampton, he picked up a facsimile edition of Whitman's original *Leaves of Grass*. He started reading the poem, hoping it would help put him to sleep, but "of course it was the wrong hour to do it because it is an incredibly stimulating work," he recalled. Obviously, he had read Whitman before this, but confronted anew with "Song of Myself," it came as a fresh revelation. Within a few days he was inspired to try to write something "like it," and he began "The Crystal Lithium."

The most noticeable borrowing from "Song of Myself" in "The Crystal Lithium" is the long line, which imparts to both poems a magisterial pace and tone. Schuyler had used longish lines before, in "The Cenotaph" and elsewhere, but never quite as long, or for their own sake, so to speak, or so consistently. In speaking of the long line of "The Crystal Lithium" in one interview, Jimmy said its length was not important "so long as the breath didn't give out." Elsewhere he describes the poem as being best read as one long, continuous breath, but disclaimed any influence of Charles Olson's ideas about "breath" from "Projective Verse." Here "breath" is imagined not as a rhythmic exchange but something to be held on to, endlessly. In fact, the poem quickly introduces an image of a held breath: "the air is emptied to an uplifting gassiness / That turns lungs to winter waterwings, buoying . . ." Following from this, there is a sense that the whole poem is aloft, suspended in air, never touching ground: indeed, there are virtually no periods in the work, even at the end.

In hindsight the several poems and diary entries that Jimmy wrote earlier that winter, evoking evanescent snowfalls and snowy air and ocean light, seem like warm-up exercises for the opening lines of "The Crystal Lithium":

> The smell of snow, stinging in nostrils as the wind lifts it from a
> beach
> Eye-shuttering, mixed with sand, or when snow lies under the street
> lamps and on all
> And the air is emptied to an uplifting gassiness
> That turns lungs to winter waterwings, buoying, and the bright
> white night
> Freezes in sight a lapse of waves, balsamic, salty, unexpected . . .

Writing the poem took almost two months of intermittent work, from late February or early March to late April. Even as he was writing, Schuyler was aware that he was onto something special. "It seemed to break through into what I wanted. It was also a breakthrough because it was turning out to be one of my best poems. I was very aware of that." "I didn't want to spoil it." When he went back to New York to stay at Kenward's at the end of March, he took the unfinished poem with him to continue it there. "And then something happened in my life," Jimmy recalled, "and I wrote the end." The "something" was that he fell in love. On Friday night, April 2, he went to the Everard Baths, and in the early hours of Saturday morning had an exciting encounter there with a man named Robert Jordan. They stayed together until early Sunday afternoon. Having been unsure how to end "The Crystal Lithium," the bathhouse encounter with Jordan, in "a room in this or that cheap dump / Where the ceiling light burns night and day," provided the answer. The poem returned to the beach, snow, and wind imagery of its beginning, but changed now by the encounter with the lover into an implied question and a command:

> . . . we stare at or into each
> Other's eyes in hope the other reads there what he reads: snow, wind
> Lifted; black water, slashed with white; and that which is, which is
> beyond
> Happiness or love or mixed with them or more than they or less,
> unchanging change,
> "Look," the ocean said (it was tumbled, like our sheets), "look in
> my eyes"

The title of the poem, as Schuyler was at pains to state in several interviews, has "nothing to do with the use of lithium as a medication," which he claimed he was not even aware of at the time. Rather, it comes from an old postcard he had thumbtacked to the wall in front of his desk showing a ramshackle roadhouse bearing the sign "Crystal Lithium." The beneficial properties of lithium, a mineral component of some spring water, have long been known. In the nineteenth and early twentieth centuries, "Lithia Water" was bottled and sold as a tonic; people bathed in lithium-rich water at spas like the one shown on the postcard. As Jimmy wrote to Kenneth, who had expressed doubts about the title, "I like the sound of it; and for me the 'crystal' connects directly with the snow imagery . . . Lithium; well, I thought everybody knew what Lithia Water was, or is. At my house they used to guzzle it like Perrier water." One cannot be certain that Jimmy really had no idea of the psychiatric use of lithium when he wrote the poem, but that usage was quite new in 1971, and he wasn't taking it himself. Lithium was only approved for use in the treatment of "mania" in 1970, and for the long-term treatment of bipolar condition in 1974.

Jimmy's reading of "Song of Myself" also brought back his earlier readings of Whitman, especially "A Winter Day on the Sea Beach" (which he had referred to in "Empathy and New Year") with its evocation of the Jersey shore as "That spread of waves and gray-white beach, salt, monotonous, senseless," which was now echoed, down to its trio of laconic adjectives, by Jimmy as "a lapse of waves, balsamic, salty, unexpected." Along with the rediscovery of Whitman himself, reading *Leaves of Grass* also reawakened Schuyler's conscious and unconscious memories of the teenage epiphany that occurred while reading *about* Whitman in Logan Pearsall Smith's *Unforgotten Years*, and the opening and closing lines of "The Crystal Lithium" retain traces not only of Whitman but of Smith's book as well. In one passage Smith recalls conversations he had as a boy with the aged Whitman, who "always from the days of his boyhood on the Long Island coasts . . . had tried and tried again to seize the meaning which the voice of the ocean was always whispering in his ear." Smith recalls with admiration Whitman's efforts to convey "the sea's voice, for instance, or the breath of its salt fragrance, or even, as he himself had said, 'the undulation of one wave.'"

One need not credit Schuyler with total recall or believe that he was consciously thinking of this passage from a book read more than thirty years earlier, but an element of his genius clearly resided in his ability to retain an almost bodily awareness of many disparate past experiences and reintegrate them into the present moment when called for. Something of Smith's cadences and imagery, and his paraphrases and quotations of Whitman, stayed latent within Jimmy all that time, to be reconstituted, as it were, by the much-later reading of Whitman while within earshot of the ocean himself. At the poem's end, it is "the sea's voice" that speaks directly to Schuyler with a life-changing command.

The poem "happens" everywhere and in every time at once. Begun in the depths of winter, it moves to "a broiling day in late September" and includes references to "the thunder of a summer's day." Nominally set in the "present," it slides in and out of the real time of the poem's period of composition as the poet reexperiences the past, always with a feeling of natural elision, with each thought or image folded into another, transforming and enriching both.

The shifts in imagery are triggered not only by what is "happening" in the poem but by words themselves, turned around and seen in new contexts. The sound of summer thunder merges with heat waves on a blacktop road, and a smell of freshly mown grass "thickens the air" like custard thickening on a wooden spoon, which turns into a gray snow-laden sky filled with a rising flock of small gray birds. Calling attention to his own writing process, the poet modifies a description of starlings from "unloved" to "Not so likeable as some" and then refers to the new description as "temperate enough"; this in turn suggests the word *temperature*, which "Drops to rise to snowability of a softness even in its scent of roses / Made of untinted butter frosting . . ."

Images of water- or airborne metamorphoses recur throughout the poem and mirror the currents of the poet's thought process, as it evokes and revokes an "unchanging change" of imagery and experience—the phrase itself reminiscent of Marc Bloch's "continuum of perpetual change." Phrases tangle and twist themselves inside out in seemingly awkward constructions such as "slow-up wings," "the gibbous rest" (of the new moon), and "shrunk into itself from cold forsythia snarl." Words (*temperate / temperature*) bump rudely into the imagery and change the poem's direction as abruptly as the fickle currents of wind and waves and thought. A reference to "lengthening short days" of a post-solstice winter morphs into a parent's plaint about a child growing out of his clothes (for whom too-short pants have to be lengthened): "'He's outgrown them / Before you can turn around,'" which phrase continues on the new line with "and see behind you the landscape of the past." And there follows a vignette from Schuyler's own past: the excursion to Positano in 1948, when "One—someone—stops to break off a bit of myrtle and recite all the lines / Of Goethe that come back, and those in French, *Connais-tu . . .* ?" Here was another one of those "lumps" of experience Jimmy wrote of having retained within himself, in his letter to Fairfield from Venice so many years before, now finally "broken apart" or "unfolded" in this poem.

References to the process or state of crystallization run through the poem—"irradiate" it, as the poet says. Salt, sand, ice, snow, lithium—the crystal imagery hints at processes of growth and change, and the way all physical matter is ultimately reducible to a few mutable elements. When he was young, Jimmy, like many boys of his era, may have had a crystal set: a basic radio that is powered solely by radio waves themselves. In such a device a piece of rock crystal detects and "hears" sounds flowing in currents of air that are otherwise, of course, inaudible: a passive receptor of data flowing in waves or currents, not unlike the poet himself. In fact, in a letter to Ron Padgett in January 1971, perhaps a month before beginning the poem, Jimmy writes (speaking of his response to the noisy crowd at a party), "I get the feeling that I've turned into an old-fashioned crystal set, very good at picking up signals from all over."

The poem by its nature could have gone on forever, but obviously it needed an ending—one commensurate with the breakthrough Jimmy knew it to be. The meeting with Bob Jordan provided the ending—or perhaps the need for an ending may have produced Bob Jordan.

Robert Jordan was a "big tall hunk" three or four years younger than Jimmy, six feet two inches tall, slender, with dark hair and "hazel" or greenish blue eyes, handsome in a certain rather slick way. "He looked sort of like a Brooks Brothers salesman, which is what he was," Ashbery recalled. Actually he was a buyer there, trying to start his own importing company. He was married, and lived with his wife in New Jersey. Jimmy preferred not to speculate too much about his wife, and knew only that Jordan had married relatively late, at age thirty-six, "so I surmise that they knew what they were doing."

The love affair took off quickly. Jordan's job meant that he was often traveling, which gave him a certain amount of cover to carry on his extramarital affair, but also took him away from both lover and wife for extended periods. Jimmy's longing for his return during his absences became a frequent refrain in references to the affair.

At first, Jimmy's friends were happy that he had begun a new relationship, but very soon after meeting Jordan, almost to a person, they began to find him strange and unappealing. He seemed "sleazy," in hard-to-define ways. Jane Freilicher claimed she "didn't know him very well, but I didn't like what I saw." "I think he wore plaid Bermuda shorts to the beach or something." She thought that "inviting him out to Fairfield and Anne's was like desecrating a church."

John Ashbery was very pleased for Jimmy when he learned that he had finally met someone he was "so passionate about." But he gradually realized that Jimmy "was in a manic state, and that Bob Jordan was not the Prince Charming Jimmy thought he was." Kenward thought that

Jordan "was an absolute jerk. A total one hundred percent jerk. Our mouths were agape: how could Schuyler fall for such a creep?" Kenward attributed the attraction to a split between Jimmy's "serene" and "intelligent" side and another dark, masochistic side of his "schizoid nature."

Many of Jimmy's friends felt there was a fictional or fictitious quality about Jordan. Ashbery felt there was "something totally phoney about him" and the "double life" he was leading. Jane thought he was "material for a short story of a disagreeable character [who] sort of wreaks havoc . . . [A] complete outsider who comes in and sort of tears the fabric of a life." Robert Dash perhaps put it best: "I think Jimmy made him up. Which is what you do when you're in love. Jimmy was very much in love and made him up. The fellow didn't really exist."

There is, of course, a famous fictional character called "Robert Jordan": the hero of Ernest Hemingway's novel of the Spanish Civil War, *For Whom the Bell Tolls*. And it is widely recognized that one of the three or four Lincoln Brigade fighters on whom this Robert Jordan was based was Bill Aalto. Whether or not Jimmy made the connection—and how could he not?—it does appear that the two relationships, although separated by some twenty-five years, shared some sexual dynamics. Aalto was a volatile, violent person who on occasion attacked and struck Jimmy; Jordan's relationship with Jimmy was known to have a sadomasochistic component. Of course, there is a huge difference between domestic violence and the head trips and role-playing of consensual sadomasochistic scenarios. However, it is probable that here the line was blurred in both cases: that the relationship with Aalto included consensual S&M-type role-playing (as John Richardson sensed), and the relationship with Jordan some borderline abuse. Either way, for Jimmy there was at least the similarity of his own masochistic response to both men.

That the relationship came to include S&M elements was understood by many of Jimmy's close friends, but for the most part they did not discuss it with him. The only outward sign of it was a heavy Danish silver chain that Jordan gave Jimmy that June and that he began to wear constantly. It was extremely conspicuous—Trevor Winkfield likened it to a "bicycle chain" and Darragh Park to a "dog collar." To his friends the chain carried a clear connotation of sexual ownership and subjugation. John Ashbery got the idea, based on conversations with Jimmy, that "Bob had commanded him to always wear this chain, or something."

Direct evidence of the relationship's sadomasochistic aspect can be found in a handful of letters and recollections of friends, while indirect references turn up in a few poems, including "The Morning of the Poem" and the story "Life, Death and Other Dreams," which was written early in the relationship. Exceptionally, Kenward recalled being an unwilling audience to Jimmy's confidences about his and Jordan's sexual practices at the time: "I think he was a deep-dyed masochist, sexually, in tastes . . . I got very prudish about [it]—he was tying up his balls and really [into] weird pain things." Much later, Jimmy also confided to Tom Carey that these practices included sewing up his foreskin with dental floss.

In a letter to his sister-in-law, Hilde Ridenour, written long after the affair with Jordan had run its course, Jimmy referred unambiguously to its sadomasochistic basis, while attributing his own need for it to his stepfather's treatment of him as a child and adolescent. "B's cruelty to me caused me to have a three year sado-masochistic episode. Chains, whips, burns, a needle and dental tape. As a matter of fact pain doesn't hurt; it's a sensation, like a kiss."

Jimmy was back at Kenward's house for an extended stay from mid-April through May, hoping to see as much of Jordan as possible. Soon he was entering a manic phase, nudged along by drugs. Marijuana, speed, and opiated hash were freely available at Kenward's, and Jimmy was partaking of all of it regularly. Joe Brainard had a habit of rolling particularly fat joints—"Brainard Bombers"—which were almost too potent. A diary entry of May 14, 1971, describing a busy day in the city, is a rare example of Jimmy's writing that seems to have been composed under the influence of—something. But at the same time, it also seems a conscious and successful attempt to render in prose the frenetic pace and stoned tenor of his city life at this juncture. The entry is typed right up to the very edges of the paper, splitting words without the benefit of hyphens wherever they fall, abbreviating many, to form a single dense block of type, a visual object.

Toward the end of May, Jordan left for a three-week business trip to Europe. Jimmy missed him desperately. Challenged by Jordan with the query "You ever write any love poems?" he wrote a number of poems exploring his love for Jordan over the next weeks, months, and years. Perhaps there was an unacknowledged need, too, to defend his love, in the face of disapproval of his choice of lover, implied or explicit, on the part of most of his friends. The eleven poems that were eventually published in *The Crystal Lithium* in the section called "Loving You" date from about April 1971 through the early fall.

After Bob left, Ashbery hosted a dinner party at the duplex apartment he and Aladar Marberger were now renting in a town house at 456 West Twenty-fifth Street. The apartment was furnished by the owner in a style Jimmy privately termed "distinctly middle-brow queer," featuring a dark brown library hung with velvet curtains and a dining room papered with a trompe l'oeil imitation of Venetian drapery. During one of the many loud arguments between Aladar and John that punctuated the dinner, Aladar slammed the dining room door so hard that even Larry Rivers said, "Man, I can't take this!" and Jimmy's patience snapped. He stood up and threw his plate of fruit compote across the room, shouting, "What do you think of that, Aladar? . . . Now you know how I feel about all this door slamming." The "willow-ware" plate did not break, but Aladar was frightened and startled into temporary silence. John was not pleased—"it was in *my* dining room"—although he agreed later, "It was very easy to get mad at Aladar. He was an annoying person, and Jimmy had not too much tolerance for such people . . . But I remember it did cast a certain pall over the evening."

Jimmy returned to Southampton on May 29, to find early summer in full green riot: "leaves, leaves, spring salad greens, and lilacs, the marvelous ones I see from this window, a tree of lilacs, taller than the low two story house, and over the forsythia—whose blooming I altogether missed this year—white dogwood; and the wine-dark of copper beech." He started working on a prose work: "Life, Death and Other Dreams." Originally subtitled "An Eclogue for Gerrit Henry," the work is divided into sixty-two sections, varying in length from a single line to more than a page. In place of the pastoral dialogue between nymphs and shepherds of the classical eclogue, Jimmy's alternates between dialogue and third-person narration describing the picaresque activities of an unnamed "they," who seem to be a male couple in a highly energized sexual and romantic relationship and are usually the presumed speakers of the intermittent dialogue.

If the story can be compared with anything else in Schuyler's oeuvre, it might be "The Infant Jesus of Prague." That work, as he said, was written in part as an attempt to convey the feeling of a nervous breakdown, while "Life, Death and Other Dreams" was written as Schuyler was leading up to another. Both works share a similar edgy intensity that reflects, or purposely harnesses, Schuyler's borderline manic state.

There are lyrical sections:

> "How many ways do I love you? Clad, half-clad, starkers, erect, recumbent, tumescent, down right limp. Snoring. Smiling—as now—eyes shut, almost asleep. I love your fingers. They unlax, they unfurl . . . I will tell you softly and more softly still of the many ways I love you and gently ease my voice to a thread, to an all but invisible strand of silk loosened—so lightly—from the cocoon of sleep, unseen, within you."

And references to sex, drugs:

> "I can't even read my palm in this murk. Put on the strobe. That's besser, baby. Says here it says, 'to ball for eight continuous hours . . . something something . . .' What it boils down to is, get a light liquor high, throw in the upper of your choice, toke away at the Nepalese Blue Streak Hash, and keep the amyl handy."

and violence:

> ". . . you can't leave hate out. It's there, like blood. Here. Take this Lady Schick injector stainless steel blade with the plutonium edge, keener than keen, and cut my arm. Right here. Flesh is flesh and flesh bleeds. I want you to see it bleed and know, for once if not for all, that blood and hate are real, red and real as roses. Take it and cut."

In the sections of the work set in an S&M milieu, Schuyler's ambivalent tone and larding with recondite cultural references (to the decadent *fin-de-siècle* graphic artist Felicien Rops, for example) suggest that he did not take too seriously the posturing that is often part of the lifestyle. Yet he did take sadomasochism itself seriously enough to read Gilles Deleuze's book *Masochism: Coldness and Cruelty*, framed as an introduction to Leopold von Sacher-Masoch's novel *Venus in Furs*. Schuyler was impressed by Deleuze's "long and groundbreaking" essay on masochism, as distinct from and in relation to sadism, in which Deleuze lays emphasis on the "contractual" nature of S&M relationships.

Once Bob returned from London on June 6, bringing the famous silver chain, Jimmy was eager for him to visit him in Southampton. But when he informed the Porters that he intended to invite Bob out, the response from Anne Porter was a firm refusal. The sticking point, as she recalled it, was Jimmy's insistence that if Jordan's wife should telephone, Anne must deny that Jordan was there—a lie she refused to tell or be a party to. This hurt and maddened Jimmy, who became "very angry" at Anne because he felt "this isn't really my home if I can't bring Bob here." He took his grievance to Bob Dash, "in tears" of frustration. Dash provided a way out of the difficulty by offering to let Jordan stay with him at his house in nearby Sagaponack, to which he had moved full-time in 1966.

Jimmy was "incandescent" in June 1971, according to Dash. "He became all rapid" in his speech and actions. "He was like an electric light that was burning too too brightly, and his face was flushed." Jimmy had a regular arrangement to eat dinner every Wednesday with Dash, who particularly remembered one time when he drew up at 49 South Main Street to pick him up, and found him out in front of the house in his bathrobe, watering the plants "but missing" while eating a peach, as Gabriel Fauré's lush Ballade for Piano and Orchestra was "*booming* out of the house" at full volume. And Dash recalled thinking, "Oh, he's very close. Very, very, very close." As soon as Jimmy got to Dash's house he "insisted on playing the same Mae West record over and over and over, all through dinner . . . I think it was 'I Like a Man Who Comes in Slow,' or something like that, real grinding, dum-dum-dum. It was difficult."

While still at work on "Life, Death and Other Dreams," Jimmy now began what he called a "collage-prose-poem," "The Fauré Ballade." "The Fauré Ballade" is composed entirely of quotations drawn from the diverse range of his reading and the casual conversation of his friends. There is nothing didactic about the idiosyncratic selections in "The Fauré Ballade," but they are all in one way or another illustrative of his sensibility, especially in the prevalence of nineteenth- and early twentieth-century diaries, letters, essays, and art writing. One is invited to share Jimmy's delight in such phrases as "When the heart speaks, it is unnecessary to speak correctly" (Delacroix), "I am a parcel of vain strivings" (Thoreau), and many more. The fact that what is "depicted" in the work—the quotations—are also its medium aligns "The Fauré Ballade" with Schuyler's conceit of the rose made out of a real rose in "Fabergé," and in that sense, his entire poetic project. Most of the work was composed in a single frantic day in Southampton, after which his room looked like a tornado had blown through it: "books everywhere." He finished a draft by June 11, but was still retyping and refining it in late July.

Gabriel Fauré's Ballade for Piano and Orchestra in F-sharp Minor, opus 19, is a piano concerto in all but name. The late-Romantic piano concerto was Frank O'Hara's favorite musical form. Threaded conspicuously throughout Schuyler's poem are twelve quotations from Frank's conversation or works, more than from any other single source, and two additional references to him by other speakers—so that one might fancifully regard Frank's voice and presence as the "piano part" of Jimmy's own "concerto." The O'Hara references come more thickly toward the end, with the effect that the other, apparently unrelated, quotations coming at that point also seem to refer to him, notably the work's closing, a paraphrase from the denouement of Ambroise Thomas's opera *Mignon* that, we are told, Frank wrote in his program during a performance: "*où suis-je? / je respire l'air nouveau / l'azur est plus profond.*" Because of this sublime closing, and the steady ostinato of O'Hara references throughout, and in view of the opening lines taken from Sir Thomas Browne's *Urn Burial*, an essay on ways in which the dead have historically been memorialized, "The Fauré Ballade" becomes, in a very real sense, a memorial—a cenotaph—to O'Hara.

The anger and violence expressed in "Life, Death and Other Dreams" may partly have been a deflection of anger Jimmy felt toward the Porters but couldn't fully acknowledge. They had recently reaffirmed their resolve to have him move out and had now set a date, at the end of the summer, for Johnny to move back in Jimmy's place. Again, Jimmy made no clear reference to the plan in his surviving letters or poems; instead, it built up inside and contributed to his growing mania.

On June 15, John Ashbery went to London and Paris for a visit of about ten days, accompanied by David Kermani; Marberger was also in Europe for the summer. While they were away, John gave Jimmy access to their apartment, and Jimmy stayed there with Jordan a couple of times in late June. When John returned from Europe around the twenty-fifth, it was to find Jimmy there, and they had a series of long and intimate conversations throughout the day and into the evening. In addition to details about Jimmy's relationship with Bob, they apparently discussed Jimmy's being asked to leave the Porters: "You could see," Schuyler wrote to him shortly afterward, "and so, really, could I—that my hysteria about Fairfield and Anne was merely that. What am I going to 'do' about it? Go on being myself."

That night, Jimmy couldn't sleep, and he wrote a poem, "The Night," beginning:

> The night is filled with indecisions
> To take a downer or an upper
> To take a walk
> To lie
> Down and relax
>
> I order you: RELAX

The poem soon evolves into another love poem to Jordan (mentioned by name in an early version, but not as published), and includes references to a recent dramatic episode, detailed more explicitly in a letter to John, when Jimmy had "nearly" tried to commit suicide by taking sleeping pills and tranquilizers ("nearly all I had") but "my unconscious made me put back a few. Yes, it was that close."

If, as Anne believed, Jimmy's coming to live with the Porters had followed one suicide attempt, it's ironic that his being asked to leave nearly prompted another. Neither, however, appeared to have been entirely serious. Jimmy, as he himself recognized, was not a suicidal personality.

As Jimmy would not be accompanying the Porters to Great Spruce Head that summer, it was arranged that he would stay on at 49 South Main Street with the Padgett family, who had again been invited to live in the house over the summer. When Jimmy returned to Southampton in late June, the Porters and Katherine Koch were all still there. Within a day or so, Johnny went back to Vermont, and Anne and Fairfield set out for Maine. Their leaving brought home painfully the fact that he was not going with them. Katie and Liz stayed behind for a few days, along with Katherine.

As soon as the girls were alone with Jimmy, his suppressed anger was uncapped and he began acting strangely and irrationally. With Katie for an audience representing the family, he took to going around the house "frantically and angrily" taking paintings off the walls and replacing them with other paintings from the studio, acting out his insistence that this was his house too, and that he was going to make it his for the summer.

At some point Jimmy took the opportunity to tell Katie that the reason Fairfield had been hit by a train while driving across a railroad crossing in 1965 was because he had been distracted by old feelings of guilt about his earlier love affair with Ilse Hamm. Jimmy's decision to tell her this now didn't make sense to Katie. She had never known about her father's old love affair, and interpreted Jimmy suddenly telling her about it, in this slightly oblique way, as an "angry action against her." "It was so disturbing," she recalled, "I didn't have the basis to recover from it." It is also possible that Jimmy's reference to this long-past extramarital love affair of her father's was a coded reference to his own more recent, long-lasting, and complex affair with Fairfield. Although they had been scrupulous about keeping the sexual aspect of their relationship private from friends and family, and Katie had no idea of it or of her father's bisexuality until after his death, she did otherwise grasp the tenor of their "very, very close relationship," and knowledge of its full extent did not seem all that surprising to her when it came.

One morning Katie came downstairs to find the dining room table covered with typed letters from Jimmy to "all sorts of people." Those that she read were "really crazy," including a rambling one to Liz that seemed "really spiteful." She didn't know what to do, so she left the letters where they were, and later they disappeared. As Katherine Koch recalled, Katie "protected us from the fact that every night Jimmy was leaving these vituperative letters on the dining room table addressed to all of us . . . She always got up earlier than we did, and so she was a little scared about what was going on." In truth, Katie felt "paralyzed" about it because as she later said, "In my family you didn't talk about anything that might embarrass or hurt anybody." She couldn't easily ask her parents for advice because there was no telephone on Great Spruce Head.

Ron and Pat Padgett had been very much looking forward to being in Southampton and spending time with Jimmy that summer. They loved the rambling old house, and its garden with its forsythia hedges and giant elm trees. Almost immediately after they arrived at the end of June, however, the Padgetts noticed the same air of "incandescence" about Jimmy that Dash described. He appeared pleased to see them, and at first they simply thought that he was acting a bit strangely, "slightly manic," and they were not overly concerned. He just seemed "very happy about everything . . . He was talking about God and the Universe and he was very expansive and very happy and it was as if he had had some kind of conversion."

On Thursday, July 1, the three girls left, after which Jimmy "deteriorated very quickly, *very* quickly, in a matter of like twenty-four hours . . . he went from being kind of a little off the wall into being absolutely out of his mind." That day, Jimmy went around the house in a heightened state, making excited comments that seemed to have religious overtones, which on the surface it was hard to disagree with, like, "It's great to experience God!" or, "You know, money is shit!" Ron, who later realized he was in a state of denial, thought to himself, "You're absolutely right, I couldn't agree more"—until he noticed that Jimmy had actually thrown all his money into wastepaper baskets around the house. Like other friends in the past, the Padgetts were caught unaware by Jimmy's odd behavior. They had never before witnessed psychotic behavior firsthand and it took a while for them to recognize it for what it was.

On the morning of Friday the 2nd, Jimmy came downstairs believing that he was Jesus Christ, and, moving from room to room, repeatedly reenacted the stages of the Passion and Crucifixion to the stunned horror of the Padgetts. As Ron Padgett saw it: "He was having these spells. He would put his arms out, as if he were Christ on the Cross, and then he would swing, and fall on the floor." During one of these spells Ron became so disturbed and desperate he fell on top of Jimmy, sobbing and begging him, "Come back!"

Over the course of the day their friend had become a frightening, alien figure to the Padgetts. Pat recalled, "It was so powerful, the vibes, like something in a movie: we were in this enormous house . . . There were people around but it was as if we were totally cut off from them. And his power was emanating though that house. Through that *whole* house, he was so powerful, the madness was *so* powerful, and it was really destructive." At one point mention was made of his being asked to leave the Porters', and Jimmy became furious and started screaming. Neither Pat nor Ron had ever heard Jimmy scream before—the idea was almost inconceivable, and extremely frightening.

Jimmy asked Pat to cook him a steak. She obliged, glad to be doing something that would perhaps restore some sense of normalcy, but while the two of them were in the kitchen together, Jimmy started to talk about how "the youngest person" was in danger. He then uttered words that to Pat sounded sinister and ominous: "Harm may befall the infant." This she and Ron interpreted as a threat of violence toward their five-year-old son, Wayne, whom Jimmy in normal times was extremely fond of. Under the influence of the intensity generated by Jimmy's condition, Pat debated with herself whether to pick up the heavy iron skillet and hit him over the head with it. The only thing that stopped her was the fear that she might not hit him hard enough, and he would come back at her infuriated and stronger than ever. Instead, she "did a Jimmy" and erupted into an angry, terrified outburst of her own. "I went kind of crazy, and it scared him." Her ploy worked and Jimmy, taken aback, said, "Oh, let's go outside, let's go outside." Outside, Pat calmed down, and the conversation took another turn so that "nothing more [was] said about who was in danger and who wasn't." But at the same time, Ron was getting a knife in case Jimmy attacked one of them.

As frightened as they were of being in the house, the Padgetts were also afraid to leave it. Finally, Ron got up the nerve to ask, "Jimmy, uh, Pat and Wayne and I are going to go for a drive. Is that OK?" and he said, "Sure, yeah, fine, why not?" The family drove to the pay phone in town and called Kenneth Koch, who then called Jane Freilicher and Joe Hazan, with whom Ashbery was also staying that weekend. Kenneth, Joe, and John met the Padgetts in the village, then they all went back to the Porters' house together and knocked on the door. Jimmy appeared at the door stark naked, with rose petals adhering to his body, having previously rolled around in the garden. Facing the delegation, which included Frank O'Hara's two closest Harvard friends, he asked, "Have you seen Frank? I hear he's in town tonight."

At this, Padgett and the rest realized the situation was hopelessly beyond them. Ron approached the next-door neighbor, Mary Johnson, who was a doctor, and she came to the house and attempted to wrap Jimmy in a blanket and talk him into going to the hospital. When he wouldn't hear of it, she advised them to call the police, and despite ingrained counterculture misgivings, they did so. Ron returned to the house with two Southampton police officers, and again knocked, and again Jimmy appeared, still naked. The police, in Padgett's words, "chatted with him a minute, and were very calm," and said something like, "We're just a little concerned about your health, and we want to take you down to have a doctor look at you and make sure you're OK." They were "very smooth, but they were kind of firm too" and Jimmy was "very compliant" with them. Jimmy went back into the house, emerged dressed, and went willingly with the police officers and Ron to Southampton Hospital. In the ambulance Jimmy, still in character as Jesus Christ, was forgiving and serenely condescending to the cops, telling them, "Everyone says that you're 'pigs' but without you this whole society would collapse."

When the group reached Southampton Hospital, Kenneth called Dr. Arnold Cooper, a psychiatrist friend. Before he got there, Ron was sitting in a room alone with Jimmy, nervously "keeping my eye on him," very aware that he had just had him brought in by the police, and wondering whether there were "any scalpels around in the room," when a young staff psychiatrist came in to question him. To Ron's horror, Jimmy responded to his questions in a totally rational manner, saying of Ron, "'Doctor, I'm shocked by my friend's behavior, I don't understand why he's called the police, it baffles me,' and he sounded completely rational, all vestiges of his previous behavior suddenly vanished! And I thought, 'Oh shit! They're going to turn him loose! But this guy looked at him a couple of minutes and turned to me and said, 'Schizophrenia.' Right in front of Jimmy. And I thought, that's not very tactful. And Jimmy didn't react, he didn't say anything, he didn't object." The psychiatrist gave Jimmy a paper to sign, committing him to a mental hospital. Jimmy looked it over and said, "I'd have to be crazy to [sign this]!" and tore it up.

Dr. Cooper arranged that he be transferred to the Pilgrim State Mental Hospital at Islip, New York, a large, grim, and somewhat chaotic public hospital in the middle of Long Island. Ron and John Ashbery visited the next day, by which time he already "didn't seem that crazy, actually, and [was] obviously wanting very much to be out." Ron recalled that he was quite medicated and as a result "a bit zombie-like." Kenneth and Jane visited Jimmy there together a day or two later and found him seeming almost himself; as was usual during his stays in mental hospitals, he had made friends among the other patients and was dispensing advice.

Ron had finally managed to get through to the Porters in Maine with the news of Jimmy's breakdown and emergency hospitalization. They were very concerned, and sent Jimmy a check for $1,000 (partly to help pay for his hospital expenses). In thanking Anne and Fairfield for the money, Jimmy added, "I may be asking for more."

While in Pilgrim State, Jimmy wrote some fragmentary poems and diary entries in a small spiral-bound notebook. One is a partial first draft of the last section of the poem that became "Beautiful Funerals," which imagines a gathering in some sort of "heaven" of departed friends and acquaintances, writers and performers, all of them in one sense or another figures in Frank O'Hara's personal pantheon, such as the jazz singer Libby Holman, Carole Lombard, James Dean, John O'Hara, Scott and Zelda Fitzgerald, John Latouche, and others. The poem includes the lines "I will / call on Frank today, / and to him say, man to man, / Libby Holman's / Dead and gone," and seems to have taken flight from his recent delusion that Frank was still alive. In a letter to Fairfield and Anne Porter written the day after he was released from the hospital, he said: "I'm sorry if I scared JA and Kenneth, by asking them, 'Is Frank in town?' Well, he wasn't. The point though is that I am certain, now, that I will see Frank again one day."

On July 12, Jane Freilicher and Barbara Guest brought him back to 49 South Main Street. At the hospital Jimmy had been put on a prescription of Thorazine, which seemed to help him. He described it to Fairfield as "a mild tranquilizer" with some side effects: it "makes one very thirsty. It makes my mouth feel parched in a way that is fairly easy to ignore, although with a vague feeling of an unearned hang-over symptom." The Padgetts had returned to the city a few days before, far too disturbed to stay with Jimmy when he got out, so he was alone at the house for about four days.

Jimmy's attitude to the Padgetts immediately after the incident was one of self-professed "understanding" that they had reacted as they did, with a reluctance to acknowledge the gravity of his mental illness. He wrote to Kenward, after he was released from Pilgrim State, "What happened was a religious experience in the guise of a psychotic—or as far as I'm concerned—psychic—episode. I was very open about it with Ron and Pat, but it did get pretty hairy. Ron panicked, the police came—now I ask you, dear, if a friend wigged out, would you gallop off to the hospital and speak to a strange—'horribly hostile': K. Koch—shrink and send the fuzz?" The question, as applied to Kenward, was prescient.

There were ongoing discussions over the next several months among the Porters, Padgetts, Bob Dash, Kenneth, Jane, and John about where Jimmy should go and what should be done about him. He had already planned to go to Vermont later that summer, and with Kenward's cooperation, the visit was brought forward. From the hospital, Jimmy had already written to assure Kenward that he "would like to make my self at *home*, & would try not to be *too* bossy, or take-overish."

Kenward's view of all this was complex and contradictory. He wrote to Ron shortly afterward that once the "Jimmy phone-calls began" he felt "caught in something inexorable." His two sisters had both experienced periods of mental instability and one had been hospitalized, and he retained a lingering fear that one day he, too, would go "bonkers." To have said no to the idea of Jimmy coming to stay with him now would have been, he felt, "giving in" to his own "fear of going nuts, plus letting Jimmy down in a crisis." Once he accepted what seemed the inevitable, he became fatalistically convinced that Jimmy would in fact have another breakdown. At the same time, he wanted to believe in the possibility of the "long shot: can someone who thinks they're Christ one week find peace and sanity in the quiet woods two weeks later?"

Jimmy left on Friday the 16th for New York, where he stayed for five days before going up to Vermont. On Monday, he had dinner with John on Twenty-fifth Street. Apparently, he came to the apartment earlier in the day while John was at work, and there wrote the poem "Letter to a Friend: Who Is Nancy Daum?"

It begins with the lines, famous to all readers of Schuyler, "All things are real / no one a symbol," and proceeds to take note of the décor and works of art in Ashbery's apartment, including silk curtains, a potted palm, an Alex Katz painted cutout of Pierre Martory, a terra-cotta bust of Marie Antoinette, a porcelain *sang de boeuf* spittoon, a glass-filled cabinet, various books, and a Daum art nouveau glass lamp bearing a crepuscular design of autumn trees on the base and "a swamp / lagoon or fen" on the shade.

In so boldly stating "All things are real / no one a symbol," Jimmy may have been thinking to challenge a line in Lévi-Strauss's essay "The Scope of Anthropology"—"everything is symbol and sign"—but the rest of the poem seems to engage with Lévi-Strauss's idea in a sense. By listing the objects in the apartment individually, Jimmy may be insisting on the quiddity of each, but in the aggregate they did constitute a set of signs, and they were speaking to him. Earlier they had said nothing more than "middle brow queer"; now they reverberated with the soul-searching conversations with John two weeks earlier. Describing the objects, Jimmy creates a fictional environment pregnant with expectation, and slightly reminiscent, as it happens, of Deleuze's description of the typical *mise-en-scène* of a Sacher-Masoch novel, "with their heavy draperies, their stuffy intimacy, boudoirs and hangings [that] create a half-light from which emerge only suspended gestures and sufferings."

The visual arts themselves "eternalize their subject, suspending a gesture or an attitude," Deleuze wrote, continuing, "The essence of masochism is the state of waiting. The masochist is one who lives a pure form of waiting." In fact, the theme of Jimmy's love affair with Bob Jordan was waiting—for Jordan to call, return from trips, or be free to see him. "'I'm not prompt' / you said, rueful / factual / 'I' I said, 'climb / walls.'" Set in suspension himself, between Southampton and Vermont, between a life with the Porters and an unknown future ("I—have lost / my place . . ."; "Where am I? / en route to / a literal / Vermont"), amid these static witnesses, Jimmy becomes aware of his own living body with its nerves, muscles, and pulsing current of blood—which "helps (is / that the word?) / propel / this ball-point / pen." He is willing to gamble on a relationship with Bob and their painful "games":

O Day!
   literal
and unsymbolic
                          day:
silken: gray: sunny:
     in salt and pepper
tweed soot storm:
guide, guard,
         be freely
               pierced
by the steel and
gold-eyed
needle passes—stitches
—of my love, my
                            lover,
                                          our love,
his lover—I
                            am he—
     (is not
at any tick
each and every life

at hazard: *faites*
vos jeux,
    messieurs)

The next day, Jimmy took "a beautiful ride on a half-empty bus" up to Vermont. On the way he wrote the short "Letter Poem #2," also addressed to Jordan, and soon after he got to Kenward's, "Letter Poem #3." It evokes a tranquil scene, with the clover-bestrewn field of "Salute" transposed to the heavens:

The night is quiet
as a kettle drum
the bull frog basses
tuning up. After
swimming, after sup-
per, a Tarzan movie,
dishes, a smoke. [. . .]

. . . The stars tonight
in pale dark space
are clover flowers
in a lawn the expanding
Universe in which
we love . . .

[17]

AFTER FIVE O'CLOCK A KIND OF ENDLESSNESS SETS IN

1971–1973

Jimmy was happy to be back in Calais, with swims in the lake, walks in the woods, and jolly evenings with Kenward and Joe around the collage table. As he had in the past, he stayed in a little guest cabin, across the small lake and down a rise from Kenward's farmhouse. The lake was a former beaver pond, fed by a gentle waterfall at the far end where a brook emerged from the woods. Kenward had recently expanded it and made it permanent by cementing up the beaver dam. The poet Anne Waldman dubbed the result "Veronica Lake." Jimmy himself now recognized that he had been "incandescent" since April, and wrote to Bob Dash that he felt the need to "relax, unwind, get back to my normal tempo (whatever that is!)."

The house was astir with creative activity. Kenward was putting final touches on his musical, *The Grass Harp*, based on Truman Capote's novel; Joe had recently returned from an extended stay in Bolinas, California, visiting Bill Berkson and others, and was editing his *Bolinas Journal*, a record of the stay, which would be published by Berkson's Big Sky Books that year. Jimmy was already writing new poems, including "Letter Poem #3."

Despite Jimmy's happiness and optimism at the beginning of the visit, Kenward remained uneasy, as he tried to convince himself that Jimmy "wasn't as nuts" as he truly was. Early in the visit, in an attempt to solve Jimmy's problems "in a 'sensible' manner," as he put it, he offered to provide him with financial assistance by setting up a modest trust fund, with the income going to Jimmy for his lifetime and the principal reverting to Kenward on his death. Before it could be set up, as a sort of down payment, he also gave Jimmy some "fritter money"—apparently a couple of thousand dollars. Jimmy took the term literally and used much of it to make gifts to friends: $500 to buy a copy of the complete *O.E.D.* for Kenneth, another $500 to Bob Jordan, and $200 to buy a large (five foot square) nude portrait of Bill Berkson by George Schneeman, whose exhibition of portraits Jimmy had seen on his way through New York. The purchase of the portrait was somewhat out of character for Schuyler, and in writing to Bill Berkson later, he apparently felt a need to set the record straight. "I think of you often—I think I've always been a bit diffident with you out of a fear you would think my interest was sexual. You're very beautiful—the world agrees on that, but really, I'm only attracted by people who are clearly attracted to me." This was somewhat disingenuous: Berkson's primary significance for Jimmy probably stemmed from the passionate attachment that O'Hara had felt for him, and buying this nude image of Frank's "muse" now was a way to connect with Frank, as he was entering another manic episode.

John Ashbery arrived for a long-planned visit on about August 1. The visit went well for several days. In the evenings they smoked "Brainard bombers" and sat around "laughing hysterically" and reading aloud from *Women's Household*. Jimmy was feeling well enough, or high enough, to stop taking his Thorazine.

On August 5, Jimmy received a letter from Fairfield, enclosing his responses to a chronology he had been hired to write for Fairfield's upcoming exhibition at the Knoedler Gallery. The contents of the letter (which has not survived), coupled with the return of the chronology, and the simultaneous receipt of his payment of $250 for it from the gallery, somehow combined with his overuse of marijuana to trigger a psychotic reaction. Fairfield's letter may also have included some reference to his moving out of Southampton; at any rate, Jimmy intended to ask Kenward if he could spend the winter with him on Greenwich Avenue, but that evening in his altered state he instead became irrationally angry at

Kenward—he "blew his cool," as he phrased it, but whatever he did or said was considerably more frightening for Kenward than a simple loss of temper.

In the middle of the night of the 6th, John, sleeping in the guest room in the main house, was awakened by strange noises coming from the bathroom next door. Water was running "a great deal," the light was on, and he could hear Jimmy, who had come up from his cabin, bustling around in there and "sort of laughing." "I began to get quite scared. Apparently what he was doing was washing all of his money. And sort of chuckling about it. I don't think I slept a wink after I woke up." Kenward and Joe also woke up and heard Jimmy going in and out of the bathroom, running the water, washing rugs, moving furniture downstairs, and "rearranging objects bizarrely."

Jimmy returned to his cabin across the lake sometime during the night. In the morning, before he returned to the house, the other three had an early conference and decided he needed to be taken to a mental hospital. John, a veteran of the Southampton breakdown, understood that they needed the help of the police. They drove into Montpelier, about twenty miles away, and spoke to the police there, who said an officer would meet them back at the house with a doctor. By the time they returned, Jimmy had come up from his cabin. They tried to convince him that he ought to go to the hospital, but Jimmy said he didn't feel he had to. At one point, Jimmy "collapsed," apparently again reenacting the Passion of Christ as he had in Southampton, and Joe held him and calmed him. Kenward was grateful for Joe's steady and compassionate presence, as well as for the cool-headedness of John, who, Kenward stated, "has quite a knack for fending off reality horrors by concentrating on 'language.'"

Finally, a state trooper arrived along with a doctor from the mental hospital in Waterbury. When they suggested to Jimmy that he accompany them to the hospital, he declined, "sensibly enough," as John later joked. Both the officer and the doctor, according to Kenward, were "unbelievably gentle, tactful and nice, and patient," and sat calmly in the living room while Jimmy served them coffee. John was sitting in the rocking chair when Jimmy "bustled" out of the kitchen and asked him if he had read "The Fauré Ballade" yet. John said he had and that he liked it very much. "Yes, but do you believe it's true?" To which John replied "in a peevish tone," "I don't have *any* idea what you mean."

When the doctor again tried to persuade Jimmy to come with them to the hospital, Jimmy turned to his friends and asked, "What do you think I should do?" It was Joe, according to Kenward's recollection, who "took command" and was finally able to persuade Jimmy to get into the police car. John rode to the hospital with Jimmy, acutely uncomfortable, and struck by the pathos of the situation, which reminded him of the last scene of *A Streetcar Named Desire*, when Blanche DuBois is finally persuaded by "the kindness of strangers" to go off to a mental institution. During the drive Jimmy turned to him and said, "John, you do believe that I'm the Resurrection and the Life, don't you?" "Sure," said John.

For Kenward, the breakdown, "horrible" as it was, was also in a way "an enormous relief" after his tense anticipation of it for the preceding two weeks. Writing shortly afterward to Ron Padgett, Kenward admitted, "This has been an 'awful' happening . . . that kind of intensity is demonic, and one can't survive with it. Not for long. Or unless one has incredible experience & training, to get one accustomed to it."

Jimmy was admitted to the Vermont State Hospital in Waterbury on August 7. Kenward handled the paperwork. Because he was brought in by the state trooper, Jimmy had to be legally "committed" to the institution, rather than allowed to enter voluntarily, and could not be released without a court hearing, which was scheduled for August 26. He blamed this on Kenward, and as the weeks went by and he remained hospitalized, Jimmy harbored a sense of bitter grievance against his friend, who in his inner psychodrama he cast in the role of Judas to his Christ. Joe, in speaking about the episode later, used to add, "It wasn't too bad for me—I got to be one of the Disciples."

The Vermont State Hospital was housed in a set of imposing Victorian brick buildings clustered around courtyards on a tree-studded campus. Jimmy responded fairly well to the institutional environment and was quite active during his three weeks there: writing poems, editing an in-house literary magazine, and making plans for the future, albeit some of them unrealistic or delusional. Bob Jordan and a partner were trying to start their own business, importing woolens and sweaters from Europe. Jimmy was very excited about it, and encouraged them to set up a retail store, which he envisioned as a combination clothing store and art gallery selling work by his friends. In addition to the $500 he had already given Jordan, he wanted to invest an additional $5,000, and wrote to the Porters to ask if they would lend it to him. Fairfield in his plainspoken way replied, "I do not want to lend you $5000," and went on to other matters. But he referred to the request in one of the many discussions with John and others about Jimmy's condition that summer, writing that such "grandiose ideas have a good side, for it is the opposite of his former complete dependency."

The daily routine at the hospital was rather loosely structured, and for long stretches of the day Jimmy and the other patients were left to their own devices in the common areas. Toward the end of his stay, Jimmy reported to Fairfield that the hospital provided "a productive therapeutic situation." But he felt that for those who were not writers, the amount of unstructured time left many people at loose ends, which was not conducive to recovery. "I was lucky, because I could keep scribbling. But the poor non-poets! . . . a weekend with utterly nothing to do is not my idea of how to make people with real problems feel any better. It makes them nervous and cross."

Jimmy made friends quickly in the hospital. A number of the young people in the hospital were there as a result of psychedelic drug reactions, including seventeen-year-old Gary Greenly, whom Jimmy described as his "buddy, friend, kid brother, troop leader, health & exercise instructor, dietician & you name it." He was "a Brainard-type 'natural'—chosen field, music, à la Bob Dylan." Learning that he had no close family, Jimmy declared to his friends, and to Greenly, that he wanted to "adopt" him, writing to Fairfield on August 7, "I popped the question & he did not say no." What Jimmy meant by this is uncertain, in practical terms, but the idea is significant in light of his own early separation from his father, his feelings of emotional distance from his stepfather, and indeed, his relationship with Fairfield. As Jimmy wrote, "I want, in general, to stand in relation to him as Fairfield has to me, someone on whom he can unquestionably rely." It was apparently not a sexual liaison and Jimmy had no further contact with Greenly after he was released.

By 1971, after the recent deaths of Jimi Hendrix, Janis Joplin, and Jim Morrison, whatever initial sense of innocence and optimism there may have been around the combination of rock music and "recreational" drugs had become inflected with a darker mood. Jimmy was saddened by the deaths of Morrison and Joplin, in particular, and wrote a short elegy to Morrison a few weeks after his death. Janis Joplin's death was referenced both in "Janis Joplin's Dead: Long Live Pearl," a poem written earlier in the summer, and in "Mike," written in Waterbury. The interest Jimmy took in "celebrity" deaths at this time, especially of young performers, is itself a recognition and possibly an "appropriation" of Frank O'Hara's obsession with the deaths of James Dean, Billie Holiday, and others.

Poems that Jimmy either wrote or completed at Waterbury are "Beautiful Funerals," "Roxy," "Our Father," "Mike," and "In the Round." The two most distinctive of them, "Mike" and "Roxy," take the new "skinny" format of the recent "Letter Poems" to an extreme, with some lines being only a single word, resulting in a staccato urgency that propels the poems forward. Jimmy, whose taste in music had earlier been centered in the classical tradition, started listening to more rock, soul, and rhythm and blues music in the '60s, and especially in the hospital, where there was little choice, thanks to the ever-present jukebox and the radio. "Roxy," in its fast-paced, four-beat lines, can seem to echo the driving beat and insistence of rock music, while the still-shorter lines of "Mike" slow the pace of the poem, or string it out—as if acknowledging the slang expression for drug addiction.

"Roxy" and "Mike" are narrative poems, although the narrative is far from clear in either case. "Roxy" interweaves references to four individuals: Linda Jean, Bob, Wayne, and Gary Greenly. Bob is Bob Jordan, usually referred to in this poem as "Bob far out." The identities of Linda Jean and Wayne are unknown. The recurring phrase "Bob far out" continually pulls the poem back to a paean to Jordan, and a plaint at missing him. "Mike" is more death-haunted, and mentions Joplin's death in the context of that of Mike Payne, a fellow patient, who died on August 20 (after being released) from a drug overdose. The poem incorporates a rather ambiguous caution against drug use, which segues into a command that has been interpreted as a summary of Schuyler's poetic credo:

> *He* paid
> the tab
> all right,
> playing
> with
> death—
> why?
> Why not,
> messer about
> with pills
> and
> artificial
> paradises?
> Look out
> the win-
> dow
> cluck:
> it's real,
> it's there,
> it's life.

"Our Father" is in a calmer register, and effectively interweaves lines of the Lord's Prayer with Jimmy's own "looking out the window" and making observations of the day and his surroundings: "This morning view / is very plain: thou art / in Heaven: modern / brick, plate glass, unhallowèd, / as yet, by time."

Jimmy noted the unusually religious tone of these new poems, writing to the poets Shelly Lustig and Jim Brodey, "Have been on heavy religious Praise God creative trip—poems pour out." After Jimmy had cooled down a bit, he told Ron Padgett he was glad his religious mood was fading. He later had a conversation with John Ashbery about the poems written in this period and the Christian ideation of the breakdowns that preceded them, telling him, "The funny thing is that I'm not all that religious." "I never thought you were," replied John. The point is arguable, though. In the poem "I Sit Down to Type," written a few years later, Jimmy sets out some of the flip-flops of his religious attitudes, writing (in sequence): "I don't believe / in God: not for myself"; "I'm a crypto-Catholic"; "In / fact, I am a Presbyterian: / but before I was / confirmed . . . / . . . became an atheist"; "And yet I am religious: I / believe implacably in / the perfectability of man"; and finally, "it has been my profoundest / prayer that God will grant / me grace and I will die / a Catholic, secure in his / all-forgiving love."

Jimmy also edited and printed a mimeo magazine in the hospital, *The Daily Planet*, gathering contributions from both within and outside the hospital. The second issue included, in addition to his own "Roxy" and "Mike," poems or prose by Joe Brainard, Clark Coolidge, Coolidge's three-year-old daughter, Celia, Ron Padgett, and Elizabeth Hazan (Jane Freilicher and Joe Hazan's ten-year-old daughter), along with those of fellow patients, a hospital employee, and some unsigned notices.

Jimmy's relationship with Fairfield and Anne Porter, already on shaky ground for the past year or two, was further strained by his behavior now. The surviving letters he wrote from the hospital range from normal and affectionate to bossy and delusional, but he apparently wrote others that verged on incoherence as well as hostility. Anne destroyed most of the letters he wrote to her in this period, feeling that their content did not represent Jimmy as she knew him to be, and as he would want to be remembered; she later wondered if this had been right. One thing she remembered from them was Jimmy telling her, "We both must write, because you are as great as Emily Dickinson and I am as great as Walt Whitman!"

As Jimmy's release date grew close, Fairfield let Jimmy's friends know that the Porter family could no longer take care of him indefinitely, and appealed to John, Kenneth, and Kenward for help in providing for his future. As Fairfield wrote to John on August 20, "Jimmy needs a wife, in short; and which of Jimmy's friends is willing to be Jimmy's wife? When he lives with us, it puts a strain on the family, which is unfair to children growing up in the family, of which Lizzie remains . . . I realize now that Jimmy has been sick for a long time, and my bad habit has been to appease him in order not to endure his anger." At the same time, Lizzie herself undoubtedly voiced the thoughts of the whole family when she told her parents, "When a person has been living with you for a long time, you can't turn them out simply because they are sick."

Kenward withdrew his offer to set up a trust fund for Jimmy during his Vermont hospitalization, when Jimmy expressed various unrealistic and grandiose ideas for spending the money, although he remained willing to renew the offer when and if he got well, or if someone was able to supervise his expenditures. There was also concern that Jimmy continue to receive psychiatric care, if not hospitalization, but this was going to be difficult, since, as Kenward wrote to Fairfield, "part of his illness is not being able to face the fact that he *is* ill."

In the end, these discussions were inconclusive, and, seemingly unaware of the behind-the-scenes maneuvering, Jimmy made his own plans to leave the hospital with Bob Jordan. As it turned out, there was no need for a hearing, and he was released on the 26th on his own recognizance. After a brief stop in New York, he returned to the Porters' house, which despite everything remained his primary residence for another two years.

When Fairfield returned from collecting his summer paintings in Maine and Jimmy was helping him stretch the canvases, he did notice a new uneasiness and irritability in Fairfield, but, writing to Joe Brainard, he blamed it on changes at the Knoedler Gallery, and added, "He's also very jealous of Bob Jordan, & is afraid (I think) that I might move from here to N. Y. C." As far as Jimmy was concerned, it was as if the painful conversation of the previous fall, not to mention his two breakdowns, had never taken place.

Nonetheless, not long after he got out of the hospital, Jimmy did start to think about finding an apartment in New York. It's not clear how hard he actually looked, until the painter Neil Welliver, who was moving out of the city to live full-time in Maine, offered to sublet Jimmy his apartment at 250 East Thirty-fifth Street. Although the one-room basement apartment was small, dark, charmless, and inconveniently located on a trafficky street near the mouth of the Queens Midtown Tunnel, it was inexpensive and provided Jimmy with a much-needed city roost where he could get together with Bob Jordan. He started using the apartment in October 1971 for overnight visits every week or two. "Now that I can see Bob Jordan sort of regularly I am as happy as the King of Norway," Jimmy wrote to Ron.

That fall, Jimmy began assembling the manuscript of a new book of poems, which he was calling *The Crystal Lithium*, and sending individual poems to various publications. The book itself he sent to Charlotte Mayerson, an editor at Random House, who had published Ron Padgett and David Shapiro's *Anthology of New York Poets* the previous year. Mayerson accepted it, on the condition that he take out the sequence "The Fireproof Floors of Witley Court," which she felt "fought" with the other poems. Jimmy obliged, and the book was published the following year.

Inspired by his experiences editing the hospital literary magazine, and all the "stapled" magazines that were being produced by young poets in New York, Jimmy now decided to edit and publish his own one-shot periodical, paying for it with money from his advance from Random House. He considered several names for the publication before settling on *49 South*, after the Porters' and his home address. The choice of this title pays homage to a place where he had found a real refuge over the past ten years, enabling him to survive as a person, grow as a poet, and publish his first books. At the same time, it reinforces none too subtly his sense of a territorial claim to the Porters' home, and by extension their very lives, just when he was under pressure to move out.

Jimmy hoped to make it a bit different from other such magazines by including as many drawings by his artist friends as there were poems. In addition to poets of (roughly) his own generation, like Anne and Fairfield Porter, Harry Mathews, Kenward Elmslie, Barbara Guest, and Rudy Burckhardt, and a generous selection of younger New York poets, such as Ron Padgett, Anne Waldman, Larry Fagin, Joe Brainard, Lewis Warsh, Clark Coolidge, Bill Berkson, Tom Clark, Alice Notley, Tony Towle, Michael Brownstein, Peter Schjeldahl, and Ted Berrigan, *49 South* included contributions from the children of some of his friends, and from one or two mental patients he had met in Waterbury. In the end, there were many more poets (45) than artists (11); nonetheless, the graphic work, by Bob Dash, Joe Brainard, Jane Freilicher, Trevor Winkfield, Edith Schloss, Pat Padgett, Fairfield Porter, Red Grooms, Alex Katz, Nell Blaine, and Neil Welliver, added to the sense of community that Jimmy was hoping to foster.

In late November 1971, Frank O'Hara's *Collected Poems*, edited by Donald Allen, was published by Alfred A. Knopf. Jimmy found himself strongly moved by the strange, Whitmanic transformation of the person, the living, laughing friend, into the solemn, solid block of a book, with "even 'a note on the type.'" Shortly thereafter he wrote the poem "To Frank O'Hara," one of his three or four great elegies to departed friends, in which with seeming casualness he encapsulates his feelings about a person in recalling events from the past. He ends the poem with vignettes from the summer of 1953, when the two poets were having tandem love affairs with Gold and Fizdale at Snedens Landing.

After the excitements of the previous year, 1972 was a period of relative calm. Schuyler was still on Thorazine, but claimed he was trying to wean himself from it. "It's odd," he wrote to Kenneth in February, "to take pills to feel one's every-day self." Apparently he didn't have a regular, local psychiatrist at this time, despite all the concern and planning evinced by his friends the previous August, but was still relying on medication prescribed at Waterbury. On the evidence of his letters, he appeared stable. But as Kenward noted, he was "very wily about appearing 'well.'"

In addition to *The Crystal Lithium*, Schuyler was also in the process of publishing a book of recent poems with the poet Larry Fagin's small press, Adventures in Poetry. Titled *A Sun Cab*, it included nine poems (all later printed in *The Crystal Lithium*), with three illustrations and a cover by Fairfield Porter. Several of the poems were ones previously published abroad in *Juillard* and *The Paris Review*, and due to arcane copyright laws, they were vulnerable to being pirated until or unless they had been printed and copyrighted in the United States.

When the book came out in February, there was a benefit reading at the Poetry Project at St. Mark's Church, where his poems were read by fellow poets and friends including Kenneth, Jane, John, Edwin Denby, Fairfield Porter, and others. By now, Jimmy had acquired an almost mythic aura among many younger poets, who saw him as a reclusive, troubled figure. On this occasion, too, he stayed in Southampton, but Janice Koch reported to him afterward, "It was one of the great Poetry Readings of the decade!" "Full house; applause; spontaneous laughter at witty points; craning of necks to see if author might not actually be in house, heavily veiled or disguised as part of the sound equipment."

On February 21, Jimmy did attend what he called a "stately banquet" hosted by Random House to celebrate Auden's sixty-fifth birthday. Auden's physical and emotional health had declined in the past three years, the accumulated result of years of excessive drinking and reliance on amphetamines, and he had recently accepted an offer to live in rooms in his old Oxford college, Christ Church. Thus the birthday banquet was also a farewell. Jimmy made the best of it, writing to his mother that "the speeches were dull, except for Wystan's response. He has a very ready wit." This was very likely the last time Jimmy saw Auden, his friend and generous patron since 1944, and he must have been saddened by Auden's physical decline, as Auden presumably noted Jimmy's own transformation from the beautiful youth of the mid-'40s to the heavy, uncomfortable, middle-aged man—Schuyler was now forty-eight—he had become. Some months after Auden's death in September of the following year, Jimmy wrote his understated elegy "Wystan Auden," which begins with a recollection of a very different birthday party, Auden's fortieth in 1947, six months before Jimmy and Bill Aalto went off to Italy, to be joined there by Chester and Wystan later.

The next month, Jimmy, John, the painter Anne Dunn Moynihan, and her twenty-year-old son, Francis Wishart, also an artist, made an excursion together to Washington, DC, and Charlottesville, Virginia. The trip was primarily to visit museums, including the National Gallery, the Phillips Gallery, with its great collection of Impressionist and modern paintings, and the Freer Gallery, home of Whistler's *Peacock Room*. The group also made outings to Arlington Cemetery, and Charlottesville to see Thomas Jefferson's Monticello and the University of Virginia's neoclassical campus. All of the group, except Francis, was suffering from some sort of ailment: John a hernia, Anne water on the knee, and Jimmy hemorrhoids. In Washington, Jimmy apparently didn't experience any Proustian epiphanies inspired by his early childhood there, except when he saw the so-called Buffalo Bridge near the Phillips Collection, whose four giant bronze buffalo by Alexander Phimister Proctor he remembered patting as a little boy.

Back in Southampton, on about March 19, Jimmy began a new long poem, "Hymn to Life," recording various signs of spring burgeoning around him, combined with evocations of his recent trip to Washington and other memories and reflections. Like "The Crystal Lithium," the line is again page-width, and the initial word of each line is capitalized, as is rarely the case in Schuyler's shorter-line poems. However, "Hymn to Life" is more than twice as long and moves at a more leisurely pace: transitions between images are less abrupt, less oblique, less "manic," than in the earlier poem. The poem was written over about three months during what he later called "a rather gloomy period." At times Jimmy feared it might be "a dud," or "the prosiest poem ever written," and every time he finished a page he "totally hated it" and put it away. But then he would return and write another page, and in the end he "didn't think it was so bad after all." To many, it is one of his greatest poems.

It opens to imagery of the personified wind, in a setting similar to "The Crystal Lithium" but transposed forward a few months:

> The wind rests its cheek upon the ground and feels the cool damp
> And lifts its head with twigs and small dead blades of grass
> Pressed into it as you might at the beach rise up and brush away
> The sand.

The next lines extend the image to include sound and Schuyler's sense of air itself as constantly flowing with meaning and message:

> The world is filled with music, and in between the music, silence
> And varying the silence all sorts of sounds, natural and man made:
> There goes a plane, some cars, geese that honk and, not here, but
> Not so far away, a scream so rending that to hear it is to be
> Never again the same.

In a continuous flow of imagery, sensation, and ideas the poem moves among manifestations of the progress of spring, recollections of his recent trip, and other "involuntary" memories: all prompting reflections on the nature of existence, consciousness, memory, and forgetting. Death and decay are presented as integral to the life force that is praised in the hymn. The idea of forgetting is mentioned several times as something of equal importance to memory, with suggestions of its connection to death and rebirth and the possibility that forgetting may bring a deeper level of consciousness.

The relationship with Jordan makes little impression in "Hymn to Life," aside from a couple of brief references to a rift that occurred between them in April and May, which Jimmy seems to have realized instinctively was temporary, and as such perhaps welcomed, for giving him the emotional space he needed to write a long poem. As another poem acknowledges, Jimmy was a different person in his relationship with Jordan, and he was briefly tempted by "An angry wish / to shake it off and be oneself / again."

Soon after finishing "Hymn to Life," Jimmy started a new novel, *What's for Dinner?*, and by August 21 he had written more than a hundred pages. It began, as he wrote to Joe, "rather like a sequel to *A Nest of Ninnies*. Which I didn't want to do; but I guess I, like John A., am indelibly stamped by the outer suburbs." He compared it to a daytime TV soap opera, only "not so melodramatic." The plot concerns two suburban families, Norris and Lottie Taylor, and the Delehanteys: Bryan and Maureen, their twins, Patrick and Michael, and Bryan's mother, Biddy. By the second chapter Lottie is in a mental hospital being treated for alcoholism, and much of the book consists of her group therapy sessions, where, as Jimmy wrote, "a cast of thousands can say whatever comes into my head." Meanwhile, her husband, Norris, is having a torrid affair with a neighboring widow, Mag.

Mostly dialogue, the novel develops organically through conversations that, like those in *A Nest of Ninnies*, are mostly quite mundane, but at the same time rich and funny because of Jimmy's sensitivity to the nuances of everyday conversation. Alice Notley rightly called the book "a comedy of manners," but, as with Jane Austen, it is not the "manners" that are the point of the book but rather the language that reveals them. James McCourt, in an afterword to a new edition, refers to the "fractal" quality of Schuyler's lyric poetry, and there is also a kind of fractal quality to these serial conversations: creating in their sameness a larger entity made up of smaller versions of itself.

Never really described is the alcoholic crisis that led Lottie to being committed to the hospital. From trauma and mess and "breakdown," Schuyler's fictional eye looked away, and the hospital is seen primarily as a place of creativity: conversation and arts and crafts, with intervals of bridge playing. The implication is that these activities are curative, as Jimmy, figuratively, was "cured" by writing "Salute" in Bloomingdale in 1951. What remains with the reader are feelings of compassion for the ordinary, troubled, middle-American characters Jimmy has created. As Lottie says about group therapy, "I find this variety of human experience fascinating. I've learned a lot of little things here that may add up to one big thing."

For the second summer in a row, Jimmy was not invited to Maine, and planned to remain at 49 South Main Street without the Porters. He invited Ron Padgett and his family to share the house with him again, but they were far too shaken by the events of the previous July to accept. Vague plans to share the house with Donald Droll (now Fairfield's dealer at the Knoedler Gallery) did not pan out, and Jimmy was left by himself in the house for most of the summer.

Although his letters still present a calm and pleasant façade, and he seemed to be working well on his new novel, Schuyler's actual condition that summer was unstable. He was drinking too much, which combined with the Thorazine to make him silent, moody, overweight, and disheveled. He saw a lot of Bob Dash, finding him "a great resource." Dash remained a loyal friend even as Jimmy grew increasingly difficult. "He had a way of moving into your heart," Dash said later, "and staying there. I mean there was no one like him, and there was no one who had been like him before, and so when you knew him, he just moved into a place that was totally unoccupied and took over." For years Jimmy went to Dash's house for dinner once a week, and this routine became especially important to him when the Porters were away. For Dash, however, these dinners could sometimes be a trial, with Jimmy either being silently impassive or acting bizarrely. He was indiscriminate about taking pills: "You could hear them rattling in his pockets." Dash learned to remove all his own pills from his bathroom cabinet before Jimmy came over. Jimmy was also drinking up to a quart of vodka a day. When Jimmy was drunk he often became immobile, tense, and impassive, with a kind of suppressed energy that caused beads of sweat to appear on his forehead. Dash was a heavy drinker himself, and on one occasion Fairfield, who recognized the problem that Jimmy's drinking had become and was trying to get him to stick to wine, became angry with Dash for letting him drink spirits at his house, telling him he "lacked moral responsibility." This infuriated Bob, who pointed out the many times he had picked Jimmy up from the Porters "reeking of booze." They didn't speak after this for three years.

One way in which Bob was "a great resource" was in bringing some new young people into Jimmy's life. In July 1972, Jimmy met the artist Darragh Park, with whom Bob had recently begun a close relationship, and who was visiting for the first of many weekends. Darragh was thirty-three, blond, tall, and dashingly good-looking, and had recently abandoned a half-hearted career in business to become a full-time painter, working in a gestural realist style related to that of Dash himself and Fairfield Porter. On later visits it would become Darragh's job to pick Jimmy up from the Porters', and during those short drives, Jimmy opened up a little bit; that was the beginning of their friendship. Darragh recalled, "I immediately gravitated toward him. He was very, very easy for me to talk to."

Most often during dinners and gatherings at Dash's house, Jimmy was silent. "It was obviously a troubled time," said Darragh. "Fairfield had persuaded him to drink only wine, because his drinking really had been a problem, although I remember actually vodka sodas too, lots of them . . . So this was a problem, together with whatever drugs he was taking then too, so he was very, very quiet socially." Yet recollecting the long years of friendship that followed, Darragh also remarked on Jimmy's genuine interest in the lives of his friends. "It was not a casual or a pro-forma kind of thing at all, and it also was not judgmental—*most* of the time—I remember having the feeling with him that he would sort of leave you alone, but be very supportive."

When he wasn't visiting Bob, life by himself at 49 South Main could be bleak and lonely. As he admitted to Fairfield, "I don't really like the days when I'm altogether alone. After five o'clock a kind of endlessness sets in. Once in a while is all right, but not several days in a row. It reminds me of something you said about Carbondale [Illinois], 'When I got back to the motel, I wanted to howl with loneliness.'"

In late August, Peter Ackroyd, a young English poet, came out to stay with Jimmy for about a week, bringing his boyfriend Brian Kuhn. Ackroyd, later well-known as a biographer and historian, was then doing graduate work at Yale, and had become friends with John Ashbery, who introduced him to Porter, who had painted his portrait earlier in the year. Ackroyd remembered little of this visit, however, except that Jimmy had stayed pretty much to himself in his room. J. J. Mitchell stopped by one day during their visit, bringing another young poet, Brad Gooch, who recalled that the gossip around Schuyler that summer centered on the fact that he was having an affair with a "straight" married man, whom not many had met.

Anne, Fairfield, and Lizzie returned to Southampton around Labor Day. By this time, *49 South* had finally been printed, after numerous delays at the printer. In addition, the fall issue of *The Paris Review* appeared, containing "Life, Death and Other Dreams." The following year, the story would be anthologized by Howard Moss in his book *The Poet's Story*. September 1972 also was the official publication date of *The Crystal Lithium*, Jimmy's second commercially published book of poems. Like his succeeding books, *The Crystal Lithium* is arranged thematically and partly chronologically, opening with "Empathy and New Year" and with sections headed "Southampton and New York," "The Island," "Fall and Winter," and ending with "Loving You," the love poems to Jordan. The cover was a watercolor by Fairfield of ocean waves, and in addition to a short blurb from James Merrill, the book jacket copy also "outed" Jimmy or, in his words, made it clear that the contents included "love poems by someone as queer as an owl. Oh well, it's true, so I can't complain about that." The book was reviewed in *The New York Times Book Review* by David Kalstone, who began by saying it "contains the best poems [Schuyler] has ever written," and praised "The Crystal Lithium" itself as "the very best poem of the book." Comparisons were being made to the work of Elizabeth Bishop, and Gold and Fizdale sent her a copy. She replied on September 28: "I hadn't read his poetry until last year when James Merrill recommended it—someone lent me *Freely Espousing* and I like some of those poems a lot. But this book is much finer, I think—

some really lovely poems—and nice love poems, which are very rare. Thank you very much and if you see him give him my congratulations."

In mid-October, Jimmy went back to Vermont to visit Kenward Elmslie, and stayed through the first week of November. It was a quiet and uneventful visit, although Kenward must have been quite nervous about it, and seems to have kept his distance. The weather was generally gray: "Louring skys, sunny days, and finally snow . . ." Jimmy took long walks when the weather was good, and when it was not he stayed upstairs in his room writing and reading while Kenward worked in the living room. As in previous years, Jimmy wrote a group of "Vermont" poems during the visit, but feared they might not be as good as "A Vermont Diary": "I may have shot my Calais wad in that." Collected in a group subheaded "Evenings in Vermont" in his next book, *Hymn to Life*, they are quieter and less varied than "A Vermont Diary" but include gems such as "The Bluet" and "Sunset."

Despite Jimmy's troubles, it had been a productive year. In December, he realized he already had enough poems for a new book, and sent the manuscript of *Hymn to Life* to Charlotte Mayerson, who told him that it was too soon to publish another book. "I suppose," he mused in a letter to Clark Coolidge, "I could burn the poems, write some new ones and thus get into proper time-synch." In the meantime he had sent the title poem to *Poetry*, which published it as the leadoff work to the April 1973 issue.

By May 1973, Jimmy seems to have reconciled himself, in a way, to the fact that he really would have to leave the Porters' house and live on his own in his apartment on Thirty-fifth Street. He began to make plans to move in the fall. Remembering Kenward's earlier offer to settle a trust fund on him, Jimmy wrote to him on May 7 to ask if he would reconsider the plan. It was a dignified letter, in which he wrote, "In the fall I'm going to be living in New York again, and the future looks a bit dim. I've worked very hard to make myself a poet, and I hate having to give it up and go back to some sort of office work—not so easy to find at fifty, for the matter of that." He added, "Whatever you decide, I don't see that it need make any difference to our friendship." Kenward did agree. The trust came into effect on July 30, 1973, and provided Jimmy with an income of about $5,000 a year to the end of his life. It was, at the beginning, just enough to get by on, thanks to the low rent on Thirty-fifth Street. Inevitably, however, the trust did make a difference to their friendship.

That summer, the Porters were again on Great Spruce Head Island, leaving the Southampton house in Jimmy's care. Not wanting to leave him alone again, Fairfield and Anne tried to think of someone who could share the house and its responsibilities with him. After approaching several of Jimmy's friends, they finally came up with Ruth Kligman.

Kligman was famous as the girlfriend of Jackson Pollock, who had been with him in 1956 when he drove, drunk, into a tree in Springs, New York, killing himself and a friend of Ruth's who was with them. Frank O'Hara cruelly dubbed her "Death Car Girl." A beautiful, vivacious, and sensual woman, she was attracted to famous and successful painters and writers, and they to her. Anne Dunn recalled meeting her around this time at Jane Freilicher and Joe Hazan's New York apartment, where she was wearing a dress of white *broderie anglaise*, and thinking she was "staggeringly beautiful." To Harry Mathews, who had a brief but intense fling with her, she was "the greatest courtesan of our times."

Ruth and Jimmy first met at a party at Larry Rivers's house in Southampton in the late '60s, when he came up to her and said, "You're ravishing. I'm Jimmy Schuyler." It was, she recalled, "a beautiful meeting." However, their acquaintance remained casual until Fairfield offered her the use of his house and a car if she would spend the summer with Jimmy at 49 South Main.

Jimmy paid for groceries out of an allowance provided by Fairfield; Ruth did most of the cooking. "What's for dinner?" became a catchphrase in the house that summer, inspired by the novel, which Jimmy was trying to finish. Ruth was an aspiring painter, and had the use of Fairfield's studio. She had recently written a memoir of her time with Jackson Pollock, *Love Affair*, and that summer she was correcting the galleys. Jimmy wrote a blurb for the dustjacket, which ends, "Unconsciously, Ruth Kligman draws a touching portrait of herself, a beautiful young woman, ambitious to be a painter, unsure of the way. Truth makes a classic, and truth is what this book is made of."

Sharing sexual confidences became a large part of their friendship. Jimmy related some of his sexual interests and history to Ruth, including his activities with Jordan, his previous promiscuity, and his visits to the baths, leading Ruth to observe later, "He was like Baudelaire, rich in his desire." They often talked about the "meaning of sexuality and the heavy influence it had" on their lives. Anne Dunn, who was also becoming a close friend at this time, said they could sound like "two bawds" in their sexual banter. Ruth sometimes saw gay men as a challenge to her skills of seduction, and regularly picked up men at the Millstone, a local gay bar. Brad Gooch, who knew Ruth well, had no reason to think that she had a sexual relationship with Schuyler himself, but speculated that her sexual aggressiveness may have struck a chord in Schuyler's masochistic psyche.

Be that as it may, their relationship that summer was for the most part fairly domestic. They had a few weekend guests, including J. J. Mitchell, who impressed even Ruth with his need to have a sexual partner every night, as though "every night was his last." They gave several dinner parties, including a "white dinner" of vichyssoise, fillet of sole Véronique (with white grapes), white rice salad, white patty pan squash, and vanilla ice cream with white crème de menthe, inviting Harry Mathews, Larry Rivers, Jane Freilicher and Joe Hazan, John Ashbery, and Eleanor Ward. Living with Ruth was never dull, and her active social life was at least diverting for Jimmy vicariously, even if he didn't take part in all her outings; they provided a good distraction from his own problems, especially the looming one of moving into the city on his own. She sprained her toe, "burned herself in the kitchen, then she fell down dancing on the slate floor in Johnny Bates's renovated barn and hurt her knee, followed by chills and fever."

Unmentioned in Jimmy's few letters of the summer were two or three manic episodes, which Ruth dealt with effectively, it seems. One night Jimmy had a meltdown and started screaming and shouting in the early hours of the morning, terrifying Ruth, who locked herself into her room. She called a friend in hysterics, asking her and her husband to come and help. Just as they were reluctantly getting ready to leave their house,

Ruth called back to say she had finally opened the door and told Jimmy, "Stop it! You're scaring me!" at which Jimmy backed off, saying, "Oh, I am so sorry."

In some ways Ruth "really was difficult," according to Darragh Park, but Jimmy was "fond of her, and not many other people were, she was really so obstreperous [and] . . . larger than life. She was a mensch, essentially, Ruth, I mean he felt that way." Much as he liked or perhaps loved Ruth, he had no illusions about her. Several years later, he sketched his feelings toward her in lines in "The Morning of the Poem":

I know someone else who looks
deep into your eyes and under
The curly hair the lies are manufactured. Mostly
it delights me, like
A farce, the need to dramatize, to make out, "Oh
I was beautiful, oh the most
Famous men all fell for me and slipped it up
my cooze. I've seen
'em all!" I believe you, dear.

That summer, Jimmy began seeing a new psychiatrist, Dr. Hyman Weitzen, who practiced both in New York and in Water Mill, where he began to see Jimmy twice a week. When Weitzen first met Jimmy, he found him to be "in terrible shape" and emotionally remote. Weitzen had trouble diagnosing him, in large part because of the cocktail of illicit and prescription drugs he was taking, in addition to alcohol, and his initial thought was that he "looked" schizophrenic and had to be hospitalized. But after he had adjusted his medications, Weitzen decided he was in fact "depressed," and sometime later resolved on a diagnosis of schizoaffective disorder. Schizoaffective disorder is defined by the National Alliance on Mental Illness as "a chronic mental health condition characterized primarily by symptoms of schizophrenia, such as hallucinations or delusions, and symptoms of a mood disorder, such as mania and depression."

Most frighteningly, Jimmy had developed a kind of physical catatonia, and was alarmed to find himself suddenly unable to type. Weitzen diagnosed the condition as an effect of long-term use of Thorazine, and told Jimmy it might be irreversible. The idea was chilling. "Can you imagine never being able to type again?" Jimmy wrote Kenward. Fortunately, Jimmy's motor skills returned after Weitzen got him off Thorazine and prescribed another medication to counteract its effects. But as he mused to Fairfield, "There's something funny about taking a pill in order to recover from another pill."

Weitzen felt that anxiety and fear were Jimmy's main problems, along with his terrific passivity and dependence on others. Since he believed Jimmy was "no candidate for" classical Freudian analysis, his treatment consisted of medication, therapy, and support. He also convinced Jimmy to cut down on his drinking. Weitzen, then in his mid-fifties, had a paternal demeanor, and Jimmy liked and trusted him.

Ron, Pat, and Wayne Padgett came to visit Jimmy and Ruth over the Labor Day weekend—the first time they dared to come see him there since his breakdown two years earlier. They found him much better than the last time they'd seen him in the city, which they credited to Ruth, noting that "he 'looked' better, which made me *feel* better, which in turn helped Jimmy forget his anxiety over scaring us with his nuttiness." Nonetheless, the Padgetts would never return to their earlier level of friendship with Jimmy.

In the three years since the Porters had first asked him to leave, when his reply had been "I'll think about it," the atmosphere at the Porter house had often been uncomfortable. According to Anne Porter, Jimmy "knew that we thought he should leave, but he just couldn't do it." And it was "very hard" for Anne and Fairfield too, waiting for Jimmy to gather his resolve. In their desperation the couple considered and immediately rejected radical options, as Anne later implied: "You can't just call the police on your friends, you know, you just don't do *that*."

In addition to the silent pressure from the Porters, several other factors finally gave Jimmy the courage to leave them in the fall of 1973. First was the support of Dr. Weitzen, whom he would be able to continue to see in the city. In addition, living in the apartment on Thirty-fifth Street, small and charmless as it was, would allow him to see Bob Jordan more often. Financially, he was slightly better off since he had recently been awarded a modest Ingram Merrill grant, and, most crucially, he now had the promise of a regular income from the proceeds of the trust that Kenward Elmslie set up for him.

Still, he did not make things easy for the Porters, or himself, when the day finally came for him to leave. Perhaps it was not completely real to him until the Home Sweet Home moving van turned up at the Porters' doorstep on the unseasonably warm morning of October 15. He was loudly and bitterly disparaging about the name of the movers. While the van was being packed he played over and over, at earsplitting volume, the final, "suicide" scene of Puccini's *Madama Butterfly*, alternating with a British protest song denouncing the cruel behavior of factory owners who profess to be Christians but show no true Christianity. To Anne, this emotional music seemed to be "an outpouring of how Jimmy felt about leaving. Some of it was like almost his own voice" emanating from the machine.

[18]

THIS DARK APARTMENT

1974–1979

Jimmy's first months at 250 East Thirty-fifth Street were quiet and lonely. A kind of anticlimax set in, and he found himself unable to write: "I sit down at the typewriter, and a big fat nothing happens," he complained to Clark Coolidge. Jimmy was also conscious of getting older: "This Friday I'll be fifty, a fact totally unreal to me. I never *thought* about getting to be fifty."

His mood improved a bit as the fall progressed and he started to socialize with Darragh and Ruth. A bright spot remained his sessions with Dr. Weitzen, whom he could now see twice a week. He felt good about the fact that he was back in analysis after a lapse of some twelve years. But all too soon came a major setback when his expectations for the continuation of his love affair with Bob Jordan were dashed early in 1974. According to Jimmy's account, related in his poem "This Dark Apartment," at some point he returned home to discover Bob in bed with another man. Bob was matter-of-fact about it, saying he wasn't cut out to be faithful, even to his extramarital lover: "I'm / not built that way." Jimmy might have accepted that, but to make matters worse, the lover turned out to be a drug addict who, using a key Jordan had given him, came back and robbed the apartment. What finally ended the relationship was the fact that Bob simply cut off all contact and stopped returning his calls.

On March 15, 1974, Jimmy wrote "This Dark Apartment," marking the end of his three-year affair with Jordan, a poem notable for its austere, pared-down narrative of facts of a personal, even "confessional," nature. The tale of Jordan's perfidy is bracketed by lyrical evocations of his neighborhood on East Thirty-fifth Street, and his realization of its relative proximity to East Forty-ninth Street, where he lived twenty years before with Frank O'Hara. The towers of New York "shine" like beacons of hope and friendship, in contrast to the dark and lonely apartment he was returning to.

> How I wish you would come
> back! I could tell
> you how, when I lived
> on East 49th, first
> with Frank and then with John,
> we had a lovely view of
> the UN building and the
> Beekman Towers. They were
> not my lovers, though.
> You were. You said so.

Jimmy still wore Jordan's silver chain for a year or two after the breakup. He was not unaware of the inconsistency and even absurdity of doing so, and was even able to laugh at the picture he sometimes presented, telling Trevor Winkfield about a time when he was prowling the halls of the Everard Baths, fat, with long tangled hair, wearing just a towel and the prominent chains, and encountered a fellow patron who exclaimed, "Brunhilde!"

Anne Dunn had recently begun renting an apartment on East Eighty-fifth Street and spending three or four months of the year in New York. Still at loose ends, Jimmy suggested that he'd like to visit her, and volunteered himself as a model. Starting early in the spring of 1974, he came to her almost every morning, ostensibly to model, but also to sit quietly and visit, and enjoy a nice lunch.

Often Jimmy was in bad shape during these visits: his face and body bloated, his hair long, lank, and dirty. His demeanor could be uncannily unresponsive, as though he were sleepwalking. He carried containers of pills—Thorazine, Stelazine, and others—in his jacket pockets, and took them at will, "popping so many pills it was very alarming . . . as if they were Smarties or something." He was also still drinking, which exacerbated the effect of the drugs. Many of their visits passed in silence. "We didn't talk, but I was easy with silence," said Anne. "That was the special quality of our relationship, being able to be silent for hours on end."

At other times, when in a communicative mood, he reminisced about his time on Ischia with Auden and Chester Kallman. He liked to feel a connection to Anne's own European life in London and Provence, where she was a good friend of John Richardson's, and mentioned his night of lovemaking with Richardson in 1949 as "the best he had ever had."

On one occasion, Jimmy was sitting in his chair being drawn when he suddenly got up and went into the bathroom, took off all his clothes, and came back and sat down again. Anne decided to pretend she hadn't noticed and simply continued to draw him, nude now. In time, without anything being said on either side, Jimmy got back up and put his clothes on and resumed his pose. Anne felt that this was both a tease and an oblique way of making a kind of pass at her. On another occasion he blurted out, "I give very good head, you know."

Anne's presence was stabilizing for Jimmy when she was in town. She left the country around May, and when she returned the following November, the sittings took up where they had left off, establishing a pattern for the next couple of years. With her return to France, Jimmy was thrown back onto his own resources, which at this time were not many. His writing silence continued.

Soon after moving to Thirty-fifth Street, Jimmy had called up the artist George Schneeman and finally arranged to have the portrait of Bill Berkson that he'd bought in 1971 delivered to him. This led to friendship with George and his wife, Katie, who occasionally had him over for meals in the years that followed. That they had three young "angelic" blond-haired sons was part of the attraction. One winter's night, after Jimmy got home from dinner there, he called George to announce that he wished to "adopt" their youngest son, twelve-year-old Emilio. As with his purported "adoption" of Gary Greenly in 1971, it is hard to know exactly what Jimmy meant by this, except that he was clearly taken with the boy's beauty. The Schneemans were amused; it never went any further.

In March 1974, *Hymn to Life* was published by Random House, with another beautiful cover illustration by Fairfield Porter, showing the pear tree behind the house at 49 South Main Street in bloom. The collection bore the same dedication as *The Crystal Lithium*: "For Bob" (Jordan), and contained another section of love poems inspired by him, although by the time the book appeared the relationship was over.

That summer was Jimmy's first in thirteen years not spent outside the city. He was able to visit friends on Long Island, however: a weekend with Bob Dash, where Darragh was spending the summer, and three weeks with the painter Mary Abbott in Southampton. Over another weekend in June, he and John Ashbery stayed with Jane Freilicher and Joe Hazan in Water Mill. There he wrote the poem "June 30, 1974" while sitting at the kitchen table, "watching the clear / day ripen." The poem is concerned with continuity and change around a stable physical environment, and is also an appreciation of the domestic refuge that Jane had created: "Home! How lucky to / have one, how arduous / to make this scene / of beauty for / your family and / friends." As such it has a certain poignancy: Jane, like many other old friends, was finding it increasingly hard to maintain her old level of intimacy with Jimmy after the changes of the past two years. She felt he had "kind of lost his spring and . . . really deteriorated," becoming "difficult and demanding" and moody. As usual, the poem suggests none of this, projecting a bulwark of domesticity and sanity. Jimmy dedicated the poem to his weekend hosts, and while Jane found the poem "wonderful," she also regarded it (perhaps unfairly) as a kind of emotional "blackmail," which she resisted. This was, in fact, the last time Jimmy would stay with Jane and Joe.

His longest time out of New York was a visit of six weeks to his mother in East Aurora. After a slightly rocky start due to his late-rising habits, which Margaret appeared to find almost immoral, things settled down between mother and son, and Jimmy enjoyed renewing his acquaintance with his niece and nephews. He also wrote at least one poem, "August first, 1974," sitting at his desk in his old bedroom, observing the view out the window and contemplating the changes in the town since his youth. The poem anticipates "The Morning of the Poem," which he would write sitting in the same spot two years later.

At the end of December, Bob Dash and Darragh Park hosted a Christmas–to–New Year's house party in Sagaponack with Schuyler,

Trevor Winkfield, Douglas Crase, and Frank Polach. Jimmy had met Douglas Crase at Bob's two years earlier at a joint birthday party he gave for Darragh and John Ashbery, who brought Crase. Doug never forgot his surprise at Jimmy's first words to him at that party, delivered with his inimitable deep-voiced solemnity, "John is always telling me about some beautiful young man he has met, and this is the first time it has turned out to be true." At that time, Doug lived in Rochester, but recently he had moved to New York with Frank Polach, his new lover. Doug, in addition to being a poet, had a day job writing corporate messaging for Kodak. Frank had been a plant pathologist at Cornell, but after he and Doug moved to New York he entered library school at Columbia, and he later took an internship at the New York Botanical Garden, leading to a job as plant information officer. Jimmy grew close to both of them, especially Frank, whose quiet nature and deep knowledge about plants appealed to him.

Jimmy spent most of the visit sitting quietly, enjoying the bustle of young men and dogs around him, reading, and writing a new poem almost every day of the visit. One of them, "Dec. 28, 1974," interweaves music (Scriabin) playing on the phonograph visualized physically as filling the air "with wildly flying notes"; plants in the room nearby; light fading across a distant field; Darragh or Dash coming down the iron spiral staircase; and the poet's reflections, which include the often quoted lines: "'Your poems,' / a clunkhead said, 'have grown / more open.' I don't want to be open, / merely to say, to see and say, things / as they are." The "clunkhead" was Dash himself, who later stood by the remark, adding, "It *had* become more open . . . He sat and observed. And his eye never swerved from anyplace that I knew of. And it could take note of everything."

Recalling the weeklong visit in Sagaponack, Crase later tried to pinpoint what Jimmy's presence was like:

> One doesn't remember so much the things that he *said*, and if you do remember something he said, you also remember that there was a great space of time around it, on either side, in which he said nothing, and that mostly you remember this—one wants to say "sphinx-like" presence, but you think of a sphinx as being

closed and ungiving, and in fact Jimmy's presence was generous—but it was quiet.

Even more exciting for Doug was watching Jimmy write a poem before his eyes. "I was just thrilled. My God, this is the way it's done. He did it and astonishingly it was good." To Trevor Winkfield it seemed that "it was done very [casually] just as you might sort of write a note to somebody; I mean there was no big drama." For his part, Jimmy may not have been unaware of the performative aspect of his writing before an appreciative audience of handsome younger poets and artists.

On January 19, a couple of weeks after he had returned to the city, Jimmy opened the Sunday *New York Times* to find an obituary of Chester Kallman, who had died the previous day, fifteen months after Auden. Jimmy's best friend and camp "sister" of the 1940s and early '50s drank himself to death in Athens at the age of fifty-three. The full details of his pathetic last days may never have been reported to Jimmy, but his futile death saddened and disturbed him. His elegy, "Chester Kallman," was apparently written later that year, and forms a pair with "Wystan Auden," written the previous year. Both poems evince strong emotions held in check by a plainspoken, slightly reportorial tone, almost in the detached manner of "This Dark Apartment." "Chester Kallman" gives a succinct character sketch of his witty friend, opera queen, gourmand, and sex addict: "with a cooking utensil in hand / and on the phonograph a pirated / recording of Fidelio, Flagstad / and Bruno Walter . . . ," then asks, "But why, so / gifted, was he so death oriented? / The plain clothes cop and dangerous / rough trade, the endless drinking, / drinking, drinking down the sunless / path to Lethe." "My tears are not from sorrow, / though a dear friend he was, / tears for a wasted life."

Within a day or two of learning of Chester's death, Jimmy had a breakdown and was admitted to Bellevue. Brought in by ambulance, he was "really out of it" for the first five days he spent there. By January 27, he had been transferred to Payne Whitney, where he remained for three or four weeks.

Outside, the weather was snowy. One day Darragh arrived to find the poets Michael Brownstein and Anne Waldman visiting Jimmy in the small cubicle where he had his bed, and he was telling them, with utter ingenuousness, "Well, I write a poem, I guess, pretty much every day or so, but of course that doesn't take any time at all." Another time, the poet Peter Schjeldahl visited with his wife, Brooke Alderson, and while they were there John Ashbery appeared. Brooke was struck by John's "tender but firm treatment of Jimmy: a model of loving concern, to visibly positive effect." Other visitors included Anne Dunn, Maxine Groffsky, and the poet Charles North. On February 12, Fairfield braved the heavy snow to visit, and while he was there Gerard Malanga turned up, bringing one of his own books as a gift. He also produced a copy of *The Crystal Lithium* for Jimmy to inscribe, which he did, writing, "We meet in strange places." Photography was forbidden in the hospital, but Malanga attempted to photograph Jimmy and Fairfield together, at which Fairfield rose to his full height and said a single word: "NO."

Schuyler once likened his writing to a process of transcription ("looking at things and trying to transcribe them"), and this is what the extraordinary sequence of eleven poems that Jimmy wrote in the hospital and came to call the Payne Whitney Poems often suggests: a mind operating without filters, in slow motion, able to observe the process of thought itself. Their pared-down quality, their brevity, the mention of medication in one of them, and their designation as the "Payne Whitney Poems" have led some readers to give undue importance to the fact that they were written under some influence of psychotropic drugs, yet they are of a piece with Jimmy's perennial engagement with the act of observation, the process of thought, and the phenomenon of time. "Claustrated," as he put it, in the circumscribed and regimented environment of the hospital, time is experienced as fluid, unreal: "Now it is / one hour later" ("We Walk"); "Is this the moment? / No, not yet. / When is the moment? / Perhaps there is none" ("Linen"). Existence is reduced to an inventory of fortuitous objects and sensations: "sunbursts. / An aluminum measure / full of water. Scentlessness . . . Pale green walls and / a white ceiling. Lamps / lit in daylight. Ice" ("Heather and Calendulas").

When he got out of Payne Whitney in late February, he felt better, and initially optimistic. Following medical advice he quit drinking. The sacrifice, while it lasted, gave him a sense of motivation. "I really love to drink," he wrote Dash. "I love the taste, I love the way it acts (*hate* the hangovers) but, considering I've been on a bender since I was 16, I guess I've had my fair share."

In April 1975, to celebrate a new edition of *A Nest of Ninnies* brought out by Kenward Elmslie's recently established Z Press, and to cheer up Darragh Park, whose brother had just died, Jimmy cooked dinner for Kenward and Darragh on Thirty-fifth Street. In the years he knew him, this was the only time Darragh ever knew Jimmy to cook for friends, and he went to some trouble to make the evening special. He made pork chops, "very nicely," and for dessert "ambrosia" fruit salad, a childhood favorite. Despite the small, dark, and "crummy" apartment itself, the evening was warm and comfortable, with "a sort of family feeling," for which Darragh was "very grateful."

After a long hiatus, Jimmy had finally resumed work on *What's for Dinner?* and by June the novel was finished. Maxine Groffsky, who had returned to New York and become a well-regarded literary agent, submitted the manuscript to Random House. Charlotte Mayerson said she liked it, and Jimmy felt there was a good chance they would accept it. On the strength of this, he made plans with Donald Droll to visit Anne Dunn and Rodrigo Moynihan at their house in Provence later that summer.

Unfortunately, Random House ended up rejecting the novel, and when he got the news, Jimmy suffered severe attacks of anxiety. After four days of "terrible mounting rage," he was able to see Dr. Weitzen and "let it all hang out" in tears of "rage and self-pity." Before this, he had been off all his medications except for Valium and Antabuse; now Dr. Weitzen put him back on Stelazine, Artane (an antispasmodic to manage the side effects of Stelazine), and sleeping pills. He decided not to go to France. "It's quite serious," he wrote Anne. "My head feels utterly weird."

But soon he was hopeful about another publisher who, he said, had verbally agreed to publish *What's for Dinner?* "I don't want to talk about it until I've signed the contract. But it's a very distinguished house," he wrote Kenneth. This editor might have been Michael di Capua at Farrar, Straus and Giroux, who did see the manuscript at some point and was interested. In the end, di Capua asked Jimmy to rewrite parts of the later chapters, which he tried to do, but he couldn't make the changes work, and di Capua rejected the novel, although he left the door open to consider his next manuscript. Groffsky did not resubmit the novel until the following summer, when it was finally accepted by Black Sparrow Press.

Instead of going to France, Jimmy returned to 49 South Main Street for a short visit with the Porters. The visit started happily enough, and Jimmy wrote two poems, "July 4th" and "Mid-afternoon" (unpublished), both seeming to express deep contentment at being back, but they may have been written in an attempt to ward off bleaker thoughts. The first poem ends:

> Will
> it be clear today? Can't
> tell yet. The completion
> of the night is over.

Three days later he suffered a bad anxiety attack, and on July 7, he asked Fairfield to take him back into the city, where he was again admitted to Bellevue. After bringing Jimmy to the hospital, Fairfield then delivered the keys of the Thirty-fifth Street apartment to Darragh Park with a note saying, "Here are Jimmy's keys. He says you know what to do with them." Darragh felt that the gesture marked "a passing of the torch." After about two weeks, Jimmy was transferred to "Bloomingdale," Payne Whitney's branch in White Plains. There he remained for the rest of the summer of 1975 and into the fall.

Twenty-four years had passed since Jimmy had last been a patient at Bloomingdale, where he began his life as a poet by writing "Salute." Perhaps more so than in 1951, he appreciated the handsome campus with its wide lawns and majestic old trees. His favorite was an enormous weeping beech, "a creature of many shimmering moods," which he could see from his room. When John came to visit, Jimmy pointed the tree out to him, saying, "Once I've noticed that there is a weeping beech there's not much else to do."

The distance from Manhattan meant he had fewer visitors than at Payne Whitney. Darragh was his mainstay, coming out almost once a week, with letters, books, cigarettes, and other necessities. At Bloomingdale, he was prescribed lithium for the first time, well after writing "The

Crystal Lithium." He continued to take it after being released, although for how long and with what effect is not clear.

Jimmy wrote at least five poems at Bloomingdale. The best of them, "Song," evoking the dying of the day, is one of his most euphonious poems, beginning with its alliterative first line, "The light lies layered in the leaves" and continuing with other sound effects, both aural and described: "Traffic sounds and / bells resound in silver clangs / the hour, a tune, my friend / Pierrot." The introduction of Pierrot brings a kind of rococo lightness of mood, as of a Watteau idyll:

A cloud boy brings the evening paper:
The Evening Sun. It sets.
Not sharply or all at once
a stately progress down the sky
(it's gilt and pink and faintly green)

The poem ends with the day ("so many and so few") as both are brought into the notebook in which the poem is being written:

and leaves are lap-held notebook leaves
discriminated barely
in light no longer layered.

On September 17, he was allowed to come into the city for dinner at Darragh's apartment with John Ashbery, David Kermani, and Trevor Winkfield, who recalled that Jimmy was uncomfortably quiet and withdrawn. The next day, September 18, brought terrible news: on his early morning walk to the coffee shop to get the newspaper, Fairfield Porter had collapsed of a heart attack and died at the age of sixty-eight.

Jimmy's immediate reaction was hard to gauge. His friends were worried that it would send him over the edge: there was a lot of "murmuring: how was Jimmy going to take this? What can we all expect?" Darragh saw John in Sagaponack that weekend, whose first reaction was "What about Jimmy?" Clearly the fact that he was already in the hospital helped cushion the blow, although it set back his release for at least another month. In fact, Darragh felt that he took the news with "great aplomb," but what that really meant was that he "internalized" it as usual.

Fairfield Porter's funeral was eclectic, as might have been expected. The coffin was laid out in the living room at 49 South Main. Placed in front of it was a vase that Fairfield had painted, containing roses from the bushes Jimmy planted. The service was held at the large Catholic church on Hill Street. Lizzie and some friends played guitar and recorder music, but there were no eulogies aside from the sermon, and as he was not a Catholic, Fairfield's body was not allowed inside. Laurence drove it from the house to the cemetery in the Porter station wagon (stopping for gas on the way). "There was a plainness to the whole thing that was difficult to come to terms with," Jane Freilicher recalled. Jimmy, of course, did not attend.

Anne wrote to Jimmy shortly before the service, using Fairfield's family nickname:

> I know that you & I & Furl's children are the ones that will miss him most, because he was part of us, so I've been thinking specially of you & worrying a little about the pain for you . . . You were one of the very dearest & most important parts of his life—which I know makes it hard for you to have him die.

Even though Fairfield had stopped supporting Jimmy two years earlier, his death brought new urgency to the ongoing discussions of his future among his friends. Full-time hospitalization was not a realistic option, if only because of the cost: a year at Bloomingdale would run about $65,000. A partial solution was hit upon by Morris Golde, who proposed that the legal framework of the Frank O'Hara Foundation, which had been set up after Frank's death to support the publication of first books by poets, and of which he was president, be repurposed to channel funds for Jimmy's support, thus allowing his friends and supporters to take a charitable tax deduction for anything they contributed for his upkeep. John and Kenneth, who, along with Jimmy himself, were the other O'Hara trustees, agreed to the plan in theory, but it would not be formalized until 1978.

Jimmy was out of the hospital by October 24, and celebrated his fifty-second birthday on November 9 with John and Darragh. He was still (or again) not drinking. He resumed his sittings with Anne Dunn. It was apparently around this time that Jimmy had his long-troublesome teeth replaced with dentures.

Jimmy was never very happy in the apartment on Thirty-fifth Street. Periodically he made half-hearted attempts to look for something else, but there was little chance of finding another apartment he could afford by himself. Finally, Darragh heard of a place in Chelsea that sounded promising: a brownstone at 348 West Twentieth Street between Eighth and Ninth Avenues, whose owner rented out rooms to congenial artist and writer types. Darragh called it "a kind of rooming house for sort of indigent intellectuals"; John Ashbery called it "a seedy *pension*." By May 1976, Jimmy had moved in. His room was at the back of the house, which made it very quiet; best of all, it faced south and was sunny for much of the day, in contrast to Thirty-fifth Street. The room boasted a marble fireplace, on which he leaned George Schneeman's portrait of Bill Berkson. The residents also shared a kitchen, so Jimmy was able to do some cooking for himself, and for a while, "he was functioning really quite well," Darragh recalled.

Perhaps the best thing about the apartment was its location in Chelsea, two or three blocks away from Darragh, John and David, and Doug Crase and Frank Polach, and within walking distance of Kenward, Ruth Kligman, Morris Golde, and Janice Koch (now separated from Kenneth) in the West Village. In a letter to Anne Dunn on May 31 he wrote: "I'm all moved and happy to be a Chelsea-ite, embowered in friends," and indeed he was soon busy with regular social engagements, including celebrations in honor of Ashbery's recent "trifecta" of winning the National Book Award, the National Book Critics' Circle Award, and the Pulitzer Prize for his latest book, *Self-Portrait in a Convex Mirror*. As Jimmy wrote to Anne, "You can't imagine the fuss that's being made of the little dear, but he's being sweet about it, only a little anxious about being drummed into the establishment." Meanwhile, John was writing to Anne that Jimmy "looks seedy and seems to do nothing at all, including the revisions on his novel. It is very disturbing to see him waste his powers," and to Kenneth: "His state seems to have its ups and downs. I don't think he does much though I've tried to get him to get a book of poems together, maybe a Selected."

Jimmy spent the months of July and August 1976 with his mother in East Aurora. The visit was the longest period of time he had spent with her since leaving home, and was marked by a recognition of her failing powers and a deliberate intention of making peace with her while she was alive. As he wrote to Anne Dunn, "When my mother dies, I don't want to feel that I treated her like an utter shit." Margaret was still living in Jimmy's childhood home, and Jimmy had his old room. Sharing the house with her was not always easy. She forgot what had been said to her from one minute to the next, yet she could also reassert her parental role, as when she walked in on him while he was shaving naked in the bathroom to scold him for keeping the water running.

Jimmy had already decided that he wanted to write a long, book-length poem of about a hundred pages during the visit. Two or three days after arriving in East Aurora, he sat down at the typewriter to begin. To himself he designated that morning as "the morning of the poem," and that became the title. From that point on, he spent most of his mornings at the typewriter.

As he had done in writing "The Crystal Lithium" and "Hymn to Life," he began by setting the margins of the typewriter as wide as they would go, and typed each line more or less to the end of the page. He soon recalled, however, that in setting the two earlier poems in type for their original publication, many of the lines had had to be broken and anything from one to four words at the end were dropped to an indented line below. It made a strong visual and rhythmic effect, and although it was not his original intention, Jimmy came to like the syncopation of the alternating longer and shorter lines. Although "The Morning of the Poem" was also begun in long unbroken lines, early on Jimmy decided to preempt the typesetter and retype the poem, making his own secondary line breaks and indenting the shorter lines. While the first part of each original line retains its initial capital letter, the second, indented part is not capitalized, a deliberate move "to indicate that it was all one line."

Not only in line width, but in the length and ambition of the poem, Jimmy was expanding on precedents established with "The Crystal Lithium" and "Hymn to Life." One might see the progression of Jimmy's long poems as becoming (superficially) more "open" (as Bob Dash claimed), with "The Crystal Lithium" the most dense and imagistically ambiguous, "Hymn to Life" less disjunctive, and "The Morning of the Poem" showing increased expansiveness and clarity. The idea of a poem being "open" can be viewed in different ways. Dash seemed to think of it as being "open" to and recording as many stimulae as possible. But one might also see it as being more self-revealing, or simply clearer in meaning. "Openness" in the case of "The Morning of the Poem" is reflected formally in a visible loosening of the line, especially beginning in about the middle of the poem, where the double lines become longer than could ever have fit on a single line. Seemingly as a result, the expression is less condensed, images and anecdotes are drawn out, the pace is more leisurely.

Jimmy recognized a difference between the tone and content of "The Morning of the Poem" and his other poems, and in one interview compared it to the letters he had written in the preceding decades to his two steadiest correspondents, Joe Brainard and John Ashbery: "It has a certain lightness of tone, gaiety that comes from that." But their own works also inspired him, specifically Joe's *I Remember* and John's "Self-Portrait in a Convex Mirror." *I Remember* is not really about the past ("it isn't nostalgic at all, because I'm not nostalgic," Joe said), but about the state of mind that produced the work, one that by being fully "present" simultaneously and paradoxically releases the past and brings it forth into conscious thought. "The Morning of the Poem" does not use Joe's catalytic phrase "I remember" more than two or three times, but is full of spontaneous memories and is situated in that same mental state of acute awareness in which the past is lived through the present.

Although Jimmy's and John's prose voices are indistinguishably blended in *A Nest of Ninnies* and nearly so in their letters to each other, their poetic voices and concerns are very different. John was always a strong supporter of Jimmy's work, and while he was not "influenced" by "Hymn to Life," he admired it and it was part of the furniture of his mind once he came to write "Self-Portrait in a Convex Mirror." Coincidentally or not, there is an "openness" of tone and narrative clarity to "Self-Portrait" that is unusual in Ashbery's work, exemplified, for example, by his incorporating "real people" into the poem, most surprisingly himself and his former lover Pierre Martory, when he wrote, "Vienna where the painting is today, where / I saw it with Pierre in the summer of 1959; New York / Where I am now, which is a logarithm / Of other cities." Whether or not Jimmy recognized any trace of his own work in "Self-Portrait in a Convex Mirror," it is likely that its ambition and narrative discursiveness partly inspired Jimmy to write his own very different long poem. (Both begin, incidentally, with an image of a painter at work.)

Between the writing of "Hymn to Life" in 1972 and "The Morning of the Poem" in 1976, Jimmy's world had been overturned. He had been ejected from what Kenward Elmslie called "Porter nirvana," had been summarily dropped by his lover, spent two extensive periods in mental hospitals, and was mourning the death of his "best friend," sometime lover, and the mainstay of a large part of his life. In a sense, the poem begins as a reaffirmation of his own identity: it opens with the date, as many do, but here with the effect of a person waking from a coma and answering a doctor's orienting questions: "July 8 or July 9, the eight surely, certainly / 1976 that I know / Awakening in western New York blurred barely / morning sopping dawn . . ."

Written in a small bedroom of his childhood house during two rainy summer months of 1976, "The Morning of the Poem" begins as an address to Darragh Park in New York, and expands to encompass, selectively, his whole life. Finding himself "claustrated" in East Aurora for an extended period was somewhat disorienting, and led to contemplation not only of his own past, but of the strangeness of being someplace and not someplace else—in space or in time. At first, the contrast is between East Aurora and New York City, but as the poem advances, increasingly it is between the present and the past, which merge in the making of the poem. The poem roves freely from East Aurora to New York City, Washington in the '30s, Paris in the '40s, Italy in the '50s, Maine in the '60s, Sagaponack in the '70s, Albert Lea, Key West, Vermont, Venice, always circling back to, or contained within, the experience of East Aurora in the present, ever-mutable moment.

In comparing "The Morning of the Poem" with his letters, Jimmy was right to point to its "tone" as the poem's distinguishing element. In a sense, beyond all its lively details, anecdotes, and sense impressions in both the present and the past, the intimate, confiding tone of the poem is arguably its subject, a tone that establishes the character of the narrator—Schuyler—as effectively and sympathetically as the characters in his fiction are created by their own words. Like the "rose made out of a real rose," the tone of voice, which is the poem, is consonant with the words that convey it.

The narrative fabric of the poem relates it not only to his letters, but also to some of the autobiographical novelists, diarists, and essayists he loved, yet to compare the poem to prose is beside the point. In the staggered longer and shorter lines, Schuyler invented the poetic form that he needed, one that in its relentless forward propulsion induces a sort of trance state in poet and reader alike. As Alice Notley has said, "It opened the space and the possibilities of what you could do inside that kind of poem."

Jimmy returned to New York at the end of August or beginning of September, where he intended to keep going with the poem, but once back he found himself unable to do so. "Everything was just too cut off, certainly everything that had been feeding the poem." Instead, he fell into old patterns of not doing much other than seeing friends once in a while.

In January 1977, Schuyler was interviewed on tape by the poet and art critic Peter Schjeldahl, who was doing research for a biography of Frank O'Hara. The lucidity of his recollections is remarkable, as is his delivery, speaking in long, perfectly structured sentences, almost as if he were still held in the same state of grace that had brought forth "The Morning of the Poem." But three months later John Ashbery began to hear reports that Jimmy was behaving "strangely." Apparently his behavior had "alarmed some of the other tenants" at his rooming house, which Dr. Weitzen had recently visited—the only person who ever did so, according to John—and described to Darragh as "unspeakable" in its disorder and squalor.

On the night of April 23, 1977, a fire broke out in Jimmy's room after he passed out while smoking in bed. The neighbor in the next room luckily heard him fall and cry out, and called the fire department. Jimmy was found unconscious; his breathing and pulse had stopped and his lungs were badly seared. When Ashbery visited him in the intensive care unit at St. Vincent's Hospital a few days later, he was unconscious from sedation and breathing through a respirator, for which he had been given a tracheotomy. He suffered third-degree burns over parts of his body, and was horribly scarred on his arms, hands, and torso. The scars would require an extensive series of skin grafts over a three-month period, after which he had to wear an airplane splint for several days, holding his arm out at a right angle from his body, to immobilize the areas. "Poor Jimmy," Ashbery wrote to Anne Dunn. "During his breakdown in Vermont he told me that life had been after him with a sledgehammer, and if it wasn't a self-fulfilling prophecy then it certainly is that now."

Jimmy spent almost a month in St. Vincent's. While he was there, Darragh Park and Frank Polach went back to his room and found it "a disaster area." Many of his belongings—his papers, letters, and works of art (including the large Schneeman portrait)—had been damaged by smoke and/or water. Fortunately, Morris Golde owned a storage warehouse not far away, and after Jimmy's wet and smoky belongings were moved there, Darragh, Frank, and David Kermani spent several days painstakingly separating and drying as many of his papers and works of art as possible, blotting them between sheets of paper towel. Thanks to their efforts, most of the papers and drawings, including works by Joe Brainard and Fairfield Porter, were saved.

Jimmy was released on June 22, and went to stay with Darragh for several days. He had lost a lot of weight and was a "sylph," Darragh remembered, "like he must have looked when he was in his twenties." Unfortunately, he then had a bad reaction to a new antischizophrenic and antispasmodic drug he was given, Haldol, which produced a "paralytic effect" that "almost killed him," and sent him to the Neurological Institute at Columbia Presbyterian Hospital. Ashbery and Douglas Crase tried to visit him there, arriving only to find him being wheeled away on a gurney for more tests, leaving them to wave as he went by. As they were leaving, Doug noticed that John's eyes were moist.

Jimmy stayed at Columbia Neurological for most of the summer, where Dr. Weitzen continued to supervise his care. The bills there were "incredible," and as soon as he was stabilized, he had to leave. Unsurprisingly, he was not welcome to return to 348 West Twentieth Street, and money was, as always, a problem. The income from Kenward Elmslie's trust fund did not begin to cover his medical and hospital bills in addition to his modest living expenses. Darragh remembered this summer as a time of "much telephoning" as he tried to raise money and organize his care. Eventually he arranged for him to be admitted to Lincoln Square Home for Adults, at the corner of Broadway and Seventy-fourth Street. This was basically an old-age home, institutional in feeling, but clean and well-run. Jimmy moved in around August 20.

Here he began to receive visitors and slowly seemed to be coming out of this lowest period to date. Frank and Doug came to see him there several times that late summer and fall, always noting how "sane and lucid" he appeared "for someone allegedly so bonkers." Whenever they did, Jimmy asked them to bring him his favorite edibles, especially the "forbidden" fatty foods that his doctor had vetoed because of his newly diagnosed diabetes. If they neglected to do so, he would immediately command Frank to go get him some ice cream—the only "socially unusual" behavior they saw from him during these visits.

Jimmy wasn't very familiar with the Upper West Side. In 1977, while gentrification was well under way, some of the blocks between Amsterdam and Columbus Avenues were intimidating. He was reluctant to venture into Central Park, "two bizarre blocks / away," because an acquaintance, Billy Nichols, had been violently mugged there a few years earlier. But on the morning of August 28, Jimmy did go to the New-York Historical Society, at Central Park West and Seventy-sixth Street, to see an exhibition of the Bella Landauer Collection of printed ephemera, and he was looking forward to going out to dinner that evening with Frank Polach and Doug Crase, so much so that when he got back to his room, he started a poem about the evening ahead, anticipating finishing it when he came home that night. He was already calling it "Dining Out with Doug and Frank."

But when he got to their apartment at Twenty-third Street and Tenth Avenue, it turned out that Doug had to stay in and work, and would not be coming with them. Jimmy looked surprised and rather affronted when told, but Doug knew he would not really mind, since he would have Frank to himself for the evening. They ate one block away at McFeely's, on the site of the old Terminal Hotel, across from what had been the Twenty-third Street ferry terminal on the Hudson River. The ferry, which had stopped running in 1967, was one of several that used to go to Hoboken, where Jimmy had often visited Alvin Novak in the late '50s. By 1977, the hotel bar had been transformed into a restaurant, retaining many of the building's original nineteenth-century details.

Jimmy was quiet during dinner, as usual. They talked a little bit about Frank's poetry writing, and Jimmy gave some advice ("experiment / more," "try collages," and "write / some skinny poems"). After they got back to the corner of Tenth Avenue, they both looked up and remarked on the moon, "the most beautiful full moon you can imagine!" as Frank later recalled.

Over the next few days Jimmy finished the poem he had started that morning, still called "Dining Out with Doug and Frank," even though Doug had stayed home and the poem is mostly concerned not with them or the dinner, but with Jimmy's memories and associations brought to mind by the waterfront setting. From a description of McFeely's, to an evocation of the vanished Hudson River ferryboats ("you / were *in* the water, *in* the shipping"), the poem segues into a long elegy for Bill Aalto, dead now for an unbelievable nineteen years. In fact, the entire Aalto "elegy" is contained in a 36-line parenthesis framed by the split phrase: "Bill / Aalto, my first lover . . . used / to ride the ferries all the / time, doing the bars along / the waterfront." The riverine poem divides around the "island" of the Aalto digression (and others) to reunite at the other end, just as the poem describes the Hudson doing "when it bifurcates from / the East River to create / Manhattan." Bill Aalto's life was now enclosed within temporal boundaries, but life flowed on obliviously around it.

As Jimmy points out in the poem and seems slightly surprised by, "Dining Out with Doug and Frank" is "full of death," beginning as it does with the mention of the deaths of two friends, both suicides—one Billy Nichols, who killed himself a year after his Central Park mugging, never having fully recovered from his injuries; the other an old flame, Peter Kemeny, who had recently jumped in front of a subway train—before moving on to the death (by cancer) of Bill Aalto. Of course, Jimmy had barely escaped death himself five months earlier. "Now it's tomorrow, / as usual," begins section II, but that "as usual" is no longer to be taken for granted. While there is no reference to the River Styx and its ferryman, the image lingers subliminally, especially in the last stanza: "It would / have been so nice after dinner / to take a ferry boat ride with Frank / across the Hudson . . . To be on / the water in the dark . . ." In the context of the deaths in the poem and its setting, mingled perhaps with thoughts of the "other" and still primary Frank, it becomes an almost shocking suggestion.

If "now" is "tomorrow," then it follows that yesterday is today, and all the days of one's life are taking place simultaneously in one's perception of them through the poem. The poet by virtue of his awareness transcends time, in a sense, or is both in it and of it, as the bygone ferry boats were "*in* the water, *in* the shipping." Like so much of Schuyler's work the depth of feeling is hidden, potential rather than explicit, sensed and alive beneath a surface of quotidian beauty. The poem ends on an upbeat, offbeat note:

> Oh. Doug and Frank. One is light,
> the other dark.
> Doug is the tall one.

Among the friends who visited Jimmy at Lincoln Square was Ada Katz, who had not seen him in several years. In telling her about the fire and the painful skin grafts he had had to undergo as a result of his burns, he "was so accustomed to being natural that he pulled off his shirt and showed me his scars," Ada recalled. "I was a little bit appalled to see them because they were so raw still." Nice as the visit was, it still felt a bit strained. Yet Jimmy had a strong urge to reconnect with the parts of his life that the Katzes represented, and Ada, sensing that, wanted to help him do so. "It was not relaxed . . . He was tense; I was tense; we both were tense, but we both seemed not to want to let it go, and tried to lengthen the day instead of running away from it. It was very strange, but I liked it."

In the first week of October, Jimmy called Darragh, told him he was "having real problems," and asked if he would take him to the psychiatric ward at Roosevelt Hospital. On arriving there, they found that the hospital staff wouldn't admit him, and wanted instead to send him to the public hospital on Wards Island. Darragh phoned Dr. Weitzen, who refused to come down to help. Jimmy was lying on a gurney staring at the ceiling, silent and inert—exhibiting a degree of passivity that was both self-destructive and, to susceptible friends, powerfully persuasive. Darragh tried to engage him, stating the situation and offering a choice: "They can't deal with you here, and Dr. Weitzen can't help this time. What do you want to do? Do you want to go back to Lincoln Square?" But Jimmy "just lay there. He didn't say one fucking word." Darragh called Weitzen again and "read the riot act to him." Finally Weitzen did come to the hospital and Jimmy was admitted. He stayed there about a week before returning to Lincoln Square.

~

Nineteen seventy-seven saw the publication of *The Home Book*, a miscellany of early uncollected poems, plays, and stories that Trevor Winkfield assembled for Z Press. And in the fall of 1978, *What's for Dinner?* was published by Black Sparrow Press, with a cover drawing by Jane Freilicher and dedicated to Anne Dunn. The book was favorably reviewed in *The New York Review of Books* by Stephen Spender, who called it a "quietly scarifying, very funny, and wonderfully compassionate novel," and perceptively by Alice Notley in the *American Book Review*.

By early 1978, Jimmy was assembling a manuscript of new poems, including "The Morning of the Poem," "Dining Out with Doug and Frank," "The Payne Whitney Poems," and others. Still smarting from Random House's rejection of *What's for Dinner?*, Jimmy decided that he wanted his next book to be published by Farrar, Straus and Giroux, partly because they published Elizabeth Bishop. He wrote a letter of inquiry directly to Michael di Capua, who he knew was an old friend of Alvin Novak's and had appreciated elements of *What's for Dinner?* Di Capua, who had long admired Schuyler's poetry, replied enthusiastically, sending a signed contract for his next, as yet untitled, book of poetry, sight unseen.

Maxine Groffsky sent the manuscript of *The Morning of the Poem* to FSG that summer, and she, di Capua, Jimmy, and Groffsky's good friend the critic David Kalstone corresponded at length over the next year about poems to be included or left out. Di Capua was a hands-on editor, and in addition to eliminating "quite a few" poems from the book, he made careful, small revisions in the title poem itself, which he felt was Schuyler's "greatest poem." The final selection was determined by the following summer, and the book appeared at the beginning of 1980.

The poet Charles North met Schuyler in 1971 or 1972. He had

admired his work since being introduced to it by Kenneth Koch, and written a poem dedicated to Jimmy in 1970, "Lights," which he showed to Tony Towle, who sent it to Jimmy. Some months later, Schuyler returned the compliment by dedicating and sending to him his poem "Light from Canada." Charles and his wife, Paula, and their infant daughter lived on West Ninety-second Street, and while Jimmy was living at Lincoln Square they saw each other regularly. As usual, Jimmy loved being included in family life, but he was not always an easy guest: he was heavy, his hair was long, matted, and dirty, and he persisted in wearing a ratty old sheepskin coat that Bob Jordan had given him. "I know he attracted attention on the street," said North. At the apartment, he tended to perspire; his mouth and tongue would be in constant motion due to dyskinesia from antidepressant medication; and often, of course, he was silent. One evening in 1978, North and Schuyler got to talking about *49 South*, the one-shot magazine Jimmy had edited and produced six years earlier, and they decided to do something similar together, and call it *Broadway* after the thoroughfare they both lived on. A mailing went out on September 25 to a roster of more than sixty poets and artists, asking them to submit their "best poem" or "best drawing." Jimmy proved to have quite strong opinions about which poets were to be invited, and North recalled that there were "some real shockers" among those he originally did not want to include. The book came out in 1979. Ten years later the process was repeated when Jimmy and Charles collaborated again on *Broadway 2*.

Jimmy moved out of Lincoln Square in October 1978. Cost must have been the main factor in the decision, since his next home, the Allerton Hotel, was even less appropriate. The single-room-occupancy hotel—a "flophouse," Darragh called it—was located at the corner of Eighth Avenue and Twenty-second Street. Here at least he was near his Chelsea friends, but in every other way it was a bad move. The writer and musician Patti Smith spent a couple of weeks at the Allerton in 1969 with her then boyfriend Robert Mapplethorpe, and described it in the bleakest terms: "dark and neglected, with dusty windows that overlooked the noisy street . . . [It] reeked of piss and exterminator fluid" and was "filled with derelicts and junkies." Almost none of Jimmy's friends ventured to the hotel to see him. Charles North, one of the few who did, described it as "pretty horrifying, the fleabag of fleabags," his room consisting of "a bed, on which . . . he lay surrounded by a sea of dirty laundry . . . And of course the smell was pretty bad."

When Jimmy's birthday came around in November, Barbara Guest gave a party. He was supposed to be on Antabuse but apparently didn't take it that day and duly got drunk. Charles North attended, and as he was leaving, Jimmy told him he wanted to write a poem for him. As they stood together by the elevator, Jimmy took a piece of paper and "wrote and wrote and wrote" and finally handed Charles a sheet covered entirely with wavy lines—"no words whatsoever."

Later that month, the plan that had been sketched out two years earlier, whereby the Frank O'Hara Foundation would be restructured to accept tax-deductible donations for Jimmy's benefit, was formally put in motion by Darragh, Morris Golde, Donald Droll, and the lawyer Richard Savitsky. To kick it off, on December 3 there was a benefit reading organized by the poet Jim Brodey in a space run by the Public Theater on Great Jones Street. The all-star list of readers included Kenneth Koch, Larry Rivers, Barbara Guest, Anne Waldman, Charles North, Joe LeSueur, Alice Notley, Jim Carroll, Donald Windham, Ted Berrigan, and Ron Padgett. Tom Carey, a young musician and actor newly arrived from Los Angeles and the brother of the poet Steve Carey, performed a song he set from "Poem (How about an oak leaf)." Jimmy did not attend.

Jimmy was admitted to Payne Whitney in March, and then again in May 1979. During these hospital stays, Anne Dunn was a frequent visitor and caregiver. When she went back to the Allerton in order to retrieve his false teeth and glasses, she was horrified by the nightmarish and "tragic" conditions she saw he had been living in, and became determined to get him out of the hotel. United by their concern, she and Ruth Kligman began to collaborate to make that happen. Anne credited Ruth with the idea of moving Jimmy to the Chelsea Hotel, where she had friends and connections and was able to arrange for him to rent a small apartment.

In late May, Ruth and Anne packed up some of Jimmy's belongings into giant black plastic garbage bags and taxied them two blocks over to the hotel. When he was released from the hospital around May 24, Schuyler moved directly into what would be his final home: room 625 in the Chelsea Hotel.

[19]

NEVER TRUST BLONDS FROM SHERMAN OAKS

1979–1985

The Chelsea Hotel was built in 1884 in the Victorian Aesthetic style. It is twelve stories high with a façade of red brick and stone, topped with peaked roofs and ornamental chimneys, fronted with rows of balconies decorated with ornamental cast-iron balustrades. Designed as one of the city's first cooperative apartment buildings, it was converted to a hotel in 1905, when most of the original apartments were subdivided into smaller rooms. After David Bard bought it in 1940, the hotel continued to house both short-term hotel guests and long-term residents. A long roster of famous writers, artists, musicians, and performers, ranging from Thomas Wolfe to Patti Smith, have lived in the hotel over the years. Schuyler's old acquaintance from Gold and Fizdale days, Virgil Thomson, still lived in one of the building's original grand apartments.

While the Chelsea was far from a full-service hotel, it fostered a sense of community through its many artist residents. In no small degree this community spirit was made possible by the owner and manager, Stanley Bard, David's son, who had grown up in the hotel working for his father. Supportive of artists and writers, although often sorely tried by their delinquencies and occasional bad behavior, Bard sometimes accepted paintings and sculptures in lieu of rent, many examples of which were installed rather haphazardly in the lobby.

Jimmy's studio apartment was tiny, perhaps about 300 or 400 square feet, and consisted of a single narrow living and sleeping space, with a

French door to the cast-iron balcony facing Twenty-third Street at one end, and a kitchenette and bathroom at the other. Bookshelves were attached to the two side walls, but books still piled up on the floor. Paintings and drawings hung above the desk and the bed.

Soon after Jimmy moved into the Chelsea, Morris Golde arranged for an "assistant" (as Jimmy came to call them) to come in every morning with his medications and any necessary shopping, stay for a couple of hours, make breakfast, help with correspondence, and keep Jimmy company. The young poet Eileen Myles was the first person hired for the job, at a salary of seven dollars an hour.

Eileen Myles came to New York from Boston in 1974 at the age of twenty-four to be a poet. She briefly enrolled in an MA program in creative writing at Queens College, where the professor brought in two poems by Schuyler, "Poem (How about an oak leaf)" and "3/23/66," and O'Hara's "To the Harbormaster," telling the class these poets were "denizens of St. Mark's Church." Eileen quickly dropped out of the class and headed to St. Mark's, joining a group of younger poets there going to all the readings and workshops by Alice Notley, Ted Berrigan, Paul Violi, and others. The general understanding was that Jimmy was impossible to meet because of his mental health, so when in 1979 Charles North told her that a job working for him might be available, Myles was thrilled. At that point, Eileen had published one mimeographed book of poems, *The Irony of the Leash* (1978), and was editing a magazine, *Dodgems*. Twenty-five books of poetry, fiction, and nonfiction have followed to date, along with performances, exhibitions of photographs, films, and political activism, making Myles one of the most visible poets of their generation. Eileen's queerness is intrinsic to their public persona and work. As Myles wrote, "I put lesbian content in the New York School poem because I wanted the poem to be there to receive me." Myles has used nonbinary pronouns since about 2018; however, in the '80s their pronouns were she/her, which is what I use in references to that period.

The first time Eileen met Jimmy at the Chelsea with Anne Dunn and Donald Droll, he was thin and had curly hair down to his shoulders and was wearing a white undershirt. He looked frail and almost paralyzed with fear: "like somebody who's spent his life in mental hospitals." Eileen herself was slender and androgynous-looking and was later told that he thought she was a cute long-haired boy. Eileen blurted out in her shy and jocular way, "I love your poems!" and suddenly found she had been hired. It was "the shortest job interview ever."

Myles arrived every morning with Jimmy's medication and *The New York Times*—a routine that would be followed by a series of assistants over the next few years. She made him breakfast—often French toast—and sat with him for several hours in silence as both of them read. As she recalled, "I would just sit down and he would read and I would read for—five hours! It was a great job!"

Many of Jimmy's possessions still remained in his old room at the Allerton, and one of Eileen's first tasks was to pack them in boxes and bags and bring them over to the Chelsea in a series of taxis. The sad, ruined room, with "dry cleaned clothes still in plastic bags, charred bits of poetry on papers, art prints books," held such strong vibes that on the final day, Eileen was inspired to masturbate in its midst.

As Jimmy responded to Eileen's warmth and youth and the sense of security and routine that her presence provided, a friendship developed. Soon he began to put on the weight he had lost in the hospital—and then some, due to the rich creamy drinks he was always so fond of. Eileen convinced him to get his long hair cut, and began to try to make sense of his chaotic practical affairs, putting his bills and correspondence in order. A significant aspect of the job was to accompany him by taxi to weekly appointments with Dr. Weitzen, as Jimmy was now having trouble with his mobility. Even though they felt comfortable with each other, Jimmy was still "*really* hard to talk to then, the silence was just incredible." When she showed him her poems, which he became a big fan of, his comments were laconic: "It's a great one, babe." One way to make a slight dent in the wall of silence, Eileen found, was to gratify his somewhat prurient curiosity about her sexual exploits, and soon a daily recounting of her previous night's adventures became part of the routine. Likewise, in his more communicative moods, Jimmy would relate gossip about his own past, telling Eileen, for example, that sex with William Burroughs had been like sleeping with a reptile. And always, beneath the silence "there was still that funny little sense of humor that would come out at weird moments."

"From his bed he ran the show," Eileen later wrote in the story "Chelsea Girls."

> The presence of his attention was so strong, so deeply passive—such a thing to bathe your tiny desperate words in that when it was gone you had to stop and hover in the silence again . . . You had to stay silent for a very long time some days. He was like music, Jimmy was, and you had to be like music too to be with him, but understand in his room he was conductor. He directed the yellow air in room 625.

There were many days too when Jimmy's behavior was erratic, baffling, and frightening to Eileen. This may have been due, in part, to inconsistencies in his medications. Dr. Weitzen, Eileen recalled, "kept changing the drugs and stuff, ultimately trying to stop them."

In the middle of the summer, Eileen went away for several weeks to the Jack Kerouac School of Disembodied Poetics in Boulder, Colorado. During her absence, other young poets filled in for her, including Rochelle Kraut, Elinor Nauen, and Steve Carey, a young poet from southern California and a close friend of Ted Berrigan's. One day Carey couldn't make it and sent his younger brother, Tom, in his place. Tom Carey was already an admirer of Schuyler's work and had performed at the benefit reading in 1978. Their first meeting was unremarkable. Tom introduced himself, and after a deep "Hello," Jimmy "was very sort of noncommittal and he didn't say much," as charming as Tom tried to be. Shortly after this, while Eileen was still away, Jimmy went to East Aurora for about two weeks.

In the three years since Jimmy had last been in East Aurora, his mother, who was in failing health, had sold her house and moved in with her younger son, Fredric Ridenour, and his wife, Hilde. Jimmy liked his younger brother but they had little in common aside from an undemonstrative manner. Hilde was much more sociable and in many ways the mainstay of the family, taking devoted care of Margaret as she declined. Jimmy's teenaged niece was away at camp this summer and he slept in her bedroom, decorated with rock star posters.

Margaret at eighty-nine was exhibiting signs of mental vagueness and slowly going blind from macular degeneration. She greeted him with "I can't see you but I know your voice." She spent much of her time in front of the television, able at least to hear its "rumble." It was no doubt in part because of her apparent deterioration that the poem Jimmy wrote during this visit, "A few days," is full of recurring images of death, his own among them: "What will it be like when there's no / more tomorrow?"

The new poem, which he began to write immediately after his arrival, intending to make it a kind of pendant to "The Morning of the Poem," shares that poem's conversational tone and real-time observation of immediate events, fluidly mixed with discursive reminiscences of the past. It is composed in the same long lines, again broken by shorter intervening ones, though this time the first word of each pair of lines is not capitalized, which indicates a somewhat looser approach.

The poem begins with a title that runs into the first line:

A few days

are all we have. So count them as they pass. They pass
    too quickly
out of breath: don't dwell on the grave, which yawns for
    one and all

Like "The Morning of the Poem," the work becomes a transcription of the movements of Schuyler's mind and consciousness, and as with other Schuyler poems, it is not so much the specifics of what he records as the state of extreme attentiveness in which it was written that makes the poem come alive. Yet paradoxically, it is the specifics—the artificial flowers on his niece's desk, the boring music on the radio, a memory of Frank O'Hara wearing chinos and sneakers in the snow—that for all their mundane qualities engage and lead the reader inexorably on, from line to line and into a state of timelessness.

Living with his brother and Hilde, who were already strained by their long-term care of Margaret, and with Margaret herself, in her diminished condition, became slightly tense. Nonetheless, Jimmy enjoyed some quiet moments with his mother, "sitting out on the terrace and discussing ancestors." During these last talks between mother and son, Jimmy apparently tried to clear up some old misunderstandings, and suggested that despite the deep-rooted antagonism between him and his stepfather, he realized now that Berton actually loved him, in his way. Margaret, "the old truth-teller," was having none of it. "He did not," she said. "Berton hated you."

He continued to work on "A few days" when he returned to New York in August, and the poem takes on a fresh energy at this point (a little under a third of the way through), more engaged in his life there than it had been with his visit to East Aurora—as he said later, there wasn't the same "involvement of place" at his brother's that he felt in the house he'd grown up in.

Jimmy was feeling better than he had in the spring, and during his first three weeks home, he continued to feel his way to a semblance of healthy life. He spent a weekend with Barbara Guest and her husband in Water Mill, and paid a call on Anne Porter, who had subdivided the lot at 49 South Main Street, sold the main house, and was about to move into a small cottage she had built for herself in the yard behind it. Although it saddened him to see the library emptied of books, he managed not to become overly depressed or disturbed—possibly because he had the ongoing poem in which to report on it: an act of simultaneous gathering and distancing.

As with "The Morning of the Poem" earlier, the writing of "A few days" was his life and his life went into the poem. There were days when he would have a burst of energy and write several pages, and he was conscious of trying to make it "good, really / good," as he told Dr. Weitzen. A short time later, however, he described taking nine sleeping pills on top of three Thorazines and a "red pill" to counter the dyskinesia from the Thorazine, sleeping only four hours, then waking up at 11:00 unable to go back to sleep and taking two more sleeping pills, all resulting in his feeling like "creamed shit" in the morning. Soon afterward, he stopped writing and put the poem aside for the next year and a half. When he returned to it, in March 1981, it would be to round it off quickly, still short of the length he had been hoping for.

Toward the end of September, Weitzen decided to try reducing Jimmy's medications, in hopes of being able to take him off the strong antidepressants altogether. It proved premature, and for the next few months he was unstable. One day Eileen arrived to find him lying on his bed in his underwear covered in sweat. In answer to her questions, he said, "I'm having anxiety attacks, babe." Eileen sat next to him and, holding his hand, "started playing this game," asking, "What was the dirtiest thing you ever did?" "What do you really like to do in bed?" in order to "match his anxiety with . . . whatever kind of anecdote would go right into the middle of the moment, stop him for a second." For the next several hours, the two of them exchanged confidences, Jimmy telling her, for example, about his masochistic urges.

She became uncomfortable leaving Jimmy alone that day and felt that he needed to be hospitalized, but, unable to get a response from Dr. Weitzen, she and her girlfriend (both in their twenties) sat up with him most of the night. In the morning Eileen returned to find Jimmy frozen in a "catatonic state." He had arranged to have lunch with Anne Dunn that day, so Eileen called Anne asking her to come early and take over. When she arrived, Dunn found Jimmy sitting on his bed, holding out a plate of scrambled eggs in front of him, frozen in place and trembling. He remained that way for what seemed several hours. She, too, couldn't reach Dr. Weitzen. Finally she called Ruth Kligman, who said, "Well, you know, no one ever touches Jimmy anymore." So Dunn put her arms around him and stroked the back of his neck and shoulders, "and he immediately put the scrambled eggs down."

Jimmy was understood to be not drinking at this time, except when he did. He calmly notes the contradiction in "A few days": "I don't drink / anymore, still I / just had four double cocktails: margaritas. At least I / stopped there." One day after a visit to Dr. Weitzen, Eileen let Jimmy take a taxi back home by himself. But he didn't go back to the hotel—he went off on a bender and was missing for the rest of the day. A few days later Eileen noticed a text in Jimmy's typewriter headed "Dear Magic Fingers" which consisted of a "fat block of prose" describing what apparently had happened when he disappeared: "this whole story of going into a bar and being thrown out and the cops coming, and them delivering him to the hotel . . . just a whole series of events that was so shocking that all this had happened, that he knew it." The paper later disappeared.

Not long after this, the cumulative effect of several such experiences caused Eileen to realize she could no longer handle Jimmy and she gave up the position. This time Golde decided to hire two people to split the responsibilities. One was Tom Carey; the other was an Anglo-Irish poet named Helena Hughes. They would each work three or four days a week.

Helena Hughes, born in Bristol, England, to Irish parents, was one of four young Britons who met Ted Berrigan when he was teaching for a term at Essex University and were inspired by him to move to New York (others being Douglas Oliver, Simon Pettet, and Marion Farrier, Steve Carey's wife). Helena had worked at the punk rock club CBGB and at the Poetry Project, which she was active in reorganizing after it was disrupted by a serious fire in 1978. A practicing Buddhist, she had worked for Allen Ginsberg before taking the job with Schuyler.

Tom Carey may not have made much of an impression on Jimmy when he substituted for Eileen Myles earlier in the year, but things were different when he came back in the fall of 1979. Carey was born in Santa Monica, California, in 1951 into a family of movie actors and vaudeville performers extending back at least three generations. His father, Harry Carey, Jr., was a character actor in many of John Ford's classic westerns including *She Wore a Yellow Ribbon* and *The Searchers*. Harry Carey, Sr., Tom's grandfather, was a famous cowboy actor in the silent era. Tom, his older brother, Steve, and their two sisters grew up in Sherman Oaks, a suburb north of Los Angeles.

Tom and Steve got involved in both poetry and drugs at an early age. Steve began writing poetry as a teenager, and when Tom also began to write, Steve was his mentor, introducing him to *The New American Poetry* and the work of Allen Ginsberg, Frank O'Hara, Ted Berrigan, Philip Whalen, and James Schuyler. Both brothers became addicted to amphetamines, which they obtained by forging doctors' prescriptions.

For several years, Tom intended to become an actor. In 1976, he moved to New York, where the following year he roomed with Jim Brodey, who introduced him to Ted Berrigan and Alice Notley, and he met Eileen Myles and other St. Mark's poets. At Ted's suggestion, he got a job at the Strand Bookstore, then worked at Weiser's Occult Bookshop with Helena Hughes, but was fired for participating in a union drive. When approached by Morris, he was unemployed, but continued to act in Off-Off-Broadway plays and write and perform songs while working for Jimmy.

Jimmy grew increasingly fond of both of his assistants, but at the beginning his focus was on Tom: handsome, blond, talented, gay, and very personable. For his part, Tom enjoyed the job. Occasionally there was a poem to type. On other days they would both sit quietly reading. Jimmy was absorbed in the Palliser novels of Anthony Trollope, while Carey made his way through the many Ross Macdonald mysteries that Jimmy had accumulated.

As had been the case with Eileen, Jimmy was curious about Tom's love life, and Tom confided in him, selectively. Around this time, Tom had fallen in love with the young poet Elio Schneeman, one of the three sons of George and Katie. The relationship was troubled: his parents, though they liked and grew close to Tom, were uneasy, partly because Elio wasn't gay, but also because of the ten-year age difference between them. Unbeknownst to George and Katie, both Tom and Elio were steadily getting deeply into drugs. For years Tom had been taking speed and diet pills, then mixing them with codeine, but sometime around the beginning of 1980, he began shooting up heroin, which Elio had also taken up in college. Although Elio developed his habit independently, his parents would later accuse Tom of being the instigator.

Jimmy took to inviting Tom to accompany him not just to the doctor, but on social visits, such as dinner at John Ashbery's and with other old friends. "Jimmy was always very strange at those parties; he was on so much medication, so he was always very taciturn," Tom recalled. "And his silences used to make me very nervous, because I am a person who oils things socially . . . Also I was usually on drugs most of the time, as much as I could manage, during all of this period."

In the fall of 1979, Jimmy abruptly stopped writing "A few days" and started to write love poems to Tom instead. They are different in tone from those written earlier to Bob Jordan, mostly because they depict unconsummated, and in that sense idealized, love. There is an effervescence and a sadness to poems such as "Suddenly" or "O Sleepless Night," and at times a silliness. The best of them, "Tom," written probably between December 1979 and March 1980, makes clear Jimmy's acceptance of the fact that Tom, while deeply fond of Jimmy, was not physically attracted to him, and therefore the relationship could never become a full-blown physical affair. As time went on, however, and Jimmy moved into a psychotic episode, this acceptance evaporated.

Early in 1980, Jimmy began making overt passes at Carey, but for Tom the idea of a physical relationship with Jimmy "was absolutely nowhere in the cards." Soon Jimmy's advances became more physical, and there were times when Tom had to "sort of like twist out of his grasp and things like that."

In February or March, Alex and Ada Katz invited Jimmy and Tom to dinner at their SoHo loft, hoping to discuss a possible production of Jimmy's play *Shopping and Waiting* for the Eye and Ear Theater, of which Ada was a director. For the Katzes, it was extremely disturbing to realize how far his "social graces had really deteriorated" by this point. Throughout the meal, Jimmy pestered Tom with kisses and embraces, embarrassing the Katzes and of course Tom himself. Schuyler piled his plate high with food, but didn't touch it. He went into the bathroom and rifled through the medicine cabinet looking for pills. In frustration at finding nothing more exciting than aspirin, he anointed himself with Ada's lipstick and perfumes before he threw them all into the bathtub, to emerge covered with lipstick and reeking of perfume.

Tom was now the lead singer and lyricist in a band, the Beeks, and getting gigs in clubs. One evening Jimmy showed up early at a club where Tom and his band were setting up to play. Jimmy had relapsed and was on a drinking binge—earlier he had been drinking at the Palm Court in the Plaza Hotel. Tom came out from backstage to find him sitting in the club, with a drink and his false teeth on the table in front of him. It was still about an hour and a half before the set was to begin. Tom was nervous about his appearance there and wondered what it portended. But he simply said, "Jimmy, you're here!" and he answered, "Yeah, babe, I'm here." Tom then announced with forced casualness, "Well, I need to go and set up with the band." And in a doom-laden voice Jimmy intoned, "No, babe, I don't think you better go set up." Tom repeated himself and Jimmy replied, "Someone told me that something terrible was going to happen to you if you set up!" As Tom was starting to protest, and repeat that he really needed to go, Jimmy suddenly got up and hit him. Tom was too shocked and horrified to fully take in the physical hurt. Jimmy, as soon as he realized what he had done, made a complete turnaround, no less terrifying than his rage. He kept repeating, "I'm sorry! I'm sorry!" and then he got down on his knees. "Oh, it was just horrible." The club manager insisted that Jimmy leave and Tom eventually reached Anne Dunn's son, Francis Wishart, who came and took him home.

The next day, Tom confronted Jimmy and told him that he had no interest in a physical relationship. Jimmy appeared to agree, but the harassment continued. He started mailing Tom some of the love poems he was writing. Tom signed up for call forwarding to screen Jimmy's calls. He stopped going to work, but Jimmy knew where he lived and came by his apartment, so Tom moved out and began staying with friends. He told Dr. Weitzen and all of Jimmy's supporting friends what was going on, and it became a kind of downtown soap opera. When Weitzen finally broke it to Jimmy that Tom was quitting, explaining, "He didn't know how to cope with your advances," Schuyler took the news with "a shock of recognition," recognizing a connection to his much earlier rejection by Paul Sipprell, who had told him, "I couldn't take it: / it was too heavy: you put on too much / Pressure," as recalled in "The Morning of the Poem."

Tom made it clear that he still hoped to remain friends with Jimmy, but decided to stop seeing him for the next couple of months. After Tom quit, Helena Hughes started working for Schuyler full-time.

In March 1980, *The Morning of the Poem* was published by Farrar, Straus and Giroux. The cover reproduced a drawing by Anne Dunn showing the view from her apartment, where Jimmy had spent so many days posing, first for her and latterly for her son, Francis, who was living in her New York apartment that year and using it as his studio. The publication should have been an occasion of great satisfaction for Jimmy, but it was offset by the news about Tom quitting.

On March 19, Jimmy came to dinner at Doug Crase and Frank Polach's apartment, bringing a copy of the new book. Soon after he arrived, he sat down to inscribe it. He started writing and did not stop, for about an hour, while Frank turned off the stove and dinner grew cold. The inscription is written as a 62-line "skinny" poem (unpublished), in response to Dr. Weitzen telling him that Tom had quit, and moves from bald statement of fact (like "This Dark Apartment"):

"Tom
isn't coming back—

He didn't know
How to cope with
your advances."

Without a sound
I sit and undergo
invisible shock

to delusional statements:

I made no advances:
It was Tom who
said, "Jim I

am going to
make love with
you: not tonight

but soon."

to lyrical outpourings and optimistic plans for a future platonic friendship:

We already plan
To write a comic novel
Next winter: we

Will have a ball. "Tom
Still buddies?" "You
Know it, Jim."

The day before, Jimmy had also sent a copy of *The Morning of the Poem* to Kenward Elmslie with another extensive inscription beginning, "I hope we have not come to some parting of the ways?" and expressing his hope that whatever silence there had lately been between them was "merely a hiatus." But for Kenward, the friendship had essentially ended a few years earlier. Assuredly the introduction of money into the relationship brought with it awkward and partially acknowledged feelings of guilt, resentment, and unmet expectations on both sides. Kenward claimed he never regretted giving Jimmy the annuity, which he had "given freely—no strings," but he did resent that Jimmy "never made a thank-you gesture of any sort," which was all the odder because of his courtesy in the earlier phase of the friendship. The last time Kenward saw Jimmy was a chance encounter at the corner of Eighth Street and Sixth Avenue, when Jimmy "puffed away at a big cigar. A poetentate," Kenward punned. "I fled, forever!"

Jimmy was in rocky shape during the first part of Helena's solo tenure, and intermittently throughout it. Whenever he was about to go into a psychotic state, his energy spiked, and he would sometimes begin writing. Helena would then arrive to find the room dark, with the curtains drawn and filled with a fug of cigarette smoke. Jimmy would be mumbling to himself and giving off "very heavy vibes . . . like a spider in his web." But on good days they sometimes collaborated on writing poems, Helena at the typewriter taking dictation and then adding her own contributions. A group of these "Collabs" was published by Misty Terrace Press in 1980.

By May 1981, Jimmy's living expenses were estimated to be about $2,000 a month, while his income from the Elmslie Trust and other sources was about $6,000 per year. Richard Savitsky had established an endowment, the Fund for James Schuyler, which at that time held about $40,000, with an additional $10,000 pledged, but he estimated that $80,000–100,000 was still needed for it to generate sufficient income to fully support Schuyler. When Morris Golde had to reduce his involvement due to medical issues, Ted Berrigan briefly carried on the work, and wrote solicitation letters.

In June 1981, Anne Porter and the Porter Family Trust began making regular monthly donations of around $1,000 to Allen Ginsberg's nonprofit, the Committee on Poetry, earmarked for Jimmy's support. Generous Anne had also given Jimmy the Joseph Cornell box sculpture that the artist had given Fairfield in the '60s, and this, too, was eventually sold through Donald Droll to help support him.

After 1982 or 1983, Savitsky and Golde became less active in their work for Schuyler, and Helena by necessity took on more responsibilities, initiating and following through on various grant applications and fundraising efforts. Because of Jimmy's constant need for money to pay doctors' and hospital bills, in addition to his ordinary living expenses, keeping him solvent was always an uphill battle, which Helena compared to "walking a tightrope." Between 1982 and 1984, she managed to secure grants for Schuyler from the Authors' League Fund, the Artists and Writers Fund at the American Academy, PEN American Center, the Academy of American Poets, the Carnegie Fund for Authors, the Ingram Merrill Foundation, and others.

Jimmy grew extremely fond of Helena, loving her "delightful beauty and disarming honesty and insight," according to one mutual friend. His affection is clear in a number of poems he wrote to her, including "Lilacs," "Tomorrow," and "November," in which he approvingly quotes Tom's moniker for her: "the Divine Miss H." At one point, Jimmy even offered to marry her, to make it possible for her to stay in the country legally as a resident alien. Helena "chickened out," which at the time he took as a personal rejection.

In March 1981, after four previous unsuccessful applications, Schuyler was finally awarded a Guggenheim Foundation grant in the amount of $20,000 (paid in quarterly installments of $5,000). The money briefly gave rise to thoughts of travel, and Jimmy dreamed of going to Venice for a month in the fall, but in fact just over half of the money would go to paying deferred medical bills. His proposal had been to write another novel, *Heck Kelly and the Kellys of Kellyville*, "a comedy of suburban life," as well as new poetry. He never got very far with *Heck Kelly*, but he did complete a number of new poems during the fellowship period.

A month later, Margaret Connor died at the age of ninety. Hilde called Jimmy with the news. Margaret's death moved him to go back to "A few days," and to conclude the poem with 39 short lines about her death, ending:

Margaret Daisy Connor Schuyler Ridenour,
rest well,
the weary journey done.

The opening pages of "A few days," steeped as they are in ideas of mortality, seem to anticipate the poem ending as it does. Yet there could have been another ending, one more like that of "The Crystal Lithium." Michael di Capua recalled that when Schuyler eventually submitted the poem to him, he told him that it originally had a different ending: a "substantial section which he had destroyed," because, Jimmy implied, it was "too sensitive or private." Di Capua conjectured that this lost ending "focused on feelings toward Tom." It is possible that elements of the alternate ending may survive in some of the love poems addressed to Tom Carey.

More good news arrived in April 1981 when Jimmy received the official notification that he had received the Pulitzer Prize for Poetry for *The Morning of the Poem*. The monetary award was only $1,000, but the recognition and prestige were of course considerable—the awards made the front page of *The New York Times*. When Jimmy learned that John Ashbery had been a member of the three-person jury, he was both grateful and disappointed, because he would have preferred that it hadn't come from someone he knew.

Tom Carey had remained deeply attached to Jimmy, and resumed visiting him at the Chelsea in the spring of 1980, but as a friend rather than an employee. Jimmy was still in love with him, but his passion had been tempered to something more manageable, and Tom was able to keep him in check by threatening to withdraw completely if he got unruly.

Unfortunately, Tom was becoming more deeply involved with heroin. He believed that Jimmy was unaware of the extent of his drug habit, and perhaps he was. On the other hand, Tom was also drinking heavily, to which Jimmy could relate all too well. He even enabled Tom's drinking by keeping a two-liter bottle of vodka on hand in his room, on the theory that if Tom drank there, he would not drink outside, but of course he did both.

That summer, Schuyler and Carey collaborated on a work of fiction, *Small Crimes*, of which the first (and only) chapter was published late that year in Dennis Cooper's journal, *Little Caesar*. Work on this provided a means for them to cement a nonsexual friendship. The title would prove prophetic.

By the winter of 1980–81, Tom was again unemployed. He was visiting Jimmy about three times a week, drawn there not only by friendship and their collaboration, but also because Jimmy was giving him regular handouts of thirty, forty, or fifty dollars. Ted Berrigan and others were furious with Tom when they found out he was cadging money from Jimmy, who was himself, of course, living on donations from a network of generous and altruistic friends. Ted and his wife, Alice Notley, were also upset by his continuing to see Elio Schneeman and shoot heroin with him.

In late spring 1981, Tom Carey walked out of his apartment over a dispute with his roommate and became essentially homeless, sleeping on friends' sofas. For a time he moved into Allen Ginsberg's apartment while Ginsberg was out of town. One night Tom, who had Jimmy's keys, found himself with no place to sleep and let himself into Jimmy's room. He slept on the floor for a couple of hours. Before he left, he slipped his hand into the pocket of a pair of Jimmy's pants, stole a couple of twenties, and left without waking him.

Soon Tom began stealing papers and manuscripts from both Ginsberg and Schuyler. While living at Allen Ginsberg's apartment, Tom noticed multiple copies of various books lying around, and started signing some of them with a passable imitation of Ginsberg's rounded signature and selling them to Bob Wilson at the Phoenix Bookstore in the Village. Then, more seriously, he graduated to stealing manuscript notebooks. It was, he admitted later, "just junkie behavior."

Meanwhile, Morris Golde contacted Helena Hughes to say that his storage space, where Jimmy's papers had been stored since the fire, was closing. Suddenly, boxes of unsorted papers, letters, manuscripts, and works of art appeared in Jimmy's small studio apartment. To pass the time, Tom took to casually browsing through them during visits. One day he came upon a letter from Frank O'Hara and quietly slipped it into his pocket. From there it quickly escalated to "just ransacking" the boxes for anything that seemed salable. Tom began to wait until Jimmy's regular afternoon nap before using his key to come into the room and steal things. "And then," Tom recalls, "I would get back on the subway and wouldn't be able to remember whether I had dreamed that I had been there, or actually I had been there. I was totally losing any kind of grip of reality."

While his brother and sister-in-law were away, Tom moved into their apartment, where he discovered Marion Farrier's checkbook and started to forge checks on her account. Everything finally came to a head in August 1981. Jimmy was planning to visit a friend on Martha's Vineyard with Helena, and wanted to take along a leather-bound notebook he had been writing in. It had survived the fire but was nowhere to be found. On a hunch, Helena called the Phoenix Bookstore, and sure enough, Bob Wilson had the notebook. At the same time, Ginsberg's secretary, Bob Rosenthal, noticed the missing Ginsberg notebooks and suspected Tom of taking them. Then, too, the places where Tom had cashed bad checks on Farrier's account started calling. On top of all that, George and Katie Schneeman finally found out that Elio and Tom were both hooked on heroin. They were bitter and furious, feeling that their generosity in welcoming Tom into their family had been betrayed.

As all these revelations were coming out, Tom fled to California on a prearranged visit to his family, letting the whole house of cards, as he later put it, collapse behind him. In Los Angeles over the next several weeks he was able to get some perspective on his derailed life. With support from his family, he managed to quit heroin. On August 10, he wrote Jimmy what he termed "a letter of apology and explanation":

> You have never been anything but lovely to me, you are a lovely, loving man and I have made the worst kind of trespass on the bounds of friendship . . . When I come back, I'll go about the business of making good, which will probably take a long time because the last 4 months seem like one blur of horror that emanated from me . . . Please believe me that I do love you, always have . . . and if you can't or don't want to see me, I'll understand but I hope you do.

Meanwhile, Helena had been working to retrieve as many of the stolen items as possible. A similar process was under way with the Ginsberg notebooks, and Marion Farrier had to be repaid. Before Tom returned from California in September, the long intricate process of restitution and repayment had been put in motion.

Jimmy's attitude to it all reflected a combination of emotions. He felt betrayed by someone he loved, he was greatly saddened to lose the letters from Frank O'Hara, the notebook, and other papers, and highly annoyed and offended by the tiresome details of getting them back. Yet one does not find in his few letters on the subject the fury one might expect, but more a kind of bemusement:

> I just had a lovely experience: someone I loved and trusted and who worked for me for a few hours a day got on heroin and ripped me off, but good . . . I'm by no means the only friend he victimized. "He" is in California, kicking the habit; I hope, for his sake. "You must feel vandalized and raped," my shrink said. Precisely. Never trust blonds from Sherman Oaks.

Later, when time had smoothed his immediate outrage, Jimmy told Tom what he thought about the episode: "You made me pretty mad, but my real concern was for you, and that you shouldn't seriously injure yourself."

Over the next few years, as Tom regained control of his life, Jimmy became less obsessive and more responsive to Tom as an individual. Jimmy loved being in the position of being able to forgive Tom, and doing so matured his feelings. His displays of affection became more moderate, and at the same time Tom was more willing to put up with them, perhaps feeling that it was a small price to pay for Jimmy's forgiveness—not to mention the genuine pleasures of his company.

In 1980, Darragh Park bought a modest shingled summer cottage near the ocean in Bridgehampton, Long Island, about a mile from Bob Dash, and began to spend his summers and weekends there. Over the next decade and until his death, Jimmy was a regular guest. He made the first of his many visits there in late August 1981, accompanied by Helena

Hughes. He grew to love the place tremendously, finding a kind of substitute for the tranquil beauty of the Porters' house. He tended to spend a lot of his time in his bedroom, which looked out into the branches of a large butternut tree, or on the porch, just sitting quietly, basking in the landscape and the trees. By this time, Darragh and Bob Dash had had a falling-out and were no longer on speaking terms, and although Jimmy continued to see and correspond with Bob, their friendship was constrained by his greater closeness to Darragh.

Eileen Myles got sober in 1983, and as part of that process, decided to make amends for times in the past when she had taken advantage of Jimmy's obliviousness to pocket small sums of money, or keep the change from buying groceries. She made some approximate calculations and came up with a figure of $500, which she suddenly gave to Schuyler all at once one day. Jimmy was caught unawares and greatly appreciative. From that day their friendship entered a new phase, and "totally blossomed." Eileen began to spend more time with Jimmy, having lunch and going to exhibitions. She loved their visits to a local florist, where Jimmy seemed to know the names of all the flowers: "He was completely in his element . . . It was like being in heaven with God." Jimmy had always admired and been supportive of her poetry, but now he would make suggestions of mainstream editors to send it to, as he would do for other younger poet friends like David Trinidad and Peter Gizzi.

Jimmy's friendship with the novelist and essayist James McCourt also expanded around this time. McCourt and his lover, Vincent Virga, first met Jimmy in December 1980, through Darragh Park, when McCourt recognized him as a "shape" he used to encounter in the hallways of the Everard Baths in the '60s. The deep affection that grew between them was fed partly by love of operatic gossip—McCourt was a good friend of the Spanish diva Victoria de los Angeles. Schuyler appears as the poet referred to as "the Skylark" in McCourt's 1984 short story collection, *Kaye Wayfaring in "Avenged,"* which ends with a scene of the opera singer Mawrdew Czgowchwz singing a musical setting of "Hymn to Life." Calling Schuyler "the Skylark" pays homage to the musical quality McCourt found in his verse, and its "singer's sense of phrasing." "The purity of the voice knocked me out," McCourt said.

In a series of four meetings, in January and February 1983, Schuyler was interviewed on tape by Ted Berrigan, who hoped to publish the result in *The Paris Review* for its ongoing series "The Art of Poetry." The interviews turned out to be rather one-sided, however, with Berrigan doing most of the talking, and after Berrigan's death, his estate decided not to release them. Five months after the last taping session, Berrigan died of hepatitis C, undiagnosed at the time, at the age of forty-eight. His premature death was widely understood to be related to his drug use, and deficiencies in the U.S. health care system, and both Tom and Jimmy saw it as a warning.

Within a year or so after quitting heroin, Tom had entered a recovery program and given up drinking and all other drugs. As part of the process and in response to Ted's illness he decided to get a complete physical checkup. When in the summer of 1983 Jimmy began experiencing alarming physical symptoms, including seeing double, Tom recommended him to his new doctor, Daniel Newman, who traced the problems to his previously diagnosed diabetes and gave him instructions to change his diet. Within weeks he was much improved.

Dr. Newman was about thirty-six, gay, and good-looking. Jimmy liked him immediately, and Newman, on his part, took a friendly professional interest in Jimmy and came to regard him as a friend. After decades of abusing his body with drink, drugs, fatty foods, and lack of exercise, Jimmy was in bad physical health for a man of sixty. Now, for perhaps the first time in his adult life, he had a regular physician who "really cared about" him as an individual, in contrast to Dr. Weitzen, who remained detached outside office hours. Dr. Newman put Jimmy on medication to lower his blood pressure, took steps to lower his blood sugar level and help him lose weight, and in collaboration with Dr. Weitzen, reduced the number and dosages of tranquilizers and other psychotropic drugs he was taking. He also enrolled Jimmy in a grant program at Beekman Downtown Hospital that offset some hospital fees for needy writers.

Despite his progress under Dr. Newman, Jimmy began to experience "continuous pain" starting about March 1984. The condition was again traced to his diabetes, which was affecting the circulation in his lower body and causing what he described as "palsy" in his right leg. The pain became so great that he would "lie on the bed and sob." In May, he underwent two surgeries on the leg, and despite their overall success, two of Jimmy's toes had become gangrenous, and in August, they were amputated. Jimmy, already a slow and awkward walker, became even more so for the rest of his life.

Jimmy paid another visit to Darragh Park in Bridgehampton over the weekend of October 11 with Tom Carey. It was "the longest continuous time" he had spent with Tom, and he loved it. The stay "awakened" in Jimmy "a great longing for country living," and reminded him of its pleasures: "to see things growing, to see blue and tumbling skies, walk on the winter shore." With this visit Jimmy also resumed his long-neglected diary, which he would now continue, with some gaps, to the end of his life.

In the fall of 1984, when Jimmy sent Michael di Capua at FSG the proposed typescript of his next book, including its title poem, "A few days," the editor balked. He did not think that "A few days" was up to the quality of "The Morning of the Poem," nor was he greatly impressed with the other poems included in the collection, many of them love poems addressed to Tom Carey. He rejected the book and advised Jimmy not to publish it. However, his previous publisher, Random House, had recently hired a new young editor, Jonathan Galassi, who was also a poet and translator. Maxine Groffsky sent the manuscript on to Galassi, who accepted it with enthusiasm. Galassi had always loved Schuyler's work, but "never dreamt he might get to publish it," he told Jimmy.

Over the weekend of July 20, 1985, during another visit to Darragh in Bridgehampton with Tom, Jimmy paid a call on Anne Porter and Liz in their new, smaller house built behind the old one. The visit went well, except that Jimmy was "put into a tantrum" by the fact that all the rosebushes he had planted in the yard had been pulled out by the new owner and the two giant horse-chestnut trees chopped down. The desecration inspired the poem "Horse-Chestnut Trees and Roses," which he wrote the day after he returned to the city.

One of the best of Schuyler's late poems, "Horse-Chestnut Trees and Roses" notes the characteristics and locations of the roses, with a restrained, matter-of-fact tone and a frank appreciation of their lovely names and their associations: "and then, oh loveliness, oh / glory, Mme.

Alfred Carrière, white, with a faintest / blush of pink, and which will bloom even on a / north wall. I used to shave and gaze down into her— / morning kisses." The poet puts a "curse" on the despoiler of the roses, then retracts it ("Oh, well, it's his house now"). Rosebushes can be replaced more easily than mature trees; he saves his ire for the loss of the horse-chestnut trees, whose annual blooming was "magic, breath-catching, eye-delighting." It is tempting, if contrary to the straightforward nature of Schuyler's work, to think of the poem as a deflected elegy to his decade living with the Porter family. The poem ends, though, "It's the horse-chestnut trees I mind," as though discovering that for all the evaporated beauties of the past, it was the stolid, un-rose-like Fairfield Porter and his too-early death that Jimmy mourned most deeply.

Back in January 1985, Helena Hughes had found that she needed someone to share the job of Schuyler's caretaking. The poet Bernadette Mayer recommended her friend Bill DeNoyelles, a poet and artist, who began working for Jimmy that month. His New Jersey blue-collar background occasionally made him feel self-conscious around some of Jimmy's friends, including Helena—but never with Jimmy, with whom he developed a comfortable relationship.

At the end of July, Helena Hughes went on a three-week vacation to Ireland, leaving DeNoyelles in charge. Over the next few days, Jimmy grew increasingly manic and reminiscent, as the entries in his diary indicate. Even though the visit to the Hamptons had gone well, it still left Jimmy with a lingering sadness and a sense of loss. There are hints of impending or past unspecified events: "I wonder whether I'll carry through what I have it in mind to do?" (July 25); "Yesterday is a day I'm not going to think about, much less discuss. Enough to say, I was as cross as two sticks" (July 28).

He left some "really crazy" messages on Tom Carey's answering machine, expressing anger at Helena Hughes and threatening to do her harm. The next time Tom visited, he found Jimmy had set up "some kind of shrine" in the living room, which had "something to do with Helena." As DeNoyelles recalled it, Jimmy had transformed the floor of the small apartment into a kind of maze, with piles of books and records stacked up on the floor and narrow pathways in between. The stacks and their configurations changed every day, and seemed to hold private meanings.

On Monday, August 5, Eileen Myles came to visit, finding Jimmy in bad shape. While Jimmy was never outgoing or their relationship easy to define, nonetheless "he was consistent in some way," but on this day, "that wasn't there . . . and you could feel something changing in the room." Looking very hot and red and "as though he was about to burst," he sat at the table near the window and wrote a poem. Even while Jimmy looked "ravaged," as though he was "going mad," the poem he wrote was one Eileen characterized as serene and observational. "It gave me this sort of window into his poetry," Eileen recalled. "It seemed to be that he was composing a universe of calm out of complete franticness . . . Those kind of calm beauties that he assembles were such a construction of his needs."

DeNoyelles arrived just as Myles was leaving, encountering a confused and disoriented Schuyler, who asked him to type the poem he had just written, which was "Shaker." As he did so, DeNoyelles found him to be "agitated, pacing and visibly not at all himself." Jimmy asked him to take the finished poem up to Jonathan Galassi. When he got back, Teddy Wilson's staccato jazz piano music was playing, and as they talked, Jimmy "started to talk in the cadences of the music and twitch." Bill turned the music down, and Jimmy sat staring into space. Then he said, "I think I need to go to the doctor." In fact, while DeNoyelles had been out, Jimmy had already made an appointment with Dr. Weitzen, but the soonest he could see him was at the end of the afternoon, around 4:30. DeNoyelles agreed to stay with him until then.

Over the course of the day Jimmy grew progressively worse. He went to the doorway and yanked a photograph of Helena off the wall and threw it on the floor. "Do you know what that witch did to me?" Jimmy asked. "The bitch took my money." This may have been about his illogical resentment of the fact that part of the money Helena raised through the many grants she obtained on his behalf went to pay her own salary.

To try to distract him, Bill asked him to talk about Frank O'Hara. At one point, however, Jimmy "had a major slip," and thought they had to go to see Frank. Later, when Jimmy asked Bill what his favorite poem was, he answered, "Apollinaire's smoking poem"—meaning "Hôtel." Jimmy said it was one of his favorite poems too, and proceeded to recite it, standing up, first in French and then in English:

My room has the shape of a cage
The sun puts its arm in at the window
But I who want to smoke to make mirages
Light my cigarette at the fire of day
I do not want to work I want to smoke

"And then," DeNoyelles recalled, he "kind of just stood, and looked like he was in it."

The reason Jimmy knew this poem by heart in both French and English was because it had been set to music by Francis Poulenc and the song was a favorite of Frank O'Hara's. Ned Rorem recalled that whenever they were together, Frank would ask Ned to sing it for him.

At another point, Jimmy went into an involved discussion of how "hot" he thought the television newsman Chuck Scarborough was. Finally, it was time to go to Weitzen's office. They got a cab, but by then it was rush hour and they became stuck in traffic. As they were sitting motionless in the car, who should cross the street directly in front of them but Chuck Scarborough. Bill was terrified that Jimmy would see him and make some sort of scene, but fortunately he was oblivious.

Dr. Weitzen saw Jimmy in his office and then asked Bill if he could stay with Jimmy in the Chelsea for the next several days. As Jimmy wasn't physically ill, he couldn't be admitted to Beekman, and for some reason Weitzen declined to have him admitted to a mental hospital. DeNoyelles agreed on the condition that he could be assisted by a visiting nurse during that time. Over the next few days, Jimmy and Bill settled into an uneasy pattern. When Helena returned, Bill met her in the lobby and they went up to the room together. For several minutes all seemed well, until Jimmy abruptly turned to DeNoyelles and said, "Excuse me, Bill, would you please get that woman out of the room!"

Helena and Tom Carey finally arranged for Jimmy to be admitted to the psychiatric unit at St. Vincent's Hospital, where he stayed for about a week and a half. Tom brought him back to the hotel on or about August 22.

One result of the breakdown and its aftermath was that Bill DeNoyelles decided he was underqualified to be managing Jimmy's care and gave notice. He did, however, stay in touch over the next month, and substituted for Helena when she went on another trip, to Maine in mid-September. When she returned on September 19, she brought details of Edwin Denby's suicide there two years previously. Denby had remained close to Rudy Burckhardt and his second wife, the painter Yvonne Jacquette, and the three of them shared a summer house in Maine. In 1983, Denby had quietly gone into the woods outside the cabin and taken his own life. Jimmy heard of this at the time, but only now, when Helena told him some of the details and described visiting his modest grave in the woods, "an unmarked stone of no great size," did it really hit him. To Helena it appeared to be a kind of "tap on the shoulder" for Jimmy, stirring up emotions long buried, at the same time increasing his awareness of his own mortality. The fact that he and Denby had never really been reconciled, in all the years since Jimmy left him for Arthur Gold, added a painful sense of unfinished business to his death. Schuyler wrote the following day in his diary, "That elegance, that genius, that strange lover: and, aged eighty—why spell it out?"

[20]

IN BELL-LIKE BLUE

1985–1991

In retrospect, Jimmy's breakdown and hospitalization of August 1985 was a watershed event, a point when, as Tom Carey later saw it, he was able to "touch bottom and come up with his personal mythology intact and integrated in some way that it hadn't been before." Tom noticed a difference right away. "It was really quite something, because you'd be sitting in his room and he'd read his poems to you, which he never, ever, ever, ever did" before. Over the next five years the changes in Jimmy's behavior continued to be striking: "He bought clothes for himself . . . he began to take care of his appearance, he started going to Darragh's hairdresser, he bought stuff for the apartment . . . kept the place clean, made his own dinner . . . he began taking over the management of his own finances . . . began to take little trips . . . Really remarkable: a miracle really."

Jimmy and Tom's relationship also evolved. Tom now came to understand that the early part of their friendship had been "born out of sickness," when Jimmy was mentally ill, on mood-altering drugs, and drinking, which Tom exploited, while Tom was a drug addict and alcoholic, which Jimmy enabled. The relationship had changed most fundamentally after Tom became sober and joined a recovery program, and wasn't as dependent on Jimmy, or as available. Jimmy himself had been advised to stop drinking by Dr. Newman, and had mostly stopped after 1985 or earlier.

To Darragh Park it appeared that "Tom's enormous contribution to

Jimmy's life was allowing himself to be loved without going crackers in the process," and that this gave Jimmy purpose and direction outside himself, which allowed him to take control of his own life again. "It was one of those experiences that you see occasionally in life where really it does appear that love, a little love in somebody's life, can really transform it. And it really was transformed . . . Just socializing with him, too, he was so outgoing and felt so much better about himself . . . And with that came the whole business of branching out and meeting new people, and these younger people . . . gathered around him."

In the fall of 1985, *A Few Days*, the last collection of new work that Schuyler would see produced in his lifetime, was published by Random House. The title poem had already come out that summer in *The Paris Review* and had won the magazine's annual prize of $1,000 for a long poem. He also learned that he had received a $25,000 Whiting Award and he asked Eileen Myles to accompany him to the presentation at the Morgan Library in October. They both found the event quite strange, with Saul Bellow giving a rambling keynote talk, after which all the honorees were corralled together for a group photograph. It was Halloween night with a full moon and there were no taxis. To Eileen it was "the longest night ever," as they walked very slowly back to the hotel, yet they were both happy because of the money. Jimmy again had fleeting thoughts of travel to Venice or Rome, but in the end the prize mostly went to pay medical bills.

For several years the AIDS crisis had been moving closer to Jimmy's life. When Rock Hudson died on October 2, 1985, at the age of fifty-nine, Jimmy was distraught and succumbed to several "tearful outbursts." O'Hara's former lover J. J. Mitchell had been hospitalized with AIDS, also in October, and at one point was thought to be dying, but he went into remission and was released. He had been an alcoholic and drug user until getting sober and joining a recovery program, where he became friends with Tom Carey. Tom came to love him for his courage and élan, and, since he had known everybody and slept with many, his juicy high-society gossip. Jimmy had harbored ambivalent feelings about him in the old days, associating him with O'Hara's alcoholism and death, but now came to appreciate his wit and charm. They had dinner together with Darragh in October, when Jimmy found him looking "still very like his startling handsomeness of so long ago; his only reference (direct) to his fatal condition was 'It's like something you read about that's happening to somebody else.' And they say gallantry is dead!" J. J. Mitchell died in 1986.

A closer friend who had become ill with HIV and whose fluctuating condition was a frequent subject of concern and gossip was John Ashbery's former lover Aladar Marberger. Aladar took an aggressive approach to his illness, enrolling in several trial therapies, and telling Anne Dunn that he was determined to be the first person to survive the disease. One of the last times Jimmy saw him was at a dinner party at Darragh Park's in January 1988, where Marberger, looking diminished and bald from chemotherapy, but somehow "distinguished," dominated the conversation. "Aladar wasn't offstage for a second," Jimmy noted. "He talked and talked and talked . . . On the other hand, he was very sweet, and he is certainly most courageous." He died in November 1988.

Jimmy was worried about Dr. Daniel Newman, on whom he had developed a crush. They had conversations about Jimmy's sexual history, and Newman's own. Jimmy had stopped going to the baths after the early '70s, and Newman claimed he had never been promiscuous but was nonetheless worried because of the long incubation period before the illness showed itself. He was cautiously in search of a boyfriend. "Poor Daniel," Jimmy mused. "Finding a lover in the age of AIDS is not so easy." The strain of caring for so many young men with AIDS told on him. "You must have a lot of strength to cope with this epidemic," Jimmy told him. "Sometimes I wonder how much strength I do have, Jim." Daniel Newman died of AIDS in 1994.

Not long after he became sober in the fall of 1982, Tom Carey had begun attending the Episcopal Church of the Good Shepherd on East Thirty-first Street, often stopping by Jimmy's apartment afterward to gossip. Jimmy observed Tom's involvement with the church with vicarious interest for several years, before he began going to church himself. Starting in January 1986, he would venture out on Sunday mornings to sample different Episcopal congregations throughout the city. Their shared religious interests brought a new element to the relationship, one in which Jimmy was following Tom's lead. In late 1988, Jimmy finally settled on the Episcopal Church of the Incarnation on Madison Avenue at Thirty-fifth Street, originally attracted there because it offered an early morning service, and staying because of the sympathetic character of the rector, Douglas Ousley.

By the spring of 1986, Tom had decided to become an Episcopal priest. Before he could enroll in a seminary, he first had to complete his BA degree, and in the fall of 1986 he started classes at Columbia. Jimmy's support for these changes in Tom's life was unstinting, even though he realized that it meant he would see less of him. "Tom *loves* going to college," he wrote to the poet David Trinidad, "but, alas it takes up an awful lot of his time."

A new friend who took up some of the slack was the freelance editor and publisher of Hanuman Books, Raymond Foye. He had been living part-time in the Chelsea Hotel since 1979 but had never met Jimmy, until one day he encountered Schuyler in the elevator, told him that he was one of his favorite poets, and asked if he could phone him sometime. "Sure." The next afternoon, he did phone him around three o'clock, reintroduced himself, and suggested a visit. Unfortunately, he had caught him during a nap, and Jimmy slammed down the phone, with an angry "No, you cannot, and I'll thank you for not waking me up!" Taken aback, Foye later spoke to Helena, who told him that Jimmy was very sorry to have been so abrupt and would like to apologize, and he should try again. The second time he called all was well, and they arranged to meet. Foye felt that Jimmy's remorse at having slammed the phone down the first time caused him to be "particularly nice" to him and uncharacteristically forthcoming. "He really bent over backwards to be pleasant, and to kind of entertain me."

Soon Foye began to stop by Jimmy's room regularly to visit. Although conversation seldom came easily, Jimmy enjoyed Raymond's wit and anecdotes and respected his judgments on literature and music, and soon Raymond became one of his regular dates for movies, meals, and concerts, including memorable performances by Peggy Lee and Roy Orbison that they both greatly enjoyed. Raymond had an early Apple computer and began typing up Jimmy's new poems and printing them out in different fonts. Jimmy loved seeing his poems that way, configured as though they were set in type.

Since his leg operations, Jimmy increasingly had a hard time getting around, and just walking to the movie theater down the block, he had to stop every few yards to rest. Standing on the sidewalk, gripping Raymond or a handy tree, his gaze would appear focused on some undefined middle distance, yet he would clearly be "taking everything in, he'd be seeing everything . . . like antennae, it was a very mediumistic way of existing in the world," said Foye. "It was like life flowing through him and . . . he was seeing something that was a deeper reality."

> He had this quality of charm to him . . . charming in the sense of enchantment: there was an aura of enchantment about him that was—about being a poet! and suddenly you realized that he kind of made poems happen. You saw what was inherently poetical about reality. You saw it through his eyes and you saw it by being with him and in his aura.

In addition to his small apartment in the Chelsea, Raymond also shared an apartment in the West Village with the curator Henry Geldzahler. He was a good friend of Allen Ginsberg, Robert Creeley, and John Wieners, as well as many visual artists and musicians, and he made himself useful in various ways to many of their careers. Soon he was helping Schuyler, too. Back in 1983, Helena Hughes had recognized the potential financial value of Jimmy's papers and contacted Michael Davidson at the Archive for New Poetry at the University of California at San Diego about their sale. The university was interested but required an inventory and an appraisal, and the project languished. Raymond now took on the job, and by June 1987 he had finished the cataloguing and hired an agent and appraiser who offered the papers to the Mandeville Special Collections Library at UCSD. Two years later, the university approved the purchase of Schuyler's archive for a total of $75,000 and the papers were shipped to San Diego.

By August 1986, Jimmy's mental and physical health had improved to the degree that he felt he no longer needed the help of Helena Hughes. Their parting was unfortunately and unnecessarily bitter. In the simplest terms, he fired her, but Helena was actually "relieved and grateful" that he did so. She felt "burned out" after seven years of caring for Jimmy, especially after the events of 1985, and had wanted to quit earlier, but was dissuaded by Hy Weitzen. With Helena no longer working for him, "Jimmy moved into control of his life for the first time in decades, total control," as Darragh put it. "He was in control of his own money, and his own drug situation, and his own medical business with the doctors, all of that, and his dress, everything, and he was fine."

The idea of publishing a book of selected poems had been in Jimmy's mind for a decade, and after the publication of *A Few Days* in 1985, Jonathan Galassi agreed that such a collection should be his next book. Even before he started making the selections, Jimmy decided to dedicate the book to Daniel Newman, in recognition of the new lease on life that his medical care had given him. Since the publication of *A Few Days*, Galassi had moved from Random House to Farrar, Straus and Giroux, and Jimmy happily came with him, returning to the house that had published *The Morning of the Poem*. Starting in May 1986 and over the next year, Galassi worked with Jimmy on choosing poems from his previously published books of poetry.

The exercise of rereading his previous books was one Jimmy was unaccustomed to, he claimed, never wanting his current work to be influenced by that of the past. Yet doing so now for the *Selected*, he found himself "surprised by the—well, say it—high level, the sheer quality" of his own poetry. Spurred on by these reflections, perhaps, in the first half of 1987 Schuyler wrote several of the poems that would later be published posthumously as "Last Poems" in his *Collected Poems*, including "On the Dresser," "The Light Within," and "Under the Hanger," the cento taken from the *Journal* of the eighteenth-century English naturalist Gilbert White. The poem, like the *Journal* itself, is written entirely in the present tense; the seasons are sped up: the twenty-four and a half years covered by the *Journal* are compressed into 120 lines. As with Jimmy's other long poems there is an "allover," or as James McCourt put it, a "fractal" quality to the poem, in the sense that any one short excerpt from it is almost as good as another, and as representative of the entire poem:

Clouds, hail, shower, gleams.
Sharp air, & fire in the parlor.
Sweet day, golden even, red horizon.
Snow-drops, & crocus's shoot.
Vast frost-work on the windows.
Longest day: a cold, harsh solstice!

Late in 1987, Tom Carey became "swept up," as he put it, in the idea of becoming a Franciscan friar. He took a leave of absence from Columbia and joined the Society of St. Francis of the Episcopal Church as a postulant, and in February 1988 he moved out of the city to live at the society's friary, Little Portion, on the north shore of Long Island.

When Tom moved into the friary, he gave Jimmy his cat, Barbara. She was a black-and-white tabby, no longer a kitten but still playful, and somewhat temperamental. Schuyler loved her—she slept with him—and enjoyed her amusing antics, as recorded in letters and his diary over the rest of his life. "What a very human cat!" he remarked after one of her passive aggressions, which often involved territorial disputes over the space on his desk near his typewriter.

Jimmy made his first visit to Tom at Little Portion Friary in early May 1988, staying for about five days. Located on a 44-acre estate near Long Island Sound, the friary housed about twenty brothers who spent their days in prayer and contemplation and working in the vegetable garden and bakery. Jimmy loved it there: the landscape, the swans on the pond, and being for a while "a part of that community, going to prayers, saying the office, taking communion at evening mass." He especially loved being with Tom and seeing him going to and fro doing his chores among his fellow friars. Jimmy wrote two poems during the visit: "Birds" and "A View" (both dated May 10). When he got home, he was sad—"things seem rather, well, empty since I came back from Little Portion." He was also dreading the fall, when Tom was due to take up residency in the society's San Francisco friary for the year.

Jimmy's relationship with John Ashbery went through a series of subtle readjustments around this time. John had been a faithful supporter to Jimmy through the many crises and hospitalizations of the '70s and early

'80s, but like everyone else had found it emotionally taxing, and had drawn slightly apart. Now that Jimmy was so much healthier, the friendship was easier, although not quite as close as it had been in the '50s and '60s. Complicating matters a bit was the fact that over the past decade, John had become a much more famous and revered figure. Jimmy was happy for his friend's well-deserved fame and honors, but at the same time maintained a slightly amused skepticism about it all, occasionally sounding off to mutual friends like Anne Dunn: "I'm afraid I've never really adapted to what my John has evolved into over the years, and I find I'm not crazy about the role of straight man."

In a decade of owning his weekend house upstate in Hudson, which he had bought in 1978, John had never invited Jimmy to visit, ostensibly because his longtime partner, David Kermani, feared he would smoke in bed and set the house on fire. John couldn't really explain this to Jimmy, however, who, although he didn't say anything, was rather hurt by the lack of an invitation. But by the spring of 1988, not only was Jimmy much more stable, but David and John had split up—temporarily—and for a while David was living with a woman whom he intended to marry. In his absence, John's assistant Eugene Richie and his wife, Rosanne Wasserman, both poets, editors, and teachers, who were renovating a house near Hudson, often lived with John. Jimmy made his first visit to John, Eugene, and Rosanne in Hudson over the Memorial Day weekend of 1988.

The house was an imposing late-Victorian mansion with a granite and gray clapboard façade, facing the main town square and courthouse. For John, its dark paneled interiors and stained-glass windows recalled his beloved grandparents' house in Rochester, and he furnished it as a kind of *Gesamtkunstwerk*, mixing Victorian antiques with paintings by artist friends. David Kermani, who came from a family of Persian rug merchants, introduced many fine and rare rugs. Jimmy slept in the front guest room, perhaps the prettiest room in the house, with a faux-bamboo bed in bird's-eye maple, a fireplace with yellow tile surround, and an inviting desk in front of the bay window overlooking the square. Waking up there on his first morning, the repeating symmetrical patterns of the William Morris wallpaper gave him at first the sensation of being "in a giant Rorschach Test," but once he was fully awake he realized how "really lovely it is."

During the whole visit, John was "sweetness itself—all solicitude." On Sunday they drove to Housatonic, Massachusetts, near Great Barrington, to eat at Embree's restaurant, where Michael and Peter Gizzi, brothers and poets, waited tables. Michael, the older, was the more established poet. Peter had moved from New York City to the Berkshires the year before, joining his brother and starting the literary magazine *o-blēk*. John especially liked Michael, while Jimmy was attracted to Peter, telling John that he was a "chunky hunk." Both of the brothers were straight but didn't mind the friendly flirting.

Back in the city, Jimmy heard Anne Porter give her first public poetry reading on June 7 as part of the Intuflo reading series, organized by the poets Marc Cohen and Susan Baran, which took place picturesquely in a hardware store on Madison Avenue. After modestly declining to publish her work or read publicly for most of her life, Anne was slowly being persuaded to do both, and eventually brought out her first book, *An Altogether Different Language*, in 1994, with an introduction by David Shapiro. Ron Padgett read with her at Intuflo. Jimmy was particularly pleased by her moving poem about Fairfield, "Four Poems in One." As he wrote to her the next day, "When you read the poem for Fairfield, I thought how pleased he must be, and how proud he always was of your beautiful gift . . . It was truly an *honor* to be there."

In August 1988, Tom Carey advanced from "postulant" to "novice," in the Society of Saint Francis, earning the title Brother Thomas and the right to wear the traditional brown Franciscan habit. A few days later he left for his new assignment at San Damiano Friary, the society's house in San Francisco, California. There he would live for the next year, teaching reading and writing skills to prisoners. Jimmy missed him tremendously and wrote to him several times a week. Still, he was gratified that Tom had found a vocation and was following through on it. "It makes me so happy that you are so happy: you sound joyous!"

Around the time Tom left New York, the Los Angeles poet David Trinidad, with whom Jimmy had enjoyed a close epistolary friendship for the past three years, moved to Brooklyn to take graduate courses at CUNY. Born in 1953, David, an active participant in the Beyond Baroque Literary Arts Center in Santa Monica, was first introduced to Schuyler's work there by the novelist and publisher Dennis Cooper. David fell in love with *The Morning of the Poem*, especially "This Dark Apartment," which he deemed "perfect . . . what a poem should be." Tom Carey, Eileen Myles, and the poet Tim Dlugos regularly came out to LA to read at Beyond Baroque, and David became good friends with all three. During a brief trip to New York in 1982, Tom arranged for him to meet Jimmy, but first David went out drinking with a friend, and when he called the Chelsea to say he would be late, Jimmy took offense and told him not to bother coming. This misadventure took on enormous dimensions for David, becoming a "huge, humiliating, embarrassing disappointment." Finally in July 1985, when his second book, *Monday, Monday*, came out and he had become sober, David sent Jimmy a copy, along with a formal letter of apology. Jimmy responded with a copy of *Hymn to Life*, bearing an inscription that almost took Trinidad's breath away: "Your beautiful poems give me the feeling I had when I first read a poem by Frank O'Hara—the poem on which I have formed my manner." Later that fall, Jimmy sent David his new poem "Mood Indigo," which he dedicated to David, and a lively correspondence began.

When they finally met in person in August 1988, they hit it off right away, and immediately began getting together about once a week, for lunch or dinner, often followed by a movie. The pair shared a taste for popular first-run rom-coms. Like everyone else, David found that conversation with Jimmy was never fluid or easy, and he was always aware of "stretches of awkwardness and silence" interrupted by "spurts" of talk. "We talked about what I was reading," Trinidad recalled. "I'd ask him questions. We talked about writing a little . . . And he would show me poems . . . He was excited for me being in New York, and I think he wanted me to have a good experience . . . There was a sense in which he was a mentor."

~

The Dia Center for the Arts was established in 1974 as the Dia Art Foundation to exhibit and collect contemporary art. In 1985, it was reorganized with a new director, Charles Wright, who added a poetry reading series. Wanting to make the program stand out, Wright made a point of offering a higher honorarium than most, $3,000, and publishing a chapbook of each poet's work to accompany the reading. In the spring of 1988, he contacted Jimmy about reading there. Although he had been told by various people that Jimmy would never do it, Wright saw no reason why he shouldn't at least be asked.

Up to then, Schuyler had never wanted to read in public, partly because of a long-standing fear of "doing things in front of a crowd of people," which he traced back to his navy interrogations, and partly because of a purist feeling that any vocalized reading, even by the poet himself, was liable to distort the "voice of the poem" itself. But when Wright visited Jimmy at the Chelsea on April 18, 1988, to make his case, he found him to be "positive about the idea" from the beginning, and the reading was scheduled for November. Tom promised moral support and he had additional encouragement from Hy Weitzen, who told him he would be there sitting in the front row ("which is not as supportive as he imagines," Jimmy commented wryly to Anne Dunn). More to the point, Weitzen promised to prescribe a beta-blocker, Inderal, to help calm his nerves. For the chapbook that would accompany the reading, Jimmy provided excerpts from his 1960s diary, which Dia printed under the title *For Joe Brainard*, in honor of his old friend, the author of *I Remember*.

As the date of the Dia reading approached, Raymond Foye organized two practice sessions at the West Village apartment he shared with Henry Geldzahler. The first took place on Friday, November 4, when the audience included David Trinidad, Darragh Park, Douglas Crase, Frank Polach, Simon Pettet, Charles North, Marc Cohen, and Susan Baran. When the guests arrived, Jimmy was already there, sitting in a blue armchair. Crase recalled how "intimate" the practice reading seemed, "everybody knee to knee," and he felt "as a result, mildly claustrophobic but transported with the significance of the whole thing." Jimmy read "To Frank O'Hara," which ends with memories of Frank from the summer of 1953. Reading it aloud caused him to choke up, so he decided not to read it at Dia, telling David Trinidad he was determined not to read anything too emotional: "No tears!"

The second rehearsal, on November 10, was for older friends, including

Jane Freilicher, Joe Hazan, John Ashbery, Joe Brainard, Morris Golde, Barbara Guest, and again Darragh Park. The practice readings went well, Jimmy felt, because "I do (ahem) read very well."

The Dia reading on November 15 has now taken on the aura of an almost mythical event. Individual memories may have exaggerated certain aspects—the final applause, for example, which people remembered as lasting "several minutes," is revealed on tape as just under one minute. But no one can gainsay the beauty, dignity, and sense of occasion of the reading. Charles North expressed the feelings of many when he said: "[Schuyler's] Dia reading was the most thrilling I think I've ever been to."

The following Sunday, Barbara Guest gave a reading at Simon's Rock College in Great Barrington, Massachusetts, and Jimmy timed another visit to John Ashbery in Hudson so they all could drive over together. But Aladar Marberger had died on November 1, and on Saturday evening, John became overwhelmed with grief, retreated to his room, and wouldn't stop crying. Since he wasn't up to attending the reading the next day, Eugene, Rosanne, and Jimmy went without him. Jimmy, as always, found Barbara's work inspirational, and afterward there was a gathering at the poet Geoffrey Young's house in Great Barrington, with Clark Coolidge, Michael and Peter Gizzi, and others. Geoffrey Young and the other younger poets felt "privileged" to have heard Barbara read and to be in Jimmy's quiet, stolid company. Young noted how Jimmy "was really sensitive to [Barbara], he was really kind of gentlemanly and I could see, courtly with her."

Twenty-seven-year-old Peter Gizzi, the youngest of the poets at Geoffrey Young's party, had pretty much stayed quietly in the background, just "taking it all in." That fall, he wrote to Jimmy to ask if he would send something for a special New York School issue of his magazine *o-blēk*, and in response, Jimmy sent him his new poem "Under the Hanger." For his part Jimmy had been impressed by what he had read of Peter's work, and as soon as he got back to New York made sure to check with Charles North that they had invited both Gizzi brothers to contribute to *Broadway 2*, which they were then in the process of editing, adding, "they are both so extra swell, and represent the School of Stockbridge so nicely."

Peter came to New York to visit Jimmy at the Chelsea two or three times, and was surprised by the smallness and spareness of his apartment:

"a single bed with a Hudson Bay blanket, the green Olivetti typewriter with his cat Barbara sitting on top of it, a plump chair, books scattered, a hot plate." After lunch there would be a very slow walk back to the hotel, stopping every fifteen feet or so for Jimmy to point out "a tree or a flower or a weed." Back in Jimmy's room during a visit in 1989, Jimmy agreed to read several of his poems to Peter, including "A Man in Blue," "Light Blue Above," and "Korean Mums."

Almost as soon as Tom moved to California, Jimmy started trying to figure out a way to visit him there, and by Thanksgiving 1988, fresh from the success of the Dia reading, he was writing to a friend: "Perhaps someone will let me give a reading to pay for [the trip]." This was a rather astonishing suggestion, considering that the notion of giving a reading anywhere, much less across the country in an unfamiliar city, would have been unthinkable for Jimmy earlier. After Jimmy recalled that Bill Berkson was teaching at the San Francisco Art Institute, and might be in a position to invite him to read there, Bill was duly approached, and he contacted the poet Robert Glück, who was head of the Poetry Center at San Francisco State University. The two of them arranged for Jimmy to give a reading at the Art Institute the following February, co-sponsored by the Poetry Center.

Jimmy arrived in San Francisco on February 7, 1989, on his first cross-country flight. Tom brought him to the San Damiano Friary, housed in a late-Victorian building facing Dolores Park, where he lived for the week with the brothers. The visit was Jimmy's only experience of California, and his impressions of San Francisco were fleeting. He did not enjoy the hills ("My legs weren't made for steeping") but he loved "the way the cute houses hold each other up as they scramble up" them. He had the impression that "people's faces are full of color (not necessarily tan—just vibrant color) and they seem to run around, going from place to place a lot, but they're really very sluggish."

The reading was on Friday, February 10, a cool evening with a crescent moon peeking out between scudding stretches of cloud. When the poets Dodie Bellamy and Kevin Killian got to North Beach, where the Art Institute was located, it seemed to be "crawling with writers" excitedly asking one another, "Are you going?" In the lecture hall, Jimmy sat on the stage at a table set like a still-life with a blue pitcher and a red-and-yellow floral-patterned mug. The writer Lucia Berlin recalled that the auditorium was "packed" and wondered what it was about the crowd that felt so unusual: perhaps "the intensity of their expectation? And when he read, their complete attention?" The fifty-minute selection was mostly the same as at Dia, with four poems omitted and five added. As before, he began with "Salute." Tom noted Jimmy's poise under pressure, his "mindfulness" of himself and who he was in front of the big, respectful audience.

The day after the reading, Tom drove Jimmy across the Golden Gate to visit Bill Berkson and his family in Bolinas. It was a sunny day, and as they drove along the winding roads of the coastal Marin Headlands, Jimmy was thrilled to look down and see the Pacific spread out below, and noted "how you see at a glance . . . how deep the Pacific is . . . and see, on a sunny winter day, its two beautiful colors (my favorite colors): light blue and dark blue."

On Sunday afternoon Kevin Killian and Dodie Bellamy visited Tom and Jimmy at the friary. Jimmy was relaxed and commented on how beautifully the light came into the room through the bay window overlooking the park. Tom was "effervescent," Dodie remembered, and entertained the group with hilarious stories of his acting past. The conversation was easy, ranging from the comparative merits of diet sodas, to Dylan Thomas readings, to the anomalies of Barbie's anatomy. Kevin asked Jimmy if he led a settled life. "Yes, very settled." Occasionally a brown-robed friar would come through and introduce himself. The churchly atmosphere gave Dodie the feeling of being in a Barbara Pym novel.

Jimmy spent another day driving around with Robert Glück. Much of their conversation during the day was about gardening, including methods of "feeding" a stone or masonry wall with fertilizer to encourage moss to grow on it. Jimmy was much taken with the notion of "feeding the wall." They paid a call on Don Allen. Jimmy had never been that close to Allen, although they had corresponded over the years, and the conversation was a fairly superficial one of determining when they each had last seen mutual friends. Jimmy later told Bill Berkson that Don had been "as aspish as ever" in his comments about other poets of their acquaintance. At John Ashbery's recommendation they drove to Berkeley to see Bernard Maybeck's eclectic architectural masterpiece, the First Church of Christ Scientist.

Jimmy flew home on February 15, to be greeted by an ecstatic Barbara, his cat: "Never did anyone get such a burst of affection and cuddling." A few days later he and Darragh Park attended a large party at Ann Lauterbach's loft downtown in celebration of Joe Brainard and Kenward Elmslie's collaborative book, *Sung Sex*. When they got there, Jimmy settled himself regally in an armchair. He was happy to have a chance to speak briefly to the Boston poet Bill Corbett, who had earlier sent him his chapbook "Runaway Pond": "It's a wonderful poem, and made me ache & pine for Vermont," Jimmy wrote to him shortly afterward.

One afternoon in the spring of 1989, coming out of his barbershop on West Fourth Street, Jimmy encountered a young man named Artie Growich and they struck up a conversation. Artie was thirty-two, good-looking and dark-haired, rather short and stocky, of partly southern-Italian heritage, with an infectious good nature and a raspy Queens accent. He lived in Queens with his mother, but spent most of his time on Eighth Avenue in Chelsea—a familiar figure in the neighborhood, playing basketball or pool, doing odd jobs, living by his wits and his charm. Not long after meeting, Jimmy and Artie were living together as lovers in Jimmy's small room. It's not clear whether the relationship began as a sexual one and then came to include Artie being paid to take on some of the domestic chores that had fallen to Jimmy's previous assistants, or the other way around, but for some time Artie was successful at balancing both roles. When after a year or so the relationship ceased to be sexual, their friendship and Jimmy's support continued.

Tom was one of the first to learn about the affair, and was overjoyed for Jimmy. "I want you to know how happy I am that you're seeing your friend Artie," he wrote on May 18, "it's a great thing to have someone who's there physically and you deserve that." Like so much else that was happening in Jimmy's life in these last years, this relationship was a kind of miracle. The idea that Jimmy might enter a romantic and physical partnership had been unthinkable only a year or two earlier.

As he almost disbelievingly told John Ashbery soon after meeting Artie, "I never thought I would get laid again in this lifetime." There was a playful aspect to the relationship, and a sweetness. Undoubtedly they both recognized its inherent unlikeliness: the sixty-five-year-old Pulitzer Prize–winning poet, not long out of a series of mental hospitals, and the thirty-two-year-old streetwise kid from the boroughs. That Jimmy's single bed was barely wide enough for his own bulk, much less that of another man, only added to the sense of comedy. They had to lie head-to-toe to sleep, and when Jimmy was about to crash down onto the bed, Artie would cry, "Timmm-berrrrrr!"

Jimmy reveled in Artie's physicality, comparing his tanned, sleeping form sprawled on the bed to a "brown starfish," and enjoyed his unselfconscious remarks and Neapolitan superstitions, noting them in his diary or relating them to friends. He got to know Artie's family and would have conversations about him with his mother. Being together so much in the small room was not always easy and when Artie went away for a few days in July to visit family in Ohio, they were both glad of the break, but then joyful at the reunion. When the weather got hot in August, they stayed ensconced in Jimmy's air-conditioned room and watched television: baseball, which Jimmy could enjoy, or horse racing, which he did not, although, fortunately, he found, "the broadcasts . . . are divinely brief."

Artie was shy around Jimmy's friends, at first, most of whom met him only in passing. That changed a bit that November 1989, when Joe Brainard organized a sixty-sixth birthday dinner for Jimmy at Chelsea Central restaurant with Darragh, John Ashbery, David Trinidad, Raymond Foye, Eileen Myles, and Artie. It was the first time Artie had been together with so many of Jimmy's friends in that kind of social situation, and Jimmy was a little uncertain how it would work. But the party was a great success: "Artie looked a treat, drank some wine and was very gay and winning, laughing and saying I don't remember what. Everyone liked him, and thought I had underplayed his good looks. That he was willing to come, and enjoyed himself and liked my friends, was what pleased me most."

In the years that were left to him, Jimmy led a rich and full life. There were visits to Darragh in Bridgehampton, to John in Hudson, and to Little Portion; regular outings for dinner and a movie or a concert with Raymond, David, Tom when he returned from California in 1990, Eileen, Simon Pettet, Jimmy McCourt, Joe Brainard, me, and other friends. For several years he had a standing arrangement to spend Thanksgiving with Darragh and Marc Cohen and Susan Baran, the two married poets who ran the Intuflo series. He renewed his friendship and correspondence with the poet Vincent Katz, whom he had known since he was a boy.

Attention came from an unexpected source when in March 1989, the president of Bethany College wrote to offer Schuyler an honorary doctorate, with Jimmy giving a lecture at the college that May. The timing didn't work out, however, and the ceremony was tentatively rescheduled for 1990, but apparently either Jimmy or the college failed to follow through.

In 1989, not long before I began to see Jimmy regularly, David Trinidad began a relationship with the editor Ira Silverberg and as a result he began to see Jimmy less often. But in August 1990, David and Ira invited him to dinner at their apartment to meet the poet Tim Dlugos, whose long poem "G-9," written while Tim was a patient in the AIDS ward of St. Luke's Roosevelt Hospital, had greatly moved him. Jimmy, like many others, was affected by Tim's death four months later, and attended his funeral at St. Mary the Virgin in midtown Manhattan.

The poet Simon Pettet, who had quietly been collecting Schuyler's art writings for several years, finally showed his findings to Jimmy in about 1990. After some initial skepticism about "skeletons in his closet," Jimmy took an interest in the project and pointed him to articles he had missed, and eventually approved the manuscript of what would be published as *Selected Art Writings* in 1998.

After San Francisco, Schuyler gave an additional seven public readings (nine in all). The first of these took place on June 8, 1989, part of the Intuflo series, now held at the Schreiber/Cutler Gallery in SoHo. He read entirely new poems, which he had up to then shown to only a few friends. In his diary the next day Jimmy noted carefully what he read and his thoughts of how various poems came across in public. Already he was becoming an old pro at reading, and he wryly noted, "One begins to understand how an actor becomes a ham, and how actors fall in love with their audiences—their 'public'—and when they try to say so, sound so phoney."

That November, he gave a reading at the Herman Melville house, Arrowhead, in Lenox, Massachusetts, part of the same series organized by Michael Gizzi in which Barbara Guest had read the year before, and again he stayed with John for the weekend. A week later on the 20th, he read with John Ashbery at the Poetry Center of the 92nd Street Y in New York City. Both poets were introduced by Jonathan Galassi, who spoke of the visual effects in Schuyler's poems as "stand-ins for linguistic effects, operations which produce profound transformations." The standing-room-only audience was enthusiastic; everyone seemed to recognize the historic significance of the event, the only time the pair—friends, colleagues, and sometime collaborators for some thirty-seven years—read publicly together.

The next morning, Jimmy woke up still in a glow from the reception the reading had received. He remembered (as he told Darragh Park that day) going in the late '50s to see Zinka Milanov in *Tosca* at the Metropolitan Opera with David Protetch, who was a friend of the Croatian diva's, and visiting her backstage after her triumphant performance, where Milanov was holding forth: "As I said to Bjoerling ze ozzer night, Bjoerling, vere do vee heff a poobleek who luffs us as zay do een New York?"

On Sunday afternoon, May 6, 1990, Jimmy read at St. Mark's with Eileen Myles, the only time he read at the Poetry Project, and the only time the two of them read together. The trees behind the parish hall were all in bloom, "the church was just *blossoming*," and filled with light, "and again, whenever Jimmy read there was so much happiness," Eileen recalled. Jimmy read again in the Intuflo series in October 1990, this time with Tom Carey. This was the only time Jimmy read publicly one of his long poems, "The Crystal Lithium," in response to a special request by Raymond. The poet Michael Brownstein, attending one of the two Intuflo readings, felt transported to an earlier era:

> I felt like I was re-entering . . . vanished time . . . legendary time, from before I was around, let's say the '40s, 1940s, the '50s and

the '30s and all that, W. H. Auden, that whole thing came to life for me emotionally as a result of the way in which Jimmy was reading . . . I got taken into where he came from and what he represented, which was, I would say, the flowering of early modernism. And even for what influenced him, I could hear it in his voice, even going back into the nineteenth century . . . and it had something to do with the quality of his poetry . . . Jimmy was very civilized. And the civilized quality . . . really came alive in the reading. I felt like I was blessed to be there. I was very moved.

Jimmy's last reading was with Barbara Guest at NYU on February 6, 1991. He asked me to accompany him, and we had a quick dinner in the neighborhood beforehand. During dinner, Jimmy told me that he had gotten together recently with a new admirer, a filmmaker in his thirties named Mark D'Auria, who had recently seen him read on public access TV, and then gotten in touch. They had an assignation in Jimmy's room which was "very sexy." Mark told Jimmy, "I guess a lot of people must have told you you are very masculine looking. When I saw you on television I couldn't get over seeing this guy who looked like a plumber reciting this beautiful poetry." Jimmy and Artie were no longer lovers, but Artie was still living in the apartment intermittently. He was out that afternoon, but Jimmy was worried that he might return early, which, he said, "put me off my stroke a bit." Jimmy used the euphemism "swinging from the chandelier" to describe sex with D'Auria.

The reading, the only time he read with Barbara Guest, attracted a relatively small audience, but John Ashbery, Jane Freilicher, Doug Crase, Frank Polach, and Eileen Myles were there, among other old friends. The poems Jimmy read were: "Salute," "An Almanac," "Empathy and New Year," "Scarlet Tanager," "A Gray Thought," "Poem (This beauty that I see)," "Just Before Fall," "In Wiry Winter," "The Bluet," "Dining Out with Doug and Frank," "At Darragh's I," "Over the Hills," and "Six Something."

The reading was taped, and in hindsight, the sense of a valedictory mood is strong, from the litany of acts of closure and change in "An Almanac" ("Shops take down their awnings"), to the ending of "Poem" ("it goes, it goes"), to the final lines of "Six Something" (and of the reading):

> Eternity
> is tireless
> surely, like:
> rest now forever
> blessed tired heart,
> wakening otherwhere
> in bell-like blue.

When I visited Jimmy on March 15, I found him not feeling well and we ordered in. I mentioned finding a first edition of Logan Pearsall Smith's *Trivia* at the Strand Bookstore, which led Jimmy to tell me of his vision while reading Pearsall Smith's *Unforgotten Years* as a boy. This anecdote thrilled me, and because of the way it came up, I thought it might be something he had never told anyone else—little did I know he had already mentioned it in several interviews. I asked to see any new work he had. He said, as he had before, "I'm not writing now, just putting things in order for a new book." However, this time he did open his filing cabinet, and showed me a new poem, "Mark," about his visionary experience as a small child in Washington, DC. He said it was about the Holy Spirit.

On April 4, Tom Carey and I had a date to have dinner with Jimmy and we met in his room at the Chelsea around 6:30. When we got there, Jimmy told us he wasn't feeling well, he had a backache that had kept him awake all the previous night, so he wasn't going to come with us, but we should go out anyway. Tom had a disposable camera with three exposures left in it, and to finish the roll, he and I took turns photographing each other with Jimmy. Afterward, as we were eating, Tom told me that he was worried about Jimmy, that he seemed vague and "wandering" lately, and that he was going to call Dr. Newman if he didn't sound better the next day on the phone.

When Tom spoke to Jimmy in the morning, he seemed much as he had the evening before. Tom was still worried, however, especially after he called him again later in the day and got no answer. At around 3:00

in the afternoon Tom went up to the room. He found Jimmy sprawled on his bed, unresponsive and unable to talk, almost unconscious. He had wet himself and everything in his room was knocked about. When Tom asked what was going on, Jimmy could only laugh and make ambiguous hand gestures. Tom then called Raymond Foye, who came down from his apartment. They called an ambulance, but while Raymond was out in the hall meeting the medics, Jimmy had a seizure and flung himself to the floor. When Jimmy had finally been loaded into the ambulance and it had begun to pull out from the front of the hotel, a car ran into it, and the first ambulance had to wait at the accident scene while another one was sent for. Finally Jimmy made it to St. Vincent's, where he was admitted to the intensive care unit. A CT scan and other tests showed that Jimmy had had a stroke and a heart attack, but the heart attack had been more than twenty-four hours earlier. That evening, he remained unconscious and was on a respirator.

Two days later, Jimmy was still in intensive care, but awake and hooked up to various drips and monitors that beeped and glowed behind him. His eyes were alert; he was moving his head, responding to questions with appropriate nods. He and Artie seemed to be able to communicate well, wordlessly on Jimmy's side, as Artie gave him a report on his apartment at the Chelsea, where he was caring for Barbara the cat with Tom.

On Thursday the 11th, Jimmy had been moved out of the intensive care wing into another building at St. Vincent's, where he shared a double room. His bed was by the window, facing a color photo of a boat in full sail on San Francisco Bay. Several friends visited him that day, including Darragh, Doug Crase, David Trinidad, and Vincent and Ada Katz. At one point, the doctor appeared in the hallway and Darragh made to go out to talk with him, but Jimmy wouldn't let go of his hand, urgently trying to communicate with both his eyes and his hand, which finally he reluctantly released. Darragh told him that he would be right back, "but his eyes still seemed to say, 'Don't leave.'" Not long after he returned to Jimmy's bedside, Anne Porter came in. She was somewhat scattered, digging around in her purse, hunting for photographs of her grandchildren to show him, all the while talking to Jimmy and making the very Anne Porter observation, "The light coming into the city this morning was beautiful. Fairfield always used to say 'The light in New York City is the most beautiful light in the world.' But of course he had never been to every place in the world."

That evening, I found Jimmy alone. He still couldn't speak but smiled and nodded in response to my greeting. As I sat there, he kept gesturing with his eyes to the window, where the last daylight still lingered. Eileen came in and was animated, or tried to be, and for want of any other news, showed him her new leather jacket. The nurse came in to give Jimmy an insulin injection. He asked us who we were, were we family?

The next morning, I called Tom when I got to work. He sounded funny. I asked how he was. "I feel as though I've been hit by a board." "Why?" "Oh, I'm sorry, didn't you hear? Jimmy died this morning at seven o'clock."

Jimmy's funeral took place at the Church of the Incarnation on the afternoon of April 16. Pink magnolia branches from Joe Brainard framed either side of the altar. Jimmy's coffin was in the nave, covered with a cloth; the body would be cremated afterward. Father Ousley led the service. Tom had become violently ill that morning and almost didn't come, but he pulled himself together, and delivered a homily, wearing his Franciscan robe. It began with a description of his first meeting with Jimmy, coming to the Chelsea Hotel, sixth floor, turning right to room 625. He also said that he could still feel Jimmy's iron grip on his arm whenever they walked together. Alice Notley read a passage from the book of Job, chosen by Tom; Darragh read a lesson from the New Testament; John Ashbery read Jimmy's poem "Our Father," and Eileen read the late poem "Six Something." Sitting behind me was a little old lady clutching a small home-picked bouquet of roses; I later learned she was Anne Porter.

Sometime in the previous year, Jimmy and Tom had talked about burying his ashes in the cemetery at Little Portion. The brothers had become fond of Jimmy and permission was granted. The interment took place on September 22, 1991, a clear crisp fall day. Eileen, Artie, David Trinidad, Tom, and I took the Long Island Rail Road out together, Tom carrying the ashes in a round tin box on his lap. Artie was wearing Jimmy's aftershave and it was as if the air of Jimmy's room were encircling us. As the train moved through the green landscape, sunlight caught between the trees and the blurred windows ran and flickered across the curved ceiling of the car. At the friary we were joined by Doug Crase and Frank Polach, Darragh, John Ashbery, Eugene Richie, Duncan Hannah and his girlfriend, Sara Fitzmaurice, Anne Porter, Lizzie Porter, Barbara Guest, and the resident friars. Brother Mark Francis led the short burial service in the chapel, and then we walked uphill to the graveyard. The remains were buried under an evergreen tree, perhaps a spruce ("new needles on the spruce"). Before the grave was covered, we each added a handful of earth onto the container. There was a simple unmarked wooden cross beside the grave—a placeholder for the permanent marker that would come. Anne Porter placed a glass jar of miniature pink roses in front of the cross. Later a cement cross was set into the earth, matching those of the dozen or so friars lying nearby, inset with a brass plaque inscribed:

JAMES MARCUS SCHUYLER
1923–1991

NOTES

ABBREVIATIONS

Abbreviations used in citations are in bold type.

JS: James Schuyler

BOOKS BY JAMES SCHUYLER CITED

AG: *Alfred and Guinevere* (New York: New York Review Books, 2001).
CP: *Collected Poems* (New York: Farrar, Straus and Giroux, 1993).
DJS: *The Diary of James Schuyler*, Nathan Kernan, ed. (Santa Rosa, CA: Black Sparrow Press, 1997).
THB: *The Home Book*, Trevor Winkfield, ed. (Calais, VT: Z Press, 1977).
JSFOH: *The Letters of James Schuyler to Frank O'Hara*, William Corbett, ed. (New York: Turtle Point Press, 2006).
JTT: *Just the Thing: Selected Letters of James Schuyler*, William Corbett, ed. (New York: Turtle Point Press, 2004; revised edition, 2023).
OF: *Other Flowers: Uncollected Poems*, James Meetze and Simon Pettet, eds. (New York: Farrar, Straus and Giroux, 2010).
SAW: *Selected Art Writings*, Simon Pettet, ed. (Santa Rosa, CA: Black Sparrow Press, 1998).
WFD: *What's for Dinner* (New York: New York Review Books, 2006).

With John Ashbery
NN: *A Nest of Ninnies* (New York: E. P. Dutton, 1969).

PUBLISHED INTERVIEWS WITH JAMES SCHUYLER CITED

Foye 1991: Raymond Foye, "Schuyler in Conversation," March 2, 1990, *XXIst Century*, no. 1 (Winter 1991–1992).
Hillringhouse 1985: Mark Hillringhouse, "James Schuyler: An Interview," *The American Poetry Review* (March/April, 1985).
Little 1993: Carl Little, October, 1986, *Agni*, no. 37 (1993).
Ross 1981: Jean W. Ross, "CA Interviews the Author," March 27, 1980, *Contemporary Authors*, vol. 101 (1981).
Thompson 1992: Robert Thompson, "An Interview with James Schuyler," October 1, 1990, *The Denver Quarterly*, no. 26 (Spring 1992).

UNPUBLISHED INTERVIEWS WITH JAMES SCHUYLER CITED

Berrigan 1983: Ted Berrigan, January 4 and 7; February 3 and 13, 1983.
Schjeldahl 1977: Peter Schjeldahl, January 3, 4, and 19, 1977.

MANUSCRIPTS AND LETTERS

James Schuyler's personal papers, including manuscripts and letters addressed to him, are held in the James Schuyler Papers, 1947–1991. The Archive for New Poetry, **Mandeville** Department of Special Collections, University of California, San Diego, La Jolla, CA.

When William Corbett was editing *Just the Thing*, his wonderful edition of James Schuyler's letters, first published in 2004, and its companion volume, *The Letters of James Schuyler to Frank O'Hara* (2006), he generously gave me copies of all the letters he had collected, including many that did not end up in the book, which I then worked from. Most of these letters came from the original recipients, as he notes in his Acknowledgments, but many have since been deposited in various archives. In addition, Joe Brainard, Darragh Park, David Trinidad, Trevor Winkfield, and others supplied me with letters that they had received, which are now in institutions. Unless otherwise noted, Schuyler's letters to the following recipients are now found in the institutions or private collections below:

John Ashbery: John Ashbery Papers. Houghton Library, Harvard University, Cambridge, MA. (**JA Houghton**)

Joe Brainard: The Joe Brainard Letters 1957–1994. Mandeville Special Collections and Archives, University of California, San Diego, La Jolla, CA. (**JB Mandeville**)

Bill Berkson: Bill Berkson Papers, Archives and Special Collections, Thomas J. Dodd Research Center, University of Connecticut, Storrs, CT. (**Dodd**)

John Button: John Button Papers. Uncatalogued Mss. Henry W. and Albert A. Berg Collection of English and American Literature, New York Public Library, New York, NY. (**JB Berg**)

Tom Carey: Tom Carey Papers, Beinecke Rare Book and Manuscript Library, Yale University, New Haven, CT. (**TC Beinecke**)

Clark Coolidge: Clark Coolidge Collection, University at Buffalo, Archival and Manuscript Collections, Buffalo, NY. (**Buffalo**)

Bill Corbett: William Corbett Papers, Rare Books and Manuscripts Library, Ohio State University, Columbus, OH. (**Ohio**)

Douglas Crase and Frank Polach Papers, Beinecke Rare Book and Manuscript Library, Yale University, New Haven, CT.

Robert Dash: Robert Dash Papers, Beinecke Rare Book and Manuscript Library, Yale University, New Haven, CT. (**RD Beinecke**)

Anne Dunn: Anne Dunn Moynihan, Lausanne, Switzerland. (**Dunn**)

Kenward Elmslie: The Kenward Elmslie Papers, Mandeville Special Collections and Archives, University of California, San Diego, La Jolla, CA. (**KGE Mandeville**)

Larry Fagin: Larry Fagin Papers, Archives and Special Collections Library, University of Connecticut Library, Storrs, CT. (**U Conn**)

Jane Freilicher: Jane Freilicher Papers, Houghton Library, Harvard University, Cambridge, MA. (**JF Houghton**)

Arthur Gold and Robert Fizdale: Gold Fizdale Papers, New York, NY. (**Gold Fizdale**)

Grace Hartigan: Grace Hartigan Papers, Syracuse University Libraries, Special Collections Research Center, Syracuse, NY. (**Syracuse**)

Kenneth Koch: Kenneth Koch Collection of Papers, ca. 1939–1995, Henry W. and Albert A. Berg Collection of English and American Literature, New York Public Library, New York, NY. (**KK Berg**)

Harry Mathews: Harry Mathews Papers, Kislak Center for Special Collections, Rare Books and Manuscripts, University of Pennsylvania, Philadelphia, PA. (**Kislak**)

Charles North: Charles North Papers, Beinecke Rare Book and Manuscript Library, Yale University, New Haven, CT. (**CN Beinecke**)

Frank O'Hara: Frank O'Hara Papers, Maureen O'Hara Granville-Smith. (**O'Hara**)

Ron Padgett: Ron Padgett Papers, Beinecke Rare Book and Manuscript Library, Yale University, New Haven, CT. (**RP Beinecke**)

Darragh Park: Darragh Park Papers, Mandeville Special Collections and Archives, University of California, San Diego, La Jolla, CA. (**DAP Mandeville**)

Fairfield and Anne Porter: Fairfield Porter Papers, 1888–2001, Archives of American Art, Washington, DC. (**AAA**)

Ridenour family: Ridenour Family Papers, Buffalo, NY. (**Ridenour**)

David Trinidad: David Trinidad Papers, Fales Library and Special Collections, New York University, New York, NY. (**Fales**)

Anne Waldman: Anne Waldman Papers, 1945–2012, University of Michigan Special Collections Research Center, University of Michigan Library, Ann Arbor, MI. (**Michigan**)

Donald Windham: Donald Windham Papers, Beinecke Rare Book and Manuscript Library, Yale University, New Haven, CT. (**DW Beinecke**)

Trevor Winkfield: Trevor Winkfield Papers, Beinecke Rare Book and Manuscript Library, Yale University, New Haven, CT. (**TW Beinecke**)

Geoffrey Young: Geoffrey Young Papers, University of Michigan Special Collections Research Center, University of Michigan Library, Ann Arbor, MI. (**Michigan**)

OTHER ARCHIVES, LIBRARIES, AND INSTITUTIONS CONSULTED

Archives and Special Collections, T. W. Phillips Memorial Library, Bethany College, Bethany, WV.

Aurora Historical Society, East Aurora, NY.

Berg: Henry W. and Albert A. Berg Collection of English and American Literature, New York Public Library, New York, NY.

CK Berg: Chester Kallman Collection of Papers

WHA Berg: W. H. Auden Collection of Papers

AA Berg: Alan Ansen Collection of Papers

HM Berg: Howard Moss Papers

Uncatalogued Berg: Judith Malina and Julian Beck Papers

Howard Griffin Collection of Papers

Dodd: The Allen Collection of Frank O'Hara Letters, 1950–1966, Archives and Special Collections, Thomas J. Dodd Research Center, University of Connecticut, Storrs, CT.

East Aurora Advertiser Archives, East Aurora, NY.

Eton College Library, Eton College, Windsor, UK.

Freeborn County Historical Museum, Albert Lea, MI.

Irma and Paul Milstein Division of United States History, Local History and Genealogy, New York Public Library.

John Simon Guggenheim Memorial Foundation Records.

London Metropolitan Archives, London, UK.

Museum of Modern Art Archives, New York.

National Archives and Records Administration, National Personnel Records Center, Military Personnel Records, St. Louis, MO.

St. Edmund's School, Canterbury, UK.

University of Illinois Archives, J. Kerker Quinn Papers.

PROLOGUE

3 *"The uptown poets"*: Author Zoom interview with Peter Gizzi, December 15, 2022.

4 *"asking advice from him"*: John Ashbery, *Selected Prose* (Ann Arbor: University of Michigan Press, 2004), 209.

4 *"When about to enter a tumbrel"*: JS to Anne Dunn, November 17, 1988. Dunn. JTT, 444.

4 *"dim, hushed, respectful"*: Duncan Hannah, email to the author, December 16, 2013.

5 *laughter from the room*: The reading is available online at PennSound Center for Programs in Contemporary Writing at the University of Pennsylvania. https://writing.upenn.edu/pennsound/x/Schuyler.php.

5 *"everyone being 'rapt'"*: Trevor Winkfield, email to the author, December 11, 2013.

5 *"with no ornament"*: Geoffrey Young, "James Schuyler Reads at Dia," unpublished reminiscence, April 21, 2008.

5 *"there was also the assurance"*: Douglas Crase, email to the author, December 12, 2013.

5 *"Everybody on the planet"*: Author interview with Eileen Myles, February 11, 2014.

5 *"Most vividly I remember"*: Crase email, 2013.

5 *"And then that famous applause"*: Myles interview, 2014.

6 *"the crowd began to clap"*: Young, "James Schuyler," 2008.

6 *"in a very good mood"*: Author interview with Harry Mathews, November 12, 2009.

6 *"I was a fucking sensation"*: JS to Anne Dunn, November 17, 1988. JTT, 444. Dunn.

6 *Rereading the novel*: Ashbery, *Prose*, 209.

7 *Ashbery's own mother*: Schjeldahl 1977.

7 *twenty-first-century*: See for example José Esteban Muñoz, *Cruising Utopia: The Then and There of Queer Futurity* (New York and London: New York University Press, 2009), 13–15, 23–26.

1. A DREAM OF THE GREAT MIDWEST

11 *"dream" of the Midwest*: "Money Musk," CP, 15.

11 *"the mystery of a flat"*: James Schuyler, "A Memory Haunts Me," *Accent* XI, no. 3 (Summer 1951): 149.

12 *The name Schuyler*: Strangely enough, the name Schuyler has died out in the Netherlands. Nor is *schuyler* a word in the Dutch language. The closest word in modern Dutch seems to be the verb *schuilen*, meaning to hide or take shelter.

13 *David Pieterse's four times*: Florence A. Christoph, *Schuyler Genealogy* . . . (Albany, Friends of the Schuyler Mansion, c. 1987–c. 1992), v. I, pp. 7, 25, 84, 167; v. II, pp. 66, 174, 294. Irma and Paul Milstein Division of United States History, Local History and Genealogy, New York Public Library.

13 *in January 1935*: *Arkansas, U.S., Marriage Index, 1933–1939* [online database], Ancestry.com Operations Inc, 2005.

13 *In 1885*: Census: 1885, Beaver, Butler Co., Iowa, Age 3, Farmer born NY; 1900 Census: 1900 Kremlin, Garfield Co., Oklahoma, Age 18, born Oct 1881. Information courtesy Lee Pound.

13 *By 1913*: Tulsa, OK, *City Directory* (1913). Terre Haute, IN, *City Directory* (1915) lists Mark J. Schuyler, "proofreader," living at 112½ So. 4th. Ancestry.com.

14 *Margaret Connor's grandfather*: Slater genealogy. Ridenour.

14 *Ella Slater became the new district's*: Rev. Edward D. Neill, *History of Freeborn County* (Minneapolis: Minnesota Historical Co., 1882), 420.

15 *Richard George Connor*: Historical information about Richard Connor obtained from London Municipal Archives, London, UK, Census of 1841, 1851, 1861; England Death Index 1867; Marriage records 1864. *Crockford's Clerical Directory*, 1860, 131.

15 *Jane sent both Richard*: Email to author from Peter Henderson, Archivist, King's School, Canterbury, July 23, 2008.

16 *In March 1882*: National Archives, Washington, DC; *Passenger Lists of Vessels Arriving at New York, New York, 1820–1897*; Microfilm Serial or NAID: *M237*; RG Title: *Records of the U.S. Customs Service*; RG: *36*; Ancestry.com.

16 *Charming and red-haired*: Ruth Blunt, "Names for Farm Picture," unpublished narrative, September 1981. Ridenour.

16 *Frederick abandoned*: Blunt narrative, 1981.

16 *Margaret retained vague*: JS to Anne Dunn, "St. Anne's Day," 1976. Dunn.

17 *as family tradition*: Blunt narrative, 1981.

17 *On the night of Saturday*: "Morphine Did It: Frederick Connor Ends His Life . . ." *Albert Lea Enterprise*, Albert Lea, MN (November 21, 1895): 8; "Life Not Worth the Living," *Freeborn County Standard*, Albert Lea, MN (November 20, 1895): 4. Freeborn County Historical Museum, Albert Lea, MN.

17 *never spoken of*: Author conversation with Fred and Hilde Ridenour, October 23, 2012.

17 *"truly a* wonderful *person"*: Blunt narrative, 1981.

18 *"Dickens and Thackeray"*: Love Cruikshank, "Leave England to Make Home Here," *Albert Lea Tribune*, May 3, 1976.

18 *"There once was a senior"*: *So and Not So*, Albert Lea College Yearbook (1913): 49; Freeborn County Historical Museum, Albert Lea, MN.

18 *Chase was an accountant*: For information on Stuart Chase (1888–1985) I am indebted to his biographer, Professor Richard Vangermeersch.

19 *he coined the phrase*: F. William Engdahl, "Some Unconventional Reflections on the Great Depression and the New Deal," Geopolitics—Geoeconomics, August 2002, http://www.oilgeopolitics.net/History/New_Deal/new_deal.html.

19 *Margaret was there*: JS, "Bombshell," typescript, Mandeville [box 7, folder 3].

19 *"a hangout for political"*: Sherwood Anderson, "Letters to Cynthia," quoted in "The Education of Sidney Adams: Anderson's 'Letters to Cynthia'" by Charles E. Modlin on the blog Mick Speer (https://blog.richmond.edu/mspear/2012/07/23/the-education-of-sidney-adams-andersons-letters-to-cynthia/).

19 *"long discussions about that Revolution"*: Kenneth Rexroth, *An Autobiographical Novel* (New York: New Directions, 1991), 273.

19 *Margaret held antimilitaristic*: JS, "Bombshell." Mandeville.

19 *Learning of this, Irma Tator wrote*: Irmagarde Tator to Margaret Connor [September 10, 1918], Ridenour.

20 *From December 1918*: University of Chicago Application Form, August 1926. Ridenour.

20 *newly founded Labor Party of Cook County*: See "Labor Party of the United States, Farmer-Labor Party of the United States, Federated Farmer-Labor Party (1918–1925)," Early American Marxism, http://www.marxisthistory.org/subject/usa/eam/farmerlaborparty.html.

20 *became an active member*: Margaret represented the local branch of the league at several of its Annual Regional Conventions in Des Moines, Iowa, and reported on it in the *Examiner* (November 24, 1921).

20 *right-wing machinations*: Richard Vangermeersch to the author, July 31, 2008. Samuel and Irmagarde Tator also left Washington at this time and established Quinnipiac University in Connecticut in 1929.

21 *"heavy, jolly, well-read man"*: "The Morning of the Poem," CP, 277.
22 *"There is no camafloge"*: "The Sales Tax," *Albert Lea Examiner* (August 1921): 1.
22 *"Smug citizens will be often shocked"*: "Main Street," *Albert Lea Examiner* (November 10, 1921): 1.
22 *"jingler, and exploiter of trite slang"*: "Imperialism," *Albert Lea Examiner* (February 2, 1922).
22 *"News Writers Wanted"*: *Albert Lea Examiner* (June 1921).
23 *"Miss Connor brings to her work"*: *Albert Lea Examiner* (October 27, 1921).
23 *In later recollections*: Schjeldahl 1977; Berrigan 1983.

2. LOVER'S LEAP LOST / ITS ROMANCE

25 *one of the local newspapers*: James Schuyler understood that this was the *Chicago Tribune*, but this cannot be verified.
25 *A "Baby Book"*: Ridenour.
25 *as one poet recalled*: Author interview with Michael Brownstein, May 8, 2012.
26 *in several interviews*: Schjeldahl 1977; Little, 154.
26 *"My earliest memory"*: JS, untitled typescript. Mandeville [box 1, folder 5].
26 *"Snapshot"*: OF 4.
26 *"My mother's name was Daisy"*: JS, untitled typescript.
26 *On the application*: "Application for Admission to Advanced Standing, The University of Chicago," August 27, 1926. Ridenour.
27 *Marcus moved to Washington*: Washington, DC, *City Directory* (1927) lists "Marcus J. Schuyler, printer, at 4520 Georgia Ave., NW, apt. 4." Ancestry.com, https://www.ancestry.com/search/collections/2469/records/1158425904?tid=&pid=&queryId=062721f3-ef82-4759-b766-ace765c6fb40&_phsrc=Ioy36&_phstart=successSource. See also correspondence addressed to the couple at 114 F Street, SW, dated August 27, 1928. Ridenour.
27 *circumstantial reasons suggest*: The front page of *The Washington Times* for March 19, 1929, included a photograph of Schuyler in his kindergarten class doing crafts at a table in Garfield Park under the heading "Summertime Joys Start Now for These Tots." Ridenour.
27 *two poems*: "I Sit Down to Type," CP, 241; "Mark," CP, 383.
28 *At the farm*: CP, 276–77.
28 *"one of the most successful"*: "Dynamite Kills Local Farmer," *Freeborn County Standard*, Albert Lea, MN, August 30, 1928: 1; Freeborn County Historical Museum, Albert Lea, MN.
28 *Ella was stoic*: Ella Connor to Margaret Schuyler, undated, August 1928. Ridenour.
28 *Jimmy, was lucky to have*: Ella Connor to JS, undated, August 1928. Ridenour.
28 *Working late nights at the paper*: Berrigan 1983.
28 *Marcus was reduced to tears*: Author interview with Bernard Oshei, June 4, 1996.
29 *Jimmy was left with a memory*: Author interview with Darragh Park, December 12, 1994.
29 *by the police*: JS to Ron Padgett [July 18, 1971]. RP Beinecke.
29 *"Then, in the asexual"*: OF, 108.
29 *The divorce agreement*: District of Columbia Supreme Court, *Margaret C. Schuyler v. Marcus J. Schuyler*, September 20, 1929. Ridenour.
29 *in later interviews*: Berrigan 1983; Schjeldahl 1977.
29 *Medical opinion is divided*: Wikipedia, "Problem gambling," last updated October 30, 2024, https://en.wikipedia.org/wiki/Problem_gambling.

30 *Dr. Edmund Bergler*: Wikipedia, "Edmund Bergler," last updated October 2, 2024, https://en.wikipedia.org/wiki/Edmund_Bergler.
30 *"To be children of a broken home"*: JS to Hilde Ridenour, April 16, 1975. Ridenour.
30 *He died from a heart attack*: Margaret Ridenour notes regarding life insurance claim, January 1946. Ridenour.
31 *"gentle Grandma Ella"*: CP, 266.
31 *"'those / birds,' she / would have said"*: CP, 179–80.
31 *a "wrinkled woman"*: "Granny's Funeral," typescript. Mandeville [box 7, folder 11].
33 *the first painting*: JS typed memo, February 5, 1983. RP Beinecke.
33 *"The Spirit of St. Louis"*: "Bombshell," typescript. Mandeville [box 7, folder 3].
33 *the only character*: Little 1993, 163.
33 *"You mustn't answer"*: AG, 19.
33 *"Nobody wants"*: AG, 18.
33 *Granny is someone*: AG, 64, 62.
33 *"We mustn't care"*: AG, 20.
34 *Ridenour was born*: "Resume Business Experience— F. Berton Ridenour," July 8, 1946. Ridenour.
35 *souvenirs from their*: Author interview with Faye Mowery Donoghue, July 2, 2013.
35 *"the first image I ever had"*: JS to Janice Koch, March 23, 1957. Katherine Koch. Mowery's label on the bottom of the fragment states that it was actually "taken from the Roman Forum in 1916." Information courtesy Eldred Mowery III, 2024.
35 *Another prized artifact:* Donoghue interview, 2013.
36 *One day Faye and Eldred*: Phone message to author from Faye Mowery Donoghue, June 30, 2013.
36 *a situation that echoes*: Eldred Mowery, Sr., left his family for a job in Marietta, Georgia, intending to send for them when he got settled. According to Faye, that separation led to her parents' eventual divorce.
37 *"from schist / to granite"*: CP, 396.
37 *Jimmy saw the encampment*: JS in conversation with the author, date unknown.
37 *"all those ugly"*: Berrigan 1983.
37 *"When I was young"*: JS to Hilde Ridenour, April 16, 1975. Ridenour.
38 *In the first period*: Schuyler's first-grade report card from the John Adams School in Washington, DC, is preserved in the James Schuyler Papers at the Mandeville Special Collections Library at UCSD. Others are in the Ridenour Family Papers.
38 *"the floor show"*: DJS, 213.
38 *"blueish people in costumes"*: JS, "Why I'm Called Jack." Mandeville [box 8, folder 9].
38 *"had a name"*: "Why I'm Called Jack." Mandeville.
38 *It was at this time*: Chevy Chase School report card, grade 3B-4A, September 1932. Ridenour.
39 *Berton's employment history*: "Resume Business Experience—F. Berton Ridenour," July 8, 1946. Ridenour.

3. THE LANDSCAPE SHIMMERED

40 *He spoke in a soft*: Author interview with Bernard Oshei, June 4, 1996.
41 *Jimmy spoke approvingly*: Oshei interview, 1996.
41 *"enjoyed" being sissified*: Oshei interview, 1996.
41 *"You're gliding!"* Oshei interview, 1996; author interview with Tom Carey, October 3, 1994.

41 *"rich cousin"*: JS to Tom Carey, February 21, 1988. JTT, 433.
41 *"I was a real* Vogue*"*: JS to David Trinidad [September 23], 1986. Fales.
42 *"Your grandmother is dying"*: JS, "Granny's Funeral," 1975, typescript. Mandeville [box 7, folder 11].
42 *As the family gathered*: "Granny's Funeral." Mandeville.
42 *"She always talked"*: Author notes from Ridenour Family Papers, 2007.
43 *"in the middle of nowhere"*: Author interview with Fred and Hilde Ridenour, October 23, 2012.
43 *the mortgage*: Ridenour.
44 *its special atmosphere*: Schjeldahl 1977.
44 *Bernie got up*: Oshei interview, 1996.
45 *"We were more friends"*: Ridenour interview, 2012.
45 *"a gardening slave"*: Hillringhouse 1985, 5.
45 *irrigation trenches*: Oshei interview, 1996.
45 *"quite nutty and very cruel"*: Berrigan 1983.
45 *David Copperfield's cruel*: Berrigan 1983.
46 *"a novel by Dostoyevsky!"*: Schjeldahl 1977.
46 *a library card*: Schuyler mentions this in several interviews (see Hillringhouse 1985, 5), but his family felt it was out of character for Berton, who had a great respect for education, and that there must be more to the story. Author notes from conversation with Hilde Ridenour, November 29, 2007.
46 *The story describes*: THB, 44.
46 *"You probably saw him"*: JS to Hilde Ridenour, April 16, 1975. Ridenour.
46 *it sometimes seemed*: Oshei interview, 1996.
47 *"I wish it was"*: CP, 282–83.
47 *quick to put a damper*: Hillringhouse 1985, 5.
48 *As Bernie later observed*: Oshei interview, 1996.
48 *From the stories of Saki*: Oshei 1996.
48 *"Just because you like Oscar Wilde"*: Author interview with Eileen Myles, April 13, 1991.
48 *"I was very affected by reading"*: Ross 1981, 3.
48 *He also traced*: Little 1993, 174.
49 *"the whole landscape shimmered"*: Little 1993, 157; see also Ross 1981, 1; Foye 1991, 46.
49 *"lying out of doors"*: Logan Pearsall Smith, *Unforgotten Years* (Boston: Little, Brown, 1939), 84–85.
49 *"receptivity to experience"*; Smith, *Unforgotten*, 105–106.
50 *"I really didn't"*: Hillringhouse 1985, 5.
50 *"very smart"*: Author phone interview with Margaret Meade, December 2007.
50 *"quiet, but not"*: Author phone interview with Russell Drosendahl, December 5, 2007.
50 *he "wore a different"*: Author phone interview with Sally Ingalls Rohrdanz, December 2007.
51 *"Class Prophecy"*: *Auroran* (East Aurora High School, 1941): 33. Aurora Historical Society, East Aurora, NY.
51 *"just too too"*: "S'nuff Stuff," *High School Highlights* (October 19, 1939). *East Aurora Advertiser* Archives, East Aurora, NY.
51 *she later achieved*: Mary Nenno (d. 2007) became associate director for policy development at the National Association of Housing and Redevelopment in Washington.
51 *essay contest*: Sipprell's rather smarmy essay, "Time Out for Youth," was published in *The Journal of Educational Sociology* (Payne Educational Sociology Foundation, NYU) 14, no. 8: 452–57. The publication was noted in *The New York Times* on April 20, 1941.

51 *"I couldn't take it"*: CP, 284.
52 *"the very first"*: CP, 284.
52 *"To go steady"*: *Auroran* (East Aurora High School, 1941): 23. Aurora Historical Society, East Aurora, NY.
52 *"very luscious with long"*: JS, "Inhaling," 1969, unpublished text. Mandeville [box 8, folder 9].
53 *Several focus*: See for example "Custodians Sweep Up Million Footprints," *High School Highlights*, October 3, 1940; "27,000 Feet of Motion Pictures Shown Since Fall," *High School Highlights*, February 6, 1941.
54 *opening "windows"*: "The Morning of the Poem," CP, 285.
54 *"When you're in college"*: CP, 286.
54 *"big white whale"*: Berrigan 1983.
55 *"complete freedom"*: Little, 167.
55 *he came to feel*: Little, 167.
55 *"sacred books"*: JS to Don Allen, September 20 [1959]. JTT, 111.
55 *"not so much"*: Little, 157.
55 *In 1940, Berton*: "Resume Business Experience—F. Berton Ridenour, July 8, 1946." Ridenour.
56 *derived, he said*: "I sit down to type," CP, 240.
56 *"it does kill people"*: JS to Hilde Ridenour, April 16, 1975. Ridenour Papers.
56 *he worked at*: JS to John Ashbery, December 12, 1969. JTT, 280.
56 *"vividly wanting to be 18"*: JS to John Ashbery, December 12, 1969. JA Houghton. JTT, 280.

4. CURSES FLAP INTO THE SKY LIKE STARLINGS

57 *"an attractive group"*: JS, "Poet and Painter Overture," in Donald M. Allen, ed., *New American Poetry* (New York: Grove Press, 1960), 444.
57 *his main activity*: Thompson, 110.
58 *In his first semester*: Bethany College Permanent Academic Record for James Schuyler Ridenour. Archives and Special Collections, T. W. Phillips Memorial Library, Bethany College, Bethany, WV.
58 *"I was very influenced"*: Little 1993, 155.
58 *"imaginative, the intellectual"*: Florence M. Hoagland, "Character and Curriculum in the Church-Related College," *The Christian-Evangelist*, June 8, 1939.
58 *"a large great* sun*"*: May Sarton, *Dear Juliette: Letters of May Sarton to Juliette Huxley* (New York: W. W. Norton, 1999), 119.
58 *"thrilled by it"*: Little 1993, 155.
58 *"quiet," "sensitive," "moody"*: Author phone interview with Jesse Barton, May 12, 2009.
59 *"a quiet, introspective"*: Author phone interview with Robert Golbey, May 13, 2009.
59 *struck by his obvious*: Author phone interview with William Stophel, May 14, 2009.
59 *"virtually ignorant"*: Golbey interview, 2009.
59 *"lighthearted . . . more like a friend"*: Stophel interview, 2009.
60 *"not knowing which bedroom"*: JS to Robert Jordan, June 27, 1991. Mandeville. JTT, 349. After leaving Bethany in 1956, Behymer went on to head the library at Long Island University, where a scholarship in library science is named in his memory. In 1981, after retiring, he donated a large collection of homoerotic literature and magazines to the Mariposa Foundation, now part of the Human Sexuality Collection at the Cornell University Library. Schuyler left his own books to Bethany College,

where they are maintained as a separate collection in a dedicated room in the college library.

60 *Alex Katz mistakenly*: Schjeldahl 1977. See also "A few days," CP, 368.

60 *drawn to since his suburban*: Foye, 46.

60 *"I was in the shower"*: CP, 368.

61 *"almost any night"*: CP, 85–86.

61 *in perfect health*: Report of Physical Examination and Induction, Armed Forces Original D. S. S. Form 221, December 29, 1942. National Archives and Records Administration, National Personnel Records Center, Military Personnel Records, St. Louis, MO.

61 *"denied the privilege"*: Ridenour, James Schuyler, Permanent Academic Record, Bethany College, February 5, 1943. Archives and Special Collections, T. W. Phillips Memorial Library, Bethany College, Bethany, WV.

61 *working-class Irish*: John G. Caulfield online exchange with Helen Graham, July 13–17, 2013. Also George Chauncey email to the author, April 15, 2009. A very blurry image of the building can be found on the NYPL website, image #707878f.

61 *Jimmy was besotted*: "Dining Out with Doug and Frank," CP, 249.

61 *he and a tall*: I date the meeting of Bill and Jim to this visit in 1943, rather than 1944 when Schuyler moved to New York, from information provided by Schuyler to U.S. consular officials in Florence in 1949, as explained in the following chapter.

62 *He was then*: Ridenour, James Schuyler, Shipping Articles, April 8, 1943. National Archives.

62 *"more or less"*: Frank O'Hara to his family, July 19, 1944, as quoted in Brad Gooch, *City Poet: The Life and Times of Frank O'Hara* (New York: Alfred A. Knopf, 1993), 62–63.

62 *"Now that we were"*: Frank O'Hara, *Early Writing* (San Francisco, CA: Grey Fox Press, 1977), 112.

63 *"Without exaggerating at all"*: O'Hara to his family, August 24, 1944, quoted in Gooch, *City Poet*, 64–65.

63 *"There are bars"*: O'Hara, *Early Writing*, 115.

63 *"Key West! / The beautiful white houses"*: "The Morning of the Poem," CP, 270.

63 *"walking under the palms"*: CP, 270.

64 *"short skinny boy"*: DJS, 49.

64 *Trainees were first taught*: H. G. Jones, *The Sonarman's War* (Jefferson, NC: McFarland, 2010), 15–16.

64 *"Even though he was but an enlisted man"*: Jones, *Sonarman's*, 16.

64 *Jimmy completed*: National Archives.

64 *The* Glennon *(DD620)*: E. Andrew Wilde, Jr., ed., *The USS Glennon (DD-620) in World War II: Documents and Photographs* (Needham, MA: Privately printed by the author, 1999, 2001), n.p. Online at: https://destroyerhistory.org/assets/pdf/wilde/620glennon_wilde.pdf

65 *On the first night out*: Wilde, *The USS Glennon.*

65 *"sparks and lights"*: Lt. D. Stix, "USS Glennon, Operational Remarks," October 21, 1943, in Wilde, *USS Glennon*.

65 *"I was brave"*: DJS, 197.

66 *While in port*: Author telephone interview with Gustavus R. Ide, March–April 2009.

66 *would have noted*: *The New Yorker*, November 20, 1943. *New Yorker* online archive.

67 *a partly gay clientele*: See Allan Bérubé, *Coming Out Under Fire* (New York: Free Press, 1990), 115. For a description of the wartime late-night ambiance around the Astor Bar, see Robert M. Coates, "Big Night," *The New Yorker*, May 27, 1944: 49–55.

67 *On the* Glennon*'s last night*: Author interview with Tom Carey, October 3, 1994.
67 *Jimmy was reported*: Memo from Commander C. A. Johnson, December 3, 1943. National Archives.
67 *In June 1944*: Wilde, *USS Glennon*, 2001.
68 *"kind of breakdown"*: Schjeldahl 1977.
68 *gay-friendly and inexpensive*: Harold Norse, *Memoirs of a Bastard Angel* (New York: William Morrow, 1989), 105.
68 *"In '43 Sidney Gittler"*: James Schuyler to Ron Padgett, August 15, 1971. RP Beinecke. (Not "Sid Catlett" as printed in JTT, 356.)
68 *who once starred*: It is possible that this was Louella Gear (1897–1980), who introduced the Harold Arlen, Ira Gershwin, and Yip Harburg song "My Paramount—Publix—Roxy—Rose," in the 1934 revue *Life Begins at 8:40*. Schuyler does not explain the connection between the song and his poem.
69 *Sydney Gittler*: "Sydney Gittler, 85, Coat Retailer Who Reproduced European Styles," *New York Times* (August 22, 1991): D22.
69 *"To Whom it May Concern"*: Charles R. Hulbeck, December 28, 1943. National Archives.
70 *any common interests*: Coincidentally, both had work (under their original names) in *C* magazine, no. 10, February 1965.
70 *persuaded a doctor friend*: Richard Huelsenbeck, *Memoirs of a Dada Drummer* (Berkeley: University of California Press, 1991), 7–8.
71 *Provocatively homosexual*: Alexander Klee, "The Sinister Mopp," in *Oppenheimer—Mahler and the Music* (Vienna: Belvedere, 2010), 73–74.
71 *imbued with homoeroticism*: One such painting, *The Flagellation* of 1913, over six feet tall, a frankly homoerotic, essentially S&M image of four muscular nude men whipping a naked Christ, was on view in Mopp's studio on Sixty-seventh Street. If Jimmy ever visited, he would have seen this arresting picture. Klee, "Sinister," 85–86.
71 *a painting in the first*: Entitled "Modern Art," the painting is now in the collection of the Museum of Modern Art, New York. Oppenheimer's reputation today rests mostly on his portraits of illustrious writers and musicians of the interwar period.
71 *"Every evening"*: Huelsenbeck, *Memoirs*, 19.
72 *his "sexual problems"*: Huelsenbeck, *Memoirs*, 19.
72 *"Homosexuality develops"*: Charles R. Hulbeck, "Emotional Conflicts in Homosexuality," *The American Journal of Psychoanalysis* 8 (1948): 72–73.
72 *"For the average brain"*: Huelsenbeck, *Memoirs*, 53.
72 *As it was, he waited*: Report of Lt. H. V. Snyder, December 29, 1943. National Archives.
73 *"emotionally unstable"*: "Harts Island Used as Prison by Navy," *New York Times* (June 12, 1944): 19.
73 *armed guards*: *NY Times*, "Harts Island."
73 *Prisoners were wakened*: *NY Times*, "Harts Island."
74 *"Across the water lies the shore"*: THB, 4.
74 *"The fairy's here"*: Author interview with Bernard Oshei, June 4, 1996.
74 *"The subject gives a history"*: Lt. Comdr. W. Bromberg to the Commanding Officer, U.S. Naval Receiving Station, Harts Island, NY. January 7, 1944. National Archives.
75 *some of the tests*: Bérubé, *Coming Out*, 152–54.
75 *"I hereby admit"*: "Statement of Ridenour, James Schuyler, 805 47 02 SOM3C USNR," January 19, 1944. National Archives.
76 *traumatic draft interview*: Karin Roffman email to the author, October 13, 2024. Karin Roffman, *The Songs We Know Best* (New York: Farrar, Straus and Giroux, 2017), 133–34.

76 *he told his psychiatrist*: Author interview with Dr. Hyman Weitzen, June 26, 1995.
76 *He also told*: Author interview with Tom Carey, October 3, 1994.
76 *a "disturbed condition"*: Margaret Ridenour to Commanding Officer, USNRS Disciplinary Barracks, Harts Island NY, March 30, 1944. National Archives.
76 *he had "the shakes"*: Author interviews with Fred and Hilde Ridenour, November 8, 2007; October 23, 2012.
77 *She was verbally cruel*: Oshei interview, 1996.
77 *"I am the mother of"*: Margaret Ridenour to Commanding Officer, Harts Island, March 30, 1944. National Archives.
78 *James's letter*: James Schuyler Ridenour to Officer in Charge, Bureau of Naval Personnel, Washington, DC, April 11, 1944. National Archives.
79 *actually written by Margaret*: She certainly typed it, as indicated by her secretarial annotation at the bottom: "JSR:mr."
79 *he was primarily "relieved"*: Schjeldahl 1977.
79 *"Your patriotic offer"*: National Archives.

5. GOSSIP AND OPERA

80 *by late April 1944*: James Schuyler Summary of Interrogation at American Consulate, Florence, Italy, August 19, 1948. U.S. State Department. Courtesy Helen Graham.
80 "my *New York*": James Schuyler to Tom Carey, April 21, 1988. TC Beinecke.
81 *Bill Aalto was a complex*: Most of the following information about Bill Aalto is due to the extensive research of Professor Helen Graham of the Royal Holloway College, University of London, who has included a chapter on Aalto in her book *In the Shadow of Defeat: Radical Lives After the Spanish Civil War*, forthcoming from Cambridge University Press, and has been unstinting in her generosity in sharing her findings with me. See Helen Graham, "The Wars of Bill Aalto: Guerrilla Soldier in Spain, 1937–39," *The Volunteer*, March 21, 2014. https://albavolunteer.org/2014/03/the-wars-of-bill-aalto-guerrilla-soldier-in-spain-1937–39/. I am also grateful to the late Donald Windham, who kindly shared with me an unpublished biography of Aalto, *A Hero of the Left*, by James W. Foss (1984).
82 *Bill and Irving are acknowledged*: See for example David Margolick, "A Hemingway Hero Embraced by Both Sides," *New York Times* (November 2, 2008).
82 *The article described*: "Departing Volunteers Run Rebel Blockade; 2,380 Convoyed from Valencia on 2 Ships," *New York Times* (January 20, 1939): 8.
83 *a trainee froze*: Helen Graham, "Crossing the Lines: Bill Aalto (1915–1958)," in *In the Shadow of Defeat: Radical Lives After the Spanish Civil War* (London: Cambridge University Press, forthcoming).
83 *the winter of 1942–43*: Walter W. Orebaugh, American Consul, Florence, Italy, to Secretary of State, Washington, DC, August 21, 1948. Confidential report of interrogation of James Marcus Schuyler. US State Department. Courtesy Helen Graham.
83 *had been reluctant*: Graham, *In the Shadow*.
84 *whose Italianate steeple*: Author conversation with Dorothy Farnan, October 17, 1995.
84 *"terrible fights"*: Foye 1991.
84 *"A dark / Finn"*: "Dining Out with Doug and Frank," CP, 249.
84 *"always on the defensive"*: Donald Windham, Diary, June 8, 1950. DW Beinecke.
84 *a chip on his shoulder*: Author conversation with Bernard Perlin, March 13, 2010.
85 *"being looked at"*: Author interview with Bernard Oshei, June 4, 1996.

85 *angrily tipping over*: Author interviews with Donald Windham, September 27, 1994, and March 5, 2008. See also Foss, *A Hero of the Left*, 22.

85 *he bodily picked up*: Dorothy Farnan, *Auden in Love* (New York: Simon & Schuster, 1984), 139. Schuyler appears under two different pseudonyms in Farnan's book: as "Ray Schultz" in the '40s when he was going by James Ridenour and living with Aalto ("Bill Armstrong"), and as "Dutch Martell" when he returned from Italy as Schuyler, living with Heilemann ("Charles Henry").

85 *derived from Hurricane Edna*: DJS, 187. The name was in use by at least 1948, six years before the hurricane.

85 *or from the volcano*: Richard Olney, *Reflexions* (New York: Brick Tower Press, 2012).

85 *"Perhaps he'll / bat me"*: "New Year," OF, 93.

85 *"All I ever found"*: Mandeville [box 6, folder 1].

86 *whom he had first*: Schuyler gave several slightly different but not necessarily conflicting accounts of meeting Kallman in interviews. In Foye 1991 (46), it was "through Bill Aalto." In Berrigan 1983, it was through a man he had an affair with while in the navy (who might have been Aalto, David Protetch, or Bill Gilmore). In Schjeldahl 1977, Jimmy was "not quite sure how I met Chester. I was introduced to him first by someone named Bill Gilmore in the Astor Bar." In Thompson 1992 (111), he attributes the connection again to Aalto. It seems safe to say that they met first casually in the Astor Bar and then became close through Aalto.

86 *In 1939, he and his*: Harold Norse, *Memoirs of a Bastard Angel* (New York: William Morrow, 1989), 61–65. See also Humphrey Carpenter, *W. H. Auden: A Biography* (Boston: Houghton Mifflin, 1981), 257.

87 *"with a bottle of red wine"*: Farnan, *Auden*, 91.

87 *a "dim and dusty blue"*: Farnan, *Auden*, 91.

87 *part of the attraction*: Carpenter, *Auden*, 261.

87 *valued Kallman's critical faculties*: James Merrill to Humphrey Carpenter, April 9, 1979. Langdon Hammer and Stephen Yenser, eds., *A Whole World: Letters from James Merrill* (New York: Alfred A. Knopf, 2021), 496.

87 *"the person who most"*: Schjeldahl 1977.

87 *Jimmy later characterized*: Foye 1991, 47; Thompson 1992, 112. The word may have come from Chester himself, who complained in a letter to Auden of a poem he was working on being "constipated." Chester Kallman to W. H. Auden, December 1 [1941], Berg.

88 *"My chief luxury"*: Carpenter, *Auden*, 261.

88 *"When Chester shared with you"*: Farnan, *Auden*, 100.

88 *mounting the stairs*: Author interview with William Weaver, April 3, 1995.

88 *"homosexuality, partygoing and the opera"*: Alan Ansen, *The Vigilantes: A Fragment* (Sudbury, MA: Water Row Press, 1987), 38.

88 *"Chester was really* dedicated": Author interview with John Hohnsbeen, May 16, 1995.

89 *"the first major poet"*: "Wystan Auden," CP, 243.

90 *Chester had a habit*: Author interview with Piero Tosi, December 29, 2005.

90 *parallels between his tumultuous*: Hammer and Yenser, *A Whole World*, 497.

90 *"I've decided that opera"*: Alan Ansen, *The Table Talk of W. H. Auden* (London and Boston: Faber and Faber, 1990), 92.

90 *He compared himself*: Carpenter, *Auden*, 315.

90 *Jimmy instinctively summoned*: James Schuyler to Piero Tosi, June 30 [1950]. Courtesy Helen Graham.

90 *"a very intimidating person"*: Foye 1991, 46.

90 *notably generous*: Edward Mendelson, "The Secret Auden," *New York Review of Books* (March 20, 2014), 4–7.
90 *believed that they had been lovers*: Author correspondence with Helen Burckhardt, via Lukas Burckhardt, February 19, 1996.
90 *"Please thank Jimmy"*: W. H. Auden to Chester Kallman, March 15 [1949]. WHA Berg.
91 *Auden intended to dedicate*: Foye 1991, 46–47.
91 *"Having enlisted in the Navy"*: W. H. Auden, *Collected Poems* (New York: Modern Library, 2007), 448–49.
91 *"The blast killed many"*: Auden, *Collected*, 455.
92 *"webs of . . . sad sound"*: Auden, *Collected*, 454–55.
92 *"The insensible ocean"* (etc.): Auden, *Collected*, 455.
92 *heard Auden's earlier*: In addition, both poems share imagery, and Schuyler's a title, with Marianne Moore's "A Grave" (1922).
93 *"roar"*: "recalling, a war ago, / walking down Third Avenue in New York / with a thin book of his [St. John of the Cross] poems while trains roared." "November," JS, unpublished poem (1960). Mandeville [box 5, folder 21].
93 *"set off a chain reaction"*: Schjeldahl 1977.
93 *His job there*: Little 1993, 158.
93 *"I remember the years"*: CP, 361.
93 *"Now it's tomorrow"*: "Dining Out with Doug and Frank," CP, 245.
93 *"Now, this moment"*: "Linen," CP, 254.
93 *"a kind of crazy place"*: Weaver interview, 1995.
94 *a two-week vacation*: Bill Aalto statement to U.S. Passport Division, Department of State, June 23, 1947. Courtesy Helen Graham.
94 *cabin near Lac St. Jean*: DJS, 33.
94 *"The truth is, the bar here"*: W. H. Auden to Rhoda Jaffe [August 26], 1946. WHA Berg.
95 *"an oasis where carefully-chosen"*: Cyril Connolly, "Introduction," *Horizon*, nos. 93–94 (October 1947): 2.
95 *"At last the luxury of poverty"*: Connolly, "Introduction," 3.
95 *the guests*: Alan Ansen Papers, October 8, 1947. AA Berg.
95 *a slightly different reminiscence*: Cyril Connolly, "Some Memories," in Stephen Spender, ed., *W. H. Auden: A Tribute* (New York: Macmillan, 1975), 73.
95 *"One cannot write about"*: DJS, 124–25.
96 *"two other fairies"*: Alan Ansen, "Bericht über einen musikalischer abend bei Chester Kallman," January 30, 1947. AA Berg.
96 *On a later visit*: Alan Ansen, May 17 [1947]. AA Berg.
96 *"Chester seems to have hit"*: Alan Ansen, May 17 [1947]. AA Berg.
96 *"made up with the sailor"*: Alan Ansen, October 18, 1947. AA Berg.
96 *"They always have vice squad"*: Alan Ansen, April 12, 1947. AA Berg.
97 *"That was when people"*: Ansen, December 10, 1947. AA Berg. *Table Talk*, 89.
97 *"There's a good deal"*: Ansen, October 20, 1947. AA Berg.
97 *"The judge was very nice"*: Ansen, January 19, 1948. AA Berg.
97 *treated with penicillin*: Dr. Giulio G. Jona to JS, January 17, 1949. Mandeville [box 1, folder 9].
97 *It brought $6,000*: Bank of Pocahontas, Arkansas to James M. Schuyler, October 6, 1947. Mandeville [box 19, folder 2].
97 *"goof off and be"*: Hillringhouse 1985, 6.

6. WE ALL LAY ON THE ISLAND BEACH TOGETHER

99 *Jimmy, Bill, Wystan, and Chester*: Alan Ansen, October 20, 1947. AA Berg.
99 *watched the water*: "Hymn to Life," CP, 215.
99 *"It's good to / have"*: CP, 375.
99 *"You're never going to write"*: Author interview with Bernie Oshei, June 4, 1996.
99 *he helped with practical*: Bill Aalto Deposition, August 18, 1948. U.S. State Department. Courtesy Helen Graham.
100 *an "astringent" orchestral*: DJS, 252.
100 *"Amsterdam belongs"*: "Amsterdam," OF, 139.
100 *"free to be a slightly"*: CP, 359.
100 *"all of the towns mentioned"*: John Ashbery to Helen Graham, June 12, 2002. Courtesy Helen Graham.
101 *"Early post-war Italy"*: Sybille Bedford, *Quicksands: A Memoir* (New York: Counterpoint, 2005), 11–12.
101 *"Rome was strange"*: Gore Vidal, *Palimpsest: A Memoir* (New York: Penguin Books, 1996), 150.
101 *The young Americans*: Author interview with Piero Tosi, December 29, 2005.
102 *"Honey, you would love"*: Donald Windham, ed., *Tennessee Williams' Letters to Donald Windham 1940–65* (New York: Penguin, 1980), 207.
102 *"superficial and boring"*: James Schuyler Deposition, August 18, 1948. U.S. State Department. Courtesy Helen Graham.
102 *"He had that facility of rapport"*: Tosi interview, 2005.
103 *their thirst "to know Italy"*: Tosi interview, 2005.
103 *went to Zürich*: Why Zürich? Possibly because penicillin, which was still a relatively new invention in 1947, was unobtainable in Florence. Compare the 1949 movie *The Third Man*.
103 *"with a river in front"*: JS to John Ashbery, October 15, 1958. JA Houghton. JTT, 89.
103 *As we learn*: CP, 301.
104 *"Drunkenly" leaning*: CP, 301.
104 *basking in the knowledge*: CP, 301.
104 *"To walk up to / Bellosguardo"*: CP, 309–10.
104 *It was Downes*: Donald Downes, *The Scarlet Thread* (New York: British Book Centre, 1953), 108.
104 *He became closely*: Franco Zeffirelli, *Zeffirelli* (New York: Weidenfeld & Nicolson, 1986), 77.
104 *"a gentleman of international"*: Tennessee Williams, *Notebooks* (New Haven, CT: Yale University Press, 2006), 472n686.
105 *"both in high and low strata"*: Tennessee Williams, *Memoirs* (New York: New Directions, 2006), 141–42.
105 *a rich gay American*: Bill Aalto Deposition, August 18, 1948. U.S. State Department. Courtesy Helen Graham; author interview with John Ashbery, June 27, 2009.
105 *"giantly ancient cypress"*: CP, 396.
105 *"After the first wild surmise"*: James Schuyler to Kenneth Koch, December 24, 1956. KK Berg.
105 *interview the novelist Elio Vittorini*: Bill Aalto Deposition, August 18, 1948. U.S. State Department. Courtesy Helen Graham.
105 *some American expatriates*: Windham, *Williams' Letters*, 215.

106 *"I get to like Chester"*: Christopher Isherwood, *Diaries Volume One: 1939–1960* (New York: HarperCollins, 1997), 402.
106 *"Italy is pure heaven"*: W. H. Auden to Rhoda Jaffe, May 8 (?), 1948. WHA Berg.
107 *"see all available operas"*: Isherwood, *Diaries*, 402.
107 *"spoke of opera constantly"*: Author interview with Piero Tosi, December 29, 2005.
107 *"Taken outside the entrance"*: JS to Margaret Ridenour, 1948. Ridenour.
107 *In the three weeks*: JS to Edward Mendelson, February 23, 1975. Courtesy Edward Mendelson.
107 *"My dear, I feel like"*: JS to Mendelson, 1975.
108 *"he was, inside"*: Marie-Jacqueline Lancaster, *Brian Howard: Portrait of a Failure* (London: Anthony Blond, 1968), ix.
108 *"an arrogant drunk"*: JS, "We All Lay on the Island Beach Together," OF, 94.
108 *"the most / bored and boring"*: "A few days," CP, 368.
108 *"one of the loveliest"*: W. H. Auden to Rhoda Jaffe, May 30, 1948. WHA Berg. Carpenter, *Auden*, 357.
109 *"blue skies, lemons"*: Sam Langford to Lura Howard, May 26, 1948. Eton College Library, Eton College, Windsor, UK.
109 *It was now that*: Carpenter, *Auden*, 357.
109 *One day Brian*: JS to Mendelson, 1975. See also Lancaster, *Howard*, 492–93.
109 *"My thanks are for you"*: "Ischia," W. H. Auden, *Collected Poems* (New York: Modern Library, 2007), 541.
109 *"though," he wrote*: Lancaster, *Howard*, 492.
109 *"They turn to face the sun"*: Lancaster, *Howard*, 598.
109 *We All Lay on the Island Beach Together*: Mandeville [box 5, folder 22]. This version differs slightly in punctuation from that published in OF, 94.
110 *Auden hated it*: W. H. Auden to Rhoda Jaffee, June 24, 1948. WHA Berg.
110 *"Lady Howard," "Madame Kallman"*: Frederic Prokosch, *Voices: A Memoir* (New York: Farrar, Straus and Giroux, 1983), 213.
110 *"a handsome young man"*: Prokosch was surely unaware that Aalto had reviewed his war novel, *Age of Thunder*, in *New Masses* in 1945, where he wrote disparagingly, "Prokosch's sentences drip. The entire journey of the hero to freedom in Switzerland occurs in a ghastly light generated by the author's style." *New Masses* (May 29, 1945): 28.
111 *"hidden from Positano"*: Zeffirelli, *Zeffirelli*, 81.
111 *Chester paused to*: "The Crystal Lithium," CP, 118.
111 *the house had three bedrooms*: Carpenter, *Auden*, 360.
111 *"less than 3 months rent"*: W. H. Auden to Rhoda Jaffe, July 6 [1948]. WHA Berg. Carpenter, *Auden*, 360.
111 *One night at Caffè*: Tosi interview, 2005.
112 *"whose striped churches"*: JS to Kenneth Koch, January, 1957. KK Berg. JTT, 71.
112 *separate written depositions*: U.S. Department of State, documents declassified November 20, 2001, under Freedom of Information Act. Courtesy Helen Graham.
112 *Bill had long since*: Helen Graham, "Crossing the Lines: Bill Aalto (1915–1958)," in *In the Shadow of Defeat: Radical Lives After the Spanish Civil War* (London: Cambridge University Press, forthcoming).
112 *"If the embassy of our country"*: JS, "A Brief Account of My Time in Italy," Enclosure no. 4, Despatch no. 218 from the American Consulate to the State Department, Washington, DC, August 18, 1948. U.S. State Department. Courtesy Helen Graham.
113 *"Mr. Schuyler appears to be"*: Walter W. Orebaugh, American Consul, Florence, Italy, to

the Secretary of State, Washington, DC, "Confidential," August 21, 1948. U.S. State Department. Courtesy Helen Graham.

113 *"Poor Bill and Jim"*: W. H. Auden to Rhoda Jaffe, July 6 [1948], WHA Berg.

113 *wrote back on September 20*: Senator Ferruccio Pari to Donald Downes, September 20, 1948, Enclosure No. 1 to Despatch No. 233 from the American Consulate, Florence, Italy, "Refusal of Residence Permits for Italy to William Eric AALTO and James Marcus SCHUYLER, Alleged Communists." U.S. State Department. Courtesy Helen Graham.

113 *In retaliation*: Helen Graham, "Crossing."

114 *they all dined together*: Donald Windham, *1948: Italy* (Verona: Sandy Campbell, 1998), 63, 65.

114 *a formal letter*: Avv. Francesco Maria Cerboni to JS, October 10, 1948. Mandeville [box 1, folder 9].

114 *mad concatenation*: Windham, *1948*, 75–76.

7. MEN ARE SUCH BOYS

115 *Set off from Via*: Humphrey Carpenter, *W. H. Auden: A Biography* (Boston: Houghton Mifflin, 1981), 360.

116 *such an "agony"*: JS, "Bombshell," typescript, Mandeville [box 7, folder 3].

116 *In late November*: See JS's unpublished poem, "Rome, December 1948." HM Berg.

116 *declaiming in his basso profondo*: Author conversation with James McCourt, January 4, 2006.

116 *"monstrous- / ly real, obscene"*: "Rome, December 1948."

116 *"tangled bob-wire"*: "Rome, December 1948."

116 *"I do hope"*: W. H. Auden to Chester Kallman, December 6, 1948. WHA Berg.

117 *"I am very glad"*: W. H. Auden to Chester Kallman, December 13, 1948. WHA Berg.

117 *drinking brought out*: JS interview with Peter Carroll, October 19, 1989. Courtesy Helen Graham.

118 *"When [Bill] was drunk"*: Dorothy Farnan, *Auden in Love* (New York: Simon & Schuster, 1984), 140.

118 *"Men are such boys"*: JS, "Chester Kallman," *Court Green* 9 (2012): 38.

118 *"any reference" to those frightening*: Farnan, *Auden*, 141.

118 *"Dear Jimmy, Just an immediate"*: W. H. Auden to JS, February 7, 1949. WHA Berg.

119 *"What do Bill and Jim respectively"*: W. H. Auden to Chester Kallman, February 13 [1949]. WHA Berg.

119 *"My desires are"*: W. H. Auden to Chester Kallman [February 21, 1949]. WHA Berg.

119 *"I want you or Jimmy"*: W. H. Auden to Chester Kallman, February 24 [1949]. WHA Berg.

119 *Auden sent the five hundred*: W. H. Auden to JS, March 3 [1949]. Mandeville.

119 *they lived a hand-to-mouth*: Bill Aalto to JS, March 28, 1951. Mandeville [box 14, folder 18].

120 *"Please do not give my address"*: JS to Piero Tosi, June 30 [1950]. Courtesy Helen Graham. Translation by the author.

120 *He was given a military*: James W. Foss, *A Hero of the Left*, 60.

120 *Jimmy did not go*: "Dining Out with Doug and Frank," CP, 248.

121 *"The English-speaking colony"*: Donald Windham, ed., *Tennessee Williams' Letters to Donald Windham 1940–65* (New York: Penguin, 1980), 237–38.

122 *"Jimmy ca-n't ca-atch"*: Author interview with Tom Carey, October 3, 1994.

122 *"the strangest, most haunting"*: Gerald Clarke, ed., *Too Brief a Treat: The Letters of Truman Capote* (New York: Random House, 2004), 72.
122 *"Well, that is a story"*: Clarke, *Too Brief*, 74.
123 *The next day was Easter*: W. H. Auden to Wayne Cogswell, April 19 [1949]. WHA Berg.
123 *"The only emotional problems"*: WHA to Rhoda Jaffe, May 17, 1949. WHA Berg.
123 *"In the house are"*: W. H. Auden to Wayne Cogswell, May 2 [1949]. WHA Berg.
125 *One day Auden and Jimmy*: JS to Edward Mendelson, February 23, 1975; also Little 1993, 160.
125 *"pottering shades"*: "Under Sirius," W. H. Auden, *Collected Poems* (New York: Modern Library, 2007), 544.
125 *Another time, Capote*: Little 1993, 160.
125 *"an act of friendship"*: Berrigan 1983.
125 *"I'm earning my pin-money"*: JS to Margaret Ridenour, May 11, 1949. Ridenour.
126 *which have been dated*: Edward Mendelson, ed., *W. H. Auden, Collected Poems* (New York: Modern Library, 2007).
126 *"almost the entire manuscript"*: JS to Mendelson, 1975; Schjeldahl 1977.
126 *"Well, if this is poetry"*: Little 1993, 161.
126 *"awed by the technical intricacy"*: Schjeldahl 1977.
126 *"It was very liberating"*: Thompson 1992, 112.
126 *"the experience of so"*: JS, John Simon Guggenheim Memorial Foundation application, October 10, 1969. John Simon Guggenheim Memorial Foundation Records.
127 *"an established poet"*: W. H. Auden, "Making, Knowing and Judging," *The Dyer's Hand and Other Essays* (New York: Vintage Books, 1968), 37.
127 *"Rather amusing"*: Truman Capote to Andrew Lyndon, May 8, 1949; Clarke, *Too Brief*, 83.
127 *"I have* never *seen"*: JS to Windham, June 23, [1949].
127 *"They say she's"*: CP, 260.
128 *a brief encounter*: Author conversation with JS, per author diary, December 28, 1990. Green was known as "Julien" in France but as "Julian" in the United States, where he lived for many years. Schuyler read him in translation as "Julian," which is how I refer to him here for consistency.
128 *Jimmy's "dazzling" beauty*: Author phone interview with John Richardson, February 9, 2005.
128 *"intense, rough sex"*: Richardson interview, 2005.
129 *"a huge part"*: Richardson interview, 2005.
129 *"Don't stop," said Jimmy*: John Richardson, *The Sorcerer's Apprentice* (London: Jonathan Cape, 1999), 62.
129 *"everybody was fucking"*: Richardson interview, 2005.
129 *Jimmy and Wystan's relationship*: Richardson interview, 2005.
130 *"We hit it off right away"*: Author interview with Morris Golde, April 27, 1995.

8. SALUTE

131 *"somewhat strained relations"*: Schjeldahl 1977.
132 *"the most* unlikely *person"*: Author interview with John Hohnsbeen, May 16, 1995.
132 *He resented the cooler*: W. H. Auden to Chester Kallman, December 27 [1949]. WHA Berg.
132 *"Have not seen Jimmy and Charlie"*: W. H. Auden to Chester Kallman, January 6 [1950]. WHA Berg.

132 *"giving my birthday party"*: W. H. Auden to Chester Kallman, February 17 [1950]. WHA Berg.
133 *good with his hands*: Author interview with Jane Freilicher, February 1, 2005.
133 *"utterly unscrupulous and awful"*: Schjeldahl 1977.
133 *a difficult employer*: W. H. Auden to Chester Kallman, March 7 [1950]. WHA Berg.
133 *Kleemann, he said*: James Schuyler to Piero Tosi, June 30 [1950]. Courtesy Helen Graham.
133 *other shady practices*: Author interview with Tom Carey, July 9, 2004.
133 *Charles fell asleep "in protest"*: W. H. Auden to Chester Kallman, March 7 [1950]. WHA Berg.
133 *In a letter to Tosi*: JS to Tosi, 1950.
134 *"Our closest period"*: Author interview with John Hohnsbeen, May 16, 1995.
134 *"sort-of an affair"*: Schjeldahl 1977.
134 *"New York, that terrible city"*: JS to Tosi, 1950.
134 *The new apartment*: Author interview with Waldeman Hansen, April 6, 2005.
135 *"a minor work"*: JS to Edward Mendelson, February 23, 1975. Courtesy Edward Mendelson.
135 *"He sort of looked at the first"*: Little 1993, 175.
135 *"He was very astute"*: Little 1993, 161.
135 *"very good endings"*: Berrigan 1983.
135 *"In White, Like a Bride"*: JS submission list, University of Illinois Archives, J. Kerker Quinn Papers [box 17, folder: Schram-Shawgo].
135 *seven poems*: The titles were "Things Seen," "Amalfi," "Amsterdam," "Mountain Crossroads," "Off Key West," "Not Here," "Evening." Submission list, University of Illinois.
136 *"I offer a bunch of pansies"*: D. H. Lawrence, *Poems Volume I* ([London?]: Heron Books in association with William Heinemann, 1964), 424.
136 *The three stories printed*: *Accent: A Quarterly of New Literature* (Urbana, IL, Summer 1951): 149–52.
138 *"You never* told *me"*: Schjeldahl 1977.
139 *"Garbo-esque simple beauty"*: Author conversation with Edith Schloss, December 30, 2005.
139 *"looked a lot like Julie Harris"*: Author telephone conversation with Jeremiah Goodman, June 17, 2009.
139 *In later recollections*: Schjeldahl 1977.
139 *"a gay salon"*: Joe LeSueur, *Digressions on Some Poems by Frank O'Hara: A Memoir* (New York: Farrar, Straus and Giroux, 2003), 41.
140 *"a little drunk"*: Schjeldahl 1977.
140 *In his recollection*: Author interviews with John Ashbery, January 26, 1995, and July 22, 2004.
140 *"whether a serious artist"*: Schjeldahl 1977.
140 *"But that was never a problem"*: Schjeldahl 1977.
141 *To Hohnsbeen's surprise*: Author interview with John Hohnsbeen, May 16, 1995. Hohnsbeen recalled that the encounter took place at the Kleemann Gallery, but by this time Schuyler was probably no longer working there and it is more likely that he visited John at the Buchholz Gallery.
141 *"very important" to tell him*: Author interview with Donald Windham, September 27, 1994. Also Windham Diary, October 23, 1951. DW Beinecke.
142 *"a rather cryptic description"*: Hillringhouse 1985, 11.
142 *"One afternoon there"*: THB, 1.
143 *Auden footed the bill*: Hohnsbeen interview, 1995.

143 *"braiding belts and Indian"*: Hohnsbeen interview, 1995.
143 *"when I get out of here"*: JS to John Hohnsbeen, December 9, 1951.
143 *boxing lessons*: JS to John Hohnsbeen, November 15, 1951. JTT, 3.
143 *his most "entrancing"*: JS to Howard Moss, December 4, "perhaps" [1951]. HM Berg.
143 *"Quite a bunch of"*: Helen Burckhardt to author, via Lukas Burckhardt, February 19, 1996.
143 *"Whatever it was it happened"*: JS to Howard Moss, November 27 [1951]. HM Berg.
144 *"If you look at ["Salute"]"*: Schjeldahl 1977.
144 *"the only writing"*: JS to Moss, November 27 [1951]. HM Berg.
145 *"one of the Young Harvard"*: JS to Moss, "Monday" [December 1951]. HM Berg.
145 *"I'm pleased about the poem"*: JS to Moss, December 31, 1951. HM Berg.
145 *Jimmy eventually received*: New American Writing Papers, NAW Beinecke.
145 *"The selections are devotedly serious"*: "Books: The Better Things," *Time*, May 12, 1952. https://time.com/archive/6608751/books-the-better-things/.
146 *"At the Beach"*: The fact that the manuscript for "At the Beach" is not with Schuyler's letters to Moss, or in the *New Yorker* Archive, also housed at the NYPL, does not necessarily rule out the possibility that it, too, could have been sent to Moss at this time.
146 *"always had a ready"*: DJS, 216.
147 *Eileen Myles points out*: Eileen Myles, *The Importance of Being Iceland: Travel Essays in Art* (Los Angeles: Semiotext(e), 2009), 204.
149 *"ever so much better"*: W. H. Auden to Chester Kallman, December 24 [1951]. WHA Berg.
149 *"It was decided in the hospital"*: Schjeldahl 1977.
149 *"somewhat to mutual regret"*: Schjeldahl 1977.
150 *Preston learned*: Schjeldahl 1977. See also JS to Howard Moss, December 31 [1951]. HM Berg.
150 *"I can't think where"*: JS to Howard Moss, "Wed." [January 1951]. HM Berg.
150 *Jimmy, according to Donald*: Donald Windham Diary, January 15, 1952. DW Beinecke.

9. I WAS A POET

151 *"Both John and Frank"*: Schjeldahl 1977.
151 *"Let's face it"*: Brad Gooch, *City Poet: The Life and Times of Frank O'Hara* (New York: Alfred A. Knopf, 1993), 136.
153 *"kind of cobble everything"*: Gooch, *City Poet*, 188.
153 *peripheral to his life*: Charles Heilemann left Parsons in the late 1960s to establish the interior design department at F.I.T. He is sometimes remembered for his watercolor illustrations of interiors, which appeared in magazines mid-century. He died in 1976 and was given a military funeral at Long Island National Cemetery in East Farmingdale, the same cemetery where Bill Aalto was buried in 1958.
153 *"I had never really gone out"*: Schjeldahl 1977.
154 *the "bird circuit"*: Charles Kaiser, *The Gay Metropolis: The Landmark History of Gay Life in America* (New York: Grove Paperback, 2019), 106.
154 *already having an affair*: Author interview with John Ashbery, January 26, 1995.
154 *"the color of silvery parchment"*: CP, 289.
154 *he spoke in a "whisper"*: Author interview with Angelo Torricini, January 19, 2005.
154 *"the most interesting"*: Edith Schloss, *The Loft Generation* (New York: Farrar, Straus and Giroux, 2021), 33.
154 *Denby's loft*: Schloss, *Loft*, 36–37.

155 *having "second feelings"*: Ashbery interview, 1995.
155 *Jimmy told Jane Freilicher*: Author interview with Jane Freilicher and Joe Hazan, October 18, 1994.
155 *"I loved Edwin"*: JS to Rudy Burckhardt, October "3 or 4," 1985. Courtesy Yvonne Jacquette.
155 *"like having an x-ray"*: DJS, 122.
155 *"a vulnerable spot"*: Anne Waldman, email to the author, August 10, 2024.
156 *a series of "dramatic occasions"*: Kenneth Koch, "James Schuyler (Very Briefly)," *Denver Quarterly* 24, no. 4 (Spring 1990): 21–22.
156 *leading Jimmy*: Schjeldahl 1977.
157 *The first time Jimmy visited*: JS, "Frank O'Hara: Poet Among Painters," in Bill Berkson and Joe LeSueur, eds., *Homage to Frank O'Hara* (Bolinas, CA: Big Sky Books, 1988), 82.
157 *"going to parties"*: Joe LeSueur, *Digressions on Some Poems by Frank O'Hara: A Memoir* (New York: Farrar, Straus and Giroux, 2003), 47.
157 *"part of life"*: LeSueur, *Digressions*, 47.
157 *Jimmy recalled an occasion*: JS, "O'Hara" in *Homage*, 82–83.
157 *"He always had charm"*: Schjeldahl 1977.
157 *"John always made me feel"*: Schjeldahl 1977.
158 *"everybody considered him"*: Author interview with John Ashbery, July 22, 2004.
158 *often taking walks*: Ashbery interview, July 22, 2004.
158 *Vanderbilt was a "generous"*: Schjeldahl 1977.
158 *a club-like atmosphere*: Author interview with Joe LeSueur, December 6, 1994; author phone interview with Gerrit Lansing, June 2, 2011.
158 *"How delightful"*: DJS, 205–206.
159 *it inspired a line*: Ashbery interview, July 22, 2004.
159 *whose coy expressions*: John Ashbery to JS, October 14 [1959].
159 *"Rome, December 1948"*: HM Berg.
159 *"Marie, Marie, hold on"*: Schjeldahl 1977.
160 *Jimmy cited his line*: Little 1993, 167.
160 *particularly "the greats"*: JS to Donald Allen, September 20 [1959]. JTT, 109.
160 *"I doubt if any very"*: JS to Allen [1959].
161 *"Marianne Moore and Elizabeth Bishop"*: Ross 1981, 1.
161 *"There were so many"*: Author interview with John Ashbery, January 26, 1995.
161 *"New York poets"*: JS, "Poet and Painter Overture," in Donald Allen, *The New American Poetry* (New York: Grove Press, 1960), 418.
161 *"The next line"*: Little 1993, 171.
161 *soon Jimmy and his friends*: Schjeldahl 1977.
161 *Jimmy heard both Frank*: JS to Donald Allen, "Notes on Frank O'Hara Poems," August 12, 1969: typescript, Mandeville [box 9, folder 14].
162 *Guest's poems had caught*: Karin Roffman, *The Songs We Know Best* (New York: Farrar, Straus and Giroux, 2021), 281n36.
162 *"the kind of non-committal trance"*: JS to Allen, "Notes on O'Hara."
162 *offended by the reference*: Little 1993, 159.
162 *On that or another*: Schjeldahl 1977.
162 *his first and longest*: The play, thought lost for many years, was rediscovered in the papers of Julian Beck in the NYPL, Berg Collection.
162 *The original title*: Author interview with John Ashbery, June 3, 2006.
163 *Michael Brownstein observed*: Author interview with Michael Brownstein, May 8, 2012.

163 *"just sat down"*: Author interview with John Ashbery, July 22, 2004.
163 *in early 1951*: Gooch, *City Poet*, 171.
163 *Poets' Theatre's first performance*: Gooch, *City Poet*, 180.
163 *"a madly funny pair"*: Judith Malina, *The Diaries of Judith Malina 1947–1957* (New York: Grove Press, 1984), 210; Roffman, *Songs*, 204.
163 *influenced him "immediately"*: JS to Allen, "Notes on O'Hara."
164 *"sort of a Dada play"*: Schjeldahl 1977.
166 *initially rather displeased*: Author interview with Kenneth Koch, May 9, 1995.
166 *When John and Frank appeared*: Schjeldahl 1977.
166 *not as much*: Schjeldahl 1977.
166 *"I thought our little crowd"*: Koch interview, May 9, 1995.
166 *"It was one of the great"*: Koch interview, May 9, 1995.
166 *"hearing about homosexual"*: Koch interview, May 9, 1995.
166 *John did not tell Kenneth*: Koch interview, May 9, 1995. However, Ashbery told Karin Roffman that he did tell Kenneth he was gay in 1947 when Koch was proposing him as literary editor of *The Harvard Advocate*, but Kenneth ignored it or didn't believe him. Karin Roffman, email to the author, October 13, 2024. See Roffman, *Songs*, 147 and 269–70n81.
167 *"Janice loved Jimmy"*: Koch interview, May 9, 1995.
167 *Latouche originally*: Author interview with Harrison Starr, May 12, 2014.
167 *the house included*: Schjeldahl 1977.
168 *"I suppose there has never"*: Schjeldahl 1977.
168 *"I think that John Latouche"*: Author interview with Jane Freilicher, February 1, 2005.
168 *"a lot of ladies' dresses"*: Schjeldahl 1977.
168 *a Halloween party*: See *The Grand Surprise: The Journals of Leo Lerman* (New York: Alfred A. Knopf, 2007), 130–31. Although a Maya Deren film was the main event, Jane Freilicher's presence may indicate that *Presenting Jane* was also screened.
169 *"a cold rich snob"*: Schjeldahl 1977.
169 *Porter "suddenly exploded"*: Schjeldahl 1977.
169 *"I'll put you to bed"*: Schjeldahl 1977.
169 *"it was fun writing them"*: Schjeldahl 1977. The two poems were published in Anne Waldman, ed., *The World Anthology: Poems from the Saint Mark's Poetry Project* (Indianapolis and New York: Bobbs-Merrill, 1969), 101–102.
169 *"It was Jimmy"*: Author interview with John Ashbery, August 13, 2004.
170 *"Alice was tired"*: NN, 9.
170 *"looking out the window"*: Foye 1991, 46.
171 *"In among the dunes"*: THB, 49.
171 *Jimmy knew most*: Edith Schloss, "Jimmy's Silences," unpublished reminiscence.
171 *a sixth-floor*: Author interview with John Ashbery, June 27, 2009. See also LeSueur, *Digressions*, xiv; Gooch, *O'Hara*, 192–93.
171 *"the nicest thing"*: Ashbery interview, June 27, 2009.
172 *"That really is the beginning"*: Schjeldahl 1977.
172 *"exhibit his prize"*: Author interview with John Ashbery, July 22, 2004.
172 *"very interested in each other"*: Ashbery interview, July 22, 2004.
172 *"Le Weekend"*: OF, 64.
173 *"Dear Jimmie, This surprises me"*: Quoted by JS in a letter to Arthur Gold, "Friday night or Saturday morning [April 17–18, 1953]. Gold Fizdale.
173 *"Absolutely everyone"*: JS to Arthur Gold, December 7 [1952]. Gold Fizdale.

10. MUSIC, SWIMMING AT NIGHT, PLAYS, POEMS, LOVE AND QUARRELS

174 *a quadruple bill*: John Bernard Myers, *Tracking the Marvelous: A Life in the New York Art World* (New York: Random House, 1983), 166; Frank O'Hara, *Selected Plays* (New York: Full Court Press, 1978), 311.

174 *"nervous excitement"*: Judith Malina, *The Diaries of Judith Malina 1947–1957* (New York: Grove Press, 1984), 270.

174 *"horrible thanks to Herbert"*: CP, 378.

174 *"he didn't have a* clue*"*: Author interview with Tony Towle, February 9, 2012.

174 *"I long to see Judith"*: JS to Julian Beck and Judith Malina, April 24 [1953]. Uncatalogued Berg.

175 *"Half the valid music"*: Author interview with Ned Rorem, March 29, 2005.

175 *"[Gold] was snippy"*: Author interview with Bernard Perlin, March 13, 2010.

175 *Fizdale* "seemed *much nicer"*: Author interview with John Ashbery, July 22, 2004.

175 *"Arthur . . . was the stern one"*: Author interview with Kenneth Koch, May 9, 1995.

176 *"I know who I want"*: JS to Arthur Gold, April 13, 1953. Gold Fizdale.

176 *"much the best"*: JS to Arthur Gold, April 16 [1953]. An excerpt from the performance can be heard at "Martha Flowers sings 'Come scoglio'—Live, 1953," YouTube, https://www.youtube.com/watch?v=kr8PotLpfDY.

176 *Even the catalogue*: JS to Arthur Gold, April 15 [1953]. Gold Fizdale.

176 *a one-page Dada play*: JS to Arthur Gold, April 15 [1953]. Gold Fizdale.

177 *could have been aware*: An (unattributed) article by Brendan Gill pointing out his dual identities appeared in *The New Yorker* on January 27, 1945.

177 *collaborated on a literally*: The unsigned poem (which appears as the frontispiece to Karin Roffman's *The Songs We Know Best*) was included in a letter from John Ashbery to Bobby Fizdale, October 20, 1952. Ashbery told Karin Roffman that it had been a collaboration. Roffman 213. Gold Fizdale.

177 *"I like an art"*: JS to Miss Batie, March 25, 1969. Mandeville. JTT, 239.

177 *Two mid-'50s works*: Little 1993, 179.

178 *"He was very white"*: Edith Schloss, *The Loft Generation*, early draft, unpublished page proofs, 91. Author interview with Edith Schloss, December 30, 2005. Schloss was under the impression it was John Ashbery whom Edwin was jealous of and hit, but Ashbery was never sexually involved with Schuyler, and confirmed that Edwin, though angry with him, never hit him. Author interview with John Ashbery, June 3, 2006.

178 *Gold told Joe LeSueur*: Author interview with Joe LeSueur, December 6, 1994.

178 *"The blazing sun"*: Edwin Denby, *The Complete Poems*, ed. Ron Padgett (New York: Random House, 1986), 121. See Mary Maxwell, "Edwin Denby's New York School," *The Yale Review* 95, no. 4 (October 2007): 65–96.

178 *an angry phone call*: Author interview with John Ashbery, June 3, 2006.

178 *Edwin "went berserk"*: Author interview with Jane Freilicher and Joe Hazan, October 18, 1994.

178 *"He could be extremely unpleasant"*: Author interview with John Ashbery, July 22, 2004.

179 *a pair of pier glasses*: Schjeldahl 1977.

179 *wasn't "included"*: Schjeldahl 1977.

179 *At breakfast the next morning*: Schjeldahl 1977.

180 *"some Rachmaninoff or Liszt"*: Schjeldahl 1977.

180 *"I didn't know Fairfield"*: Schjeldahl 1977.

181 *"how ravishing Jane looked"*: Schjeldahl 1977.

181 *"the most brilliant driver"*: Schjeldahl 1977.
181 *"What a very good time"*: Schjeldahl 1977.
181 *"warm and rather tearful"*: Schjeldahl 1977.
181 *"reminded her of friends"*: James Schuyler, "Fall," 1960. Mandeville [box 7, folder 8].
182 *"like Pierrots and that kind"*: Schjeldahl 1977.
182 *"entrancingly warm"*: Frank O'Hara to Bobby Fizdale, November 3, 1953. Gold Fizdale.
182 *Fairfield Porter was born*: For information on Fairfield Porter and his family I am indebted to Justin Spring's biography, *Fairfield Porter: A Life in Art* (New Haven: Yale University Press, 1999).
183 *In 1955, she would convert*: Spring gives 1954 (178), but epistolary evidence points to June 1955: (Frank O'Hara to Kenneth Koch, June 23, 1955, KK Berg; JS to Fairfield Porter, June 30 [1955], AAA). Only two people told Anne they were happy for her at the time: James Schuyler and "a ninety-year-old Episcopal lady who lived down the street" in Southampton. Author interview with Anne Porter, May 5, 2004.
183 *"very domestic and very quiet"*: Author interview with Ron and Pat Padgett, February 1, 1995.
183 *Fairfield was "relieved"*: Spring, *Porter*, 86.
183 *"poured himself out"*: Author interview with Anne Porter, May 5, 2004.
184 *a serious extramarital love affair*: See Spring, *Porter*, 133–51.
185 *He began writing*: Fairfield Porter, *The Collected Poems with Selected Drawings* (New York: Tibor de Nagy Editions, 1985). The book includes one poem dated 1930–31 but the rest are undated, and most were written after meeting the New York poets and painters in 1952 (Little 1993, 166). Fairfield became especially adept at the sestina form.
185 *suggested that he should try*: Hillringhouse 1985, 12.
185 *"the rhymes, the writing"*: Schjeldahl 1977.
185 *"very easy to do"*: Thompson 1992, 114.
186 *"If I Could Tell You"*: Edward Mendelson, ed., *W. H. Auden, Collected Poems* (New York: Modern Library, 2007), 312.
186 *later mimeographed typescript*: Courtesy Christopher Foss.
186 *a strong case*: Wayne Koestenbaum, *My 1980s & Other Essays* (New York: Farrar, Straus and Giroux, 2013), 107.
187 *"Have you written* anything*"*: Little 1993, 180.
187 *"no diminishment of enjoyment"*: JS to Frank O'Hara, January 15, 1954. O'Hara. JSFOH, 2.
187 *The two works*: The album cover features an amusing illustration incorporating photographs of all the principals, and on the back Schuyler's full text. Schuyler sometimes categorized this on his CV as his first "book" publication.
187 *"bright enough to matter"*: Paul Bowles to Tennessee Williams, March 28, 1954. Jeffrey Miller, ed., *In Touch: The Letters of Paul Bowles* (New York: Farrar, Straus and Giroux, 1994), 254.
188 *"This sophisticated and rather"*: *Musical Courier* (April 14, 1954).
188 *"the Bowles Cantata"*: Frank O'Hara to Ned Rorem, April 20, 1954. Dodd.
188 *an "exchange of affection"*: Frank O'Hara to Jane Freilicher [c. March 26, 1954]. JF Houghton.
188 *Thomson's belief*: Virgil Thomson, *Virgil Thomson* (New York: Da Capo Press, 1967), 217, 231, 239, 241–42.
188 *"very much aware"*: Author phone interview with Martha Flowers, June 29, 2005.

189 *at pains later*: JS to Dan Wickenden, December 19 [1956], JTT, 65–66.
189 *"scarcely more than"*: Richard H. Ullman, "Four Plays on a Plain Stage," *Harvard Crimson* (March 26, 1954).
190 *another of his helpful*: Author interview with John Ashbery, July 22, 2004.
190 *With Gold's support*: Hillringhouse 1985, 7.
190 *"Mostly it was a weather report"*: Author telephone interview with Grace Hartigan, January 24, 2005.
190 *"Arthur and I liked visiting"*: JS to Fairfield and Anne Porter, June 24 [1954]. AAA.
191 *"the implied story"*: JS to Fairfield Porter, "Bastille Day Eve" [July 13, 1954]. AAA. JTT, 7–8.
191 *"I keep forgetting"*: JS to Porter [July 13, 1954]. AAA. JTT, 8.
191 *"very beautiful, especially"*: JS to Fairfield Porter, October 16 [1954]. AAA. JTT, 9.
192 *"You didn't* visit*"*: CP, 13–14.
192 *"I'm really so foolishly"*: JS to Frank O'Hara, "Tuesday" [August 31, 1954]. O'Hara. JSFOH, 12.
192 *"It's marvelous to have"*: JS to Frank O'Hara, October 8, 1954. O'Hara. JSFOH, 18.
192 *"I am so delighted"*: JS to Fairfield Porter, September 27, 1954. AAA.
192 *"Venice itself"*: JS to Fairfield Porter, October 16, 1954. AAA. JTT, 9.
193 *"looked so much 'quieter'"*: JS to Frank O'Hara, "Tuesday" [1954]. O'Hara. JSFOH, 31.
193 *"I meant my gloom"*: JS to Jane Freilicher, November 3, 1954. JF Houghton. JTT, 11.
193 *"the cheeriest thing"*: JS to Jane Freilicher, November 9 [1954]. JF Houghton.
193 *"I met Respighi's"*: JS to Frank O'Hara, "Tuesday" [1954]. O'Hara. JSFOH, 30.
194 *"finally a feeling"*: JS to Fairfield Porter, December 2 [1954]. AAA. JTT, 14.
194 *"A Head"*: Dated on the typescript "11/29/54 // Villa Aurelia Rome." Mandeville.
194 *apparently precipitated*: Schuyler said that Frank first showed him "Poem" ("There I could never be a boy") in February 1955, after he had returned from Italy. JS to Donald Allen, "Notes on Frank O'Hara Poems," August 12, 1969, Mandeville [box 9, folder 14].
194 *"The boy who walks"*: O'Hara. JSFOH, 15–16.
194 *"I like writing"*: JS to Fairfield Porter, December 2 [1954]. AAA. JTT, 14.
195 *a sestina, "Genoa"*: Fairfield Porter, *The Collected Poems with Selected Drawings* (New York: Tibor de Nagy Editions, 1985), 60–61.
195 *"as beautiful as any work"*: JS to Fairfield Porter, January 3, 1955. AAA. JTT, 15.
195 *"squat temples"*: JS, "Reciprocity," Mandeville [box 5, folder 28].
195 *"My impressions of Sicily"*: JS to Fairfield Porter, January 3, 1955. AAA. JTT, 15.

11. BETWEEN THESE LINES I WRITE YOUR NAME

196 *social events almost every*: See JS appointment book, Mandeville [box 8, folder 3].
196 *"new ease, a directness"*: JS to Fairfield Porter, "Thursday" [February 17, 1955]. AAA.
196 *the "first thing"*: JS to Barbara Guest, July 7 [1955]. JTT, 21.
196 *"turned out laborious"*: JS to Miss Batie, March 25, 1969. JTT, 240. Mandeville.
197 *They both "made fun"*: Schjeldahl 1977.
197 *An account of its writing*: JS to Batie. JTT, 239–40.
197 *"Often a poem 'happens'"*: JS to Batie. JTT, 240.
198 *"In Rivers language"*: JS to Guest, July 7 [1955]. JTT, 20.
198 *"the most musical poet"*: Little 1993, 181.
198 *"blind rests the night"*: "The Setting of the Moon," OF, 196.
198 *Jimmy identified*: He was undoubtedly familiar with Iris Origo's biography, *Leopardi: A Study in Solitude* (London: Hamish Hamilton, 1953).

198 *"Distraction: An Ode"*: OF, 24.
198 *"enjoying a domesticity"*: John Ashbery to Kenneth Koch, April 13, 1955. Berg.
199 *Jimmy advised Frank*: Frank O'Hara to JS, February 11, 1956, in William Corbett and Geoffrey Young, eds., *That Various Field for James Schuyler* (Great Barrington, MA: The Figures, 1991), 14; JS to Donald Allen, "Notes on Frank O'Hara Poems," August 12, 1969: typescript, Mandeville [box 9, folder 14].
199 *"clippers, pruners"*: O'Hara to JS, *Various Field*, 14.
199 *a certain amount of intrigue*: See Karin Roffman, *The Songs We Know Best* (New York: Farrar, Straus and Giroux, 2021), 236.
199 *"The Instruction Manual"*: John Ashbery, *Collected Poems 1956–1987* (New York: Library of America, 2008), 5.
199 *a letter to Kenneth Koch*: JS to Kenneth Koch, August 15 [1955]. KK Berg. JTT, 21.
199 *They were not lovers*: Joe LeSueur, *Digressions on Some Poems by Frank O'Hara* (New York: Farrar, Straus and Giroux, 2003), 50.
200 *Great Spruce Head*: Justin Spring, *Fairfield Porter: A Life in Art* (New Haven, CT: Yale University Press, 1999), 15–20.
200 *"chafed, constipated, cranky"*: JS to Frank O'Hara, July 26, 1955. O'Hara. JSFOH, 41.
201 *"Little did I suspect"*: JS to Tom Carey, May 28, 1988. TC Beinecke.
201 *"one of the most beautiful"*: JS to Frank O'Hara, July 18, 1955. O'Hara. JSFOH, 38.
201 *"A week here"*: JS to Frank O'Hara, July 28, 1955. O'Hara. JSFOH, 40.
201 *"I won't attempt"*: JS to Frank O'Hara, July 18, 1955. O'Hara. JSFOH, 38.
201 *"Jimmy is writing"*: Fairfield Porter to Frank O'Hara, August 1, 1955. Ted Leigh, ed., *Material Witness: The Selected Letters of Fairfield Porter* (Ann Arbor: University of Michigan Press, 2005), 132–33.
202 *"Jim and FP seem"*: Richard Stankiewicz, journal entry, August 3, 1955. AAA; Spring, *Porter*, 215.
202 *"It's really impossible"*: JS to Fairfield Porter, "Wednesday" [August 1955]. AAA. JTT, 23.
202 *"The vision goes untold"*: JS, *Presenting Jane*, Uncatalogued Berg.
202 *"Often, when it has been you"*: JS to Fairfield Porter, "Thursday" [Fall 1955], AAA. JTT, 24.
203 *"knew damn well"*: JS to Porter, Thursday" [Fall 1955], AAA. JTT, 26.
203 *"Just report"*: Fairfield Porter interviewed by Paul Cummings, June 6, 1968, AAA. https://www.aaa.si.edu/collections/interviews/oral-history-interview-fairfield-porter-12873.
203 *introducing Ashbery*: Author interview with John Ashbery, January 26, 1995.
204 *"Al Jensen [Tanager]"*: JS, "Reviews and Previews," *Art News* (December 1955), 57.
204 *"Johnny and Alvin are going"*: Donald Allen, ed., *The Collected Poems of Frank O'Hara* (New York: Alfred A. Knopf, Inc., 1971), 225.
204 *"Slight, wiry, of medium"*: Joe LeSueur, *Digressions on Some Poems by Frank O'Hara* (New York: Farrar, Straus and Giroux, 2003), 136.
205 *"He was the life"*: Author interviews with Alex and Ada Katz, November 17, 1995; May 4, 2011.
205 *a "Pirandelloesque touch"*: Frank O'Hara to Grace Hartigan, January 11, 1956. Syracuse.
205 *Wieners, then twenty-two*: For information on John Wieners I am grateful to his biographer, Robert Dewhurst; his email to Raymond Foye, September 23, 2024.
206 *O'Hara sent his poems*: Frank O'Hara to Kenneth Koch, April 12, 1956. KK Berg.
206 *he "looks rested"*: O'Hara to Koch, April 12, 1956. KK Berg.
206 *it was in the bar*: Schjeldahl 1977.
206 *"sat on rocks"*: JS to John Button, "Wednesday" [April 11, 1956]. JB Berg.

206 *Montgomery took photographs*: JS to Fairfield Porter, "Wednesday" [April 11, 1956]; Frank O'Hara to Kenneth Koch, April 12, 1956. KK Berg.
207 *"I do seem to have"*: JS to Alfred Leslie, March 3, 1960, published in Alfred Leslie, *The Hasty Papers: Special Millennium Edition* (Austin, TX: Host Publications, 1999), 47.
208 *"Having My Say-So"*: OF, 47.
208 *"tired, rather tan"*: JS to Frank O'Hara, May 14, 1956. O'Hara. JSFOH, 60.
209 *"I don't know why"*: JS to John Button, undated. JB Berg. JTT, 29.
209 *"[Jimmy] was* mad *for him!"*: Author interview with Bernard Perlin, March 13, 2010.
209 *had "no comment"*: JS to O'Hara, May 14, 1956. O'Hara. JSFOH, 61.
209 *"I hope that poem"*: JS to John Button, "Friday" [June, 1956]. JB Berg.
210 *"'That poem,' you forced"*: John Button to JS, "Friday" [June 1956]. Mandeville [box 2, folder 13].
210 *"a young and somewhat snotty"*: John Button to Trevor Winkfield, August 30, 1976. TW Beinecke.
210 *"I think in the fall"*: JS to John Button, "Sunday" [June 1956]. JB Berg.
211 *"I sent my letter"*: Fairfield Porter to JS, undated [Summer 1956]. Mandeville [box 3, folder 39].
211 *"You have the power"*: Fairfield Porter to JS, "Saturday" [August 1956]. Mandeville [box 3, folder 39]. Leigh, *Witness*, 154.
211 *Schuyler, Porter, O'Hara*: For example, Frank O'Hara wrote to Schuyler on June 15, 1956, "I think Proust is ruining me, since when one is not actively reading him one seems to be unconsciously scrutinising one's own experiences and particularly one's motives (ugh!) and finding them unworthy." Brad Gooch, *City Poet: The Life and Times of Frank O'Hara* (New York: Alfred A. Knopf, 1993), 281.
212 *"The letter I wrote"*: Fairfield Porter to JS, undated [Summer 1956]. Mandeville [box 3, folder 39]. Leigh, *Witness*, 215.
212 *"They do tell"*: JS to John Button, "Friday" [June 1956]. JB Berg.
212 *"I'm in the dog house"*: JS to John Button, "Tuesday" [June 1956]. JB Berg.
212 *"Everything about the house"*: JS to Fairfield Porter, July 7 [1956]. AAA. JTT, 39.
213 *"I want to talk"*: John Button to JS [June 18, 1956]. Mandeville [box 14, folder 17].
213 *"We never spoke"*: JS to John Button, July 3 [1956]. JB Berg. JTT, 38.
213 *"Jimmy, I can't even"*: John Button to JS, undated [July 1956]. Mandeville [box 2, folder 12].
213 *"the most marvelous devil's"*: JS to John Button, "Sunday" [July 15, 1956]. JB Berg. JTT, 47.
213 *"I feel so certain"*: JS to John Button, "Sunday" [July 15, 1956]. JB Berg. JTT, 48.
213 *a very silly and camp*: John Button and Frank O'Hara to JS, undated [July 1956]. Mandeville [box 3, folder 30].
214 *"No matter what"*: JS to John Button, "Sunday" [July 15, 1956]. JB Berg. JTT, 47.
214 *"I feel like a dirigible"*: JS to John Button, "Sunday" [July 15, 1956]. JB Berg. JTT, 48.
214 *"There's been a real"*: JS to John Button, "Saturday" [July 21, 1956]. JB Berg. JTT, 50.
214 *"Just received"*: Frank O'Hara to JS, July 24, 1956. Mandeville [box 3, folder 30].
214 *"Frank cried and cried"*: Schjeldahl 1977.
215 *"full of gas"*: Schjeldahl 1977.
215 *"took care of him"*: Gooch, *City Poet*, 287.
215 *"quite strange"*: Author interview with John Ashbery, January 26, 1995.
215 *"I am thrilled"*: John Ashbery to JS, August 25, 1956. Mandeville.
216 *"Your physical rejection"*: JS to John Button, "Labor Day" [September 2, 1956]. JTT, 58. JB Berg.

216 *"Since last September"*: JS to Margaret Ridenour, November 20, 1956. Ridenour. JTT, 63.
216 *"How shy one is"*: JS to Kenneth Koch, December 11 [1956]. JTT, 69. KK Berg.
216 *gave up both drinking*: Joe LeSueur to JS, September 19, 1956. Mandeville [box 3, folder 16].
216 *Over lunch to discuss*: JS to Kenneth Koch, "Wednesday" [Summer 1956]. KK Berg. JTT, 54.
217 *"warm, witty, immensely"*: LeSueur, *Digressions*, 115.
217 *"As soon as I found"*: Schjeldahl 1977.
218 *"I am clinging"*: Frank O'Hara to Kenneth Koch, KK Berg. Gooch, *City Poet*, 292.
218 *"mildly, keeping my voice"*: LeSueur, *Digressions*, 116.

12. YOU SEE ALL THESE FRUSTRATING THINGS HAPPEN

219 *A week into the new year*: Frank O'Hara to Larry Rivers, January 7, 1957. Fales.
219 *"And then it was"*: Schjeldahl 1977.
219 *"had not done anything"*: Schjeldahl 1977.
219 *"Frank was capable"*: Joe LeSueur, *Digressions on Some Poems by Frank O'Hara* (New York: Farrar, Straus and Giroux, 2003), 116.
219 *Osgood "had the feeling"*: Author interview with Lawrence Osgood, October 13, 2010.
220 *his own fear and mistrust*: Schjeldahl 1977.
220 *"Your December news"*: JS to Kenneth Koch, January 1957. KK Berg. JTT, 71.
220 *"By that point"*: JS to Dan Wickenden, March 19, 1957. Mandeville.
221 *"the Hudson instead"*: "Hoboken," JS, *May 24th or So* (New York: Tibor de Nagy Editions, 1966), 4. The variant version published in *Other Flowers* as "So That's Why," OF, 40–41, lacks the first three stanzas.
221 *"you can't talk"*: "Hudson Ferry," CP, 21.
221 *"you can't just say"*: "Hoboken," *May 24th or So*, 4. "So That's Why," OF, 40.
222 *"I was going to write"*: JS, *May 24th or So*, 3.
222 *visited the Porters*: Anne Porter, notes from a letter to her mother, April 1957. AAA.
222 *"Radio's Oldest"*: The former title is crossed out and replaced with "Rachmaninoff's Third" on the typescript. Mandeville. Another typescript is dated "4/2/57."
223 *"And one* can *say"*: John Wieners to JS, June 11, 1957. Mandeville [box 4, folder 4].
223 *In his comments*: John Wieners to JS, April 22, 1957. Mandeville [box 4, folder 4].
223 *he did acknowledge*: Hillringhouse 1985, 8.
224 *"For the first time"*: Charles Olson, "Projective Verse," in Donald M. Allen, ed., *The New American Poetry* (New York: Grove Press, 1960), 393.
224 *Schuyler also acknowledged*: JS to Arthur Gold (in reference to *Grand Duo* specifically), "Thursday" [June 9, 1960]. Gold Fizdale.
224 *Working at the front desk*: Author interview with Jeanne Keyes Youngson, March 7, 2011.
224 *"We used it"*: Author interview with Alvin Novak, May 3, 2004.
224 *Fairfield Porter, who was there*: Youngson interview, March 7, 2011.
225 *"tried to cover"*: Novak interview, May 3, 2004.
225 *"Everyone except one"*: JS to John Ashbery, August 16, 1957. Houghton. JTT, 81.
225 *He had decided*: Author interview with John Ashbery, August 13, 2004.
226 *"I hope you are feeling"*: John Ashbery to JS, "Monday" [1958], Mandeville.
226 *"took often the form"*: Ashbery interview, August 13, 2004.
226 *"It's really very easy!"*: Author interview with John Ashbery May 6, 2013.
226 *feeling "sort of excluded"*: Ashbery interview, May 6, 2013.

227 *"one of the most horrible"*: Schjeldahl 1977.
227 *Later that day*: Ashbery interview, May 6, 2013.
227 *"I only saved"*: Schjeldahl 1977.
227 La Grande Jatte *barely*: Ashbery interview, 2013.
227 *One workman*: Schjeldahl 1977.
227 *"some rather random"*: Schjeldahl 1977.
228 *He had a liking*: Novak interview, May 3, 2004; author interview with Kynaston McShine, December 16, 2010.
228 *"quite pleasant"*: JS to John Ashbery, June 6, 1958. JA Houghton.
228 *"It's fantastic how"*: JS to John Button, July, 14, 1958. JB Berg.
228 *Esta at this time*: Author interviews with Alvin Novak, September 28, 1994, and May 3, 2004.
229 *"tops in the taste"*: Ashbery interview, May 3, 2004.
229 *"very unlikely"*: Ashbery interview, May 3, 2004.
229 *a collaborative play*: Memories differ about where and when the play was put on. Michael Goldberg (interview with the author, June 3, 2004) remembered it as being at Joan Mitchell's studio, and Maxine Groffsky at Elaine de Kooning's (interview with the author, December 12, 2011). A typescript of the play gives the location as Goldberg's studio, implying that that was also where it was presented, which Goldberg denied was the case. Joe LeSueur in his introduction to *Selected Plays of Frank O'Hara* (xvi) states that the play was produced to celebrate Schuyler's thirty-third birthday, in November 1956, which is also inaccurate. The play was produced a second time at the Artists' Club, according to Goldberg. Appearing in the play, either as themselves or as one another, were Irma Hurley, Mike Goldberg, Kenneth Koch, John Ashbery, Frank O'Hara, Hal Fondren, Jane Freilicher, and Larry Rivers. John Ashbery's name is crossed out in the typescript included among his papers at Harvard, indicating that perhaps he was not in it after all.
229 *Jane Cobb*: Jane Cobb, "Things Kept Happening," *New York Times Book Review* (April 20, 1958): 154.
229 *was not written in*: Kenneth Koch, "Poetry as Prose," *Poetry* 93, no. 5 (February 1959): 321–23.
230 *"Do you suppose"*: JS to John Ashbery, July 22, 1958. JA Houghton.
230 *He was greatly relieved*: JS to John Ashbery, October 15, 1958. JA Houghton. JTT, 90.
230 *Two he identified*: James Schuyler to David Trinidad, June 12, 1987. Fales. JTT, 430.
231 *"How the thing said"*: CP, 268.
231 *a "hearty spread"*: JS to John Ashbery, November 11, 1958. JA Houghton. JTT, 91.
231 *a "stuatory tenant"*: JS to John Ashbery, April 23, 1959. JA Houghton. JTT, 99.
232 *"one of those lovely"*: Frank O'Hara to John Ashbery, July 14, 1959. JA Houghton.
232 *a rambling, six-page*: JS to Leland Bell, July 17, 1959. Museum of Modern Art Archives, New York.
232 *on one occasion*: Author interview with John Ashbery, August 13, 2004.
232 *"Anyone who combines"*: JS to John Ashbery, September 10 [1959]. JA Houghton. JTT, 104.
232 *"an insomniac's torture"*: JS to John Ashbery, October 13, 1959. JA Houghton. JTT, 115.
232 *"a simply staggering"*: John Ashbery to JS, August 28 [1959]. Mandeville.
233 *"It is sublime"*: JS to John Ashbery, September 10 [1959]. JA Houghton. JTT, 105.
233 *"the roaches and silverfish"*: JS to John Ashbery, November 2, 1959. JA Houghton. JTT, 117.

234 *"made enough noise"*: JS to John Ashbery, November 16, 1959. JA Houghton. JTT, 122.
234 *"simply marvelous"*: John Ashbery to JS, December 28, 1959. Mandeville.
235 *"Of course the father"*: JS, "Poet and Painter Overture," *The New American Poetry* (New York: Grove Press, 1960), 418–19.
235 *the front page*: Marianne Moore, "The Ways Our Poets Have Taken Since the War," in *A Marianne Moore Reader* (New York: Viking Press, 1961), 237–43.
235 *John and Kenneth encouraged*: Author telephone interview with Harry Mathews, November 12, 2009.
236 *Mathews had recently*: Mathews interview, November 12, 2009.
236 *"he was less severe"*: Mathews interview, November 12, 2009.
236 *"to leaven the New York"*: JS to Robin Blaser, March 23, 1960. Courtesy William Corbett.
236 *"Current Events"*: THB, 75–82.
236 *a "book of sketches"*: JS to John Ashbery, "Wednesday" [December 1961]. JA Houghton. JTT, 139.
237 *"the poets were assigned"*: Author phone interview with Grace Hartigan, January 24, 2005.
237 *"One wonders about"*: Fairfield Porter, *Art in Its Own Terms: Selected Criticism 1935–1975*, Rackstraw Downes, ed. (Cambridge, MA: Zoland Books, 1979), 225.
237 *"contemplative and compressed"*: Porter, *Art*, 221.
238 *"The more things change"*: JS to John Ashbery, "Monday" [December 1959]. JA Houghton.
238 *For the past two years*: Fairfield Porter interviewed by Paul Cummings, June 6, 1968, Archives of American Art. https://www.aaa.si.edu/collections/interviews/oral-history-interview-fairfield-porter-12873.

13. NOW AND THEN A HUMAN BEING

239 *One Eighty-One Avenue A*: Author telephone interview with Philip and Dorothy Pearlstein, May 19, 2011.
239 *took anything of value*: Such is the inference to be drawn from Ashbery's letter to JS of August 28, 1959, in which he suggests his furniture and clothes be discarded rather than stored, but asks JS to hang on to books, records, and artworks. Mandeville.
239 *"bad like me"*: Fairfield Porter to JS, July 7, 1960. Ted Leigh, ed., *Material Witness: The Selected Letters of Fairfield Porter* (Ann Arbor: University of Michigan Press, 2005), 203–204.
240 *"An easy way"*: JS to Fairfield Porter, July 8, 1960. AAA.
240 *"I love to get"*: Fairfield Porter to JS, July 14 [1960]. Mandeville [box 3, folder 39].
240 *Dash was born*: A vignette of Bob Dash as a graduate student at the University of New Mexico appears in Lucia Berlin's story "Dear Conchi": "He looks like a handsome author on a book jacket. A pipe, patches on his elbows. He lives in an adobe house filled with Indian pots and rugs and modern art. We drink gin and tonics with lime in them, listen to Bartok's Sonata for Two Pianos and Percussion." Lucia Berlin, *Instructions for Cleaning Women* (New York: Farrar, Straus and Giroux, 2016), 214.
241 *an instant rapport*: Author interview with Robert Dash, October 21, 1995.
242 *in February wrote*: JS to Porter McCray, February 19, 1960. Museum of Modern Art Archives, New York.
242 *The show debuted*: MoMA Archives, NY.
242 *a "period of megalomania-paranoia"*: Frank O'Hara to John Ashbery, October 14, 1960. JA Houghton.

243 *"wanted to slap him"*: O'Hara to Ashbery, October 14, 1960.
243 *"Sometimes, though it seems"*: O'Hara to Ashbery, October 14, 1960.
243 *"Did you see"*: JS to Anne Porter, "Tuesday" [June 28, 1960]. AAA.
243 *"putting him in the shade"*: Frank O'Hara to John Ashbery, May 1, 1961. JA Houghton.
243 *"couldn't bring himself"*: O'Hara to John Ashbery, May 1, 1961.
244 *"Frank O'Hara will be"*: Author interview with Bill Berkson, March 22, 2005.
244 *"For the last few"*: JS to John Ashbery, September 30, 1960. JA Houghton.
245 *"My life has not"*: JS to Ashbery, September 30, 1960.
245 *"petite, fairly attractive"*: Author interview with Kynaston McShine, December 16, 2010.
245 *"merry and sad"*: Author interview with Robert Dash, October 22, 1995.
245 *The fact that Fairfield*: Berkson interview, March 22, 2005.
246 *"Jimmy has been spending"*: Fairfield Porter to John Button, October 1, [1960]. JB Berg.
246 *"The Yvonne Clare Story"*: RD Beinecke.
246 *On September 2*: JS to John Ashbery [September 19, 1960], JA Houghton; JS to Chester Kallman, September 3, 1960. CK Berg.
247 *"J Is for My Name"*: OF, 74.
247 *"Do you feel like"*: Author interview with Robert Dash, October 21, 1995.
247 *"mushy" as poetry*: Frank O'Hara to Vincent Warren, January 19–22, 1962. Dodd.
248 *"I'm still a director"*: JS to Robin Blaser, undated [c. September 30, 1960]. Courtesy Bill Corbett.
248 *"Fairfield has more"*: Frank O'Hara to John Ashbery, October 14, 1960. JA Houghton.
248 *Old friends*: Carl Morse to Bill Corbett, April 15, 1997. Author interview with Jane Freilicher, October 18, 1994.
248 *was sent downtown*: Berkson interview, March 22, 2005.
248 *he called the former*: Pearlstein interview, May 19, 2011.
249 *"full of pins"*: JS to Harry Mathews, October 25, 1961. Kislak. JTT, 138.
249 *"alternately been working"*: JS to Margaret Ridenour, February 11, 1961. Ridenour.
249 *"looked terrible"*: Frank O'Hara to Vincent Warren, January 23, 1961. Dodd.
249 *"digging him out"*: JS to Robert Dash, July 29, 1971. RD Beinecke. JTT, 352.
249 *"uneasy" about the possible*: Langdon Hammer, *James Merrill: Life and Art* (New York: Alfred A. Knopf, 2015), 175.
249 *he was his patient*: James Merrill's autobiography, *Another Person*, includes many examples of his insightful compassion.
249 *"While the Medical Center"*: Thomas Detre to John Bernard Myers, March 1, 1961. Mandeville.
250 *because of his "artistry"*: John Bernard Myers to JS, March 17, 1961. Mandeville.
250 *"Patients in the manic"*: Thomas P. Detre and Henry G. Jarecki, *Modern Psychiatric Treatment*, 113.
250 *"may have been"*: Justin Spring, *Fairfield Porter: A Life in Art* (New Haven, CT: Yale University Press, 1999), 258.
250 *his mother and stepfather*: Author interview with Hilde Ridenour, November 8, 2007.
250 *remarkably changed*: Author interview with Alex and Ada Katz, November 17, 1995.
250 *"quite a hate"*: Frank O'Hara to John Ashbery, May 1, 1961. JA Houghton.
251 *"I don't think"*: O'Hara to Ashbery, May 1, 1961.
251 *"A Blue Shadow Painting"*: OF, 76.
252 *"well, cheerful and fat"*: Fairfield Porter to Howard Griffin, June 20, 1961; quoted in Spring, *Porter*, 258.
252 *"I'll never let"*: DJS, 189.

252 *In the evenings*: Fairfield Porter to Robert Dash, July 27, 1961. RD Beinecke. Leigh, *Witness*, 223.
252 *From there he*: JS to Robert Dash, August 11, 1961. RD Beinecke. JTT, 136.
252 *"I don't know when"*: JS to Dash, August 11, 1961.
252 *"quite expressionless"*: Anne Porter to author, undated [May 2004].
252 *Evening readings*: Leigh, *Witness*, 225; Fairfield Porter to Bob Dash, August 10, 1961. RD Beinecke. Leigh, *Witness*, 226.
253 *"I gather you"*: JS to John Ashbery, December 1, 1961. JA Houghton.
253 *the article is written*: SAW, 37–43.
253 *"Jimmy just took"*: Author interview with Alex and Ada Katz, November 17, 1995.
253 *his "long vacation"*: JS to Donald Allen, November 28, 1961. Mandeville [Ms. 3, box 68, folder 40].
253 *"friendly and charming"*: Frank O'Hara to John Ashbery, December 7, 1961. JA Houghton.
254 *One of the first*: Edward J. Ennis, Trustee, to JS, December 22, 1960. Mandeville.
254 *the "demon game"*: JS to John Ashbery, December, 1961. JA Houghton. JTT, 139.
255 *"having birth pains"*: JS to John Ashbery, January 1, 1962. JA Houghton.
255 *"writing poems very"*: JS to Harry Mathews, January 21, 1962. Kislak.

14. BUT THIS IS NOT / YOUR POEM, YOUR POEM I MAY / NEVER WRITE

256 *"Jimmy came for the weekend"*: Author interview with Robert Dash, October 21, 1995.
256 *"Is Mr. Schuyler"*: Dash interview, October 21, 1995.
256 *By mid-1962*: Fairfield named Jimmy as a dependent in a letter to his dealer, John Myers, dated February 15, 1963. Justin Spring, *Fairfield Porter: A Life in Art* (New Haven, CT: Yale University Press, 1999), 266.
256 *"much the happiest"*: Ross 1981, 4.
256 *"almost* pathologically *generous"*: Author interview with Larry Fagin, February 11, 2013.
257 *"Anne and Fairfield were"*: Author interview with Robert Dash, October 22, 1995.
257 *"I hear that in the city"*: Anne Porter to her mother, April 28, 1953. AAA. Spring, *Porter*, 197.
258 *Before their marriage*: Author interview with Anne Porter, May 5, 2004.
258 *in a few cases*: Author interview with Joe LeSueur, December 6, 1994; author interview with Robert Dash, May 4, 2004.
258 *"I had a wonderful"*: Anne Porter interview, May 5, 2004.
258 *a "romantic fixation"*: Author phone interview with Laurence Porter, January 12, 2009.
258 *Fairfield in particular*: Author interview with James McCourt, January 4, 2006.
258 *"but this is not"*: CP, 262.
259 *"touching or intimacy"*: Laurence Porter interview, January 12, 2009.
259 *Whatever sexual activity*: Author interview with Tom Carey, October 3, 1994.
259 *"F[airfield] and Jimmy"*: Anne Porter to the author, September 14, 1994.
259 *liked to be awakened*: Anne Porter to the author, undated [October 14, 1994].
259 *it "never occurred"*: Author interview with Anne Porter, September 9, 1994.
259 *"didn't think of it"*: Anne Porter interview, May 5, 2004.
259 *"I understood a little"*: Anne Porter interview, May 5, 2004.
260 *"saved" the marriage*: Anne Porter to the author, undated [May 2004].
260 *hosts would blithely*: Author interview with Katharine Porter, May 11, 2013.
260 *"Oh Fairfield, Fairfield"*: DJS, 134.

261 *wide-eyed unflinching*: Author interview with Robert Dash, May 4, 2004; author interview with Ron and Pat Padgett, February 1, 1995. Both Dash and the Padgetts independently compared the girls' eerie stares to the camp 1960 British horror movie *Village of the Damned.*
261 *"the older brother"*: Author interview with Jane Freilicher, February 1, 2005.
261 *"avuncular kindness"*: Dash interview, May 4, 2004.
261 *"When I was a kid"*: Katharine Porter interview, May 11, 2013.
261 *"He was sort of"*: Author interview with Elizabeth Porter, October 22, 1995.
261 *"Neither of my parents"*: Elizabeth Porter interview, October 22, 1995; Anne Porter interview, May 5, 2004.
261 *a disarming childishness*: Author interview with Katherine Koch, March 25, 2013.
261 *fascination with corny puns*: Elizabeth Porter interview, October 22, 1995.
261 *"raw and intoxicating"*: Anne Porter interview, May 5, 2004.
262 *Jimmy added to*: Elizabeth Porter interview, October 22, 1995.
262 *the patience and empathy*: Author interviews with Anne Porter, September 9, 1994; May 5, 2004.
262 *He loved to stand*: Anne Porter interview, September 9, 1994.
262 *"varying it with whoops"*: "For My Son Johnny," in Anne Porter, *Living Things: Collected Poems* (Hanover, NH: Zoland Books, 2006), 85–88.
262 *Jimmy "felt for him"*: Anne Porter interview, May 5, 2004.
262 *"living on the margins"*: Anne Porter interview, September 9, 1994.
262 *"the* enormous *relief"*: Anne Porter interview, May 5, 2004.
262 *almost a "trade off"*: Katharine Porter interview, May 11, 2013.
262 *"Nothing about the Porters"*: Author interview with Jane Freilicher, February 1, 2005.
262 *Jimmy was "probably"*: Author interview with Ron and Pat Padgett, February 1, 1995.
263 *still-rural character*: Anne Porter interview, September 9, 1994.
263 *The house was furnished*: Author interviews with Robert Dash, May 4, 2004; with Anne Porter, September 9, 1994; with Cornelia Foss, December 27, 2022.
263 *"in the middle"*: Author interview with Robert Dash, October 22, 1995.
263 *a "tiny, tiny" electric*: Ron and Pat Padgett interview, February 1, 1995.
263 *a "wonderfully undisciplined"*: Author interview with Robert Dash, October 22, 1995.
263 *"I remember a third day"*: Dash interview, October 22, 1995.
263 *Lizzie enjoyed*: Elizabeth Porter interview, October 22, 1995.
264 *"wondrous" white blossoms*: CP, 372.
264 *"full of books"*: Katherine Koch interview, March 25, 2013.
264 *Jimmy contributed*: Author interview with Katherine Koch, March 25, 2013, relating information from Kenneth Koch.
264 *brought a broad range*: Anne Porter interview, September 9, 1994.
264 *"could get kind of inside"*: Katherine Koch interview, March 25, 2013.
264 *After Jimmy compared*: Anne Porter interview, September 9, 1994.
264 *"tried to write poems"*: Hillringhouse 1985, 7.
265 *"Under a Storm Washed"*: OF, 157. For date, OF, 206, n157.
265 *"for some years"*: Berrigan 1983.
267 *primitive living conditions*: Edith Schloss, *The Loft Generation* (New York: Farrar, Straus and Giroux, 2021), 76–79.
267 *"acoustically it's like"*: Anne Porter interview, September 9, 1994.
267 *"His penchant for natural"*: Author interview with Jane Freilicher, October 18, 1994.
267 *"The result is sometimes"*: Fairfield Porter to Lucien and Poppy Day, July 23, 1962. Leigh, *Witness*, 232.

267 *did not enter*: Author interview with Alex and Ada Katz, November 17, 1995.
267 *"Jimmy asks to be"*: Fairfield Porter to Robert Dash, August 21, 1962. Beinecke. Leigh, *Witness*, 227 [where misdated 1961].
267 *"I hear applause"*: Fairfield Porter to Lucien and Poppy Day, July 23, 1962. Leigh, *Witness*, 232.
268 *"I would love"*: John Ashbery to JS, February 21, 1963. Mandeville.
268 *"Would [writing] alternate"*: JS to John Ashbery, March 29, 1963. JA Houghton. JTT, 143.
268 *missing a Porter*: Spring, *Porter*, 267.
268 *"I'm sorry you weren't"*: JS to John Ashbery, July 4, 1963. JA Houghton.
268 *"Woman's work"*: Anne Porter interview, September 9, 1994.
268 *"certain knacks"*: Author interview with Jane Freilicher, February 1, 2005.
268 *"that would have satisfied"*: JS to Arthur Gold, July 30, 1963. Gold Fizdale.
269 *began as a way*: Berrigan 1983.
270 *John Ashbery was jealous*: John Ashbery to JS, December 12 [1964]. Mandeville.
270 *gave Schuyler pause*: JS to John Ashbery [July 15, 1964]. JA Houghton.
271 *got an early start*: JS to Carl Morse, August 29, 1964. Courtesy William Corbett.
271 *"There are Quaker Ladies"*: Fairfield Porter to Anne Porter, June 5, 1964. AAA. Spring, *Porter*, 271.
271 *The Porter family*: Spring, *Porter*, 273.
271 *His disappearance left Anne*: JS letter to Jane Freilicher, July 4, 1964. JF Houghton.
271 *"After so long"*: JS to Margaret Ridenour, July 18 [1964]. Ridenour.
272 *"It's made me feel"*: JS to Robert Dash, July 21, 1964. RD Beinecke. JTT, 149.
272 *"I'm gardening quite a lot"*: JS to Dash, July 21, 1964. RD Beinecke. JTT, 148.
272 *"a very good"*: Anne Porter interview, May 5, 2004.
272 *Another time*: Anne Porter interview, May 5, 2004.
272 *"The house seemed"*: Margaret Ridenour to JS, January, 21, 1965. Mandeville [box 19, folder 2].
273 Unpacking the Black Trunk: In Kenward Elmslie, *Album* (New York: Kulchur Press, 1969), 125–32.
273 *"The timing and action"*: Diane di Prima, *Recollections of My Life as a Woman* (New York: Penguin Books, 2002), 407.
273 *The accident inspired*: Spring, *Porter*, 274–75.
273 *"not without a touch"*: JS to Arthur Gold, July 11, 1965. Gold Fizdale.
273 *"The island is dry"*: JS to Gold, July 11, 1965. Gold Fizdale.
274 *also a relief*: JS to Ron Padgett, January 16, 1966. RP Beinecke. JTT, 158.
275 *"living in a storm-swept"*: JS to John Ashbery, December 24, 1964. JA Houghton. JTT, 151.
275 *a goal of finishing*: JS to John Ashbery, August 7, 1966. JA Houghton. JTT, 166.
275 *Paul Bowles wrote to Jimmy*: JS to Arthur Gold, January 21, 1966. Gold Fizdale.
275 *English gardening magazines*: Little 1993, 179.
276 *The Friday before*: Author interview with John Ashbery, January 26, 1995.
276 *"like a dream"*: JS to John Ashbery, July 28, 1966. JA Houghton. JTT, 165.
276 *"loved the island"*: Author interview with John Ashbery, August 13, 2004.
276 *"pines, lichen, crabs"*: Kenward Elmslie to Ron and Pat Padgett [July 18, 1966]. RP Beinecke.
276 *"And then I was very worried"*: Author interview with John Ashbery, January 26, 1995.
277 *"stunned by Frank's death"*: JS to John Ashbery, July 28, 1966. JA Houghton. JTT, 164.

277 *stopped "with a thump"*: JS to Kenward Elmslie, August 24, 1966. KGE Mandeville. JTT, 168.
277 *Later Anne agonized*: Author interview with Anne Porter, September 9, 1994.
277 *"I too have been"*: John Ashbery to JS, August 2 [1966]. Mandeville.
277 *"of the slow and stately"*: JS to Elmslie, August 24, 1966.
277 *"She was somehow"*: JS to Elmslie, August 24, 1966.
277 *On August 27*: JS to John Ashbery, August 27, 1966. JA Houghton. JTT, 170.

15. VAGABOND SHOES

279 *she "ran off"*: Author interview with Maxine Groffsky, December 12, 2011.
279 *Groffsky approached George Plimpton*: Groffsky interview, December 12, 2011.
280 *"The paint is not"*: SAW, 15–16.
280 *the piece borrows*: SAW, 73–80.
280 *"I hope . . . you aren't"*: JS to Ron Padgett, May 23 [1967: misdated 1966 by JS]. RP Beinecke. JTT, 177.
280 *"When I described"*: Ron Padgett to JS, May 26, 1967. Mandeville [box 3, folder 31].
281 *of its time*: The selection was finalized in 1968. Ron Padgett later stated (email to the author, August 4, 2024) that "there were a number of visible women poets of that time—confessional, formalist, Beat—but *very* few of the NY poets variety . . . Had it been just a few years later, we would have included any number of the new young women poets who were proving their strength."
281 *"I guess it's time"*: JS to John Ashbery, "Mothering Sunday" [March 24], 1968. JA Houghton. JTT, 190.
281 *the first time*: Author interview with Ron and Pat Padgett, February 1, 1995.
281 *"Joe has got everybody"*: JS to Fairfield Porter, August 29, 1967. AAA.
281 *"we used to smoke"*: Author interview with John Ashbery, August 13, 2004.
282 *likened to the "jukes"*: Author interview with Larry Fagin, February 11, 2013.
283 *"extraordinary freedom"*: James Merrill to JS, January 15, 1969. Mandeville. Langdon Hammer, *James Merrill: Life and Art* (New York: Alfred A. Knopf, 2015), 456.
283 *"the most magical"*: Ron and Pat Padgett interview, 1995.
283 *One day Jimmy*: Ron Padgett email to the author, May 9, 2016.
284 *"A notion like that of empathy"*: Claude Lévi-Strauss, *The Scope of Anthropology* (London: Jonathan Cape, 1967), 16.
284 *"A Winter Day"*: Walt Whitman, *Complete Poetry and Collected Prose* (New York: Library of America, 1982), 795–96.
284 *"Are You The New"*: Whitman, *Complete*, 277.
285 *"reticence of intimacy"*: DJS, 28.
285 *went on a diet*: JS to John Ashbery, January 1, 1968. JA Houghton.
285 *"too touchy lately"*: DJS, 32.
285 "*to write* something": JS to Geoffrey Young, August 19, 1981. Geoffrey Young. JTT, 406.
285 *"People," Jimmy said*: JS to Joe Brainard, July 6, 1968. JB Mandeville. JTT, 194.
286 *Returning to the city*: Author interview with John Ashbery, January 26, 1995.
286 *"It's bliss"*: JS to Joe Brainard, June 29, 1968. JB Mandeville.
286 *"memorable currant-cardamom"*: JS to John Ashbery, July 13, 1968. JA Houghton. JTT, 200.
287 *originally separate poems*: Little 1993, 166; Berrigan 1983.
287 *"There sure are"*: Berrigan 1983.

287 *Jimmy had been reading*: Berrigan 1983. Spring, *Porter*, 295.
288 *"a continuum" and also*: Marc Bloch, *The Historian's Craft* (New York: Vintage 1953), 27–29.
288 *"There really isn't anything"*: JS to Joe Brainard, July 1, 1969. JB Mandeville. JTT, 249.
289 *the island was "magic"*: Author interview with Katherine Koch, March 25, 2013.
289 *"The thought of Kenneth"*: JS to Ron Padgett, July 21, 1968. RP Beinecke. JTT, 205.
289 *Jimmy especially liked*: JS to Joe Brainard, July 31, 1968. JB Mandeville. JTT, 210.
289 *"I wish I could"*: Author interview with Kenneth Koch, May 9, 1995.
290 *he "could get angry"*: Katherine Koch interview, March 25, 2013.
290 *"For the landscape"*: JS to John Ashbery, August 21, 1968. JA Houghton. JTT, 216.
290 *"shuffling along the hall"*: Author interview with James McCourt, January 4, 2006.
290 *"total eclectic looks"*: JS to John Ashbery, October 14, 1968. JA Houghton. JTT, 223.
291 *"He was a great"*: Author interview with Kenward Elmslie, November 18, 2004.
291 *"Coming upon a mature"*: John Koethe, "Freely Espoused," *Poetry* (October 1970): 54.
291 *an unfavorable review*: Guy Davenport, "Dependent On a Private Understanding of the World," *New York Times Book Review* (December 14, 1969): 55.
291 *"Things to Do When You Get a Bad Review"*: OF, 186.
291 *"Things to Do"*: CP, 59.
291 *the appreciative one*: W. H. Auden, "A Piece of Pure Fiction in the Firbank Mode," *New York Times Book Review* (May 4, 1969): 5.
291 *"unruffled, sec and witty"*: Thomas Lask, "The Saving Grace," *New York Times* (March 3, 1969): 33.
292 *"happy and* beaming*"*: Author interview with Lewis Warsh, May 23, 2012.
292 *aiming an enormous telephoto*: DJS, 50.
292 *"Tomorrow," he wrote*: JS to John Ashbery, July 8, 1969. JA Houghton. JTT, 251–52.
292 *"John P[orter] seems"*: JS to Ashbery, July 8, 1969.
293 *When Fairfield pointed*: Author interview with Alex and Ada Katz, November 17, 1995.
293 *"kind of a Sunday"*: Alex and Ada Katz interview, 1995.
293 *an "easier guest"*: JS letter to Joe Brainard, August 5, 1969. JB Mandeville.
293 *"There was always somewhat"*: Author interview with John Ashbery, August 13, 2004.
293 *"Jimmy was not looked upon"*: Ashbery interview, August 13, 2004.
294 *when John visited in August*: JS to John Ashbery [August 7, 1969]. JA Houghton. JTT, 262.
294 *"Voodoo Darkskin Love Beans"*: JS to Joe Brainard, August 10, 1969. JB Mandeville. JTT, 263.
294 *On August 27*: DJS, 65.
294 *a large clapboard*: Justin Spring, *Fairfield Porter: A Life in Art* (New Haven, CT: Yale University Press, 1999), 302.
294 *"I haven't come to light"*: JS to Ron Padgett, October 7, 1969. RP Beinecke.
294 *Jimmy liked Amherst*: JS to Arthur Gold, October 3, 1969. Gold Fizdale.
295 *"such an English thing"*: Author interview with Trevor Winkfield, June 2, 1995.
295 *"liked Jimmy enormously"*: Winkfield interview, June 2, 1995.
295 *"I already feel"*: JS to John Ashbery, July 8, 1969. JA Houghton. JTT, 251.
295 *"I think James Schuyler"*: John Ashbery, "Report," December 19, 1969. John Simon Guggenheim Memorial Foundation Records.
295 *All of the other*: Guggenheim Foundation.
295 *"a Vermont version"*: Winkfield interview, June 2, 1995.
296 *"I think about"*: JS to Joe Brainard, October 7, 1969. JB Mandeville.
296 *Jimmy spent Thanksgiving*: DJS, 74.
296 *"ten years younger"*: JS to John Ashbery, October, 30, 1969. JA Houghton.

296 *"We've had ice storms"*: JS to Joe Brainard, December 29, 1969. JB Mandeville.
296 *"The sun is shining"*: JS to Kenward Elmslie, June 19, 1970. KGE Mandeville. JTT, 296.
296 *He resolved that summer*: JS to Elmslie, June 19, 1970. KGE Mandeville.
296 *"instantly . . . gained 800"*: JS to Larry Fagin, August 2, 1970. U Conn. JTT, 308.
297 *Jimmy made*: JS to Joe Brainard, June 28, 1970. JB Mandeville. JTT, 298.
297 *John and Jimmy had intended*: JS to Kenward Elmslie, August 2, 1970. KGE Mandeville.
297 *"He and John have evolved"*: JS to Kenward Elmslie, August 17, 1970. KGE Mandeville. JTT, 310.
297 *"Yes, when we travel"*: JS to Kenward Elmslie, August 31, 1970. KGE Mandeville. JTT, 316.
298 *pleased to be back*: JS to Joe Brainard, September 20, 1970. JB Mandeville.
298 *a quick, informal drawing*: Collection of the author.
298 *"Kenward is right behind"*: CP, 107.
299 *she now took*: Author interview with Katharine Porter, May 11, 2013.
299 *"so much to give"*: Katharine Porter interview, May 11, 2013.
299 *Anne was particularly*: Author interview with Anne Porter, May 5, 2004.
299 *She would come home*: Author interview with Elizabeth Porter, October 22, 1995.
299 *Katie who was the catalyst*: Katharine Porter interview, May 11, 2013.
299 *"turn white"*: Katharine Porter interview, May 11, 2013.
299 *"We didn't want"*: Anne Porter interview, May 5, 2004.
300 *"I'll think about it"*: Anne Porter to the author, undated [May 2004]. Justin Spring dates this conversation to 1968. However, Anne stated that the conversation took place "3 years before he actually left," which was in October 1973.

16. PAIN DOESN'T HURT; IT'S A SENSATION, LIKE A KISS

301 *"December 24, 1970"*: DJS, 101.
301 *He proposed collaborating*: JS to Trevor Winkfield, August 26, 1970. TW Beinecke.
302 *he "seemed in a"*: JS to Trevor Winkfield, June 11, 1971. TW Beinecke.
302 *having a simultaneous*: JS to Harry Mathews, March 16, 1971. Kislak.
302 *"very beautiful"*: John Ashbery to JS, July 8, 1970. Mandeville.
302 *the two relationships*: Author interviews with John Ashbery, August 13, 2004; June 3, 2006.
302 *a facsimile edition*: Little 1993, 157.
302 *"it was the wrong hour"*: Thompson 1992, 120.
302 *"so long as the breath"*: Little 1993, 171.
303 *one long, continuous breath*: Thompson 1992, 121.
303 *disclaimed any influence*: Hillringhouse 1985, 8.
303 *"It seemed to break"*: Hillringhouse 1985, 10.
303 *"I didn't want"*: Little 1993, 170.
303 *"And then something"*: Hillringhouse 1985, 10. See also JS to Kenneth Koch, May 27, 1971. KK Berg. JTT, 334.
303 *On Friday night*: DJS, 114.
304 *"nothing to do"*: Little 1993, 171.
304 *an old postcard*: JS to Darragh Park [August 4, 1985]. DAP Mandeville.
304 *"I like the sound"*: JS to Kenneth Koch, May 27, 1971. KK Berg. JTT, 333.
304 *Lithium was only*: Author interview with (Dr.) Katharine Porter, May 11, 2013.
304 *"That spread of waves"*: Walt Whitman, *Complete Poetry and Collected Prose* (New York: Library of America, 1982), 796.

305 *"always from the days"*: Logan Pearsall Smith, *Unforgotten Years* (Boston: Little, Brown, 1939), 104–105.
305 *"the sea's voice"*: Smith, *Unforgotten*, 106.
307 *"I get the feeling"*: JS to Ron Padgett, January 12, 1971. RP Beinecke.
307 *"big tall hunk"*: Author interview with Jane Freilicher, February 1, 2005.
307 *"He looked sort of"*: Author interview with John Ashbery, August 13, 2004.
307 *he was a buyer*: JS to Harry Mathews, June 2, 1971. Kislak. JTT, 342.
307 *"so I surmise"*: JS to Harry Mathews, June 2, 1971. Kislak. JTT, 343.
307 *He seemed "sleazy"*: Author interview with Jane Freilicher, October 18, 1994.
307 *"inviting him out to Fairfield"*: Author interview with Jane Freilicher, October 18, 1994.
307 *"so passionate about"*: Author interviews with John Ashbery, August 13, 2004; January 26, 1995.
308 *"was an absolute jerk"*: Author interview with Kenward Elmslie, November 18, 2004.
308 *"something totally phoney"*: Ashbery interview, January 26, 1995.
308 *"material for a short story"*: Freilicher interview, February 1, 2005.
308 *"I think Jimmy made"*: Author interview with Robert Dash, October 22, 1995.
308 *one of the three or four*: David Margolick, "A Hemingway Hero Embraced by Both Sides," *New York Times* (November 2, 2008).
308 *a "bicycle chain"*: Author interview with Trevor Winkfield, April 8, 2021.
308 *a "dog collar"*: Author interview with Darragh Park, May 6, 2004.
309 *"Bob had commanded"*: Ashbery interview, August 13, 2004.
309 *"I think he was a deep-dyed"*: Elmslie, November 18, 2004.
309 *these practices included*: Author interview with Tom Carey, March 16, 2011. One of Jimmy's assistants in the '80s heard tales from Lewis Warsh about Jimmy engaging in this practice, not unknown in the S&M subculture, whereby "at the moment of climax [the suture] would break apart, thus merging pleasure and pain." Bill DeNoyelles, email to the author, January 23, 2013.
309 *"B's cruelty to me"*: JS to Hilde Ridenour, March 6, 1980. Ridenour.
309 *A diary entry*: DJS, 115–16.
310 *"You ever write"*: Epigraph to "Janis Joplin's Dead: Long Live Pearl," CP, 120, which I attribute to Bob Jordan.
310 *"distinctly middle-brow"*: JS to Harry Mathews, November 15, 1970. Kislak. JTT, 319.
310 *even Larry Rivers*: JS to Ron Padgett, undated. RP Beinecke.
310 *"it was in* my *dining room"*: Author interview with John Ashbery, June 3, 2006.
310 *"leaves, leaves, spring salad"*: DJS, 119.
310 *"Life, Death and Other Dreams"*: *The Paris Review* 55 (Fall 1972): 29–66; reprinted in Howard Moss, ed., *The Poet's Story* (New York: Touchstone, 1973), 183–213. Gerrit Henry was a poet and an art writer, a student and friend of John Ashbery.
312 *"long and groundbreaking"*: JS to Clark Coolidge, June 21, 1972. Buffalo. JTT, 382.
312 *the "contractual" nature*: Gilles Deleuze, *Présentation de Sacher-Masoch* (Paris: Editions de Minuit, 1967), 76.
312 *The sticking point*: Author interview with Anne Porter, May 5, 2004.
312 *"in tears" of frustration*: Author interview with Robert Dash, May 21, 2012.
312 *Jimmy was "incandescent"*: Author interview with Robert Dash, October 21, 1995.
312 *watering the plants*: Author interview with Robert Dash, May 4, 2004.
313 *a "collage-prose-poem"*: JS to Joe Brainard, July 16, 1971. JB Mandeville.
313 *"books everywhere"*: Little 1993, 176.
313 *was still retyping*: JS to Joe Brainard, June 11 and July 16, 1971. JB Mandeville.
313 "où suis-je?": The actual lines are: "Où suis-je? Je respire plus librement! L'air me semble

plus doux et plus pur! . . . Ah le ciel! Comme il est profond!" O'Hara's version can be translated, "Where am I? / I breathe a new air / the blue firmament is more vast."

314 *They had recently reaffirmed*: Author interview with Ron and Pat Padgett, February 1, 1995; author interview with Katharine Porter, May 11, 2013.

314 *"You could see"*: JS to John Ashbery, undated [c. June 25, 1971] and possibly unsent. Mandeville.

314 *an early version*: See below.

314 *a letter to John*: JS to John Ashbery, undated [c. June 25, 1971]. The letter contains the draft of "The Night" that includes Jordan's name. Mandeville.

315 *not a suicidal*: CP, 123.

315 *he began acting strangely*: Author interview with Katharine Porter, May 11, 2013.

315 *an "angry action"*: Katharine Porter interview, May 11, 2013.

316 *covered with typed letters*: Katharine Porter interview, May 11, 2013.

316 *Katie "protected us"*: Author interview with Katherine Koch, March 25, 2013.

316 *"In my family"*: Katharine Porter interview, May 11, 2013.

316 *the same air of "incandescence"*: Author interview with Ron and Pat Padgett, February 1, 1995.

316 *"deteriorated very quickly"*: Padgett interview, February 1, 1995.

317 *"He was having"*: Padgett interview, February 1, 1995.

317 *During one of these*: Ron Padgett to Joe Brainard, July 4, 1971. RP Beinecke.

317 *"It was so powerful"*: Padgett interview, February 1, 1995.

317 *started screaming*: Padgett interview, February 1, 1995.

317 *"the youngest person"*: Padgett interview, February 1, 1995.

317 *"Harm may befall"*: JTT, 350n752.

317 *"I went kind of"*: Padgett interview, February 1, 1995.

318 *Kenneth, Joe, and John*: Author interview with John Ashbery, August 13, 2004.

318 *"Have you seen Frank"*: See also JS to Fairfield and Anne Porter, July 13, 1971. AAA.

318 *"chatted with him"*: Padgett interview, February 1, 1995.

318 *"Everyone says"*: Author interview with Kenneth Koch, May 9, 1995.

319 *"I'd have to be"*: Author interview with Jane Freilicher, October 18, 1994.

319 *"didn't seem"*: Author interview with John Ashbery August 13, 2004.

319 *made friends*: Kenneth Koch interview, May 9, 1995; author interview with Robert Dash, October 22, 1995.

319 *"I may be asking"*: JS to Fairfield and Anne Porter, July 13, 1971. AAA.

319 *spiral-bound notebook*: Mandeville.

320 *"I'm sorry"*: JS to Porter, July 13, 1971. AAA.

320 *"a mild tranquilizer"*: JS to Fairfield Porter, July 14, 1971. AAA.

320 *"What happened was"*: JS to Kenward Elmslie, July 13, 1971. KGE Mandeville. JTT, 350.

320 *"would like to make"*: JS to Kenward Elmslie, July 8, 1971. KGE Mandeville.

320 *"Jimmy phone-calls"*: Kenward Elmslie to Ron Padgett [August 13, 1971]. RP Beinecke.

321 *Daum art nouveau glass*: Daum was a famous art glass studio in Nancy, France. Schuyler knew this and didn't really think there was a person named "Nancy Daum."

321 *"everything is symbol"*: Claude Lévi-Strauss, *The Scope of Anthropology* (London: Jonathan Cape, 1967), 20.

321 *"with their heavy draperies"*: Deleuze, *Sacher-Masoch*, 34. Translation by the author.

322 *"eternalize their subject"*: Deleuze, *Sacher-Masoch*, 70.

322 *"The essence of"*: Deleuze, *Sacher-Masoch*, 71.

323 *"a beautiful ride"*: JS to Fairfield and Anne Porter, [July] 21, 1971. AAA. JTT, 351.

17. AFTER FIVE O'CLOCK A KIND OF ENDLESSNESS SETS IN

324 *"relax, unwind"*: JS to Robert Dash, July 29, 1971. RD Beinecke. JTT, 352.
324 *"wasn't as nuts"*: Elmslie to Padgett [August 13, 1971]. RP Beinecke.
325 *"fritter money"*: JS to Kenneth Koch, February 7, 1972. KK Berg.
325 *"I think of you"*: JS to Bill Berkson, September 24, 1971. Dodd.
325 *"laughing hysterically"*: Author interview with John Ashbery, August 13, 2004.
326 *"blew his cool"*: JS to Ron Padgett, August 7 (?), 1971. RP Beinecke. JTT, 355.
326 *awakened by strange*: Author interview with John Ashbery, January 26, 1995.
326 *"rearranging objects"*: Kenward Elmslie to Ron Padgett [August 13, 1971]. RP Beinecke. Author interview with John Ashbery, August 13, 2004.
326 *Kenward was grateful*: Elmslie to Padgett [August 13, 1971].
326 *he declined*: Ashbery interview, January 26, 1995.
326 *"unbelievably gentle"*: Elmslie to Padgett [August 13, 1971].
326 *Jimmy "bustled" out*: Elmslie to Padgett [August 13, 1971].
327 *"took command"*: Kenward Elmslie, *Bare Bones* (Flint, MI: Bamberger Books, 1995), 13.
327 *During the drive*: Ashbery interview, August 13, 2004.
327 *"This has been"*: Elmslie to Padgett [August 13, 1971].
327 *had to be legally*: State of Vermont, "In Re: James M. Schuyler, New York City, New York," *Notice of Application for Admission to a Mental Hospital*, August 10, 1971. Courtesy Ron Padgett.
327 *Joe, in speaking*: Author interview with Tom Carey, October 3, 1994.
328 *"I do not want"*: Fairfield Porter to JS, August 19, 1971. Mandeville. Ted Leigh, ed., *Material Witness: The Selected Letters of Fairfield Porter* (Ann Arbor: University of Michigan Press, 2005), 288.
328 *"grandiose ideas"*: Fairfield Porter to John Ashbery, August 20, 1971. JA Houghton.
328 *"a productive therapeutic"*: JS to Fairfield Porter, August 19, 1971. AAA. JTT, 366.
328 *"I was lucky"*: JS to Trevor Winkfield, October 7, 1971. TW Beinecke.
328 *"buddy, friend"*: JS to Fairfield Porter, August 7, 1971. AAA. JTT, 354.
328 *"a Brainard-type 'natural'"*: JS to Harry Mathews, August 16, 1971. Kislak. JTT, 362.
328 *"I popped the question"*: JS to Porter, August 7, 1971. AAA. JTT, 354.
328 *"I want, in general"*: JS to Fairfield and Anne Porter, August 19, 1971. AAA. JTT, 365.
329 *who died*: JS to Winkfield, October 7, 1971. TW Beinecke.
330 *has been interpreted*: See Douglas Crase, "A Voice Like the Day," Douglas Crase, *On Autumn Lake: The Collected Essays* (New York: Nightboat Books, 2022), 13–14.
330 *"This morning view"*: The poem may have been influenced by William Blake's "The Lord's Prayer," which JS would have known from its inclusion in W. H. Auden's commonplace book *A Certain World*, 308.
330 *"Have been on"*: JS to Shelly Lustig, August 12, 1971. Courtesy Bill Corbett.
330 *he told Ron Padgett*: JS to Ron Padgett, August 18, 1971. RP Beinecke.
331 *"The funny thing is"*: JS to Kenneth Koch, February 7, 1972. KK Berg.
331 The Daily Planet: Courtesy Clark Coolidge.
331 *Anne destroyed*: Author interview with Anne Porter, May 5, 2004.
331 *"Jimmy needs a wife"*: Fairfield Porter to John Ashbery, August 20, 1971. JA Houghton.
332 *"When a person"*: Porter to Ashbery, August 20, 1971.
332 *"part of his illness"*: Kenward Elmslie to Fairfield Porter [August 1971]. AAA.
332 *"He's also very"*: JS to Joe Brainard, October 6, 1971. JB Mandeville.
332 *Jimmy did start*: JS to Joe Brainard, September 18, 1971. JB Mandeville.
332 *offered to sublet*: JS to Barbara Guest, October 15, 1971. Courtesy Bill Corbett.

332 *small, dark, charmless*: JS to Kenneth Koch, February 7, 1972. KK Berg.
332 *"Now that I can"*: JS to Ron Padgett, September 15, 1971. RP Beinecke. JTT, 376.
333 *on the condition*: Little 1993, 179.
333 *as many drawings*: JS to Harry Mathews, September 13, 1971. Kislak; JS to Anne Waldman, November 8, 1971. Michigan; JS to Clark Coolidge, November 5, 1971. Buffalo.
333 *In addition to poets*: *49 South* (Southampton, NY: James Schuyler, n.d. [1972]).
334 *"even 'a note on the type'"*: CP, 154.
334 *"It's odd"*: JS to Kenneth Koch, February 7, 1972. KK Berg.
334 *"very wily"*: Kenward Elmslie to Fairfield Porter, undated [August 1971]. AAA.
334 *When the book*: JS to Larry Fagin, March 7, 1972. U Conn.
334 *"It was one"*: Janice Koch to JS, February 10 [1972]. Mandeville.
335 *a "stately banquet"*: JS to Margaret Ridenour, March 7, 1972. Ridenour.
335 *All of the group*: JS to Larry Fagin, March 21, 1972. U Conn.
335 *he remembered patting*: CP, 219.
336 *"a rather gloomy"*: Berrigan 1983.
336 *"the prosiest poem"*: JS to Harry Mathews, May 22, 1972. Kislak.
336 *"totally hated it"*: Berrigan 1983.
337 *"An angry wish"*: "Was It," CP, 182.
337 *"rather like a sequel"*: JS to Joe Brainard, August 21, 1972. JB Mandeville.
337 *"a comedy of manners"*: Alice Notley, *American Book Review* (date unknown), quoted on cover of WFD.
337 *"fractal" quality*: James McCourt, "Afterword," WFD, 200.
338 *"I find this"*: WFD, 123.
338 *He invited Ron*: JS to Ron Padgett, April 14, 1972. RP Beinecke.
338 *"a great resource"*: JS to Fairfield Porter, July 17, 1972. AAA.
338 *"He had a way"*: Author interview with Robert Dash, May 4, 2004.
338 *"You could hear them"*: Dash interview, May 4, 2004.
339 *"lacked moral responsibility"*: Dash interview, May 4, 2004.
339 *a close relationship*: Both Dash and Park denied that it was a love affair, although many assumed it was.
339 *"I immediately gravitated"*: Author interview with Darragh Park, May 6, 2004.
339 *"It was obviously"*: Author interview with Darragh Park, December 12, 1994.
339 *"It was not a casual"*: Park interview, December 12, 1994.
339 *"I don't really like"*: JS to Fairfield Porter, July 17, 1972. AAA.
340 *Jimmy had stayed*: Peter Ackroyd email to author, May 13, 2012.
340 *who recalled*: Author conversation with Brad Gooch, June 7, 2012.
340 *"love poems by someone"*: JS to Trevor Winkfield, September 4, 1972. Beinecke. JTT, 385.
340 *"contains the best"*: David Kalstone, "A Poetry of Nouns and Adjectives," *New York Times Book Review* (November 5, 1972): 6.
340 *"I hadn't read"*: Elizabeth Bishop to Arthur Gold and Robert Fizdale, September 28, 1972. *One Art* (New York: Farrar, Straus and Giroux, 1994), 572.
341 *"Louring skys"*: JS to Clark Coolidge, December 14, 1972. Buffalo. JTT, 386, where mistranscribed as "lowering."
341 *Kenward worked*: JS to Fairfield Porter, October 25, 1972. AAA.
341 *"I may have shot"*: JS to Robert Dash, October 30, 1972. RD Beinecke.
341 *"I suppose"*: JS to Clark Coolidge, December 14, 1972. Buffalo. JTT, 387.
341 *"In the fall"*: JS to Kenward Elmslie, May 7, 1973. KGE Mandeville.

341 *The trust*: Kidder Peabody statements dated November 26, 1982 to March 31, 1983. Mandeville [box 28, folder 10].
342 *Anne Dunn recalled*: Author interview with Anne Dunn, March 17, 2004.
342 *"the greatest courtesan"*: JS to Kenward Elmslie, October 6, 1973. KGE Mandeville.
342 *"You're ravishing"*: Author interview with Ruth Kligman, October 25, 1995.
342 *"Unconsciously, Ruth Kligman"*: Ruth Kligman, *Love Affair: A Memoir of Jackson Pollock* (New York: William Morrow, 1974), endleaf.
343 *"He was like"*: Kligman interview, October 25, 1995.
343 *"two bawds"*: Author interview with Anne Dunn, March 30, 2011.
343 *gay men*: Gooch conversation, June 7, 2012.
343 *her sexual aggressiveness*: Gooch conversation, June 7, 2012.
343 *"every night was"*: Kligman interview, October 25, 1995.
343 *sprained her toe*: JS to Joe Brainard, August 20, 1973. JB Mandeville.
343 *called a friend*: Author interview with Cornelia Foss, December 27, 2022.
344 *"really was difficult"*: Author interview with Darragh Park, May 6, 2004.
344 *"I know someone"*: CP, 264-65.
344 *"in terrible shape"*: Author interview with Hyman Weitzen, June 26, 1995.
344 *"looked" schizophrenic*: Weitzen interview, June 26, 1995.
344 *later resolved*: Hyman Weitzen to "Whom it May Concern" on behalf of JS, June 13, 1984. Mandeville [box 28, folder 7].
344 *"a chronic mental"*: "Schizoaffective Disorder," National Alliance on Mental Illness, https://www.nami.org/about-mental-illness/mental-health-conditions/schizoaffective-disorder.
344 *a kind of physical*: JS to Kenward Elmslie, October 6, 1973. KGE Mandeville.
345 *"Can you imagine"*: JS to Kenward Elmslie, October 6, 1973.
345 *"There's something funny"*: JS to Fairfield Porter, July 19, 1973. AAA.
345 *"no candidate for"*: Weitzen interview, June 26, 1995.
345 *convinced Jimmy*: JS to Fairfield Porter, August 31, 1973. AAA.
345 *Jimmy liked*: JS to Kenward Elmslie, October 6, 1973.
345 *"he 'looked' better"*: Ron Padgett to Fairfield Porter, November 7, 1973. AAA.
345 *Jimmy "knew"*: Author interview with Anne Porter, May 5, 2004.
345 *"You can't just call"*: Anne Porter interview, May 5, 2004.
346 *While the van*: Anne Porter interview, May 5, 2004.

18. THIS DARK APARTMENT

347 *"I sit down"*: JS to Clark Coolidge, November 4, 1973. Buffalo.
347 *"I'm / not built that way"*: "This Dark Apartment," CP, 227.
347 *On March 15*: Dated on the typescript, Mandeville.
348 *prowling the halls*: Author interview with Trevor Winkfield, April 8, 2021.
348 *Starting early*: Author interviews with Anne Dunn, March 17, 2004; March 30, 2011.
349 *"popping so many"*: Dunn interview, March 17, 2004.
349 *"We didn't talk"*: Author interview with Anne Dunn, May 26, 2015.
349 *"the best"*: Author interview with Anne Dunn, June 20, 2022.
349 *On one occasion*: Author interview with Anne Dunn, October 13, 1994.
349 *"I give very good"*: Dunn interview, March 17, 2004.
349 *establishing a pattern*: Dunn interview, March 17, 2004.
349 *One winter's night*: Author interview with George and Katie Schneeman, December 4, 2006.

350 *"kind of lost"*: Author interview with Jane Freilicher, October 18, 1994.
351 "*John is always"*: Author interview with Douglas Crase, May 21, 2008.
351 *a new poem*: Poems written during this visit are: "December 28, 1974" (CP, 233); "Can I Tempt You to a Pond Walk" [December 29], published in *Poetry* (February 1976), 255 (uncollected); "Growing Dark" [December 30] (CP, 232); "Chabrier" (OF, 97); an untitled poem beginning "The Airdales sleep . . ." [December 31] (unpublished); and "New Year" [January 1, 1975] (OF, 93). Manuscript notebook, Berg.
351 "*It* had *become"*: Author interview with Robert Dash, October 22, 1995.
351 *"One doesn't remember"*: Author interview with Douglas Crase, May 21, 2008.
352 *"I was just thrilled"*: Crase interview, May 21, 2008.
352 *"it was done"*: Author interview with Trevor Winkfield, June 2, 1995.
352 *The full details*: Dorothy Farnan, *Auden in Love* (New York: Simon & Schuster, 1984), 250–53.
352 *"Chester Kallman"*: Published in *Court Green* 9 (2012): 38 (uncollected).
352 *"really out of it"*: JS to Anne and Fairfield Porter, April 16, 1975. AAA.
352 *By January 27*: Darragh Park agenda, DAP Mandeville.
353 *"Well, I write"*: Author interview with Darragh Park, May 6, 2004.
353 *"tender but firm"*: Peter Schjeldahl email to author, July 24, 2021.
353 *"We meet in strange"*: JS to Kenward Elmslie, February 15, 1975. KGE Mandeville.
353 *"looking at things"*: Ross 1981, 1.
353 *"Claustrated"*: "Trip," CP, 252.
353 *"I really love"*: JS to Robert Dash, February 4, 1975. RD Beinecke.
354 *Jimmy cooked dinner*: Author interview with Darragh Park, May 6, 2004.
354 *he made plans*: JS to Margaret Ridenour, April [misdated August] 18, 1975. Ridenour. JS to Anne Dunn, June 13, 1975. Dunn.
354 *"terrible mounting rage"*: JS to Anne Dunn, June 24, 1975. Dunn.
354 *"I don't want"*: JS to Kenneth Koch, July 1, 1975. KK Berg.
354 *did see the manuscript*: Author phone interview with Michael Di Capua, ca. 1995; Berrigan interview, 1983.
355 *"July 4th"*: JS manuscript notebook. NYPL Berg Collection.
355 *on July 7*: Author interview with Darragh Park, December 12, 1994.
355 *"Here are Jimmy's"*: Park interview, December 12, 1994.
355 *"a creature of"*: JS to Darragh Park, July 26, 1975. DAP Mandeville.
355 *"Once I've noticed"*: Author interview with John Ashbery, May 6, 2013.
355 *was prescribed lithium*: JS to Fairfield Porter, August 5, 1975. AAA; JS to Robert Dash, August 23, 1975. RD Beinecke.
356 *at least five poems*: These are: "Good Morning" (CP, 234); "Men Cut Down Old Trees" (unpublished; included in a letter to Barbara Guest, September 9, 1975, Berg Collection); "The Weeping Beech" (OF, 171); "Poem" (The day gets slowly started) (OF, 178); and "Song" (CP, 235).
356 *On September 17*: Darragh Park agenda, DAP Mandeville.
356 *uncomfortably quiet*: Author interview with Trevor Winkfield, June 6, 2013.
356 *how was Jimmy*: Author interview with Darragh Park, May 6, 2004.
357 *funeral was eclectic*: Anne Porter to JS [September 20, 1975]. Mandeville [box 3, folder 37]. Justin Spring, *Fairfield Porter: A Life in Art* (New Haven, CT: Yale University Press, 1999), 344–45.
357 *"There was a plainness"*: Spring, *Porter*, 345.
357 *"I know that you"*: Anne Porter to JS [September 20, 1975]. Mandeville. Spring, *Porter*, 344.

357 *a year at Bloomingdale*: John Ashbery to Anne Dunn, September 3, 1975. Dunn.
357 *A partial solution*: Ashbery to Dunn, September 3, 1975.
358 *It was apparently*: JS to Anne Dunn, "Decoration Day" [May 31], 1976. Dunn. JTT, 397.
358 *"a kind of rooming"*: Author interview with Darragh Park, December 12, 1994.
358 *"a seedy* pension": John Ashbery to Anne Dunn, June 1, 1976. Dunn.
358 *"he was functioning"*: Author interview with Darragh Park, May 6, 2004.
358 *"I'm all moved"*: JS to Dunn, "Decoration Day" [May 31], 1976. JTT, 397.
358 *"You can't imagine"*: JS to Dunn, "Decoration Day" [May 31], 1976. JTT, 400.
358 *"looks seedy"*: John Ashbery to Anne Dunn, June 1, 1976. Dunn.
358 *"His state seems"*: John Ashbery to Kenneth Koch, May 23, 1976. KK Berg.
359 *"When my mother"*: JS to Dunn, "Decoration Day" [May 31], 1976. JTT, 400.
359 *a long, book-length*: Thompson 1992, 117; Little 1993, 178.
359 *begun in long*: JS to Kenward Elmslie, August 13, 1976. KGE Mandeville.
359 *"to indicate that"*: Berrigan 1983. In the Hillringhouse interview (p. 9), Schuyler says that the broken lines in "The Morning of the Poem" were "changed for typesetting," implying that the secondary line breaks were randomly established by the typographer. He may have been thinking of the first printing of "Hymn to Life" in *Poetry*, where that had been the case. (In the wider page format of *Collected Poems* it was mostly not necessary.) However, the lineation of "The Morning of the Poem" was his own and is consistent between its first publication in the eponymous book and in *Collected Poems*.
360 *"It has a certain lightness"*: Thompson 1992, 17–18.
360 *"it isn't nostalgic"*: Tim Dlugos, "The Joe Brainard Interview," September 26, 1977, *Little Caesar* 10 (1980).
361 *"Vienna where the painting"*: John Ashbery, *Collected Poems 1956–1987*, Mark Ford, ed. (New York: Library of America, 2008), 480. The poem was first published in *Poetry* in August 1974.
361 *"Porter nirvana"*: Kenward Elmslie to the author, December 8, 1995.
362 *"It opened the space"*: Author interview with Alice Notley, October 17, 2022.
362 *"Everything was just too"*: Thompson 1992, 117.
362 *behaving "strangely"*: John Ashbery to Anne Dunn, April 30 [1977]. Dunn.
362 *"unspeakable"*: Ashbery to Dunn, April 30 [1977].
362 *On the night*: Ashbery to Dunn, April 30 [1977].
363 *an extensive series*: Author interview with Darragh Park, December 12, 1994.
363 *"Poor Jimmy"*: Ashbery to Dunn, April 30 [1977].
363 *"a disaster area"*: Park interview, December 12, 1994.
363 *"like he must"*: Park interview, December 12, 1994.
363 *a "paralytic effect"*: John Ashbery to Anne Dunn, July 10 [1977]. Dunn.
363 *being wheeled away*: Author interview with Douglas Crase and Frank Polach, January 30, 1996.
363 *most of the summer*: Park interview, December 12, 1994.
364 *"much telephoning"*: Darragh Park, notes to the author, undated.
364 *basically an old-age*: Author interview with Darragh Park, May 6, 2004; Crase and Polach interview, January 30, 1996.
364 *"sane and lucid"*: Douglas Crase email to the author, May 31, 2022.
364 *"two bizarre"*: "Dining Out with Doug and Frank," CP, 245.
364 *surprised and rather affronted*: Crase and Polach interview, January 30, 1996.
365 *"experiment / more"*: CP, 250.
365 *"the most beautiful"*: Author interview with Frank Polach, June 2, 2011.

365 *"full of death"*: CP, 250. See also the title essay in Howard Moss, *Whatever Is Moving* (Boston / Toronto: Little, Brown and Company, 1981): 54-69.
366 *"was so accustomed"*: Author interview with Alex and Ada Katz, November 17, 1995.
366 *"having real problems"*: Author interview with Darragh Park, December 12, 1994.
367 The Home Book: The poems included in *The Home Book* were later republished in *Collected Poems*, but the stories and plays have not been reprinted.
367 *"quietly scarifying"*: Stephen Spender, "Meat Loaf," *New York Review of Books* (October 11, 1979).
367 *replied enthusiastically*: Author phone interview with Michael di Capua, undated, c. 1995.
367 *eliminating "quite a few"*: Di Capua interview, c. 1995.
367 *He had admired*: Author interview with Charles North, November 6, 1995.
368 *"I know he attracted"*: Justin Jamail and Andrew McCarron, "James Schuyler: Charles North Interview," *Pataphysics* (Publishing Issue, 2005): 6.
368 *One evening*: Author interview with Charles and Paula North, November 6, 1995.
368 *"some real shockers"*: Charles North email to the author, January 30, 2004. North later said he could not remember any examples (email to author, September 30, 2024).
368 *a "flophouse"*: Author interview with Darragh Park, December 12, 1994.
368 *"dark and neglected"*: Patti Smith, *Just Kids* (New York: Ecco, 2010), 86–87.
369 *"pretty horrifying"*: North interviewed by Jamail and McCarron, 4.
369 *"wrote and wrote"*: North interviewed by Jamail and McCarron, 6. Michael Lally recalled a similar experience at the same or a different party, when Schuyler simply signed his name numerous times in progressively smaller and smaller script.
369 *Later that month*: Richard D. Savitsky, "Memorandum to the Friends of Jimmy Schuyler," September 25, 1980. Mandeville.
369 *The all-star list*: *A Reading from James Schuyler*, December 3, 1978. Flyer collection Charles North.
369 *nightmarish and "tragic"*: Author interview with Anne Dunn, October 13, 1994.

19. NEVER TRUST BLONDS FROM SHERMAN OAKS

371 *"I put lesbian content"*: Maggie Nelson, *Women, the New York School, and Other True Abstractions* (Iowa City: University of Iowa Press, 2007), 173.
371 *"like somebody who's spent"*: Author interview with Eileen Myles, October 10, 1994.
372 *"the shortest job interview"*: Eileen Myles, email to the author, July 8, 2024.
372 *"I would just sit"*: Myles interview, October 10, 1994.
372 *"dry cleaned clothes"*: Eileen Myles, *Chelsea Girls* (Santa Rosa, CA: Black Sparrow Press, 1994), 274.
372 *"It's a great one"*: Myles interview, October 10, 1994. Schuyler included Myles among his favorite contemporary poets in at least two interviews: Ross 1981 (2) (along with Barbara Guest, Frank O'Hara, Ron Padgett, and Gary Snyder) and Hillringhouse 1985 (8) (with Ron Padgett, Michael Brownstein, Anne Waldman, Gary Snyder, Geoffrey Young, and Helena Hughes).
372 *sleeping with a reptile*: Myles interview, October 10, 1994.
372 *"there was still"*: Myles interview, October 10, 1994.
373 *"The presence of his"*: Myles, *Chelsea Girls*, 274.
373 *"kept changing"*: Myles interview, October 10, 1994.
373 *"sort of noncommittal"*: Author interview with Tom Carey, July 9, 2004.
374 *"I can't see you"*: "A few days," CP, 355.

374 *"What will it be"*: CP, 358.
375 *"sitting out on"*: JS to Margaret Ridenour, September 2, 1979. Ridenour.
375 *"Berton hated you"*: "A few days," CP, 379.
375 *there wasn't the same*: Little 1993, 178.
375 *"good, really / good"*: CP, 377.
375 *"creamed shit"*: CP, 376.
376 *Weitzen decided*: Myles interview, October 10, 1994.
376 *"I'm having anxiety"*: Myles interview, October 10, 1994.
376 *"catatonic state"*: Myles interview, October 10, 1994.
376 *"Well, you know"*: Author interview with Anne Dunn, April 20, 2013.
376 *One day after a visit*: Myles interview, October 10, 1994.
378 *"Jimmy was always"*: Carey interview, July 9, 2004.
379 *"was absolutely nowhere"*: Carey interview, July 9, 2004.
379 *his "social graces"*: Author interview with Alex and Ada Katz, November 17, 1995.
379 *"Jimmy, you're here!"*: Carey interview, July 9, 2004.
380 *"He didn't know how"*: JS Manuscript poem, "For Frank" (March 19, 1980). Douglas Crase and Frank Polach Papers, Series I, box 34, Beinecke.
380 *"I couldn't take it"*: CP, 284.
381 *"Tom / isn't coming back"*: JS, "For Frank."
382 *"I hope we have"*: Collection of the author.
382 *"given freely"*: Kenward Elmslie to the author, December 8, 1995.
382 *"very heavy vibes"*: Author interview with Helena Hughes, March 1, 1995.
382 *By May 1981*: Richard D. Savitsky to "Friends and Interested Parties," May 27, 1981. Mandeville.
382 *Ted Berrigan briefly*: Author interview with Bob Rosenthal, June 24, 2022.
382 *In June 1981*: Rosenthal interview, June 24, 2022.
383 *Between 1982 and 1984*: Mandeville.
383 *"delightful beauty"*: Author interview with Michael Lally, June 13, 2022.
383 *Jimmy even offered*: Author telephone interview with Helena Hughes, October 1995.
383 *after four previous*: The successful 1980 application is the only one of the eight total that includes an outright lie: in it Jimmy awarded himself a BA in English from Bethany College in 1945. John Simon Guggenheim Memorial Foundation Records.
383 *just over half*: JS to John Simon Guggenheim Memorial Foundation, June 9, 1982. Guggenheim Foundation.
384 *a "substantial section"*: Author phone interview with Michael di Capua, undated, c. 1995.
384 *When Jimmy learned*: Author interview with John Ashbery, July 22, 2004.
385 Small Crimes: Tom Carey later reused the title for an unrelated novel published in 2011.
385 *Ted and his wife*: Author interview with Alice Notley, October 17, 2022.
385 *Tom began stealing*: Author interview with Tom Carey, October 3, 1994.
385 *"just junkie behavior"*: Carey interview, October 3, 1994.
385 *it quickly escalated*: Carey interview, October 3, 1994.
386 *"You have never"*: Tom Carey to JS, August 10, 1981. Mandeville.
387 *"I just had a lovely"*: JS to Geoffrey Young, August 19, 1981. Young. JTT, 406.
387 *"You made me"*: JS to Tom Carey, April 30, 1988. TC Beinecke.
388 *"totally blossomed"*: Myles interview, October 10, 1994.
388 *"He was completely"*: Myles interview, October 10, 1994.
388 *McCourt recognized him*: Author interview with James McCourt, January 4, 2006.
388 *a scene of the opera*: James McCourt, *Kaye Wayfaring in "Avenged"* (New York: Penguin Books, 1985), 186–87.

388 *"singer's sense"*: McCourt interview, January 4, 2006.
389 *"really cared"*: Author interview with Helena Hughes, March 1, 1995.
389 *He also enrolled*: Hughes interview, March 1, 1995.
389 *"lie on the bed"*: D, 147.
390 *"the longest continuous"*: D, 133.
390 *"to see things growing"*: D, 134.
390 *He did not think*: Author telephone interview with Michael di Capua, undated, c. 1995.
390 *"never dreamt"*: D, 146.
390 *"put into a tantrum"*: JS to Joe Brainard, July 29, 1985. Mandeville. JTT, 410; D, 164.
390 *which he wrote*: D, 164.
391 *Bernadette Mayer recommended*: Author phone interview with Bill DeNoyelles, January 9, 2013.
391 *"really crazy" messages*: Author interview with Tom Carey, October 3, 1994.
391 *"some kind of shrine"*: Author interview with Tom Carey, July 9, 2004.
391 *Jimmy had transformed*: DeNoyelles interview, January 9, 2013.
392 *"he was consistent"*: Myles interview, October 10, 1994.
392 *as though he was*: Author interview with Eileen Myles, February 11, 2014.
392 *"It gave me this"*: Myles interview, October 10, 1994.
392 *"agitated, pacing"*: Bill DeNoyelles email to the author, January 19, 2013.
392 *"started to talk"*: DeNoyelles interview, January 9, 2013.
392 *"Do you know"*: DeNoyelles interview, January 9, 2013. (DeNoyelles couldn't remember whether the word was *witch* or *bitch* or both.)
392 *"had a major slip"*: DeNoyelles interview, January 9, 2013.
393 *"My room has"*: Guillaume Apollinaire, "Hôtel," translated by Fairfield Porter. Fairfield Porter, *The Collected Poems with Selected Drawings* (New York: Tibor de Nagy Editions, 1985), 84.
393 *Ned Rorem recalled*: Author interview with Ned Rorem, March 29, 2005.
393 *how "hot"*: DeNoyelles interview, January 9, 2013.
393 *"Excuse me, Bill"*: DeNoyelles interview, January 9, 2013.
393 *about a week*: One or both of Jimmy's Diary entries, dated August 18 and 23, may be misdated. Both appear to have been written after he returned from the hospital, but the one dated the 23rd refers to his having returned the day before, which seems possible.
394 *"an unmarked stone"*: DJS, 180.
394 *"tap on the shoulder"*: Author interview with Helena Hughes, March 1, 1995.
394 *"That elegance"*: DJS, 180.

20. IN BELL-LIKE BLUE

395 *"touch bottom"*: Author interview with Tom Carey, October 3, 1994.
395 *"It was really quite"*: Carey interview, October 3, 1994.
395 *"born out of sickness"*: Carey interview, October 3, 1994.
395 *"Tom's enormous contribution"*: Author interview with Darragh Park, December 12, 1994.
396 *"It was one of those"*: Park interview, December 12, 1994.
396 *Whiting Award*: This was the inaugural year of the award, established by the Mrs. Giles Whiting Foundation to support "emerging" poets and fiction writers (of any age).
396 *"the longest night"*: Author interview with Eileen Myles, October 10, 1994.

396 *to several "tearful outbursts"*: JS to David Trinidad, October 5, 1985. JTT, 418.
396 *his courage and élan*: Carey interview, October 3, 1994.
397 *"still very like"*: JS to David Trinidad, October 5, 1985. Fales. JTT, 421.
397 *the first person*: DJS, 204.
397 *"Aladar wasn't offstage"*: DJS, 204.
397 *"Poor Daniel"*: DJS, 156; 136.
397 *"You must have"*: DJS, 216.
398 "*Tom* loves *going*": JS to David Trinidad: "First day of fall" [September 23], 1986. Fales.
398 "*No, you cannot*": Author interview with Raymond Foye, October 20, 2013.
398 *"He really bent over"*: Foye interview, October 20, 2013.
399 *"taking everything in"*: Foye interview, October 20, 2013.
399 *Back in 1983*: Michael Davidson, Archive for New Poetry, UCSD to Helena Hughes, November 30, 1983. Mandeville.
399 *the university approved*: George Robert Minkoff (Agent) to Raymond Foye, June 26, 1989. Mandeville.
400 *"relieved and grateful"*: Author interview with Helena Hughes, March 1, 1995.
400 *"Jimmy moved into"*: Park interview, December 12, 1994.
400 *"surprised by the"*: DJS, 191.
401 *"What a very human"*: DJS, 243.
401 *"a part of that"*: DJS, 220.
401 *"things seem rather"*: JS to Tom Carey, May 16, 1988. Beinecke.
402 *"I'm afraid I've"*: JS to Anne Dunn, April 20, 1987. Dunn. JTT, 426.
402 *was rather hurt*: Author interview with John Ashbery, January 26, 1995.
403 *"a giant Rorschach Test"*: JS to Anne Dunn, May 28, 1988. Dunn.
403 *a "chunky hunk"*: Author zoom interview with Peter Gizzi, December 15, 2022.
403 *"When you read"*: JS postcard to Anne Porter, June 8, 1988. AAA.
403 *"It makes me so"*: JS to Tom Carey, September 12, 1988. Beinecke.
404 *"perfect . . . what a poem"*: Author interview with David Trinidad, March 30, 2005.
404 *"huge, humiliating"*: Trinidad interview, March 30, 2005.
404 *"Your beautiful poems"*: JS to David Trinidad, August 1, 1985. Fales.
404 *"stretches of awkwardness"*: Trinidad interview, March 30, 2005.
405 *"doing things in front"*: Thompson 1992: 106.
405 *he traced back*: Author interview with Hyman Weitzen, June 26, 1995.
405 *"voice of the poem"*: Thompson 1992: 106.
405 *"positive about the idea"*: Author interview with Charles Wright, October 24, 2013.
405 *"which is not"*: JS to Anne Dunn, June 30, 1988. Dunn. JTT, 440.
405 *how "intimate"*: Douglas Crase email to author, December 13, 2013. Memories differ in some cases about who was there.
405 *"No tears!"*: David Trinidad email to the author, December 12, 2013.
405 *older friends*: Darragh Park agenda, November 10, 1988. DAP Mandeville.
406 *"I do (ahem)"*: JS to Anne Dunn, July 11, 1988. Dunn.
406 *"[Schuyler's] Dia reading"*: Justin Jamail and Andrew McCarron, "James Schuyler: Charles North Interview," *Pataphysics* (Publishing Issue, 2005): 8.
406 *a gathering*: DJS, 242.
406 *Young and the other*: Author interview with Geoffrey Young, July 11, 2022.
406 *"taking it all in"*: Author zoom interview with Peter Gizzi, December 15, 2022.
406 *"they are both"*: JS to Charles North, December 1, 1988. CN Beinecke.
407 *"a single bed"*: Gizzi interview, December 15, 2022.
407 *"Perhaps someone"*: JS to Anne Dunn, "Thanksgiving" [November 24], 1988. Dunn.

407 *"My legs weren't made"*: JS to Peter Gizzi, February 13, 1989. JS wrote two poems in San Francisco, both on Ash Wednesday, February 8, "Blossoming Oakwood" and "A Chapel."
408 *"crawling with writers"*: Dodie Bellamy, "James Schuyler Gives His Second Poetry Reading Ever," courtesy Dodie Bellamy. Published in the *Archive for New Poetry Newsletter*, UCSD, 1989.
408 *"the intensity"*: Chip Livingston, ed., *Love, Loosha: The Letters of Lucia Berlin & Kenward Elmslie* (Albuquerque: High Road Books, 2022), 318.
408 *"mindfulness" of himself*: Author interview with Tom Carey, March 16, 2011.
408 *"how you see"*: DJS, 251.
408 *Tom was "effervescent"*: Bellamy, "Second Reading," 1989.
408 *"feeding" a stone*: Author interview with Robert Glück, December 13, 2006.
409 *"as aspish as ever"*: Bill Berkson email to the author, April 19, 2005.
409 *"Never did anyone"*: JS to Tom Carey, February 19, 1989. TC Beinecke. JTT, 445.
409 *a large party*: Author interview with David Trinidad, March 30, 2005.
409 *"It's a wonderful"*: JS to William Corbett, March 5, 1989. Ohio.
409 *coming out of his barbershop*: Author interview with Darragh Park, December 12, 1994.
409 *"I want you to know"*: Tom Carey to JS, May 18, 1989. Mandeville.
410 *"I never thought"*: Author diary, March 26, 1990.
410 *"Timmm-berrrrrr!"*: Author diary, March 26, 1990.
410 *a "brown starfish"*: DJS, 257.
410 *He got to know*: Author interview with Darragh Park, May 6, 2004.
410 *Artie went away*: DJS, 265.
410 *"the broadcasts"*: JS to Anne Dunn, August 21, 1989. Dunn. JTT, 451.
410 *"Artie looked a treat"*: DJS, 269.
411 *the president of Bethany College*: D. Duane Cummins to JS, March 24, 1989. Mandeville [box 14, folder 18].
411 *"skeletons in his closet"*: Author interview with Simon Pettet, March 22, 2023.
411 *"One begins to understand"*: DJS, 264.
412 *"stand-ins for"*: Jonathan Galassi, "Introduction to a Reading at the 92nd Street Y, November 20, 1989." The reading can be heard on the Penn Sound website.
412 *"As I said to Bjoerling"*: Darragh Park, agenda, November 23, 1989. DAP Mandeville.
412 *"I felt like I was"*: Author interview with Michael Brownstein, May 8, 2012.
413 *"I guess a lot of people"*: Author diary, February 7, 1991. Jimmy did not tell me the man's name but I discovered it later among his papers in the Mandeville Library. In 1993, D'Auria would release the movie *Smoke*, which he wrote, directed, and starred in. The protagonist is a thirty-five-year-old man who, "seeking a father figure as a result of childhood abandonment, carries on with older men a mix of affairs, one-night stands, and casual sex in public toilets" until a reunion with his family sparks "a crisis and a resolution." *Smoke*, IMBd, https://www.imdb.com/title/tt0108166/.
413 *The reading was taped*: Penn Sound: https://media.sas.upenn.edu/pennsound/authors/Schuyler/Schuyler-Tapes/Schuyler-James_Complete-Recording_Date-Location-Unknown.mp3. I identify this tape as the NYU reading because of the trouble Schuyler had with his new bifocals at 16:10, which I made a note of at the time.
414 *When I visited*: Author diary, March 16, 1991.
414 *When we got there*: Author diary, April 4, 1991.
414 *When Tom spoke*: Author conversations with Tom Carey, per author diary, April 6–7, 1991.
415 *A CT scan*: Author conversation with Raymond Foye, per author diary, April 6, 1991.

415 *Two days later*: Author diary, April 7, 1991.
415 *His bed was by*: Author diary, April 13, 1991.
415 *"but his eyes still"*: Darragh Park, agenda, June 15, 1991. DAP Mandeville.
415 *"The light coming"*: Author conversation with Darragh Park, per author diary, April 12, 1991.
416 *He asked us*: Author diary, April 15, 1991.
416 *"I feel as though"*: Author diary, April 12, 1991.
416 *Jimmy's funeral*: Author diary, April 17, 1991. Joe Brainard was in Venice at the time on a long-planned visit, but asked me to send flowers on his behalf. I chose pink magnolias, thinking of "Hymn to Life."
416 *Tom had become*: Author interview with Tom Carey, January 24, 2023.
416 *Eileen, Artie, David*: Author diary, September 22, 1991.

SELECTED BIBLIOGRAPHY

BOOKS BY JAMES SCHUYLER

Alfred and Guinevere (New York: Harcourt, Brace and Company, 1958; repr., New York: New York Review Books, 2001)

Salute (New York: Tiber Press, 1960)

May 24th Or So (New York: Tibor de Nagy Editions, 1966)

Freely Espousing (Garden City, NY: Doubleday Paris Review Editions, 1969; repr., New York: Sun, 1979)

A Sun Cab (with illustrations by Fairfield Porter) (New York: Adventures in Poetry, 1972)

The Crystal Lithium (New York: Random House, 1972)

Hymn to Life (New York: Random House, 1974)

The Fireproof Floors of Witley Court (Newark West Burke, VT: Janus Press, 1976)

The Home Book, Trevor Winkfield, ed. (Calais, VT: Z Press, 1977)

What's for Dinner? (Santa Rosa, CA: Black Sparrow Press, 1978; repr., New York: New York Review Books, 2006)

The Morning of the Poem (New York: Farrar, Straus and Giroux, 1980)

Early in '71 (Berkeley: The Figures, 1982)

A Few Days (New York: Random House, 1985)

Selected Poems (New York: Farrar, Straus and Giroux, 1988; repr., with a new introduction by John Ashbery, New York: Farrar, Straus and Giroux, 2007)

For Joe Brainard (New York: Dia Art Foundation, 1988)

James Schuyler Poems / Andrew Lord Sculptures (Zürich: Edition Bruno Bischofberger, 1992)

Collected Poems (New York: Farrar, Straus and Giroux, 1993)

Two Journals (with illustrations by Darragh Park) (New York: Tibor de Nagy Editions, 1995)

The Diary of James Schuyler, Nathan Kernan, ed. (Santa Rosa, CA: Black Sparrow Press, 1997)

Selected Art Writings, Simon Pettet, ed. (Santa Rosa, CA: Black Sparrow Press, 1998)

Last Poems (London: Slow Dancer Press, 1999)

Just the Thing: Selected Letters of James Schuyler, William Corbett, ed. (New York: Turtle Point Press, 2004; rev. ed., 2023)

The Letters of James Schuyler to Frank O'Hara, William Corbett, ed. (New York: Turtle Point Press, 2006)

Other Flowers: Uncollected Poems, James Meetze and Simon Pettet, eds. (New York: Farrar, Straus and Giroux, 2010)

TRANSLATIONS

Hymne an das Leben, Gedichte, Erwin Einzinger, trans. (Salzburg, Austria: Residenz Verlag, 1991)

Il est douze heures plus tard, Stéphane Bouquet, trans. (Nantes, France: éditions joca seria, 2014)

WITH JOHN ASHBERY

A Nest of Ninnies (New York: E. P. Dutton, 1969; repr., Calais, VT: Z Press, 1975; New York: Ecco Press, 1997; Champaign, IL, and London: Dalkey Archive Press, 2008). Translation: *Ein Haufen Idioten*, Erwin Einzinger, trans. (Salzburg, Austria: Residenz Verlag, 1990)

WITH KENWARD ELMSLIE AND KENNETH KOCH

Penguin Modern Poets 24: Kenward Elmslie, Kenneth Koch, James Schuyler; John Ashbery, Guest Editor (Harmondsworth, UK: Penguin Books, 1974)

EDITED BY JAMES SCHUYLER

49 South (Southampton NY: James Schuyler, 1972)

EDITED BY JAMES SCHUYLER AND CHARLES NORTH

Broadway: A Poets and Painters Anthology (New York: Swollen Magpie Press, 1979)

Broadway 2: A Poets and Painters Anthology (New York: Hanging Loose Press, 1989)

SECONDARY SOURCES

Donald M. Allen, *The New American Poetry 1945–1960* (New York: Grove Press, 1960)

Alan Ansen, *The Table Talk of W. H. Auden* (London and Boston: Faber and Faber, 1990)

Alan Ansen, *The Vigilantes: A Fragment* (Sudbury, MA: Water Row Press, 1987)

John Ashbery, *Collected Poems 1956–1987*, Mark Ford, ed. (New York: Library of America, 2008)

John Ashbery, *Collected Poems 1991–2000*, Mark Ford, ed. (New York: Library of America, 2017)

John Ashbery, *Selected Prose*, Eugene Richie, ed. (Ann Arbor: University of Michigan Press, 2004)

John Ashbery, *Three Plays* (Calais, VT: Z Press, 1978)

W. H. Auden, *A Certain World* (New York: Viking, 1970)

W. H. Auden, *Collected Poems*, Edward Mendelson, ed. (New York: Modern Library, 2007)

W. H. Auden, *The Dyer's Hand and Other Essays* (New York: Vintage Books, 1968)

Sybille Bedford, *Quicksands: A Memoir* (New York: Counterpoint, 2005)

Bill Berkson and Joe LeSueur, eds., *Homage to Frank O'Hara* (Bolinas, CA: Big Sky Books, 1978)

Bill Berkson, *Since When: A Memoir in Pieces* (Minneapolis: Coffee House Press, 2018)

Lucia Berlin, *Instructions for Cleaning Women* (New York: Farrar, Straus and Giroux, 2016)

Lucia Berlin and Kenward Elmslie, *Love, Loosha: The Letters of Lucia Berlin & Kenward Elmslie*, Chip Livingston, ed. (Albuquerque: High Road Books, 2022)

Allan Bérubé, *Coming Out Under Fire* (New York: Free Press, 1990)

Elizabeth Bishop, *One Art: Letters*, Robert Giroux, ed. (New York: Farrar, Straus and Giroux, 1994)

Marc Bloch, *The Historian's Craft* (New York: Vintage 1953)

Paul Bowles, *In Touch: The Letters of Paul Bowles*, Jeffrey Miller, ed. (New York: Farrar, Straus and Giroux, 1994)

Joe Brainard, *The Collected Writings of Joe Brainard*, Ron Padgett, ed. (New York: Library of America, 2012)

Truman Capote, *Portraits and Observations* (New York: Random House, 2007)

Truman Capote, *Too Brief a Treat: The Letters of Truman Capote*, Gerald Clarke, ed. (New York: Random House, 2004)

Humphrey Carpenter, *W. H. Auden: A Biography* (Boston: Houghton Mifflin, 1981)

George Chauncey, *Gay New York: Gender, Urban Culture, and the Making of the Gay Male World, 1890–1940* (New York: Basic Books, 1994)

Thekla Clark, *Wystan and Chester: A Personal Memoir of W. H. Auden and Chester Kallman* (London: Faber and Faber, 1995)

William Corbett and Geoffrey Young, eds., *That Various Field for James Schuyler* (Great Barrington, MA: The Figures, 1991)

Douglas Crase, *On Autumn Lake: The Collected Essays* (New York: Nightboat Books, 2022)

Douglas Crase and Jenni Quilter, eds., *Painters & Poets. Tibor de Nagy Gallery* (New York: Tibor de Nagy Gallery, 2011)

Cathy Curtis, *Restless Ambition: Grace Hartigan, Painter* (New York: Oxford University Press, 2015)

Charles Darwin, *The Autobiography of Charles Darwin and Selected Letters* (New York: Dover Publications, 1958)

Gilles Deleuze, *Présentation de Sacher-Masoch* (Paris: Editions de Minuit, 1967)

Edwin Denby, *The Complete Poems*, Ron Padgett, ed. (New York: Random House, 1986)

Thomas P. Detre and Henry G. Jarecki, *Modern Psychiatric Treatment* (Philadelphia and Toronto: J. B. Lippincott, 1971)

Diane di Prima, *Recollections of My Life as a Woman* (New York: Penguin Books, 2002)

Donald Downes, *The Scarlet Thread* (New York: British Book Centre, 1953)

Kenward Elmslie, *Album* (New York: Kulchur Press, 1969)

Kenward Elmslie, *Bare Bones* (Flint, MI: Bamberger Books, 1995)

Kenward Elmslie, *Blast from the Past* (Austin, TX: Skanky Possum Press, 2000)

Andrew Epstein, *Attention Equals Life: The Pursuit of the Everyday in Contemporary Poetry and Culture* (Oxford: Oxford University Press, 2018)

Dorothy Farnan, *Auden in Love* (New York: Simon & Schuster, 1984)

Russell Ferguson, *In Memory of My Feelings: Frank O'Hara and American Art* (Los Angeles: Museum of Contemporary Art, 1999)

James W. Foss, *A Hero of the Left* (unpublished typescript, 1984. Courtesy Donald Windham)

Brad Gooch, *City Poet: The Life and Times of Frank O'Hara* (New York: Alfred A. Knopf, 1993)

John Gruen, *The Party's Over Now: Reminiscences of the Fifties—New York's Artists, Writers, Musicians, and Their Friends* (New York: Viking Press, 1972)

Barbara Guest, *The Collected Poems of Barbara Guest*, Hadley Haden Guest, ed. (Middletown, CT: Wesleyan University Press, 2008)

Donald Hall, Robert Pack, and Louis Simpson, eds., *The New Poets of England and America* (New York: Meridian Books, 1957)

Langdon Hammer, *James Merrill: Life and Art* (New York: Alfred A. Knopf, 2015)

Langdon Hammer and Stephen Yenser, eds., *A Whole World: Letters from James Merrill* (New York: Alfred A. Knopf, 2021)

Grace Hartigan, *The Journals of Grace Hartigan, 1951–1955*, William T. La Moy and Joseph P. McCaffrey, eds. (Syracuse: Syracuse University Press, 2009)

Richard Huelsenbeck, *Memoirs of a Dada Drummer* (Berkeley: University of California Press, 1991)
Agnes Husslein-Arco and Alexander Klee, eds., *Oppenheimer—Mahler and the Music* (Vienna: Belvedere, 2010)
Christopher Isherwood, *Diaries Volume One: 1939–1960*, Katherine Bucknell, ed. (New York: HarperCollins, 1997)
H. G. Jones, *The Sonarman's War* (Jefferson, NC: McFarland, 2010)
Kenneth Koch, *The Collected Poems of Kenneth Koch* (New York: Alfred A. Knopf, 2005)
Chester Kallman, *Storm at Castelfranco* (New York: Grove Press, 1956)
Ruth Kligman, *Love Affair: A Memoir of Jackson Pollock* (New York: William Morrow, 1974)
Wayne Koestenbaum, *My 1980s & Other Essays* (New York: Farrar, Straus and Giroux, 2013)
Marie-Jacqueline Lancaster, *Brian Howard: Portrait of a Failure* (London: Anthony Blond, 1968)
V. R. Lang, *Poems & Plays* (New York: Random House, 1975)
D. H. Lawrence, *Poems Volume I* ([London?]: Heron Books in association with William Heinemann, 1964)
David Lehman, *The Last Avant-Garde: The Making of the New York School of Poets* (New York: Doubleday, 1998)
Ted Leigh, ed., *Material Witness: The Selected Letters of Fairfield Porter* (Ann Arbor: University of Michigan Press, 2005)
Alfred Leslie, *The Hasty Papers: Special Millennium Edition* (Austin, TX: Host Publications, 1999)
Joe LeSueur, *Digressions on Some Poems by Frank O'Hara: A Memoir* (New York: Farrar, Straus and Giroux, 2003)
Claude Lévi-Strauss, *The Scope of Anthropology* (London: Jonathan Cape, 1967)
Joan Ludman, *Fairfield Porter: A Catalogue Raisonné of the Paintings, Watercolors, and Pastels* (New York: Hudson Hills Press, 2001)
Judith Malina, *The Diaries of Judith Malina 1947–1957* (New York: Grove Press, 1984)
James McCourt, *Kaye Wayfaring in "Avenged"* (New York: Penguin Books, 1985)
James McCourt, *Queer Street: Rise and Fall of an American Culture, 1947–1985* (New York and London: W. W. Norton, 2004)
Edward Mendelson, *Later Auden* (New York: Farrar, Straus and Giroux, 1999)
James Merrill, *Another Person: A Memoir* (New York: Alfred A. Knopf, 1993)
Marianne Moore, *A Marianne Moore Reader* (New York: Viking Press, 1961)
Howard Moss, ed., *The Poet's Story* (New York: Touchstone, 1973)
Howard Moss, *Whatever Is Moving* (Boston and Toronto: Little, Brown, 1981)
José Esteban Muñoz, *Cruising Utopia: The Then and There of Queer Futurity* (New York and London: New York University Press, 2009)
John Bernard Myers, *The Poets of the New York School* (Philadelphia: Graduate School of Fine Arts, University of Pennsylvania, 1969)
John Bernard Myers, *Tracking the Marvelous: A Life in the New York Art World* (New York: Random House, 1983)
Eileen Myles, *Chelsea Girls* (Santa Rosa, CA: Black Sparrow Press, 1994)
Eileen Myles, *The Importance of Being Iceland: Travel Essays in Art* (Los Angeles: Semiotext(e), 2009)
Eileen Myles, *I Must Be Living Twice: New and Selected Poems* (New York: Ecco, 2015)
Maggie Nelson, *Women, the New York School, and Other True Abstractions* (Iowa City: University of Iowa Press, 2007)
Harold Norse, *Memoirs of a Bastard Angel* (New York: William Morrow, 1989)

Frank O'Hara, *Art Chronicles 1954–1966* (New York: George Braziller, 1975)
Frank O'Hara, *The Collected Poems of Frank O'Hara*, Donald M. Allen, ed. (New York: Alfred A. Knopf Inc., 1971)
Frank O'Hara, *Early Writing* (San Francisco, CA: Grey Fox Press, 1977)
Frank O'Hara, *Selected Plays* (New York: Full Court Press, 1978)
Iris Origo, *Leopardi: A Study in Solitude* (London: Hamish Hamilton, 1953)
Ron Padgett, *Joe: A Memoir of Joe Brainard* (Minneapolis: Coffee House Press, 2004)
Ron Padgett, *Ted: A Personal Memoir of Ted Berrigan* (Great Barrington, MA: The Figures, 1993)
Ron Padgett and David Shapiro, eds., *An Anthology of New York Poets* (New York: Random House, 1970)
Boris Pasternak, *Safe Conduct: An Autobiography and Other Writings* (New York: New Directions Paperback, 1958)
Jed Perl, *New Art City: Manhattan at Mid-Century* (New York: Alfred A. Knopf, 2005)
Marjorie Perloff, *Frank O'Hara: Poet Among Painters* (Chicago and London: University of Chicago Press, 1998)
Howard Pollack, *The Ballad of John Latouche: An American Lyricist's Life and Work* (New York: Oxford University Press, 2017)
Anne Porter, *Living Things: Collected Poems* (Hanover, NH: Zoland Books, 2006)
Eliot Porter, *Summer Island* (San Francisco: Sierra Club, 1966)
Fairfield Porter, *Art in Its Own Terms: Selected Criticism 1935–1975*, Rackstraw Downes, ed. (Cambridge MA: Zoland Books, 1979)
Fairfield Porter, *The Collected Poems with Selected Drawings* (New York: Tibor de Nagy Editions, 1985)
Frederic Prokosch, *Voices: A Memoir* (New York: Farrar, Straus and Giroux, 1983)
Jenni Quilter, *New York School Painters & Poets: Neon in Daylight* (New York: Rizzoli, 2014)
John Richardson, *The Sorcerer's Apprentice* (London: Jonathan Cape, 1999)
Larry Rivers, *What Did I Do: The Unauthorized Autobiography* (New York: HarperCollins, 1992)
Karin Roffman, *The Songs We Know Best: John Ashbery's Early Life* (New York: Farrar, Straus and Giroux, 2021)
Ned Rorem, *The Paris Diary of Ned Rorem* (New York: George Braziller, 1966)
Edith Schloss, *The Loft Generation* (New York: Farrar, Straus and Giroux, 2021)
Logan Pearsall Smith, *Unforgotten Years* (Boston: Little, Brown, 1939)
Patti Smith, *Just Kids* (New York: Ecco, 2010)
Stephen Spender, ed., *W. H. Auden: A Tribute* (New York: Macmillan, 1975)
Justin Spring, *Fairfield Porter: A Life in Art* (New Haven, CT: Yale University Press, 1999)
Mark Strand, ed., *The Contemporary American Poets: American Poetry Since 1940* (New York: Meridian Books, 1969)
Gertrude Stein, *Last Operas and Plays* (New York: Rinehart & Co., 1949)
Virgil Thomson, *Virgil Thomson* (New York: Da Capo Press, 1967)
Tony Towle, *Memoir 1960–1963* (Cambridge, MA: Faux Press, 2001)
David Trinidad, *Dear Prudence: New and Selected Poems* (New York: Turtle Point Press, 2011)
Florence Turner, *At the Chelsea* (San Diego, New York, and London: Harcourt Brace Jovanovich, 1986)
Mark Van Doren, ed., *An Anthology of World Poetry* (New York: Albert & Charles Boni, 1929)
Gore Vidal, *Palimpsest: A Memoir* (New York: Penguin Books, 1996)
Anne Waldman, *Bard, Kinetic* (Minneapolis: Coffee House Press, 2023)
Anne Waldman and Lewis Warsh, eds., *The Angel Hair Anthology* (New York: Granary Books, 2001)

Anne Waldman, ed., *The World Anthology: Poems from the Saint Mark's Poetry Project* (Indianapolis and New York: Bobbs-Merrill, 1969)
Douglas Waller, *Wild Bill Donovan* (New York: Free Press, 2011)
William Watkin, *In the Process of Poetry: The New York School and the Avant-Garde* (Lewisburg, PA: Bucknell University Press; London: Associated University Presses, 2001)
William Fense Weaver, *A Tent in This World* (Kingston, NY: McPherson, 1999)
Walt Whitman, *Complete Poetry and Collected Prose* (New York: Library of America, 1982)
John Wieners, *Yours Presently: The Selected Letters of John Wieners*, Michael Seth Stewart, ed. (Albuquerque: University of New Mexico Press, 2020)
E. Andrew Wilde, Jr., ed., *The USS Glennon (DD-620) in World War II: Documents and Photographs* (Needham, MA: Privately printed by the author, 1999, 2001; online at https://destroyerhistory.org/assets/pdf/wilde/620glennon_wilde.pdf)
Tennessee Williams, *Memoirs* (New York: New Directions, 2006)
Tennessee Williams, *Notebooks* (New Haven, CT: Yale University Press, 2006)
Tennessee Williams, *Tennessee Williams' Letters to Donald Windham 1940–65*, Donald Windham, ed. (New York: Penguin Books, 1980)
Donald Windham, *1948: Italy* (Verona: Sandy Campbell, 1998)
John Yau, *Joe Brainard: The Art of the Personal* (New York: Rizzoli Electa, 2022)
Franco Zeffirelli, *Zeffirelli* (New York: Weidenfeld & Nicolson, 1986)

SELECTED PERIODICALS

Accent: A Quarterly of New Literature (Urbana, IL, Summer 1951)
Agni 37 (1993)
The American Poetry Review (March/April 1985)
Art and Literature, nos. 1–12 (1964–1967)
Art News (1955–1970)
C, A Journal of Poetry, nos. 1–13 (1963–1966)
Contemporary Authors (v. 101, 1981)
Denver Quarterly (University of Denver) 24, no. 4 (Spring 1990); 26, no. 4 (Spring 1992)
Folder, nos. 1–4 (1953–1956)
Horizon, nos. 93–94 (October 1947)
Little Caesar 10 (1980)
Locus Solus, nos. I–V (1961–1962)
New Directions 14 (February 11, 1953)
New World Writing, no. 1 (April 1952)
The Paris Review 40 (Winter–Spring 1967); 43 (Summer 1968); 53 (Winter 1972); 55 (Fall 1972); 96 (Summer 1985)
Poetry 93, no. 5 (February 1959); 113, no. 1 (October 1968); 121, no. 3 (December 1972); 127, no. 5 (February 1976)
Semi-Colon 1, nos. 1–6; 2, nos. 1–4 (1950–1970)
XX!st Century, no. 1 (New York: Rizzoli International Publications, Winter 1991–1992)

ACKNOWLEDGMENTS

This book could never have been written without the help and generosity of many people. In trying to thank them all I don't know where to start, except at the beginning, with Jonathan Galassi, who commissioned the book in 2003 and has been a support and inspiration during the entire period of its research and writing. The book would not exist without his faith and vision. I wish to thank my friend the late great Joe Brainard for introducing me to Jimmy in 1989, and for the gift of a transcription of Jimmy's letters to him after he died, which may have been what started me thinking about a biography. I owe a huge debt to the late poet William Corbett, who provided me with unstinting help from the days I was editing Schuyler's diary and compiling the chronology that accompanied it, welcoming me into his home and family in Boston and sharing with me the letters he collected. Darragh Park, Schuyler's first executor and a much-missed friend, took a big chance in entrusting me with the editing of Schuyler's diary. The current executor, Raymond Foye, has been a steady support and wise counselor. Schuyler's late brother and sister-in law, Fredric and Hilde Ridenour, were kind and patient in answering questions and lending me family papers and photographs. The late Anne Porter, as well as Katharine, Elizabeth, and Laurence Porter, have my particular gratitude for their frank and searching answers to difficult questions, not to mention their family's longtime assistance to Schuyler himself. John Ashbery, Jimmy's good friend from 1952 until his death, submitted to hours of interviews over many years with unfailing good humor and amazing recall. Through Jimmy I have been fortunate to know Tom Carey, his close friend, muse, and legatee, whose openness in answering what were sometimes intrusive questions has greatly enriched the book. Eileen Myles also became a valued friend and mentor through Jimmy and provided invaluable insights over many years. Ron and Pat Padgett helped in multiple ways, not only answering questions about their own close friendship with Jimmy, but Ron also in his capacity as artistic and literary executor of the Estate of Joe Brainard and executor of the Estate of Kenward Gray Elmslie. Karin Roffman, the biographer of John Ashbery, has been over-the-top generous in sharing information, insights, and documentation. I wish I could go back and take her courses at Yale and learn how to do this properly. Helen Graham, the historian of the Spanish Civil War and biographer of Bill Aalto, first approached me in 2001, sparking a long and fruitful correspondence. In particular, her research at the US Department of State through the Freedom of Information Act, so generously shared with me, immeasurably enhanced my knowledge of Schuyler's and Aalto's years in Italy. I am grateful to the late Peter Schjeldahl for loaning me the tapes of his 1977 interview with Schuyler, which I was able to transcribe and which proved especially valuable in helping me understand Schuyler's relationship with Frank O'Hara. Tragically, the tapes were subsequently lost in a fire, but fortunately the transcription remains. I also thank Alice Notley for giving me a transcription of her husband Ted Berrigan's unpublished 1983 interview with Schuyler, which revealed important details.

Julia Ringo deftly helped edit the early 375,000-word version of this manuscript to manageable size, and discovered the title. Thank you, Julia. At Farrar, Straus and Giroux, Oona Holahan was enormously helpful and always there when I needed her; while Gretchen Achilles, Nina Frieman, Carrie Hsieh, Katie Liptak, and Joshua Porter made the book a reality. For reading the book at various stages and providing invaluable suggestions and important corrections I thank Tom Carey, Douglas Crase, Raymond Foye, Maxine Groffsky, Eileen Myles, Charles North, Ron Padgett, Karin Roffman, David Trinidad, and Tom Whitridge. Of course any remaining errors are my own.

In addition to the persons mentioned above, many others helped me in my research. Not all of the approximately 134 interviews I conducted "got into" the book, but all of them helped me to enter imaginatively into Schuyler's world, person, and work, and I am grateful to everyone who took the time to speak with me, or to help in other ways:

Mary Abbott, Peter Ackroyd, Don Bachardy, Susan Baran, Jesse Barton, Jay Beber, Sibyl Bedford, Dodie Bellamy, Bill Berkson, Michael Brownstein, Helen Burckhardt, Jacob Burckhardt, Lukas Burckhardt, Rudy Burckhardt, Ada Calhoun, Marc Cohen, Clark Coolidge, Susan Coolidge, Beverly Corbett, Robert Dash, Ronald de Leeuw, Christophe de Menil, Bill DeNoyelles, Michael di Capua, Fay Mowery Donoghue, Kenward Elmslie, Larry Fagin, Dorothy Farnan, Martha Flowers, Hal Fondren, Christopher Foss, Cornelia Foss, Jane Freilicher, Peter Gizzi, Robert Glück, Robert Golbey, Michael Goldberg, Morris Golde, Brad Gooch, Jeremiah Goodman, Maureen Granville-Smith, Barbara Guest, Forrester Hammer, Langdon Hammer, Duncan Hannah, Waldemar Hansen, Robert Harms, Grace Hartigan, Joe Hazan, Richard Hennessy, John Hohnsbeen, Helena Hughes, Gustavus Ide, Yvonne Jacquette, Gerlof Janzen, Ada Katz, Alex Katz, Vincent Katz, David Kermani, Lisa Kernan, Kevin Killian, Ruth Kligman, Karen Koch, Katherine Koch, Kenneth Koch, Esta Kramer, Michael Lally, Gerrit Lansing, Joe LeSueur, James Lord, Robin Magowan, Ned Maloof, Harry Mathews, Charlotte Mayerson, James McCourt, Kynaston McShine, Edward Mendelson, Eldred Mowery III, Anne Dunn Moynihan, Eleanor Munro, Paula North, Alvin Novak, Larry Osgood, Bernard Oshei, Douglas Ousley, Maggie Paley, Philip Pearlstein, Claude Peck, Bernard Perlin, Simon Pettet, Frank Polach, Howard Pollack, Stuart Preston, John Richardson, Eugene Richie, Sally Ingalls Rohrdanz, Ned Rorem, Bob Rosenthal, John Saumarez Smith, Edith Schloss, George Schneeman, Katie Schneeman, Charles Shively, Justin Spring, Harrison Starr, William Stophel, Harold Talbot, Yvonne Thomas, Angelo Torricini, Piero Tosi, Tony Towle, Vincent Virga, Anne Waldman, Lewis Warsh, Rosanne Wasserman, William Weaver, Susan Weil, Hyman Weitzen, Megan Wilson, Donald Windham, Trevor Winkfield, Francis Wishart, Charles Wright, Geoffrey Young, Jeanne Keyes Youngson, Bill Zavatsky. A special thanks to my partner, Tom Whitridge, who makes it all possible.

Grateful acknowledgment is made for permission to reprint the following material:

Quotations from James Schuyler's Farrar, Straus and Giroux editions courtesy of Farrar, Straus and Giroux, and the James Schuyler Literary Trust, Raymond Foye, executor.

Excerpts from unpublished or uncollected poems, letters, and other writings by James Schuyler are used with the permission of the James Schuyler Literary Trust, Raymond Foye, executor.

I thank Ruth Greenstein and Turtle Point Press for permission to quote from published letters of James Schuyler included in William Corbett, editor, *Just the Thing: Selected Letters of James Schuyler, 1951–1991, Revised Anniversary Edition*. Copyright © 2023 by the Estate of William Corbett and the Estate of James Schuyler. Original edition copyright © 2004 by William Corbett and the Estate of James Schuyler. Used by permission of Turtle Point Press; and William Corbett, editor,

The Letters of James Schuyler to Frank O'Hara. Copyright © 2006 by William Corbett and the Estate of James Schuyler. Copyright © 2020 by the Estate of William Corbett and the Estate of James Schuyler. Used by permission of Turtle Point Press.

Excerpts from Frank O'Hara's out-of-print writings and letters are copyright by Maureen Granville-Smith and used with the permission of Maureen Granville-Smith.

Excerpts from John Ashbery's unpublished interviews, diaries, letters, and texts quoted herein are copyright © 2025 John Ashbery. All rights reserved. Used by arrangement with Georges Borchardt, Inc., for the author.

Excerpts from John Ashbery's published texts quoted herein are copyright © 2025 John Ashbery. All rights reserved. Used by arrangement with Georges Borchardt, Inc., for the author.

For permission to quote from his own letters and those of Kenward Elmslie, and to reproduce the drawing of James Schuyler by Joe Brainard, I thank Ron Padgett, executor of the Estate of Kenward Gray Elmslie and literary and artistic executor of the Estate of Joe Brainard.

For permission to quote from the unpublished letters of W. H. Auden I am grateful to Edward Mendelson, executor, the Estate of W. H. Auden.

"Ischia," copyright 1950 by W. H. Auden and © renewed 1978 by the Estate of W. H. Auden; *The Age of Anxiety*, copyright 1947 by W. H. Auden and © renewed 1975 by the Estate of W. H. Auden; and "If I Could Tell You," copyright 1934 and © renewed 1962 by W. H. Auden; from *Collected Poems* by W. H. Auden, edited by Edward Mendelson. Used by permission of Random House, an imprint and division of Penguin Random House LLC. All rights reserved.

"Making, Knowing and Judging," copyright © 1956 by W. H. Auden and renewed 1984 by the Estate of W. H. Auden; from *The Dyer's Hand and Other Essays* by W. H. Auden. Used by permission of Random House, an imprint and division of Penguin Random House LLC. All rights reserved.

Excerpts from *The Age of Anxiety: A Baroque Eclogue*, "If I Could Tell You," and "Ischia," by W. H. Auden, copyright © 1947, 1940, 1948 by the Estate of W. H. Auden, are used in the ebook by permission of Curtis Brown, Ltd. All rights reserved.

Excerpt from *Chelsea Girls* by Eileen Myles. Copyright © 1994 Eileen Myles. Used by permission of HarperCollins Publishers.

Excerpt from Christopher Isherwood, *Diaries Volume One: 1939–1960* by

Christopher Isherwood. Copyright © 1997 by Christopher Isherwood, used by permission of the Wylie Agency LLC.

Excerpt from *Tennessee Williams' Letters to Donald Windham*, edited by Donald Windham, is used by permission of the Beinecke Rare Book and Manuscript Library, Yale University, New Haven, CT.

For permission to quote from letters of Fairfield and Anne Porter I thank Katharine Porter.

For permission to quote from *Material Witness: The Selected Letters of Fairfield Porter*, edited by Ted Leigh (Ann Arbor: The University of Michigan Press, 2005), I thank the University of Michigan Press.

For permission to quote from the unpublished papers of Alan Ansen, I am grateful to Rachel Hadas, executor of the Estate of Alan Ansen.

For permission to quote from the works of Cyril Connolly I thank Cresida Connolly and the Estate of Cyril Connolly.

For permission to quote from the work of Kenneth Koch I thank Karen Koch, executor of the Kenneth Koch Literary Estate.

Excerpts from *Too Brief a Treat* by Truman Capote, edited by Gerald Clarke, copyright © 2004 by Gerald Clarke; Truman Capote material copyright © 2004 by the Truman Capote Literary Trust. Used by permission of Penguin Random House LLC and the Truman Capote Literary Trust.

At libraries and other institutions my first debt is to Lynda Corey Claassen, director and chief curator, the Mandeville Special Collections Library, University of California, San Diego, who has been a support to the project from the beginning. I also thank Nina Mamikunian, curator, Archive for New Poetry, UC San Diego Library. At the New York Public Library I was helped over the years by Rodney Phillips, and by Dr. Isaac Gewirtz, the then curators of the Henry W. and Albert A. Berg Collection of English and American Literature, New York Public Library Astor, Lenox and Tilden Foundations.

I also wish to thank Melissa Barton, curator, Yale Collection of American Literature, Beinecke Library, Yale University, New Haven, CT; D. Duane Cummins, president emeritus, R. Jeanne Cobb, archivist, and Heather Ricciuti, the

Mary Cutlip Director of Libraries and Learning Resources, Bethany College, Bethany, WV; Jeremy Morlock, *East Aurora Advertiser*, East Aurora, NY; East Aurora Historical Society, East Aurora, NY; Michael Meredith, curator of the modern collections, Eton College Library, Eton College, Windsor, England; Linda Evenson, the Freeborn County Historical Museum, Albert Lea, MN; Gold and Fizdale Collection, Peter Jay Sharp Special Collections, Juilliard School Library, New York, NY; André Bernard, the John Simon Guggenheim Foundation, New York, NY; Leslie A. Morris, Gore Vidal Curator of Modern Books and Manuscripts, Houghton Library, Harvard University, Cambridge, MA; Bridget Howlett, senior archivist, London Metropolitan Archives, London, England; the Museum of Modern Art Archives, New York, NY; Bryan Whitledge, University Archives, University of Illinois at Urbana-Champaign, IL; Christopher Pennington, Jerome Robbins Foundation, New York, NY; Martin Clifford, archivist, St. Edmund's School, Canterbury, England; Shannon O'Neill, curator for Tamiment-Wagner Collections, NYU Special Collections, New York University, NY; Linda Taylor, researcher, Waseca County Historical Society, MN; Westminster City Archives, London, England.

Portions of this book previously appeared, in slightly different form, in *Tether* 1 (Sienese Shredder Editions, 2015) and online in *Jacket2* (Kelly Writers House, Philadelphia, June 30, 2012: https://jacket2.org/article/past-past).

INDEX